Dennis
Each day bring
us closer to Home
Happy five oh!
y

Rudy

Power-Filled
LIVING

Power-Filled LIVING

R. A. Torrey

Whitaker House

POWER-FILLED LIVING

ISBN: 0-88368-550-7
Printed in the United States of America
Copyright © 1998 by Whitaker House

Whitaker House
30 Hunt Valley Circle
New Kensington, PA 15068

Library of Congress Cataloging-in-Publication

Torrey, R. A. (Reuben Archer), 1856–1928.
    Power-filled living / by R. A. Torrey.
       p.   cm.
    ISBN 0-88368-550-7 (pbk.)
    1. Christian life.   I. Title
BV5401.2.T655   1999
243—dc21   99-11399

2 3 4 5 6 7 8 9 10 11 12 13 14 / 09 08 07 06 05 04 03 02 01 00

Contents

About the Author

R euben Archer Torrey was born in Hoboken, New Jersey, on January 28, 1856. He graduated from Yale University in 1875 and from Yale Divinity School in 1878.

Upon his graduation, R. A. Torrey became a Congregational minister. A few years later, he joined Dwight L. Moody in his evangelistic work in Chicago and became the pastor of the Chicago Avenue Church. He was selected by D. L. Moody to become the first dean of the Moody Bible Institute of Chicago. Under his direction, Moody Institute became a pattern for Bible institutes around the world.

Torrey is respected as one of the greatest evangelists of modern times. At the turn of the century, Torrey began his evangelistic tours and crusades. He spent the years of 1903–1905 in a worldwide revival campaign, along with the famous song leader Charles McCallon Alexander. Together they ministered in many parts of the world and reportedly brought nearly one hundred thousand souls to Jesus. Torrey continued worldwide crusades for the next fifteen years, eventually reaching Japan and China. During those same years, he served as Dean of the Bible Institute of Los Angeles and pastored the Church of the Open Door in that city.

Torrey longed for more Christian workers to take an active part in bringing the message of salvation through Christ to a lost and dying world. His straightforward style of evangelism has shown thousands of Christian workers how to become effective soulwinners.

R. A. Torrey died on October 26, 1928. He is well-remembered today for his inspiring devotional books on the Christian life, which have been translated into many different languages. In *How to Bring Men to Christ*, the evangelistic message that sent Torrey around the world is still ministering to all whose hearts yearn to lead men, women, and children to salvation through Jesus Christ.

How to Obtain Fullness of Power

Contents

———◆———

Preface

◆

A cry for more power in our personal conflict with the world, the flesh, and the Devil is rising from many earnest hearts; also, there is a need for more power in our service for others. The Bible makes very plain the way to obtain this greatly desired power. There is no presumption in undertaking to tell how to obtain fullness of power in Christian life and service. The Bible itself tells how, and the Bible was intended to be understood.

The Bible statement of the way is not mystical or mysterious; it is very plain and straightforward. If we will only practice personally the power of the Word of God, the power of the blood of Christ, the power of the Holy Spirit, the power of prayer, and the power of a surrendered life, we will then experience the fullness of power in Christian life and service. The following chapters make this clear.

The present volume has been written partly in response to a request from readers of the author's book *How to Bring Men to Christ,* suggesting a follow-up book for use in the training of those who have just accepted Christ. But this book has another and far more important purpose. Many do not even know that there is a life of abiding rest, joy, satisfaction, and power in Jesus. Many others, while they think there must be something beyond the life they know, are in ignorance as to how to obtain it. This book is written to help them.

Chapter 1

The Power of the Word of God

◆——————

The power that belongs to God is stored in the great reservoir of His own Word: the Bible. *"Power belongs to God"* (Ps. 62:11). If we wish to make it ours, we must go to the Bible. Yet people who are praying for power but neglecting the Bible abound in the church. Many long to have power for fruit-bearing in their own lives, yet they forget that Jesus has said, *"The seed is the word of God"* (Luke 8:11). They long to have power to melt the cold heart and break the stubborn will, yet they forget that God has said, *"Is not My word like a fire?...And like a hammer that breaks the rock in pieces?"* (Jer. 23:29).

If we are to obtain fullness of power in life and service, we must feed on the Word of God. No other food is so strengthening. If we will not take time to study the Bible, we cannot have power anymore than we can have physical strength if we will not take time to eat nutritious food. Let us see what the Word of God has the power to do.

Conviction of Sin

First of all, the Word of God has the power to convict of sin. In Acts 2:37, we read: *"Now when they heard this, they were cut to the heart, and said to Peter and the rest of the apostles, 'Men and brethren, what shall we do?'"* If we look to see what they heard that produced this deep conviction, we find that it was simply the Word of God. If we will read Peter's sermon, we will find it to be one of the most biblical sermons ever preached. It was Scripture from beginning to end. It was the Word of God, carried home by the Spirit of God, that pricked their minds and hearts.

If we wish to produce conviction, we must give people the Word of God. Once, I heard a man pray this prayer, "O God, convict us of sin." That was a very good prayer, but unless we bring our souls into contact with the instrument God designed for the conviction of sin, we will feel nothing. And if we desire to produce conviction in others, we must use the Word.

The Greatest Sin

Not long ago, a fine-looking young man came up to me after a meeting. I asked him, "Are you a Christian?"

He answered, "No, sir."

"Why not?"

"I think Christianity is a first-rate thing, but I don't have much feeling about it."

"But, " I said, "do you realize that you are a sinner?"

He said, "Yes, sir, I suppose I am, but I am not very much of a sinner. I am a pretty good sort of fellow."

"So, my friend, you do not have very much conviction of sin. I have something in my hand that is a divinely appointed instrument to produce conviction of sin." Opening my Bible, I asked him to read Matthew 22:37–38.

He read: *"You shall love the LORD your God with all your heart, with all your soul, and with all your mind. This is the first and great commandment.'"*

Then I asked him, "In light of this Scripture, what is the first and greatest sin?"

He replied, "It must be to neglect to keep that commandment."

"Have you kept it?" I asked. At this point, the Spirit of God took it home to his heart. Not long after that, we were kneeling as he asked God for mercy through Christ.

Life-Giving Power

The Word of God has the power to regenerate. In 1 Peter 1:23, we read: *"Having been born again, not of corruptible seed but incorruptible, through the word of God which lives and abides forever."* James 1:18 says, *"Of His own will He brought us forth by the word of truth, that we might be a kind of firstfruits of His creatures."*

If you wish to be born again, the way is very simple. Take the Word of God concerning Christ crucified and risen, and store it in your heart by meditating on it. Look to God by His Holy Spirit to quicken it. Believe it with your heart, and the work will be done.

If you wish to see someone else born again, give him the Word of God. Although God's part in the process of regeneration is a mystery to us, our part is quite simple: The human heart is the soil; you and I are sowers; the Word of God is the seed that we plant in that soil; God quickens it by His Holy Spirit and gives the increase (1 Cor. 3:6); the heart closes around the Word by faith; and the new life is the product.

The new birth is simply the impartation of a new nature—God's nature. But how are we made partakers of God's nature? Read 2 Peter 1:4: *"That through these ['exceedingly great and precious promises'] you may be partakers of the divine nature."* That is all there is to it. The Word of God is the seed out of which the divine nature springs up in the human soul.

Saving Faith

The Word of God also has the power to produce faith. In Romans 10:17, we read: *"Faith comes by hearing, and hearing by the word of God."* You can never get faith by merely praying. You can never get it by an effort of the will. You can never get it by trying to "pump it up" in any way. Faith is the effect of a certain cause, and that cause is the Word of God.

Such is the case, for example, with saving faith. Suppose you want a man to have saving faith. Simply give him something definite from God's Word on which he can rest. The Philippian jailer asked, *"Sirs, what must I do to be saved?"* (Acts 16:30), and Paul and Silas answered, *"Believe on the Lord Jesus Christ, and you will be saved, you and your household"* (v. 31).

But they did not stop there. Read verse 32: *"Then they spoke the word of the Lord to him and to all who were in his house."* They did not merely tell the Philippian jailer to believe in the Lord Jesus Christ, and then leave him there floundering

17

in the dark without giving him something to believe or something for his faith to rest on. They gave him what God has ordained to produce faith.

It is at this point that we often make a mistake. We tell people, "Believe, believe, believe," but do not show them how or give them anything definite to believe. The biblical way, and the intelligent way as well, is when you tell a person to believe and give him something in which to believe. Give him, for example, Isaiah 53:6, and thus hold up Christ crucified, or give him 1 Peter 2:24. Here he has something for his faith to rest on. Faith must have a foundation; it cannot float in thin air. It is disheartening to see people told to believe when they are not given anything in which to believe.

Prevailing Faith

Not only does saving faith come through the Word of God, but also prevailing faith in prayer. Suppose I read Mark 11:24: *"Whatever things you ask when you pray, believe that you receive them, and you will have them."* I used to say, "The way to get anything I want is to believe I am going to get it." I would kneel down and pray, trying to believe, but I did not get the things that I asked for. I had no real faith.

Real faith must have a guarantee. Before I can truly believe I am to receive what I ask for, I must have a definite promise from God's Word or a definite leading of the Holy Spirit to rest my faith on. What, then, should we do?

We go into God's presence with the thing we desire. Next, we ask ourselves this question: Is there any promise in God's Word regarding what we desire? We look into the Word of God and find the promise. Then all we have to do is to present that promise to God. For example, we say, "Heavenly Father, we desire the Holy Spirit. You say in Your Word, *'If you then, being evil, know how to give good gifts to your children, how much more will your heavenly Father give the Holy Spirit to those who ask Him!'* (Luke 11:13). And again in Acts 2:39 that *'the promise is to you and to your children, and to all who are afar off, as many as the Lord our God will call.'* I have been called; I am saved; and here in Your Word is Your promise. So please fill me now with the Holy Spirit."

We then take 1 John 5:14–15 and say, "Father, I have confidence in You that if I ask anything according to Your will—and I know that this petition is according to Your will—You hear me, and since I know that You hear me, I know that I have the request that I have asked of You."

Then we stand on God's promise and say, "It is mine," and it will be. The only way to have a faith that prevails in prayer is to study your Bible, know the promises, and present them to God. George Müller, one of the church's mightiest men of prayer, always prepared for prayer by studying the Word.

Christian Evidence

The Word of God also gives us the faith we need to dispel doubt. Suppose you have a skeptic to deal with, and you desire that he will receive faith. What will you do with him? To begin with, turn to John 20:31: *"But these are written that you may believe that Jesus is the Christ, the Son of God, and that believing you may have life in His name."* Clearly, then, this book of John was given that through *"those things which are written in it"* (Rev. 1:3), men *"may believe that Jesus is the Christ, the Son of God, and that believing* [they] *may have life in His name."* The gospel of John is an inspired book on Christian evidence.

Then, find out whether the skeptic's will is surrendered or not. *"If anyone wants to do His will, he shall know concerning the doctrine, whether it is from God or whether I speak on My own authority"* (John 7:17). After the will has been surrendered, just say, "Take this Book and read it thoughtfully and honestly. Then come back and tell me the result." The result is absolutely sure.

No person—agnostic, infidel, or whatever you please—can read the Bible, asking the Holy Spirit to give him light, without believing in Jesus as the Christ, the Son of God, provided his will is surrendered to the truth. I have tried this with many men and women, and there has never been one exception to the rule laid down by Christ. It has always come out the same way.

Victorious Faith

Faith that wins mighty victories for God—that gets the victory over the world, the flesh, and the Devil—comes through the

Word. (See 1 John 5:4; Ephesians 6:16; Hebrews 11:33–34.) Very early in my ministry, I read a sermon by Dwight Moody in which he said that a man would not amount to anything if he did not have faith. I said, "That sermon is true. I must have faith." I went to work and tried to generate some faith, with no success. The more I tried, the less I had. But one day, I ran across this text: *"Faith comes by hearing, and hearing by the word of God"* (Rom. 10:17). In it, I learned the great secret of faith, one of the greatest secrets I have ever learned.

I began to feed my faith on the Word of God, and it has been growing ever since. So, in every respect, we see that *"faith comes by hearing, and hearing by the word of God."* If we are to have faith, we must feed steadily, largely, and daily on the Word of God.

Cleansing

The Word of God has the power to cleanse. In Ephesians 5:25–26, we read: *"Husbands, love your wives, just as Christ also loved the church and gave Himself for her, that He might sanctify and cleanse her with the washing of water by the word."* The Word of God has the power not only to take impurities out of the heart, but to cleanse the outward life as well. If you want a clean outward life, you must wash it often by bringing your life into contact with the Word of God.

If one lives in a city whose atmosphere is polluted with smoke, his hands will get black when he goes into the street. He must wash frequently if he wishes to keep clean. We all live in a very dirty world, whose spiritual atmosphere is polluted. As we go out from day to day, coming into contact with it, there is only one way to keep clean: by taking frequent baths in the Word of God. You must bathe every day and take plenty of time to do it. A daily, prolonged, thoughtful bath in the Word of God is the only thing that will keep a life clean. (See Psalm 119:9.)

Character Building

The Word of God has the power to build up. In Acts 20:32, we read: *"I commend you to God and to the word of His grace, which is able to build you up.*" Character building should be done according to the Word of God. In 2 Peter 1:5–7, we have a picture of a seven-story Christian built on the foundation of faith. The great trouble today is that we have too many one-story Christians because of their neglect of the Word.

In 1 Peter 2:2, we have a similar thought expressed in a different way: *"As newborn babes, desire the pure milk of the word, that you may grow thereby."* If we are to grow, we must have wholesome, nutritious food and plenty of it.

The only spiritual food that contains all the elements necessary for balanced Christian growth is the Word of God. A Christian can no more grow up in good health without feeding frequently, regularly, and largely on the Word of God than a baby can grow up in good health without proper nutrition.

Wisdom

The Word of God has the power to give wisdom. Psalm 119:130 is worthy of the most careful attention: *"The entrance of Your words gives light; it gives understanding to the simple."* There is more wisdom in the Bible than there is in all the other literature of the ages. The man who studies the Bible, even if he does not study any other book, will possess more real wisdom—wisdom that counts for eternity as well as time, wisdom that this perishing world needs, wisdom for which hungry hearts today are starving—than the man who reads every other book and neglects his Bible.

This has been illustrated over and over again in the history of the church. Men who have greatly affected the spiritual history of this world, those who have brought about great reformations in morals and doctrines, men whom others have flocked to hear and on whose words people have hung, have been men of the Bible in every instance. In many cases, they knew little besides the Bible.

I have known unsophisticated men and women who knew little more than their Bibles. I would rather sit at their feet and learn the wisdom that falls from their lips than listen to the man well-versed in philosophy, science, and even theology, if he does not know anything about the Word of God. There is wonderful force in the words of Paul to Timothy:

21

All Scripture is given by inspiration of God, and is profitable for doctrine, for reproof, for correction, for instruction in righteousness, that the man of God may be complete, thoroughly equipped for every good work. (2 Tim. 3:16–17)

Through what? Through the study of the Bible.

Eternal Life

The Word of God has the power to give assurance of eternal life. In 1 John 5:13, we read: *"These things I have written to you who believe in the name of the Son of God, that you may know that you have eternal life, and that you may continue to believe in the name of the Son of God."* That is, the assurance of eternal life comes through what is *"written."*

What should we do with someone who is not sure of his salvation? Tell him to pray until he gets assurance? Not at all. Instead, take him to a passage such as John 3:36, *"He who believes in the Son has everlasting life."* Make him focus on that point until he takes God's Word as truth and knows he has everlasting life because he believes on the Son and because God says, *"He who believes in the Son has everlasting life."*

The Peace of the Lord

The Word of God has the power to bring peace into the heart. In Psalm 85:8, we read: *"I will hear what God the LORD will speak, for He will speak peace to His people and to His saints."* Many people today are looking for peace, longing for peace, and praying for peace. But deep peace of heart comes only from the study of the Word of God.

There is, for example, one passage in the Bible that, if fed on daily until it becomes indelibly written on our hearts, will banish all anxiety forever. It is Romans 8:28, *"And we know that all things work together for good to those who love God, to those who are the called according to His purpose."* Nothing can come to us that is not one of the *"all things."* If we really believe this passage and it really takes hold of us, nothing will disturb our peace.

Joy! Joy! Joy!

The Word of God has the power to produce joy. Jeremiah 15:16 says, *"Your words were found, and I ate them, and Your word was to me the joy and rejoicing of my heart."* And Jesus said in John 15:11, *"These things I have spoken to you, that My joy may remain in you, and that your joy may be full."* Clearly, then, fullness of joy comes through the Word of God.

There is no joy on this earth, from any worldly source, like the joy that kindles and glows in the heart of a believer in Jesus Christ. This joy comes as he feeds on the Word of God and as the Word of God is engraved on his heart by the power of the Holy Spirit.

Patience, comfort, and hope also come through the Word of God. Romans 15:4 says, *"For whatever things were written before were written for our learning, that we through the patience and comfort of the Scriptures might have hope."*

The Power to Protect

Finally, the Word of God has the power to protect us from error and sin. In Acts 20:29–32, the apostle Paul warned the elders at Ephesus of the errors that would creep in among them. He commended them, in closing, *"to God and to the word of His grace"* (v. 32). In a similar way, Paul, writing to Timothy, the bishop of the same church, said:

> *But evil men and impostors will grow worse and worse, deceiving and being deceived. But you must continue in the things which you have learned and been assured of, knowing from whom you have learned them, and that from childhood you have known the Holy Scriptures, which are able to make you wise for salvation through faith which is in Christ Jesus.* (2 Tim. 3:13–15)

The one who feeds constantly on the Word of God is protected from committing errors. It is simple neglect of the Word that has left so many believers prey to the many false doctrines with which the Devil, in his subtlety, is endeavoring to infiltrate the church of Christ today.

23

The Word of God not only has the power to protect from error, but from sin as well. In Psalm 119:11, we read: *"Your word I have hidden in my heart, that I might not sin against You!"* The man who feeds daily on the Word of God will be protected against the temptations of the Devil. Any day we neglect to feed on the Word of God, we leave an open door through which Satan is sure to enter our hearts and lives. Even the Son of God Himself met and overcame the temptations of the Adversary by the Scriptures. To each of Satan's temptations, Jesus replied, *"It is written"* (Matt. 4:4, 7, 10). Satan left the field completely vanquished.

Study the Word

It is evident from what has been said that the first step in obtaining fullness of power in Christian life and service is the study of the Word. There can be no fullness of power in life and service if the Bible is neglected. In much that is now written on power, this fact is overlooked. The work of the Holy Spirit is magnified, but the instrument through which the Holy Spirit works is largely forgotten. The result is transient enthusiasm and activity but no steady continuance and increase in power and usefulness.

We cannot obtain or maintain power in our own lives or in our work for others unless there is deep and frequent meditation on the Word of God. If our leaf is not to wither and whatever we do is to prosper, our delight must be in the law of the Lord, and we must meditate on it day and night (Ps. 1:2–3).

Of course, it is much easier and more agreeable to our spiritual laziness to go to a revival meeting claiming a "filling with the Holy Spirit" than it is to inch along day after day, month after month, year after year, digging into the Word of God. But a filling with the Spirit that is not maintained by persistent study of the Word will soon vanish. Precisely the same results that Paul in one place ascribed to being *"filled with the Spirit"* (Eph. 5:18), in another place he attributed to letting *"the word of Christ dwell in you richly"* (Col. 3:16). Evidently Paul knew of no filling with the Holy Spirit divorced from deep and constant meditation on the Word. To sum it all up, anyone who wishes to obtain and maintain fullness of power in Christian life and service must feed constantly on the Word of God.

Chapter 2

The Power of the Blood of Christ

◆

Because *"power belongs to God"* (Ps. 62:11), it is at man's disposal. But there is one thing that separates man and God, and that is sin. We read in Isaiah:

Behold, the Lord's hand is not shortened, that it cannot save; nor His ear heavy, that it cannot hear. But your iniquities have separated you from your God; and your sins have hidden His face from you, so that He will not hear.
(Isa. 59:1–2)

Before we can know God's power in our lives and service, sin must be removed in order to get rid of the separation between God and us.

It is Christ's blood that removes sin. (See Hebrews 9:26.) We must know the power of the blood if we are to know the power of God. Our experience of the power of the Word, the power of the Holy Spirit, and the power of prayer is dependent on our knowing the power of the blood of Christ. Let us see what the blood of Christ has the power to do.

Christ's Atoning Sacrifice

First of all, the blood of Christ is an offering to God for sin. In Romans 3:25, we read: *"Whom God set forth as a propitiation by His blood, through faith, to demonstrate His righteousness, because in His forbearance God had passed over the sins that were previously committed."* In the earlier verses of this chapter, Paul proved all men to be sinners—*"every mouth may be stopped, and all the world may become guilty before God"* (v. 19).

26

But God is holy, a God who hates sin. God's hatred of sin is no false hatred. It is real; it is living; it is active. Somehow, it must manifest itself. God's wrath at sin must strike somewhere. What hope then is there for any of us, for *"all have sinned and fall short of the glory of God"* (v. 23)?

The Blood of Jesus

God gives us His own answer to this tremendously important question. There is hope for us because God Himself has provided an appeasement: the shed blood of Christ. God has *"set forth [Christ] as a propitiation by His blood, through faith"* (v. 25). The wrath of God at sin strikes Him instead of striking us.

The prophet Isaiah glimpsed this great truth several hundred years before the birth of Christ. *"All we like sheep have gone astray; we have turned, every one, to his own way; and the LORD has laid [literally, made to strike] on Him the iniquity of us all"* (Isa. 53:6).

The first power of Christ's blood is as a sin offering, providing a target for and satisfying God's holy wrath at sin. He is *"our Passover"* (1 Cor. 5:7). When God sees His blood, He will pass over and spare us, even though we are sinners. (See Exodus 12:13, 23.)

This propitiation is chiefly for the believer, *"a propitiation...through faith"* (Rom. 3:25). All of God's wrath at the believer's sins is fully appeased or satisfied in the blood of Christ. What a wonderfully comforting thought it is when we remember how often and how greatly we have sinned, to know how infinitely holy God is, how He hates sin, and how His wrath has already been fully appeased in the shed blood of His own Son, the propitiation that He Himself provided!

Believers and Unbelievers

The blood of Christ covers unbelievers as well as believers, the vilest sinner and the most stubborn unbeliever and blasphemer. In 1 John 2:2, we read: *"And He Himself is the propitiation for our sins, and not for ours only but also for the whole world."* By the shed blood of Christ, a basis is provided on which God can deal mercifully with the whole world.

All of God's dealings in mercy with man are on the ground of the shed blood of Christ. And more, His dealings with those who ridicule the doctrine of the Atonement are on the ground of that shed blood. All the mercy of God on man since the fall of Adam is on the ground of that shed blood. Without the shed blood, God would cut the sinner off at once in his sin.

Someone may ask, "How then could God have dealt in mercy with sinners before Christ came and died?" The answer is simple. Jesus is the Lamb who was *"slain from the foundation of the world"* (Rev. 13:8).

From the moment sin entered the world, God had His eyes on that sacrifice that He Himself had prepared *"from the foundation of the world."* In the very Garden of Eden, the blood of sacrifices that pointed to the true sacrifice began to flow. It is the power of the blood that has given men the security of God's mercy since sin arrived. The most determined rejecter of Christ owes all he has that is good to Christ's blood.

Forgiveness

Again in Ephesians 1:7, we read: *"We have redemption through His blood, the forgiveness of sins."* Forgiveness of sins is not something the believer in Christ is to look for in the future; it is something he already has. *"We have,"* said Paul, *"...the forgiveness of* [our] *sins."*

Forgiveness of sin is not something we are to do; it is not something to secure. It is something that the blood of Christ has already secured, which our faith simply appropriates and enjoys. Forgiveness has already been secured for every believer in Christ by the power of His blood. Oh, blessed is the one who has learned to rest in the peace Christ gives, who counts his sins forgiven because Christ's blood was shed and God says so! *"We have redemption through His blood, the forgiveness of sins."*

Continuous Cleansing

Another passage very closely related to this one reveals the power of Christ's blood even further: *"But if we walk in the light as He is in the light, we have fellowship with one another, and the blood of Jesus Christ His Son cleanses us from all sin"* (1 John 1:7). This describes the completeness of the forgiveness we get through the blood. The blood of Christ has the power to cleanse the believer from *"all sin."* And it cleanses continuously, keeping him clean every minute, every day, and every hour.

The cleansing here is from the guilt of sin. When cleansing is mentioned in the Bible in connection with the blood, it is always cleansing from guilt. Cleansing from the power of sin and the presence of sin is by the Word of God, the Holy Spirit, and the living and indwelling Christ. Christ on the cross saves from the guilt of sin; Christ on the throne saves from the power of sin; and Christ coming again will save from the presence of sin.

White as Snow

When one is walking in the light, submitting to the light, and walking in Christ who is the Light, then the blood of Christ cleanses from *all* the guilt of sin. His past may be as bad as a past can be, laden with countless, enormous sins, but they are all—every one, the greatest and the smallest—washed away. His record is absolutely white in God's sight. It is as white as the record of Jesus Christ Himself. His sins that were as scarlet are as white as snow; though they were red like crimson, they are as wool. (See Isaiah 1:18.)

The blood of Christ has the power to wash the blackest record white. We all have had a black past, for if we could see our past as God sees it before it is washed, the record of the best of us would be black, black, black. But if we are walking in the light, submitting to the truth of God, believing in the light—in Christ—our record today is as white as Christ's garments were when the disciples saw Him on the Mount of Transfiguration. (See Matthew 17:2; Mark 9:3; Luke 9:29.) No one can lay anything to the charge of God's elect (Rom. 8:33); there is no condemnation to those who are in Christ Jesus (Rom. 8:1).

Saved from Wrath

In Romans 5:9, we read: *"Much more then, having now been justified by His blood, we shall be saved from wrath through*

Him." The blood of Christ has the power to justify. Every believer in Christ is already justified in Christ's blood. This means that he is more than forgiven and cleansed.

Forgiveness, as glorious as it is, is a negative thing. It means merely that our sins are put away, and we are regarded as if we had not sinned. But justification is positive. It means that we are counted as positively righteous; that positive and perfect righteousness, the perfect righteousness of Christ, is credited to our account.

It is a good thing to be stripped of vile and filthy rags, but it is far better to be clothed with garments of glory and beauty. In forgiveness, we are stripped of the vile and stinking rags of our sin. In justification, we are clothed with the glory and beauty of Christ. The power of the blood secures this experience.

In shedding His blood as a penalty for sin, Christ took our place; when we believe in Him, we step into His place. *"For He made Him who knew no sin to be sin for us, that we might become the righteousness of God in Him"* (2 Cor. 5:21).

No More Dead Works

Now let us look at Hebrews 9:14: *"How much more shall the blood of Christ, who through the eternal Spirit offered Himself without spot to God, cleanse your conscience from dead works to serve the living God?"* The blood of Christ has the power to cleanse the conscience from dead works to serve the living God. Do you understand what that means? It is a glorious truth, and I will try to make it plain.

When a man awakens to the fact that he is a sinner and that God is holy, he feels that he must do something to please God and atone for sin. He must somehow make restitution or give away money to atone for his sins. All these self-efforts to please God and atone for sins are *"dead works."* They can never accomplish what they aim at and can never bring peace. For many weary years, Martin Luther sought peace in this way and did not find it. But when we see, as Luther finally did, how the power of the blood washed away our sins and justified us before God, making us pleasing and acceptable in God's sight by reason of that shed blood, then our consciences are not only relieved from the burden of guilt, but also from the burden of our self-efforts. We are now at liberty to serve the living God, not in the slavery of fear, but in the liberty of the freedom and joy of those who know they are accepted and beloved sons.

It is the blood that delivers us from the awful bondage of thinking we must do something to atone for sins and please God. The blood shows us that it is already done.

Do or Done?

A friend of mine once said to someone who was seeking peace through his own works, "You have a two-letter religion, and I have a four-letter one."

"How is that?" asked the other man.

"Your religion is *do*. My religion is *done*. You are trying to rest in what you do. I am resting in what Christ has done."

Many Christians today have not permitted the blood of Christ to cleanse their consciences from dead works. They are constantly feeling they must do something to atone for sin. Look at what God looks at—the blood—and see that it is already done! God is satisfied; sin is atoned for; you are justified! Don't do *"dead works"* (Heb. 9:14) to commend yourself to God. Realize that you are already commended by the blood; then serve Him in the freedom of love, not in the bondage of fear.

There are three kinds of men. First, there are those who are not at all burdened by sin, who, on the contrary, love it. That is wholly bad. Second, there are those who are burdened by sin and seek to get rid of it by their own works. That is better, but there is something infinitely better. Third, there are those who saw the hideousness of sin and were burdened by it, but who have been brought to see the power of the blood, settling sin forever and putting it away (Heb. 9:26). They are no longer burdened and no longer work to commend themselves to God. Rather, out of joyous gratitude, they serve Him who perfectly justifies the ungodly through His shed blood.

God's Own

In Acts 20:28, we read: *"Take heed to yourselves and to all the flock, among which the Holy Spirit has made you overseers, to shepherd the church of God which He purchased with His own blood."* Revelation 5:9 says, *"And they sang a new song, saying: 'You are worthy to take the scroll, and to open its seals; for You were slain, and have redeemed us to God by Your blood out of every tribe and tongue and people and nation.'"* The blood of Christ has the power to purchase us, to make us God's own. The blood of Christ makes me God's own property.

That thought brings me a feeling of responsibility. If I belong to God, I must serve Him wholly; body, soul, and spirit must be surrendered completely to Him. But the thought that I am God's property also brings a feeling of security. God can and will take care of His own property. The blood of Christ has power to make me eternally secure.

Holy Boldness

We learn still more about the power of the blood in Hebrews 10:19–20: *"Therefore, brethren, [we have] boldness to enter the Holiest by the blood of Jesus, by a new and living way which He consecrated for us, through the veil, that is, His flesh."* The blood of Christ has the power to give the believer boldness to enter into the Holy Place, the very presence of God.

In the old Jewish days of the tabernacle and temple, God manifested Himself in the Most Holy Place. This was the place to meet God. Only one Jew in all the nation was allowed to enter this hallowed place—the high priest. He could go in only once a year, on the Day of Atonement, and then only with blood.

God was teaching the Jews—and through them, the world—three great truths: that God is unapproachably holy, that man is sinful, and that sinful man can approach a holy God only through atoning blood. That is, *"without shedding of blood there is no remission"* of sin (Heb. 9:22), consequently, no approach to God.

But the blood of the Old Testament sacrifices was only a symbol of the true sacrifice, Jesus Christ. Because of His shed blood, the vilest sinner who believes on Him has the right to approach God boldly, going into His very presence whenever he desires without fear, *"in full assurance of faith"* (Heb. 10:22).

The wondrous power of the blood of Christ removes all fear

when I draw near to the *"consuming fire"* (Heb. 12:29) of my most holy God. Yes, I am a sinner. But by that wondrous offering of Christ *"once for all"* (Heb. 9:12), my sin is forever put away. I am *"perfected"* (Heb. 10:14) and *"justified"* (Rom. 3:24). On the ground of that blood so precious and satisfying to God, I can march boldly into the very presence of God.

The Tree of Life

But the blood of Christ has still further power. Read Revelation 22:14: *"Blessed are those who do His commandments, that they may have the right to the tree of life, and may enter through the gates into the city."* Then read Revelation 7:14: *"These are the ones who come out of the great tribulation, and washed their robes and made them white in the blood of the Lamb."* We see that it is in the blood of Christ that robes are washed. The blood of Christ, therefore, has the power to give those who believe in Him a right to the Tree of Life and entrance into the City of God.

Sin shut men away from the Tree of Life and out of Eden. (See Genesis 3:22–24.) The shed blood of Christ reopens the way to the Tree of Life and to the New Jerusalem. The blood of Christ regains all that Adam lost by sin and brings us much more than was lost.

We Need His Atoning Blood

Do you fully appreciate the blood of Christ? Have you let it have the power that it ought to have? Some today try to devise a theology that leaves out the blood of Christ. But Christianity without the atoning blood is a Christianity without mercy for the sinner, without settled peace for the conscience, without genuine forgiveness, without justification, without cleansing, without boldness in approaching God, *without power*. It is not Christianity, but the Devil's own counterfeit.

If we desire fullness of power in Christian life and service, we must know the power of the blood of Christ, for it is what brings us pardon, justification, and boldness in our approach to God. We cannot experience the power of the Spirit until we know the power of the blood. We certainly cannot experience the power of prayer until we know the power of that blood by which alone we can approach God.

Those who ignore the fundamental truth about the blood are trying to build a lofty superstructure without a firm foundation. It is bound to tumble. We must begin with the blood if we are to go on to the "Holy of Holies." Every priest who entered the Holy Place first met the bronze altar where blood was shed. There is no other way of entrance there.

If we do not learn the lesson of this chapter, it is useless for us to try to learn the lessons of chapters three and four. To everyone who wishes to know the power of the Spirit, we first put the question: "Do you know the power of the blood?"

Chapter 3

The Power of the Holy Spirit

◆

The Holy Spirit is the Person who imparts to believers the power that *"belongs to God"* (Ps. 62:11). The Holy Spirit's work in believers is to take what belongs to God and make it theirs. All the manifold power of God belongs to the children of God as their birthright in Christ: *"For all things are yours"* (1 Cor. 3:21). But all that belongs to believers as their birthright in Christ becomes theirs in actual possession through the Holy Spirit's work in them as individuals.

Claim the Spirit

We obtain the fullness of power that God has provided for us in Christ to the same extent that we understand and claim the Holy Spirit's work for ourselves. Many in the church claim for themselves only a small part of what God has made possible for them in Christ because they know so little of what the Holy Spirit can do—and longs to do—for us. To find out what the Holy Spirit has the power to do in men, let us study the Word of God.

We will not go far before we discover that the same work that we see ascribed in one place to the power of the Word is in other places credited to the Holy Spirit. The explanation of this is simple. The Word of God is the instrument through which the Holy Spirit does His work. The Word of God is *"the sword of the Spirit"* (Eph. 6:17).

The Word of God is also the seed the Spirit sows and quickens. (See Luke 8:11; 1 Peter 1:23.) The Word of God is the instrument of all the varied operations of the Holy Spirit (as seen in Chapter 1). Therefore, if we wish the Holy Spirit to do His work in our hearts, we must study the Word. If we wish Him to do His work in the hearts of others, we must give them the Word.

The Sword of the Spirit

The Word will not do the work alone. The Spirit Himself must use the Word because when He uses His own sword, its real strength, keenness, and power are manifested. God's work is accomplished by the Spirit through the Word.

The secret of effective Christian living is knowing the power of the Spirit through the Word. The secret of effective Christian service is using the Word in the power of the Spirit.

Some believers magnify the Spirit but neglect the Word. This will not do because fanaticism and groundless enthusiasm are the result. Others seek to magnify the Word but largely ignore the Spirit. This will not do either. It leads to dead orthodoxy and to truth without life and power. The true course is to recognize both the instrumental power of the Word through which the Holy Spirit works and the living, personal power of the Holy Spirit who acts through the Word.

But let us get directly to the consideration of our subject: What does the Holy Spirit have the power to do?

The Spirit Reveals Christ

Read 1 Corinthians 12:3: *"Therefore I make known to you that no one speaking by the Spirit of God calls Jesus accursed, and no one can say that Jesus is Lord except by the Holy Spirit."* The Holy Spirit has the power to reveal Jesus Christ and His glory to man. When Jesus spoke of the Spirit's coming, He said, *"But when the Helper comes, whom I shall send to you from the Father, the Spirit of truth who proceeds from the Father, He will testify of Me"* (John 15:26). It is only by His testimony that men will ever come to a true knowledge of Christ.

You can send men to the Word to get knowledge of Christ. But it is only through the Holy Spirit's illumination of the Word that men can get a real, living knowledge of Christ. *"No one can say that Jesus is Lord except by the Holy Spirit"* (1 Cor. 12:3).

For men to get a true knowledge of Jesus Christ so that they will believe in Him and be saved, seek the testimony of the Holy Spirit for them. Neither your testimony nor that of the Word alone will suffice, though it is your testimony or that of the Word that the Spirit uses.

The Spirit Bears Witness

Unless your testimony is illuminated by the Holy Spirit and He Himself testifies, they will not believe. It was not merely Peter's words about Christ that convinced the Jews at Pentecost. It was the Spirit Himself bearing witness. If you wish men to know the truth about Jesus, do not depend on your own powers of explanation and persuasion, but give yourself to the Holy Spirit and ask for His testimony.

If you desire to know Jesus with a true and living knowledge, seek the witness of the Spirit through the Word. Many people have correct doctrinal conceptions of Christ through studying the Word long before they have true, personal knowledge of Christ through the testimony of the living Spirit.

The Spirit Convicts of Sin

Now let us read John 16:8–11:

And when He has come, He will convict the world of sin, and of righteousness, and of judgment: of sin, because they do not believe in Me; of righteousness, because I go to My Father and you see Me no more; of judgment, because the ruler of this world is judged.

The Holy Spirit has the power to convict the world of sin. This is closely connected with His power to reveal Jesus, for it is by showing Christ's glory and His righteousness that the Holy Spirit convicts us of sin, righteousness, and judgment. Note the sin of which the Holy Spirit convicts: *"of sin, because they do not believe in Me."* It was so at Pentecost, as we see in Acts 2:36–37. You can never convict any man of sin because that is the work of the Holy Spirit. You can reason and reason, but you will fail.

The Holy Spirit, however, can do it very quickly. Have you ever had the experience of wondering why, after showing a man passage after passage of Scripture, he remained unmoved? You were trying to convict the man of sin by yourself, rather than looking in your powerlessness to the mighty Spirit of God to do it. When you let the Spirit of God do the work, conviction comes. The Spirit can convince the most indifferent person, as experience has proven again and again.

But it is through us that the Spirit produces conviction. In John 16:7–8, we read:

> *Nevertheless I tell you the truth. It is to your advantage that I go away; for if I do not go away, the Helper will not come to you; but if I depart, I will send Him to you. And when He has come, He will convict the world of sin, and of righteousness, and of judgment.*

It was the Spirit sent to Peter and the rest who convicted the three thousand on the Day of Pentecost. (See Acts 2:4–37.) It is ours to preach the Word and to look to the Holy Spirit to produce conviction.

The Spirit Renews

In Titus 3:5, we read: *"Not by works of righteousness which we have done, but according to His mercy He saved us, through the washing of regeneration and renewing of the Holy Spirit."*

The Holy Spirit has the power to renew men. Regeneration is His work. He can take a man dead in trespasses and sins and make him alive. He can transform the man whose mind is blind to the truth of God, whose will is at enmity with God and set on sin, and whose affections are corrupt and vile. He imparts God's nature to him so that he thinks God's thoughts, wills what God wills, loves what God loves, and hates what God hates.

I never lose hope for a man when I remember the regenerative power of the Holy Spirit, for I have seen it manifested again and again in the most hardened and hopeless cases. But it is through us that the Holy Spirit regenerates others. (See 1 Corinthians 4:15.)

As we learned in Chapter 1, the Word has the power to re-generate, but not on its own. It must be made a living thing in the heart by the power of the Holy Spirit. No amount of preaching and no amount of mere study of the Word will regen-erate without the assistance of the Holy Spirit. Just as we are utterly dependent on the work of Christ for our justification, so we are utterly dependent on the work of the Holy Spirit for re-generation.

The Indwelling Spirit

When one is born of the Spirit, the Spirit takes up His abode in him. (See 1 Corinthians 3:16; 6:19.) The Holy Spirit dwells in everyone who belongs to Christ (Rom. 8:9). We may not have surrendered our lives utterly to this indwelling Spirit, we may be very far from being full of the Spirit, and we may be very imperfect Christians. But if we have been born again, the Spirit dwells in us, just as He did in the Corinthians, who were certainly far from being perfect Christians.

What a glorious thought it is that the Holy Spirit dwells in me! But it is also a very solemn thought as well. If my body is the temple of the Holy Spirit (1 Cor. 6:19), I certainly should not defile it, as many professed Christians do. Bearing in mind that our bodies are temples of the Holy Spirit would solve many problems that perplex young Christians.

The Spirit Gives Satisfaction

We find a further thought about the power of the Holy Spirit in John 4:14: *"But whoever drinks of the water that I shall give him will never thirst. But the water that I shall give him will become in him a fountain of water springing up into ever-lasting life."* You may not see at first that this verse has any-thing to do with the Holy Spirit, but compare it with the seventh chapter of John, verses thirty-seven and thirty-nine, and it will be evident that the water here symbolizes the Holy Spirit. So the Holy Spirit then has the power to give abiding and everlasting satisfaction.

Of every worldly joy, it must be said, *"Whoever drinks of this water will thirst again"* (John 4:13). The world can never satisfy. But the Holy Spirit has the power to satisfy every longing of the soul. The Holy Spirit, and He alone, can satisfy the human heart. If you give yourself up to the Holy Spirit's inflowing—or rather upspringing—in your heart, you will never thirst. You will not long for worldly gain or honor.

The Holy Spirit has poured the unutterable joy and indescribable satisfaction of His living water into many souls. Have you felt this living fountain within you? Is it springing up without restraint into everlasting life?

The Spirit Offers Freedom

In Romans 8:2, we read: *"For the law of the Spirit of life in Christ Jesus has made me free from the law of sin and death."* The Holy Spirit has the power to set us *"free from the law of sin and death."* What *"the law of sin and death"* is can be found in the preceding chapter. (See Romans 7:9–24.) Read this description carefully. We all know this *"law of sin and death"*; we have all been in bondage to it. Some of us are still in bondage to it, but we do not need to be.

God has provided a way of escape by the Holy Spirit's power. When we give up the hopeless struggle of trying to overcome *"the law of sin and death"* with our own strength and in utter helplessness surrender to the Holy Spirit to do everything for us—when we walk in His blessed power rather than in the power of the flesh—then He sets us *"free from the law of sin and death."*

Many professing Christians today live as is described in Romans 7. Some go so far as to maintain that the normal Christian life is a life of constant defeat. This would be true if we were left to ourselves, for in ourselves, we are *"carnal, sold under sin"* (v. 14). But we are not left to ourselves. The Holy Spirit undertakes for us what we fail to do ourselves (Rom. 8:2–4).

The True Christian Life

Romans 8 gives us a picture of the true Christian life. This life is possible, and God expects it from each one of us. The commandment comes to this life (see Romans 7), but the mighty Spirit comes also, working obedience and victory.

The flesh is still in us, but we are not in the flesh. (See Romans 8:9, 12–13.) We do not live after it. We walk *"according to the Spirit"* (v. 4). *"By the Spirit* [we] *put to death the deeds of the body"* (v. 13). We *"walk in the Spirit"* and do *"not fulfill the lust of the flesh"* (Gal. 5:16).

It is our privilege, in the Spirit's power, to have daily, hourly, and constant victory over the flesh and over sin. But the victory is not in ourselves, not in any strength of our own. Left to ourselves, deserted by the Spirit of God, we would be as helpless as ever. It is all in the Spirit's power. If we try to take one step in our own strength, we will fail.

Has the Holy Spirit set you *"free from the law of sin and death"* (Rom. 8:2)? Will you let Him do it now? Simply give up all self-effort to stop sinning. Believe in the divine power of the Holy Spirit to set you free, and give yourself to Him to do it. He will not fail you. Then you can triumphantly cry with Paul: *"The law of the Spirit of life in Christ Jesus has made me free from the law of sin and death"* (Rom. 8:2).

The Spirit Strengthens the Believer

We find a closely allied but larger thought about the Holy Spirit's power in Ephesians 3:16: *"That He would grant you, according to the riches of His glory, to be strengthened with might through His Spirit in the inner man."*

The Holy Spirit strengthens the believer with power in the inner man. The result of this strengthening is seen in Ephesians 3:17–19. Here, the power of the Spirit manifests itself not merely in giving us victory over sin, but in Christ's dwelling in our hearts (v. 17); our being *"rooted and grounded in love"* (v. 17); and our being made *"able to comprehend with all the saints what is the width and length and depth and height; to know the love of Christ which passes knowledge"* (vv. 18–19). It culminates in our being *"filled with all the fullness of God"* (v. 19).

The Spirit Guides the Life

We find a further thought about the Holy Spirit's power in Romans 8:14: *"For as many as are led by the Spirit of God, these are sons of God."* The Holy Spirit has the power to lead us into a holy life—a life as *"sons of God,"* a godlike life. Not only does the Holy Spirit give us the power to live a holy life that is pleasing to God, He takes us by the hand and leads us into that life.

All we must do is simply surrender ourselves completely to His leading and molding. Those who do this are not merely God's offspring (which all men are, according to Acts 17:28); neither are they merely God's children—these are *"sons of God."*

Later in the chapter, there is a new thought: *"The Spirit Himself bears witness with our spirit that we are children of God"* (Rom. 8:16). The Holy Spirit bears witness with the spirit of the believer that he is a child of God. Note that Paul did not say that the Spirit bears witness *to* our spirit, but *with* it—*"with our spirit"* is the exact force of the words used.

In other words, there are two who bear witness to our sonship: our spirits and the Holy Spirit bear witness together that we are children of God. How does the Holy Spirit bear His testimony to this fact? Galatians 4:6 answers this question: *"Because you are sons, God has sent forth the Spirit of His Son into your hearts, crying out, 'Abba, Father!'"* The Holy Spirit Himself enters our hearts and cries, *"Abba, Father."*

Note the order of the Spirit's work in Romans 8:2, 4, 13–14, 16. He bears witness in us (v. 16) only when *"the law of the Spirit of life in Christ Jesus has made* [us] *free from the law of sin and death"* (v. 2), so that *"the righteous requirement of the law might be fulfilled in us who do not walk according to the flesh but according to the Spirit"* (v. 4); only when we *"by the Spirit...put to death the deeds of the body"* (v. 13) and when we are surrendered to the Spirit's leading (v. 14) can we expect to experience the promise in verse 16 and have the clear assurance that comes from the Spirit of God testifying together with our spirits *"that we are children of God"* (v. 16).

Many believers expect this witness of the Holy Spirit to precede their surrendering wholly to God and their confessing Jesus Christ as their Savior and Lord, which is incorrect. The testimony of the Holy Spirit to our sonship comes only after all this is done.

The Spirit Gives Christlikeness

An exceedingly important thought about the Holy Spirit's power is found in Galatians 5:22–23: *"But the fruit of the Spirit is love, joy, peace, longsuffering, kindness, goodness, faithfulness, gentleness, self-control. Against such there is no law."*

The Holy Spirit brings forth Christlike graces of character in the believer. (See Romans 14:17; 15:13; 5:5.) All real beauty of character—all real Christlikeness in us—is the Holy Spirit's work. It is His *"fruit."* He bears it; not we. Note that these graces are not said to be the *fruits* of the Spirit; they are the *"fruit."* All the various manifestations of the Holy Spirit have the same origin. Therefore, not just some of them, but all, will appear in everyone in whom the Holy Spirit is given full control.

It is a beautiful life that is set forth in these verses. Every word is worthy of earnest study and profound meditation: *love, joy, peace, longsuffering, kindness, goodness, faithfulness, gentleness, self-control.* The Christ-life is the life we long for. It is not natural to us, and it is not attainable by any effort of the flesh. The life that is natural for us is described in the three preceding verses (vv. 19–21).

But when we give the indwelling Spirit full control, realizing the evilness of the flesh and giving up ever attaining anything good in its power—when we come to the end of self—then these holy graces of character become His fruit in us.

If you desire these graces in your character and in your life, renounce yourself and all your attempts at holiness. Then let the Holy Spirit, who dwells in you, take full control and bear His own glorious fruit. Live in the reality expressed (from another point of view) in Galatians 2:20:

> *I have been crucified with Christ; it is no longer I who live, but Christ lives in me; and the life which I now live in the flesh I live by faith in the Son of God, who loved me and gave Himself for me.*

The Flesh Never Bears Christlikeness

Realize from the start that the flesh can never bear the fruit of the Spirit, that you can never attain these things on your own. Those who study ethical philosophy would like us to believe that the flesh can be cultivated until it bears this fruit. But it cannot be done until thorns can be made to bear figs, and a bramble bush bear grapes. (See Luke 6:44; Matthew 12:33.)

Others talk about character building. Nothing is essentially wrong with this, but if you let the Holy Spirit do the building, it becomes not so much building as fruit-bearing. There is also a good deal said about cultivating graces of character. But we must always bear in mind that the way to cultivate the true graces of character is by submitting ourselves entirely to the Spirit. This is *"sanctification of the Spirit"* (1 Pet. 1:2).

We turn now to another aspect of the power of the Holy Spirit.

The Spirit Guides into Truth

However, when He, the Spirit of truth, has come, He will guide you into all truth; for He will not speak on His own authority, but whatever He hears He will speak; and He will tell you things to come. (John 16:13)

The Holy Spirit has the power to guide the believer *"into all truth."* This promise was originally made to the apostles, but the apostles themselves applied it to all believers (1 John 2:20, 27).

It is the privilege of each of us to be *"taught by God"* (John 6:45). Each believer is independent of human teachers. *"You do not need that anyone teach you"* (1 John 2:27). This does not mean, of course, that we may not learn much from others who are themselves taught by the Holy Spirit. If John had thought that, he never would have written this epistle to teach others.

The man who can be most fully taught by God is the one who is most ready to listen to what God has taught others. This does not mean that when we are taught by God we are independent of the Word of God. The Word is the very place to which the Spirit leads His pupils, and the instrument through which He teaches them. (See John 6:63; Ephesians 5:18–19; 6:17; Colossians 3:16.)

But we should not be dependent on men, even though we can learn much from them. We have a divine teacher: the Holy

Spirit. We will never truly know the truth until we are taught by Him. No amount of mere human teaching, no matter who our teachers may be, will give us a correct understanding of the truth. Not even a diligent study of the Word, either in English or in the original languages, will give us a real understanding of the truth. We must be taught by the Holy Spirit.

The one who is thus taught, even if he does not know a word of Greek or Hebrew, will understand the truth of God better than someone who does know the original languages but who is not taught by the Spirit. The Spirit will guide the one He teaches *"into all truth"* (John 16:13)—not in a day, a week, or a year, but one step at a time.

There are two especially important aspects of the Spirit's teaching: *"He will tell you things to come"* (John 16:13). Many say we can know nothing about the future, that all our thoughts on that subject are nothing but guesswork. Anyone taught by the Spirit knows better than that. Second, *"He will glorify Me, for He will take of what is Mine and declare it to you"* (v. 14). The Holy Spirit's special area of instruction, with the believer as well as the unbeliever, is to reveal Christ and glorify Him. Many fear to emphasize this truth about the Holy Spirit because it might overshadow Christ. Actually, though, no one magnifies Christ as the Holy Spirit does.

We will never understand Christ, nor see His glory, until the Holy Spirit reveals Him to us. Merely listening to sermons and lectures, even studying the Word, will never present Christ as He can. And He is longing to do so. Let the Holy Spirit do His glorious work in you. Christ is so different when the Holy Spirit magnifies Him by taking the things of Christ and showing them to us (John 16:15).

The Spirit Teaches Christ's Words

Turning to John 14:26, we again find the Holy Spirit's power to teach, but with an added thought: *"But the Helper, the Holy Spirit, whom the Father will send in My name, He will teach you all things, and bring to your remembrance all things that I said to you."* The Holy Spirit has the power to bring to our remembrance the words of Christ.

This promise was made primarily to the apostles, and it guarantees the accuracy of their report of what Jesus said. But the Holy Spirit works similarly in each believer who expects it of Him and looks to Him to do it.

He brings to mind the teachings and the words of Christ, just when we need them, for either the necessities of our own life or our Christian service. How often have we been distressed about something or lost as to what to say to someone we wanted to help. Just then, the Scripture we needed—probably some passage we had not thought of for a long time, perhaps never thought of in this connection—was brought to mind. It was the Holy Spirit who did this, and He is ready to do it even more when we expect it of Him.

It is not without significance that in the next verse, after making this great promise, Jesus said, *"Peace I leave with you, My peace I give to you"* (John 14:27). Look to the Holy Spirit to bring the right words to remembrance at the right time, and you will have peace. This is the way to remember Scripture just when you need it and just the Scripture you need.

The Spirit Reveals Mysteries

Closely related to what has been said in the two preceding sections is the power of the Holy Spirit as seen in 1 Corinthians 2:10–14:

But God has revealed them to us through His Spirit. For the Spirit searches all things, yes, the deep things of God. For what man knows the things of a man except the spirit of the man which is in him? Even so no one knows the things of God except the Spirit of God. Now we have received, not the spirit of the world, but the Spirit who is from God, that we might know the things that have been freely given to us by God. These things we also speak, not in words which man's wisdom teaches but which the Holy Spirit teaches, comparing spiritual things with spiritual. But the natural man does not receive the things of the Spirit of God, for they are foolishness to him; nor can he know them, because they are spiritually discerned.

In these verses, we see a twofold work of the Spirit: First, the Holy Spirit reveals to us the deep things of God that are hidden from, and foolishness to, the natural man. It is preeminently to the apostles the Spirit did this, but His work is not limited to them. Second, the Holy Spirit interprets His own revelation, or imparts power to discern, know, and appreciate what He has taught.

Not only is the Holy Spirit the Author of revelation—the written Word of God—He is also the Interpreter of what He has revealed. How much more interesting and useful any profound book becomes when we have the author of the book right at hand to interpret it for us!

This is what we may always have when we study the Bible. The Author—the Holy Spirit—is right at hand to interpret. To understand the Bible, we must look to Him. Then, even the darkest places become clear. We need to pray often with the psalmist, *"Open my eyes, that I may see wondrous things from Your law"* (Ps. 119:18).

It is not enough for us to have the objective revelation of the written Word. We must also have the inward illumination of the Holy Spirit to enable us to comprehend it. Trying to comprehend a spiritual revelation with the natural understanding is a great mistake.

Consider a man who has no sense of aesthetics expecting to appreciate a fine painting simply because he is not color blind. It would be the same for a man who was not filled with the Spirit to try to understand the Bible simply because he understood the grammar and the vocabulary of the language in which the Bible was written.

I would no more think of allowing a man to teach art merely because he understood paints than of allowing him to teach the Bible merely because he understood Greek or Hebrew.

Utter Insufficiency

Not only must we recognize the utter insufficiency and worthlessness of our own righteousness (the lesson of the opening chapters of Romans), but also the utter insufficiency and worthlessness of our own wisdom in comprehending the things of God (the lesson of the first epistle to the Corinthians).

The Jews had a revelation from the Spirit, but they failed to depend on Him to interpret it for them, so they went astray. The whole evangelical church realizes the utter insufficiency of man's righteousness, theoretically at least. Now it needs to be taught, and made to feel, the utter insufficiency of man's wisdom. That is perhaps the lesson this century of arrogant, intellectual conceit needs more than any other. To understand God's Word, we must totally disregard our own wisdom and rest in utter dependence on the Spirit of God to interpret it for us. (See Matthew 11:25.)

Only when we put away our own righteousness will we find the righteousness of God. (See Philippians 3:4–9; Romans 10:3.) Only when we put away our own wisdom will we find the wisdom of God. (See 1 Corinthians 3:18; Matthew 11:25; 1 Corinthians 1:25–28.) And only when we put away our own strength will we find the strength of God. (See Isaiah 40:29; 2 Corinthians 12:9; 1 Corinthians 1:27–28.)

Emptying must precede filling. Self must be poured out so that Christ may be poured in. We must be taught daily by the Holy Spirit to understand the Word of God. I cannot depend today on the fact that the Spirit taught me yesterday. Each new contact with the Word must be in the power of the Spirit. That the Holy Spirit once illumined our minds to grasp a certain passage is not enough. He must do so each time we confront that passage.

Andrew Murray, in his book *The Spirit of Christ,* states this truth well. He said, "Each time you come to the Word in study, in hearing a sermon or reading a religious book, there should be a definite act of self-relinquishment denying your own wisdom and yielding yourself in faith to the Divine Teacher."

The Spirit Helps Us Communicate

The Holy Spirit not only has the power to teach us the truth, but He also helps us communicate that truth to others. We see this brought out again and again:

And I, brethren, when I came to you, did not come with excellence of speech or of wisdom declaring to you the testimony of God. For I determined not to know anything among you except Jesus Christ and Him crucified. I was with you in weakness, in fear, and in much trembling. And my speech and my preaching were not with persuasive words of human wisdom, but in demonstration of the Spirit and of power, that your faith should not be in the wisdom of men but in the power of God. (1 Cor. 2:1–5)

Our gospel did not come to you in word only, but also in power, and in the Holy Spirit. (1 Thess. 1:5)

But you shall receive power when the Holy Spirit has come upon you. (Acts 1:8)

The Holy Spirit enables the believer to communicate powerfully to others the truth he himself has been taught. We not only need the Holy Spirit to reveal and then to interpret the truth He has revealed, we also need Him to enable us to effectively communicate that truth to others. We need Him every step of the way.

One great cause of real failure in the ministry, even when there is apparent success (not only in the ministry, but in all forms of Christian service), is the attempt to teach what the Holy Spirit has taught us by *"persuasive words of human wisdom"* (1 Cor. 2:4), human logic, rhetoric, or eloquence. What is needed is Holy Spirit power, a *"demonstration of the Spirit and of power"* (v. 4).

Causes of Failure

There are three causes of failure in Christian work. First, a message other than the message that the Holy Spirit has revealed in the Word is taught. Men will preach science, art, philosophy, sociology, history, experience, etc., but not the Word of God as found in the Holy Spirit's Book—the Bible. Second, the Spirit's message, the Bible, is studied without the Spirit's illumination. Third, the Bible is taught to others with *"persuasive words of human wisdom"* and not *"in demonstration of the Spirit and of power"* (1 Cor. 2:4).

We must be absolutely dependent on the Holy Spirit when it comes to God's Word. He must teach us how to speak as well as what to speak. His must be the power as well as the message.

The Spirit Teaches Prayer

The Holy Spirit has the power to teach us how to pray. In Jude 20, we read: *"But you, beloved, building yourselves up on your most holy faith, praying in the Holy Spirit."* And again in Ephesians 6:18: *"Praying always...in the Spirit."*

The Holy Spirit guides the believer in prayer. The disciples did not know how to pray as they should, so they came to Jesus and said, *"Lord, teach us to pray"* (Luke 11:1). *"We do not know what we should pray for as we ought"* (Rom. 8:26), but we have another Helper right at hand to help us (John 14:16–17). *"The Spirit also helps in our weaknesses"* (Rom. 8:26).

He teaches us to pray. True prayer is prayer *"in the Spirit"* (Eph. 6:18), the prayer that the Spirit inspires and directs. When we come into God's presence to pray, we should recognize our ignorance of what we should pray for or how we should pray. With this awareness, we should then look to the Holy Spirit and cast ourselves utterly on Him to direct our prayers.

Pray in the Spirit

Rushing heedlessly into God's presence and asking the first thing that comes to our minds, or what someone asks us to pray for, is not praying *"in the Spirit"* and is not true prayer. We must wait for and surrender ourselves to the Holy Spirit. The prayer that the Holy Spirit inspires is the prayer that God the Father answers.

From Romans 8:26–27, we learn that the longings the Holy Spirit creates in our hearts are often too deep for utterance; too deep, apparently, for clear and definite comprehension on the part of the believer himself, in whom the Holy Spirit is working. God Himself must search the heart to know *"what the mind of the Spirit is"* (v. 27) in these unuttered and unutterable longings. But God does know *"what the mind of the Spirit is."* He does know what those Spirit-given longings mean, even if we do not.

These longings are *"according to the will of God"* (v. 28), and He grants them. He is *"able to do exceedingly abundantly above all that we ask or think, according to the power that works in us"* (Eph. 3:20). Other times, the Spirit's leadings in prayer are so plain that we *"pray with the spirit, and...with the understanding"* (1 Cor. 14:15).

The Spirit Offers Thanks

The Holy Spirit also has the power to lead our hearts in acceptable thanksgiving to God. Paul said:

> *Be filled with the Spirit, speaking to one another in psalms and hymns and spiritual songs, singing and making melody in your heart to the Lord, giving thanks always for all things to God the Father in the name of our Lord Jesus Christ.* (Eph. 5:18–20)

Not only does the Spirit teach us to pray, He also teaches us to give thanks. One of the most prominent characteristics of the Spirit-filled life is thanksgiving. True thanksgiving is *"to God the Father in the name of our Lord Jesus Christ"* and in the Holy Spirit.

The Spirit Inspires Worship

The Holy Spirit has the power to inspire worship that is acceptable to God in the heart of the believer. *"For we are the circumcision, who worship God in the Spirit, rejoice in Christ Jesus, and have no confidence in the flesh"* (Phil. 3:3). Prayer is not worship; thanksgiving is not worship. Worship is a definite act of the believer in relation to God. Worship is bowing before God in adoring acknowledgment and contemplation of Him.

Someone has said, "In our prayers we are taken up with our needs, in our thanksgivings we are taken up with our blessings, and in our worship we are taken up with Himself." There is no true and acceptable worship except what the Holy Spirit inspires and guides. *"For the Father is seeking such to worship Him"* (John 4:23).

The flesh seeks to enter every sphere of life. It has its worship as well as its lust. The worship that the flesh prompts is an abomination to God. Not all earnest and honest worship is worship *"in the Spirit"* (Phil. 3:3). A person's worship may be very

51

honest and earnest; still, it may not be led by the Holy Spirit, so it remains in the flesh. Even where there is great loyalty to the letter of the Word, worship may not be *"in the Spirit."*

To worship properly, we must *"have no confidence in the flesh"* (Phil. 3:3). We must recognize the utter inability of the flesh (the natural self, as contrasted with the divine Spirit, who dwells in and molds the believer) to worship acceptably. We must also realize the danger of the flesh—self—intruding into our worship. In complete self-distrust and self-denial, we must ask the Holy Spirit to lead us to worship correctly. Just as we must renounce our self-worth and look to the crucified Christ for justification, we must renounce our self-righteousness and give ourselves completely to the Holy Spirit for His guidance in praying, giving thanks, worshipping, living, and in everything else that we do.

The Spirit Calls to the Ministry

Let us consider the Holy Spirit's power as a guide. In Acts 13:2–4, we read:

> As they ministered to the Lord and fasted, the Holy Spirit said, "Now separate to Me Barnabas and Saul for the work to which I have called them." Then, having fasted and prayed, and laid hands on them, they sent them away. So, being sent out by the Holy Spirit, they went down to Seleucia, and from there they sailed to Cyprus.

People are called and sent forth by the Holy Spirit to particular types of work. He not only calls in a general way into Christian work but also selects the specific work and points it out. "Should I go to China, to Africa, or to India?" a believer might ask. You cannot answer that question for yourself, and no one else can answer it for you. Besides, not every Christian is called to China or Africa or any other foreign field. God alone knows whether He wishes you to go to any of these places, and He is willing to show you.

How does the Holy Spirit call? The passage before us does not say. It is, presumably, intentionally silent on this point to prevent our thinking that He must always call in precisely the same way. Nothing indicates that He spoke in an audible voice, much less that He made His will known in any of the fantastic ways in which some profess to discern His leading (as by opening the Bible at random). But the important point is that He made His will clearly known.

He is as willing to make His will clearly known to us today. The great need in present-day Christian work is men and women whom the Holy Spirit calls and sends forth. We have plenty of people whom *men* have called and sent forth, and we have far too many *who have called themselves.* How do we receive the Holy Spirit's call? By desiring it, seeking it, waiting on the Lord for it, and expecting it. *"As they ministered to the Lord and fasted"* (v. 2), the record reads.

Many Christians say they have never been called by the Spirit. How do they know that? Have they been listening for it? God often speaks in a still, small voice, which only the attentive ear can perceive. Have you definitely offered yourself to God to be used by Him? While no one should go to China or Africa unless he is clearly called, he should definitely offer himself to God to be used *somehow* by Him. He should then be ready for a call and listen carefully so that he hears it when it comes.

The Spirit Guides Us

In these verses, we learn something further about the Holy Spirit's power to guide us.

> *So he arose and went. And behold, a man of Ethiopia, a eunuch of great authority under Candace the queen of the Ethiopians, who had charge of all her treasury, and had come to Jerusalem to worship, was returning. And sitting in his chariot, he was reading Isaiah the prophet. Then the Spirit said to Philip, "Go near, and overtake this chariot."*
> (Acts 8:27–29)

And in Acts 16:6–7, we read:

> *Now when they had gone through Phrygia and the region of Galatia, they were forbidden by the Holy Spirit to preach*

the word in Asia. After they had come to Mysia, they tried to go into Bithynia, but the Spirit did not permit them.

The Holy Spirit guides us in our daily life and service, showing us where to go and where not to go, what to do and what not to do. It is possible for us to have the unerring guidance of the Holy Spirit at every turn in our lives.

For example, God does not expect an evangelist to speak to every person he meets. There are some to whom we should not speak. Time spent on them could be time taken from work that would be more to the glory of God. Doubtless, Philip met many people as he journeyed toward Gaza, before he met the one of whom the Spirit said, *"Go near, and overtake this chariot."*

In the same way, the Holy Spirit is ready to guide us in our personal work. He is also ready to guide us in all of our affairs—business, school, social life—everything. We can have God's wisdom if we desire it. There is no promise more simple and explicit than James 1:5: *"If any of you lacks wisdom, let him ask of God, who gives to all liberally and without reproach, and it will be given to him."*

The Way to Wisdom

How do we gain this wisdom? James 1:5–7 answers this question. There are really five steps:

(1) We must be conscious of and fully admit our own inability to decide wisely. Not only the sinfulness, but the wisdom of the flesh, must be renounced.

(2) We must sincerely desire to know God's way and be willing to do God's will. This is a point of fundamental importance. Here we find the reason why many believers do not know God's will and do not have the Spirit's guidance. They are simply not willing to do whatever the Spirit leads them to do. It is the *"humble He guides in justice, and the humble He teaches His way"* (Ps. 25:9). The Christian who *"wants to do His will"* is the Christian who *"shall know"* (John 7:17).

(3) We must definitely *ask* for guidance.

(4) We must confidently *expect* guidance. *"Let him ask in faith, with no doubting"* (James 1:6).

(5) We must follow, step by step, as the guidance comes. Just how it will come, no one can tell, but it will come. It may come with only one step made clear at a time. But that is all we really need to know. Too many believers remain in darkness because they do not know what God wants them to do next week, next month, or next year. To know just the next step is enough. Take it, and then He will show you the next. (See Numbers 9:17–23.)

God's Way Is Made Clear

God's guidance is clear guidance (John 1:5). You may, at some point, believe the Spirit is leading you to do a particular thing, but you are not certain. As God's child, you have a right to be sure. Go to Him and say, "Heavenly Father, please let me know if this is Your will, and I will gladly do it." He will answer you, and you should do nothing until He does.

However, we have no right to dictate to God how He should give His guidance to us. Although we may ask for and expect wisdom, we may not dictate how it is to be given. (See 1 Corinthians 12:11.)

The Spirit Gives Boldness

There is one more dimension to the Holy Spirit's power. Read Acts 4:31: *"And when they had prayed, the place where they were assembled together was shaken; and they were all filled with the Holy Spirit, and they spoke the word of God with boldness."* The Holy Spirit has the power to give us boldness in our testimony for Christ.

Many people are naturally shy. They long to do something for Christ, but they are afraid. The Holy Spirit can make you bold if you will look to Him and trust Him to do it. It was He who turned the cowardly Peter into the one who fearlessly faced the Sanhedrin and rebuked their sin. (See Acts 4:8–12.)

The Power of the Spirit

Two things stand out in what has been said about the power of the Holy Spirit in the believer. First, we are utterly dependent on Him in every aspect of Christian life and service. Second, because of the Holy Spirit's work, God's provision for that life and service is a fullness of privilege that is open to even the humblest believer.

It is not of much importance what we are by nature—either intellectually, morally, spiritually, or even physically. What matters is what the Holy Spirit can do for us and what we will let Him do. The Holy Spirit often takes the one who seems the least promising and uses him far more than those who seem the most promising.

Christian life is not to be lived in the realm of natural temperament but in the realm of the Spirit. And Christian work is not to be done in the power of natural endowment but in the power of the Spirit. The Holy Spirit eagerly desires to do His whole work for each of us. He will do for us everything we will let Him do.

Chapter 4

The Power of Prayer

◆————————————◆

"**P**ower *belongs to God"* (Ps. 62:11), but all that belongs to God, we can have for the asking. God holds out His full hands and says:

Ask, and it will be given to you....If you then, being evil, know how to give good gifts to your children, how much more will your Father who is in heaven give good things to those who ask Him! (Matt. 7:7, 11)

The poverty and powerlessness of the average Christian find their explanation in the words of the apostle James: *"You do not have because you do not ask"* (James 4:2).

Because You Do Not Ask

"Why is it," a Christian may ask, "that I make such poor progress in my Christian life?"

"Neglect of prayer," God answers. *"You do not have because you do not ask."*

"Why is it there is so little fruit in my ministry?" asks many a discouraged minister.

"Neglect of prayer," God answers again. *"You do not have because you do not ask."*

"Why is it," both ministers and laymen are asking, "that there is so little power in my life and service?"

And again God answers: "Neglect of prayer. *'You do not have because you do not ask.'"*

God has provided a life of power for every child of His. He has put His own infinite power at our disposal and has proclaimed

57

over and over in a great variety of ways in His Word, *"Ask, and it will be given to you"* (Matt. 7:7; Luke 11:9). Thousands upon thousands have taken God at His word in this matter, and they have always found it true.

Power

The first Christians were men and women of tremendous power. For example, what power Peter and John had in their lives! What power they had in their work! There was opposition in those days—most determined, bitter, and relentless opposition, that, in comparison, would make any that we might encounter appear like child's play—but the work went right on.

We constantly read such statements as these: *"The Lord added to the church daily those who were being saved"* (Acts 2:47). *"However, many of those who heard the word believed; and the number of the men came to be about five thousand"* (Acts 4:4). *"And believers were increasingly added to the Lord, multitudes of both men and women"* (Acts 5:14).

The apostles themselves explained the secret of their irresistible power when they said, *"We will give ourselves continually to prayer and to the ministry of the word"* (Acts 6:4). But it was not only the leaders of that early church who had power in life and service, so did the rank and file. What a beautiful picture we have of their abounding love and fruitfulness! (See Acts 2:44–47; 4:32–37; 8:4; 11:19, 21.) The secret of this fullness of power in life and service is found in Acts 2:42: *"They continued steadfastly...in prayers."*

In the Lord's Presence

God delights to answer prayer: *"Call upon Me in the day of trouble,"* He cries. *"I will deliver you, and you shall glorify Me"* (Ps. 50:15). There is a place where strength can always be renewed; that place is the presence of the Lord: *"Those who wait on the LORD shall renew their strength; they shall mount up with wings like eagles, they shall run and not be weary, they shall walk and not faint"* (Isa. 40:31).

How little time the average Christian spends in prayer! We are too busy to pray, and so we are too busy to have power. We have a great deal of activity, but we accomplish little; there are many services, but few conversions. The power of God is lacking in our lives and in our work. We do not have because we do not ask (James 4:2).

Many Christians confess that they do not believe in the power of prayer. Some go so far as to contemptuously contrast the pray-ers with the doers—forgetting that in the history of the church, the real doers have been pray-ers. Without exception, those who have made the church's history glorious have been people of prayer.

A Mighty Weapon

Of those who do believe theoretically in the power of prayer, not one in a thousand realizes its power. How much time does the average Christian spend daily in prayer? How much time do you spend daily in prayer?

It was a masterstroke of the Devil to get the church and the ministry to lay aside the mighty weapon of prayer. He does not mind at all if the church expands her organizations and her deftly contrived machinery for the conquest of the world for Christ if she will only give up praying. He laughs softly as he looks at the church of today and says under his breath: "You can have your Sunday schools, your social organizations, your grand choirs, and even your revival efforts, as long as you do not bring the power of almighty God into them by earnest, persistent, and believing prayer."

The Devil is not afraid of organizations; he is only afraid of God, and organizations without prayer are organizations without God.

Our day is characterized by the increase of man's machinery and the decrease of God's power sought and obtained by prayer. But when men and women arise who believe in prayer and who pray in the way the Bible teaches us to pray, prayer accomplishes as much as it ever did. Today's prayer can do as much as the early church's prayer. All the infinite resources of God are at its command.

The Key to God's Grace

Prayer can do anything God can do, for the arm of God responds to its touch. Prayer is the key that opens the inexhaustible storehouses of divine grace and power. *"Ask, and it will be given to you"* (Matt. 7:7), cries our heavenly Father, as He swings the doors of His treasure-house open wide. The only limit to what prayer can do is what God can do. But all things are possible with God (Matt. 19:26); therefore, prayer is omnipotent.

Christian history and Christian biography demonstrate the truth of what the Word of God teaches about prayer. All through the history of the church, men and women have arisen in all ranks of life who believed with simple, childlike faith what the Bible teaches about prayer. They have asked, and they have received. But what are some of the definite things that prayer has the power to do?

Prayer Brings Knowledge

Prayer has the power to bring us a true knowledge of ourselves and our needs. Nothing is more necessary than for us to know ourselves: our weaknesses, our sinfulness, our selfishness; how that in us (that is to say, in our flesh) *"nothing good dwells"* (Rom. 7:18). Lives of power have usually begun with a revelation of the utter powerlessness and worthlessness of self.

So it was with Isaiah. In the year that King Uzziah died, he was brought face-to-face with God, saw himself, and cried out: *"Woe is me, for I am undone! Because I am a man of unclean lips"* (Isa. 6:5). Then a life of power began for Isaiah as God sent him forth to a mighty work. (See Isaiah 6:8–9.)

So it was with Moses. He met God at the burning bush, where he was emptied of his former self-confidence and saw his utter unfitness for the Lord's work. Then the Lord sent him to Pharaoh as a mighty man of power. (See Exodus 3:2, 5, 11; compare with his former self-confidence in Exodus 2:12–15.)

And so it was with Job. It was after Job met God and cried concerning himself, *"I abhor myself, and repent in dust and ashes"* (Job 42:6), that the Lord released him from captivity, giving him power to intercede for his friends and to bear abundant fruit.

If we are to have fullness of power, it is necessary that we see ourselves as we are by nature in the flesh. This is accomplished through prayer. If we sincerely pray the psalmist's prayer, *"Search me, O God, and know my heart; try me, and know my anxieties"* (Ps. 139:23), He will do it.

But to pray this prayer just once is not enough; it needs to be repeated daily. Then we will come to see ourselves as God sees us. There will be a consequent emptying of self, making room for the incoming of the power of God.

Prayer Cleanses from Sin

Prayer has the power to cleanse our hearts from sin—from secret sins and from known sins (Ps. 19:12–13). In answer to David's prayer after his disastrous fall, God washed him thoroughly from his iniquity and cleansed him from his sin (Ps. 51:2).

Many have fought for days, months, and years against sins that have been marring their lives and sapping their spiritual power. David finally went to God in prayer, persisting in that prayer until God blessed him, and he emerged a victor from the place of prayer.

In this way, sins that seem unconquerable have been laid in the dust. In this way, sins unknown to the sinner, which have robbed him of power, have been discovered in all their real hideousness and rooted out. Of course, as seen in the previous chapter, it is the Holy Spirit who sets us free from sin's power, but the Holy Spirit works in our lives in answer to our prayers (Luke 11:13).

Prayer Gives the Victory

Prayer has the power to hold us up in our goings and give us victory over temptation. *"Uphold my steps in Your paths, that my footsteps may not slip"* (Ps. 17:5), cried David. That is a prayer God is always ready to hear.

In His last hours, Jesus Himself said to His disciples: *"Pray that you may not enter into temptation"* (Luke 22:40). But the disciples did not heed the warning. They slept when they should have prayed, and when the temptation came in a few hours, they failed utterly. But Jesus Himself spent that night in prayer. The next day, when the fiercest temptation that ever attacked a man swept down on Him, He gloriously triumphed.

We can be victorious over every temptation if we will prepare for it and meet it with prayer. Many of us are led into defeat and denial of our Lord, as Peter was, by sleeping when we should have been praying.

Prayer Governs the Tongue

Prayer has the power to govern our tongues. Many Christians who have desired fullness of power in Christian life and service have found themselves kept from it by unruly tongues. They have learned by bitter experiences the truth of the words of James: *"No man can tame the tongue"* (James 3:8). But while no man can tame it, God can and will, in answer to believing prayer.

If one will earnestly pray in faith with David: *"Set a guard, O LORD, over my mouth; keep watch over the door of my lips"* (Ps. 141:3), God will do it. Many unruly tongues have been brought into subjection through this prayer.

Tongues that were as sharp as a sword have learned to speak words of gentleness and grace. True prayer can tame the unruliest tongue by which man or woman was ever cursed because true prayer brings into play the power of Him with whom nothing is impossible (Luke 1:37).

Prayer Brings Wisdom

Prayer has the power to bring us wisdom. The Word of God is very explicit on this point: *"If any of you lacks wisdom, let him ask of God, who gives to all liberally and without reproach, and it will be given to him"* (James 1:5). No promise could be more explicit than that. We can have wisdom, the wisdom of God Himself, whenever we ask for it.

God does not intend for His children to grope in darkness. He puts His own infinite wisdom at our disposal. All He desires is that we ask, and *"ask in faith"* (v. 6). Many of us are stumbling in our own foolishness, instead of walking in His wisdom, simply because we do not ask.

We can all have the joy of knowing and walking in God's way. It is His great desire to make it known to us. All we have to do is ask. (See Psalms 25:4; 86:11; 119:33; 143:10.)

Prayer Reveals the Word

Prayer has the power to open our eyes to behold wondrous things out of God's Word (Ps. 119:18). It is wonderful how the Bible opens up to someone who looks to God in earnest, believing prayer to interpret it for him. Difficulties vanish, obscure passages become clear as day, and old, familiar portions become luminous with new meaning, living with new power.

Prayer will do more than a theological education to make the Bible an open book. Only people of prayer can understand the Bible.

Prayer Brings the Spirit

Prayer has the power to bring the Holy Spirit in all His blessed power and manifold works into our hearts and lives. Jesus said, *"If you then, being evil, know how to give good gifts to your children, how much more will your heavenly Father give the Holy Spirit to those who ask Him!"* (Luke 11:13).

It was after the first disciples had *"continued with one accord in prayer and supplication"* (Acts 1:14) that *"they were all filled with the Holy Spirit"* (Acts 2:4). On another occasion *"when they had prayed, the place where they were assembled together was shaken; and they were all filled with the Holy Spirit"* (Acts 4:31).

When Peter and John came down to Samaria and found a company of young converts who had not yet experienced the fullness of the Holy Spirit's power, they *"prayed for them that they might receive the Holy Spirit....Then they laid hands on them, and they received the Holy Spirit"* (Acts 8:15, 17).

It was in answer to prayer that Paul expected the saints in Ephesus *"to be strengthened with might through His Spirit in the inner man"* (Eph. 3:16), and that *"the God of our Lord Jesus Christ, the Father of glory,"* would give them *"the spirit of wisdom and revelation in the knowledge of Him"* (Eph. 1:17).

Prayer brings the fullness of the Spirit's power into our hearts and lives. One great reason why so many of us have so little of the Holy Spirit's power in our lives and service is that we spend so little time and thought in prayer. We *"do not have because* [we] *do not ask"* (James 4:2).

Every precious, spiritual blessing in our own lives is given by our heavenly Father in answer to true prayer. Prayer promotes our spiritual growth and our likeness to Christ as almost nothing else can. The more time we spend in real, true prayer, the more we will grow in likeness to our Master.

One of the saintliest, most Christlike men who ever lived was John Welch, the son-in-law of John Knox, the great Scottish reformer. Welch is said to have given one-third of his time to prayer, and he often spent a whole night in prayer. Someone who knew him well, speaking of him after he had gone to be with Christ, said of him: "He was a type of Christ."

Many illustrations could be given of the power of prayer to bring our lives into conformity with Christ. In prayer, we gaze into the face of God and *"beholding as in a mirror the glory of the Lord, are being transformed into the same image from glory to glory"* (2 Cor. 3:18).

The Fullness of Power

But prayer has more to offer than the power to mold us spiritually into the likeness of Christ. It also has the power to bring the fullness of God's power into our work. When the apostolic church saw themselves confronted by obstacles that they could not surmount, *"they raised their voice to God with one accord"* (Acts 4:24). *"And when they had prayed"* (v. 31), the power came that swept away all obstacles.

Do you desire the power of God in your personal work, in your preaching, or in the training of your children? Pray for it. Hold on to God until you get it: *"Men always ought to pray and not lose heart"* (Luke 18:1).

I will never forget a sight I once witnessed. A woman of limited experience in public speaking was called on to address an audience filling the old Tremont Temple in Boston. It was a notable audience in its makeup as well as in its number. Many leading clergymen of all evangelical denominations were there, as well as men prominent in philanthropic and political affairs.

As the woman spoke, the audience was hushed, swayed, melted, and molded. Tears coursed down cheeks that were unaccustomed to them. The impression made on many was not only good, but permanent. It was an address of marvelous power. The secret of her success lay in the fact, known only to a few, that the woman had spent the whole of the previous night on her face before God in prayer.

Another example of the power of prayer happened in the 1630s. John Livingstone, a Scottish minister, is said to have spent a full night with several fellow Christians in prayer and discussion of spiritual matters. The next day, he preached in the kirk (church) of Shotts with such power that five hundred souls were saved.

Once, a mother came to me in great distress about her boy, one of the most incorrigible children I ever knew.

"What should I do?" she cried.

"Pray," I answered.

She did so, with new determination, sincerity, and faith. The change came soon, if not immediately, and the change continues to this day.

We can all have power in our work, if we will only believe God's promise regarding prayer. Go to Him often, with a holy boldness that knows He desires to answer you.

Prayer Brings Salvation

The man of prayer can have power in his own life and service as well as power in the life and service of others. Prayer has the power to bring salvation to others. *"If anyone sees his brother sinning a sin which does not lead to death, he will ask, and He will give him life for those who commit sin not leading to death"* (1 John 5:16). Prayer succeeds in attaining the salvation of others where every other effort fails.

There is little doubt that Saul of Tarsus, the most dangerous human enemy the church ever had, became Paul the apostle in answer to prayer. There have been countless instances where men and women, seemingly beyond all hope, have been converted in quite direct and unmistakable answer to prayer.

The Call for Revival

Prayer will bring blessing on a church. It will settle church quarrels, allay misunderstandings, root out heresy, and bring revivals down from God. Dr. Spencer, in his *Pastor's Sketches,* tells how a great revival was brought to his church by the prayers of a godly old man who was confined to his room due to lameness.

In Philadelphia during the pastorate of Dr. Thomas Skinner, three men of God came together in his study to pray. They wrestled in prayer. As a result, a powerful revival sprang up in that city.

One of the most notable, widespread, and enduring revivals ever known, according to an account given by Charles Finney, rose from the prayers of a humble woman who had never seen a revival but was led to ask God for one.

One of the church's greatest needs is to persevere in calling on God until He visits her again with a mighty outpouring of His Spirit. In past times, there have been great revivals with very little preaching or human effort, but there has never been a great and true revival without abundant prayer. Many modern so-called revivals are contrivances of man's self-effort. Genuine revivals are brought down by prayer.

Prayer Strengthens Ministers

Prayer will bring wisdom and power to ministers of the Gospel. Paul was a tremendous preacher and worker, but he so deeply felt the need of the prayers of God's people that he asked for them from every church to which he wrote, except for one (the backslidden church in Galatia).

It has been demonstrated again and again that prayer can transform a poor preacher into a good one. If you are not satisfied with your pastor, pray for him. Keep on praying for him, and you will soon have a better minister. If you think your present minister is a good one, you can make him even better with more prayer. Little do many Christians realize how much they can influence the powerful or powerless preaching their pastor gives them by their prayer or neglect of prayer.

The power of prayer reaches across the sea and around the earth. We can contribute to the conversion of the heathen and the evangelization of the world by our prayers. The prayers of believers in America have brought down the power of the Spirit in India and China.

Although more men and more money could certainly be used for mission work, its greatest need is prayer. It is a sad fact that much money given to mission work has been largely wasted, simply because there has not been enough prayer behind the giving.

Wait upon the Lord

There is mighty power in prayer. It has much to do with our obtaining fullness of power in Christian life and service. Whoever will not take time for prayer may as well give up all hope of obtaining the fullness of power God has for him. It is *"those who wait on the LORD"* who will *"renew their strength"* (Isa. 40:31).

Waiting on God means something more than spending a few minutes at the beginning and close of each day running through some memorized form of request. *"Wait on the LORD."* True prayer takes time and thought, but ultimately, it is the great time-saver.

No matter what the time or the place, if we are to know fullness of power, we must be men and women of prayer.

Chapter 5

The Power of a Surrendered Life

◆

"**P**ower belongs to God" (Ps. 62:11), but there is one condition on which that power is given to us. That condition is absolute surrender to Him. In Romans 6:13, we read: *"Do not present your members as instruments of unrighteousness to sin, but present yourselves to God as being alive from the dead, and your members as instruments of righteousness to God."* Again in Romans 6:22, we read: *"Having been set free from sin, and having become slaves of God, you have your fruit to holiness, and the end, everlasting life."* The great secret of blessedness and power is found in these verses.

Surrender to God

"Present yourselves to God"—the whole secret is found in those words. The word translated *"present"* means "to put at one's disposal." Put yourselves at God's disposal is the thought. In other words, surrender yourselves absolutely to God— become His property—and allow Him to use you however He wills. This is the wisest thing anyone can do for himself. It secures all the blessedness that is possible to man. Day by day, year by year, God's blessings will be given to him in ever increasing measure.

If anyone asks, "What is the one thing I can do in order to discover everything that God has for me?" the answer is very simple: surrender absolutely to God. Say to Him, "Heavenly Father, from now on, I have no will of my own. Let Your will be done in me, through me, by me, and regarding me, in all things. I put myself unreservedly in Your hands. Please do whatever You desire with me."

In response, God, who is infinite love, infinite wisdom, and infinite power, will do His very best with you. You may not immediately see that it is His best, but trust that it is, and sooner or later you will see it. God floods the heart of the believer who surrenders absolutely to Him with light and joy and fills his life with power. Absolute surrender to God is the secret of blessedness and power.

Results of Absolute Surrender

Look at what the Bible says will definitely result from absolute surrender. John 7:17 says, *"If anyone wants to do His will, he shall know concerning the doctrine."* Knowledge of the truth comes with the surrender of the will. There is nothing like it to clear one's spiritual vision. *"God is light and in Him is no darkness at all"* (1 John 1:5). Surrendering to Him opens our eyes to the light that He Himself is. It brings us at once in harmony with all truth.

Nothing blinds the spiritual vision like self-will or sin. I have seen questions that bothered men for years solved in a very short time when those men simply surrendered to God. What was as dark as night before became as light as day.

The Unsurrendered Will

An unsurrendered will lies behind almost all the skepticism in the world. Are you filled with doubts and questions? Would you like certainty instead of doubt? Yield yourself to God. Would you like to get your feet on the solid rock? Yield yourself to God. Are you trying to feel your way along in the dark? Would you rather see your path clearly before you? Yield yourself to God.

The greatest truths—eternal truths—cannot be learned by mere investigation and study. They cannot be reasoned out. They must be seen. And the only one who can see them is the one whose eye is cleared by absolute surrender to God. *"If therefore your eye is good,"* said Jesus, *"your whole body will be full of light. But if your eye is bad, your whole body will be full of darkness"* (Matt. 6:22–23). A surrendered life and will is the secret of light and knowledge.

Many people have confided in me that they were wandering in the dark, not knowing what to believe and not quite sure they believed anything. I asked them these questions: "Will you surrender your will to God? Will you give yourself up to God and allow Him to do what He chooses with you?" When their answer was yes, they soon said, "My doubts, my uncertainties, and my darkness are gone. There is nothing but light now."

The Secret of Prevailing Prayer

The next result of a surrendered will and life is power in prayer. The greatest secret of prevailing prayer is what John records from his own joyous experience in 1 John 3:22: *"Whatever we ask we receive from Him, because we keep His commandments and do those things that are pleasing in His sight."* Notice those wonderful words: *"Whatever we ask we receive from Him."* Think of it! Not one prayer, great or small, goes unanswered.

Then notice the reason: *"because we keep His commandments and do those things that are pleasing in His sight."* A life entirely surrendered to doing God's will as revealed in His Word and to doing the things that are pleasing in His sight—a life completely at God's disposal—is the secret of prevailing prayer.

Do you wonder why you do not get what you ask for, why you cannot, like John, say: "Whatever I ask I get"? It is not because he was an apostle and you are just an ordinary Christian. It is because he could say, "I keep His commandments and do those things (and only those things) that are pleasing in His sight," while you cannot. It is because his life was entirely surrendered to God, while yours is not.

Many people are greatly puzzled because their prayers never seem to reach the ears of God, but fall back, unanswered, to the earth. There is no mystery about it. It is because they have not met the one great, fundamental condition of prevailing prayer—a surrendered will and a surrendered life. It is when we make God's will ours that He makes our will His. *"Delight yourself also in the LORD, and He shall give you the desires of your heart"* (Ps. 37:4).

Jesus said to the Father, *"I know that You always hear Me"* (John 11:42). Why did God always hear Him? You say, "Because

Jesus was His only begotten Son." But this is not the reason. It was because Jesus could say: *"I have come down from heaven, not to do My own will, but the will of Him who sent Me"* (John 6:38); and *"My food is to do the will of Him who sent Me"* (John 4:34); and again, *"Behold, I have come...to do Your will, O God"* (Heb. 10:7).

The great secret of prevailing prayer is a surrendered will and a surrendered life. George Müller was preeminent as a powerful man of prayer. Why? Because many years ago, he set out to be and do just what God wanted him to be and do. He pondered God's Word daily and deeply in order to know His will. He yielded himself to God. There is not one of us who cannot become a mighty prince of God if we will do the same thing.

Joy Overflowing

The next result of a surrendered will is a heart overflowing with joy. In the face of the horrible trial and agony through which He was to pass, Jesus said to His disciples:

> *If you keep My commandments, you will abide in My love, just as I have kept My Father's commandments and abide in His love. These things I have spoken to you, that My joy may remain in you, and that your joy may be full.*
>
> (John 15:10–11)

Jesus had found joy in keeping His Father's commandments by completely surrendering to His will. If the disciples would follow that path, His joy would remain in them, and their joy would be *"full."*

The only way to find fullness of joy is through complete, unconditional surrender to God. *"Present yourselves to God"* (Rom. 6:13). There is no great joy in a half-hearted Christian life. Many Christians have just enough religion to make them miserable. They can no longer enjoy the world, and they have not yet entered the *"joy of the Lord"* (Neh. 8:10). There they stand, deprived of the *"leeks, the onions, and the garlic"* (Num. 11:5) of Egypt, yet they are without the milk and honey of Canaan (Exod. 3:8). That is an unhappy place to be. The way out is simple, absolute surrender to God. Then their joy will be fulfilled.

71

I have known so many who have experienced this fullness of joy. Sometimes it followed a great struggle in which they were afraid to yield absolutely to God; so afraid to say: "O God, I put myself unreservedly into Your hands; do with me what You please." They were afraid God would ask them to do something hard, afraid God might whisper, "China," "India," or "Africa."

Indeed, sometimes He has, and there has been what to the world seemed great sacrifice—giving up cherished ambitions, loved ones, or a great sum of money. But the underlying joy of the Lord made it all worthwhile. A will and life completely surrendered to the God of love will bring joy under all circumstances.

Christ Manifested

The next result of a surrendered life is Christ manifesting Himself to us. On the night in which Jesus was betrayed, He said to His disciples: *"He who has My commandments and keeps them, it is he who loves Me. And he who loves Me will be loved by My Father, and I will love him and manifest Myself to him"* (John 14:21). Surrendering ourselves to Christ brings Christ to us.

It is true that the full manifestation of Jesus lies in that future glad day when *"the Lord Himself will descend from heaven with a shout, with the voice of an archangel, and with the trumpet of God"* (1 Thess. 4:16). But there is a manifestation of Jesus possible to us now, when the Son and the Father come to us and make their home with us (John 14:23).

You say you don't know what it means for Christ to manifest Himself to you. Have you yielded yourself to Him? Are you keeping His commandments? Do not ask which commandment is great and which is small, which is important and which is unimportant, but only ask which commandment is His and keep that. If you are obeying His words, you will know what it is to have Him manifest Himself to you; your joy will be full.

We are told in one place, *"Then the disciples were glad when they saw the Lord"* (John 20:20). You will be glad, also, when you see the Lord. And you will see Him when you go to Him and say, "I surrender my life completely to You. Please manifest Yourself to me, according to Your promise."

Receive the Spirit

One more result of the surrendered will and life is revealed by Peter in Acts 5:32: *"the Holy Spirit whom God has given to those who obey Him."* A surrendered will and life is the great key to receiving the Holy Spirit. Everything hinges on this. We may plead with God for the filling of the Holy Spirit, but unless we are yielded to Him to the very center of our beings, nothing is likely to come of it.

Perhaps He comes with great surging waves of power and joy; perhaps in a gentle calm that steals over our whole beings; perhaps in a still, small voice that whispers, *"If we ask anything according to His will, He hears us. And if we know that He hears us, whatever we ask, we know that we have the petitions that we have asked of Him"* (1 John 5:14–15).

Regardless of the way He comes, it is with power. The great secret of power for God is the Holy Spirit upon us (Acts 1:8). And the great secret of the Holy Spirit's coming upon us is a surrendered will, a yielded life. The Holy Spirit's power is so wondrous, so blessed, and so glorious! Would you like to have it? *"Present yourselves to God as being alive from the dead, and your members as instruments of righteousness to God"* (Rom. 6:13).

Obtaining Power

We have seen in previous chapters the power of the Word of God, the power of the Holy Spirit, and the power of prayer. But the one great condition of obtaining this power in and through our lives and service is a surrendered will, lives given absolutely, unreservedly, and totally to God. Will you surrender to Him?

How foolish it is not to! You are robbing yourself of everything that makes life really worth living and of the joy, beauty, and glory of eternity. Will you yield today?

The Person and Work
of the Holy Spirit

CONTENTS

———◆———

Chapter 1

The Personality of the Holy Spirit

◆————

Before one can correctly understand the work of the Holy Spirit, he must first of all know the Spirit Himself. A frequent source of error and fanaticism about the work of the Holy Spirit is the attempt to study and understand His work without first of all coming to know Him as a person.

It is of the highest importance from the standpoint of worship that we decide whether the Holy Spirit is a divine person, worthy to receive our adoration, our faith, our love, and our entire surrender to Himself, or whether the Spirit is simply an influence emanating from God or a power or an illumination that God imparts to us. If the Holy Spirit is a divine person and we do not know Him as such, then we are robbing a divine being of the worship, the faith, the love, and the surrender to Himself that are His due.

It is also of the highest importance from a practical standpoint that we decide whether the Holy Spirit is merely some mysterious and wonderful power that we, in our weakness and ignorance, are somehow to get hold of and use or whether the Holy Spirit is a real person, infinitely holy, infinitely wise, infinitely mighty, and infinitely tender, who is to get hold of and use us. The former conception is utterly heathenish, not essentially different from the thought of the African fetish worshipper who has his god whom he uses. The latter conception is sublime and Christian. If we think of the Holy Spirit, as so many do, as merely a power or influence, our constant thought will be, "How can I get more of the Holy Spirit?" But if we think of Him in the biblical way as a divine person, our thought will instead be, "How can the Holy Spirit have more of me?"

The conception of the Holy Spirit as being a divine influence or power that we are somehow to get hold of and use leads to self-exaltation and self-sufficiency. One who thinks of the Holy Spirit in this way and who at the same time imagines that he has received the Holy Spirit will almost inevitably be full of spiritual pride and strut about as if he belonged to some superior order of Christians. One frequently hears such people say, "I am a Spirit-filled man" or "I am a Spirit-filled woman."

But if we once grasp the thought that the Holy Spirit is a divine person of infinite majesty, glory, holiness, and power, who in marvelous condescension has come into our hearts to make His abode there and take possession of our lives and make use of them, it will put us in the dust and keep us in the dust. I can think of no thought more humbling or more overwhelming than the thought that a person of divine majesty and glory dwells in my heart and is ready to use even me.

It is of the highest importance from the standpoint of experience that we know the Holy Spirit as a person. Thousands and tens of thousands of men and women can testify to the blessing that has come into their own lives as they have come to know the Holy Spirit. They have come to know the Holy Spirit not merely as a gracious influence (emanating, it is true, from God), but as a real person, just as real as Jesus Christ Himself. He is an ever present, loving Friend, and a mighty Helper who is not only always by their sides, but who dwells in their hearts every day and every hour and who is ready to undertake for them in every emergency of life. Thousands of ministers, Christian workers, and Christians in the humblest spheres of life have spoken to me or written to me of the complete transformation of their Christian experience that came to them when they grasped the thought (not merely in a theological but in an experiential way) that the Holy Spirit is a person and consequently came to know Him.

There are at least four distinct proofs in the Bible that the Holy Spirit is a person.

All the distinctive characteristics of personality are ascribed to the Holy Spirit in the Bible.

What are the distinctive characteristics, or marks, of personality? Knowledge, feeling or emotion, and will. Any entity that thinks, feels, and wills is a person. When we say that the Holy Spirit is a person, there are those who understand us to mean that the Holy Spirit has hands, feet, eyes, ears, a mouth, and so on, but these are not the characteristics of personality but of bodily substance. All of these characteristics or marks of personality are repeatedly ascribed to the Holy Spirit in the Old and New Testaments.

We read in 1 Corinthians:

But God has revealed them to us through His Spirit. For the Spirit searches all things, yes, the deep things of God. For what man knows the things of a man except the spirit of the man which is in him? Even so no one knows the things of God except the Spirit of God. (1 Cor. 2:10–11)

Here knowledge is ascribed to the Holy Spirit. We are clearly taught that the Holy Spirit is not merely an influence that illuminates our minds to comprehend the truth, but a being who Himself knows the truth.

We also read: *"But one and the same Spirit works all these things, distributing to each one individually as He wills"* (1 Cor. 12:11). Here, will is ascribed to the Spirit, and we are taught that the Holy Spirit is not a power that we get hold of and use according to our desires, but a person of sovereign majesty who uses us according to His will. This distinction is of fundamental importance in our establishing a right relationship with the Holy Spirit. It is at this very point that many honest seekers after power and effectiveness in service go astray. They are reaching for and struggling to get possession of some mysterious and mighty power that they can make use of in their work according to their own desires. They will never get possession of the power they seek until they come to recognize that there is not some divine power for them to get hold of and use in their blindness and ignorance, but that there is a Person, infinitely wise as well as infinitely mighty, who is willing to take possession of them and use them according to His own perfect will.

When we stop to think of it, we must rejoice that there is no divine power we beings, so ignorant and so liable to err as we are, can get hold of and use. How appalling the results might be if there were. But what a holy joy must come into our hearts when we grasp the thought that there is a divine person, One who never errs, who is willing to take possession of us and impart to us such gifts as He sees best and to use us according to His wise and loving will.

We read in Romans 8:27: *"Now He who searches the hearts knows what the mind of the Spirit is, because He makes intercession for the saints according to the will of God."* In this passage, mind is ascribed to the Holy Spirit. The Greek word translated *"mind"* is a comprehensive word, including the ideas of thought, feeling, and purpose. It is the same word that is used in Romans 8:7, where we read that *"the carnal mind is enmity against God; for it is not subject to the law of God, nor indeed can be."* So in this verse, all the distinctive marks of personality are included in the word *mind* and are ascribed to the Holy Spirit.

We find the personality of the Holy Spirit brought out in a most touching, significant way in Romans 15:30: *"Now I beg you, brethren, through the Lord Jesus Christ, and through the love of the Spirit, that you strive together with me in prayers to God for me."* Here we have *"love"* ascribed to the Holy Spirit. The reader would do well to stop and ponder those five words: *"the love of the Spirit."*

We dwell often on the love of God the Father. It is the subject of our daily thought. We meditate often on the love of Jesus Christ the Son. Who would think of calling himself a Christian who passed a day without meditating on the love of his Savior, but how often have we meditated on *"the love of the Spirit"*?

Each day of our lives, if we are living as Christians should, we kneel down in the presence of God the Father, look into His face, and say, "I thank you, Father, for Your great love that led You to give Your only begotten Son to die upon the cross of Calvary for me." Each day of our lives we also look into the face of our Lord and Savior, Jesus Christ, and say, "Oh, glorious Lord and Savior, Jesus the Son of God, I thank You for Your great love that led You not to *'consider it robbery to be equal with God'* (Phil. 2:6), but You emptied Yourself, forsaking all the glory of heaven. You came down to earth with all its shame in order to take my sins upon Yourself and die in my place upon the cross of Calvary." But how often do we kneel and say to the Holy

Spirit, "Oh, eternal and infinite Spirit of God, I thank You for Your great love that led You to come into this world of sin and darkness and to seek me out and to follow me so patiently until You brought me to see my utter ruin and need of a Savior and to reveal to me my Lord and Savior, Jesus Christ, as just the Savior whom I need"? Yet we owe our salvation just as truly to the love of the Spirit as we do to the love of the Father and the love of the Son.

If it had not been for the love of God the Father looking down on me in my utter ruin and providing a perfect atonement for me in the death of His own Son on the cross of Calvary, I would have been in hell today. If it had not been for the love of Jesus Christ, the eternal Word of God, looking on me in my utter ruin and, in obedience to the Father, putting aside all the glory of heaven for all the shame of earth and taking my place, the place of the curse, upon the cross of Calvary and pouring out His life utterly for me, I would have been in hell today. But if it had not been for the love of the Holy Spirit, sent by the Father in answer to the prayer of the Son (see John 14:16), leading Him to seek me out in my utter blindness and ruin, I would have been in hell today. He followed me day after day, week after week, and year after year when I persistently turned a deaf ear to His pleadings, followed me through paths of sin, where it must have been agony for that Holy One to go, until at last I listened. He opened my eyes to see my utter ruin and then revealed Jesus to me as the Savior who would meet my every need. Then, He enabled me to receive Jesus as my own Savior. If it had not been for this patient, longsuffering, never tiring, infinitely tender love of the Holy Spirit, I would have been in hell today. Oh, the Holy Spirit is not merely an influence, a power, or an illumination, but is a person—just as real as God the Father or Jesus Christ His Son.

The personality of the Holy Spirit comes out in the Old Testament as truly as in the New, for we read in Nehemiah 9:20, *"You also gave Your good Spirit to instruct them, and did not withhold Your manna from their mouth, and gave them water for their thirst."* Here both intelligence and goodness are ascribed to the Holy Spirit. Some tell us that while it is true the personality of the Holy Spirit is found in the New Testament, it

83

is not found in the Old. However, it is certainly found in this passage. As a matter of course, the doctrine of the personality of the Holy Spirit is not as fully developed in the Old Testament as in the New, but the doctrine is there.

There is perhaps no passage in the entire Bible in which the personality of the Holy Spirit comes out more tenderly and touchingly than in the following: *"And do not grieve the Holy Spirit of God, by whom you were sealed for the day of redemption"* (Eph. 4:30). Here grief is ascribed to the Holy Spirit. The Holy Spirit is not a blind, impersonal influence or power that comes into our lives to illuminate, sanctify, and empower us. No, He is immeasurably more than that. He is a holy person who comes to dwell in our hearts, One who sees clearly every act we perform, every word we speak, every thought we entertain, even the most fleeting fancy that is allowed to pass through our minds. If there is anything in act or word or deed that is impure, unholy, unkind, selfish, mean, petty, or untrue, this infinitely Holy One is deeply grieved by it. I know of no thought that will help one more than this to lead a holy life and to walk softly in the presence of the Holy One.

How often a young man is kept from yielding to the temptations that surround young manhood by the thought that if he should yield to the temptation that now assails him, his dear mother might hear of it and would be grieved beyond expression. How often some young man has had his hand on the door of some place of sin that he was about to enter and the thought has come to him, "If I should enter here, my mother might hear of it, and it would nearly kill her." Then, he has turned his back on that door and gone away to lead a pure life so that he might not hurt his mother.

There is One who is holier than any mother, One who is more sensitive against sin than the purest woman who ever walked this earth, and who loves us as even no mother ever loved. This One dwells in our hearts, if we are really Christians, and He sees every act we do by day or under cover of night. He hears every word we utter in public or in private. He sees every thought we entertain. He observes every fancy and imagination that is permitted even a momentary lodging in our minds. If there is anything unholy, impure, selfish, mean, petty, unkind, harsh, unjust, or in any way evil in act or word or thought, He is grieved by it. If we will allow those words, *"do not grieve the Holy Spirit of God"* (Eph. 4:30), to sink into our hearts and become the motto of our lives, they will keep us from many sins. How often some thought has knocked for an entrance into my own mind and was about to find entrance when the thought has come, "The Holy Spirit sees that thought and will be grieved by it." With that reminder, the improper thought has been banished.

Many acts that only a person can perform are ascribed to the Holy Spirit.

If we deny the personality of the Holy Spirit, many passages of Scripture become meaningless and absurd. For example, we read in 1 Corinthians 2:10: *"But God has revealed them to us through His Spirit. For the Spirit searches all things, yes, the deep things of God."* This passage sets before us the Holy Spirit not merely as an illumination whereby we are enabled to grasp the deep things of God, but as a person who Himself searches the deep things of God and then reveals to us the precious discoveries that He has made.

We read in Revelation 2:7: *"He who has an ear, let him hear what the Spirit says to the churches. To him who overcomes I will give to eat from the tree of life, which is in the midst of the Paradise of God."* Here the Holy Spirit is presented not merely as an impersonal enlightenment that comes to our minds, but as a person who speaks and, out of the depths of His own wisdom, whispers into the ears of His listening servants the precious truths of God.

Galatians 4:6 states, *"And because you are sons, God has sent forth the Spirit of His Son into your hearts, crying out, 'Abba, Father!'"* Here the Holy Spirit is represented as crying out in the heart of the individual believer. The Holy Spirit is not merely a divine influence producing in our own hearts the assurance of our sonship, but One who cries out in our hearts, who bears witness together with our spirits that we are children of God (Rom. 8:16).

The Holy Spirit is also represented in the Scripture as one who prays:

> *Likewise the Spirit also helps in our weaknesses. For we do not know what we should pray for as we ought, but the Spirit Himself makes intercession for us with groanings which cannot be uttered.* (Rom. 8:26)

It is plain from this passage that the Holy Spirit is not merely an influence that moves us to pray, not merely an illumination that teaches us how to pray, but a person who Himself prays in and through us.

There is wondrous comfort in the thought that every true believer has two divine persons praying for him. One is Jesus Christ, the Son who was once on this earth, who knows all about our temptations, who sympathizes with our weaknesses (Heb. 4:15), and who is now ascended to the right hand of the Father (Mark 16:19). In that place of authority and power, He ever lives to make intercession for us. (See Hebrews 7:25; 1 John 2:1.) There is another person, just as divine as Christ, who walks by our side each day, who dwells in the innermost depths of our beings, who knows our needs even as we do not know them ourselves, and who from these depths makes intercession to the Father for us. The position of the believer is indeed one of perfect security with these two divine persons praying for him.

We read in John 15:26: *"But when the Helper comes, whom I shall send to you from the Father, the Spirit of truth who proceeds from the Father, He will testify of Me."* Here the Holy Spirit is set before us as a person who gives His testimony to Jesus Christ, not merely as an illumination that enables the believer to testify of Christ, but as a person who Himself testifies. A clear distinction is drawn in this and in the following verse between the testimony of the Holy Spirit and the testimony of the believer to whom He has borne His witness, for we read: *"And you also will bear witness, because you have been with Me from the beginning"* (v. 27). So there are two witnesses, the Holy Spirit bearing witness to the believer and the believer bearing witness to the world.

The Holy Spirit is also spoken of as a teacher: *"But the Helper, the Holy Spirit, whom the Father will send in My name,*

He will teach you all things, and bring to your remembrance all things that I said to you" (John 14:26). And in a similar way, we read:

> *I still have many things to say to you, but you cannot bear them now. However, when He, the Spirit of truth, has come, He will guide you into all truth; for He will not speak on His own authority, but whatever He hears He will speak; and He will tell you things to come. He will glorify Me, for He will take of what is Mine and declare it to you.* (John 16:12–14)

In the Old Testament, we read: *"You also gave Your good Spirit to instruct them"* (Neh. 9:20). In all these passages, it is perfectly clear that the Holy Spirit is not a mere illumination that enables us to apprehend the truth. He is a person who comes to teach us day by day the truth of God. It is the privilege of the humblest believer in Jesus Christ not merely to have his mind illumined to comprehend the truth of God, but to have a divine Teacher to daily teach him the truth he needs to know. (See 1 John 2:20, 27.)

The Holy Spirit is also represented as the Leader and Guide of the children of God. We read in Romans 8:14: *"For as many as are led by the Spirit of God, these are the sons of God."* He is not merely an influence that enables us to see the way that God would have us go, nor merely a power that gives us strength to go that way, but a person who takes us by the hand and gently leads us in the paths in which God would have us walk.

The Holy Spirit also has authority to command men in their service of Jesus Christ. We read of the apostle Paul and his companions:

> *Now when they had gone through Phrygia and the region of Galatia, they were forbidden by the Holy Spirit to preach the word in Asia. After they had come to Mysia, they tried to go into Bithynia, but the Spirit did not permit them.*
>
> (Acts 16:6–7)

Here the Holy Spirit directs the conduct of Paul and his companions. He is a person whose authority they recognized and to whom they instantly submitted.

87

Further, the Holy Spirit is represented as the One who is the supreme authority in the church, who calls men to work and appoints them to office. We read in Acts 13:2: *"As they ministered to the Lord and fasted, the Holy Spirit said, 'Now separate to Me Barnabas and Saul for the work to which I have called them.'"* Later in Acts, we read: *"Take heed to yourselves and to all the flock, among which the Holy Spirit has made you overseers, to shepherd the church of God which He purchased with His own blood"* (Acts 20:28). There can be no doubt to a candid seeker after truth that the Holy Spirit is a person of divine majesty and sovereignty. From all the passages here quoted, it is evident that many acts that only a person can perform are ascribed to the Holy Spirit.

An office is asserted by the Holy Spirit that can only be asserted by a person.

Jesus said:

> *And I will pray the Father, and He will give you another Helper, that He may abide with you forever; the Spirit of truth, whom the world cannot receive, because it neither sees Him nor knows Him; but you know Him, for He dwells with you and will be in you.* (John 14:16–17)

Our Lord had announced to the disciples that He was about to leave them. An awful sense of desolation took possession of them. Sorrow filled their hearts (John 16:6) at the contemplation of their loneliness and absolute helplessness when Jesus would leave them alone. To comfort them, the Lord told them that they would not be left alone, that in leaving them He was going to the Father and that He would pray the Father and would give them another Comforter to take the place of Himself during His absence.

Is it possible that Jesus Christ could have used such language if the other Comforter who was coming to take His place was only an impersonal influence or power? Still more, is it possible that Jesus could have said as He did in John 16:7, *"Nevertheless I tell you the truth. It is to your advantage that I*

go away; for if I do not go away, the Helper will not come to you;
but if I depart, I will send Him to you," if this Comforter whom
He was to send was simply an impersonal influence or power?

No, one divine person was going; another person just as divine was coming to take His place. For the disciples, it was necessary that the One go to represent them before the Father because another just as divine and sufficient was coming to take His place. This promise of our Lord and Savior of the coming of the other Comforter and of His abiding with us is the greatest and best of all for the present dispensation. This is the promise of the Father (Acts 1:4), the promise of promises. We will take it up again when we come to study the names of the Holy Spirit.

A treatment is asserted by the Holy Spirit that could only be asserted by a person.

We read in Isaiah 63:10: *"But they rebelled and grieved His*
Holy Spirit; so He turned Himself against them as an enemy,
and He fought against them." Here we are told that the Holy
Spirit is rebelled against and grieved. (Compare Ephesians
4:30.) Only a person, and only a person of authority, can be rebelled against. Only a person can be grieved. You cannot grieve a mere influence or power.

In Hebrews, we read:

> *Of how much worse punishment, do you suppose, will he*
> *be thought worthy who has trampled the Son of God un-*
> *derfoot, counted the blood of the covenant by which he was*
> *sanctified a common thing, and insulted the Spirit of*
> *grace?* (Heb. 10:29)

Here we are told that the Holy Spirit is treated with contempt. There is but one kind of entity in the universe who can be treated with contempt (or insulted), and that is a person. It is absurd to think of treating an influence or a power or any kind of being except a person with contempt.

We also read: *"But Peter said, 'Ananias, why has Satan*
filled your heart to lie to the Holy Spirit and keep back part of the
price of the land for yourself?'" (Acts 5:3). Here we have the

Holy Spirit represented as one who can be lied to. One cannot lie to anything but a person.

Matthew recorded these verses:

> *Therefore I say to you, every sin and blasphemy will be forgiven men, but the blasphemy against the Spirit will not be forgiven men. Anyone who speaks a word against the Son of Man, it will be forgiven him; but whoever speaks against the Holy Spirit, it will not be forgiven him, either in this age or in the age to come.* (Matt. 12:31–32)

Here we are told that the Holy Spirit is blasphemed against. It is impossible to blaspheme anything but a person. If the Holy Spirit is not a person, it certainly cannot be a more serious and decisive sin to blaspheme Him than it is to blaspheme the Son of Man, our Lord and Savior, Jesus Christ Himself.

We have examined four distinctive and decisive lines of proof that the Holy Spirit is a person. Theoretically, most of us believe this, but do we, in our real thoughts of Him and in our practical attitudes toward Him, treat Him as if He were indeed a person?

At the close of an address on the personality of the Holy Spirit at a Bible conference some years ago, one who had been a church member many years, a member of one of the most orthodox of our modern denominations, said to me, "I never thought of the Holy Spirit before as a person." Undoubtedly, this Christian woman had often sung,

> Praise God from whom all blessings flow,
> Praise Him all creatures here below,
> Praise Him above, ye heavenly host,
> Praise Father, Son, and Holy Ghost.

Undoubtedly, she had often sung,

> Glory be to the Father,
> and to the Son,
> and to the Holy Ghost,
> As it was in the beginning,
> is now, and ever shall be,
> World without end, Amen, Amen.

However, it is one thing to sing words; it is quite another thing to realize the meaning of what we sing. If this Christian woman had been questioned in regard to her doctrine, she would doubtless have said that she believed that there were three persons in the Godhead: Father, Son, and Holy Spirit. But a theological confession is one thing; a practical realization of the truth we confess is quite another. So the question is altogether necessary, no matter how orthodox you may be in your doctrinal statements: Do you indeed regard the Holy Spirit as real a person as Jesus Christ; as loving, wise, and strong; as worthy of your confidence, love, and surrender as Jesus Christ Himself?

The Holy Spirit came into this world to be to the disciples of our Lord after His departure, and to us, what Jesus Christ had been to them during the days of His personal companionship with them. (See John 14:16–17.) Is He that to you? Do you know Him? Although you often hear the apostolic benediction, *"The grace of the Lord Jesus Christ, and the love of God, and the communion of the Holy Spirit be with you all"* (2 Cor. 13:14), do you take in its significance? Do you know the communion of the Holy Spirit? The fellowship of the Holy Spirit? The partnership of the Holy Spirit? The companionship of the Holy Spirit? The intimate personal friendship of the Holy Spirit?

Here lies the whole secret of a real Christian life, a life of liberty, joy, power, and fullness. To be conscious that one has the Holy Spirit as his ever present friend, and to surrender one's life entirely to His control—this is true Christian living.

The doctrine of the personality of the Holy Spirit is as distinctive of the religion that Jesus taught as the doctrines of the deity and the Atonement of Jesus Christ Himself. But it is not enough to believe the doctrine; one must know the Holy Spirit Himself. The whole purpose of this chapter (God help me to say it reverently) is to introduce you to my friend, the Holy Spirit.

Chapter 2

The Deity of the Holy Spirit

n the preceding chapter, we saw clearly that the Holy Spirit is a person, but what sort of a person is He? Is He a finite person or an infinite person? Is He God? These questions are plainly answered in the Bible. In the Scriptures of the Old and New Testaments, five distinct and decisive pieces of evidence of the deity of the Holy Spirit are presented.

Each of the four distinctively divine attributes is ascribed to the Holy Spirit.

What are the distinctively divine attributes? Eternity, omnipresence, omniscience, and omnipotence. All of these are ascribed to the Holy Spirit in the Bible. We find eternity ascribed to the Holy Spirit: *"How much more shall the blood of Christ, who through the eternal Spirit offered Himself without spot to God, cleanse your conscience from dead works to serve the living God?"* (Heb. 9:14).

Omnipresence is ascribed to the Holy Spirit:

Where can I go from Your Spirit? Or where can I flee from Your presence? If I ascend into heaven, You are there; if I make my bed in hell, behold, You are there. If I take the wings of the morning, and dwell in the uttermost parts of the sea, even there Your hand shall lead me, and Your right hand shall hold me. (Ps. 139:7–10)

Omniscience is ascribed to the Holy Spirit in several passages. For example, we read the following passages from Scripture:

92

> *But God has revealed them to us through His Spirit. For the Spirit searches all things, yes, the deep things of God. For what man knows the things of a man except the spirit of the man which is in him? Even so no one knows the things of God except the Spirit of God.* (1 Cor. 2:10–11)

> *But the Helper, the Holy Spirit, whom the Father will send in My name, He will teach you all things, and bring to your remembrance all things that I said to you.*
> (John 14:26)

> *I still have many things to say to you, but you cannot bear them now. However, when He, the Spirit of truth, has come, He will guide you into all truth; for He will not speak on His own authority, but whatever He hears He will speak; and He will tell you things to come.* (John 16:12–13)

Omnipotence is ascribed to the Holy Spirit.

> *And the angel answered and said to her, "The Holy Spirit will come upon you, and the power of the Highest will overshadow you; therefore, also, that Holy One who is to be born will be called the Son of God."* (Luke 1:35)

Three distinctively divine works are ascribed to the Holy Spirit.

When we think of God and His work, the first work of which we always think is that of creation. In the Scriptures, creation is ascribed to the Holy Spirit. We read in Job 33:4: *"The Spirit of God has made me, and the breath of the Almighty gives me life."* Psalm 104:30 states, *"You send forth Your Spirit, they are created; and You renew the face of the earth."* The activity of the Spirit is referred to in connection with the description of creation in the first chapter of Genesis. (See Genesis 1:1–3.)

The impartation of life is also a divine work, and this is ascribed in the Scriptures to the Holy Spirit. We read in John 6:63: *"It is the Spirit who gives life; the flesh profits nothing."* We read also in Romans 8:11: *"But if the Spirit of Him who raised Jesus from the dead dwells in you, He who raised Christ from the dead will also give life to your mortal bodies through His Spirit who dwells in you."* In the description of the creation of man in Genesis 2:7, it is the breath of God, that is, the Holy Spirit, who imparts life to man, and man becomes a living soul. The exact words are, *"And the LORD God formed man of the dust of the ground, and breathed into his nostrils the breath of life; and man became a living being."* Although the Holy Spirit as a person does not come out distinctly in this early reference to Him in Genesis 2:7, this passage interpreted in the light of the fuller revelation of the New Testament clearly refers to the Holy Spirit because the Greek word that is rendered "spirit" means "breath."

The authorship of divine prophecies is also ascribed to the Holy Spirit. We read in 2 Peter 1:21: *"For prophecy never came by the will of man, but holy men of God spoke as they were moved by the Holy Spirit."* Even in the Old Testament, there is a reference to the Holy Spirit as the author of prophecy. We read in 2 Samuel 23:2–3:

> *The Spirit of the LORD spoke by me, and His word was on my tongue. The God of Israel said, the Rock of Israel spoke to me: "He who rules over men must be just, ruling in the fear of God."*

So we see that the three distinctly divine works—creation, impartation of life, and prophecy—are ascribed to the Holy Spirit.

Statements in the Old Testament that distinctly name the LORD or Jehovah as their subject are applied to the Holy Spirit in the New Testament. Thus, the Holy Spirit occupies the position of deity in New Testament thought.

A striking illustration of this point is found in a comparison of passages from Isaiah and Acts.

> *My eyes have seen the King, the LORD of hosts....And He said, "Go, and tell this people, 'Keep on hearing, but do not understand; keep on seeing, but do not perceive.' Make the*

> *heart of this people dull, and their ears heavy, and shut*
> *their eyes; lest they see with their eyes, and hear with their*
> *ears, and understand with their heart, and return and be*
> *healed."*   (Isa. 6:5, 9–10)

In verse five, we are told that it was Jehovah (whenever the word *LORD* is spelled in capitals in the Old Testament, it stands for Jehovah in the Hebrew) whom Isaiah saw and who spoke to Him. But in Acts, there is a reference to this passage from Isaiah, and we are told that it was the Holy Spirit who was the speaker. The passage in Acts reads as follows:

> *So when they did not agree among themselves, they de-*
> *parted after Paul had said one word: "The Holy Spirit*
> *spoke rightly through Isaiah the prophet to our fathers,*
> *saying, 'Go to this people and say: "Hearing you will hear,*
> *and shall not understand; and seeing you will see, and not*
> *perceive; for the hearts of this people have grown dull.*
> *Their ears are hard of hearing, and their eyes they have*
> *closed, lest they should see with their eyes and hear with*
> *their ears, lest they should understand with their hearts*
> *and turn, so that I should heal them."'"*   (Acts 28:25–27)

So we see that what is distinctly ascribed to Jehovah in the Old Testament is ascribed to the Holy Spirit in the New; thus, the Holy Spirit is identified with Jehovah. It is a noteworthy fact that in the gospel of John, chapter twelve verses thirty-eight to forty-one, where another reference to this passage in Isaiah is made, this same passage is ascribed to Christ (note carefully the forty-first verse). So in different parts of Scripture, we have the same passage referred to Jehovah, referred to the Holy Spirit, and referred to Jesus Christ. May we not find the explanation of this in the threefold "Holy" of the angelic cry in Isaiah 6:3, where we read: *"And one cried to another and said, 'Holy, holy, holy is the LORD of hosts; the whole earth is full of His glory!'"* In this we have a distinct suggestion of the tri-personality of the Jehovah of Hosts and hence the propriety of the threefold application of the vision. A further suggestion of this tri-personality of Jehovah of Hosts is found in Isaiah 6:8, where the Lord is represented as saying, *"Whom shall I send, and who will go for Us?"*

Another striking illustration of the application of passages that in the Old Testament distinctly name Jehovah as their subject and in the New Testament name the Holy Spirit is found in Exodus 16:7: *"And in the morning you shall see the glory of the LORD; for He hears your complaints against the LORD. But what are we, that you complain against us?"* Here the murmuring of the children of Israel is distinctly said to be against Jehovah. But in Hebrews 3:7–9, where this instance is referred to, we read:

> *Therefore, as the Holy Spirit says: "Today, if you will hear His voice, do not harden your hearts as in the rebellion, in the day of trial in the wilderness, where your fathers tested Me, tried Me, and saw My works forty years."*

In the book of Exodus, the *"complaints"* that Moses said were against Jehovah, we are told in Hebrews were against the Holy Spirit. This leaves it beyond question that the Holy Spirit occupies the position of Jehovah, or deity, in the New Testament. (Compare Psalm 95:8–11.)

The name of the Holy Spirit is coupled with that of God in a way that would be impossible for a reverent, thoughtful mind to couple the name of any finite being with that of deity.

We have an illustration of this in 1 Corinthians:

> *There are diversities of gifts, but the same Spirit. There are differences of ministries, but the same Lord. And there are diversities of activities, but it is the same God who works all in all.* (1 Cor. 12:4–6)

Here we find God, the Lord, and the Spirit associated together in a relation of equality that would be shocking to contemplate if the Spirit were a finite being. We have a still more striking illustration of this in Matthew 28:19: *"Go therefore and make disciples of all the nations, baptizing them in the name of the Father and of the Son and of the Holy Spirit."* What person who had grasped the biblical concept of God the Father would think for a moment of coupling the name of the Holy Spirit with that of the Father if the Holy Spirit were a finite being, even the most exalted of angelic beings?

Another striking illustration is found in 2 Corinthians 13:14: *"The grace of the Lord Jesus Christ, and the love of God, and the communion of the Holy Spirit be with you all. Amen."* Can anyone ponder these words and catch their real importance without seeing clearly that it would be impossible to couple the name of the Holy Spirit with that of God the Father unless the Holy Spirit were Himself a divine being?

The Holy Spirit is called God.

The final and decisive proof of the deity of the Holy Spirit is found in the fact that He is called God in the New Testament. We read in Acts 5:3–4:

> *But Peter said, "Ananias, why has Satan filled your heart to lie to the Holy Spirit and keep back part of the price of the land for yourself? While it remained, was it not your own? And after it was sold, was it not in your own control? Why have you conceived this thing in your heart? You have not lied to men but to God."*

In the first part of this passage, we are told that Ananias lied to the Holy Spirit. When this is further explained, we are told it was not to men but to God that he had lied in lying to the Holy Spirit; in other words, the Holy Spirit to whom he lied is called God.

To sum it up, by the ascription of all the distinctively divine attributes and several distinctly divine works, by comparing statements that clearly name Jehovah, the LORD, or God as their subject in the Old Testament with passages that name the Holy Spirit in the New Testament, by coupling the name of the Holy Spirit with that of God in a way that would be impossible to couple that of any finite being with that of deity, and by plainly calling the Holy Spirit God—in all these unmistakable ways, God in His own Word distinctly proclaims that the Holy Spirit is a divine person.

Chapter 3

The Holy Spirit's Distinction

◆————————

We have seen thus far that the Holy Spirit is a person and a divine person. And now another question arises: Is He, as a divine person, separate and distinct from the Father and from the Son? One who carefully studies the New Testament statements cannot but discover that beyond a question He is. We read in Luke 3:21–22:

> *When all the people were baptized, it came to pass that Jesus also was baptized; and while He prayed, the heaven was opened. And the Holy Spirit descended in bodily form like a dove upon Him, and a voice came from heaven which said, "You are My beloved Son; in You I am well pleased."*

Here the clearest possible distinction is drawn between Jesus Christ, who was on earth, and the Father, who spoke to Him from heaven, as one person speaks to another person, and the Holy Spirit, who descended in a bodily form as a dove. The Holy Spirit came from the Father (who was speaking) to the Son (to whom He was speaking) and rested upon the Son as a person separate and distinct from Himself.

We see a clear distinction drawn between the name of the Father and the Son and the Holy Spirit in Matthew 28:19, where we read: *"Go therefore and make disciples of all the nations, baptizing them in the name of the Father and of the Son and of the Holy Spirit."* The distinction of the Holy Spirit from the Father and the Son comes out again with exceeding clearness in John 14:16: *"And I will pray the Father, and He will give you another Helper, that He may abide with you forever."* Here we see one person, the Son, praying to another person, the Father, and the Father to whom He is praying giving another person, *"another Helper,"* in answer to the prayer of the second person, the Son. If words mean anything, and certainly in the Bible they mean what they say, there can be no mistaking that the Father, the Son, and the Spirit are three distinct, separate persons.

Again in John 16:7, a clear distinction is drawn between Jesus, who goes away to the Father, and the Holy Spirit, who comes from the Father to take His place. Jesus said, *"Nevertheless I tell you the truth. It is to your advantage that I go away; for if I do not go away, the Helper will not come to you; but if I depart, I will send Him to you."* A similar distinction is drawn in Acts 2:33, where we read: *"Therefore being exalted to the right hand of God, and having received from the Father the promise of the Holy Spirit, He [Jesus] poured out this which you now see and hear."* In this passage, the clearest possible distinction is drawn between the Son, exalted to the right hand of the Father; the Father, to whose right hand He is exalted; and the Holy Spirit whom the Son receives from the Father and pours out on the church.

Again and again, the Bible draws the clearest possible distinction among the three persons: the Holy Spirit, the Father, and the Son. They are three separate personalities, having mutual relations to one another, acting upon one another, speaking of or to one another, and applying the pronouns of the second and third persons to one another.

Chapter 4

The Subordination of the Spirit

◆——————————◆

From the fact that the Holy Spirit is a divine person, it does not follow that the Holy Spirit is in every sense equal in His roles to the Father. While the Scriptures teach that in Jesus Christ *"dwells all the fullness of the Godhead bodily"* (Col. 2:9) and that He was so truly and fully divine that He could say, *"I and My Father are one"* (John 10:30) and *"He who has seen Me has seen the Father"* (John 14:9), they also teach with equal clearness that Jesus Christ was subordinate to the Father in many ways.

In a similar way, the Scriptures teach us that though the Holy Spirit is a divine person, He is subordinate to the Father and to the Son. We are taught that the Holy Spirit is sent by the Father and in the name of the Son. Jesus declares very clearly:

> *But the Helper, the Holy Spirit, whom the Father will send in My name, He will teach you all things, and bring to your remembrance all things that I said to you.*
>
> (John 14:26)

In John 15:26, we are told that it is Jesus who sends the Spirit from the Father. The exact words are, *"But when the Helper comes, whom I shall send to you from the Father, the Spirit of truth who proceeds from the Father, He will testify of Me."* Just as we are elsewhere taught that Jesus Christ was sent by the Father (see John 6:29; 8:29, 42), we are here taught that the Holy Spirit in turn is sent by Jesus Christ.

The subordination of the Holy Spirit to the Father and the Son comes out also in the fact that He derives some of His names from the Father and from the Son. We read in Romans 8:9: *"But you are not in the flesh but in the Spirit, if indeed the Spirit of God dwells in you. Now if anyone does not have the Spirit of Christ, he is not His."* Here we have two names of the Spirit, one derived from His relation to the Father, *"the Spirit of God,"* and the other derived from His relation to the Son, *"the Spirit of Christ."*

The subordination of the Spirit to the Son is also seen in the fact that the Holy Spirit speaks not from Himself but speaks the words that He hears. We read in John:

> *However, when He, the Spirit of truth, has come, He will guide you into all truth; for He will not speak on His own authority, but whatever He hears He will speak; and He will tell you things to come.* (John 16:13)

In a similar way, Jesus said of Himself, *"My doctrine is not Mine, but His who sent Me"* (John 7:16). (See also John 8:26, 40.)

The subordination of the Spirit to the Son comes out again in the clearly revealed fact that it is the work of the Holy Spirit not to glorify Himself but to glorify Christ. Jesus says in John 16:14, *"He will glorify Me, for He will take of what is Mine and declare it to you."* In a similar way, Christ sought not His own glory, but the glory of Him who sent Him, that is, the Father. (See John 7:18.)

From all these passages, it is evident that the Holy Spirit in His present work, while possessed of all the attributes of deity, is subordinated to the Father and to the Son. On the other hand, we will see later that in His earthly life, Jesus lived, taught, and worked in the power of the Holy Spirit.

Chapter 5

The Names of the Holy Spirit

◆────────

A t least twenty-five different names are used in the Old and New Testaments in speaking of the Holy Spirit. There is the deepest significance in these names. By carefully studying them, we find a wonderful revelation of the person and work of the Holy Spirit.

The Spirit

The simplest name by which the Holy Spirit is mentioned in the Bible is that which stands at the head of this paragraph: "The Spirit." This name is also used as the basis of other names, so we begin our study with this name. The Greek and Hebrew words so translated mean literally, "Breath" or "Wind." Both thoughts are in the name as applied to the Holy Spirit.

The thought of Breath is brought out in John 20:22, where we read: *"And when He had said this, He breathed on them, and said to them, 'Receive the Holy Spirit.'"* It is also suggested in Genesis 2:7: *"And the LORD God formed man of the dust of the ground, and breathed into his nostrils the breath of life; and man became a living being."* This becomes more evident when we look at Psalm 104:30: *"You send forth Your Spirit, they are created; and You renew the face of the earth,"* and Job 33:4: *"The Spirit of God has made me, and the breath of the Almighty gives me life."* What is the significance of this name from the standpoint of these passages? It is that the Spirit is the outbreathing of God, His inmost life going forth in a personal form to enliven.

When we receive the Holy Spirit, we receive the inmost life of God Himself to dwell in a personal way in us. When we really grasp this thought, it is overwhelming in its solemnity. Just stop and think what it means to have the inmost life of that infinite and eternal being whom we call God dwelling in a personal way in you. How solemn, how awesome, and yet unspeakably glorious life becomes when we realize this.

The thought of the Holy Spirit as the Wind is brought out in the following Scripture:

> *That which is born of the flesh is flesh, and that which is born of the Spirit is spirit. Do not marvel that I said to you, "You must be born again." The wind blows where it wishes, and you hear the sound of it, but cannot tell where it comes from and where it goes. So is everyone who is born of the Spirit.* (John 3:6–8)

In the Greek, the same word that is translated in one part of this passage "Spirit" is translated in the other part of the passage "wind." And it would seem as if the word should be translated the same way in both parts of the passage. It would then read: "That which is born of the flesh is flesh, and that which is born of the Wind is wind. Do not marvel that I said to you, 'You must be born again.' The wind blows where it wishes, and you hear the sound of it, but cannot tell where it comes from and where it goes. So is everyone who is born of the Wind." The full significance of this name as applied to the Holy Spirit (or Holy Wind) may be beyond us to fathom, but we can see at least this much of its meaning through the following sections.

The Spirit, like the wind, is sovereign.

"The wind blows where it wishes" (v. 8). You cannot dictate to the wind. It does as it wills. Just so with the Holy Spirit—He is sovereign—we cannot dictate to Him. He distributes *"to each one individually as He wills"* (1 Cor. 12:11). When the wind is blowing from the north, you may long to have it blow from the south, but cry as noisily as you may to the wind, "Blow from the south," it will keep right on blowing from the north. While you cannot dictate to the wind, while it blows as it will, you may learn the laws that govern the wind's motions. By bringing yourself into harmony with these laws, you can get the wind to

do your work. You can erect your windmill so that, whichever way the wind blows, the wheels will turn, and the wind will grind your grain or pump your water. Just so, while we cannot dictate to the Holy Spirit, we can learn the laws of His operations. By bringing ourselves into harmony with those laws, above all by submitting our wills absolutely to His sovereign will, the sovereign Spirit of God will work through us and accomplish His own glorious work through us.

Like the wind, the Spirit is invisible, yet it is perceptible, real, and mighty.

You hear the sound of the wind (see John 3:8), but the wind itself you never see. You hear the voice of the Spirit, but He is invisible. (The word translated *"sound"* in John 3:8 is the word translated *voice* elsewhere in Scripture and here in other versions.) We not only hear the voice of the wind, but we see its mighty effects. We feel the breath of the wind on our cheeks; we see the dust and the leaves blowing before the wind; we see the vessels at sea driven swiftly toward their ports; but the wind itself remains invisible. It is the same with the Spirit. We feel His breath on our souls and see the mighty things He does, but we do not see Him. He is invisible, but He is real and perceptible.

I will never forget a solemn hour in Chicago Avenue Church. Dr. W. W. White was making a farewell address before going to India to work among the students there. Suddenly, without any apparent warning, the place was filled with an awesome and glorious Presence. To me it was very real, but the question arose in my mind, "Is this merely subjective, just a feeling of my own, or is there an objective Presence here?" After the meeting was over, I asked different people whether they were conscious of anything and found that at the same point in the meeting, they, too, though they saw no one, became distinctly conscious of an overwhelming Presence, the presence of the Holy Spirit. Though many years have passed, there are those who speak of that hour to this day.

On another occasion in my own home in Chicago, when kneeling in prayer with an intimate friend, it seemed as if an unseen and awesome Presence entered the room as we prayed. I realized what Eliphaz meant when he said, *"Then a spirit passed before my face; the hair on my body stood up"* (Job 4:15). The moment was overwhelming but as glorious as it was awesome.

These are but two illustrations from many that might be given. None of us has seen the Holy Spirit at any time, but we have been distinctly conscious again and again of His presence. We have witnessed His mighty power, and His reality we cannot doubt. There are those who tell us that they do not believe in anything that they cannot see. Not one of them has ever seen the wind, but they all believe in the wind. They have felt the wind, and they have seen its effects. Likewise, we, beyond a question, have felt the mighty presence of the Spirit and witnessed His mighty workings.

Like the wind, the Spirit is inscrutable.

"You hear the sound of it, but cannot tell where it comes from and where it goes" (John 3:8). Nothing in nature is more mysterious than the wind. Even more mysterious still is the Holy Spirit in His operations. We hear of how suddenly and unexpectedly in widely separated communities, He begins to work His mighty work. Doubtless, there are hidden reasons why He begins His work, but often these reasons are completely undiscoverable by us. We do not know where He comes from or where He goes. We cannot tell where He will display His mighty, gracious power next.

Like the wind, the Spirit is indispensable.

Without wind, that is, air in motion, there is no life, and so Jesus says, *"Most assuredly, I say to you, unless one is born of water and the Spirit, he cannot enter the kingdom of God"* (John 3:5). If the wind should absolutely cease to blow for a single hour, most of the life on this earth would cease to be. Time and again when health reports of different cities of the United States are issued, it has been found that the five healthiest cities in the United States were five cities located on the Great Lakes. Many have been surprised at this report when they have

105

visited some of these cities and found that they were far from being the cleanest cities or the most sanitary in their general appearance. Yet year after year this fact has been reported. The explanation is simply this: it is the wind blowing from the lakes that has brought life and health to the cities. Just so, when the Spirit ceases to blow in any heart, in any church, or in any community, death ensues, but when the Spirit blows steadily on the individual, the church, or the community, there is abounding spiritual life and health.

Closely related to the foregoing thought, like the wind, the Holy Spirit is life-giving.

This thought comes out repeatedly in the Scriptures. For example, we read in John 6:63: *"It is the Spirit who gives life,"* and in 2 Corinthians 3:6: *"The letter kills, but the Spirit gives life."* Perhaps the most suggestive passage on this point is Ezekiel 37:8–10. (Compare John 3:5.)

> *Indeed, as I looked, the sinews and the flesh came upon them, and the skin covered them over; but there was no breath in them. Also He said to me, "Prophesy to the breath, prophesy, son of man, and say to the breath, 'Thus says the Lord GOD: "Come from the four winds, O breath, and breathe on these slain, that they may live."'"*
> *So I prophesied as He commanded me, and breath came into them, and they lived, and stood upon their feet, an exceedingly great army.*

Israel, in the prophet's vision, was only bones, *"very many"* and *"very dry"* (v. 2), until the prophet proclaimed to them the word of God. Then there was a noise and a shaking, and the bones came together; bone joined to bone, and the sinews and the flesh came upon the bones. Still there was no life, but when the wind blew the breath of God's Spirit, then they *"stood upon their feet, an exceedingly great army"* (v. 10).

All life in the individual believer, the teacher, the preacher, and the church is the Holy Spirit's work. You will sometimes make the acquaintance of a man, and as you hear him talk and observe his conduct, you are repelled and disgusted. Everything about him declares that he is a dead man, a moral corpse, not only dead but rapidly decaying. You get away from him as quickly as you can. Months afterwards, you meet him again. You hesitate to speak to him; you want to get out of his very presence. But you do speak to him, and he has not spoken many words before you notice a marvelous change. His conversation is sweet and wholesome and uplifting; everything about his manner is attractive and delightful. You soon discover that the man's whole conduct and life has been transformed. He is no longer a decaying corpse but a living child of God. What has happened? The Wind of God has blown on him; he has received the Holy Spirit, the Holy Wind.

Some quiet Sabbath day you visit a church. Everything about the outward appearance of the church is all that could be desired. There is an attractive sanctuary, an expensive organ, a gifted choir, a scholarly preacher. The service is well arranged, but you have not been there long before you are forced to see that there is no life, that it is all form, and that there is nothing really being accomplished for God or for man. You go away with a heavy heart. Months later, you have occasion to visit the church again. The outward look of the church is much as it was before, but the service has not proceeded far before you note a great difference. There is a new power in the singing, a new spirit in the prayer, a new force in the preaching; everything about the church is teeming with the life of God. What has happened? The Wind of God has blown on that church; the Holy Spirit, the Holy Wind, has come.

You go some day to hear a preacher of whose abilities you have heard great reports. As he stands up to preach, you soon learn that almost all of what has been said in praise of his abilities has been from the merely intellectual and rhetorical standpoint. His diction is faultless, his style beautiful, his logic unimpeachable, his orthodoxy beyond criticism. It is an intellectual treat to listen to him. Yet after all, as he preaches, you cannot avoid a feeling of sadness, for there is no real strength, no real power, indeed, no life in the man's preaching. You go away with a heavy heart at the thought of this waste of magnificent abilities. Months, perhaps years, pass by. You again find yourself listening to this celebrated preacher, but what a change! The same faultless diction, the same beautiful style, the same unimpeachable logic, the same skillful articulation, the same sound orthodoxy, but now there is something more. There is reality, life, force, and power in the preaching. Men and women sit breathless as he speaks; sinners bow with tears of contrition, pricked to their hearts with conviction of sin. Men and women and boys and girls renounce their selfishness, their sins, their worldliness, and accept Jesus Christ. They surrender their lives to Him. What has happened? The Wind of God has blown on that man. He has been filled with the Holy Wind.

Like the wind, the Holy Spirit is irresistible.

We read in Acts 1:8:

But you shall receive power when the Holy Spirit has come upon you; and you shall be witnesses to Me in Jerusalem, and in all Judea and Samaria, and to the end of the earth.

When this promise of our Lord was fulfilled in Stephen, we read: *"And they were not able to resist the wisdom and the Spirit by which he spoke"* (Acts 6:10). A man filled with the Holy Spirit is transformed into a cyclone. What can stand before the wind? When St. Cloud, Minnesota, was visited with a cyclone years ago, the wind picked up loaded freight cars and carried them off the track. It wrenched an iron bridge from its foundations, twisted it together, and hurled it away. When a cyclone later hit St. Louis, Missouri, it snapped off telegraph poles a foot in diameter as if they had been twigs. It leveled enormous trees close to the root, and it cut off the corners of brick buildings as though they had been cut by a knife. Nothing could stand before it, just as nothing can stand before a Spirit-filled preacher of the Word. None can resist the wisdom and the Spirit by which he speaks.

The Wind of God took possession of Charles G. Finney, an obscure country lawyer, and sent him through New York, then through New England, then through England, mowing down strong men by his Spirit-given logic. One night in Rochester, scores of lawyers, led by the justice of the Court of Appeals, filed out of the pews, bowed in the aisles, and yielded their lives to God.

The Wind of God took possession of D. L. Moody, an uneducated young businessman in Chicago. In the power of this irresistible Wind, men, women, and young people were brought in humble confession and renunciation of sin to the feet of Jesus Christ and filled with the life of God. They were the pillars in the churches of Great Britain and throughout the world after that. The great need today in individuals, in churches, and in preachers is that the Wind of God would blow upon us.

Much of the difficulty that many find with John 3:5, *"Jesus answered, 'Most assuredly, I say to you, unless one is born of water and the Spirit, he cannot enter the kingdom of God,'"* would disappear if we would only bear in mind that *"Spirit"* means "Wind" and translate the verse literally all through: "Unless one is born of water and Wind [there is no *the* in the original], he cannot enter the kingdom of God." The thought would then seem to be, "Unless one is born of the cleansing and quickening power of the Spirit [or else of the cleansing Word—compare John 15:3; Ephesians 5:26; James 1:18; 1 Peter 1:23—and the quickening power of the Holy Spirit]."

The Spirit of God

The Holy Spirit is frequently spoken of in the Bible as the Spirit of God. For example: *"Do you not know that you are the temple of God and that the Spirit of God dwells in you?"* (1 Cor. 3:16). In this name, we have the same essential thought as in the former name but with this addition, that His divine origin, nature, and power are emphasized. He is not merely the "Wind," but "the Wind of God."

The Spirit of Jehovah

This name of the Holy Spirit is used in Isaiah 11:2 (ASV): *"And the Spirit of Jehovah shall rest upon him."* The thought of the name is, of course, essentially the same as the preceding with the exception that God is here thought of as the Covenant

God of Israel. He is thus spoken of in the connection in which the name is found, and, of course, the Bible, following that unerring accuracy that it always exhibits in its use of the different names for God, in this connection speaks of the Spirit as the Spirit of Jehovah and not merely as the Spirit of God.

The Spirit of the Lord Jehovah

The Holy Spirit is called the Spirit of the Lord Jehovah in Isaiah 61:1 (ASV):

The Spirit of the Lord Jehovah is upon me; because Jehovah hath anointed me to preach good tidings unto the meek; he hath sent me to bind up the broken-hearted, to proclaim liberty to the captives.

Here the Holy Spirit is spoken of not merely as the Spirit of Jehovah but as the Spirit of the Lord Jehovah because of the relation in which God Himself is spoken of in this connection. He is not merely Jehovah, the Covenant God of Israel, but Lord Jehovah, Israel's Lord as well as their covenant-keeping God. This name of the Spirit is even more expressive than the name the Spirit of God.

The Spirit of the Living God

The Holy Spirit is called the Spirit of the living God in 2 Corinthians 3:3:

Clearly you are an epistle of Christ, ministered by us, written not with ink but by the Spirit of the living God, not on tablets of stone but on tablets of flesh, that is, of the heart.

What is the significance of this name? It is made clear by the context. The apostle Paul is contrasting the Word of God written with ink on parchment and the Word of God written on *"tablets of flesh"* by the Holy Spirit. In this connection, the Holy Spirit is called the Spirit of the living God because He makes God a living reality in our personal experience instead of a mere intellectual concept.

Many believe in God and are perfectly orthodox in their conception of God, but God is to them only an intellectual, theological proposition. It is the work of the Holy Spirit to make God something vastly more than a theological notion, no matter how orthodox. He is the Spirit of the living God, and it is His work to make God a living God to us, a being whom we know, with whom we have personal acquaintance, a being more real to us than the most intimate human friend we have. Do you have a real God? Well, you can have. The Holy Spirit is the Spirit of the living God, and He is able and ready to give to you a living God, to make God real in your personal experience.

Many have a God who once lived and acted and spoke, a God who lived and acted at the creation of the universe, who perhaps lived and acted in the days of Moses, Elijah, Jesus Christ, and the apostles, but who no longer lives and acts. If He exists at all, He has withdrawn Himself from any active part in nature or the history of man. He created nature and gave it its laws and powers but now leaves it to run itself. He created man and endowed him with his various faculties but now has left him to work out his own destiny. They may go further than this; they may believe in a God who spoke to Abraham, to Moses, to David, to Isaiah, to Jesus, and to the apostles but who speaks no longer. We may read in the Bible what He spoke to these various men, but we cannot expect Him to speak to us.

In contrast to these, it is the work of the Holy Spirit, the Spirit of the living God, to enable us to know a God who lives and acts and speaks today, a God who is ready to come as near to us as He came to Abraham, Moses, Isaiah, the apostles, or to Jesus Himself. Not that He has any new revelations to make, for He guided the apostles into all the truth (see John 16:13), but though there has been a complete revelation of God's truth made in the Bible, God still lives today and will speak to us as directly as He spoke to His chosen ones of old. Happy is the one who knows the Holy Spirit as the Spirit of the living God, and who, consequently, has a real God, a God who lives today, a God on whom he can depend to undertake for him, a God with whom he enjoys intimate personal fellowship, a God to whom he may raise his voice in prayer and who answers him.

The Spirit of Christ

"But you are not in the flesh but in the Spirit, if indeed the Spirit of God dwells in you. Now if anyone does not have the Spirit of Christ, he is not His" (Rom. 8:9). The Holy Spirit is called the Spirit of Christ. The Spirit of Christ in this passage does not mean a Christlike spirit. It means something far more than that—it is a name of the Holy Spirit. Why is the Holy Spirit called the Spirit of Christ? For several reasons.

Because He is Christ's gift.

The Holy Spirit is not merely the gift of the Father, but the gift of the Son as well. We read in John 20:22 that Jesus *"breathed on them, and said to them, 'Receive the Holy Spirit.'"* The Holy Spirit is therefore the breath of Christ as well as the breath of God the Father. It is Christ who breathes on us and imparts the Holy Spirit to us.

In John 14:15–26, Jesus teaches that it is in answer to His prayer that the Father gives the Holy Spirit to us. In Acts 2:33, we read that Jesus, *"being exalted to the right hand of God, and having received from the Father the promise of the Holy Spirit,"* poured out the Spirit on believers. That verse says that Jesus, having been exalted to the right hand of God, in answer to His prayer, received the Holy Spirit from the Father and shed forth upon the church Him whom He had received from the Father. In Matthew 3:11, we read that it is Jesus who baptizes with the Holy Spirit. In John 7:37–39, Jesus invites all who are thirsty to come to Him and drink, and the context makes it clear that the water that He gives is the Holy Spirit, who becomes in those who receive Him a source of life and power flowing out to others. It is the glorified Christ who gives to the church the Holy Spirit. In John 4:10, Jesus declares that He is the One who gives the living water, the Holy Spirit. In all these passages, Christ is set forth as the One who gives the Holy Spirit, so the Holy Spirit is called the Spirit of Christ.

There is a deeper reason why the Holy Spirit is called the Spirit of Christ—it is the work of the Holy Spirit to reveal Christ to us.

In John 16:14, we read: *"He* [the Holy Spirit] *will glorify Me, for He will take of what is Mine and declare it to you."* In a similar way, it is written, *"But when the Helper comes, whom I shall send to you from the Father, the Spirit of truth who proceeds from the Father, He will testify of Me"* (John 15:26). The work of the Holy Spirit is to bear witness of Christ and reveal Jesus Christ to men. And as the revealer of Christ, He is called the Spirit of Christ.

There is a still deeper reason why the Holy Spirit is called the Spirit of Christ—it is His work to form Christ as a living presence within us.

In Ephesians 3:16–17, the apostle Paul prays to the Father:

That He would grant you, according to the riches of His glory, to be strengthened with might through His Spirit in the inner man, that Christ may dwell in your hearts through faith.

This then is the work of the Holy Spirit, to cause Christ to dwell in our hearts, to form the living Christ within us. Just as the Holy Spirit literally and physically formed Jesus Christ in the womb of the Virgin Mary (see Luke 1:35), so the Holy Spirit spiritually but really forms Jesus Christ within our hearts today. Jesus told His disciples that when the Holy Spirit came, He Himself would come; that is, the result of the coming of the Holy Spirit to dwell in their hearts would be the coming of Christ Himself.

And I will pray the Father, and He will give you another Helper, that He may abide with you forever; the Spirit of truth, whom the world cannot receive, because it neither sees Him nor knows Him; but you know Him, for He dwells with you and will be in you. I will not leave you orphans; I will come to you.   (John 14:16–18)

It is the privilege of every believer in Christ to have the living Christ formed by the power of the Holy Spirit in his own heart; therefore, the Holy Spirit who forms Christ within the heart is called the Spirit of Christ. How wonderful! How glorious is the significance of this name. Let us ponder it until we understand it, as far as it is possible to understand, and until we rejoice exceedingly in the glory of it.

The Spirit of Jesus Christ

The Holy Spirit is called the Spirit of Jesus Christ in Philippians 1:19: *"For I know that this will turn out for my deliverance through your prayer and the supply of the Spirit of Jesus Christ."* The Spirit is not merely the Spirit of the eternal Word, but the Spirit of the Word incarnate; not merely the Spirit of Christ, but the Spirit of Jesus Christ. It is the Man Jesus exalted to the right hand of the Father who receives and sends the Spirit. So we read in Acts 2:32–33:

> *This Jesus God has raised up, of which we are all witnesses. Therefore being exalted to the right hand of God, and having received from the Father the promise of the Holy Spirit, He poured out this which you now see and hear.*

The Spirit of Jesus

The Holy Spirit is called the Spirit of Jesus:

> *And they went through the region of Phrygia and Galatia, having been forbidden of the Holy Spirit to speak the word in Asia; and when they were come over against Mysia, they assayed to go into Bithynia; and the Spirit of Jesus suffered them not.* (Acts 16:6–7 ASV)

By using this name, the Spirit of Jesus, the thought of the relation of the Spirit to the Man Jesus is still clearer than in the name preceding this, the Spirit of Jesus Christ.

The Spirit of His Son

The Holy Spirit is called the Spirit of His Son in Galatians 4:6: *"And because you are sons, God has sent forth the Spirit of*

His Son into your hearts, crying out, 'Abba, Father!'" We see from the context of the preceding verses that this name is given to the Holy Spirit in special connection with His testifying to the sonship of the believer:

> *But when the fullness of the time had come, God sent forth His Son, born of a woman, born under the law, to redeem those who were under the law, that we might receive the adoption as sons.* (Gal. 4:4–5)

It is the Spirit of His Son who testifies to our sonship. The thought is that the Holy Spirit is a filial Spirit, a Spirit who produces a sense of sonship in us. If we receive the Holy Spirit, we no longer think of God as if we were serving under constraint and bondage, but we are His children living in joyous liberty. We do not fear God; we trust Him and rejoice in Him. When we receive the Holy Spirit, we do not receive a *"spirit of bondage again to fear"* (Rom. 8:15) but *"the Spirit of adoption by whom we cry out, 'Abba, Father'"* (v. 15). This name of the Holy Spirit is one of the most suggestive of all. We do well to ponder it long until we realize the glad fullness of its significance. We will take it up again when we come to study the work of the Holy Spirit.

The Holy Spirit

This name is frequently used, and it is the name with which most of us are familiar. One of the most well-known passages in which the name is used is Luke 11:13: *"If you then, being evil, know how to give good gifts to your children, how much more will your heavenly Father give the Holy Spirit to those who ask Him!"* This name emphasizes the essential moral character of the Spirit. He is holy in Himself. We are so familiar with the name that we neglect to consider its significance. Oh, if we only realized more deeply and constantly that He is the Holy Spirit! We would do well if we, like the seraphim in Isaiah's vision, would bow in His presence and cry, *"Holy, holy, holy"* (Isa. 6:3). Yet how thoughtlessly we often talk about Him and pray for Him. We pray for Him to come into our churches and into our hearts, but what would He find if He would come there? Would He find much that would be painful and agonizing to Him?

What would we think if vile women from the lowest den of iniquity would go to the purest woman in their city and invite her to come and live with them in their disgusting corruption with no intention of changing their evil ways? But that would not be as shocking as for you and me to ask the Holy Spirit to come and dwell in our hearts when we have no intention of giving up our impurity, our selfishness, our worldliness, or our sins. It would not be as shocking as it is for us to invite the Holy Spirit to come into our churches when they are full of worldliness, selfishness, contention, envy, pride, and all that is unholy.

However, if the inhabitants of the vilest den of infamy would go to the purest, most Christlike woman, asking her to go and live with them with the intention of putting away everything that was vile and evil and giving to this holy and Christlike woman the entire control of the place, she would go. As sinful, selfish, and imperfect as we may be, the infinitely holy Spirit is ready to come and take His dwelling in our hearts if we will surrender to Him the absolute control of our lives and allow Him to bring everything—our thoughts and our actions—into conformity with His will. The infinitely holy Spirit is ready to come into our churches, however imperfect and worldly they may be now, if we are willing to put the absolute control of everything in His hands. But let us never forget that He is the Holy Spirit; when we pray to Him, let us pray to Him as such.

The Holy Spirit of Promise

The Holy Spirit is called the Holy Spirit of promise in Ephesians 1:13: *"In Him you also trusted, after you heard the word of truth, the gospel of your salvation; in whom also, having believed, you were sealed with the Holy Spirit of promise."* We have here the same name as that given above with the added thought that this Holy Spirit is the great promise of the Father and of the Son. The Holy Spirit is God's great all-inclusive promise for the present dispensation. The one thing Jesus commanded the disciples to wait for after His ascension before they undertook His work was *"the Promise of the Father"* (Acts 1:4), that is, the Holy Spirit.

The great promise of the Father, until the coming of Christ was the coming atoning Savior and King. When Jesus came and died His atoning death on the cross of Calvary and arose and ascended to the right hand of the Father, then the second great promise of the Father was the Holy Spirit to take the place of our absent Lord. (See Acts 2:33.)

The Spirit of Holiness

The Holy Spirit is called the Spirit of holiness in Romans 1:4: *"And declared to be the Son of God with power according to the Spirit of holiness, by the resurrection from the dead."* At first glance, it may seem as if there were no essential difference between the two names, the Holy Spirit and the Spirit of holiness, but there is a marked difference. The name of the Holy Spirit, as already said, emphasizes the essential moral character of the Spirit as holy, but the name the Spirit of holiness brings out the thought that the Holy Spirit is not merely holy in Himself, but He imparts holiness to others. To those who receive Him, He imparts the perfect holiness that He Himself possesses. (See 1 Peter 1:2.)

The Spirit of Judgment

The Holy Spirit is called the spirit of judgment in Isaiah 4:4: *"When the Lord has washed away the filth of the daughters of Zion, and purged the blood of Jerusalem from her midst, by the spirit of judgment and by the spirit of burning."* There are two names of the Holy Spirit in this passage. The first is the spirit of judgment. The Holy Spirit is so called because it is His work to bring sin to light, to convict of sin. (See John 16:7–9.) When the Holy Spirit comes to us, the first thing that He does is to open our eyes to see our sins as God sees them. He judges our sins. (We will go into this more at length in studying John 16:7–11 when considering the work of the Holy Spirit.)

The Spirit of Burning

This name is used in the passage just quoted above. This name emphasizes His searching, refining, rubbish-consuming, illuminating, and energizing work. The Holy Spirit is like a fire in the heart in which He dwells, and as fire tests, refines, consumes, illuminates, warms, and energizes, so does He. In the context, it is the cleansing work of the Holy Spirit that is especially emphasized. (See Isaiah 4:3–4.)

The Spirit of Truth

The Holy Spirit is called the Spirit of truth in John 14:17: *"The Spirit of truth, whom the world cannot receive, because it neither sees Him nor knows Him; but you know Him, for He dwells with you and will be in you."* (See John 15:26; 16:13.) The Holy Spirit is called the Spirit of truth because it is the work of the Holy Spirit to communicate and to impart truth to those who receive Him. This comes out in the passage given above, and, if possible, it is revealed even more clearly in John 16:13: *"However, when He, the Spirit of truth, has come, He will guide you into all truth; for He will not speak on His own authority, but whatever He hears He will speak; and He will tell you things to come."* All truth is from the Holy Spirit. It is only as He teaches us that we come to know the truth.

The Spirit of Wisdom and Understanding

The Holy Spirit is called the Spirit of wisdom and understanding in Isaiah 11:2: *"The Spirit of the LORD shall rest upon Him, the Spirit of wisdom and understanding, the Spirit of counsel and might, the Spirit of knowledge and of the fear of the LORD."* The significance of the name is so plain that it needs no explanation. It is evident both from the words used and from the context that it is the work of the Holy Spirit to impart wisdom and understanding to those who receive Him. Those who receive the Holy Spirit receive the Spirit *"of power and of love and of a sound mind* [or sound sense]" (2 Tim. 1:7).

The Spirit of Counsel and Might

We find this name used of the Holy Spirit in the passage given in the preceding section. The meaning of this name is also obvious; the Holy Spirit is called *"the Spirit of counsel and might"* (Isa. 11:2) because He gives us counsel in all our plans and strength to carry them out. (Compare Acts 1:8; 8:29; 16:6–7.) It is our privilege to have God's own counsel in all our plans and God's strength in all the work that we undertake for Him. We receive them by receiving the Holy Spirit, the Spirit of counsel and might.

The Spirit of Knowledge and of the Fear of the LORD

This name also is used in the passage given above (Isa. 11:2). The significance of this name is also obvious. It is the work of the Holy Spirit to impart knowledge to us and to place in us a reverence for Jehovah, a reverence that reveals itself above all in obedience to His commandments. The one who receives the Holy Spirit finds his delight *"in the fear of the LORD"* (v. 3). The three suggestive names just given refer especially to the gracious work of the Holy Spirit in the servant of the Lord, that is, Jesus Christ. (See Isaiah 11:1–5.)

The Spirit of Life

The Holy Spirit is called the Spirit of life in Romans 8:2: *"For the law of the Spirit of life in Christ Jesus has made me free from the law of sin and death."* The Holy Spirit is called the Spirit of life because it is His work to impart life. (Compare John 6:63; Ezekiel 37:1–10.) Beginning back in Romans 7:7, Paul drew a contrast between the law of Moses outside a man— holy and just and good, it is true, but impotent—and the living Spirit of God in the heart, imparting spiritual and moral life to the believer and enabling him to meet the requirements of the law of God. He draws this contrast to show that *"what the law could not do in that it was weak through the flesh"* (Rom. 8:3), the Spirit of God imparting life to the believer and dwelling in the heart enables him to do. Therefore, the righteousness of the law is fulfilled in those who do not walk after the flesh but after the Spirit (v. 4):

> *For the law of the Spirit of life in Christ Jesus has made me free from the law of sin and death. For what the law*

> *could not do in that it was weak through the flesh, God did*
> *by sending His own Son in the likeness of sinful flesh, on*
> *account of sin: He condemned sin in the flesh, that the*
> *righteous requirement of the law might be fulfilled in us*
> *who do not walk according to the flesh but according to the*
> *Spirit.* (Rom. 8:2–4)

The Holy Spirit is therefore called the Spirit of life, because He imparts spiritual life, consequently victory over sin, to those who receive Him.

The Oil of Gladness

The Holy Spirit is called *"the oil of gladness"* in Hebrews 1:9: *"You have loved righteousness and hated lawlessness; therefore God, Your God, has anointed You with the oil of gladness more than Your companions."* Someone may ask what reason we have for supposing that *"the oil of gladness"* in this passage is a name of the Holy Spirit. The answer is found in a comparison of Hebrews 1:9 with Acts 10:38 and Luke 4:18. In Acts 10:38, we read about *"how God anointed Jesus of Nazareth with the Holy Spirit and with power."* In Luke 4:18, Jesus Himself is recorded as saying, *"The Spirit of the LORD is upon Me, because He has anointed Me to preach the gospel to the poor."* In both these passages, we are told that Jesus was anointed with the Holy Spirit. As in the passage in Hebrews, we are told that it was with *"the oil of gladness"* that He was anointed; therefore, the only possible conclusion is that *"the oil of gladness"* means the Holy Spirit. What a beautiful, significant name it is for Him whose fruit is first, *"love"* and then, *"joy"* (Gal. 5:22).

The Holy Spirit becomes a source of boundless joy to those who receive Him. He fills and satisfies the soul, so that the soul who receives Him *"will never thirst"* (John 4:14). No matter how great the afflictions with which the believer receives the Word, still he will have the *"joy of the Holy Spirit"* (1 Thess. 1:6).

On the Day of Pentecost, when the disciples were baptized with the Holy Spirit, they were so filled with ecstatic joy that others looking at them thought they were intoxicated. They said, *"They are full of new wine"* (Acts 2:13). Paul drew a comparison between intoxication that comes through excess of wine and the wholesome exhilaration that comes through being filled with the Spirit:

> *And do not be drunk with wine, in which is dissipation; but be filled with the Spirit, speaking to one another in psalms and hymns and spiritual songs, singing and making melody in your heart to the Lord, giving thanks always for all things to God the Father in the name of our Lord Jesus Christ.* (Eph. 5:18–20)

When God anoints one with the Holy Spirit, it is as if He breaks a precious alabaster box of oil of gladness above his head until it runs down to the hem of his garments and the whole person is suffused *"with joy inexpressible and full of glory"* (1 Pet. 1:8).

The Spirit of Grace

The Holy Spirit is called the Spirit of grace in Hebrews 10:29:

> *Of how much worse punishment, do you suppose, will he be thought worthy who has trampled the Son of God underfoot, counted the blood of the covenant by which he was sanctified a common thing, and insulted the Spirit of grace?*

This name emphasizes the Holy Spirit's work to administer and apply the grace of God. He Himself is gracious, it is true, but the name means far more than that. The name means that He makes the manifold grace of God ours experientially. It is only by the work of the Spirit of grace in our hearts that we are enabled to appropriate to ourselves that infinite fullness of grace that God has bestowed on us from the beginning in Jesus Christ. It is ours from the beginning, as far as belonging to us is concerned, but it is only ours experientially as we claim it by the power of the Spirit of grace.

The Spirit of Grace and of Supplication

The Holy Spirit is called the Spirit of grace and supplication in Zechariah 12:10:

> *And I will pour on the house of David and on the inhabitants of Jerusalem the Spirit of grace and supplication; then they will look on Me whom they pierced. Yes, they will mourn for Him as one mourns for his only son, and grieve for Him as one grieves for a firstborn.*

The phrase *"the Spirit of grace and supplication"* in this passage is beyond a doubt a name of the Holy Spirit.

The name the Spirit of grace we have already studied in the previous section, but here there is a further thought of that operation of grace that leads us to pray intensely. The Holy Spirit is so called because it is He who teaches us to pray. All true prayer is in the Spirit: *"But you, beloved, building yourselves up on your most holy faith, praying in the Holy Spirit"* (Jude 20). In ourselves, *"we do not know what we should pray for as we ought, but the Spirit Himself makes intercession for us with groanings which cannot be uttered"* (Rom. 8:26). He leads us to pray *"according to the will of God"* (v. 27). The secret of all true and effective praying is knowing the Holy Spirit as the Spirit of grace and supplication.

The Spirit of Glory

The Holy Spirit is called *"the Spirit of glory"* in 1 Peter 4:14: *"If you are reproached for the name of Christ, blessed are you, for the Spirit of glory and of God rests upon you. On their part He is blasphemed, but on your part He is glorified."* This name does not merely teach that the Holy Spirit is infinitely glorious Himself, but rather that He imparts the glory of God to us, just as the Spirit of truth imparts truth to us. The Spirit of life imparts life to us; the Spirit of wisdom and understanding imparts wisdom and understanding; the Spirit of counsel and might imparts counsel and might; the Spirit of knowledge and of the fear of the Lord imparts to us knowledge and the fear of the Lord; the Spirit of grace applies and administers to us the manifold grace of God; likewise, the Spirit of glory is the administrator to us of God's glory.

In the preceding verse, we read: *"Rejoice to the extent that you partake of Christ's sufferings, that when His glory is revealed, you may also be glad with exceeding joy"* (v. 13). It is in this connection that He is called the Spirit of glory. We find a similar connection between the sufferings that we endure and the glory that the Holy Spirit imparts to us:

The Spirit Himself bears witness with our spirit that we are children of God, and if children, then heirs; heirs of God and joint heirs with Christ, if indeed we suffer with Him, that we may also be glorified together.

(Rom. 8:16–17)

The Holy Spirit is the administrator of glory as well as of grace, or rather of the grace that culminates in glory.

The Eternal Spirit

The Holy Spirit is called the eternal Spirit in Hebrews 9:14: *"How much more shall the blood of Christ, who through the eternal Spirit offered Himself without spot to God, cleanse your conscience from dead works to serve the living God?"* The eternity, the deity, and infinite majesty of the Holy Spirit are brought out by this name.

The Helper

The Holy Spirit is called the Helper over and over again in the Scriptures. For example in John 14:26, we read: *"But the Helper, the Holy Spirit, whom the Father will send in My name, He will teach you all things, and bring to your remembrance all things that I said to you."* And in John 15:26: *"But when the Helper comes, whom I shall send to you from the Father, the Spirit of truth who proceeds from the Father, He will testify of Me."* (See also John 16:27.)

The word translated *"Helper"* in these passages means that, but it means much more. It is difficult to adequately translate the Greek word into any one word in English. The word translated *"Helper"* means literally, "one called to another's side," the idea being, one right at hand to take another's part. It is the same word that is translated *"Advocate"* in 1 John 2:1: *"My little children, these things I write to you, so that you may not sin. And if anyone sins, we have an Advocate with the Father, Jesus Christ the righteous."* The word *advocate,* as we now understand it, does not give the full force of the Greek word. Etymologically, *advocate* means nearly the same thing. *Advocate* is from the Latin, "advocatus," and means "one called to another to take his part," but in our modern usage, the word has acquired a restricted meaning. The Greek word, *Parakletos,* is translated "Helper" and means "one called alongside," that is, one called to stand constantly by one's side and who is ever ready to stand by us and take our part in everything in which his help is needed. It is a wonderfully tender and expressive name for the Holy One. Sometimes when we think of the Holy Spirit, He seems to be so far away, but when we think of the *Parakletos,* or in plain English, our "Standbyer" or our "Part-taker," how near He is.

Up to the time that Jesus made this promise to the disciples, He Himself had been their *Parakletos.* When they were in any emergency or difficulty, they turned to Him. On one occasion, for example, the disciples were in doubt as to how to pray, and they turned to Jesus and said, *"Lord, teach us to pray"* (Luke 11:1). And the Lord taught them this wonderful prayer that has come down through the ages:

> *So He said to them, "When you pray, say: Our Father in heaven, Hallowed be Your name. Your kingdom come. Your will be done on earth as it is in heaven. Give us day by day our daily bread. And forgive us our sins, for we also forgive everyone who is indebted to us. And do not lead us into temptation, but deliver us from the evil one."*
>
> (Luke 11:2–4)

On another occasion, Peter was sinking in the waves of Galilee and cried, *"Lord, save me!"* (Matt. 14:30), and *"immediately Jesus stretched out His hand and caught him"* (v. 31). In every extremity, they turned to Him. Likewise, now that Jesus is gone to the Father, we have another person, just as divine as He is, just as wise as He, just as strong as He, just as loving as He, just as tender as He, just as ready, and just as able to help, who is always right by our side. Yes, better yet, He dwells in our hearts and will take hold and help if we only trust Him to do it.

If the truth of the Holy Spirit as set forth in the name *Parakletos* once gets into our hearts and abides there, it will banish all loneliness forever, for how can we ever be lonely when this best of all friends is ever with us? In the last eight years, I have been called on to endure what would naturally be a very lonely life. Most of the time, I am separated from my wife and children by the call of duty. For eighteen months consecutively, I was separated from almost all my family by many thousands of miles. The loneliness would have been unendurable were it not for the one all-sufficient Friend, who was always with me.

I recall one night walking up and down the deck of a storm-tossed steamer in the South Seas. Most of my family were eighteen thousand miles away; the remaining member of my family was not with me. The officers were busy on the bridge. I was pacing the deck alone, and the thought came to me, "Here you are all alone." Then another thought came, "I am not alone; as I walk this deck in the loneliness and the storm, the Holy Spirit walks by my side," and He was enough.

I said something like this once at a Bible conference in St. Paul. A doctor came to me at the close of the meeting and gently said, "I want to thank you for that thought about the Holy Spirit always being with us. I am a doctor. Often in stormy weather, late at night, I have to drive far out in the country to attend to a case. I have often been so lonely, but I will never be lonely again. I will always know that by my side in my carriage, the Holy Spirit goes with me."

If this thought of the Holy Spirit as the ever present Paraclete once gets into your heart and abides there, it will banish all fear forever. How can we be afraid in the face of any peril, if this divine One is by our side to counsel us and to take our part? There may be a howling mob about us or a threatening storm; it does not matter. He stands between us and anything that would alarm us.

One night I had promised to walk four miles to a friend's house after an evening session of a conference. As I started for my friend's house, a thunderstorm was coming up. I had not counted on this, but since I had promised, I felt I should go. The path led along the edge of the lake, often very near to the edge. Sometimes the lake was near the path and sometimes many feet below. The night was so dark that I could not see ahead. Now and then, there would be a blinding flash of lightning in which I could see where the path was washed away, and then it would be blacker than ever. I could hear the lake booming below. It seemed a dangerous place to walk. But that very week, I had been speaking on the personality of the Holy Spirit and about the Holy Spirit as an ever present friend. The thought came to me, "What was it you were telling the people in the message about the Holy Spirit as an ever present friend?" And then I said to myself, "Between me and the churning lake and the edge of the path walks the Holy Spirit," and I pushed on, fearless and glad.

When we were in London, a young lady attended the meeting one afternoon in the Royal Albert Hall. She had an abnormal fear of the dark. It was absolutely impossible for her to go into a dark room alone, but the thought of the Holy Spirit as an ever present friend sank into her mind. She went home and told her mother what a wonderful thought she had heard that day and how it had banished forever all fear from her. It was already growing very dark in the London winter afternoon, and her mother looked up and said, "Very well, let us see if it is real. Go up to the top of the house and shut yourself alone in a dark room." She instantly sprang to her feet, bounded up the stairs, went into a room that was totally dark, shut the door, and sat down. All fear was gone, and as she wrote the next day, the whole room seemed to be filled with a wonderful glory, the glory of the presence of the Holy Spirit.

In the thought of the Holy Spirit as the Paraclete, there is also a cure for insomnia. For two awful years, I suffered from insomnia. Night after night, I would go to bed feeling nearly dead from lack of sleep. It seemed as though I must sleep, but I could not sleep. Oh, the agony of those two years! I thought I would lose my mind if I did not get relief. Relief came at last, and for years I went on without the suggestion of trouble from insomnia. Then one night, I retired to my room in the institute and lay down expecting to fall asleep in a moment as I usually did. But scarcely had my head touched the pillow when I became aware that insomnia was back again. If one has ever had it, he never forgets it and never mistakes it. It seemed as if insomnia were sitting on the footboard of my bed, grinning at me and saying, "I am back again for another two years." "Oh," I thought, "two more awful years of insomnia."

However, that very morning, I had been lecturing to our students in the institute about the personality of the Holy Spirit and about the Holy Spirit as an ever present friend. At once the thought came to me, "What were you talking to the students about this morning? What were you telling them?" I looked up and said, "Blessed Spirit of God, You are here. I am not alone. If You have anything to say to me, I will listen," and He began to open to me some of the deep and precious things about my Lord and Savior, things that filled my soul with joy and rest. The next thing I knew, I fell asleep and did not awaken until morning. So whenever insomnia has come my way since, I have simply remembered that the Holy Spirit was there, and I have looked up to Him to speak to me and to teach me. He has done so, and insomnia has taken its flight.

In the thought of the Holy Spirit as the Paraclete, there is a cure for a breaking heart. How many aching, breaking hearts there are in this world of ours, so full of death and separation from those we most dearly love. Example after example could be given of a woman who, a few months or a few weeks ago, had no care or no worry, for by her side was a Christian husband who was so wise and strong that the wife rested all responsibility on him and walked carefree through life, happy in his love and companionship. But one awful day, he was taken from her. She was left alone, and all the cares and responsibilities rested on her. How empty that heart has been ever since; how empty the whole world has been. She has just dragged through her life and her duties as best she could with an aching and almost breaking heart. There is One, if she only knew it, wiser and more loving than the tenderest husband, One willing to bear all the care and responsibilities of life for her, One who is able, if she will only let Him, to fill every nook and corner of her empty, broken heart. That One is the Paraclete.

I said something like this in St. Andrews' Hall in Glasgow. At the close of the meeting, a sad-faced Christian woman wearing a widow's garb came to me as I stepped out of the hall into the reception room. She hurried to me and said, "Dr. Torrey, this is the anniversary of my dear husband's death. Just one year ago today he was taken from me. I came today to see if you could not speak some word to help me. You have given me just the word I need. I will never be alone again." A year and a half passed by. I was on the yacht of a friend on the lochs of the Clyde. One day a little boat put out from shore and came alongside the yacht. One of the first to come up the side of the yacht was this widow. She hurried to me, and the first thing she said was, "The thought that you gave me that day in St. Andrews' Hall on the anniversary of my husband's leaving me has been with me ever since, and the Holy Spirit does satisfy me and fill my heart."

It is in our work for our Master that the thought of the Holy Spirit as the Paraclete comes with greatest helpfulness. I think it may be permissible to illustrate it from my own experience. I entered the ministry because I was literally forced to. For years I refused to become a Christian because I was determined that I would not be a preacher, and I feared that if I surrendered to Christ, I would have to enter the ministry. My conversion turned upon my yielding to Him at this point. The night I yielded, I did not say, "I will accept Christ" or "I will give up sin" or anything of that sort. I simply cried, "Take this awful burden off my heart, and I will preach the Gospel." But no one could be less fitted by natural temperament for the ministry than I.

From early boyhood, I was extraordinarily timid and bashful. Even after I had entered Yale College, when I would go home in the summer and my mother would call me in to meet her friends, I was so frightened that when I thought I spoke, I did not make an audible sound. When her friends had gone, my mother would ask, "Why didn't you say something to them?" I would reply that I supposed I had, but my mother would say, "You did not utter a sound." Think of a young fellow like that entering the ministry. I never mustered courage even to speak in a public prayer meeting until after I was in the theological seminary. Then I felt, if I were to enter the ministry, I must be able to at least speak in a prayer meeting. I memorized a little piece to say, but when the hour came, I forgot much of it in my terror. At the critical moment, I grasped the back of the pew in front of me, pulled myself hurriedly to my feet, and held on. One Niagara seemed to be going up one side and another down another; my voice faltered. I repeated as much as I could remember and sat down. Think of a man like that entering the ministry.

In the early days of my ministry, I would write my sermons out in full, commit them to memory, stand up and twist a button until I had repeated it as best I could, and then sink back into the pulpit chair with a sense of relief that that was over for another week. I cannot tell you what I suffered in those early days of my ministry. But the glad day came when I came to know the Holy Spirit as the Paraclete. The thought got possession of me that when I stood up to preach there was Another who stood by my side. While the audience saw me, God saw Him. The responsibility was all on Him. He was abundantly able to meet it and care for it all. All I had to do was to stand back as far out of sight as possible and let Him do the work.

I have no dread of preaching now. Preaching is the greatest joy of my life. Sometimes when I stand up to speak and realize that He is there, that all the responsibility is on Him, such a joy fills my heart that I can scarcely restrain myself from shouting and leaping. He is just as ready to help us in all our work, in our Sunday school classes, in our personal work, and in every other line of Christian effort.

Many hesitate to speak to others about accepting Christ. They are afraid they will not say the right thing; they fear that they will do more harm than good. You certainly will if you do it alone, but if you will just believe in the Paraclete and trust Him to say it and to say it in His way, you will never do harm but always good. It may seem at the time that you have accomplished nothing, but perhaps years later, you will find out you have accomplished much. Even if you do not find it out in this world, you will find it out in eternity.

There are many ways in which the Paraclete stands by us and helps us, which we will examine at length when we come to study His work. He stands by us when we pray (Rom. 8:26–27); when we study the Word (John 14:26; 16:12–14); when we do personal work (Acts 8:29); when we preach or teach (1 Cor. 2:4); when we are tempted (Rom. 8:2); and when we leave this world (Acts 7:54–60). Let us get this thought firmly fixed now and for all time that the Holy Spirit is One called to our side to take our part.

> Ever present, truest Friend,
> Ever near, Thine aid to lend.

Chapter 6

The Holy Spirit in the Material Universe

◆

M any think of the work of the Holy Spirit as limited to
man, but God reveals to us in His Word that the Holy
Spirit's work has a far wider scope than this. We are
taught in the Bible that the Holy Spirit has a threefold work in
the material universe.

The creation of the material universe and of man is effected through the agency of the Holy Spirit.

We read in Psalm 33:6: *"By the word of the LORD the heavens were made, and all the host of them by the breath of His
mouth."* We have already seen in our study of the names of the
Holy Spirit that the Holy Spirit is the breath of Jehovah, so this
passage teaches us that all the hosts of heaven, all the stellar
worlds, were made by the Holy Spirit. We are taught explicitly
in Job 33:4 that the creation of man is the Holy Spirit's work.
We read: *"The Spirit of God has made me, and the breath of the
Almighty gives me life."* Here both the creation of the material
frame and the impartation of life are attributed to the agency of
the Holy Spirit.

In other passages of Scripture, we are taught that Creation
was in and through the Son of God. For example, we read in Colossians 1:16:

> *For by Him all things were created that are in heaven and
> that are on earth, visible and invisible, whether thrones or
> dominions or principalities or powers. All things were cre-
> ated through Him and for Him.*

In a similar way, we read in Hebrews 1:2 that God *"has in these last days spoken to us by His Son, whom He has appointed heir of all things, through whom also He made the worlds* [ages].*"* In the passage given above (Ps. 33:6), the Word as well as the Spirit are mentioned in connection with Creation. In the account of the creation and the rehabilitation of this world to be the abode of man, Father, Word, and Holy Spirit are all mentioned. (See Genesis 1:1–3.) It is evident from a comparison of these passages that the Father, Son, and Holy Spirit are all active in the creative work. The Father works in His Son through His Spirit.

The maintenance of living creatures is attributed to the agency of the Holy Spirit in the Bible.

The original creation of the material universe is not the only matter attributed to the agency of the Holy Spirit, as we can see in the following verses:

> *You hide Your face, they are troubled; You take away their breath, they die and return to their dust. You send forth Your Spirit, they are created; and You renew the face of the earth.* (Ps. 104:29–30)

The clear indication of this passage is that not only are things brought into being through the agency of the Holy Spirit, but also they are maintained by the Holy Spirit. Not only is spiritual life maintained by the Spirit of God, but material existence as well. Things exist and continue by the presence of the Spirit of God in them. This does not mean for a moment that the universe is God, but it does mean that the universe is maintained in its being by the immanence of God in it. This is the great and solemn truth that lies at the foundation of the awful and debasing perversions of pantheism in its countless forms.

The development of the material universe into higher states of order is attributed to the agency of the Holy Spirit.

The universe is created and maintained in its existence through the agency of the Holy Spirit. Also, the development of the earlier, chaotic states of the material universe into higher orders of being is effected through the working of the Holy Spirit. We read in Genesis:

The earth was without form, and void; and darkness was on the face of the deep. And the Spirit of God was hovering over the face of the waters. Then God said, "Let there be light"; and there was light. (Gen. 1:2–3)

We may take this account to refer either to the original Creation of the universe, or as the deeper students of the Word are more inclined to take it, as the account of the rehabilitation of the earth after its plunging into chaos through sin after the original Creation described in verse one. In either case, we have set before us here the development of the earth from a chaotic and unformed condition into its present highly developed condition through the agency of the Holy Spirit.

We see the process carried still further in Genesis 2:7: *"And the LORD God formed man of the dust of the ground, and breathed into his nostrils the breath of life; and man became a living being."* Here again it is through the agency of the breath of God that a higher thing, human life, comes into being. Naturally, as the Bible is the history of man's redemption, it does not dwell on this phase of truth, but seemingly each new and higher impartation of the Spirit of God brings forth a higher order of being: first, inert matter; then motion; then light; then vegetable life; then animal life; then man; and as we will see later, then the new man; and then Jesus Christ, the supreme Man, the completion of God's thought of man, the Son of Man. This is the biblical thought of development from the lower to the higher by the agency of the Spirit of God as distinguished from the godless evolution that has been so popular in the present generation. It is, however, only hinted at in the Bible. The more important phases of the Holy Spirit's work, His work in redemption, are those that are emphasized, stated, and reiterated. The Word of God is even more plainly active in each state of progress of creation. *"God said"* occurs ten times in the first chapter of Genesis.

Chapter 7

The Holy Spirit Convicts the World

◆

Our salvation begins experientially with our being brought to a profound sense that we need a Savior. The Holy Spirit is the One who brings us to this realization of our need. We read in John 16:8–11:

> *And when He has come, He will convict the world of sin, and of righteousness, and of judgment: of sin, because they do not believe in Me; of righteousness, because I go to My Father and you see Me no more; of judgment, because the ruler of this world is judged.*

We see in this passage that it is the work of the Holy Spirit to convict men of sin.

That is, to so convince men of their error in respect to sin as to produce a deep sense of personal guilt. We have the first recorded fulfillment of this promise in Acts:

> *"Therefore let all the house of Israel know assuredly that God has made this Jesus, whom you crucified, both Lord and Christ." Now when they heard this, they were cut to the heart, and said to Peter and the rest of the apostles, "Men and brethren, what shall we do?"* (Acts 2:36–37)

The Holy Spirit had come just as Jesus had promised He would, and when He came, He convicted the world of sin. He pricked their hearts with a sense of their awful guilt in the rejection of their Lord and their Christ. If the apostle Peter had spoken the same words the day before Pentecost, no such results would have followed. But now Peter was filled with the Holy Spirit (see Acts 2:4), and the Holy Spirit convicted the hearers through the instrumentality of Peter and his words. The Holy Spirit is the only One who can convince men of sin.

"The [natural] *heart is deceitful above all things, and desperately wicked"* (Jer. 17:9), and there is nothing in which the inbred deceitfulness of our hearts comes out more clearly than in our estimations of ourselves. We are all of us sharp-sighted enough to the faults of others, but we are all blind by nature to our own faults. Our blindness to our own shortcomings is often just short of ludicrous. We have a strange power of exaggerating our imaginary virtues and utterly losing sight of our defects. The longer and more thoroughly one studies human nature, the more clearly he will see how hopeless the task is of convincing other men of sin. We cannot do it, nor has God left it for us to do. He has put this work into the hands of One who is abundantly able to do it—the Holy Spirit.

One of the worst mistakes that we can make in our efforts to bring men to Christ is to try to convince them of sin through any power of our own. Unfortunately, it is one of the most common mistakes. Preachers will stand in the pulpit and argue and reason with men to make them see that they are sinners. They make it as plain as day. It is a wonder that their hearers do not see it, but they do not. Personal workers sit down beside an inquirer and reason with him and bring forward passages of Scripture in a most skillful way—the very passages that are calculated to produce the desired effect—and yet there is no result. Why? Because we are trying to do the Holy Spirit's work—the work that He alone can do—to convince men of sin. If we would only bear in mind our own inability to convince men of sin and cast ourselves on Him in utter helplessness to do the work, we would see results.

At the close of an inquiry meeting in our church in Chicago, one of our best workers brought to me an engineer on the Pan Handle Railway with the remark, "I wish that you would speak to this man. I have been talking to him two hours with no result." I sat down by his side with my open Bible, and in less than ten minutes that man, under deep conviction of sin, was on his knees crying to God for mercy.

The worker who had brought him to me said when the man had gone out, "That is very strange."

"What is strange?" I asked.

"Do you know," the worker said, "I used exactly the same passages in dealing with that man that you did, and though I had worked with him for two hours with no result, in ten minutes with the same passages of Scripture, he was brought under conviction of sin and accepted Christ."

What was the explanation? Simply this: for once that worker had forgotten something that she seldom forgot, namely, that the Holy Spirit must do the work. She had been trying to convince the man of sin. She had used the right passages; she had reasoned wisely; she had made out a clear case; but she had not looked to the only One who could do the work. When she brought the man to me and said, "I have worked with him for two hours with no result," I thought to myself, "If this expert worker has dealt with him for two hours with no result, what is the use of my dealing with him?" In a sense of utter helplessness, I cast myself on the Holy Spirit to do the work, and He did.

While we cannot convict men of sin, the Holy Spirit can. He can convince the most hardened and blinded man of sin. He can change men and women from utter carelessness and indifference to a place where they are overwhelmed with a sense of their need of a Savior. How often we have seen this illustrated.

Some years ago, the officers of the Chicago Avenue Church were burdened with the fact that there was so little profound conviction of sin manifested in our meetings. There were conversions, a good many were being added to the church, but very few were coming with an apparently overwhelming conviction of sin. One night one of the officers of the church said, "Fellow believers, I am greatly troubled by the fact that we have so little conviction of sin in our meetings. While we are having conversions and many accessions to the church, there is not that deep conviction of sin that I like to see. I propose that we, the officers of the church, meet from night to night to pray that there may be more conviction of sin in our meetings." The suggestion was taken up by the entire committee.

We had not been praying many nights when one Sunday evening I saw in the front seat underneath the gallery a showily dressed man with a very hard face. A large diamond was blazing from his shirtfront. He was sitting beside one of the deacons. As I looked at him as I preached, I thought to myself, "That man is a gambling man, and Deacon Young has been fishing today." It turned out that I was right. The man was the son of a woman who kept a gambling house in a Western city. I think he had never been in a Protestant service before. Deacon Young had gotten hold of him that day on the street and had brought him to the meeting. As I preached, the man's eyes were riveted on me. When we went downstairs to the after-meeting, Deacon Young took the man with him. I was late dealing with the anxious that night. As I finished with the last one about eleven o'clock and almost everybody had gone home, Deacon Young came over to me and said, "I have a man over here I wish you would come and speak with." It was this big gambler. He was deeply agitated.

"Oh," he groaned, "I don't know what is the matter with me. I never felt this way before in all my life," and he sobbed and shook like a leaf. Then he told me this story: "I started out this afternoon to go down to Cottage Grove Avenue to meet some men and spend the afternoon gambling. As I passed by the park over yonder, some of your young men were holding an open-air meeting, and I stopped to listen. I saw one man testifying whom I had known in a life of sin, and I waited to hear what he had to say. When he finished, I went on down the street. I had not gone far when some strange power took hold of me and brought me back, and I stayed through the meeting. Then this gentleman spoke to me and brought me over to your church, to your Yokefellows' Meeting. I stayed for supper with them, and he brought me up to hear you preach. Then he brought me down to this meeting." Here he stopped and sobbed, "Oh, I don't know what is the matter with me. I feel awful. I never felt this way before in all my life," and his great frame shook with emotion.

"I know what is the matter with you," I said. "You are under conviction of sin; the Holy Spirit is dealing with you," and I pointed him to Christ. He knelt down and cried to God for mercy to forgive his sins for Christ's sake.

Not long after, one Sunday night I saw another man sitting in the gallery almost exactly above where this man had sat. A diamond flashed also from this man's shirtfront. I said to myself, "There is another gambling man." He turned out to be a traveling man who was also a gambler. As I preached, he leaned further and further forward in his seat. In the midst of my sermon, without any intention of giving out the invitation, simply wishing to drive a point home, I said, "Who will accept Jesus Christ tonight?" Quick as a flash the man sprang to his feet and shouted, "I will." His words rang through the building like the crack of a revolver. I dropped my sermon and instantly gave out the invitation; men and women and young people rose all over the building to yield themselves to Christ. God was answering prayer, and the Holy Spirit was convincing men of sin.

The Holy Spirit can convince men of sin. We need not despair of anyone, no matter how indifferent they may appear, no matter how worldly, no matter how self-satisfied, no matter how irreligious. The Holy Spirit can convince men of sin.

A young minister of very rare culture and ability once came to me and said, "I have a great problem on my hands. I am the pastor of the church in a university town. My congregation is largely made up of university professors and students. They are the most delightful people. They have very high moral ideals and are living most exemplary lives. Now," he continued, "if I had a congregation in which there were drunkards and outcasts and thieves, I could convince them of sin, but my problem is how to make people like that, the most charming people in the world, believe that they are sinners—how to convict them of sin."

I replied, "It is impossible. You cannot do it, but the Holy Spirit can." And so He can. Some of the deepest manifestations of conviction of sin I have ever seen have been on the part of men and women of most exemplary conduct and attractive personality. But they were sinners, and the Holy Spirit opened their eyes to the fact.

While it is the Holy Spirit who convinces men of sin, He does it through us. This comes out very clearly in the context of the passage before us (John 16:8–11). Jesus said in the preceding verse, *"Nevertheless I tell you the truth. It is to your advantage that I go away; for if I do not go away, the Helper will not come to you; but if I depart, I will send Him to you."* (v. 7). Then

He goes on to say, *"And when He has come, He will convict the world of sin, and of righteousness, and of judgment"* (v. 8). That is, our Lord Jesus sends the Holy Spirit to us believers, and when He comes to us, He convinces the world through us. On the Day of Pentecost, it was the Holy Spirit who convinced the three thousand of sin, but the Holy Spirit came to the group of believers and through them convinced the outside world.

As far as the Holy Scriptures definitely tell us, the Holy Spirit has no way of getting at the unsaved world except through the agency of those who are already saved. Every conversion recorded in the Acts of the Apostles was through men or women already saved. Take, for example, the miraculous conversion of Saul of Tarsus. The glorified Jesus appeared visibly to Saul on his way to Damascus, but before Saul could come out clearly into the light as a saved man, human instrumentality had to be brought in. Prostrate on the ground, Saul cried to the risen Christ asking what he must do, and the Lord told him to go into Damascus. There he would be told what he must do. And then Ananias, *"a certain disciple"* (Acts 9:10), was brought on the scene as the human instrument through whom the Holy Spirit could do His work. (See Acts 9:17; 22:16.)

Take the case of Cornelius. Here again was a most remarkable conversion through supernatural agency. An angel appeared to Cornelius, but the angel did not tell him what to do to be saved. Instead, the angel said to Cornelius, *"Send men to Joppa, and call for Simon whose surname is Peter, who will tell you words by which you and all your household will be saved"* (Acts 11:13–14). So we may go right through the record of the conversions in the Acts of the Apostles, and we will see they were all effected through human instrumentality.

How solemn, how almost overwhelming, is the thought that the Holy Spirit has no way of getting at the unsaved with His saving power except through the instrumentality of those of us who are already Christians. If we realized that, would we not be more careful to offer to the Holy Spirit a more free and unobstructed channel for His all-important work? The Holy Spirit needs human lips to speak through. He needs yours, and He needs lives so clean and so utterly surrendered to Him that He can work through them.

Notice which sin it is that the Holy Spirit convinces men—the sin of unbelief in Jesus Christ. *"Of sin, because they do not believe in Me"* (John 16:9), says Jesus. Not the sin of stealing, not the sin of drunkenness, not the sin of adultery, not the sin of murder, but the sin of unbelief in Jesus Christ. The one thing that the eternal God demands of men is that they *"believe in Him whom He sent"* (John 6:29). The one sin that reveals man's rebellion against God and daring defiance of Him is the sin of not believing in Jesus Christ, and this is the one sin that the Holy Spirit emphasizes and of which He convicts men. This was the sin of which He convicted the three thousand on the Day of Pentecost. Undoubtedly, there were many other sins in their lives, but the one point that the Holy Spirit brought to the front through the apostle Peter was that the One whom they had rejected was their Lord and Christ, attested to be so by His resurrection from the dead. (See Acts 2:22–36.) *"Now when they heard this* [namely, that He whom they had rejected was Lord and Christ], *they were cut to the heart"* (Acts 2:37). This is the sin of which the Holy Spirit convinces men today.

In regard to the comparatively minor moralities of life, there is a wide difference among men, but the thief who rejects Christ and the honest man who rejects Christ are alike—condemned at the great point of what they do with God's Son. This is the point that the Holy Spirit presses home. The sin of unbelief is the most difficult of all sins of which to convince men. The average unbeliever does not look on unbelief as a sin. He looks on his unbelief as a mark of intellectual superiority. Not infrequently, he is all the more proud of it because it is the only mark of intellectual superiority that he possesses. He tosses his head and says, "I am an agnostic," "I am a skeptic," or "I am an infidel," and assumes an air of superiority on that account. If he does not go so far as that, the unbeliever frequently looks on his unbelief as, at the very worst, a misfortune. He looks for pity rather than for blame. He says, "Oh, I wish I could believe. I am so sorry I cannot believe," and then appeals to us for pity because he cannot believe. But when the Holy Spirit touches a man's heart, he no longer looks on unbelief as a mark of intellectual superiority. He does not look on unbelief as a mere misfortune. He sees it as the most daring, decisive, and damning of all sins and is overwhelmed with a sense of his awful guilt in that he had not believed on the name of the only begotten Son of God.

The Holy Spirit not only convicts of sin, but also convicts in respect to righteousness.

He convicts the world of righteousness because Jesus Christ has gone to the Father. That is, He convicts (convinces with a convincing that is self-condemning) the world of Christ's righteousness, which is attested to by His going to the Father. The coming of the Spirit is in itself a proof that Christ has gone to the Father (see Acts 2:33), and the Holy Spirit thus opens our eyes to see that Jesus Christ, whom the world condemned as an evildoer, was indeed the righteous One. The Father sets the stamp of His approval on His character and claims by raising Him from the dead, exalting Him to His own right hand, and giving to Him a name that is above every name.

The world at large today claims to believe in the righteousness of Christ, but it does not really believe in the righteousness of Christ. It has no adequate conception of the righteousness of Christ. The righteousness that the world attributes to Christ is not the righteousness that God attributes to Him, but a poor human righteousness, perhaps a little better than our own. The world loves to put the names of other men that it considers good alongside the name of Jesus Christ. But when the Spirit of God comes to a man, He convinces him of the righteousness of Christ. He opens his eyes to see Jesus Christ standing absolutely alone, not only far above all men, but *"far above all principality and power and might and dominion, and every name that is named, not only in this age but also in that which is to come"* (Eph. 1:21).

The Holy Spirit also convicts the world of judgment.

The Holy Spirit convinces men of judgment on the grounds that *"the ruler of this world is judged"* (John 16:11). When Jesus Christ was nailed to the cross, it seemed as if He were judged there, but in reality, it was the Prince of this world who was judged at the cross. By raising Jesus Christ from the dead, the Father made it plain to all coming ages that the cross was not the judgment of Christ, but the judgment of the Prince of Darkness. The Holy Spirit opens our eyes to see this fact and so convinces us of judgment.

There is a great need today for the world to be convinced of judgment. Judgment is a doctrine that has fallen into the background, that has indeed almost disappeared from sight. It is not popular today to speak about judgment, retribution, or hell. One who emphasizes judgment and future retribution is not thought to be quite up-to-date; he is considered medieval or even archaic. But when the Holy Spirit opens the eyes of men, they believe in judgment.

In the early days of my Christian experience, I had great difficulties with the Bible doctrine of future retribution. I came again and again up to what it taught about the eternal penalties of persistent sin. It seemed as if I could not believe it: it must not be true. Time and again I would back away from the stern teachings of Jesus Christ and the apostles concerning this matter. But one night, I was waiting on God that I might know the Holy Spirit in a fuller manifestation of His presence and His power. God gave me what I sought that night. With this larger experience of the Holy Spirit's presence and power, there came such a revelation of the glory, the infinite glory of Jesus Christ, that I no longer had any difficulties with what the Book said about the stern and endless judgment that would be visited on those who persistently rejected this glorious Son of God. From that day to this, while I have had many heartaches over the Bible doctrine of future retribution, I have had no intellectual difficulty with it. I have believed it. The Holy Spirit has convinced me of judgment.

Chapter 8

The Holy Spirit Bears Witness to Jesus

◆

When our Lord was talking to His disciples on the night before His crucifixion about the Comforter who, after His departure, was to come to take His place, He said:

But when the Helper comes, whom I shall send to you from the Father, the Spirit of truth who proceeds from the Father, He will testify of Me. And you also will bear witness, because you have been with Me from the beginning.
(John 15:26–27)

The apostle Peter and the other disciples, when they were strictly commanded by the Jewish Council not to teach in the name of Jesus, said, *"We are His witnesses to these things, and so also is the Holy Spirit"* (Acts 5:32). It is clear from these words of Jesus Christ and the apostles that it is the work of the Holy Spirit to bear witness concerning Jesus Christ.

We not only find the Holy Spirit's testimony to Jesus Christ in the Scriptures, but also the Holy Spirit bears witness directly to the individual heart concerning Jesus Christ. He takes His own Scriptures, interprets them to us, and makes them clear to us. All truth is from the Spirit, for He is *"the Spirit of truth"* (John 15:26), but it is especially His work to bear witness to Him who is the truth, that is Jesus Christ. (See John 14:6.) It is only through the testimony of the Holy Spirit directly to our hearts that we ever come to a true, living knowledge of Jesus Christ. (See 1 Corinthians 12:3.) No amount of mere reading the Bible and no amount of listening to man's testimony will ever bring us to a living knowledge of Christ. It is only when the

Holy Spirit Himself takes the written Word, or takes the testimony of our fellowman, and interprets it directly to our hearts that we really come to see and know Jesus as He is.

On the Day of Pentecost, Peter gave all his hearers the testimony of the Scriptures regarding Christ and also gave them his own testimony. He told them what he and the other apostles knew by personal observation regarding His resurrection. Unless the Holy Spirit Himself had taken the Scriptures that Peter spoke and taken the testimonies of Peter and the other disciples, the three thousand would not on that day have seen Jesus as He really was, received Him, and been baptized in His name. The Holy Spirit added His testimony to Peter's and to that of the written Word. Mr. Moody used to say in his terse and graphic way that when Peter said, *"Therefore let all the house of Israel know assuredly that God has made this Jesus, whom you crucified, both Lord and Christ"* (Acts 2:36), the Holy Spirit said, "Amen," and the people saw and believed. It is certain that unless the Holy Spirit had come that day, and through Peter and the other apostles had borne His direct testimony to the hearts of their hearers, there would have been no saving vision of Jesus on the part of the people.

If you wish people to get a true view of Jesus Christ, such a view of Him that they may believe and be saved, it is not enough that you give them the Scriptures concerning Him; it is not enough that you give them your own testimony. You must seek for them the testimony of the Holy Spirit and put yourself into such a relationship with God that the Holy Spirit may bear His testimony through you. Neither your testimony nor that of the written Word alone will effect this, even though it is your testimony or that of the Word that the Holy Spirit uses. Unless your testimony and that of the Word is taken up by the Holy Spirit and He Himself testifies, they will not believe.

This explains something that every experienced worker must have noticed. We sit down beside an inquirer and open our Bibles and give him those Scriptures that clearly reveal Jesus as his atoning Savior on the cross, a Savior from the guilt of sin, and as his risen Savior, a Savior from the power of sin. It is just the truth the man needs to see and believe in order to be saved, but he does not see it. We go over these Scriptures repeatedly, which to us are as plain as day, and the inquirer sits there in blank darkness. He sees nothing; he grasps nothing. Sometimes we almost wonder if the inquirer is ignorant because he cannot see the truth. No, he is not slow-witted, except with that spiritual blindness that possesses every mind unenlightened by the Holy Spirit: *"But the natural man does not receive the things of the Spirit of God, for they are foolishness to him; nor can he know them, because they are spiritually discerned"* (1 Cor. 2:14). We go over it again, and still he does not see it. We go over it again, and his face lightens up as he exclaims, "I see it. I see it." He sees Jesus and believes and is saved and knows he is saved there on the spot. What has happened? Simply this: the Holy Spirit has borne His testimony, and what was as dark as midnight before is as clear as day now.

This explains also why it is that one who has long been in darkness concerning Jesus Christ so quickly comes to see the truth when he surrenders his will to God and seeks light from Him. In surrendering to God, he has put himself into that attitude toward God where the Holy Spirit can do His work. (See Acts 5:32.) Jesus says in John 7:17, *"If anyone wants to do His will, he shall know concerning the doctrine, whether it is from God or whether I speak on My own authority."* When a man wills to do the will of God, then the conditions are right for the Holy Spirit to be able to do His work, and He illuminates the mind to see the truth about Jesus and to see that His teaching is the very Word of God.

John wrote, *"But these are written that you may believe that Jesus is the Christ, the Son of God, and that believing you may have life in His name"* (John 20:31). John penned his gospel for this purpose: that men might see Jesus as the Christ, the Son of God, through what he recorded and that they might believe that He is the Christ, the Son of God; and that, thus believing, they might have life through His name. The best book in the world to put into the hands of one who desires to know about Jesus and to be saved is the gospel of John. However, many have read the gospel of John over and over and over again and have not seen and believed that Jesus is the Christ, the Son of God. But let the same man surrender his will absolutely to God and ask God for light as he reads this gospel and promise God that he will take his stand on everything in the gospel that He shows him to be true, and before the man has finished reading, he will see clearly that Jesus is the Christ, the Son of God, and will believe and have eternal life. Why? Because he has put himself into the place where the Holy Spirit can take the things written in the gospel and interpret them and bear His testimony. I have seen this tested and proven time and time again all around the world.

Many have come to me and have said that they did not believe that Jesus is the Christ, the Son of God. They have gone further and said that they were agnostics and did not even know whether there was a personal God. Then I have told them to read the gospel of John, where John presented the evidence that Jesus was the Christ, the Son of God. Often, they have told me they have read it repeatedly and yet were not convinced that Jesus was the Christ, the Son of God.

Then I have said to them, "You have not read it the right way," and I have urged them to surrender their wills to God (or in the case where they were not sure there was a God, have gotten them to take their stand to follow it wherever it might carry them). Then I have had them agree to read the gospel of John slowly and thoughtfully, and each time before they read to look to God, if there were any God, to help them to understand what they were to read and to promise Him that they would take their stand on whatever He showed them to be true and follow it wherever it would carry them. In every instance, before they have finished the gospel, they have come to see that Jesus was the Christ, the Son of God, and have believed and been saved. They had put themselves in that position where the Holy Spirit could bear His testimony to Jesus Christ, and He had done it. Through His testimony, they saw and believed.

If you wish men to see the truth about Christ, do not depend on your own powers of expression and persuasion, but cast yourself on the Holy Spirit, seek for them His testimony, and see to it that they put themselves in the place where the Holy Spirit can testify. This is the cure for both skepticism and ignorance concerning Christ. If you yourself are not clear concerning the truth about Jesus Christ, seek the testimony of the Holy Spirit regarding Christ. Read the Scriptures; read especially the gospel of John, but do not depend on the mere reading of the

Word. Before you read it, put yourself in such an attitude toward God by the absolute surrender of your will to Him that the Holy Spirit may bear His testimony in your heart concerning Jesus Christ. What we all need most is a clear and full vision of Jesus Christ, and this comes through the testimony of the Holy Spirit.

One night a number of our students came back from the Pacific Garden Mission in Chicago and said to me, "We had a wonderful meeting at the mission tonight. There were many drunkards and outcasts at the front who accepted Christ."

The next day I met Mr. Harry Monroe, the superintendent of the mission, on the street, and I said, "Harry, the boys say you had a wonderful meeting at the mission last night."

"Would you like to know how it came about?" he replied.

"Yes."

"Well," he said, "I simply held up Jesus Christ, and it pleased the Holy Spirit to illumine the face of Jesus Christ so that men saw and believed."

It was a unique way of putting it, but it was an expressive way and true to the essential facts in the case. It is our part to hold up Jesus Christ. We must then look to the Holy Spirit to illuminate His face or to take the truth about Him and make it clear to the hearts of our hearers. He will do it, and men will see and believe. Of course, we need to be walking toward God so that the Holy Spirit may use us as the instruments through whom He will bear His testimony.

Chapter 9

The Regenerating Work of the Holy Spirit

◆━━━━━━━━━━━━

The apostle Paul wrote, *"Not by works of righteousness which we have done, but according to His mercy He saved us, through the washing of regeneration and renewing of the Holy Spirit"* (Titus 3:5). In these words, we are taught that the Holy Spirit renews men, or makes men new, and that through this renewing of the Holy Spirit, we are saved. Jesus taught the same in John 3:3–5:

> *Jesus answered and said to him, "Most assuredly, I say to you, unless one is born again, he cannot see the kingdom of God." Nicodemus said to Him, "How can a man be born when he is old? Can he enter a second time into his mother's womb and be born?" Jesus answered, "Most assuredly, I say to you, unless one is born of water and the Spirit, he cannot enter the kingdom of God."*

What is regeneration? Regeneration is the impartation of life, spiritual life, to those who are dead, spiritually dead, through their trespasses and sins (Eph. 2:1). It is the Holy Spirit who imparts this life. It is true that the written Word is the instrument that the Holy Spirit uses in regeneration. We read in 1 Peter 1:23: *"Having been born again, not of corruptible seed but incorruptible, through the word of God which lives and abides forever."* We read in James 1:18: *"Of His own will He brought us forth by the word of truth, that we might be a kind of firstfruits of His creatures."* These passages make it plain that the Word is the instrument used in regeneration, but it is only as the Holy Spirit uses the instrument that the new birth results. *"It is the Spirit who gives life"* (John 6:63).

148

In 2 Corinthians 3:6, we are told that *"the letter kills, but the Spirit gives life."* This is sometimes interpreted to mean that the literal interpretation of Scripture, the interpretation that takes it in its strict grammatical sense and makes it mean what it says, kills. It then means that some spiritual interpretation—an interpretation that "gives the spirit of the passage" by making it mean something it does not say—gives life, and those who insist on Scripture meaning exactly what it says are called "deadly literalists." This is a favorite perversion of Scripture with those who do not like to take the Bible as meaning just what it says and who find themselves driven into a corner looking about for some convenient way of escape. If one will read the words in their context, he will see that this thought was utterly foreign to the mind of Paul. Indeed, one who will carefully study the epistles of Paul will find that he himself was a literalist of the literalists.

If literalism is deadly, then the teachings of Paul are among the most deadly ever written. Paul built an argument on the turn of a word, on a number or a tense. What does the passage mean? The way to find out what any passage means is to study the words used in their context. Paul drew a contrast between the Word of God outside of us, written with ink on parchment or engraved on tablets of stone, and the Word of God written within us in tablets that are hearts of flesh with the Spirit of the living God (2 Cor. 3:3). He told us if we merely had the Word of God outside us in a book or on parchment or on tablets of stone, that it would kill us, that it would only bring condemnation and death, but that if we had the Word of God made a living thing in our hearts, written on our hearts by the Spirit of the living God, that it would bring us life. No number of Bibles on our tables or in our libraries will save us, but the truth of the Bible written by the Spirit of the living God in our hearts will save us.

To put the matter of regeneration in another way: regeneration is the impartation of a new nature, God's own nature, to the one who is born again. (See 2 Peter 1:4.) Every human being is born into this world with a perverted nature; his whole intellectual, emotional, and discretionary nature is perverted by sin. No matter how excellent our human ancestry, we come into this world with a mind that is blind to the truth of God: *"The natural man does not receive the things of the Spirit of God, for they are foolishness to him; nor can he know them, because they are spiritually discerned"* (1 Cor. 2:14). We come with affections that are alienated from God, loving the things that we should hate and hating the things that we should love:

> *Now the works of the flesh are evident, which are: adultery, fornication, uncleanness, lewdness, idolatry, sorcery, hatred, contentions, jealousies, outbursts of wrath, selfish ambitions, dissensions, heresies, envy, murders, drunkenness, revelries, and the like.* (Gal. 5:19–21)

We come with a will that is perverted, set on pleasing itself, rather than pleasing God: *"Because the carnal mind is enmity against God; for it is not subject to the law of God, nor indeed can be"* (Rom. 8:7).

A new intellectual, emotional, and discretionary nature is imparted to us in the new birth. We receive the mind that sees as God sees, that thinks God's thoughts after Him. (See 1 Corinthians 2:12–14.) We receive affections in harmony with the affections of God: *"The fruit of the Spirit is love, joy, peace, longsuffering, kindness, goodness, faithfulness, gentleness, self-control. Against such there is no law"* (Gal. 5:22–23). We receive a will that is in harmony with the will of God, that delights to do the things that please Him. Like Jesus we say, *"My food is to do the will of Him who sent Me, and to finish His work"* (John 4:34). It is the Holy Spirit who creates this new nature in us. No amount of preaching, no matter how orthodox it may be, and no amount of mere study of the Word will regenerate a heart unless the Holy Spirit works. It is He and He alone who makes a person a *"new creation"* (2 Cor. 5:17).

The new birth is compared in the Bible to growth from a seed. The human heart is the soil; *"the seed is the word of God"* (Luke 8:11). (Compare 1 Peter 1:23; James 1:18; 1 Corinthians 4:15.) Every preacher or teacher of the Word is a sower, but the Spirit of God is the One who quickens the seed that is sown. The divine nature then springs up as the result. There is abundant soil everywhere in which to sow the seed in the human hearts that are around us. There is abundant seed to be sown; any of us can find it in the granary of God's Word. There are many sowers today, but unless as we sow the seed, the Spirit of God quickens it and the heart of the hearer grasps it by faith, there will be no harvest. Every sower needs to realize his dependence on the Holy Spirit to enliven the seed he sows, and he needs to be in a close relationship with God so that the Holy Spirit may work through him and quicken the seed he sows.

The Holy Spirit does regenerate men. He has power to raise the dead. He has power to impart life to those who are morally dead or decaying. He has power to impart an entirely new nature to those whose nature now is so corrupt that to men they appear to be beyond hope. How often I have seen it proven. How often I have seen men and women utterly lost and ruined and vile come into a meeting scarcely knowing why they came. As they have sat there, the Word was spoken, the Spirit of God has quickened the Word thus sown in their hearts, and in a moment, that man or woman, by the mighty power of the Holy Spirit, has become a new creation.

I know a man who seemed as completely abandoned and hopeless as men ever become. He was about forty-five years of age. He had gone off in evil directions in early boyhood. He had run away from home, had joined the navy and afterwards the army, and had learned all the vices of both. He had been dishonorably discharged from the army because of his extreme dissipation and disorderliness. He had found his companions among the lowest of the low and the vilest of the vile. When he would go up the street of a Western town at night, merchants would hear his yell and would close their doors in fear. One night, out of curiosity, this man went into a revival meeting in a country church. He made fun of the meeting with a companion who sat by his side, but he went again the next night. The Spirit of God touched his heart. He went forward and bowed at the altar. He arose a new creation. He was transformed into one of the noblest, truest, purest, most unselfish, most gentle, and most Christlike men I have ever known.

I am sometimes asked, "Do you believe in sudden conversion?" I believe in something far more wonderful than sudden conversion. I believe in sudden regeneration. Conversion is merely an outward thing, the turning around. Regeneration goes down to the deepest depths of the inmost soul, transforming thoughts, affections, will, the whole inward man. I believe in sudden regeneration because the Bible teaches it and because I have seen it countless times. I believe in sudden regeneration because I have experienced it. We are sometimes told that the religion of the future will not teach sudden, miraculous conversion. If the religion of the future does not teach sudden, miraculous conversion, if it does not teach meaningful, sudden, miraculous regeneration by the power of the Holy Spirit, then the religion of the future will not be in conformity with the facts of experience and will not be scientific. It will miss one of the most certain and glorious of all truths.

Man-devised religions in the past have often missed the truth, and man-devised religions in the future will doubtless do the same. However, the religion God has revealed in His Word and that He confirms in experience teaches sudden regeneration by the mighty power of the Holy Spirit. If I did not believe in regeneration by the power of the Holy Spirit, I would quit preaching. What would be the use in facing great audiences in which there were multitudes of men and women hardened and seared, caring for nothing but the things of the world and the flesh, with no high and holy aspirations, with no outlook beyond money and fame and power and pleasure, if it were not for the regenerating power of the Holy Spirit?

But with the regenerating power of the Holy Spirit, there is every use, for the preacher can never tell where the Spirit of God is going to strike and do His mighty work. Before you sits a man who is a gambler, a drunkard, or a philanderer. There does not seem to be much use in preaching to him. But you can never tell. That very night, the Spirit of God may touch that man's heart and transform him into one of the holiest and most useful of men. It has often occurred in the past and will doubtless often occur in the future. Before you sits a woman who is a mere butterfly of fashion. She seems to have no thought beyond society, pleasure, and adulation. Why preach to her? Without the regenerating power of the Holy Spirit, it would be foolishness and a waste of time. But you can never tell. Perhaps this very night, the Spirit of God will shine in that darkened heart and open the eyes of that woman to see the beauty of Jesus Christ, and she may receive

Him. Then and there, the life of God will be imparted by the power of the Holy Spirit to her trifling soul.

The doctrine of the regenerating power of the Holy Spirit is a glorious doctrine. It sweeps away false hopes. It comes to the one who is trusting in education and culture and says, "Education and culture are not enough. You must be born again." It comes to the one who is trusting in mere external morality and says, "External morality is not enough; you must be born again." It comes to the one who is trusting in the externals of religion—in going to church, reading the Bible, saying prayers, being confirmed, being baptized, partaking of the Lord's Supper—and says, "The mere externals of religion are not enough; you must be born again." It comes to the one who is trusting in turning over a new leaf, in outward reform, in quitting his meanness; it says, "Outward reform and quitting your meanness are not enough. You must be born again." But in place of the vague, shallow hopes that it sweeps away, it brings in a new hope, a good hope, a blessed hope, a glorious hope. It says, "You may be born again." It comes to the one who has no desire higher than the desire for things animal or selfish or worldly and says, "You may become a partaker of the divine nature and love the things that God loves and hate the things that God hates. You may become like Jesus Christ. You may be born again."

Chapter 10

The Satisfaction from the Indwelling Spirit

The Holy Spirit takes up His abode in the one who is born of the Spirit. The apostle Paul said to the believers in Corinth, *"Do you not know that you are the temple of God and that the Spirit of God dwells in you?"* (1 Cor. 3:16). This passage refers not so much to the individual believer as to the whole body of believers, the church. The church as a body is indwelt by the Spirit of God. But in 1 Corinthians 6:19, we read: *"Do you not know that your body is the temple of the Holy Spirit who is in you, whom you have from God?"* It is evident in this passage that Paul is not speaking of the body of believers, of the church as a whole, but of the individual believer. In a similar way, the Lord Jesus said to His disciples on the night before His crucifixion:

> *And I will pray the Father, and He will give you another Helper, that He may abide with you forever; the Spirit of truth, whom the world cannot receive, because it neither sees Him nor knows Him; but you know Him, for He dwells with you and will be in you.* (John 14:16–17)

The Holy Spirit dwells in everyone who is born again.

We read in Romans 8:9: *"If anyone does not have the Spirit of Christ, he is not His."* The Spirit of Christ in this verse, as we have already seen, does not mean merely a Christlike spirit, but is a name of the Holy Spirit. One may be a very imperfect believer, but if he really is a believer in Jesus Christ, if he has really been born again, the Spirit of God dwells in him. It is very evident from the First Epistle to the Corinthians that the believers in Corinth were very imperfect believers; they were full

154

of imperfection, and there was gross sin among them. Nevertheless, Paul told them, even when dealing with them concerning gross immoralities, that they were temples of the Holy Spirit. (See 1 Corinthians 6:15–19.)

The Holy Spirit dwells in every child of God. In some, however, He dwells way back of consciousness in the hidden sanctuary of their spirits. He is not allowed to take possession as He desires of the whole man—spirit, soul, and body. Some, therefore, are not distinctly conscious of His indwelling, but He is there nonetheless. What a solemn, and yet, what a glorious thought, that in me dwells this august person, the Holy Spirit!

If we are children of God, we are not so much to pray that the Spirit may come and dwell in us, for He does that already. We are rather to recognize His presence, His gracious and glorious indwelling, give to Him complete control of the house He already inhabits, and strive to live so as not to grieve this holy One, this divine Guest. We will see later, however, that it is right to pray for the filling or baptism with the Spirit. What a thought it gives of the hallowedness and sacredness of the body to think of the Holy Spirit dwelling within us. How considerately we should treat these bodies, and how sensitively we should shun everything that will defile them. How carefully we ought to walk in all things so as not to grieve Him who dwells within us.

This indwelling Spirit is a source of full and everlasting satisfaction and life. Jesus said in John 4:14, *"Whoever drinks of the water that I shall give him will never thirst. But the water that I shall give him will become in him a fountain of water springing up into everlasting life."* Jesus was talking to the woman of Samaria by the well at Sychar. She had said to Him, *"Are You greater than our father Jacob, who gave us the well, and drank from it himself, as well as his sons and his livestock?"* (v. 12). Then Jesus answered and said to her, *"Whoever drinks of this water will thirst again"* (v. 13). How true that is of every earthly fountain. No matter how deeply we drink, we will thirst again.

No earthly spring of satisfaction ever fully satisfies. We may drink of the fountain of wealth as deeply as we can, but it will not satisfy for long. We will thirst again. We may drink of the fountain of fame as deeply as we can, yet the satisfaction is fleeting.

We may drink of the fountain of worldly pleasure, of human science and philosophy, and of earthly learning. We may even drink of the fountain of human love, but none will satisfy for long. We will thirst again.

Jesus went on to say, *"But whoever drinks of the water that I shall give him will never thirst. But the water that I shall give him will become in him a fountain of water springing up into everlasting life"* (v. 14). The water that Jesus Christ gives is the Holy Spirit. This John tells us in the most explicit language:

> *On the last day, that great day of the feast, Jesus stood and cried out, saying, "If anyone thirsts, let him come to Me and drink. He who believes in Me, as the Scripture has said, out of his heart will flow rivers of living water." But this He spoke concerning the Spirit, whom those believing in Him would receive.* (John 7:37–39)

The Holy Spirit fully and forever satisfies the one who receives Him. He becomes within him a well of water ever springing up into everlasting life. It is a great thing to have a well that you can carry with you, that is within you; to have your source of satisfaction and joy not in the things outside yourself, but in a well within. You are then independent of your environment. It matters little whether you have health or sickness, prosperity or adversity; your source of joy is within and is ever springing up. It matters comparatively little even whether your friends are with you or are separated from you, separated even by what men call death. This fountain within is always gushing up, and your soul is satisfied.

Sometimes this fountain within gushes up with greatest power and fullness in the days of deepest bereavement. At such times, all earthly satisfactions fail. What satisfaction is there in money or worldly pleasure, in the theater or the opera or the dance, in fame or power or human learning, when some loved one is taken from you? But in the hours when those whom we loved most dearly on earth are taken from us, then it is that the spring of joy of the indwelling Spirit of God bursts forth with fullest flow. Sorrow and sighing flee away (Isa. 35:10), and our own spirits are filled with peace and ecstasy. We have *"beauty for ashes, the oil of joy for mourning, the garment of praise for the spirit of heaviness"* (Isa. 61:3). If the experience were not too sacred to put in print, I could tell of a moment of sudden and overwhelming bereavement and sorrow when it seemed as if I would be crushed, when I cried aloud in an agony that seemed unendurable, when suddenly and instantly, this fountain of the Holy Spirit within burst forth, when I knew such a rest and joy as I had rarely known before, and my whole being was suffused with the oil of gladness.

The one who has the Spirit of God dwelling within as a well springing up into everlasting life is independent of the world's pleasures. He does not need to run after worldly entertainment, without which life does not seem worth living to those who have not received the Holy Spirit. He gives these things up, not so much because he thinks they are wrong as because he has something so much better. He loses all taste for them.

A lady once came to Mr. Moody and said, "Mr. Moody, I do not like you."

He asked, "Why not?"

She said, "Because you are too narrow."

"Narrow! I did not know that I was narrow."

"Yes, you are too narrow. You don't believe in the theater; you don't believe in cards; you don't believe in dancing."

"How do you know I don't believe in the theater?" he asked.

"Oh," she said, "I know you don't."

Mr. Moody replied, "I go to the theater whenever I want to."

"What," cried the woman, "you go to the theater whenever you want to?"

"Yes, I go to the theater whenever I want to."

"Oh," she said, "Mr. Moody, you are a much broader man than I thought you were. I am so glad to hear you say it, that you go to the theater whenever you want to."

"Yes, I go to the theater whenever I want to. I don't want to."

Anyone who has really received the Holy Spirit, and in whom the Holy Spirit dwells and is unhindered in His working, will not place great importance in worldly pleasures. Why is it then that so many professed Christians do seek after worldly amusements? For one of two reasons: either because they have never definitely received the Holy Spirit or else because the fountain is choked. It is quite possible for a fountain to become choked. The best well in one of our inland cities was choked and dry for many months because an old rag carpet had been thrust into the opening from which the water flowed. When the rag was pulled out, the water flowed again, pure and cool and invigorating. Many in the church today once knew the matchless joy of the Holy Spirit, but some sin or worldly conformity, some act of disobedience, more or less conscious disobedience, to God has come in, and the fountain is choked. Let us pull out the old rags so that this wondrous fountain may burst forth again, springing up every day and hour into everlasting life.

Chapter 11

The Holy Spirit Sets the Believer Free

◆——————

I n Romans 8:2, the apostle Paul wrote, *"The law of the Spirit of life in Christ Jesus has made me free from the law of sin and death."* We learn from Romans 7:9–24 what the law of sin and death is. Paul tells us that there was a time in his life when he *"was alive once without the law"* (v. 9), but the time came when he was brought face-to-face with the law of God. He saw that this law was holy, and the commandment holy, just, and good (v. 12). And he made up his mind to keep this holy, just, and good law of God. But he soon discovered that in addition to this law of God outside him, there was another law inside him directly contrary to this law of God outside him. While the law of God outside him said, "This good thing and this good thing and this good thing you should do," the law within him said, "You cannot do this good thing that you want to do" (v. 15).

A fierce combat ensued between this holy, just, and good law without him, which Paul himself approved after the inward man, and this other law in his members that warred against the law of his mind and kept constantly saying, "You cannot do the good that you want to do." But this law in his members, the law that *"the good that I will to do, I do not do; but the evil I will not to do, that I practice"* (v. 19), gained the victory. Paul's attempt to keep the law of God resulted in total failure. He found himself sinking deeper and deeper into the mire of sin, constrained and dragged down by this law of sin in his members, until at last he cried out, *"O wretched man that I am! Who will deliver me from this body of death?"* (v. 24).

Then Paul made another discovery. He found that in addition to the two laws that he had already found—the law of God

159

outside of him, holy, just, and good, and the law of sin and death within him, the law that the good he wanted to do he could not do and the evil he did not want to do he kept on doing—there was a third law: *"the law of the Spirit of life in Christ Jesus"* (Rom. 8:2). This law is about the righteousness that you cannot achieve in your own strength by the power of your own will approving the law of God, the righteousness that the law of God outside of you, holy, just, and good though it is, cannot accomplish in you, because it is weak through your flesh. The Spirit of life in Christ Jesus can produce this righteousness in you so *"that the righteous requirement of the law might be fulfilled in us who do not walk according to the flesh but according to the Spirit"* (v. 4).

In other words, when we come to the end of ourselves, when we fully realize our own inability to keep the law of God and in utter helplessness look to the Holy Spirit in Christ Jesus to do for us what we cannot do for ourselves, and when we surrender our every thought, every purpose, every desire, and every affection to His absolute control and thus walk after the Spirit, the Spirit does take control and set us free from the power of sin that dwells in us. He brings every hour of our lives into conformity to the will of God. It is the privilege of the child of God in the power of the Holy Spirit to have victory over sin every day, every hour, and every moment.

Many professed Christians today live in the experience that Paul described in Romans 7:9–24. Each day is a day of defeat, and at the close of the day, if they review their lives, they must cry as Paul did, *"O wretched man that I am! Who will deliver me from this body of death?"* (Rom. 7:24). Some even go so far as to reason that this is the normal Christian life, but Paul told us distinctly that this was *"when the commandment came"* (v. 9), not when the Spirit came—that it is the experience under law and not in the Spirit. The pronoun *I* occurs twenty-seven times in these fifteen verses and the *Holy Spirit* is not found once, whereas in the eighth chapter of Romans, the pronoun *I* is found only twice in the whole chapter, and the *Holy Spirit* appears constantly. Again Paul tells us in Romans 7:14 that this was his experience as *"carnal, sold under sin."* Certainly, that does not describe the normal Christian experience.

On the other hand, in Romans 8:9, we are told how not to be in the flesh but in the Spirit. In the eighth chapter of Romans, we have a picture of the true Christian life, the life that is possible to each one of us and that God expects from each one of us. Here we have a life where not merely the commandment comes, but the Spirit comes and works obedience to the commandment and brings us complete victory over the law of sin and death. Here we have life, not in the flesh but in the Spirit, where we not only see the beauty of the law (see Romans 7:22), but where the Spirit imparts power to keep it. (See Romans 8:4.) We still have the flesh, but we are not in the flesh and do not live after the flesh. We *"by the Spirit...put to death the deeds of the body"* (v. 13). The desires of the body are still there, desires which, if made the rule of our lives, would lead us into sin. But day by day, by the power of the Spirit, we put to death the deeds to which the desires of the body would lead us. We walk by the Spirit and therefore do *"not fulfill the lust of the flesh"* (Gal. 5:16). We *"have crucified the flesh with its passions and desires"* (v. 24).

It would be going too far to say we still had a carnal nature, for a carnal nature is a nature governed by the flesh. We have the flesh but in the Spirit's power, and it is our privilege to get daily, hourly, constant victory over the flesh and over sin. But this victory is not in ourselves, nor in any strength of our own. Left to ourselves, deserted of the Spirit of God, we would be as helpless as ever. It is still true that in us, that is, in our flesh, *"nothing good dwells"* (Rom. 7:18). The victory is all in the power of the indwelling Spirit, but the Spirit's power may be in such fullness that one is not even conscious of the presence of the flesh. It seems as if the flesh were dead and gone forever, but it is only kept in the place of death by the Holy Spirit's power. If for one moment we were to take our eyes off Jesus Christ, if we were to neglect the daily study of the Word and prayer, down we would go. We must live in the Spirit and walk in the Spirit if we would have continuous victory. (See Galatians 5:16, 25.) The life of the Spirit within us must be maintained by the study of the Word and prayer.

One of the saddest things ever witnessed is the way in which some people who have entered by the Spirit's power into

161

a life of victory become self-confident and imagine that the victory is in themselves and that they can safely neglect the study of the Word and prayer. The depths to which such people sometimes fall is appalling. Each of us needs to take to heart the inspired words of the apostle, *"Therefore let him who thinks he stands take heed lest he fall"* (1 Cor. 10:12).

I once knew a man who seemed to make extraordinary strides in the Christian life. He became a teacher of others and was a great blessing to thousands. It seemed to me that he was becoming self-confident, and I trembled for him. I invited him to my room, and we had a long heart-to-heart conversation. I told him frankly that it seemed as if he were going perilously near exceedingly dangerous ground. I said that I found it safer at the close of each day not to be too confident that there had been no failures or defeats that day but to go alone with God and ask Him to search my heart and show me if there was anything in my outward or inward life that was displeasing to Him. Very often failures were brought to light that must be confessed as sin.

"No," he replied, "I do not need to do that. Even if I should do something wrong, I would see it at once. I keep very short accounts with God, and I would confess it at once."

I said it seemed to me as if it would be safer to take time alone with God for God to search us through and through. While we might not know anything against ourselves, God might know something against us (see 1 Corinthians 4:4), and He would bring it to light. Our failure could be confessed and put away.

He said he did not feel that was necessary. Satan took advantage of his self-confidence. He fell into most appalling sin, and though he has since confessed and professed repentance, he has been utterly set aside from God's service.

In John 8:32, we read: *"You shall know the truth, and the truth shall make you free."* In this verse, it is the truth, or the Word of God, that sets us free from the power of sin and gives us victory. In Psalm 119:11, we read: *"Your word I have hidden in my heart, that I might not sin against You!"* Here again it is the indwelling Word that keeps us free from sin. In this matter, as in everything else, what in one place is attributed to the Holy Spirit is elsewhere attributed to the Word. The explanation, of course, is that the Holy Spirit works through the Word, and it is futile to talk of the Holy Spirit dwelling in us if we neglect the Word. If we are not feeding on the Word, we are not walking after the Spirit, and we will not have victory over the flesh and over sin.

Chapter 12

The Holy Spirit Forms Christ within Us

◆————————————◆

Paul offered a wonderful and deeply significant prayer for the believers in Ephesus and for all believers who read the epistle. Paul wrote:

For this reason I bow my knees to the Father of our Lord Jesus Christ, from whom the whole family in heaven and earth is named, that He would grant you, according to the riches of His glory, to be strengthened with might through His Spirit in the inner man, that Christ may dwell in your hearts through faith; that you, being rooted and grounded in love, may be able to comprehend with all the saints what is the width and length and depth and height; to know the love of Christ which passes knowledge; that you may be filled with all the fullness of God. (Eph. 3:14–19)

We have here an advance in the thought over what we have just been studying in the preceding chapter. It is the carrying out of the former work to its completion. Here the power of the Spirit manifests itself, not merely in giving us victory over sin, but in four things: in Christ dwelling in our hearts; in our being rooted and grounded in love; in our being made strong to comprehend with all the saints what is the width, length, depth, and height, and to know the love of Christ that passes knowledge; and in our being *"filled with all the fulness of God."*

Christ dwelling in our hearts

The word translated *"dwell"* in this passage is a very strong word. It means literally, "to dwell down," "to settle," "to dwell

164

deep." It is the work of the Holy Spirit to form the living Christ within us, dwelling deep down in the deepest depths of our beings. We have already seen that this was a part of the significance of the name sometimes used of the Holy Spirit, "the Spirit of Christ." In Christ on the cross of Calvary, making an atoning sacrifice for sin, bearing the curse of the broken law in our place, we have Christ *for* us. But by the power of the Holy Spirit bestowed on us by the risen Christ, we have Christ *in* us. Herein lies the secret of a Christlike life.

We hear a great deal in these days about doing what Jesus would do. Certainly, as Christians, we ought to live like Christ. *"He who says he abides in Him ought himself also to walk just as He walked"* (1 John 2:6). But any attempt on our part to imitate Christ in our own strength will only result in utter disappointment and despair. There is nothing more futile that we can possibly attempt than to imitate Christ in the power of our own will. If we imagine that we succeed, it will simply be because we have a very incomplete knowledge of Christ. The more we study Him, and the more perfectly we understand His conduct, the more clearly we will see how far short we have come from imitating Him. But God does not demand of us the impossible; He does not demand of us that we imitate Christ in our own strength. He offers to us something infinitely better. He offers to form Christ in us by the power of His Holy Spirit. And when Christ is thus formed in us by the Holy Spirit's power, all we have to do is to let this indwelling Christ live out His own life in us, and then we will be like Christ without struggles and efforts of our own.

A woman, who had a deep knowledge of the Word and a rare experience of the fullness that there is in Christ, stood one morning before a body of ministers as they plied her with questions. "Do you mean to say, Mrs. H——," one of the ministers asked, "that you are holy?"

Quickly but very meekly and gently, the elect lady replied, "Christ in me is holy."

No, we are not holy. To the end of our lives, in and of ourselves, we are full of weaknesses and failures, but the Holy Spirit is able to form within us the Holy One of God, the indwelling Christ. He will live out His life through us in all the humblest relations of life as well as in those that are considered greater. He will live out His life through the mother in the home, through the laborer in the factory, through the business person in an office—everywhere.

Our being rooted and grounded in love

In Ephesians 3:17, Paul used several images. The first analogy is taken from a tree shooting its roots down deep into the earth and taking fast hold of it. The second idea comes from a great building with its foundation laid deep in the earth on the rock. Paul therefore told us that by the strengthening of the Spirit in the inward man, we send the roots of our lives down deep into the soil of love and also that the foundations of the superstructure of our characters are built on the rock of love. Love is the sum of holiness, *"the fulfillment of the law"* (Rom. 13:10). Love is what we all need most in our relationships to God, to Jesus Christ, and to one another, and it is the work of the Holy Spirit to root and ground our lives in love. There is the most intimate relation between Christ being formed within us, or made to dwell in us, and our being rooted and grounded in love, for Jesus Christ Himself is the absolutely perfect embodiment of divine love.

Our being made strong to comprehend with all the saints what is the width, length, depth, and height; and to know the love of Christ that passes knowledge

It is not enough that we love; we must know the love of Christ. But that love passes knowledge. It is so broad, so long, so high, so deep, that no one can comprehend it. But we can *"grasp"* (Eph. 3:18 NIV) it; we can lay hold of it; we can make it our own; we can hold it before us as the object of our meditation, our wonder, and our joy. But it is only in the power of the Holy Spirit that we can thus comprehend it. The mind cannot grasp it at all in its own strength. A man who is not taught or strengthened by the Spirit of God may talk about the love of Christ, he may write poetry about it, he may go into rhapsodies over it, but it is only words. There is no real apprehension. But the Spirit of God enables us to really understand Christ's love it in all its dimensions.

Our being filled with the fullness of God

It is an easy matter to fill a pint cup with ocean water; a single dip will do it. But it would be an impossibility to fill a pint cup with all the fullness of the ocean until all the fullness that there is in the ocean is in that pint cup. It is seemingly a more impossible task that the Holy Spirit undertakes to do for us, to fill us *"with all the fullness"* (Eph. 3:19) of the infinite God, to fill us until all the intellectual and moral fullness that there is in God is in us.

This is the believer's destiny; we are *"heirs of God and joint heirs with Christ"* (Rom. 8:17). In other words, we are heirs of God to the extent that Jesus Christ is an heir of God; we are heirs to all God is and all God has. It is the work of the Holy Spirit to apply to us what is already ours in Christ. It is His work to make ours experientially all God has and all God is until the work is consummated in our being *"filled with all the fullness of God"* (Eph. 3:19). This is not the work of a moment, a day, a week, a month, or a year, but the Holy Spirit day by day puts His hand, as it were, into the fullness of God and conveys to us what He has taken from there and puts it into us. Then again He puts His hand into the fullness that there is in God and conveys to us what is taken from there and puts it into us, and this wonderful process goes on day after day, week after week, month after month, and year after year, and never ends until we are *"filled with all the fullness of God."*

Chapter 13

The Holy Spirit Brings Forth Christlike Graces

◆

There is a singular charm, a charm that one can scarcely explain, in the words of Paul in Galatians 5:22–23: *"The fruit of the Spirit is love, joy, peace, longsuffering, kindness, goodness, faithfulness, gentleness, self-control."* What a catalog we have here of lovely moral characteristics. Paul tells us that they are the fruit of the Spirit; that is, if the Holy Spirit is given control of our lives, this is the fruit that He will bear. All real beauty of character, all real Christlikeness in us, is the Holy Spirit's work; it is His fruit. He produces it. He bears it, not we. It is well to notice that these graces are not said to be the *fruits* of the Spirit, but the *fruit*. In other words, if the Spirit is given control of our lives, He will not bear one of these as fruit in one person and another as fruit in another person, but this will be the one fruit of many flavors that He produces in each one.

A unity of origin runs throughout all the multiplicity of manifestation. It is a beautiful life that is set forth in these verses. Every word is worthy of earnest study and profound meditation. Think of these words one by one: *"love," "joy," "peace," "longsuffering," "kindness," "goodness," "faithfulness," "gentleness," "self-control."* Here is a perfect picture of the life of Jesus Christ Himself. Is not this the life that we all long for, the Christlike life? However, this life is not natural to us and is not attainable by any effort of what we are in ourselves. The life that is natural to us is set forth in the three preceding verses:

Now the works of the flesh are evident, which are: adultery, fornication, uncleanness, lewdness, idolatry, sorcery, hatred, contentions, jealousies, outbursts of wrath, selfish ambitions, dissensions, heresies, envy, murders, drunkenness, revelries, and the like.   (Gal. 5:19–21)

All these works of the flesh will not manifest themselves in each individual. Some will manifest themselves in one person; others will be seen in other people, but they have one common source, the flesh. If we live in the flesh, this is the kind of a life that we will live. It is the life that is natural to us. But when the indwelling Spirit is given full control in the one He inhabits, when we are brought to realize the utter badness of the flesh and give up in hopeless despair of ever attaining to anything in its power, when we come to the end of ourselves and give over the whole work of making us what we ought to be to the indwelling Holy Spirit, then and only then can these holy graces of character that are set forth in Galatians 5:22–23 become His fruit in our lives. Do you desire these graces in your character and life? Do you really want them? Then renounce self utterly and all its strivings after holiness; give up any thought that you can ever attain to anything really morally pure in your own strength; and let the Holy Spirit, who already dwells in you if you are a child of God, take full control and bear His own glorious fruit in your daily life.

We get very much the same thought from a different point of view in Galatians 2:20:

I have been crucified with Christ; it is no longer I who live, but Christ lives in me; and the life which I now live in the flesh I live by faith in the Son of God, who loved me and gave Himself for me.

We hear a great deal in these days about the ethical culture, which usually means the cultivation of the flesh until it bears the fruit of the Spirit. It cannot be done, no more than thorns can be made to bear figs and the bramble bush grapes. (See Luke 6:44; Matthew 12:33.)

We also hear a great deal about character building. That may be all very well if you bear constantly in mind that the Holy Spirit must do the building, and even then it is not so much building as fruit-bearing.

We also hear a great deal about cultivating graces of character, but we must always bear it clearly in mind that the way to cultivate true graces of character is by submitting ourselves utterly to the Spirit to do His work and bear His fruit. (See 2 Peter 1:5–7.) This is *"sanctification of the Spirit"* (1 Pet. 1:2). There is a sense, however, in which cultivating graces of character is right; namely, we should look at Jesus Christ to see what He is and what we therefore should be. Then we look to the Holy Spirit to make us what we ought to be and thus, *"beholding as in a mirror the glory of the Lord, are being transformed into the same image from glory to glory, just as by the Spirit of the Lord"* (2 Cor. 3:18). Settle it, clearly and forever, that the flesh can never bear this fruit, that you can never attain to these things by your own efforts, that they are *"the fruit of the Spirit"* (Gal. 5:22).

Chapter 14

The Holy Spirit Guides the Believer

---◆---

The apostle Paul wrote in Romans 8:14, *"For as many as are led by the Spirit of God, these are sons of God."* In this passage, we see the Holy Spirit taking control of the believer's life. A true Christian life is a personally conducted life, conducted at every turn by a divine Person. It is the believer's privilege to be absolutely set free from all cares, worries, and anxieties as to the decisions that must be made at any turn of life. The Holy Spirit undertakes that responsibility for us. A true Christian life is not one governed by a long set of rules outside of us, but led by a living and ever present Person within us.

It is in this connection that Paul said, *"For you did not receive the spirit of bondage again to fear"* (Rom. 8:15). A life governed by rules outside of one's self is a life of bondage. There is always fear that we haven't made quite enough rules, and there is always the dread that in an unguarded moment, we may have broken some of the rules that we have made. The life that many professed Christians lead is one of awful bondage, for they have put on themselves a yoke more grievous to bear than that of the ancient Mosaic law, concerning which Peter said to the Jews of his time, that *"neither our fathers nor we were able to bear"* (Acts 15:10).

Many Christians have a long list of self-made rules: "Thou shalt do this," and "Thou shalt not do that." If by any chance they break one of these self-made rules, or forget to keep one of them, they are at once filled with an awful dread that they have brought on themselves the displeasure of God (and even sometimes imagine that they have committed the unpardonable sin). This is not Christianity; this is legalism. *"You did not receive the spirit of bondage again to fear"* (Rom. 8:15); we have received the Spirit who gives us the place of sons.

Our lives should not be governed by a set of rules outside of us, but by the loving Spirit of Adoption within us. We should believe the teaching of God's Word that the Spirit of God's Son dwells within us. We should surrender the absolute control of our lives to Him and look to Him to guide us at every turn of life. He will do it only if we surrender to Him and trust Him to do it. If in a moment of thoughtlessness we go our own way instead of His, we will not be filled with an overwhelming sense of condemnation and of fear of an offended God, but we will go to God as our Father, confess our going astray, believe that He forgives us fully because He says so (see 1 John 1:9), and go on free of guilt and happy of heart to obey Him and be led by His Spirit.

Being led by the Spirit of God does not mean for a moment that we will do things that the Bible tells us not to do. The Holy Spirit never leads men contrary to the Book that He Himself authored. If there is some spirit that is leading us to do something that is contrary to the explicit teachings of Jesus, we may be perfectly sure that this spirit is not the Holy Spirit. This point needs to be emphasized in our day, for many give themselves over to the leading of some spirit whom they say is the Holy Spirit but who is leading them to do things explicitly forbidden in the Word. We must always remember that many false spirits and false prophets are out in the world. (See 1 John 4:1.) Many are so anxious to be led by some unseen power that they are ready to surrender the conduct of their lives to any spiritual influence or unseen person. In this way, they open their lives to the malevolent influence of evil spirits to the utter wreck and ruin of their lives.

A man who made great professions of piety once came to me and said that the Holy Spirit was leading him and "a sweet Christian woman" whom he had met to contemplate marriage.

I said in astonishment, "You already have one wife."

"Yes," he said, "but you know we are not congenial, and we have not lived together for years."

"Yes," I replied, "I know you have not lived together for years, and I have looked into the matter, and I believe that the blame for that lies largely at your door. In any event, she is your wife. You have no reason to suppose she has been untrue to you, and Jesus Christ explicitly teaches that if you marry another while she lives, you commit adultery." (See Luke 16:18.)

"Oh, but the Spirit of God is leading us to love one another and to see that we should marry one another."

"You lie, and you blaspheme," I replied. "Any spirit that is leading you to disobey the plain teaching of Jesus Christ is not the Spirit of God, but some spirit of the Devil."

This perhaps was an extreme case, but cases of essentially the same character are not rare. Many professed Christians seek to justify themselves in doing things that are explicitly forbidden in the Word by saying that they are led by the Spirit of God. Not long ago, I protested to the leaders in a Christian assembly where at each meeting many professed to speak with tongues in distinct violation of the teaching of the Holy Spirit through the apostle Paul in 1 Corinthians 14:27–28:

> *If anyone speaks in a tongue, let there be two or at the most three, each in turn, and let one interpret. But if there is no interpreter, let him keep silent in church, and let him speak to himself and to God.*

The defense that they made was that the Holy Spirit led them to speak several at a time and many in a single meeting and that they must obey the Holy Spirit. In such a case as this, they felt they were not subject to the Word.

The Holy Spirit never contradicts Himself. He never leads the individual to do what in the written Word He has commanded us not to do. Any leading of the Spirit must be tested by what we know to be the leading of the Spirit in the Word. But while we need to be on our guard against the leading of false spirits, it is our privilege to be led by the Holy Spirit and to lead a life free from the bondage of rules and free from the anxiety that we will go wrong. Our Father has sent an unerring Guide to lead us all the way. Those who are thus led by the Spirit of God are *"sons of God"* (Rom. 8:14). That is, they are not merely children of God, born it is true of the Father but immature, but they are the grown children, the mature children of God. They are no longer babes but sons.

The apostle Paul drew a contrast in Galatians 4:1–7 between the babe under the tutelage of the law, differing nothing from a servant, and the full-grown son who is no longer a servant but a son walking in joyous liberty. It sometimes seems as if comparatively few Christians today have really thrown off the bondage of laws, rules outside themselves, and entered into the joyous liberty of sons.

Chapter 15

The Holy Spirit Bears Witness to Our Sonship

◆

One of the most precious passages in the Bible regarding the work of the Holy Spirit is found in Romans 8:15–16:

> *For you did not receive the spirit of bondage again to fear, but you received the Spirit of adoption by whom we cry out, "Abba, Father." The Spirit Himself bears witness with our spirit that we are children of God.*

There are two witnesses to our sonship. First, our own spirits, taking God at His Word (*"As many as received Him, to them He gave the right to become children of God"* John 1:12), bear witness to our sonship. Our own spirits unhesitatingly affirm that what God says—that we are sons of God—is true because God says so. But there is another witness to our sonship, namely, the Holy Spirit. He bears witness together with our spirits. "Together with" is the force of the Greek used in this passage. It does not say that He bears witness to our spirits but "together with" them. How He does this is explained in Galatians 4:6: *"Because you are sons, God has sent forth the Spirit of His Son into your hearts, crying out, 'Abba, Father!'"* When we have received Jesus Christ as our Savior and accepted God's testimony concerning Christ that through Him we have become sons, the Spirit of His Son comes into our hearts, filling them with an overwhelming sense of sonship and crying through our hearts, *"Abba, Father!"*

The natural attitude of our hearts toward God is not that of sons. We may call Him Father with our lips, as when, for example, we repeat in a formal way the prayer that Jesus taught us,

175

"Our Father in heaven" (Matt. 6:9), but there is no real sense that He is our Father. Our calling Him so is mere words. We do not really trust Him. We do not love to come into His presence; we do not love to look into His face with a sense of wonderful joy and trust because we are talking to our Father. We dread God. We come to Him in prayer because we think we should and perhaps we are afraid of what might happen if we did not. However, when the Spirit of His Son bears witness together with our spirits to our sonship, then we are filled and thrilled with the sense that we are sons. We trust Him as we have never trusted even our earthly fathers. There is less fear of Him than there was of our earthly fathers. We reverence Him while experiencing such a sense of wonderful childlike trust.

Notice when it is that the Spirit bears witness with our spirits that we are the children of God. We find the order of experience in Romans 8. First, we see the Holy Spirit setting us free from the law of sin and death. Consequently, the righteousness of the law is fulfilled in us who walk not after the law but after the Spirit (vv. 2–4). Next, we have the believer not focusing on the things of the flesh but on the things of the Spirit (v. 5). Next, we have the believer day by day through the Spirit putting to death the deeds of the body (v. 13). Then, we have the believer led by the Spirit of God (v. 14). Then and only then, we have the Spirit bearing witness to our sonship (vv. 16–17).

Many seek the witness of the Spirit to their sonship in the wrong way. They practically demand the witness of the Spirit to their sonship before they have even confessed their acceptance of Christ and certainly before they have surrendered their lives fully to the control of the indwelling Spirit of God. No, let us seek things in their right order. Let us accept Jesus Christ as our Savior and surrender to Him as our Lord and Master because God commands us to do so. Let us confess Him before the world because God commands that. (See Matthew 10:32–33; Romans 10:9–10.) Let us assert that our sins are forgiven, that we have eternal life, that we are sons of God because God says so in His Word, and we are unwilling to make God a liar by doubting Him. (See John 1:12; 5:24; Acts 10:43; 13:38–39; and 1 John 5:10–13.) Let us surrender our lives to the control of the Spirit of life, looking to Him to set us free from the law of sin and death. Let us set our minds not on the things of the flesh, but the things of the Spirit. Let us through the Spirit day by day put to death the deeds of the body. Let us give our lives up to be led by the Spirit of God in all things. Then, let us simply trust God to send the Spirit of His Son into our hearts, filling us with a sense of sonship, crying, *"Abba, Father"* (Gal. 4:6), and He will do it.

God, our Father, longs that we would know and realize that we are His sons. He longs to hear us call Him "Father" from hearts that realize what they say and that trust Him without fear or anxiety. He is our Father; He alone in all the universe realizes the fullness of meaning that there is in that wonderful word "Father," and it brings joy to Him to have us realize that He is our Father and to call Him so.

Some years ago there was a father in the state of Illinois who had a child who had been deaf and unable to speak from the time of her birth. It was a sad day in that home when they came to realize that their little child was deaf and would never hear and, as they thought, would never speak. The father heard of an institution in Jacksonville, Illinois, where deaf children were taught to speak. He took this little child to the institution and put her in the superintendent's charge. After the child had been there some time, the superintendent wrote telling the father that he should come and visit his child. A day was appointed, and the child was told that her father was coming. As the hour approached, she sat by the window, watching the gate for her father to pass through. The moment he entered the gate, she saw him, ran down the stairs and out on the lawn, met him, looked up into his face, and lifted her hands and said, "Papa." When that father heard the lips of his child speak for the first time and frame that sweet word, "Papa," such a throb of joy passed through his heart that he literally fell to the ground and rolled on the grass in ecstasy.

There is a Father who loves as no earthly father, who longs to have His children realize that they are His children. When we look into His face from a heart that the Holy Spirit has filled with a sense of sonship and call Him *"Abba* [Papa], *Father,"* no language can describe the joy of God.

Chapter 16

The Holy Spirit Teaches

◆

"*But the Helper, the Holy Spirit, whom the Father will send in My name, He will teach you all things, and bring to your remembrance all things that I said to you*" (John 14:26). Our Lord Jesus said these words in His last conversation with His disciples before His crucifixion.

Here we have a twofold work of the Holy Spirit: teaching and bringing to remembrance the things that Christ had already taught. Let us look at them in the reverse order.

The Holy Spirit brings to remembrance the words of Christ.

This promise was made primarily to the apostles and is the guarantee of the accuracy of their report of what Jesus said, but the Holy Spirit does a similar work with each believer who expects it of Him and who looks to Him to do it. The Holy Spirit brings to our minds the teachings of Christ and of the Word just when we need them for either the necessities of our lives or of our service. Many of us could tell of occasions when we were in great distress of soul or great questioning as to duty or great extremity as to what to say to one whom we were trying to lead to Christ or to help, and at that exact moment the very Scripture we needed—some passage that we had not thought of for a long time or perhaps one that we had never thought of in that connection—was brought to mind. Who did it? The Holy Spirit did it. He is ready to do it even more frequently, if we only expect it of Him and look to Him to do it. It is our privilege every time we sit down beside an inquirer to point him to the way of life to look to the Holy Spirit and say, "Just what should I say to this inquirer? Just what Scripture should I use?"

178

There is a deep significance in the fact that in the verse immediately following this precious promise Jesus said, *"Peace I leave with you, My peace I give to you"* (John 14:27). It is by the Spirit bringing His words to remembrance and teaching us the truth of God that we obtain and abide in this peace. If we will simply look to the Holy Spirit to bring to mind Scripture just when we need it, and just the Scripture we need, we will indeed have Christ's peace every moment of our lives.

One who was preparing for Christian work came to me in great distress. He said he must give up his preparation for he could not memorize the Scriptures. "I am thirty-two years old," he said, "and have been in business now for years. I have gotten out of the habit of study, and I cannot memorize anything." The man longed to be in his Master's service, and the tears stood in his eyes as he spoke. "Don't be discouraged," I replied. "Take your Lord's promise that the Holy Spirit will bring His words to remembrance. Learn one passage of Scripture, fix it firmly in your mind, then another and then another, and look to the Holy Spirit to bring them to your remembrance when you need them."

He went on with his preparation. He trusted the Holy Spirit. Afterwards he took up work in a very difficult field, a field where all sorts of error abounded. They would gather around him on the street like bees, and he would take his Bible and trust the Holy Spirit to bring to remembrance the passages of Scripture that he needed. The Holy Spirit did it. His adversaries were filled with confusion as he met them at every point with the sure Word of God, and many of the most hardened were won for Christ.

The Holy Spirit will teach us all things.

There is a still more explicit promise to this effect two chapters further on in John. Here Jesus said:

I still have many things to say to you, but you cannot bear them now. However, when He, the Spirit of truth, has come, He will guide you into all truth; for He will not speak on His own authority, but whatever He hears He will

179

speak; and He will tell you things to come. He will glorify Me, for He will take of what is Mine and declare it to you.
(John 16:12–14)

This promise was made in the first instance to the apostles, but the apostles themselves applied it to all believers. (See 1 John 2:20, 27.)

It is the privilege of each believer in Jesus Christ, even the humblest, to be *"taught by God"* (John 6:45). The humblest believer is independent of human teachers: *"You do not need that anyone teach you"* (1 John 2:27). This, of course, does not mean that we may not learn much from others who are taught by the Holy Spirit. If John had thought that, he would never have written this epistle to teach others. The man who is the most fully taught by God is the very one who will be most ready to listen to what God has taught others. Much less does it mean that when we are taught by the Spirit, we are independent of the written Word of God, for the Word is the very place to which the Spirit, who is the Author of the Word, leads His pupils and is the instrument through which He instructs them. (See John 6:63; Ephesians 5:18–19; 6:17; Colossians 3:16.) But while we may learn much from men, we are not dependent on them. We have a divine Teacher, the Holy Spirit.

We will never truly know the truth until we are thus taught directly by the Holy Spirit. No amount of mere human teaching, no matter who our teachers may be, will ever give us a correct and exact and full apprehension of the truth. Not even a diligent study of the Word, either in English or in the original languages, will give us a real understanding of the truth. We must be taught directly by the Holy Spirit, and we may be thus taught, each one of us. The one who is taught by the Spirit will understand the truth of God better, even if he does not know one word of Greek or Hebrew, than the one who knows Greek and Hebrew thoroughly, and all the cognate languages as well, but who is not taught by the Spirit.

The Spirit will guide the one whom He thus teaches *"into all truth"* (John 16:13). The whole sphere of God's truth is for each one of us, but the Holy Spirit will not guide us into all the truth in a single day or in a week or in a year, but step by step. There are two special areas of the Spirit's teaching mentioned:

"He will tell you things to come" (John 16:13).

There are many who say we can know nothing of the future, that all our thoughts on that subject are guesswork. It is true that we cannot know everything about the future. Some things God has seen fit to keep to Himself, secret things that belong to Him. (See Deuteronomy 29:29.) For example, we cannot *"know times or seasons"* (Acts 1:7) of our Lord's return, but there are many things about the future that the Holy Spirit will reveal to us.

"He will glorify Me [that is, Christ], for He will take of what is Mine and declare it to you" (John 16:14).

This is the Holy Spirit's special way of teaching the believer, as well as the unbeliever, about Jesus Christ. It is His work above all else to reveal Jesus Christ and to glorify Him. His whole teaching centers in Christ. From one point of view or the other, He is always bringing us to Jesus Christ. Some fear to emphasize the truth about the Holy Spirit lest Christ Himself be disparaged and put in the background, but there is no one who magnifies Christ as the Holy Spirit does. We will never understand Christ, or see His glory, until the Holy Spirit interprets Him to us. No amount of listening to sermons and lectures, no matter how able, no amount of mere study of the Word even, would ever enable us to see the things of Christ. The Holy Spirit must show us, and He is willing and able to do it. He is longing to do it. The Holy Spirit's most intense desire is to reveal Jesus Christ to men.

On the Day of Pentecost when Peter and the rest of the company were *"filled with the Holy Spirit"* (Acts 2:4), they did not talk much about the Holy Spirit; they talked about Christ. Study Peter's sermon on that day. Jesus Christ was his one theme, and Jesus Christ will be our one theme if we are taught by the Spirit. Jesus Christ will occupy the whole horizon of our vision. We will have a new Christ, a glorious Christ. Christ will be so glorious to us that we will long to go and tell everyone about this glorious One whom we have found. Jesus Christ is so different when the Spirit glorifies Him by taking of His things and showing them to us.

The Holy Spirit reveals to us the deep things of God that are hidden from and are foolishness to the natural man.

> *But as it is written: "Eye has not seen, nor ear heard, nor have entered into the heart of man the things which God has prepared for those who love Him." But God has revealed them to us through His Spirit. For the Spirit searches all things, yes, the deep things of God. For what man knows the things of a man except the spirit of the man which is in him? Even so no one knows the things of God except the Spirit of God. Now we have received, not the spirit of the world, but the Spirit who is from God, that we might know the things that have been freely given to us by God. These things we also speak, not in words which man's wisdom teaches but which the Holy Spirit teaches, comparing spiritual things with spiritual.* (1 Cor. 2:9–13)

This passage, of course, refers primarily to the apostles, but we cannot limit this work of the Spirit to them. The Spirit reveals to the individual believer the deep things of God, things that the human eye has not seen, nor ear heard, things that have not entered into the hearts of men, the things that God has prepared for those who love Him. It is evident from the context that this does not refer solely to heaven or the things to come in the life hereafter. The Holy Spirit takes the deep things of God that God has prepared for us, even in the life that now is, and reveals them to us.

The Holy Spirit interprets His own revelation. He imparts power to discern, know, and appreciate what He has taught.

In the next verse after those just quoted, we read: *"But the natural man does not receive the things of the Spirit of God, for they are foolishness to him; nor can he know them, because they are spiritually discerned"* (1 Cor. 2:14). Not only is the Holy Spirit the author of revelation, the written Word of God, He is also the interpreter of what He has revealed. Any profound book is immeasurably more interesting and helpful when we have the author of the book right at hand to interpret it for us, and it is

182

always our privilege to have the Author of the Bible right at hand when we study it. The Holy Spirit is the Author of the Bible, and He stands ready to interpret its meaning to every believer every time he opens the Book. To understand the Bible, we must look to Him; then the darkest places become clear. We often need to pray with the psalmist: *"Open my eyes, that I may see wondrous things from Your law"* (Ps. 119:18).

It is not enough that we have the revelation of God before us in the written Word to study; we must also have the inward illumination of the Holy Spirit to enable us to apprehend it as we study. It is a common mistake, but a most apparent one, to try to comprehend a spiritual revelation with the natural understanding. It is the foolish attempt to do this that has landed so many in the bog of so-called "higher criticism."

In order to understand art, a man must have an aesthetic sense as well as the knowledge of colors and of paint. To understand a spiritual revelation, a man must be taught by the Spirit. A mere knowledge of the languages in which the Bible was written is not enough. A man with no aesthetic sense might as well expect to appreciate the Sistine Chapel because he is not color blind, as a man who is not filled with the Spirit to understand the Bible simply because he knows the vocabulary and the laws of Hebrew and Greek grammar. We might as well think of appointing a man to teach art because he understands paints as to expect a man to teach the Bible because he has a thorough understanding of Greek and Hebrew. In our day, we need not only recognize the utter insufficiency and worthlessness before God of our own righteousness, which is the lesson of the opening chapters of the epistle to the Romans, but also the utter insufficiency and worthlessness in the things of God of our own wisdom, which is the lesson of the First Epistle to the Corinthians, especially the first three chapters. (See, for example, 1 Corinthians 1:19–21, 26–27.)

Ancient Jews had a revelation by the Spirit, but they failed to depend on the Spirit Himself to interpret it to them, so they went astray. So Christians today have a revelation by the Spirit, and many are failing to depend on the Holy Spirit to interpret it to them; thus, they go astray. The whole evangelical church recognizes theoretically at least the utter insufficiency of man's own righteousness. What it needs to be taught in the present hour, and what it needs to be made to feel, is the utter insufficiency of man's wisdom. That is perhaps the lesson that this twentieth century of towering intellectual conceit needs most of all to learn.

To understand God's Word, we must empty ourselves of our own wisdom and rest in complete dependence on the Spirit of God to interpret it to us. We do well to take to heart the words of Jesus Himself in Matthew 11:25: *"I thank You, Father, Lord of heaven and earth, that You have hidden these things from the wise and prudent and have revealed them to babes."*

A number of Bible students were once discussing the best methods of Bible study. One man, who was a learned and scholarly man, said, "I think the best method of Bible study is the baby method." When we have entirely put away our own righteousness, then and only then, we receive the righteousness of God. (See Romans 10:3; Philippians 3:4–7, 9.) When we have entirely put away our own wisdom, then and only then do we find the wisdom of God. *"Let no one deceive himself,"* said the apostle Paul. *"If anyone among you seems to be wise in this age, let him become a fool that he may become wise"* (1 Cor. 3:18). Emptying must precede filling; the self must be poured out so that God may be poured in.

We must daily be taught by the Spirit to understand the Word. We cannot depend today on the fact that the Spirit taught us yesterday. Each new time that we come in contact with the Word, it must be in the power of the Spirit for that specific occasion. That the Holy Spirit once illumined our minds to grasp a certain truth is not enough. He must do it each time we confront that passage. Andrew Murray has well said, "Each time you come to the Word in study, in hearing a sermon, or reading a religious book, there ought to be as distinct as your intercourse with the external means, the definite act of self-abnegation, denying your own wisdom and yielding yourself in faith to the divine Teacher" (*The Spirit of Christ*).

The Holy Spirit enables the believer to communicate to others in power the truth he himself has been taught.

Paul said in 1 Corinthians 2:1–5:

And I, brethren, when I came to you, did not come with excellence of speech or of wisdom declaring to you the testimony of God. For I determined not to know anything among you except Jesus Christ and Him crucified. I was with you in weakness, in fear, and in much trembling. And my speech and my preaching were not with persuasive words of human wisdom, but in demonstration of the Spirit and of power, that your faith should not be in the wisdom of men but in the power of God.

In a similar way, Paul wrote to the believers in Thessalonica: *"For our gospel did not come to you in word only, but also in power, and in the Holy Spirit and in much assurance, as you know what kind of men we were among you for your sake"* (1 Thess. 1:5).

We not only need the Holy Spirit to reveal the truth to chosen apostles and prophets in the first place and in the second place to interpret to us as individuals the truth He has thus revealed, but in the third place, we need the Holy Spirit to enable us to effectively communicate to others the truth that He Himself has interpreted to us. We need Him all along the way. One great cause of real failure in the ministry, even when there is seeming success—not only in the regular ministry but in all forms of service as well—comes from the attempt to teach by *"persuasive words of human wisdom"* (1 Cor. 2:4), that is, by the arts of human logic, rhetoric, persuasion, and eloquence, what the Holy Spirit has taught us. What is needed is Holy Spirit power, *"demonstration of the Spirit and of power"* (v. 4).

There are three causes of failure in preaching today. First, some other message is taught than the message that the Holy Spirit has revealed in the Word. Men preach science, art, literature, philosophy, sociology, history, economics, experience, etc., and not the simple Word of God as found in the Holy Spirit's Book, the Bible. Second, the Spirit-taught message of the Bible is studied and sought to be apprehended by the natural understanding, that is, without the Spirit's illumination. How common that is even in seminaries where people are being trained for the ministry, even institutions that may be altogether orthodox. Third, the Spirit-given message, the Word, studied and apprehended under the Holy Spirit's illumination, is given out to others with *"persuasive words of human wisdom"* and not in *"demonstration of the Spirit and of power"* (1 Cor. 2:4). We need, and are absolutely dependent on, the Spirit all along the way. He must teach us how to speak as well as what to speak. His must be the power as well as the message.

Chapter 17

Praying, Praising, and Worshipping

◆

T wo of the most deeply significant passages in the Bible on the subject of the Holy Spirit and on the subject of prayer are found in Jude and Ephesians. In Jude, we read: *"but you, beloved, building yourselves up on your most holy faith, praying in the Holy Spirit"* (v. 20), and in Ephesians 6:18: *"praying always with all prayer and supplication in the Spirit, being watchful to this end with all perseverance and supplication for all the saints."* These passages distinctly teach us that the Spirit helps us to pray.

The Holy Spirit guides the believer in prayer.

· The disciples did not know how to pray as they should, so they came to Jesus and said, *"Lord, teach us to pray"* (Luke 11:1). We do not know how to pray as we should—we do not know what to pray for, nor how to ask for it—but there is One who is always at hand to help (see John 14:16–17), and He knows what we should pray for. He helps our infirmities in this matter of prayer as in other matters (Rom. 8:26). He teaches us to pray. True prayer is prayer in the Spirit, prayer that the Holy Spirit inspires and directs.

The prayer in which the Holy Spirit leads us is the prayer *"according to the will of God"* (v. 27). When we ask anything according to God's will, we know that He hears us, and we know that He has granted the things that we ask. (See 1 John 5:14–15.) We may know it is ours at the moment when we pray just as surely as we know it afterwards when we have it in our actual possession. But how can we know the will of God when we pray?

In two ways. First of all, by what is written in His Word. All the promises in the Bible are sure, and if God promises anything in the Bible, we may be sure it is His will to give us that thing. But many things that we need are not specifically promised in the Word, yet even in that case, it is our privilege to know the will of God. It is the work of the Holy Spirit to teach us God's will and lead us in prayer in agreement with God's will.

Some object to the Christian doctrine of prayer, for they say that it teaches that we can go to God in our ignorance and change His will and subject His infinite wisdom to our erring foolishness, but that is not the Christian doctrine of prayer at all. The Christian doctrine of prayer is that it is the believer's privilege to be taught by the Spirit of God Himself to know what the will of God is and not to ask for things that our foolishness would prompt us to ask for; instead, we are to ask for things that the never-erring Spirit of God prompts us to ask for. True prayer is prayer *"in the Spirit"* (Eph. 6:18), that is, prayer that the Spirit inspires and directs.

When we come into God's presence, we should recognize our infirmities: our ignorance of what is best for us, our ignorance of what we should pray for, and our ignorance of how we should pray for it. In the consciousness of our utter inability to pray correctly, we should look to the Holy Spirit to teach us to pray and cast ourselves utterly on Him to direct our prayers, to discover our desires, and guide our utterance of them. There is no place where we need to recognize our ignorance more than we do in prayer. Rushing heedlessly into God's presence and asking the first thing that comes into our minds, or that some other thoughtless one asks us to pray for, is not *"praying in the Holy Spirit"* (Jude 20) and is not true prayer. We must wait for the Holy Spirit and surrender ourselves to Him. The prayer that God the Holy Spirit inspires is the prayer that God the Father answers.

The longings that the Holy Spirit creates in our hearts are often too deep for words, too deep apparently for clear and definite comprehension on the part of the believer himself in whom the Spirit is working: *"The Spirit Himself makes intercession for us with groanings which cannot be uttered"* (Rom. 8:26). God Himself *"searches the hearts"* to know what *"the mind of the*

Spirit is" (v. 27) in these unuttered and inexpressible longings. But God does know what the mind of the Spirit is. He does know what these Spirit-given longings that we cannot put into words mean even if we do not. These longings are *"according to the will of God"* (v. 27), and God grants them. It is in this way that it comes to pass that God *"is able to do exceedingly abundantly above all that we ask or think, according to the power that works in us"* (Eph. 3:20). There are other times when the Spirit's leadings are so clear that we pray with the Spirit and with the understanding also (1 Cor. 14:15). We distinctly understand what it is that the Holy Spirit leads us to pray for.

The Holy Spirit inspires the believer and guides him in thanksgiving as well as in prayer.

> *And do not be drunk with wine, in which is dissipation; but be filled with the Spirit, speaking to one another in psalms and hymns and spiritual songs, singing and making melody in your heart to the Lord, giving thanks always for all things to God the Father in the name of our Lord Jesus Christ.* (Eph. 5:18–20)

Not only does the Holy Spirit teach us to pray, but also to give thanks. One of the most prominent characteristics of the Spirit-filled life is thanksgiving. On the Day of Pentecost when the disciples were filled with the Holy Spirit and spoke as the Spirit gave them utterance (Acts 2:4), we hear them telling *"the wonderful works of God"* (v. 11). Today when any believer is filled with the Holy Spirit, he always becomes filled with thanksgiving and praise. True thanksgiving is *"to God the Father in the name of our Lord Jesus Christ"* (Eph. 5:20) through the Holy Spirit.

The Holy Spirit inspires worship on the part of the believer.

We read in Philippians 3:3: *"For we are the circumcision, who worship God in the Spirit, rejoice in Christ Jesus, and have no confidence in the flesh."* Prayer is not worship; thanksgiving is not worship. Worship is a definite act of the creature in relation to God. Worship is bowing before God in adoring acknowledgment and contemplation of Him and the perfection of His being. Someone has said, "In our prayers, we are taken up with our needs; in our thanksgiving, we are taken up with our blessings; in our worship, we are taken up with Him." There is no true and acceptable worship except what the Holy Spirit prompts and directs. *"God is Spirit, and those who worship Him must worship in spirit and truth"* (John 4:24). *"For the Father is seeking such to worship Him"* (v. 23). The flesh seeks to intrude into every sphere of life. The flesh has its worship as well as its lusts. The worship that the flesh prompts is an abomination to God. In this we see the folly of any attempt at a conference of religions where the representatives of radically different religions attempt to worship together.

Not all earnest and honest worship is worship in the Spirit. A man may be very honest and earnest in his worship and still not have submitted himself to the guidance of the Holy Spirit in the matter, and so his worship is in the flesh. Often even when there is great loyalty to the letter of the Word, worship may not be in the Spirit—in other words, inspired and directed by Him. To worship correctly, as Paul said, we must have *"no confidence in the flesh"* (Phil. 3:3); that is, we must recognize the complete inability of the flesh (our natural self as contrasted to the divine Spirit that dwells in and should mold everything in the believer) to worship acceptably. We must also realize the danger that exists that the flesh may intrude itself into our worship. In utter self-distrust and self-denial, we must cast ourselves on the Holy Spirit to lead us properly in our worship. Just as we must renounce any merit in ourselves and cast ourselves on Christ and His work for us on the cross for justification, so we must renounce any supposed capacity for good in ourselves and cast ourselves totally on the Holy Spirit and His work in us, in holy living, knowing, praying, thanking, worshipping, and all else that we are to do.

Chapter 18

The Holy Spirit's Calling

I t is evident that the Holy Spirit calls people into definite lines of work and sends them forth into that work. He not only calls in a general way into Christian service, but selects the specific work and points it out. Look at this passage from Acts:

> As they ministered to the Lord and fasted, the Holy Spirit said, "Now separate to Me Barnabas and Saul for the work to which I have called them." Then, having fasted and prayed, and laid hands on them, they sent them away. So, being sent out by the Holy Spirit, they went down to Seleucia, and from there they sailed to Cyprus. (Acts 13:2–4)

Many Christians are asking today, and many others should be asking, "Shall I go to China, to Africa, to India?" There is only one person who can rightly settle that question for you, and that person is the Holy Spirit. You cannot settle the question for yourself, much less can any other man answer it for you. Not every Christian is called to go to China; not every Christian is called to go to Africa; not every Christian is called to go to a foreign field at all. God alone knows whether He wishes you in any of these places, but He is willing to show you. In a day like today, when there is such a need of the right men and the right women ministering on foreign fields, all young, healthy, and intellectually competent Christians should definitely offer themselves to God for the foreign field and ask Him if He wants them to go, but they should not go until He, by His Holy Spirit, makes the call plain.

The great need in all areas of Christian work today is for men and women whom the Holy Spirit has called and sent forth.

We have plenty of people whom men have called and sent forth. We have plenty of men and women who have called themselves, for many today object strenuously to being sent forth by men or by any organization of any kind. But, in fact, these men and women who are sent forth by themselves and not by God are immeasurably worse.

How does the Holy Spirit call? The passage before us does not tell us how the Holy Spirit spoke to the group of prophets and teachers in Antioch, telling them to separate Barnabas and Saul to the work to which He had called them. It is presumably purposely silent on this point. Possibly it is silent on this point lest we would think that the Holy Spirit must always call in precisely the same way. There is nothing whatever to indicate that He spoke by an audible voice. Much less is there anything to indicate that He made His will known in any of the fantastic ways in which some in these days profess to discern His leading—as for example, by twitchings of the body, by shuddering, by opening the Bible at random and putting a finger on a passage that may be construed into some entirely different meaning than what the inspired author intended by it. The important point is, He made His will clearly known, and He is willing to make His will clearly known to us today. Sometimes He makes it known in one way and sometimes in another, but He will make it known.

But how do we receive the Holy Spirit's call? First of all, by desiring it; second, by earnestly seeking it; third, by waiting on the Lord for it; fourth, by expecting it. The record reads, *"As they ministered to the Lord and fasted"* (Acts 13:2). They were waiting on the Lord for His direction. For the time being, they had turned their backs utterly on worldly cares and enjoyments, even on those things that were perfectly proper in their places.

Many are saying today to justify staying home from the foreign field, "I have never had a call." How do you know that? Have you been listening for a call? God usually speaks in a still, small voice, and it is only the listening ear that can catch it. Have you ever definitely offered yourself to God to send you where He will? While no man or woman should go to China or Africa or other foreign fields unless they are clearly and definitely called, they should offer themselves to God for this work, be ready for the call, and be listening intently so that they may hear the call if it comes. Keep in mind that a man needs no more definite call to Africa than to Boston, New York, London, or any other desirable field at home.

The Holy Spirit not only calls men and sends them forth into definite areas of work, but He also guides in the details of daily life and service as to where to go and where not to go, what to do and what not to do. We read in Acts 8:27–29:

> *So he* [Philip] *arose and went. And behold, a man of Ethiopia, a eunuch of great authority under Candace the queen of the Ethiopians, who had charge of all her treasury, and had come to Jerusalem to worship, was returning. And sitting in his chariot, he was reading Isaiah the prophet. Then the Spirit said to Philip, "Go near and overtake this chariot."*

Here we see the Spirit guiding Philip in the details of service into which He had called him. In a similar way, we read in Acts 16:6–7:

> *Now when they had gone through Phrygia and the region of Galatia, they were forbidden by the Holy Spirit to preach the word in Asia. After they had come to Mysia, they tried to go into Bithynia, but the Spirit did not permit them.*

Here we see the Holy Spirit directing Paul where not to go.

It is possible for us to have the unerring guidance of the Holy Spirit at every turn of life. Take, for example, our personal work. It is clearly not God's intention that we speak to everyone we meet. To attempt to do so would be to attempt the impossible, and we would waste much time in trying to speak to people where we could do no good that might be used in speaking to people where we could accomplish something. There are some to whom it would be wise for us to speak. There are others to whom it would be unwise for us to speak. Time spent on them would be taken from work that would be more to God's glory. Undoubtedly, as Philip journeyed toward Gaza, he met many before he met the one of whom the Spirit said, *"Go near and overtake this chariot"* (Acts 8:29). The Spirit is as ready to guide us as He was to guide Philip.

Some years ago, a Christian worker in Toronto had the impression that he should go to the hospital and speak to someone there. He thought to himself, "Whom do I know at the hospital at this time?" There came to his mind one whom he knew was at the hospital, and so he hurried there. But as he sat down by his side to talk with him, he realized it was not for this man that he was sent. He got up to open a window. What did it all mean? There was another man lying across the aisle from the man he knew, and the thought came to him that this might be the man to whom he should speak. He turned and spoke to this man and had the privilege of leading him to Christ. There was apparently nothing serious in the man's case. He had suffered some injury to his knee and there was no thought of a serious issue, but that man passed into eternity that night.

Many instances of a similar character could be recorded, and they prove from experience that the Holy Spirit is as ready to guide those who seek His guidance today as He was to guide the early disciples. He is ready to guide us, not only in our more definite forms of Christian work, but in all the affairs of life, business, study, and everything we have to do. There is no promise in the Bible more plainly explicit than the following:

> *If any of you lacks wisdom, let him ask of God, who gives to all liberally and without reproach, and it will be given to him. But let him ask in faith, with no doubting, for he who doubts is like a wave of the sea driven and tossed by the wind. For let not that man suppose that he will receive anything from the Lord.* (James 1:5–7)

This passage not only promises God's wisdom, but tells us specifically just what to do to obtain it. There are really five steps stated or implied in the passage.

We lack wisdom.

We must be conscious of and fully admit our own inability to decide wisely. Here is where we often fail to receive God's wisdom. We think we are able to decide for ourselves, or at least we are not ready to admit our own utter inability to decide. There must be an entire renunciation of the wisdom of the flesh.

We must really desire to know God's way and be willing at any cost to do His will.

This is implied in the word *"ask."* The asking must be sincere, and if we are not willing to do God's will, whatever it may be, at any cost, the asking is not sincere. This is a point of fundamental importance. Nothing goes so far to make our minds clear in the discernment of the will of God as revealed by His Spirit as an absolutely surrendered will. Here we find the reason why people often do not know God's will and do not have the Spirit's guidance. They are not willing to do whatever the Spirit leads at any cost. Those who want to do His will will know not only of the doctrine but their daily duties. Men often come to me and say, "I cannot find out the will of God," but when I put the question to them, "Are you willing to do the will of God at any cost?" they admit that they are not. The way that is very obscure when we hold back from an absolute surrender to God becomes as clear as day when we make that surrender.

We must definitely ask for guidance.

It is not enough to desire; it is not enough to be willing to obey; we must ask, definitely ask, God to show us the way.

We must confidently expect guidance.

"Let him ask in faith, with no doubting" (James 1:6). Many cannot find the way, though they ask God to show it to them, simply because they have not the absolutely undoubting expectation that God will show them the way. God promises to show it if we expect it confidently. When you come to God in prayer to show you what to do, know for a certainty that He will show you. In what way He will show you, He does not tell, but He promises that He will show you, and that is enough.

We must follow step by step as the guidance comes.

Just how God's direction will come, no one can tell, but it will come. Often only a step will be made clear at a time; that is all we need to know—the next step. Many are in darkness because they do not know and cannot find what God would have them do next week or next month or next year.

A college man once came to me and told me that he was in great darkness about God's guidance, that he had been seeking to find the will of God and learn what his life's work should be, but he could not find it. I asked him how far along he was in his college course. He said his sophomore year. I asked, "What is it you desire to know?"

"What I should do when I finish college."

"Do you know that you should complete your college education?"

"Yes."

This man not only knew what he ought to do next year, but the year after; still, he was in great perplexity because he did not know what he should do when those two years were ended. God delights to lead His children a step at a time. He leads us as He led the children of Israel:

> *Whenever the cloud was taken up from above the tabernacle, after that the children of Israel would journey; and in the place where the cloud settled, there the children of Israel would pitch their tents. At the command of the LORD the children of Israel would journey, and at the command of the LORD they would camp; as long as the cloud stayed above the tabernacle they remained encamped. Even when the cloud continued long, many days above the tabernacle, the children of Israel kept the charge of the LORD and did not journey. So it was, when the cloud was above the tabernacle a few days: according to the command of the LORD they would remain encamped, and according to the command of the LORD they would journey. So it was, when the cloud remained only from evening until morning: when the cloud was taken up in the morning, then they would journey; whether by day or by night, whenever the cloud was taken up, they would journey. Whether it was two days, a month, or a year that the cloud remained above the tabernacle, the children of Israel would remain encamped and not journey; but when it was taken up, they would journey. At the command of the LORD they remained encamped, and*

at the command of the LORD they journeyed; they kept the charge of the LORD, at the command of the LORD by the hand of Moses. (Num. 9:17–23)

Many who have given themselves up to the leading of the Holy Spirit get into a place of great bondage and are tortured because they have leadings that they fear may be from God but of which they are not sure. If they do not obey these leadings, they are fearful they have disobeyed God and sometimes imagine that they have grieved the Holy Spirit because they did not follow His leading. This is all unnecessary. Let us settle it in our minds that God's guidance is clear guidance. *"God is light and in Him is no darkness at all"* (1 John 1:5). Any leading that is not perfectly clear is not from Him, that is, if our wills are absolutely surrendered to Him. Of course, the uncertainty may arise from an unsurrendered will. But if our wills are absolutely surrendered to God, we have the right as God's children to be sure that any guidance is from Him before we obey it.

We have a right to go to our Father and say, "Heavenly Father, here I am. I desire above all things to do Your will. Now make it clear to me, Your child. If this thing that I have a leading to do is Your will, I will do it, but make it as clear as day if it is Your will." If it is His will, the heavenly Father will make it plain. You need not and should not do that thing until He does make it clear, and you need not and should not condemn yourself because you did not do it. God does not want His children to be in a state of condemnation before Him. He wishes us to be free from all care, worry, anxiety, and self-condemnation. Any earthly parent would make the way clear to his child who asked to know it. How much more will our heavenly Father make it clear to us? Until He does make it clear, we need have no fears that in not doing it we are disobeying God. We have no right to dictate to God as to how He should give His guidance—as, for example, by asking Him to close off every way, by asking Him to give a sign, by asking Him to guide us in putting our finger on a text, or in any other way. It is ours to seek and to expect wisdom, but it is not ours to dictate how it will be given. The Holy Spirit divides *"to each one individually as He wills"* (1 Cor. 12:11).

Two things are evident from what has been said about the work of the Holy Spirit: first, how utterly dependent we are on the work of the Holy Spirit at every turn of Christian life and service; second, how perfect the provision for life and service is that God has made. How wonderful is the fullness of privilege that is open to the humblest believer through the Holy Spirit's work. It is not so much what we are by nature—either intellectually, morally, physically, or even spiritually—that is important. The important matter is what the Holy Spirit can do for us and what we will let Him do. Not infrequently, the Holy Spirit takes the one who seems to have the least natural promise and uses him far beyond those who have the greatest natural promise. Christian life is not to be lived in the realm of natural temperament, and Christian work is not to be done in the power of natural endowment. Christian life is to be lived in the realm of the Spirit, and Christian work is to be done in the power of the Spirit. The Holy Spirit is willing and eagerly desirous of doing for each one of us His whole work, and He will do in each one of us all that we will let Him do.

Chapter 19

The Holy Spirit and the Believer's Body

◆

T he Holy Spirit does a work for our bodies as well as for our minds and hearts. We read in Romans 8:11: *"But if the Spirit of Him who raised Jesus from the dead dwells in you, He who raised Christ from the dead will also give life to your mortal bodies through His Spirit who dwells in you."*

The Holy Spirit quickens the mortal body of the believer. It is very evident from the context that this refers to the future resurrection of the body. (See Romans 8:21–23.) The resurrection of the body is the Holy Spirit's work. The glorified body is from Him; it is *"a spiritual body"* (1 Cor. 15:44). At the present time, we have only the firstfruits of the Spirit and are waiting for the full harvest, *"the redemption of our body"* (Rom. 8:23).

There is, however, a sense in which the Holy Spirit even now quickens our bodies. Jesus tells us in Matthew 12:28 that He *"cast out demons by the Spirit of God."* We read in Acts 10:38 *"how God anointed Jesus of Nazareth with the Holy Spirit and with power, who went about doing good and healing all who were oppressed by the devil, for God was with Him."* In James 5:14, the apostle wrote, *"Is anyone among you sick? Let him call for the elders of the church, and let them pray over him, anointing him with oil in the name of the Lord."* The oil in this passage as elsewhere is a type of the Holy Spirit, and the truth is set forth that the healing is the Holy Spirit's work.

By His Holy Spirit, God does impart new health and vigor to these mortal bodies in the present life. To go to the extreme that many do and take the ground that the believer who is walking in fellowship with Christ never needs to be ill is to go further than the Bible warrants us in going. It is true that the redemption of our bodies is secured by the atoning work of Christ, but until the Lord comes, we only enjoy the firstfruits of that redemption.

We are waiting and sometimes groaning for our full place as sons manifested in the redemption of our bodies (Rom. 8:23). But while this is true, it is the clear teaching of Scripture, as well as a matter of personal experience on the part of thousands, that the life of the Holy Spirit does sweep through these bodies of ours in moments of weakness, pain, and sickness, imparting new health to them, delivering them from pain, and filling them with abounding life. It is our privilege to know the quickening touch of the Holy Spirit in these bodies as well as in our minds, affections, and wills. It would be a great day for the church and for the glory of Jesus Christ if Christians would renounce forever all the Devil's counterfeits of the Holy Spirit's work—Christian Science, mental healing, hypnotism, and the various other forms of occultism—and depend on God by the power of His Holy Spirit to work in these bodies of ours what He in His unerring wisdom sees that we need most.

Chapter 20

The Baptism with the Holy Spirit

◆

One of the most deeply significant phrases used in connection with the Holy Spirit in the Scriptures is "baptized with the Holy Spirit." John the Baptist was the first to use this phrase. In speaking of himself and the coming One, he said:

> *I indeed baptize you with water unto repentance, but He who is coming after me is mightier than I, whose sandals I am not worthy to carry. He will baptize you with the Holy Spirit and fire.* (Matt. 3:11)

There are not two different baptisms spoken of, one with the Holy Spirit and one with fire, but one baptism with the Holy Wind and Fire. Jesus afterwards used the same expression. In Acts 1:5, He said, *"John truly baptized with water, but you shall be baptized with the Holy Spirit not many days from now."* When this promise of John the Baptist and our Lord was fulfilled in Acts 2:3–4, we read: *"Then there appeared to them divided tongues, as of fire, and one sat upon each of them. And they were all filled with the Holy Spirit."* Here we have another expression, *"filled with the Holy Spirit,"* used synonymously with *"baptized with the Holy Spirit."*

We read again in Acts:

> *While Peter was still speaking these words, the Holy Spirit fell upon all those who heard the word. And those of the circumcision who believed were astonished, as many as came with Peter, because the gift of the Holy Spirit had been poured out on the Gentiles also. For they heard them speak with tongues and magnify God.* (Acts 10:44–46)

Peter himself, afterwards describing this experience in Jerusalem, told the story in this way:

> *And as I began to speak, the Holy Spirit fell upon them, as upon us at the beginning. Then I remembered the word of the Lord, how He said, "John indeed baptized with water, but you shall be baptized with the Holy Spirit." If therefore God gave them the same gift as He gave us when we believed on the Lord Jesus Christ, who was I that I could withstand God?*   (Acts 11:15–17)

Here Peter distinctly calls the experience that came to Cornelius and his household, being *"baptized with the Holy Spirit,"* so we see that the expressions *"the Holy Spirit fell"* and *"the same gift"* of the Holy Spirit are practically synonymous expressions with *"baptized with the Holy Spirit."* Still other expressions are used to describe this blessing, such as *"receive the Holy Spirit"* (Acts 19:2); *"the Holy Spirit came upon them"* (Acts 19:6); *"gift of the Holy Spirit"* (Acts 2:38; see also Hebrews 2:4); *"I send the Promise of My Father upon you"* (Luke 24:49); and *"endued with power from on high"* (v. 49).

What Is the Baptism with the Holy Spirit?

The baptism with the Holy Spirit is a definite experience that one may and should know whether he has received.

This is evident from our Lord's command to His disciples in Luke 24:49 and in Acts 1:4 that they should not depart from Jerusalem to undertake the work that He had commissioned them to do until they had received this promise of the Father. It is also evident from Acts 8:15–16, where we are distinctly told: *"the Holy Spirit...as yet He had fallen upon none of them."* It is evident also from Acts 19:2, where Paul questioned the little group of disciples at Ephesus: *"Did you receive the Holy Spirit when you believed?"*

It is evident that the receiving of the Holy Spirit was an experience so definite that one could answer yes or no to the question whether he had received the Holy Spirit. In this case, the disciples definitely answered, *"We have not so much as heard whether there is a Holy Spirit"* (Acts 19:2). It was not that they did not know about the existence of the Holy Spirit. Furthermore, they knew that there was a definite promise of the baptism with the Holy Spirit, but they had not heard that the promise had been as yet fulfilled. Paul told them that it had and took steps whereby they were definitely baptized with the Holy Spirit before that meeting closed.

It is equally evident from Galatians 3:2 that the baptism with the Holy Spirit is a definite experience of which one may know whether he has received it or not. In this passage Paul said to the believers in Galatia, *"This only I want to learn from you: Did you receive the Spirit by the works of the law, or by the hearing of faith?"* Their receiving the Spirit had been so definite as a matter of personal consciousness that Paul could appeal to it as a ground for his argument.

In our day, there is much talk about the baptism with the Holy Spirit and prayer for the baptism with the Spirit that is altogether vague and indefinite. Men stand up in meetings and pray that they may be baptized with the Holy Spirit. If you should go afterwards to the one who offered the prayer and put to him the question, "Did you receive what you asked? Were you baptized with the Holy Spirit?" it is quite likely that he would hesitate and falter and say, "I hope so." But there is none of this indefiniteness in the Bible. The Bible is clear on this, as on every other point. It sets forth an experience so definite and so real that one may know whether or not he has received the baptism with the Holy Spirit and can answer yes or no to the question, "Have you received the Holy Spirit?"

Second, it is evident that the baptism with the Holy Spirit is an operation of the Holy Spirit distinct from, and additional to, His regenerating work.

This fact is evident from Acts 1:5: *"For John truly baptized with water, but you shall be baptized with the Holy Spirit not many days from now."* It is clear, then, that the disciples had not as yet been baptized with the Holy Spirit, that they were to be thus baptized not many days from then, but the men to whom Jesus spoke these words were already new men. They had been so pronounced by our Lord Himself. He had said to them in John 15:3, *"You are already clean because of the word which I have spoken to you."* What does *"clean because of the word"* mean? The question is answered in 1 Peter 1:23: *"Having been born again, not of corruptible seed but incorruptible, through the word of God which lives and abides forever."*

A little earlier on the same night, Jesus had said to them in John 13:10, *"He who is bathed needs only to wash his feet, but is completely clean; and you are clean, but not all of you."* The Lord Jesus had pronounced that apostolic company clean—reborn men—with the exception of the one who never was a reborn man, Judas Iscariot, who would betray Him. (See verse 11.) The remaining eleven Jesus Christ had pronounced reborn men. Yet He tells these same men in Acts 1:5 that the baptism with the Holy Spirit was an experience that they had not as yet realized, that still lay in the future. So it is evident that it is one thing to be born again by the Holy Spirit through the Word and something distinct from this and additional to it to be baptized with the Holy Spirit.

The same thing is evident from Acts 8:12, compared with the fifteenth and sixteenth verses of the same chapter. In the twelfth verse we read that a large company of disciples had believed the preaching of Philip concerning the kingdom of God and the name of Jesus Christ, and had been *"baptized in the name of the Lord Jesus"* (v. 16). Certainly in this company of baptized believers there were at least some reborn people. Whatever the true form of water baptism may be, they undoubtedly had been baptized by it because the baptizing had been done by a Spirit-commissioned man, but we read:

> *Peter and John...had come down,* [and] *prayed for them that they might receive the Holy Spirit. For as yet He had fallen upon none of them. They had only been baptized in the name of the Lord Jesus.* (Acts 8:14–16)

Baptized believers they were; they had been baptized into the name of the Lord Jesus. Reborn men some of them most assuredly were, and yet not one of them as yet had received, or been baptized with, the Holy Spirit. So again, it is evident that the baptism with the Holy Spirit is an operation of the Holy Spirit distinct from and additional to His regenerating work. A man may be reborn by the Holy Spirit and still not be baptized with the Holy Spirit. In being reborn, there is the impartation of life by the Spirit's power, and the one who receives it is saved. In the baptism with the Holy Spirit, there is the impartation of power, and the one who receives it is fitted for service.

The baptism with the Holy Spirit, however, may take place at the moment of rebirth. It did, for example, in the household of Cornelius. We read in Acts 10:43 that, while Peter was preaching, he came to the point where he said concerning Jesus: *"To Him all the prophets witness that, through His name, whoever believes in Him will receive remission of sins."* At that point Cornelius and his household believed, and we immediately read:

> *While Peter was still speaking these words, the Holy Spirit fell upon all those who heard the word. And those of the circumcision who believed were astonished, as many as came with Peter, because the gift of the Holy Spirit had been poured out on the Gentiles also.* (Acts 10:44–45)

The moment they believed the testimony about Jesus, they were baptized with the Holy Spirit, even before they were baptized with water. Rebirth and the baptism with the Holy Spirit took place practically at the same moment, and so they do in many an experience today. It would seem as if, in a normal condition of the church, this would be the usual experience. But the church is not in a normal condition today. A very large part of the church is in the place where the believers in Samaria were before Peter and John came and where the disciples in Ephesus were before Paul came and told them of their larger privilege— baptized believers, baptized into the name of the Lord Jesus, baptized unto repentance and remission of sins, but not as yet baptized with the Holy Spirit. Nevertheless, the baptism with the Holy Spirit is the birthright of every believer. It was purchased for us by the atoning death of Christ. When He ascended to the right hand of the Father, He received the promise of the Father and shed Him forth upon the church. If anyone today has not received the baptism with the Holy Spirit as a personal experience, it is because he has not claimed his birthright.

Potentially, every member of the body of Christ is baptized with the Holy Spirit: *"For by one Spirit we were all baptized into one body; whether Jews or Greeks, whether slaves or free; and have all been made to drink into one Spirit"* (1 Cor. 12:13). But there are many believers with whom what is potentially theirs has not become a matter of real, actual, personal experience. All men are potentially justified in the atoning death of Jesus Christ on the cross; that is, justification is provided for them and belongs to them. (See Romans 5:18.) What potentially belongs to every man, each man must appropriate for himself by faith in Christ. Then justification is actually and experientially his. While the baptism with the Holy Spirit is potentially the possession of every believer, each individual believer must appropriate it for himself before it is experientially his. We may go still further than this and say that it is only by the baptism with the Holy Spirit that one becomes in the fullest sense a member of the body of Christ because it is only by the baptism with the Spirit that he receives power to perform those functions for which God has appointed him as a part of the body.

As we have already seen, every true believer has the Holy Spirit (see Romans 8:9), but not every believer has the baptism with the Holy Spirit (though every believer may have, as we have just seen). It is one thing to have the Holy Spirit dwell within us, perhaps dwelling within us way back in some hidden sanctuary of our beings, back of definite consciousness, and something far different, something vastly more, to have the Holy Spirit take complete possession of the one whom He inhabits. There are those who press the fact that every believer potentially has the baptism with the Spirit to such an extent that they clearly teach that every believer has the baptism with the Spirit as an actual experience. But unless the baptism with the Spirit today is something radically different from what the baptism with the Spirit was in the early church, indeed, unless it is something not at all real, then either a very large proportion of those whom we ordinarily consider believers are not believers or else one may be a believer and be reborn without having been baptized with the Holy Spirit. Certainly, the latter was the case in the early church. It was the case with the apostles before Pentecost; it was the case with the church in Ephesus; it was the case with the church in Samaria. And there are thousands today who can testify to having received Christ and been born again, and then afterwards, sometimes long afterwards, having been baptized with the Holy Spirit as a definite experience.

This is a matter of great practical importance. Many are not enjoying the fullness of privilege that they might enjoy because by pushing individual verses in the Scriptures beyond what they will bear and against the plain teaching of the Scriptures as a whole, they are trying to persuade themselves that they have already been baptized with the Holy Spirit when they have not. If they would only admit to themselves that they had not been filled, they could then take the steps whereby they would be baptized with the Holy Spirit as a matter of definite, personal experience.

The baptism with the Holy Spirit is always connected with and primarily for the purpose of testimony and service.

Our Lord, in speaking of this baptism that they were soon to receive, said in Luke 24:49, *"Behold, I send the Promise of My Father upon you; but tarry in the city of Jerusalem until you are endued with power from on high."* And again He said:

> For John truly baptized with water, but you shall be baptized with the Holy Spirit not many days from now....But you shall receive power when the Holy Spirit has come upon you; and you shall be witnesses to Me in Jerusalem, and in all Judea and Samaria, and to the end of the earth.
> (Acts 1:5, 8)

In the record of the fulfillment of this promise of our Lord, we read: *"And they were all filled with the Holy Spirit and began to speak with other tongues, as the Spirit gave them utterance"* (Acts 2:4). Then follows the detailed account of what Peter said and of the result. The result was that Peter and the other apostles spoke with such power that three thousand people were convicted of sin, renounced their sins, confessed

their acceptance of Jesus Christ in baptism, and continued steadfastly in the apostles' doctrine and fellowship and in the breaking
of bread and in prayer ever afterwards. (See Acts 2:41–42.)

In Acts 4:31–33, we read that when the apostles on another
occasion were filled with the Holy Spirit, the result was that
they *"spoke the word of God with boldness"* (v. 31) and that
*"with great power the apostles gave witness to the resurrection of
the Lord Jesus"* (v. 33). The following is a description of when
Paul was baptized with the Holy Spirit:

> *And Ananias went his way and entered the house; and lay-
> ing his hands on him he said, "Brother Saul, the Lord Je-
> sus, who appeared to you on the road as you came, has sent
> me that you may receive your sight and be filled with the
> Holy Spirit." Immediately there fell from his eyes some-
> thing like scales, and he received his sight at once; and he
> arose and was baptized. So when he had received food, he
> was strengthened....Immediately he preached the Christ in
> the synagogues, that He is the Son of God.* (Acts 9:17–20)

And in the twenty-second verse we read that he *"confounded the
Jews who dwelt in Damascus, proving that this Jesus is the
Christ."*

In 1 Corinthians chapter twelve, we have the fullest discussion of the baptism with the Holy Spirit found in any passage in
the Bible. This is the classical passage on the whole subject. The
results there recorded are gifts for service. The baptism with
the Holy Spirit is not primarily intended to make believers
happy but to make them useful. It is not intended merely for the
ecstasy of the individual believer; it is intended primarily for his
efficiency in service. I do not say that the baptism with the Holy
Spirit will not make the believer happy, for part of the fruit of
the Spirit is joy. If one is baptized with the Holy Spirit, joy must
inevitably result. I have never known one to be baptized with
the Holy Spirit into whose life there did not come, sooner or
later, a new joy, a higher and purer and fuller joy than he had
ever known before.

But this is not the primary purpose of the baptism nor the
most important and prominent result. Great emphasis needs to

be placed on this point, for there are many Christians who, in seeking the baptism with the Spirit, are seeking personal ecstasy and rapture. They go to conventions and conferences for the deepening of the Christian life and come back and tell what a wonderful blessing they have received, referring to some new ecstasy that has come into their hearts. However, when you watch them, it is difficult to see that they are any more useful to their pastors or their churches than they were before, and one is compelled to think that whatever they have received, they have not received the real baptism with the Holy Spirit.

Ecstasies and raptures are all right in their places. When they come, thank God for them—I know something about them—but in a world such as we live in today, where sin and self-righteousness and unbelief are so rampant, where there is such an awful tide of men, women, and young people sweeping toward eternal perdition, I would rather go through my whole life and never have one touch of ecstasy but have power to witness for Christ. I would rather have power to win others for Christ and thus to save them than to have rapture 365 days in the year but have no power to stem the awful tide of sin and bring men, women, and children to a saving knowledge of my Lord and Savior Jesus Christ.

The purpose of the baptism with the Holy Spirit is not primarily to make believers individually holy. I do not say that it is not the work of the Holy Spirit to make believers holy, for as we have already seen, He is the Spirit of holiness, and the only way we will ever attain holiness is by His power. I do not even say that the baptism with the Holy Spirit will not result in a great spiritual transformation and uplift and cleansing, for the promise is, *"He will baptize you with the Holy Spirit and fire"* (Matt. 3:11). The thought of fire as used in this connection is the thought of searching, refining, cleansing, and consuming. A wonderful transformation took place in the apostles at Pentecost and has taken place in thousands who have been baptized with the Holy Spirit since Pentecost, but the primary purpose of the baptism with the Holy Spirit is effectiveness in testimony and service. It has to do more with gifts for service than with graces of character. It is the impartation of spiritual power or gifts in service, and sometimes one may have rare gifts by the

Spirit's power and yet manifest few of the graces of the Spirit. (See 1 Corinthians 13:1–3; Matthew 7:22–23.) In every passage in the Bible in which the baptism with the Holy Spirit is mentioned, it is connected with testimony or service.

Chapter 21

The Results of the Baptism

◆

We will perhaps get a clearer idea of just what the baptism with the Holy Spirit is if we stop to consider what the results of the baptism with the Holy Spirit are.

The specific manifestations of the baptism with the Holy Spirit are not precisely the same in all people.

This point is clear in this passage from 1 Corinthians:

There are diversities of gifts, but the same Spirit. There are differences of ministries, but the same Lord. And there are diversities of activities, but it is the same God who works all in all. But the manifestation of the Spirit is given to each one for the profit of all: for to one is given the word of wisdom through the Spirit, to another the word of knowledge through the same Spirit, to another faith by the same Spirit, to another gifts of healings by the same Spirit, to another the working of miracles, to another prophecy, to another discerning of spirits, to another different kinds of tongues, to another the interpretation of tongues. But one and the same Spirit works all these things, distributing to each one individually as He wills. For as the body is one and has many members, but all the members of that one body, being many, are one body, so also is Christ. For by one Spirit we were all baptized into one body; whether Jews or Greeks, whether slaves or free; and have all been made to drink into one Spirit. (1 Cor. 12:4–13)

Here we see one baptism but a great variety of manifestations of the power of that baptism. There are diversities of gifts but the same Spirit. The gifts vary with the different areas of service to which God calls different people. The church is a body, and different members of the body have different functions. The Spirit imparts to the one who is baptized with the Spirit those gifts that fit him for the service to which God has called him. It is very important to bear this in mind. Through the failure to see this, many have gone entirely astray on the whole subject.

In my early study of the subject, I noticed the fact that in many instances those who were baptized with the Holy Spirit spoke with tongues (for example, see Acts 2:4; 10:46; 19:6), and I wondered if everyone who was baptized with the Holy Spirit would speak with tongues. I did not know of anyone who was speaking with tongues then, so I wondered still further whether the baptism with the Holy Spirit was for the present age. But one day I was studying 1 Corinthians chapter twelve and noticed what Paul said to the believers in that wonderfully gifted church in Corinth, all of whom had been pronounced to be baptized with the Spirit (v. 13):

> *And God has appointed these in the church: first apostles, second prophets, third teachers, after that miracles, then gifts of healings, helps, administrations, varieties of tongues. Are all apostles? Are all prophets? Are all teachers? Are all workers of miracles? Do all have gifts of healings? Do all speak with tongues? Do all interpret?*
>
> (1 Cor. 12:28–30)

So I saw it was clearly taught in the Scriptures that one might be baptized with the Holy Spirit and still not have the gift of tongues. I saw further that the gift of tongues, according to the Scriptures, was the last and the least important of all the gifts and that we were urged to desire earnestly the greater gifts. (See 1 Corinthians 12:31; 14:5, 12, 14, 18–19, 27–28.)

A little later, I was tempted to fall into another error, more specious but in reality just as unscriptural as this, namely, that if one were baptized with the Holy Spirit, he would receive the gift relating to an evangelist. I had read the stories of D. L. Moody, of Charles G. Finney, and of others who were baptized with the Holy Spirit, and of the power that came to them as evangelists. The thought was suggested that if anyone is baptized with the Holy Spirit, he should also obtain power as an evangelist. This was also unscriptural. If God has called a man to be an evangelist and that man is baptized with the Holy Spirit, he will receive power as an evangelist, but if God has called him to be something else, he will receive power to become something else. Three great evils come from the error of thinking that everyone who is baptized with the Holy Spirit will receive power as an evangelist.

The first evil is the evil of disappointment. Many seek the baptism with the Holy Spirit expecting power as an evangelist, but God has not called them to that work. Though they really meet the conditions of receiving the baptism with the Spirit and do receive the baptism with the Spirit, power as an evangelist does not come. In many cases, this results in bitter disappointment and sometimes even in despair. The one who has expected the power of an evangelist and has not received it sometimes even questions whether he is a child of God. If he had properly understood the matter, he would have known that the fact that he had not received power as an evangelist is no proof that he has not received the baptism with the Spirit, and much less is it a proof that he is not a child of God.

This second evil is graver still, namely, the evil of presumption. A man whom God has not called to do the work of an evangelist or a minister often rushes into it because he has received, or imagines he has received, the baptism with the Holy Spirit. He thinks all he needs to become a preacher is the baptism with the Holy Spirit. This is not true. In order to succeed as a minister, a man needs a call to that specific work, and furthermore, he needs the knowledge of God's Word that will prepare him for the work. If a man is called to the ministry and studies the Word until he has something to preach, if then he is baptized with the Holy Spirit, he will have success as a preacher. But if he is not called to that work, or if he has not the knowledge of the Word of God that is necessary, he will not succeed in the work even though he receives the baptism with the Holy Spirit.

The third evil is greater still, namely, the evil of indifference. Many know that they are not called to the work of preaching. If then they think that the baptism with the Holy Spirit simply imparts power as an evangelist, or power to preach, the matter of the baptism with the Holy Spirit is one of no personal concern to them. For example, consider a mother with a large family of children. She knows perfectly well that she is not called to do the work of an evangelist. She knows that her duty lies with her children and her home. If she reads or hears about the baptism with the Holy Spirit and gets the impression that the baptism with the Holy Spirit simply imparts power to do the work of an evangelist or to preach, she will think, "The evangelist needs this blessing, my minister needs this blessing, but it is not for me."

But if she understands the matter as it is taught in the Bible, that while the baptism with the Spirit imparts power, the way in which the power will be manifested depends entirely on the area of work to which God calls us; if she understands that no effective work can be done without it and sees still further that there is no function in the church of Jesus Christ today more holy and sacred than that of sanctified motherhood, she will say, "The evangelist may need this baptism, my minister may need this baptism, but I must have it to bring up my children *'in the training and admonition of the Lord'"* (Eph. 6:4).

While there are diversities of gifts and manifestations of the baptism with the Holy Spirit, everyone who is baptized will receive a gift of the Holy Spirit.

We read in 1 Corinthians 12:7: *"But the manifestation of the Spirit is given to each one for the profit of all."* The most insignificant member of the body of Christ has some function to perform in that body. The body grows *"by what every joint supplies"* (Eph. 4:16), and to the least significant joint, the Holy Spirit imparts power to perform the function that belongs to him.

The Holy Spirit decides how the baptism with the Spirit will manifest itself in any given case.

We read in 1 Corinthians 12:11: *"But one and the same Spirit works all these things, distributing to each one individually as He wills."* The Holy Spirit is absolutely sovereign in deciding how—that is, in what special gift, operation, or power— the baptism with the Holy Spirit will manifest itself. It is not for us to pick out some field of service and then ask the Holy Spirit to qualify us for that service. It is not for us to select some gift and then ask the Holy Spirit to impart to us this self-chosen gift. It is for us to simply put ourselves entirely at the disposal of the Holy Spirit to send us where He will, to select for us what kind of service He will, and to impart to us what gifts He will. He is absolutely sovereign, and our position is that of unconditional surrender to Him.

I am glad that this is so. I rejoice that He, in His infinite wisdom and love, is to select the field of service and the gifts, and that this is not to be left to me in my short-sightedness and folly. It is because of the failure to recognize this absolute sovereignty of the Spirit that many fail to obtain the blessing and meet with disappointment. They are trying to select their own gift and so get none.

I once knew an earnest child of God in Scotland who, hearing of the baptism with the Holy Spirit and the power that resulted from it, gave up at a great sacrifice his work as a ship plater for which he was receiving large wages. He heard that there was a great need for ministers in the Northwest in America. He came to the Northwest. He met the conditions of the baptism with the Holy Spirit, and I believe he was really baptized with the Holy Spirit. But God had not chosen him for the work of an evangelist, and the power as an evangelist did not come to him. No field seemed to open, and he was in great despondency. He even questioned his acceptance before God. One morning he came into our church in Minneapolis and heard me speak on the baptism with the Holy Spirit. As I pointed out that the baptism with the Holy Spirit manifested itself in many different ways and the fact that one did not have power as an evangelist was no proof that he had not received the baptism with the Holy Spirit, light came into his heart. He put himself unreservedly into God's hands for Him to choose the field of labor and the gifts. An opening soon came to him as a Sunday school missionary. Then, when he had given up choosing for himself and left it with the Holy Spirit to divide to him as He would, a strange thing happened; he did receive power as an evangelist and went through the country districts in one of our Northwestern states with mighty power as an evangelist.

While the power may be of one kind in one person and of another kind in another person, there will always be power, the very power of God, when one is baptized with the Holy Spirit.

> *For John truly baptized with water, but you shall be baptized with the Holy Spirit not many days from now....But you shall receive power when the Holy Spirit has come upon you; and you shall be witnesses to Me in Jerusalem, and in all Judea and Samaria, and to the end of the earth.*
> (Acts 1:5, 8)

As truly as anyone who reads these pages who has not already received the baptism with the Holy Spirit seeks it in God's way, he will obtain it. Then, there will come into his service a power that was never there before, power for the very work to which God has called him. This is not only the teaching of Scripture; it is the teaching of religious experience throughout the centuries. Religious biographies abound in instances of those who have worked as best they could until one day they were led to see that there was such an experience as the baptism with the Holy Spirit and to seek it and obtain it. From that hour, there came into their service a new power that utterly transformed its character.

In this matter, one thinks first of such men as Finney, Moody, and Brainerd, but cases of this nature are not confined to a few exceptional men. They are common. I have personally met and corresponded with thousands of people around the globe who could testify definitely to the new power that God has granted them through the baptism with the Holy Spirit. These thousands of men and women were in all branches of Christian service; some of them were ministers of the Gospel, some evangelists, some mission workers, some YMCA secretaries, Sunday school teachers, fathers, mothers, personal workers, etc. Nothing could possibly exceed the clearness, the confidence, and the joyfulness of many of these testimonies.

I will not soon forget a minister whom I met some years ago at a State Convention of the Young People's Society of Christian Endeavor at New Britain, Connecticut. I was speaking on the subject of personal work, and as I drew the address to a close, I said that in order to do effective personal work, we must be baptized with the Holy Spirit. In a very few sentences, I explained what I meant by that.

At the close of the address, this minister came to me on the platform and said, "I do not have this blessing you have been speaking about, but I want it. Will you pray for me?"

I said, "Why not pray right now?"

He said, "I will."

We put two chairs side by side and turned our backs on the crowd as they passed out of the auditorium. He prayed and I prayed that he might be baptized with the Holy Spirit. Then we separated. Some weeks after that, one who had witnessed the scene came to me at a convention in Washington and told me how this minister had gone back to his church a transformed man, that now his congregation filled the church, that it was largely composed of young men, and that there were conversions at every service. Some years after that, this minister was called to another field of service. His most spiritually-minded friends advised him not to go because all the ruling elements in the church to which he had been called were against aggressive evangelistic work, but for some reason or other, he felt it was the call of God and accepted it. In six months, there were sixty-nine conversions, and thirty-eight of them were businessmen of the town.

After attending an Convention of the Young Men's Christian Association (YMCA) of the Provinces of Canada in Montreal some years ago, I received a letter from a young man. He wrote, "I was present at your last meeting in Montreal. I heard you speak on the baptism with the Holy Spirit. I went to my room and sought that baptism for myself and received it. I am chairman of the Lookout Committee of the Christian Endeavor Society of our church. I called together the other members of the committee. I found that two of them had been at the meeting and had already been baptized with the Holy Spirit. Then we prayed for the other members of the committee, and they were baptized with the Holy Spirit. Now we are going out into the church, and the young people of the church are being brought to Christ right along."

A lady and gentleman once came to me at a convention and told me how, though they had never seen me before, they had read the report of an address on the baptism with the Holy Spirit delivered in Boston at a Christian workers' convention and that they had sought this baptism and had received it. The man then told me the blessing that had come into his service as superintendent of the Sunday school. When he had finished, his wife broke in and said, "Yes, and the best part of it is, I have been able to reach the hearts of my own children, which I was never able to do before."

Here were three distinctly different areas of service, but there was power in each case. The results of that power may not, however, be clear at once in conversion. Stephen was filled with the Holy Spirit, but as he witnessed in the power of the Holy Spirit for his risen Lord, he saw no conversions at the time. All he saw was gnashing of teeth, angry looks, and the merciless rocks, and so it may be with us. However, there was a conversion, even in that case, though it was a long time before it was seen, and that conversion, the conversion of Saul of Tarsus, was worth more than hundreds of ordinary conversions.

Another result of the baptism with the Holy Spirit will be boldness in testimony and service.

We read in Acts 4:31: *"And when they had prayed, the place where they were assembled together was shaken; and they were all filled with the Holy Spirit, and they spoke the word of God with boldness."* The baptism with the Holy Spirit imparts to those who receive it new liberty and fearlessness in testimony for Christ. It converts cowards into heroes.

On the night of our Lord's crucifixion, Peter proved himself a defeated coward. With oaths and curses, he denied that he knew the Lord. But after Pentecost, this same Peter was brought before the very council that had condemned Jesus to death, and he himself was threatened. This is what happened:

> *Then Peter, filled with the Holy Spirit, said to them, "Rulers of the people and elders of Israel: If we this day are judged for a good deed done to a helpless man, by what means he has been made well, let it be known to you all, and to all the people of Israel, that by the name of Jesus Christ of Nazareth, whom you crucified, whom God raised from the dead, by Him this man stands here before you whole. This is the 'stone which was rejected by you builders, which has become the chief cornerstone.' Nor is there salvation in any other, for there is no other name under heaven given among men by which we must be saved."*
> (Acts 4:8–12)

A little later when the council commanded him and his companion, John, not to speak or teach in the name of Jesus, they answered, *"Whether it is right in the sight of God to listen to you more than to God, you judge. For we cannot but speak the things which we have seen and heard"* (vv. 19–20). On a still later occasion, when they were threatened and commanded not to speak and when their lives were in jeopardy, Peter told the council to their faces:

> *We ought to obey God rather than men. The God of our fathers raised up Jesus whom you murdered by hanging on a tree. Him God has exalted to His right hand to be Prince and Savior, to give repentance to Israel and forgiveness of sins. And we are His witnesses to these things, and so also is the Holy Spirit whom God has given to those who obey Him.*
> (Acts 5:29–32)

The natural timidity of many people today vanishes when they are filled with the Holy Spirit. With great boldness and liberty, with utter fearlessness of consequences, they give their testimonies for Jesus Christ.

The baptism with the Holy Spirit causes the receiver to be occupied with God, Christ, and spiritual things.

In the record of the Day of Pentecost, we read:

They were all filled with the Holy Spirit and began to speak with other tongues, as the Spirit gave them utterance....Then they were all amazed and marveled, saying to one another, "Look, are not all these who speak Galilaeans? And how is it that we hear, each in our own language in which we were born?...We hear them speaking in our own tongues the wonderful works of God." (Acts 2:4, 7, 11)

Then follows Peter's sermon, a sermon that from start to finish is entirely taken up with Jesus Christ and His glory:

Then Peter, filled with the Holy Spirit, said to them, "Rulers of the people and elders of Israel: If we this day are judged for a good deed done to a helpless man, by what means he has been made well, let it be known to you all, and to all the people of Israel, that by the name of Jesus Christ of Nazareth, whom you crucified, whom God raised from the dead, by Him this man stands here before you whole." (Acts 4:8–10)

Regarding a later day, we read:

And when they had prayed, the place where they were assembled together was shaken; and they were all filled with the Holy Spirit, and they spoke the word of God with boldness....And with great power the apostles gave witness to the resurrection of the Lord Jesus. And great grace was upon them all. (Acts 4:31, 33)

We read of Saul of Tarsus, that when he had been filled with the Holy Spirit, *"immediately he preached the Christ in the synagogues, that He is the Son of God"* (Acts 9:20). We read of the household of Cornelius:

While Peter was still speaking these words, the Holy Spirit fell upon all those who heard the word. And those of the circumcision who believed were astonished, as many as came with Peter, because the gift of the Holy Spirit had

*been poured out on the Gentiles also. For they heard them
speak with tongues and magnify God.*   (Acts 10:44–46)

Here we see the whole household of Cornelius, as soon as they
were filled with the Holy Spirit, magnifying God.

In Ephesians 5:19, we are told that the result of being filled
with the Spirit is that those who are thus filled will speak *"to
one another in psalms and hymns and spiritual songs, singing
and making melody in* [their hearts] *to the Lord."* Those who
are filled with the Holy Spirit will not be singing sentimental
ballads, not comic ditties, nor operatic airs while the power of
the Holy Spirit is upon them. If the Holy Spirit should come
upon anyone while listening to one of the most innocent of the
world's songs, he would not enjoy it and would long to hear
something about Christ. Men who are baptized with the Holy
Spirit do not talk much about self but much about God and especially much about Christ. This is necessarily so, as it is the
Holy Spirit's office to bear witness to the glorified Christ. (See
John 15:26; 16:14.)

To sum up everything that has been said about the results
of the baptism with the Holy Spirit: the baptism with the Holy
Spirit is the Spirit of God coming upon the believer, filling his
mind with a real apprehension of truth, especially of Christ,
taking possession of his faculties, and imparting to him gifts not
otherwise his but which qualify him for the service to which
God has called him.

Chapter 22

The Necessity of the Baptism

◆────────────

The New Testament has much to say about the necessity for the baptism with the Holy Spirit. When our Lord was about to leave His disciples to go to be with the Father, He said, *"Behold, I send the Promise of My Father upon you; but tarry in the city of Jerusalem until you are endued with power from on high"* (Luke 24:49). He had just commissioned them to be His witnesses to all nations, beginning at Jerusalem (see verses 47–48), but He tells them that before they undertake this witnessing, they must wait until they receive the Promise of the Father. They were thus endued with power from on high for the work of witnessing that they were to undertake. There is no doubt as to what Jesus meant by *"the Promise of My Father,"* for which they were to wait before beginning the ministry that He had laid on them, for in Acts we read:

> *And being assembled together with them, He commanded them not to depart from Jerusalem, but to wait for the Promise of the Father, "which," He said, "you have heard from Me; for John truly baptized with water, but you shall be baptized with the Holy Spirit not many days from now."*
> (Acts 1:4–5)

It is evident, then, that the Promise of the Father through which the endowment of power was to come was the baptism with the Holy Spirit. Jesus told His disciples in Acts 1:8:

> *You shall receive power when the Holy Spirit has come upon you; and you shall be witnesses to Me in Jerusalem, and in all Judea and Samaria, and to the end of the earth.*

Now who were the men to whom Jesus said this? The men were the disciples whom He Himself had trained for the work. For more than three years, they had lived in the closest intimacy with Him; they had been eyewitnesses of His miracles, of His death, of His resurrection, and in a few moments were to be eyewitnesses of His ascension as He was taken up into heaven right before their eyes. And what were they to do? Simply go and tell the world what their own eyes had seen and what their own ears had heard from the lips of the Son of God.

Were they not equipped for the work? With our modern ideas of preparation for Christian work, we would say that they were thoroughly equipped. But Jesus said, "No, you are not equipped. There is another preparation in addition to the preparation already received, so absolutely necessary for effective work that you must not make one step until you receive it. This other preparation is the Promise of the Father, the baptism with the Holy Spirit." If the apostles with their altogether exceptional fitting for the work that they were to undertake needed this preparation for work, how much more do we?

In the light of what Jesus required of His disciples before undertaking the work, does it not seem like the most daring presumption for any of us to undertake to witness and work for Christ until we also have received the Promise of the Father, the baptism with the Holy Spirit? There was apparently imperative need that something be done at once. The whole world was perishing, and they alone knew the saving truth. Nevertheless, Jesus strictly charged them to *"wait"* (Acts 1:4). Could there be a stronger testimony to the absolute necessity and importance of the baptism with the Holy Spirit as a preparation for work that will be acceptable to Christ?

But this is not all. In Acts 10:38, we read *"how God anointed Jesus of Nazareth with the Holy Spirit and with power, who went about doing good and healing all who were oppressed by the devil, for God was with Him."* To what does this refer in the recorded life of Jesus Christ? If we read Luke 3:21–22 and Luke 4:1, 14, 17–19, we will get our answer. In Luke 3:21–22, we read that after Jesus had been baptized and was praying, *"The heaven was opened. And the Holy Spirit descended in bodily form like a dove upon Him, and a voice came from heaven which said, 'You are My beloved Son; in You I am well pleased.'"*

Then the next thing that we read, with nothing intervening but the human genealogy of Jesus, is the following: *"Then Jesus, being filled with the Holy Spirit, returned from the Jordan and was led by the Spirit into the wilderness"* (Luke 4:1). Then follows the story of His temptation. Then we read: *"Then Jesus returned in the power of the Spirit to Galilee, and news of Him went out through all the surrounding region"* (v. 14). Further, we read:

> *And He was handed the book of the prophet Isaiah. And when He had opened the book, He found the place where it was written: "The Spirit of the LORD is upon Me, because He has anointed Me to preach the gospel to the poor; He has sent Me to heal the brokenhearted, to proclaim liberty to the captives and recovery of sight to the blind, to set at liberty those who are oppressed; to proclaim the acceptable year of the LORD."* (Luke 4:17–19)

Evidently then, it was at the Jordan, in connection with His baptism, that Jesus was anointed with the Holy Spirit and power, and He did not enter His public ministry until He was baptized with the Holy Spirit. And who was Jesus? It is the common belief of Christendom that He had been supernaturally conceived through the Holy Spirit's power, that He was the only begotten Son of God, that He was divine, very God of very God, and yet truly man. If such a One, *"leaving us an example, that* [we] *should follow His steps"* (1 Pet. 2:21), did not venture upon His ministry for which the Father had sent Him until He was definitely baptized with the Holy Spirit, how can we dare to do it? If in the light of these recorded facts we do it, does it not seem like the most unpardonable presumption? Doubtless it has been done in ignorance by many of us, but can we plead ignorance any longer?

It is evident that the baptism with the Holy Spirit is an absolutely necessary preparation for effective work for Christ in every line of service. We may have a very clear call to minister, as clear as the apostles had, but the charge is laid on us as on them, that before we begin that service, we must tarry until we are clothed with power from on high. This endowment of power is through the baptism with the Holy Spirit.

Even yet, this is not all. We read in Acts 8:14–16:

Now when the apostles who were at Jerusalem heard that Samaria had received the word of God, they sent Peter and John to them, who, when they had come down, prayed for them that they might receive the Holy Spirit. For as yet He had fallen upon none of them. They had only been baptized in the name of the Lord Jesus.

There was a great company of happy converts in Samaria, but when Peter and John came to inspect the work, they evidently felt that there was something so essential that these young disciples had not received that before they did anything else, they must see to it that they received it.

In a similar way, we read:

And it happened, while Apollos was at Corinth, that Paul, having passed through the upper regions, came to Ephesus. And finding some disciples he said to them, "Did you receive the Holy Spirit when you believed?"

(Acts 19:1–2)

When he found that they had not received the Holy Spirit, the first thing that he saw to was that they would receive the Holy Spirit. He did not go on with the work with the outsiders until that little group of twelve disciples had been equipped for service. So we see that when the apostles found believers in Christ, the first thing that they always did was to ask whether they had received the Holy Spirit as a definite experience, and if not, they saw to it at once that the steps were taken whereby they should receive the Holy Spirit.

It is evident then that the baptism with the Holy Spirit is absolutely necessary in every Christian for the service that Christ demands and expects of him. There are certainly few greater mistakes that we are making today in our various Christian enterprises than that of appointing men to teach Sunday school classes and do personal work and even to preach the Gospel because they have been converted and received a certain amount of education, including perhaps a college and seminary degree, but they have not as yet been baptized with the Holy Spirit. We think that if a man is pious and has had a college and seminary education and comes out of it reasonably orthodox, he is now ready for our hands to be laid upon him and to be ordained to preach the Gospel. But Jesus Christ said, "No." There is another preparation so essential that a man must not undertake this work until he has received it. *"Tarry* [literally "sit down"]...*until you are endued with power from on high"* (Luke 24:49).

A distinguished theological professor has said that the question, "Have you met God?" should be asked every candidate for the ministry. Yes, but we ought to go further than this and be even more definite. To every candidate for the ministry we should put the question, "Have you been baptized with the Holy Spirit?" If not, we should say to him as Jesus said to the first preachers of the Gospel, "Sit down until you are endued with power from on high."

Not only is this true of ordained ministers, but also it is true of every Christian, for all Christians are called to ministry of some kind. Anyone who is in Christian work who has not received the baptism with the Holy Spirit ought to stop his work right where he is and not go on with it until he has been *"endued with power from on high"* (v. 49).

What will our work do while we are waiting? The question can be answered by asking another, "What did the world do during these ten days while the early disciples were waiting?" They knew the saving truth; they alone knew it, yet in obedience to the Lord's command, they were silent. The world was no loser. Beyond a doubt, when the power came, they accomplished more in one day than they would have accomplished in years if they had gone on in self-confident defiance and disobedience to Christ's command.

We, too, after we have received the baptism with the Spirit, will accomplish more real work for our Lord in one day than we ever would in years without this power. Even if it were necessary to spend days in waiting, they would be well spent, but we will see later that there is no need that we spend days in waiting, that the baptism with the Holy Spirit may be received today.

Someone may say that the apostles had gone on missionary tours during Christ's lifetime, even before they were baptized with the Holy Spirit. This is true, but that was before the Holy Spirit was given and before the command was given, *"Tarry ...until you are endued with power from on high"* (Luke 24:49). After that, it would have been disobedience and folly and presumption to have gone forth without this endowment, and we are living today after the Holy Spirit has been given and after the charge has been given to tarry until we are empowered.

Who can be baptized with the Holy Spirit?

We come now to the question of extreme importance, namely, who can be baptized with the Holy Spirit? At a convention some years ago, a very intelligent Christian woman, a well-known worker in educational as well as Sunday school work, sent me this question, "You have told us of the necessity of the baptism with the Holy Spirit, but who can have this baptism? The church to which I belong teaches that the baptism with the Holy Spirit was confined to the apostolic age. Will you not tell us who can have the baptism with the Holy Spirit?" Fortunately, this question is answered in the most explicit terms in the Bible:

> *Then Peter said to them, "Repent, and let every one of you be baptized in the name of Jesus Christ for the remission of sins; and you shall receive the gift of the Holy Spirit. For the promise is to you and to your children, and to all who are afar off, as many as the Lord our God will call."*
> (Acts 2:38–39)

What is the promise to which Peter refers in the thirty-ninth verse? There are two interpretations of the passage: one is that the promise of this verse is the promise of salvation; the other is that the promise of this verse is the promise of the gift of the Holy Spirit (or the baptism with the Holy Spirit—a comparison of Scripture passages will show that the two expressions are synonymous).

Which is the correct interpretation? There are two laws of interpretation universally recognized among Bible scholars.

These two laws are the law of usage and the law of context. Many a verse in the Bible standing alone might have two or three or even more possible interpretations, but when these two laws of interpretation are applied, it is settled to a certainty that only one of the various possible interpretations is the true interpretation.

The law of usage is this: when you find a word or phrase in any passage of Scripture and you wish to know what it means, do not go to a dictionary, but go to the Bible itself. Look up the various passages in which the word is used, especially how the particular writer being studied uses it and how it is used in that particular book in which the passage is found. Thus, you can determine what the precise meaning of the word or phrase is in the passage in question.

The law of context is this: when you study a passage, you should not take it out of its context but should look at what goes before it and what comes after it. While it might mean various things if it stood alone, it can only mean one thing in the context in which it is found.

Now let us apply these two laws to the passage in question. First of all, let us apply the law of usage. We are trying to discover what the expression *"the promise"* means in Acts 2:39. Turning back to Acts 1:4–5, we read:

> *He commanded them not to depart from Jerusalem, but to wait for the Promise of the Father, "which," He said, "you have heard from Me; for John truly baptized with water, but you shall be baptized with the Holy Spirit not many days from now."*

It is evident, then, that here the promise of the Father means the baptism with the Holy Spirit.

Turn now to Acts 2:33: *"Therefore being exalted to the right hand of God, and having received from the Father the promise of the Holy Spirit, He poured out this which you now see and hear."* We are told in so many words that the promise is the promise of the Holy Spirit. If this distinctive expression means the baptism with the Holy Spirit in Acts 1:4–5, and the same thing in Acts 2:33, by what same law of interpretation can it possibly mean something entirely different six verses further down in Acts 2:39? So the law of usage establishes it that the promise of Acts 2:39 is the promise of the baptism with the Holy Spirit.

Now let us apply the law of context, and we will find that, if possible, this is even more decisive. Read the following verses:

> *Then Peter said to them, "Repent, and let every one of you be baptized in the name of Jesus Christ for the remission of sins; and you shall receive the gift of the Holy Spirit. For the promise is to you and to your children, and to all who are afar off, as many as the Lord our God will call."*
>
> (Acts 2:38–39)

It is evident here that the promise is the promise of the gift of the baptism with the Holy Spirit. It is settled then by both laws that the promise of Acts 2:39 is that of the gift of the Holy Spirit or baptism with the Holy Spirit. Let us then read the verse in that way, substituting this synonymous expression for the expression *"the promise."* "For the baptism with the Spirit is to you and to your children, and to all who are afar off, as many as the Lord our God will call."

"The promise is to you," said Peter, that is, to the crowd assembled before him. There is nothing in that for us. We were not there. That crowd was all Jews, and we are not Jews. But Peter did not stop there. He went further and said, *"and to your children,"* that is, to the next generation of Jews or all future generations of Jews. Still there is nothing in it for us, for we are not Jews. But Peter did not stop even there. He went further and said, *"and to all who are afar off."* That does take us in. We are the Gentiles who were once *"afar off"* but now *"have been brought near by the blood of Christ"* (Eph. 2:13). Lest there be any mistake about it, Peter added *"as many as the Lord our God will call"* (Acts 2:39). So, on the very Day of Pentecost, Peter declared that the baptism with the Holy Spirit is for every child of God in every coming age of the church's history.

Some years ago at a ministerial conference in Chicago, a minister of the Gospel from the Southwest came to me after a lecture on the baptism with the Holy Spirit and said, "The church to which I belong teaches that the baptism with the Holy Spirit was for the apostolic age alone."

"I do not care," I replied, "what the church to which you belong teaches or what the church to which I belong teaches. The only question with me is, what does the Word of God teach?"

"That is right," he said.

Then I handed him my Bible and asked him to read Acts 2:39, and he read: *"'For the promise is to you and to your children, and to all who are afar off, as many as the Lord our God will call.'"*

"Has He called you?" I asked.

"Yes, He certainly has."

"Is the promise for you then?"

"Yes, it is." He took it, and the result was a transformed ministry.

Some years ago at a students' conference, the gatherings were presided over by a prominent Episcopalian minister, a man greatly honored and loved. I spoke at this conference on the baptism with the Holy Spirit and dwelt on the significance of Acts 2:39. That night as we sat together after the meetings were over, this servant of God said to me, "Mr. Torrey, I was greatly interested in what you had to say today on the baptism with the Holy Spirit. If your interpretation of Acts 2:39 is correct, you have your case, but I doubt your interpretation of Acts 2:39. Let us talk it over."

We did talk it over. Several years later, in July 1894, I was at the students' conference at Northfield. As I entered the back door of Stone Hall that day, an Episcopalian minister entered the front door. Seeing me, he hurried across the hall and held out his hand and said, "You were right about Acts 2:39 at Knoxville, and I believe I have a right to tell you something better yet—that I have been baptized with the Holy Spirit."

I am glad that I was right about Acts 2:39, not that it is of any importance that I should be right, but the truth thus established is of immeasurable importance. It is glorious to be able to go literally around the world and face audiences of believers all over the United States, in the Hawaiian Islands, in Australia, Tasmania, and New Zealand, in China, Japan, and India, in England, Scotland, Ireland, Germany, France, and Switzerland and to be able to tell them (and to know that I have God's sure

Word under my feet when I say), "You may all be baptized with the Holy Spirit."

But that unspeakably joyous and glorious thought has its solemn side. If we are able to be baptized with the Holy Spirit, then we must be. If we are baptized with the Holy Spirit, then souls will be saved through our instrumentality who will not be saved if we are not baptized. If we are not willing to pay the price of this baptism and therefore are not baptized, we will be responsible before God for every soul who might have been saved but was not saved because we did not pay the price and therefore did not obtain the blessing.

I often tremble for myself and for my peers in the ministry, and not only for my peers in the ministry, but for my peers in all forms of Christian work, even the most humble and obscure. Why? Because we are preaching error? No, alas, there are many in these dark days who are doing that, and I do tremble for them, but that is not what I mean now. Do I mean that I tremble because we are not preaching the truth? It is quite possible not to preach error and yet not preach the truth; many a man has never preached a word of error in his life but still is not preaching the truth. I do tremble for them, but that is not what I mean now. I mean that I tremble for those of us who are preaching the truth, the very truth as it is in Jesus, the truth as it is recorded in the written Word of God, the truth in its simplicity, its purity, and its fullness, but who are preaching it in *"persuasive words of human wisdom"* (1 Cor. 2:4) and not *"in demonstration of the Spirit and of power"* (v. 4), preaching it in the energy of the flesh and not in the power of the Holy Spirit. There is nothing more death-dealing than the Gospel without the Spirit's power. *"The letter kills, but the Spirit gives life"* (2 Cor. 3:6). It is awfully solemn business preaching the Gospel either from the pulpit or in more quiet ways. It means death or life to those who hear, and whether it means death or life depends very largely on whether we preach it with or without the baptism of the Holy Spirit.

We need repeated refillings with the Holy Spirit.

Even after one has been baptized with the Holy Spirit, no matter how definite that baptism may be, he needs to be filled again and again with the Spirit. This is the clear teaching of the New Testament. We read in Acts 2:4: *"They were all filled with the Holy Spirit and began to speak with other tongues, as the Spirit gave them utterance."* Now, one of those who was present on this occasion and who therefore was filled at this time with the Holy Spirit was Peter. Indeed, he stands forth most prominently in the chapter as a man baptized with the Holy Spirit. We read in Acts 4:8: *"Then Peter, filled with the Holy Spirit, said to them...."* Here we read again that Peter was filled with the Holy Spirit. Further down we read that being assembled together and praying, *"they were all filled with the Holy Spirit, and they spoke the word of God with boldness"* (Acts 4:31). We are expressly told in the context that two of those present were John and Peter. Here, then, was a third instance in which Peter was filled with the Holy Spirit.

It is not enough that one be filled with the Holy Spirit once. We need a new filling for each new emergency of Christian service. The failure to realize this need of constant refillings with the Holy Spirit has led to many a man, who at one time was greatly used of God, being utterly laid aside. Many today once knew what it was to work in the power of the Holy Spirit, but they have lost their anointing and their power. I do not say that the Holy Spirit has left them—I do not believe He has—but the manifestation of His presence and power has gone.

One of the saddest sights among us today is that of the men and women who once toiled for the Master in the mighty power of the Holy Spirit who are now practically of no use, or even a hindrance to the work, because they are trying to go in the power of the blessing received a year or five years or twenty years ago. For each new service that is to be conducted, for each new soul that is to be dealt with, for each new work for Christ that is to be performed, for each new day and each new emergency of Christian life and service, we should seek and obtain a new filling with the Holy Spirit. We must not *"neglect"* the gift that is in us (1 Tim. 4:14), but on the contrary *"stir up the gift of God"* (2 Tim. 1:6). Repeated fillings with the Holy Spirit are necessary to continued, increased power.

The question may arise: Should we call these new fillings with the Holy Spirit "fresh baptisms" with the Holy Spirit? To this we would answer that the expression "baptism" is never used in the Scriptures of a second experience, and there is something of an initial character in the very thought of baptism. So, if one wishes to be precisely biblical, it would seem to be better not to use the term "baptism" of a second experience, but to limit it to the first experience.

On the other hand, *"filled with the Holy Spirit"* is used in Acts 2:4 to describe the experience promised in Acts 1:5, where the words used are *"you shall be baptized with the Holy Spirit."* And it is evident from this and from other passages that the two expressions are to a large extent practically synonymous. However, if we confine the expression "baptism with the Holy Spirit" to our first experience, we will be more exactly biblical, and it would be well to speak of one baptism but many fillings.

However, I would much prefer that one should speak about new or fresh baptisms with the Holy Spirit, standing for the all-important truth that we need repeated fillings with the Holy Spirit, than that he should so insist on exact phraseology that he would lose sight of the truth that repeated fillings are needed. In other words, I would rather have the right experience by a wrong name than the wrong experience by the right name. This much is clear: we need to be filled again and again and again with the Holy Spirit. I am sometimes asked, "Have you received the second blessing?" Yes, and the third, and the fourth, and the fifth, and hundreds besides, and I am looking for a new blessing today.

Chapter 23

Obtaining the Baptism

◆

We come now to a question of practical importance, namely, what must a person do in order to be baptized with the Holy Spirit? This question is answered in the clearest and most positive way in the Bible. A definite path is laid down in the Bible consisting of a few simple steps that anyone can take, and it is absolutely certain that anyone who takes these steps will enter into the blessing. This is, of course, a very positive statement, and we would not dare be so confident if the Bible were not equally positive. But what right have we to be uncertain when the Word of God is unmistakable? There are seven steps in this path.

Accept Jesus Christ as Lord and Savior

The first step is that we accept Jesus Christ as our Savior and Lord. We read in Acts 2:38: *"Repent, and let every one of you be baptized in the name of Jesus Christ for the remission of sins; and you shall receive the gift of the Holy Spirit."* Is not this statement as positive as what we made above? Peter said that if we do certain things, the result will be, *"You shall receive the gift of the Holy Spirit."* All seven steps are in this passage, but we will refer later to other passages as throwing light on this.

The first two steps are in the word *repent*. "Repent," said Peter. What does it mean to repent? The Greek word for repentance means "an afterthought" or "change of mind." To repent, then, means to change your mind. But change your mind about what? About three things: about God, about Jesus Christ, and about sin. What the change of mind is about in any given instance must be determined by the context. In the present case, the change of mind is primarily about Jesus Christ. Peter had just said:

> *"Let all the house of Israel know assuredly that God has made this Jesus, whom you crucified, both Lord and Christ." Now when they heard this, they were cut to the heart, and said to Peter and the rest of the apostles, "Men and brethren, what shall we do?"* (Acts 2:36–37)

Then it was that Peter said, *"Repent"* (v. 38). "Change your mind about Jesus; change your mind from that attitude of mind that rejected Him and crucified Him to that attitude of mind that accepts Him as Lord and King and Savior." This then is the first step toward receiving the baptism with the Holy Spirit. Receive Jesus as Savior and Lord; first of all receive Him as your Savior. Have you done that?

What does it mean to receive Jesus as Savior? It means to accept Him as the One who bore our sins in our place on the cross (see 2 Corinthians 5:21; Galatians 3:13) and to trust God to forgive us because Jesus Christ died in our place. It means to rest all our hope of acceptance before God on the finished work of Christ on the cross of Calvary. Many who profess to be Christians have not done this.

When you go to some who call themselves Christians and ask them if they are saved, they reply, "Yes." Then, if you put to them the question: "On what are you resting as the ground of your salvation?" they will reply something like this: "I go to church, I say my prayers, I read my Bible, I have been baptized, I have united with the church, I partake of the Lord's Supper, I attend prayer meetings, and I am trying to live as near right as I know how." If these things are what you are resting on as the ground of your acceptance before God, then you are not saved, for all these things are your own works (all proper in their places but still your own works), and we are distinctly told in Romans 3:20 that *"by the deeds of the law no flesh will be justified in His sight."*

However, if you go to others and ask them if they are saved, they will reply, "Yes." Then, if you ask them on what they are resting as the ground of their acceptance before God, they will reply something to this effect: "I am not resting on anything I ever did, or on anything I am ever going to do; I am resting on what Jesus Christ did for me when He bore my sins in His own body on the cross. I am resting in His finished work of the Atonement." If this is what you are really resting on, then you are saved; you have accepted Jesus Christ as your Savior and have taken the first step toward the baptism with the Holy Spirit.

The same thought is taught elsewhere in the Bible, for example in Galatians 3:2. Here Paul asked the believers in Galatia, *"Did you receive the Spirit by the works of the law, or by the hearing of faith?"* Just what did he mean? On one occasion when Paul was passing through Galatia, he was detained there by some physical infirmity. We are not told what it was, but he was not so ill that he could not preach the Gospel to the Galatians, that Jesus Christ had redeemed them from the curse of the law by becoming a curse in their place by dying on the cross of Calvary (Gal. 3:13). These Galatians believed this testimony. This was the hearing of faith, and God set the stamp of His endorsement on their faith by giving them the Holy Spirit.

But after Paul had left Galatia, certain Judaizers came down from Jerusalem, men who were substituting the law of Moses for the Gospel, and taught them that it was not enough that they simply believe in Jesus Christ. In addition to this, the Judaizers taught that they must keep the law of Moses, especially the law of Moses regarding circumcision, and that without circumcision they could not be saved. In other words, they could not be saved by simple faith in Jesus. (See also Acts 15:1.) These young converts in Galatia became all upset. They did not know whether they were saved or not. They did not know what they should do, and all was confusion. It was just as when modern Judaizers come around and get after young converts and tell them that in addition to believing in Jesus Christ, they must keep the Mosaic seventh day Sabbath or they cannot be saved. This is simply the old controversy breaking out at a new point.

When Paul heard what had happened in Galatia, he was very indignant and wrote the epistle to the Galatians simply for the purpose of exposing the utter error of these Judaizers. He showed them how Abraham himself was justified before he was circumcised by simply believing God (see Galatians 3:6) and how he was circumcised after he was justified as a seal of the faith that he already had while he was uncircumcised. In addition to this proof of the error of the Judaizers, Paul appealed to their own personal experience. He asked them if they had received the Holy Spirit, and they replied that they had. He then asked them how they had received the Holy Spirit: by keeping the law of Moses or by the hearing of faith, the simple accepting of God's testimony about Jesus Christ that their sins were laid on Him, and that they are thus justified and saved. The Galatians had had a very definite experience of receiving the Holy Spirit, and Paul appealed to it and recalled to their minds how it was by the simple hearing of faith that they had received the Holy Spirit.

The gift of the Holy Spirit is God's seal on the simple acceptance of God's testimony about Jesus Christ, that our sins were laid on Him, while trusting God to forgive us and justify us. This, then, is the first step toward receiving the Holy Spirit. But we must not only receive Jesus as Savior, but also receive Him as Lord. Of this we will speak further in connection with another passage in the fourth step.

Renounce Sin

The second step in the path that leads into the blessing of being baptized with the Holy Spirit is renunciation of sin. Repentance, as we have seen, is a change of mind about sin as well as a change of mind about Christ: a change of mind from that attitude that loves sin and indulges sin to that attitude that hates sin and renounces sin. This, then, is the second step—renunciation of sin. The Holy Spirit is a *Holy* Spirit, and we cannot have both Him and sin. We must make our choice between the Holy Spirit and unholy sin. We cannot have both. He who will not give up sin cannot have the Holy Spirit. It is not enough that we renounce one sin or two sins or three sins or many sins; we must renounce all sin. If we cling to one single known sin, it will prevent us from receiving the blessing.

Here we find the cause of failure in many people who are praying for the baptism with the Holy Spirit, going to conventions and hearing about the baptism with the Holy Spirit, reading books about the baptism with the Holy Spirit, perhaps spending whole nights in prayer for the baptism with the Holy Spirit, and yet obtaining nothing. Why? Because there is some sin to which they are clinging. People often say to me or write to me, "I have been praying for the baptism with the Holy Spirit for a year (five years, ten years, one man said twenty years). Why do I not receive?" In many such cases, I feel led to reply, "It is sin, and if I could look down into your heart this moment as God looks into your heart, I could put my finger on the specific sin." It may be what you are pleased to call a small sin, but there are no small sins. There are sins that concern small things, but every sin is an act of rebellion against God; therefore, no sin is a small sin. A controversy with God about the smallest thing is sufficient to shut one out of the blessing.

Mr. Finney tells of a woman who was greatly in earnest about the baptism with the Holy Spirit. Every night after the meetings, she would go to her room and pray late into the night. Her friends were afraid she would go insane, but no blessing came. One night as she prayed, some little matter of head adornment, a matter that would probably not trouble many Christians today, but a matter of controversy between her and God, came up (as it had often come up before) as she knelt in prayer. She put her hand to her head and took the pins out of her hair and threw them across the room and said, "There go!" Instantly the Holy Spirit fell on her. It was not so much the matter of head adornment as the matter of controversy with God that had kept her out of the blessing.

If there is anything that always comes up when you get nearest to God, that is the thing to deal with. Some years ago at a convention in a Southern state, the presiding officer, a minister in the Baptist church, called my attention to a man and said, "That man is 'the pope' of our denomination in ——; everything he says goes, but he is not at all with us in this matter, but I am glad to see him here." This minister kept attending the meetings. At the close of the last meeting where I had spoken on the conditions of receiving the baptism with the Holy Spirit, I found this man waiting for me in the vestibule.

He said, "I did not stand up on your invitation today."

I replied, "I saw you did not."

"I thought you said," he continued, "that you only wanted those to stand who could say they had absolutely surrendered to God?"

"That is what I did say," I replied.

"Well, I could not say that."

"Then you did perfectly right not to stand. I did not want you to lie to God."

"Say," he continued, "you hit me pretty hard today. You said if there was anything that always comes up when you get nearest to God, that is the thing to deal with. Now, there is something that always comes up when I get nearest to God. I am not going to tell you what it is. I think you know."

"Yes," I replied. (I could smell it.)

"Well, I simply wanted to say this to you."

This was on Friday afternoon. I had occasion to go to another city, and returning through that city the following Tuesday morning, the minister who had presided at the meeting was at the station. "I wish you could have been in our Baptist ministers' meeting yesterday morning," he said. "That man I pointed out to you from the Northern part of the state was present. He got up in our meeting and said, 'Fellow Christians, we have been all wrong about this matter,' and then he told what he had done. He had settled his controversy with God, had given up the thing that had always come up when he got close to God. Then he continued and said, 'Fellow Christians, I have received a more definite experience than I had when I was converted.'"

Just such an experience is awaiting many others, both minister and layman, just as soon as he will judge his sin, just as soon as he will put away the thing that is a matter of controversy between him and God, no matter how small the thing may seem. If anyone sincerely desires the baptism with the Holy Spirit, he should go alone with God and ask God to search him and bring to light anything in his heart or life that is displeasing to Him. When He brings it to light, he should put it away. If after sincerely waiting on God, nothing is brought to light, then we may proceed to take the other steps. But there is no use praying, no use going to conventions, no use in reading books about the baptism with the Holy Spirit, no use in doing anything else, until we judge our sins.

Openly Confess Your Renunciation of Sin and Your Acceptance of Jesus Christ

The third step is an open confession of our renunciation of sin and our acceptance of Jesus Christ. After telling his hearers to repent in Acts 2:38, Peter continued and told them to be *"baptized in the name of Jesus Christ for the remission of sins."* Heart repentance alone was not enough. There must be an open confession of that repentance, and God's appointed way of confession of repentance is baptism. None of those to whom Peter was speaking had ever been baptized, and, of course, what Peter meant in that case was water baptism. But suppose one has already been baptized, what then? Even in that case, there must be that for which baptism stands, namely, an open confession of our renunciation of sin and our acceptance of Jesus Christ. The baptism with the Spirit is not for the secret disciple but for the openly confessed disciple.

Undoubtedly, many today are trying to be Christians in their hearts. Many really believe that they have accepted Jesus as their Savior and their Lord and have renounced sin, but they are not willing to make an open confession of their renunciation of sin and their acceptance of Christ. Such people cannot have the baptism with the Holy Spirit. Someone may ask, "Do not the Friends (Quakers), who do not believe in water baptism, give evidence of being baptized with the Holy Spirit?" Undoubtedly, many of them do, but this does not alter the teaching of God's Word. God doubtless condescends in many instances where people are misled as to the teaching of His Word by their ignorance, if they are sincere, but that fact does not alter His Word. Even with a member of the congregation of Friends, who sincerely does not believe in water baptism, there must be that for which baptism stands before the blessing is received, namely, the open confession of acceptance of Christ and of renunciation of sin.

Surrender Absolutely to God

The fourth step is absolute surrender to God. This comes out in what has already been said, namely, that we must accept Jesus as Lord as well as Savior. It is stated explicitly in Acts 5:32: *"And we are His witnesses to these things, and so also is the Holy Spirit whom God has given to those who obey Him."* That is the fourth step: *"obey Him,"* obedience.

But what does obedience mean? Some will say, doing as we are told. Right, but doing how much that we are told? Not merely one thing, two things, three things, or four things, but obedience is doing all things. The heart of obedience is in the will; the essence of obedience is the surrender of the will to God. It is going to God our heavenly Father and saying, "Heavenly Father, here I am. I am Your property. You have bought me with a price. I acknowledge Your ownership and surrender myself and all that I am absolutely to You. Send me where You will; do with me what You will; use me as You will." This is in most instances the decisive step in receiving the baptism with the Holy Spirit.

In the Old Testament typology, it was when the whole burnt offering was laid on the altar, nothing kept back within or without the sacrificial animal, that the fire came forth from the Holy Place where God dwelt and accepted and consumed the gift on the altar. So it is today. In the fulfillment of the type, when we lay ourselves, a whole burnt offering, on the altar, keeping nothing back, that the fire of God, the Holy Spirit, descends from the real Holy Place, heaven (of which the Most Holy Place in the tabernacle was simply a type), and accepts the gift on the altar. When we can truly say, "My all is on the altar," then we will not have long to wait for the fire. The lack of this absolute surrender is shutting many out of the blessing today. People turn the keys of almost every closet in their heart over to God, but there is some small closet of which they wish to keep the key themselves. Then the blessing does not come.

At a convention in Washington, D.C., on the last night, I had spoken on how to receive the baptism with the Holy Spirit. The Spirit Himself was present in mighty power that night. The chaplain of one of the houses of Congress had said to me at the close of the meeting, "It almost seemed as if I could see the Holy Spirit in this place tonight."

There were many to be dealt with. About two hours after the meeting closed (about eleven o'clock), a worker came to me and said, "Do you see that young woman over to the right with whom Miss W—— is speaking?"

"Yes."

"Well, she has been dealing with her for two hours, and she is in awful agony. Won't you come and see if you can help?"

I went into the seat behind this woman in distress and asked what was troubling her.

"Oh," she said, "I came from Baltimore to receive the baptism with the Holy Spirit, and I cannot go back to Baltimore until I have received Him."

"Is your will laid down?" I asked.

"I am afraid not."

"Will you lay it down now?"

"I cannot."

"Are you willing that God should lay it down for you?"

"Yes."

"Ask Him to do it."

She bowed her head in prayer and asked God to empty her of her will, to lay it down for her, to bring it into conformity to His will, in absolute surrender to His own. When the prayer was finished, I said, "Is it laid down?"

She said, "It must be. I have asked something according to His will. Yes, it is done."

I said, "Ask Him for the baptism with the Holy Spirit."

She bowed her head again in brief prayer and asked God to baptize her with the Holy Spirit and in a few moments looked up with peace in her heart and in her face. Why? Because she had surrendered her will. She had met the conditions, and God had given the blessing.

Intensely Desire the Baptism with the Holy Spirit

The fifth step is an intense desire for the baptism with the Holy Spirit. Jesus said in John 7:37–39:

"If anyone thirsts, let him come to Me and drink. He who believes in Me, as the Scripture has said, out of his heart will flow rivers of living water." But this He spoke concerning the Spirit, whom those believing in Him would receive; for the Holy Spirit was not yet given, because Jesus was not yet glorified.

Here again we have belief in Jesus as the condition of receiving the Holy Spirit, but we also have this: *"If anyone thirsts."* Doubtless, when Jesus spoke these words, He had in mind the Old Testament promise in Isaiah 44:3: *"For I will pour water on him who is thirsty, and floods on the dry ground; I will pour My Spirit on your descendants, and My blessing on your offspring."* In both of these passages, thirst is the condition of receiving the Holy Spirit. What does it mean to thirst? When a person really thirsts, it seems as if every pore in his body has just one cry: "Water! Water! Water!" Apply this to the matter in question; when a man thirsts spiritually, his whole being has but one cry: "The Holy Spirit! The Holy Spirit!

As long as one thinks he can get along somehow without the baptism with the Holy Spirit, he is not going to receive that baptism. As long as one is casting about for some new kind of church, machinery, new style of preaching, or anything else by which he hopes to accomplish what the Holy Spirit only can accomplish, he will not receive the baptism with the Holy Spirit. As long as one tries to find some subtle system of interpretation to read out of the New Testament what God has put into it—namely, the absolute necessity that each believer receives the baptism with the Holy Spirit as a definite experience—he is not going to receive the baptism with the Holy Spirit. As long as a man tries to persuade himself that he has received the baptism with the Holy Spirit when he really has not, he is not going to receive the baptism with the Holy Spirit. But when one gets to the place where he sees the absolute necessity that he needs to be baptized with the Holy Spirit as a definite experience and desires this blessing at any cost, he is far on the way toward receiving it.

At a state YMCA Convention, where I had spoken on the baptism with the Holy Spirit, two ministers went out of the meeting side by side. One said to the other, "That kind of teaching leads either to fanaticism or despair." He did not attempt to show that it was unscriptural. He felt condemned and was not willing to admit his deficiency and seek to have it supplied. He tried to avoid the condemnation that came from the Word by this sarcastic remark: "That kind of teaching leads either to fanaticism or despair." Such a man will not receive the baptism with the Holy Spirit until he is brought to himself and acknowledges honestly his need and intensely desires to have it supplied.

How different was another minister of the same denomination who came to me one Sunday morning at Northfield. I was to speak that morning on how to receive the baptism with the Holy Spirit. He said, "I have come to Northfield from ——— for just one purpose, to receive the baptism with the Holy Spirit, and I would rather die than go back to my church without receiving it."

I said, "My brother, you are going to receive it."

The following morning he came very early to my house. He said, "I have to go away on the early train, but I came around to tell you before I went that I have received the baptism with the Holy Spirit."

Pray Specifically for the Baptism with the Holy Spirit

The sixth step is definite prayer for the baptism with the Holy Spirit. Jesus said in Luke 11:13, *"If you then, being evil, know how to give good gifts to your children, how much more will your heavenly Father give the Holy Spirit to those who ask Him!"* This is very explicit. Jesus teaches us that the Holy Spirit is given in answer to definite prayer—just ask Him. There are many who tell us that we should not pray for the Holy Spirit, and they reason it out very inaccurately. They say that the Holy Spirit was given as an abiding gift to the church at Pentecost, and why pray for what is already given? To this the late Rev. Dr. A. J. Gordon well replied that Jesus Christ was given as an abiding gift to the world at Calvary (see John 3:16), but what was given to the world as a whole, each individual in the world must appropriate for himself. Just so, the Holy Spirit was given to the church as an abiding gift at Pentecost, but what was given to the church as a whole, each individual in the church must appropriate for himself. God's way of appropriation is prayer.

Those who say we should not pray for the Holy Spirit go further still than this. They tell us that every believer already has the Holy Spirit (which we have already seen is true in a sense), and why pray for what we already have? To this, the very simple answer is that it is one thing to have the Holy Spirit dwelling way back of consciousness in some hidden sanctuary of the being and something quite different, and vastly more, to have Him take possession of the whole house that He inhabits. But against all these inaccurate arguments we place the simple words of Jesus Christ: *"How much more will your heavenly Father give the Holy Spirit to those who ask Him!"* (Luke 11:13).

It will not do to say, as has been said, that this promise was for the time of the earthly life of our Lord, and to go back to the promise of Luke 11:13 is to forget Pentecost and to ignore the truth that now every believer has the indwelling Spirit. We find that after Pentecost as well as before, the Holy Spirit was given to believers in answer to definite prayer. For example, we read in Acts 4:31: *"When they had prayed, the place where they were assembled together was shaken; and they were all filled with the Holy Spirit, and they spoke the word of God with boldness."*

Again in Acts 8:15–16, we read that when Peter and John had come down and had seen the believers in Samaria, they *"prayed for them that they might receive the Holy Spirit. For as yet He had fallen upon none of them. They had only been baptized in the name of the Lord Jesus."* Again, in the epistle of Paul to the Ephesians, Paul told the believers in Ephesus that he was praying for them that they might be strengthened with power through His Spirit. (See Ephesians 3:16.) So right through the New Testament after Pentecost, as well as before, by specific teaching and illustrative example, we are taught that the Holy Spirit is given in answer to definite prayer.

At a Christian workers' convention in Boston, a believer came to me and said, "I notice that you are on the program to speak on the baptism with the Holy Spirit."

"Yes."

"I think that is the most important subject on the program. Now be sure and tell them not to pray for the Holy Spirit."

I replied, "My friend, I will be sure and not tell them that, for Jesus said, 'How much more will your heavenly Father give the Holy Spirit to those who ask Him!'" (Luke 11:13).

"Yes, but that was before Pentecost."

"How about Acts 4:31; was that before Pentecost or after?"

He said, "It was certainly after."

"Well," I said, "take it and read it."

"*'And when they had prayed, the place where they were assembled together was shaken; and they were all filled with the Holy Spirit, and they spoke the word of God with boldness.'*"

"How about Acts 8:15–16, was that before Pentecost or after?"

"Certainly, it was after."

"Take it and read it."

"*'Who, when they had come down, prayed for them that they might receive the Holy Spirit. For as yet He had fallen upon none of them. They had only been baptized in the name of the Lord Jesus.'*"

He had nothing more to say. What was there to say? But with me, it is not a matter of mere interpretation that the Holy Spirit is given in answer to definite prayer. It is a matter of personal and certain experience. I know just as well that God gives the Holy Spirit in answer to prayer as I know that water quenches thirst and food satisfies hunger. My first experience of being baptized with the Holy Spirit was while I waited on God in prayer. Since then, time and again as I have waited on God in prayer, I have been definitely filled with the Holy Spirit. Often as I have knelt in prayer with others, as we prayed, the Holy Spirit has fallen on us just as perceptibly as the rain ever fell on the earth.

I will never forget one experience in our church in Chicago. We were holding a noon prayer meeting of the ministers at the YMCA auditorium, in preparation of an expected visit to Chicago by Mr. Moody. At one of these meetings, a minister sprang to his feet and said, "What we need in Chicago is an all-night meeting of the ministers."

"Very well," I said. "If you will come up to Chicago Avenue Church Friday night at ten o'clock, we will have a prayer meeting, and if God keeps us all night, we will stay all night."

At ten o'clock on Friday night, four or five hundred people gathered in the lecture rooms of the Chicago Avenue Church. They were not all ministers. They were not all men. Satan made a mighty attempt to ruin the meeting. First of all, three men got down by the door and knelt down by chairs and pounded and shouted until some of our heads seemed almost to be splitting.

Some felt they must retire from the meeting, and when a brother went to urge them that things be done decently and in order, they swore at the brother who made the protest. Still later, a man sprang up in the middle of the room and announced that he was Elijah. The poor man was insane. These things were distracting, and there was more or less of confusion until nearly midnight. Some thought they would go home. But it is a poor meeting that the Devil can spoil, and some of us were there for a blessing and were determined to remain until we received it. About midnight, God gave us complete victory over all the discordant elements. Then for two hours there was such praying as I have rarely heard in my life.

A little after two o'clock in the morning a sudden hush fell on the whole gathering; we were all on our knees at the time. No one could speak; no one could pray; no one could sing; all you could hear was the subdued sobbing of joy, unspeakable and full of glory. The very air seemed trembling with the presence of the Spirit of God. It was now Saturday morning. The following morning, one of my deacons came to me and said, with bated breath, "I will never forget yesterday morning until the last day of my life." But it was not by any means all emotion. There was solid reality that could be tested by practical tests.

A man went out of that meeting in the early morning hours and took a train for Missouri. When he had transacted his business in the town that he visited, he asked the proprietor of the hotel if there was any meeting going on in the town at the time. The proprietor said, "Yes, there is a protracted meeting going on at the Cumberland Presbyterian Church." The man was himself a Cumberland Presbyterian. He went to the church, and when the meeting was opened, he arose in his place and asked the minister if he could speak. Permission was granted, and with the power of the Holy Spirit on him, he so spoke that fifty-eight or fifty-nine people professed to accept Christ on the spot.

A young man went out of the meeting in the early morning hours and took a train for a city in Wisconsin, and I soon received word from that city that thirty-eight young men and boys had been converted while he spoke. Another young man, one of our students in the Institute, went to another part of Wisconsin, and soon I began to receive letters from ministers in that neighborhood inquiring about him and telling how he had gone into the schoolhouses and churches and soldiers' home and how there were conversions wherever he spoke.

In the days that followed, men and women from that meeting went out over the earth, and I doubt if there was any country that I visited in my tour around the world, Japan, China, Australia, New Zealand, India, etc., in which I did not find someone who had gone out from that meeting with the power of God on them. For me to doubt that God fills men with the Holy Spirit in answer to prayer would be thoroughly unscientific and irrational. I know He does. And in a matter like this, I would rather have one ounce of believing experience than ten tons of unbelieving interpretation.

Have Faith

The seventh and last step is faith. We read in Mark 11:24: *"Therefore I say to you, whatever things you ask when you pray, believe that you receive them, and you will have them."* No matter how definite God's promises are, we only realize these promises experientially when we believe. For example, we read in James 1:5: *"If any of you lacks wisdom, let him ask of God, who gives to all liberally and without reproach, and it will be given to him."* Now that promise is as positive as a promise can be, but we read in the following verses:

> *But let him ask in faith, with no doubting, for he who doubts is like a wave of the sea driven and tossed by the wind. For let not that man suppose that he will receive anything from the Lord; he is a double-minded man, unstable in all his ways.* (James 1:6–8)

The baptism with the Spirit, as we have already seen, is for those believers in Christ who have put away all sin and surrendered absolutely to God and who ask for it. But even though we ask, there will be no receiving if we do not believe. Many have met the other conditions of receiving the baptism with the Holy Spirit and yet do not receive simply because they do not believe. They do not expect to receive, and they do not receive.

But there is a faith that goes beyond expectation, a faith that puts out its hand and takes what it asks on the spot. This comes out in Mark 11:24: *"Therefore I say to you, whatever things you ask when you pray, believe that you receive them, and you will have them."* When we pray for the baptism with the Holy Spirit, we should believe that we have received (that is, that God has granted our prayer, and therefore it is ours), and then we will have the actual experience of what we have asked.

Another verse that clarifies this passage in Mark is 1 John 5:14–15, which reads:

Now this is the confidence that we have in Him, that if we ask anything according to His will, He hears us. And if we know that He hears us, whatever we ask, we know that we have the petitions that we have asked of Him.

Do you see it? If not, let me explain it a little further. When we come to God in prayer, the first question to ask is, Is what I have asked of God according to His will? If it is promised in His Word, of course, we know it is according to His will. Then we can say with 1 John 5:14: I have asked something according to His will, and I know He hears me. Then we can go further and say with the fifteenth verse: Because I know He hears what I ask, I know I have the petition that I asked of Him. I may not have it in actual possession, but I know it is mine because I have asked something according to His will and He has heard me and granted what I have asked. What I thus believe that I have received because the Word of God says so, I will afterwards have in actual experience.

Now apply this to the matter before us. When I ask for the baptism with the Holy Spirit, I have asked something according to His will, for Luke 11:13 and Acts 2:39 say so; therefore, I know my prayer is heard. Still further, I know because the prayer is heard that I have the petition that I have asked of Him; in other words, I know I have the baptism with the Holy Spirit. I may not feel it yet, but I have received. What I thus count mine resting on the naked word of God, I will afterwards have in actual experience.

Some years ago I went to the students' conference at Lake Geneva, Wisconsin, with Mr. F. B. Meyer of London. Mr. Meyer spoke that night on the baptism with the Holy Spirit. At the conclusion of his address, he said, "If any of you wish to speak with Mr. Torrey or myself after the meeting is over, we will stay and speak with you." A young man came to me who had just graduated from one of the Illinois colleges. He said, "I heard of this blessing thirty days ago and have been praying for it ever since but do not receive. What is the trouble?"

"Is your will laid down?" I asked.

"No," he said, "I am afraid it is not."

"Then," I said, "there is no use praying until your will is laid down. Will you lay down your will?"

He said, "I cannot."

"Are you willing that God should lay it down for you?"

"I am."

"Let us kneel and ask Him to do it."

We knelt side by side, and I placed my Bible open at 1 John 5:14–15 on the chair before him. He asked God to lay down his will for him and empty him of his self-will and to bring his will into conformity with the will of God. When he had finished the prayer, I said, "Is it done?"

He said, "It must be. I have asked something according to His will, and I know He hears me, and I know I have the petition I have asked. Yes, my will is laid down."

"What is it you desire?"

"The baptism with the Holy Spirit."

"Ask for it."

Looking up to God, he said, "Heavenly Father, baptize me with the Holy Spirit now."

"Did you get what you asked?" I asked.

"I don't feel it," he replied.

"That is not what I asked you," I said. "Read the verse before you," and he read: "*Now this is the confidence that we have in Him, that if we ask anything according to His will, He hears us*" (1 John 5:14).

"What do you know?" I asked.

He said, "I know if I ask anything according to His will He hears me."

"What did you ask?"

"I asked for the baptism with the Holy Spirit."

"Is that according to His will?"

"Yes, Acts 2:39 says so."

"What do you know then?"

"I know He has heard me."

"Read on."

"*'And if we know that He hears us, whatever we ask, we know that we have the petitions that we have asked of Him'*" (1 John 5:15).

"What do you know?" I asked.

"I know I have the petition I asked of Him."

"What was the petition you asked of Him?"

"The baptism with the Holy Spirit."

"What do you know?"

"I know I have the baptism with the Holy Spirit. I don't feel it, but God says so."

We arose from our knees and after a short conversation separated. I left Lake Geneva the next morning but returned in a few days. I met the young man and asked if he had really received the baptism with the Holy Spirit. He did not need to answer. His face told the story, but he did answer. He went into a theological seminary the following autumn, was given a church his junior year in the seminary, and had conversions from the outset. The next year on the Day of Prayer for Colleges, largely through his influence, there came a mighty outpouring of the Spirit upon the seminary. The president of the seminary wrote to a denominational paper that it was a veritable Pentecost, and it all came through this young man who had received the baptism with the Holy Spirit through simple faith in the Word of God.

Anyone who will accept Jesus as his Savior and his Lord, put away all sin out of his life, publicly confess his renunciation of sin and acceptance of Jesus Christ, surrender absolutely to God, ask God for the baptism with the Holy Spirit, and take it by simple faith in the naked Word of God, can receive the baptism with the Holy Spirit right now. There are some who so emphasize the matter of absolute surrender that they ignore, or even deny, the necessity of prayer. It is always unfortunate when one emphasizes one side of truth and loses sight of another side that may be equally important. In this way, many lose the blessing that God has provided for them.

The seven steps given above lead with absolute certainty into the blessing. However, several questions arise.

Must we not wait until we know we have received the baptism with the Holy Spirit before we take up Christian work?

Yes, but how will we know? There are two ways of knowing anything in the Christian life. First, by the Word of God; second, by experience or feeling. God's order is to know things first of all by the Word of God. How one may know by the Word of God that he has received the baptism with the Holy Spirit has just been told. We have a right when we have met the conditions and have definitely asked for the baptism with the Holy Spirit to say, "It is mine," and to get up and go on in our work leaving the matter of experience to God's time and place. We get assurance that we have received the baptism with the Holy Spirit in precisely the same way that we get assurance of our salvation.

When an inquirer comes to you, whom you have reason to believe really has received Jesus but who lacks assurance, what do you do with him? Do you tell him to kneel down and pray until he gets assurance? Not if you know how to deal with a soul. You know that true assurance comes through the Word of God, that it is through what is "written" that we are to know that we have eternal life. (See 1 John 5:13.) So you take the inquirer to the written Word. For example, you take him to John 3:36. You tell him to read it.

He reads, *"He who believes in the Son has everlasting life."*

You ask him, "Who has everlasting life?"

He replies from the passage before him, *"He who believes in the Son."*

"How many who believe in the Son have everlasting life?"

"Everyone who believes in the Son."

"Do you know this to be true?"

"Yes."

"Why?"

"Because God says so."

"What does God say?"

"God says, *'He who believes in the Son has everlasting life.'*"

"Do you believe in the Son?"

"Yes."

"What have you then?"

He should say, "Everlasting life," but quite likely he will not. He may say, "I wish I had everlasting life." You point him again to the verse and by questions bring out what it says, and you hold him to it until he sees that he has everlasting life, sees that he has everlasting life simply because God says so. After he has assurance on the ground of the Word, he will have assurance by personal experience, by the testimony of the Spirit in his heart.

Now you should deal with yourself in precisely the same way about the baptism with the Holy Spirit. Hold yourself to the word found in 1 John 5:14–15 and know that you have the baptism with the Spirit simply because God says so in His Word, whether you feel it or not. Afterwards, you will know it by experience.

God's order is always: first, His Word; second, belief in His Word; third, experience or feeling. We desire to change God's order and first have His Word, then feeling, then we will believe, but God demands that we believe in His revealed Word. *"Abraham 'believed God, and it was accounted to him for righteousness'"* (Gal. 3:6). (Compare Genesis 15:6.) Abraham had as yet no feeling in his body of new life and power. He just believed God, and feeling came afterwards. God demands of us today, as He did of Abraham of old, that we simply take Him at His Word and count the thing ours that He has promised simply because He has promised it. Afterwards, we get the feeling and the realization of what He has promised.

Will we receive no manifestation of the baptism with the Spirit?

Will everything be just as it was before, and if so, where is the reality and use of the baptism? Yes, there will be very definite manifestation, but bear in mind what the character of the manifestation will be and when the manifestation is to be expected. When is the manifestation to be expected? After we believe in, after we have received by simple faith, the revealed Word of God.

And what will be the character of the manifestation? Here many go astray. They have read the wonderful experiences of Charles G. Finney, John Wesley, D. L. Moody, and others. These men tell us that when they were baptized with the Holy Spirit they had wonderful sensations. Finney, for example, describes it as great waves of electricity sweeping over him so that he was compelled to ask God to withhold His hand lest he die on the spot. Mr. Moody, on rare occasions, described a similar experience. That these men had such experiences, I do not question for a moment. The words of such men as Charles G. Finney, D. L. Moody, and others are to be believed. While these men doubtless had these experiences, there is not a passage in the Bible that describes such an experience. I am inclined to think the apostles had them, but if they did, they kept them to themselves. It is well that they did, for if they had put them on record, that is what we would be looking for today.

But what are the manifestations that actually occurred in the case of the apostles and the early disciples? New power in the Lord's work. We read at Pentecost that they were *"all filled with the Holy Spirit and began to speak with other tongues, as the Spirit gave them utterance"* (Acts 2:4). Similar accounts are given of what occurred in the household of Cornelius and what occurred in Ephesus. All we read in the case of the apostle Paul is that Ananias came in and said, *"Brother Saul, the Lord Jesus, who appeared to you on the road as you came, has sent me that you may receive your sight and be filled with the Holy Spirit"* (Acts 9:17). Then Ananias baptized him, and the next thing we read is that Paul went straight down to the synagogue and preached Christ so mightily in the power of the Spirit that he *"confounded the Jews who dwelt in Damascus, proving that this Jesus is the Christ"* (Acts 9:22).

So right through the New Testament, the manifestation that we are taught to expect, and the manifestation that actually occurred, is new power in Christian work, and that is the manifestation that we may expect today. We need not look too carefully for that. The thing for us to do is to claim God's promise and let God take care of the mode of manifestation.

May we have to wait for the baptism with the Holy Spirit?

Did not the apostles have to wait ten days, and may we have to wait ten days or even more? No, there is no necessity that we wait. We are told distinctly in the Bible why the apostles had to wait ten days. In Acts 2:1, we read: *"When the Day of Pentecost had fully come"* (literally, "When the Day of Pentecost was being fulfilled"). Way back in the Old Testament, and back of that in the eternal counsels of God, the Day of Pentecost was set for the coming of the Holy Spirit and the gathering of the church, and the Holy Spirit could not be given until the Day of Pentecost was fully come. Therefore, the apostles had to wait until the Day of Pentecost was fulfilled, but there was no waiting after Pentecost.

There was no waiting, for example, in Acts 4:31. Scarcely had they finished the prayer when the place where they were gathered together was shaken, and *"they were all filled with the Holy Spirit."* There was no waiting in the household of Cornelius. They were listening to their first gospel sermon, and Peter said as the climax of his argument, *"To Him* [that is, Jesus] *all the prophets witness that, through His name, whoever believes in Him will receive remission of sins"* (Acts 10:43). No sooner had Peter spoken these words than they believed, and *"the Holy Spirit fell upon all those who heard the word"* (v. 44). There was no waiting in Samaria after Peter and John came down and told them about the baptism with the Holy Spirit and prayed with them. There was no waiting in Ephesus after Paul came and told them that there was not only the baptism of John unto repentance but the baptism of Jesus in the Holy Spirit. It is true that they had been waiting some time until then, but it was simply because they did not know that there was such a baptism for them.

Many may wait today because they do not know that there is the baptism with the Spirit for them, or they may have to wait because they are not resting in the finished work of Christ or because they have not put away sin or because they have not surrendered fully to God or because they will not definitely ask and believe and take. But the reason for the waiting is not in God; it is in ourselves. Anyone who will lay this book down at this point and take the steps that have been stated can immediately receive the baptism with the Holy Spirit.

I would not say a word to dissuade men from spending much time in waiting on God in prayer, for *"those who wait on the LORD shall renew their strength"* (Isa. 40:31). There are few of us indeed in these days who spend as many hours as we should in waiting on God. I can bear joyful testimony to the manifest outpourings of the Spirit that have come time and again as I have waited on God through the hours of the night with fellow believers, but the point I would emphasize is that the baptism with the Holy Spirit may be had at once. The Bible proves this; experience proves it.

There are many waiting for feelings who ought to be claiming by faith. In these days we hear of many who say they are "waiting for their Pentecost." Some have been waiting weeks, some have been waiting months, some have been waiting years. This is not scriptural, and it is dishonoring to God. These Christians have an unscriptural view of what constitutes Pentecost. They have fixed it in their minds that certain manifestations are to occur. Since these particular manifestations, which they themselves have prescribed, do not come, they think they have not received the Holy Spirit. Many have been led into the error, already refuted in this book, that the baptism with the Holy Spirit always manifests itself in the gift of tongues. They have not received the gift of tongues; therefore, they conclude that they have not received the baptism with the Holy Spirit. But as already seen, one may receive the baptism with the Holy Spirit and not receive the gift of tongues. Others still are waiting for some ecstatic feeling. We do not need to wait at all. We may meet the conditions; we may claim the blessing at once on the ground of God's sure Word.

There was a time in my ministry when I was led to say that I would never enter my pulpit again until I had been definitely baptized with the Holy Spirit and knew it or until God in some way told me to go. I shut myself up in my study and day by day waited on God for the baptism with the Holy Spirit. It was a time of struggle. The thought would arise, "Suppose you do not receive the baptism with the Holy Spirit before Sunday. How will it look for you to refuse to go into your pulpit?" But, I held fast to my resolution. I had a more or less definite thought in my mind of what might happen when I was baptized with the

Holy Spirit, but it did not come that way at all. One morning as I waited on God, one of the quietest and calmest moments of my life, it was just as if God said to me, "The blessing is yours. Now go and preach."

If I had known my Bible then as I know it now, I might have heard that voice the very first day speaking to me through the Word. But I did not know it, and God in His infinite condescension, looking on my weakness, spoke it directly to my heart. There was no particular ecstasy or emotion, simply the calm assurance that the blessing was mine. I went into my work, and God manifested His power in that work. Some time passed, I do not remember just how long, and I was sitting in that same study. I do not remember that I was thinking about this subject at all, but suddenly it was just as if I had been knocked out of my chair onto the floor. I lay on my face crying, "Glory to God! Glory to God!" I could not stop. Some power, not my own, had taken possession of my lips and my whole person. I am not of an excitable, hysterical, or even emotional temperament, but I lost control of myself absolutely. I had never shouted before in my life, but I could not stop. When after a while I got control of myself, I went to my wife and told her what had happened. I tell this experience, not to magnify it, but to say that the time when this wonderful experience came, which I cannot really fully describe, was not the moment when I was baptized with the Holy Spirit. The moment when I was baptized with the Holy Spirit was in that calm hour when God said, "It is yours. Now go and preach."

There is an afternoon that I will never forget. It was July 8, 1894. It was at the Northfield Students' Convention. I had spoken that morning in the church on how to receive the baptism with the Holy Spirit. As I drew to a close, I took out my watch and noticed that it was exactly twelve o'clock. Mr. Moody had invited us to go up on the mountain that afternoon at three o'clock to wait on God for the baptism with the Holy Spirit. As I looked at my watch, I said, "Gentlemen, it is exactly twelve o'clock. Mr. Moody has invited us to go up on the mountain at three o'clock to wait on God for the baptism with the Holy Spirit. It is three hours until three o'clock. Some of you cannot wait three hours, nor do you need to wait. Go to your tent, go to your room in the hotel or in the buildings, go out into the woods, go anywhere where you can get alone with God, meet the conditions of the baptism with the Holy Spirit, and claim it at once."

At three o'clock, we gathered in front of Mr. Moody's mother's house, four hundred fifty-six of us in all, all men from the Eastern colleges. (I know the number because Mr. Paul Moody counted us as we passed through the gates down into the lots.) We started to climb the mountainside. After we had gone some distance, Mr. Moody said, "I do not think we need to go farther. Let us stop here." We sat down, and Mr. Moody said, "Have any of you anything to say?" One after another, perhaps seventy-five men arose and said words to this effect, "I could not wait until three o'clock. I have been alone with God, and I have received the baptism with the Holy Spirit." Then Mr. Moody said, "I can see no reason why we should not kneel right down here now and ask God that the Holy Spirit may fall on us as definitely as He fell on the apostles at Pentecost. Let us pray." We knelt down on the ground; some of us lay on our faces on the pine needles.

As we had gone up the mountainside, a cloud had been gathering over the mountain. As we began to pray, the cloud broke, and the raindrops began to come down on us through the overhanging pine trees. However, another cloud, big with mercy, had been gathering over Northfield for ten days, and our prayers seemed to pierce that cloud, allowing the Holy Spirit to fall on us. It was a wonderful hour. There are many who will never forget it.

Anyone who reads this book may have a similar hour alone by himself now. He can take the seven steps one by one, and the Holy Spirit will fall on him.

Chapter 24

The Holy Spirit's Work
in Prophets and Apostles

◆————————

T he work of the Holy Spirit in apostles and prophets is an entirely distinctive work. He imparts to apostles and prophets a special gift for a special purpose.

> *There are diversities of gifts, but the same Spirit....For to one is given the word of wisdom through the Spirit, to another the word of knowledge through the same Spirit, to another faith by the same Spirit, to another gifts of healings by the same Spirit, to another the working of miracles, to another prophecy, to another discerning of spirits, to another different kinds of tongues, to another the interpretation of tongues. But one and the same Spirit works all these things, distributing to each one individually as He wills....And God has appointed these in the church: first apostles, second prophets, third teachers, after that miracles, then gifts of healings, helps, administrations, varieties of tongues. Are all apostles? Are all prophets? Are all teachers? Are all workers of miracles? Do all have gifts of healings? Do all speak with tongues? Do all interpret?*
> (1 Cor. 12:4, 8–11, 28–30)

It is evident from these verses that the work of the Holy Spirit in apostles and prophets is of a distinctive character.

The doctrine is becoming very common and popular in our day that the work of the Holy Spirit in preachers and teachers and in ordinary believers, illuminating them and guiding them into the truth and opening their minds to understand the Word of

259

God, is the same in kind and differs only in degree from the work of the Holy Spirit in prophets and apostles. It is evident from the passage just cited that this doctrine is thoroughly unscriptural and untrue. It overlooks the fact so clearly stated and carefully elucidated that while there is *"the same Spirit"* (1 Cor. 12:4), there are *"diversities of gifts"* (v. 4), *"differences of ministries"* (v. 5), *"diversities of activities"* (v. 6), and that not all are prophets and not all are apostles. (See 1 Corinthians 12:29.)

A very scholarly and brilliant preacher seeking to minimize the difference between the work of the Holy Spirit in apostles and prophets and His work in other men calls attention to the fact that the Bible says of Bezalel that God *"filled him with the Spirit of God"* (Exod. 31:3) to devise the work of the tabernacle. (See Exodus 31:1–11.) The preacher gives this as a proof that the inspiration of the prophet does not differ from the inspiration of the artist or architect. However, in doing this, he loses sight of the fact that the tabernacle was to be built after the *"pattern of the tabernacle"* (Exod. 25:9) *"which was shown* [to Moses] *on the mountain"* (v. 40), and that, therefore, it was itself a prophecy and an exposition of the truth of God. It was not mere architecture. It was the Word of God done into wood, gold, silver, brass, cloth, skin, etc. And Bezalel needed as much special inspiration to reveal the truth in wood, gold, silver, brass, etc., as the apostle or prophet needed it to reveal the Word of God with pen and ink on parchment.

There is much reasoning in these days about inspiration that appears at first sight very learned but that will not bear much rigid scrutiny or candid comparison with the exact statements of the Word of God. There is nothing in the Bible more inspired than the tabernacle, and if the destructive critics would study it more, they would give up their ingenious but groundless theories as to the composite structure of the Pentateuch.

Truth hidden from men for ages, which they had not discovered and could not discover by the unaided processes of human reasoning, has been revealed to apostles and prophets in the Spirit.

By revelation He made known to me the mystery (as I have briefly written already, by which, when you read, you may understand my knowledge in the mystery of Christ), which in other ages was not made known to the sons of men, as it has now been revealed by the Spirit to His holy apostles and prophets. (Eph. 3:3–5)

The Bible contains truth that men had never discovered before the Bible stated it. It contains truth that men never could have discovered if left to themselves. Our heavenly Father, in great grace, has revealed this truth to us His children through His servants, the apostles and the prophets. The Holy Spirit is the agent of this revelation.

Many say that we should test the statements of Scripture by the conclusions of human reasoning or by the "Christian consciousness." The folly of all this is evident when we remember that the revelation of God transcends human reasoning, and that any consciousness that is not the product of the study and absorption of Bible truth is not really a Christian consciousness.

We know that the Bible does contain truth that man has never discovered not merely because it is so stated in the Scriptures, but we know it also as a matter of fact. There is not one of the most distinctive and precious doctrines taught in the Bible that men have ever discovered apart from the Bible. If our consciousness differs from the statements of this Book, which is so plainly God's Book, it is not yet fully Christian, and the thing to do is not to try to pull God's revelation down to the level of our consciousness but to lift our consciousness to the level of God's Word.

The revelations made to the prophets were independent of their own thinking and were made to them by the Spirit of Christ that was in them.

These revelations were subjects of inquiry to their own minds as to their meaning. They were not their own thoughts, but His.

Of this salvation the prophets have inquired and searched carefully, who prophesied of the grace that would come to

261

> *you, searching what, or what manner of time, the Spirit of Christ who was in them was indicating when He testified beforehand the sufferings of Christ and the glories that would follow. To them it was revealed that, not to themselves, but to us they were ministering the things which now have been reported to you through those who have preached the gospel to you by the Holy Spirit sent from heaven; things which angels desire to look into.*
>
> (1 Pet. 1:10–12)

These words make it plain that a Person in the prophets, and independent of the prophets, the Holy Spirit, revealed truth that was independent of their own thinking, which they did not altogether understand themselves, and regarding which it was necessary that they make diligent search and study. Another Person than themselves was thinking and speaking, and they were seeking to comprehend what He said.

No prophet's utterance was of the prophet's own will, but he spoke from God, and the prophet was led in his prophecy by the Holy Spirit.

We read in 2 Peter 1:21: *"For prophecy never came by the will of man, but holy men of God spoke as they were moved by the Holy Spirit."* Clearly then, the prophet was simply an instrument in the hands of another. As the Spirit of God led him, so he spoke.

It was the Holy Spirit who spoke in the prophetic utterances. It was His word that was on the prophet's tongue.

We read in Hebrews 3:7: *"Therefore, as the Holy Spirit says: 'Today, if you will hear His voice.'"* Further, we read:

> *But the Holy Spirit also witnesses to us; for after He had said before, "This is the covenant that I will make with them after those days, says the LORD: I will put My laws into their hearts, and in their minds I will write them."*
>
> (Heb. 10:15–16)

We read again in Acts 28:25: *"So when they did not agree among themselves, they departed after Paul had said one word: 'The Holy Spirit spoke rightly through Isaiah the prophet to our fathers.'"* Still again we read in 2 Samuel 23:2: *"The Spirit of the* LORD *spoke by me, and His word was on my tongue."*

Over and over again in these passages, we are told that it was the Holy Spirit who was the speaker in the prophetic utterances and that it was His word, not theirs, that was on the prophet's tongue. The prophet was simply the mouth by which the Holy Spirit spoke. As a man, that is, except as the Spirit taught him and used him, the prophet might be as fallible as other men are. However, when the Spirit was on him and he was taken up and led by the Holy Spirit, he was infallible in his teachings, for his teachings in that case were not his own, but the teachings of the Holy Spirit. When thus directed by the Holy Spirit, it was God who was speaking and not the prophet.

For example, there can be little doubt that Paul had mistaken notions about many things, but when he taught as an apostle in the Spirit's power, he was infallible. Rather, the Spirit who taught through him was infallible, and the consequent teaching was infallible, as infallible as God Himself. We do well, therefore, to carefully distinguish what Paul may have thought as a man and what he actually taught as an apostle. In the Bible, we have the record of what he taught as an apostle. There are those who think that Paul admitted that he was not sure that he had the word of the Lord in 1 Corinthians 7:6, 25: *"But I say this as a concession, not as a commandment"* (1 Cor. 7:6), and *"yet I give judgment as one whom the Lord in His mercy has made trustworthy"* (v. 25). If this is the true interpretation of the passage (which is more than doubtful), we see how careful Paul was to note the fact when he was not sure he was speaking for the Lord, and this gives us additional certainty in all other passages.

It is sometimes said that Paul taught in his early ministry that the Lord would return during his lifetime and that in this he was, of course, mistaken. But Paul never taught anywhere that the Lord would return in his lifetime. It is true he said in 1 Thessalonians 4:17, *"Then we who are alive and remain shall be caught up together with them in the clouds to meet the Lord in the air. And thus we shall always be with the Lord."* As he was still living when he wrote the words, he naturally and properly did not include himself with those who had already fallen asleep in speaking of the Lord's return. However, this is not to assert that he would remain alive until the Lord came. Quite probably at this period of his ministry, he entertained the hope that he might remain alive and consequently lived in an attitude of expectancy. But the attitude of expectancy is the true attitude in all ages for each believer. It is quite probable that Paul expected that he would be alive at the coming of the Lord, but if he expected to be, he did not teach that way. The Holy Spirit kept him from this as from all other errors in his teachings.

The Holy Spirit in the apostles taught not only the thoughts, or "concepts," but also the words in which the thoughts were to be expressed.

We read in 1 Corinthians 2:13: *"These things we also speak, not in words which man's wisdom teaches but which the Holy Spirit teaches, comparing spiritual things with spiritual."* This passage clearly teaches that the words, as well as the thoughts, were chosen and taught by the Holy Spirit. This is also a necessary inference from the fact that thoughts are conveyed from mind to mind by words, and it is the words that express the thoughts. If the words were imperfect, the thoughts expressed in these words would necessarily be imperfect and to that extent be untrue. Nothing could be plainer than Paul's statement, *"in words...which the Holy Spirit teaches."* The Holy Spirit has Himself anticipated all the modern, wholly unbiblical, and false theories regarding His own work in the apostles.

The more carefully and minutely we study the wording of the statements of this wonderful Book, the more we will become convinced of the marvelous accuracy of the words used to express the thoughts. Very often the solution of an apparent difficulty is found in studying the exact words used. The accuracy, precision, and inerrancy of the exact words used is amazing. To the superficial student, the doctrine of verbal inspiration may appear questionable or even absurd. Any regenerated and Spirit-taught person who ponders the words of the Scripture day after day and year after year will become convinced that the wisdom of God is in the very words, as well as in the thought that the words endeavor to convey. A change of word, letter, tense, case, or number in many instances would land us into contradiction or untruth, but when taking the words exactly as written, difficulties disappear and truth shines forth. The divine origin of nature shines forth more clearly in the use of a microscope as we see the perfection of form and adaptation of means to an end of the minutest particles of matter. In a similar manner, the divine origin of the Bible shines forth more clearly under the microscope as we notice the perfection with which the turn of a word reveals the absolute thought of God.

Someone may ask, "If the Holy Spirit is the author of the words of Scripture, how do we account for variations in style and diction? How do we explain, for instance, that Paul always used Pauline language and John Johannine language, etc.?" The answer to this is very simple. If we could not account at all for this fact, it would have but little weight against the explicit statement of God's Word with anyone who is humble enough and wise enough to recognize that there are a great many things that he cannot account for at all that could easily be accounted for if he knew more. However, these variations are easily accounted for. The Holy Spirit is quite wise enough and has quite enough facility in the use of language in revealing truth to and through any given individual to use words, phrases, forms of expression, and idioms in that person's vocabulary and forms of thought and to make use of that person's peculiar individuality. Indeed, it is a mark of the divine wisdom of this Book that the same truth is expressed with absolute accuracy in such widely variant forms of expression.

The utterances of the apostles and the prophets were the Word of God. When we read these words, we are listening not to the voice of man, but to the voice of God.

We read in Mark 7:13: *"Making the word of God of no effect through your tradition which you have handed down. And many such things you do."* Jesus had been setting up the law given through Moses against the Pharisaic traditions. In doing this, He expressly said in this passage that the law given through

Moses was *"the word of God."* In 2 Samuel 23:2, we read: *"The Spirit of the LORD spoke by me, and His word was on my tongue."* Here again, we are told that the utterance of God's prophet was the word of God. In a similar way, God said in 1 Thessalonians 2:13:

> *For this reason we also thank God without ceasing, because when you received the word of God which you heard from us, you welcomed it not as the word of men, but as it is in truth, the word of God, which also effectively works in you who believe.*

Here Paul declared that the word that he spoke, taught by the Spirit of God, was the very word of God.

Chapter 25

The Holy Spirit's Work in Jesus

J esus Christ Himself is the one perfect manifestation in history of the complete work of the Holy Spirit in man.

Jesus Christ was begotten of the Holy Spirit.

And the angel answered and said to her, "The Holy Spirit will come upon you, and the power of the Highest will overshadow you; therefore, also, that Holy One who is to be born will be called the Son of God." (Luke 1:35)

As we have already seen, the believer is begotten of God in regeneration, but Jesus Christ was begotten of God in His original generation. He is the only begotten Son of God. (See John 3:16.) It was entirely by the Spirit's power working in Mary that the Son of God was formed within her. The regenerated man has a carnal nature received from his earthly father and a new nature imparted by God. Jesus Christ had only the one holy nature that in man is called the new nature. Nevertheless, He was a real man since He had a human mother.

Jesus Christ led a holy, spotless life and offered Himself without blemish to God through the working of the Holy Spirit.

We read in Hebrews 9:14: *"How much more shall the blood of Christ, who through the eternal Spirit offered Himself without spot to God, cleanse your conscience from dead works to serve the living God?"* Jesus Christ met and overcame temptations, as other men may meet and overcome them, in the power of the Holy Spirit. He was tempted and suffered through temptation (Heb. 2:18). He was tempted in every way that we are (Heb. 4:15), but never once did He yield to temptation. He was tempted entirely apart from sin (Heb. 4:15), but He won His victories in a way that is open for all of us to win victory in the power of the Holy Spirit.

Jesus Christ was anointed and fitted for service by the Holy Spirit.

We read in Acts 10:38: *"God anointed Jesus of Nazareth with the Holy Spirit and with power, who went about doing good and healing all who were oppressed by the devil, for God was with Him."* In a prophetic vision of the coming Messiah in the Old Testament, we read:

> *The Spirit of the Lord God is upon Me, because the LORD has anointed Me to preach good tidings to the poor; He has sent Me to heal the brokenhearted, to proclaim liberty to the captives, and the opening of the prison to those who are bound.* (Isa. 61:1)

In Luke's record of the earthly life of our Lord, we read: *"Then Jesus returned in the power of the Spirit to Galilee, and news of Him went out through all the surrounding region"* (Luke 4:14). In a similar way, Jesus said of Himself when speaking in the synagogue in Nazareth:

> *The Spirit of the LORD is upon Me, because He has anointed Me to preach the gospel to the poor; He has sent Me to heal the brokenhearted, to proclaim liberty to the captives and recovery of sight to the blind, to set at liberty those who are oppressed; to proclaim the acceptable year of the LORD.* (Luke 4:18–19)

All these passages contain the one lesson that it was by the special anointing with the Holy Spirit that Jesus Christ was qualified for the service to which God had called Him. As He stood in the Jordan after His baptism, *"the Holy Spirit descended in bodily form like a dove upon Him"* (Luke 3:22). It was then and there that He was anointed with the Holy Spirit, baptized with the Holy Spirit, and equipped for the service that lay before Him. Jesus Christ received His equipment for service in the same way that we receive ours—by a definite baptism with the Holy Spirit.

Jesus Christ was led by the Holy Spirit in His movements here on earth.

We read in Luke 4:1: *"Then Jesus, being filled with the Holy Spirit, returned from the Jordan and was led by the Spirit into the wilderness."* Living as a man here on earth and setting an example for us, each step of His life was under the Holy Spirit's guidance.

Jesus Christ was taught by the Spirit who rested on Him. The Spirit of God was the source of His wisdom in the days of His flesh.

In the Old Testament prophecy of the coming Messiah, we read:

> The Spirit of the LORD shall rest upon Him, the Spirit of wisdom and understanding, the Spirit of counsel and might, the Spirit of knowledge and of the fear of the LORD. His delight is in the fear of the LORD, and He shall not judge by the sight of His eyes, nor decide by the hearing of His ears.   (Isa. 11:2–3)

Further on in Isaiah 42:1, we read: *"Behold! My Servant whom I uphold, My Elect One in whom My soul delights! I have put My Spirit upon Him; He will bring forth justice to the Gentiles."* In Matthew 12:17–18, we see that this prophecy was fulfilled in Jesus of Nazareth.

The Holy Spirit abode upon Jesus in all His fullness; consequently, the words He spoke were the very words of God.

We read in John 3:34: *"For He whom God has sent speaks the words of God, for God does not give the Spirit by measure."*

Through the Holy Spirit, Jesus Christ gave commandments after His resurrection to His apostles whom He had chosen.

"Jesus began both to do and teach, until the day in which He was taken up, after He through the Holy Spirit had given commandments to the apostles whom He had chosen" (Acts 1:1–2). This relates to the time after His resurrection, and so we see that Jesus was still working in the power of the Holy Spirit even after His resurrection from the dead.

Jesus Christ performed His miracles here on earth in the power of the Holy Spirit.

In Matthew 12:28, we read: *"I cast out demons by the Spirit of God."* It is through the Spirit that miracle-working power was given to some in the church after our Lord's departure from this earth (see 1 Corinthians 12:9–10), and in the power of the same Spirit, Jesus Christ worked His miracles.

It was by the power of the Holy Spirit that Jesus Christ was raised from the dead.

We read in Romans 8:11: *"But if the Spirit of Him who raised Jesus from the dead dwells in you, He who raised Christ from the dead will also give life to your mortal bodies through His Spirit who dwells in you."* The same Spirit who is to quicken our mortal bodies and is to raise us up in some future day raised up Jesus.

The following things are plainly evident from this study of the work of the Holy Spirit in Jesus Christ.

First of all, we see the completeness of His humanity. He lived, He thought, He worked, He taught, and He conquered sin and won victories for God in the power of that very same Spirit whom it is our privilege also to have.

Second, we see our own utter dependence on the Holy Spirit. If it was in the power of the Holy Spirit that Jesus Christ, the only begotten Son of God, lived and worked, achieved and triumphed, how much more dependent are we on Him at every turn of life and in every phase of service and every experience of conflict with Satan and sin!

The third thing that is evident is the wondrous world of privilege, blessing, victory, and conquest that is open to us. The same Spirit by which Jesus was originally begotten is at our disposal for us to be begotten again of Him. The same Spirit by which Jesus offered Himself without spot to God is at our disposal so that we also may offer ourselves without spot to Him. The same Spirit by which Jesus was anointed for service is at our disposal so that we may be anointed for service. The same Spirit who led Jesus Christ in His activities here on earth is ready to lead us today. The same Spirit who taught Jesus and imparted to Him wisdom and understanding, counsel and might, and knowledge and the fear of the Lord is here to teach us.

Jesus Christ is our pattern: *"He who says he abides in Him ought himself also to walk just as He walked"* (1 John 2:6), *"the firstborn among many brethren"* (Rom. 8:29). Whatever He realized through the Holy Spirit is for us also to realize today.

How to Pray

CONTENTS

Chapter 1

The Importance of Prayer

◆

In Ephesians 6:18, the tremendous importance of prayer is expressed with startling and overwhelming force: *"Praying always with all prayer and supplication in the Spirit, being watchful to this end with all perseverance and supplication for all the saints."* When the perceptive child of God stops to weigh the meaning of these words, then notes the connection in which they are found, he or she is driven to say, "I must pray, pray, pray. I must put all my energy and heart into prayer. Whatever else I do, I must pray."

Notice the *alls*: *"all prayer and supplication...all perseverance...for all the saints."* Note the piling up of strong words: *"prayer," "supplication," "perseverance."* Also notice the strong expression, *"being watchful,"* more literally, "in this, be not lazy." Paul realized the natural apathy of man, especially his natural neglect in prayer. How seldom we pray things through! How often the church and the individual get right up to the verge of a great blessing in prayer and then let go, become lazy, and quit. I wish that these words "in this, be not lazy" might burn into our hearts. I wish that the whole verse would burn into our hearts.

The Necessity of Persistent Prayer

Why is this constant, persistent, sleepless, overcoming prayer so necessary? Because there is a Devil. He is cunning; he is mighty; he never rests; he is continually plotting the downfall of the children of God. If the children of God relax in prayer, the Devil will succeed in ensnaring them.

Ephesians 6:12–13 reads:

For we do not wrestle against flesh and blood, but against principalities, against powers, against the rulers of the darkness of this age, against spiritual hosts of wickedness in the heavenly places. Therefore take up the whole armor of God, that you may be able to withstand in the evil day, and having done all, to stand.

Next follows a description of the different parts of the Christian's armor that we are to put on if we are to stand against Satan and his mighty schemes. Paul brings his message to a climax in Ephesians 6:18, telling us that to all else we must add prayer—constant, persistent, untiring, sleepless prayer in the Holy Spirit—or all will be in vain.

Prayer is God's appointed way for obtaining things. The reason we lack anything in life is due to a neglect of prayer. James pointed this out very forcibly: *"You do not have because you do not ask"* (James 4:2). The secret behind the poverty and powerlessness of the average Christian is neglect of prayer.

Many Christians are asking, "Why is it that I progress so little in my Christian life?"

"Neglect of prayer," God answers. "You do not have because you do not ask."

Many ministers are asking, "Why is it I see so little fruit from my labors?"

Again, God answers, "Neglect of prayer. You do not have because you do not ask."

Many Sunday school teachers are asking, "Why is it that I see so few converted in my Sunday school class?"

Still, God answers, "Neglect of prayer. You do not have because you do not ask."

Both ministers and churches are asking, "Why is it that the church of Christ makes so little headway against unbelief, error, sin, and worldliness?"

Once more, we hear God answering, "Neglect of prayer. You do not have because you do not ask."

Those men whom God set forth as a pattern of what He expected Christians to be—the apostles—regarded prayer as the most important business of their lives. When the multiplying responsibilities of the early church crowded in upon them, this was the response of the twelve disciples:

> [They] *summoned the multitude of the disciples and said, "It is not desirable that we should leave the word of God and serve tables. Therefore, brethren, seek out from among you seven men of good reputation, full of the Holy Spirit and wisdom, whom we may appoint over this business; but we will give ourselves continually to prayer and to the ministry of the word."* (Acts 6:2–4)

From what Paul wrote to both churches and individuals, it is evident that much of his time, strength, and thought were devoted to prayer for them. (See Romans 1:9; Ephesians 1:15–16; Colossians 1:9; 1 Thessalonians 3:10; and 2 Timothy 1:3.) All the mighty men of God outside the Bible have been men of prayer. They have differed from one another in many things, but in this practice of faithful praying, they have been alike.

The Ministry of Intercession

Prayer occupied a very prominent place and played a very important part in the earthly life of our Lord. Turn, for example, to Mark 1:35. *"In the morning, having risen a long while before daylight, He went out and departed to a solitary place; and there He prayed."* The preceding day had been a very busy and exciting one, but Jesus shortened the hours of needed sleep so that He could rise early and give Himself to more sorely needed prayer.

Turn to Luke 6:12, where we read: *"Now it came to pass in those days that He went out to the mountain to pray, and continued all night in prayer to God."* Our Savior occasionally found it necessary to spend a whole night in prayer.

The words *pray* and *prayer* are used at least twenty-five times in connection with our Lord in the brief record of His life in the four Gospels, and His praying is mentioned in places where these words are not used. Evidently prayer took much of Jesus' time and strength. A man or woman who does not spend much time in prayer cannot properly be called a follower of Jesus Christ.

279

Praying is the most important part of the present ministry of our risen Lord. This reason for constant, persistent, sleepless, overcoming prayer seems, if possible, even more forcible than the others.

Christ's ministry did not end with His death. His atoning work was finished then, but when He rose and ascended to the right hand of the Father, He entered into other work for us, work just as important in its place as His atoning work. It cannot be separated from His Atonement because it rests on that as its basis and is necessary to our complete salvation.

We read what that great, present work is by which He carries our salvation on to completeness: *"Therefore He is also able to save to the uttermost those who come to God through Him, since He always lives to make intercession for them"* (Heb. 7:25). This verse tells us that Jesus is able to save us to the uttermost, not merely *from* the uttermost, but *to* the uttermost—to entire completeness and absolute perfection. He is able to do this not only because He died, but also because He *"always lives."*

The verse also tells us why He now lives: *"to make intercession"*—to pray. Praying is the principal thing He is doing in these days. It is by His prayers that He is saving us.

The same thought is found in Paul's remarkable, triumphant challenge: *"Who is he who condemns? It is Christ who died, and furthermore is also risen, who is even at the right hand of God, who also makes intercession for us"* (Rom. 8:34).

If we are to have fellowship with Jesus Christ in His present work, we must spend much time in prayer. We must give ourselves to earnest, constant, persistent, sleepless, overcoming prayer.

I know of nothing that has so impressed me with a sense of the importance of praying at all seasons—being much and constantly in prayer—as the thought that this is the principal occupation of my risen Lord even now. I want to have fellowship with Him. For that reason I have asked the Father, whatever else He may make me, to make me an intercessor. I pray that He will make me a man who knows how to pray and who spends much time in prayer.

This ministry of intercession is glorious and mighty, and we can all have a part in it. The man or woman who cannot attend a prayer meeting because of illness can have a part in it. The busy mother and the woman who works outside the home can have a part. They can mingle prayers for the saints, for their pastor, for the unsaved, and for missionaries with their day's work. The hard-driven man of business can have a part in it, praying as he hurries from duty to duty. But we must, if we want to maintain this spirit of constant prayer, take time—and plenty of it—when we shut ourselves up in the secret place alone with God for nothing but prayer.

Receiving Mercy, Grace, and Joy

Prayer is the means that God has appointed for our receiving mercy and obtaining grace. Hebrews 4:16 is one of the simplest, sweetest verses in the Bible: *"Let us therefore come boldly to the throne of grace, that we may obtain mercy and find grace to help in time of need."* These words make it very clear that God has appointed a way by which we can seek and obtain mercy and grace. That way is prayer—a bold, confident, outspoken approach to the throne of grace, the Most Holy Place of God's presence. There our sympathizing High Priest, Jesus Christ, has entered in our behalf. (See Hebrews 4:14–15.)

Mercy is what we need, and grace is what we must have; otherwise, all our lives and efforts will end in complete failure. Prayer is the way to obtain mercy and grace. Infinite grace is at our disposal, and we make it ours by prayer. It is ours for the asking. Oh, if we only realized the fullness of God's grace—its height, depth, length, and breadth—I am sure we would spend more time in prayer. The measure of our appropriation of grace is determined by the measure of our prayers.

Who does not feel that he needs more grace? Then ask for it. Be constant and persistent in your asking. Be diligent and untiring in your asking. God delights in our persistence in prayer, for it shows our faith in Him, and He is mightily pleased with faith. Because of our perseverance, He will rise and give us as much as we need. (See Luke 11:8.) What little streams of mercy and grace most of us know when we might know rivers overflowing their banks!

Prayer in the name of Jesus Christ is the way He Himself has appointed for His disciples to obtain fullness of joy. He states this simply and beautifully: *"Until now you have asked nothing in My name. Ask, and you will receive, that your joy may be full"* (John 16:24). Who does not wish for joy? Well, the way to have full joy is by praying in the name of Jesus. We all know people who are full of joy. Indeed, it is just running over, shining from their eyes, bubbling out of their very lips, and running off their fingertips when they shake your hand. Coming in contact with them is like coming in contact with an electrical machine charged with gladness. People of that sort are always people who spend much time in prayer.

Why is it that prayer in the name of Christ brings such fullness of joy? In part, because we get what we ask. But that is not the only reason, nor is it the greatest. Prayer makes God real. When we ask something definite of God, and He gives it, how real God becomes! He is right there! It is blessed to have a God who is real and not merely an idea. I remember once when I suddenly and seriously fell ill all alone in my study. I dropped on my knees and cried to God for help. Instantly, all pain left me, and I was perfectly well. It seemed as if God stood right there, reached out His hand, and touched me. The joy of the healing was not as great as the joy of meeting God.

No joy on earth or in heaven is greater than communion with God. Prayer in the name of Jesus brings us into communion with God. The psalmist was surely not speaking only of future blessedness, but also of present blessedness, when he said, *"In Your presence is fullness of joy"* (Ps. 16:11). Oh, the unutterable joy of those moments when, in our prayers, we really enter into the presence of God!

Does someone say, "I have never known joy like that in prayer"? Do you take enough leisure for prayer to actually sense God's presence? Do you really give yourself up to prayer in the time that you do take?

Freedom from Anxiety

In every care, anxiety, and need of life, prayer with thanksgiving is the means that God has appointed for our obtaining freedom from all anxiety and the peace of God that passes all understanding. Paul said:

Be anxious for nothing, but in everything by prayer and supplication, with thanksgiving, let your requests be made known to God; and the peace of God, which surpasses all understanding, will guard your hearts and minds through Christ Jesus. (Phil. 4:6–7)

To many, this initially seems like the picture of a life that is beautiful but beyond the reach of ordinary mortals. This is not so at all. The verse tells us how this life of peace is attainable by every child of God: *"Be anxious for nothing"* (v. 6). The remainder of the verse tells us how to do this. It is very simple: *"But in everything by prayer and supplication, with thanksgiving, let your requests be made known to God."*

What could be plainer or more simple than that? Just keep in constant touch with God. When troubles or afflictions—great or small—occur, speak to Him about it, never forgetting to return thanks for what He has already done. What will the result be? *"The peace of God, which surpasses all understanding, will guard your hearts and minds through Christ Jesus"* (v. 7).

That is glorious, and it is as simple as it is glorious! Thank God, many are trying it. Do you know anyone who is always serene? Perhaps this person has a very temperamental nature. Nevertheless, when troubles, conflicts, opposition, and sorrow sweep around him, the peace of God that is beyond all understanding will keep his heart and his thoughts in Christ Jesus.

We all know people like that. How do they do it? By prayer, that is how. They know the deep peace of God, the unfathomable peace that surpasses all understanding, because they are men and women of much prayer.

Some of us let the hurry of our lives crowd prayer out; what a waste of time, energy, and emotion there is in this constant worry! One night of prayer will save us from many nights of insomnia. Time spent in prayer is not wasted; it is time invested at a big interest.

Vehicle for the Holy Spirit

Prayer is the method that God Himself has appointed for our obtaining the Holy Spirit. The Bible is very plain on this point. Jesus said, *"If you then, being evil, know how to give good gifts to your children, how much more will your heavenly Father give the Holy Spirit to those who ask Him!"* (Luke 11:13).

I know this as definitely as I know that my thirst is quenched when I drink water. Early one morning in the Chicago Avenue Church prayer room, where several hundred people had been assembled a number of hours in prayer, the Holy Spirit fell so fully that no one could speak or pray. The whole place was so filled with His presence that sobs of joy filled the place. Men left that room and went to different parts of the country, taking trains that very morning, and the effects of the outpouring of God's Holy Spirit in answer to prayer were soon reported. Others went into the city with the blessing of God on them. This is only one instance among many that might be cited from personal experience.

If we would only spend more time in prayer, there would be more fullness of the Spirit's power in our work. Many who once worked unmistakably in the power of the Holy Spirit now fill a room with empty shoutings, beating the air with meaningless gestures, because they have neglected prayer. We must spend much time on our knees before God if we are to continue in the power of the Holy Spirit.

Be Ready for His Return

Prayer is the means that Christ has appointed so that our hearts will not be overcome with indulgences, drunkenness, and the cares of this life, so that the day of Christ's return will not come upon us suddenly as a snare (Luke 21:34–35). We are warned in Scripture: *"Watch therefore, and pray always that* [we] *may be counted worthy to escape all these things that will come to pass, and to stand before the Son of Man"* (v. 36). According to this passage, there is only one way that we can be prepared for the coming of the Lord when He appears: through much prayer.

The second coming of Jesus Christ is a subject that is awakening much interest and discussion in our day. It is one thing to be interested in the Lord's return and to talk about it, but it is another thing to be prepared for it. We live in an atmosphere that has a constant tendency to make us unsuitable for Christ's coming. The world tends to draw us down by its self-indulgences and cares. There is only one way by which we can triumphantly rise above these things—by constant watching in prayer, that is, by sleeplessness in prayer. *"Watch"* in this passage is the same strong word used in Ephesians 6:18, and *"always"* means to pray at all times. The man who spends little time in prayer, who is not steadfast and constant in prayer, will not be ready for the Lord when He comes. But we can be ready. How? Pray! Pray! Pray!

We Need to Pray

Prayer is necessary because of what it accomplishes. Much has been said about that already, but more should be added. Prayer promotes our spiritual growth as almost nothing else, indeed, as nothing else except Bible study. Prayer and Bible study go hand in hand.

Through prayer, my sin—my most hidden sin—is brought to light. As I kneel before God and pray, *"Search me, O God, and know my heart; try me, and know my anxieties; and see if there is any wicked way in me"* (Ps. 139:23–24), God directs the penetrating rays of His light into the innermost recesses of my heart. The sins I never suspected to be present are brought to light. In answer to prayer, God washes away my iniquity and cleanses my sin (Ps. 51:2). My eyes are opened to behold wondrous things out of God's Word (Ps. 119:18). I receive wisdom to know God's way (James 1:5) and strength to walk in it. As I meet God in prayer and gaze into His face, I am changed into His image *"from glory to glory"* (2 Cor. 3:18). Each day of true prayer life finds me more like my glorious Lord.

John Welch, the son-in-law of John Knox, was one of the most faithful men of prayer this world has ever seen. He counted any day in which seven or eight hours were not devoted solely to God in prayer and the study of His Word as wasted time. An old man speaking of him after his death said, "He was a type of Christ." How did he become so like his Master? His prayer life explains the mystery.

Prayer also brings power into our work. If we wish power for any work to which God calls us, whether it is preaching, teaching, personal work, or the raising of our children, we can receive it by earnest prayer.

A woman, with a little boy who was perfectly incorrigible, once came to me in desperation and said, "What should I do with him?"

I asked, "Have you ever tried prayer?"

She said that she had prayed for him, she thought. I asked if she had made his conversion and his character a matter of specific, expectant prayer. She replied that she had not been definite in the matter. She began that day, and at once there was a marked change in the child. As a result, he grew up into Christian manhood.

How many Sunday school teachers have taught for months and years and seen no real fruit from their labors. Then, they learn the secret of intercession; by earnest pleading with God, they see their students, one by one, brought to Christ! How many poor teachers have become mighty people of God by casting away their confidence in their own abilities and gifts and giving themselves up to God to wait on Him for the *"power from on high"* (Luke 24:49)! Along with other believers, the Scottish evangelist John Livingstone spent a night in prayer to God. When he preached the next day, five hundred people were either converted or marked some definite uplift in their spiritual lives. Prayer and power are inseparable.

Prayer avails for the conversion of others. Few people are converted in this world in any other way than in connection with someone's prayers. I previously thought that no human being had anything to do with my own conversion, for I was not converted in church or Sunday school or in personal conversation with anyone. I was awakened in the middle of the night and converted. As far as I can remember, I did not have the slightest thought of being converted, or of anything of that nature, when I went to bed and fell asleep. But I was awakened in the middle of the night and converted probably within five minutes. A few minutes before, I was about as near eternal damnation as one gets. I had one foot over the brink and was trying to get the other one over. As I said, I thought no human being had anything to do with it, but I had forgotten my mother's prayers. Later, I learned that one of my college classmates had decided to pray for me until I was saved.

Prayer often avails where everything else fails. How utterly all of Monica's efforts and entreaties failed with her son! But her prayers prevailed with God, and the immoral youth became St. Augustine, the mighty man of God. By prayer, the bitterest enemies of the Gospel have become its most valiant defenders, the most wicked the truest sons of God, and the most contemptible women the purest saints. Oh, the power of prayer to reach down, where hope itself seems vain, and lift men and women up into fellowship with and likeness to God! It is simply wonderful! How little we appreciate this marvelous weapon!

Prayer brings blessings to the church. The history of the church has always been full of grave difficulties to overcome. The Devil hates the church and seeks in every way to block its progress by false doctrine, by division, and by inward corruption of life. But by prayer, a clear way can be made through everything. Prayer will root out heresy, smooth out misunderstanding, sweep away jealousies and animosities, obliterate immoralities, and bring in the full tide of God's reviving grace. History abundantly proves this. In the darkest hour, when the state of the church has seemed beyond hope, believing men and women have met together and cried to God, and the answer has come.

It was so in the days of Knox, and in the days of Wesley, Whitefield, Edwards, and Brainerd. It was so in the days of Finney and in the days of the great revival of 1857 in this country and of 1859 in Ireland. And it will be so again in your day and mine! Satan has organized his forces. Some people, claiming great apostolic methods, are merely covering the rankest dishonesty and hypocrisy with their loud and false assurance. Christians equally loyal to the great fundamental truths of the Gospel are scowling at one another with a Devil-sent suspicion. The world, the flesh, and the Devil are holding a merry carnival. It is a dark day, but now *"it is time for You to act, O LORD, for they have regarded Your law as void"* (Ps. 119:126). He is getting ready to work, and now He is listening for the voice of prayer. Will He hear it? Will He hear it from you? Will He hear it from the church as a body? I believe He will.

Chapter 2

Praying to God

———◆———

After having seen some of the tremendous importance and irresistible power of prayer, we now come directly to the lesson—how to pray with power.

In the Acts 12, we have the record of a prayer that prevailed with God and also brought about great results. In the fifth verse of this chapter, the manner and method of this prayer are described in a few words: *"Constant prayer was offered to God for him by the church"* (Acts 12:5). The first thing to notice in this verse is the brief expression *"to God."* The prayer that has power is the prayer that is offered to God.

But some will say, "Is not all prayer offered to God?" No. Much of so-called prayer, both public and private, is not directed to God. In order for a prayer to really be to God, there must be a definite and conscious approach to Him when we pray. We must have an explicit and vivid realization that He is bending over us and listening as we pray. In too many of our prayers, God is thought of too little. Our minds are taken up with thoughts of what we need and are not occupied with thoughts of the mighty and loving Father from whom we are seeking our requests. Often, we are neither occupied with the need nor with the One to whom we are praying. Instead, our minds are wandering here and there. There is no power in that sort of prayer. But when we really come into God's presence, really meet Him face-to-face in the place of prayer, really seek the things that we desire from Him, then there is power.

Coming into God's Presence

If we want to pray correctly, the first thing we should do is to make sure that we really seek an audience with God—that we really come into His very presence. Before a word of petition is offered, we should have the definite and vivid consciousness that we are talking to God. Also, we should believe that He is listening to our requests and is going to grant the things that we ask of Him. This is only possible by the Holy Spirit's power, so we should look to the Holy Spirit to lead us into the presence of God. And we should not be hasty in words until He has actually brought us there.

One night, a very active Christian man dropped into a prayer meeting that I was leading. Before we knelt to pray, I said something like the above, telling all the friends to be sure that before they prayed, they were really in God's presence. I also explained that while they were praying, they should have thoughts of God definitely in mind and be more taken up with Him than with their petitions. A few days later, I met this same gentleman. He said that this simple thought was entirely new to him. It had made prayer a completely new experience for him. If we want to pray correctly, these two little words must sink deep into our hearts: *"to God."*

Pray without Ceasing

The second secret of effective praying is found in the same verse in the words, *"constant prayer."* The word *constant* does not convey the full force of the original Greek. The word literally means "stretched-out-ed-ly." It is a pictorial word and wonderfully expressive. It represents the soul on a stretch of earnest and intense desire. *Intensely* would perhaps be as close a translation as any English word. It is the same word used to speak of our Lord in Luke 22:44, where it is said, *"He prayed more earnestly. Then His sweat became like great drops of blood falling down to the ground."*

We read in Hebrews 5:7 that Christ *"in the days of His flesh...offered up prayers and supplications, with vehement cries and tears."* In Romans 15:30, Paul begged the saints in Rome to *"strive together"* with him in their prayers. The word translated *strive* means primarily to contend as in athletic games or in a fight. In other words, prayer that prevails with God is prayer into which we put our whole souls, stretching out toward God in intense and agonizing desire. Much of our modern prayer lacks power because it lacks heart. We rush into God's presence, run through a string of petitions, jump up, and go out. If someone asks us an hour later what we prayed for, often we cannot remember. If we put so little heart into our prayers, we cannot expect God to put much heart into answering them.

We hear much in our day about the *rest* of faith, but there is not much said about the *fight* of faith in prayer. Those who want us to think that they have attained to some great height of faith and trust because they have never known any agony or conflict in prayer have surely gone beyond their Lord. They have even gone beyond the mightiest victors for God, both in effort and prayer, that the ages of Christian history have known. When we learn to come to God with an intensity of desire that wrings the soul, then we will know a power in prayer that most of us do not yet know.

Prayer and Fasting

How will we achieve this earnestness in prayer? Not by trying to work ourselves up into it. The true method is explained in Romans 8:26:

> *Likewise the Spirit also helps in our weaknesses. For we do not know what we should pray for as we ought, but the Spirit Himself makes intercession for us with groanings which cannot be uttered.*

The earnestness that we work up in the energy of the flesh is a repulsive thing. The earnestness created in us by the Holy Spirit is pleasing to God. Here again, if we desire to pray correctly, we must look to the Spirit of God to teach us how to pray.

It is in this connection that fasting enters in. In Daniel 9:3, we read that Daniel set his face *"toward the Lord God to make request by prayer and supplications, with fasting, sackcloth, and ashes."* There are those who think that fasting belongs to the old dispensation. But when we look at Acts 14:23 and Acts 13:2–3, we find that it was practiced by earnest men of the apostolic day.

If we want to pray with power, we should pray with fasting. This, of course, does not mean that we should fast every time we pray. But there are times of emergency or special crisis, when sincere believers will withdraw even from the gratification of natural appetites that would be perfectly proper under other circumstances in order to give themselves up solely to prayer. There is a mysterious power in such prayer. Every great crisis in life and work should be met in that way. There is nothing pleasing to God in our giving up things that are pleasant in a purely Pharisaic or legalistic way. But there is power in that downright earnestness and determination to obtain, in prayer, the things that we strongly feel are needs. This feeling of urgency leads us to put away everything, even things that are normal and necessary, that we may set our faces to find God and obtain blessings from Him.

Unity in Prayer

Another secret of proper praying is found in Acts 12:5. It appears in the three words: *"by the church."* There is power in united prayer. Of course, there is power in the prayer of an individual, but there is much more power in united prayer. God delights in the unity of His people and seeks to emphasize it in every way. Thus, He pronounces a special blessing on corporate prayer. We read in Matthew 18:19: *"If two of you agree on earth concerning anything that they ask, it will be done for them by My Father in heaven."* This unity, however, must be real. The passage just quoted does not say that if two will agree in asking, but if two will agree as *"concerning anything that they ask."* Two people might agree to ask for the same thing, and yet there may be no real agreement concerning the thing they asked. One might ask it because he really desired it; the other might ask simply to please his friend. But where there is real agreement, where the Spirit of God brings believers into perfect harmony concerning what they ask of God, where the Spirit lays the same burden on two or more hearts, there is absolutely irresistible power in prayer.

Chapter 3

Obeying and Praying

◆

One of the most significant verses in the Bible on prayer is 1 John 3:22. John said, *"And whatever we ask we receive from Him, because we keep His commandments and do those things that are pleasing in His sight."* What an astounding statement! John said, in so many words, that he received everything he asked for. How many of us can say the same? But John explains why this was so: *"Because we keep His commandments and do those things that are pleasing in His sight."* In other words, the one who expects God to do as he asks Him must do whatever God bids him. If we give a listening ear to all God's commands to us, He will give a listening ear to all our petitions to Him. If, on the other hand, we turn a deaf ear to His precepts, He will be likely to turn a deaf ear to our prayers. Here we find the secret of much unanswered prayer. We are not listening to God's Word; therefore, He is not listening to our petitions.

I was once speaking to a woman who had been a professed Christian but had given it all up. I asked her why she was not a Christian any longer. She replied, because she did not believe the Bible. I asked her why she did not believe the Bible.

"Because I have tried its promises and found them untrue."

"Which promises?"

"The promises about prayer."

"Which promises about prayer?"

"Does it not say in the Bible, *'Whatever things you ask in prayer, believing, you will receive'"* (Matt. 21:22)?

"It does say that."

"Well, I asked fully expecting to get and did not receive, so the promise failed."

"Was the promise made to you?"

"Why, certainly, it is made to all Christians, is it not?"

"No, God carefully defines who the *you*s are whose believing prayers He agrees to answer."

I then directed her to 1 John 3:22, and read the description of those whose prayers had power with God.

"Now," I said, "were you keeping His commandments and doing those things that are pleasing in His sight?"

She frankly confessed that she was not, and she soon came to see that the real difficulty was not with God's promises, but with herself. That is the reason for many unanswered prayers today—the one who offers them is not obedient.

Knowing and Doing God's Will

If we want power in prayer, we must be earnest students of His Word to find out what His will regarding us is. Then having found it, we must do it. One unconfessed act of disobedience on our part will shut the ear of God against many petitions. But this verse goes beyond the mere keeping of God's commandments. John tells us that we must *do those things that are pleasing in His sight*" (1 John 3:22).

There are many things that would please God, but which He has not specifically commanded. A true child is not content with merely doing those things that his father specifically commands him to do. He tries to know his father's will, and if he thinks that there is anything that he can do that would please his father, he does it gladly. He does so even if his father has never given him any specific order to do it. So it is with the true child of God. He does not merely ask whether certain things are commanded or certain things forbidden. He tries to know his Father's will in all things.

Many Christians today are doing things that are not pleasing to God. Many also neglect to do things that would be pleasing to God. When you speak to them about these things, they will confront you at once with the question, "Is there any command in the Bible not to do this thing?" If you cannot show them the verse in which their action is plainly forbidden, they think they are under no obligation whatever to give it up. But a true child of God does not demand a specific command. If we make it our desire to find out and do the things that are pleasing to God, He will make it His desire to do the things that are pleasing to us. Here again we find the explanation of much unanswered prayer. We are not making it our desire to know what pleases our Father; thus, our prayers are not answered.

Praying in Truth

Psalm 145:18 throws a great deal of light on the question of how to pray: *"The LORD is near to all who call upon Him, to all who call upon Him in truth."* That little expression *"in truth"* is worthy of further study. If you take your concordance and go through the Bible, you will find that this expression means "in reality," "in sincerity." The prayer that God answers is the prayer that is real, the prayer that asks for something that is sincerely desired.

Much of our prayer is insincere. People ask for things that they do not wish. Many women pray for the conversion of their husbands, but do not really wish their husbands to be converted. They think they do, but if they knew what would be involved in the conversion of their husbands, they would think again. It would necessitate an entire revolution in their manner of doing business and would consequently reduce their income, making it necessary to change their entire way of living. If they were sincere with God, the real prayer of their hearts would be: "O God, do not convert my husband." Some women do not wish their husbands' conversion at so great a cost.

Many churches are praying for a revival but do not really desire a revival. They think they do, for in their minds, a revival means an increase of membership, income, and reputation among the churches. But if they knew what a real revival meant, they would not be so eager. Revival brings the searching of hearts on the part of professed Christians, a radical transformation of individual, home, and social life, when the Spirit of God is poured out in reality and power. If all this were known, the real cry of the church would be: "O God, keep us from having a revival."

Many ministers are praying for the filling with the Holy Spirit, yet they do not really desire it. They think they do, for the filling with the Spirit means new joy and power in preaching the Word, a wider reputation among men, and a larger prominence in the church of Christ. But if they understood what a filling with the Holy Spirit really involved, they would think less about its rewards. They would think more of how it would necessarily bring them into antagonism with the world, with unspiritual Christians, how it would cause their name to be "cast out as evil" (see Luke 6:22), and how it might necessitate their leaving a good, comfortable living to go to work in the slums or even in some foreign land. If they understood all this, their prayer most likely would be—if they were to express the real wish of their hearts—"O God, save me from being filled with the Holy Spirit."

When we do come to the place where we really desire the conversion of friends at any cost, really desire the outpouring of the Holy Spirit whatever it may involve, really desire anything *"in truth"* and then call upon God for it *"in truth,"* God is going to hear.

Chapter 4

Praying in the Name of Christ

◆

J esus spoke a wonderful word about prayer to His disciples on the night before His crucifixion: *"Whatever you ask in My name, that I will do, that the Father may be glorified in the Son. If you ask anything in My name, I will do it"* (John 14:13–14). Prayer in the name of Christ has power with God. God is well pleased with His Son Jesus Christ. He always hears Him, and He also always hears the prayer that is really in His name. There is a fragrance in the name of Christ that makes every prayer that bears it acceptable to God. But what is it to pray in the name of Christ?

Many explanations have been attempted that make little sense to the average person. But there is nothing mystical or mysterious about this expression. If you go through the Bible and examine all the passages in which the expressions "in My name" or "in His name" are used, you will find that they mean just about what they do in everyday language.

If I go to a bank and hand in a check with my name signed to it, I ask of that bank in my own name. If I have money deposited in that bank, the check will be cashed; if not, it will not be. If, however, I go to a bank with somebody else's name signed to the check, I am asking in his name, and it does not matter whether I have money in that bank or any other. If the person whose name is signed to the check has money there, the check will be cashed. For example, if I were to go to the First National Bank of Chicago and present a check that I had signed for $500.00, the teller would say to me: "Why, Mr. Torrey, we cannot cash that. You have no money in this bank."

But if I were to go to the First National Bank with a check for $500.00 made payable to me and signed by one of the large depositors in that bank, they would not ask whether I had money in that bank or in any bank. Instead, they would honor the check at once.

When I go to God in prayer, it is like going to the bank of heaven. I have nothing deposited there. I have absolutely no credit there. If I go in my own name, I will get absolutely nothing. But Jesus Christ has unlimited credit in heaven, and He has granted me the privilege of going to the bank with His name on my checks. When I thus go, my prayers will be honored to any extent.

To pray in the name of Christ is to pray on the ground of His credit, not mine. It is to renounce the thought that I have any claims on God whatever and approach Him on the ground of Christ's claims. Praying in the name of Christ is not done by merely adding the phrase, "I ask these things in Jesus' name," to my prayer. I may put that phrase in my prayer and really be resting in my own merit all the time. On the other hand, I may omit that phrase but really be resting in the merit of Christ all the time. When I really do approach God on the ground of Christ's merit and His atoning blood (Heb. 10:19), God will hear me. Many of our prayers are in vain because men approach God imagining that they have some claim that obligates Him to answer their prayers.

Forgiveness in His Name

Years ago when D. L. Moody was young in Christian work, he visited a town in Illinois. A judge in the town was not a Christian. This judge's wife asked Mr. Moody to call on her husband, but he replied: "I cannot talk with your husband. I am only an uneducated, young Christian, and your husband is a scholarly non-believer."

But the wife would not take no for an answer, so Mr. Moody made the call. The clerks in the outer office giggled as the young salesman from Chicago went in to talk with the scholarly judge. The conversation was short. Mr. Moody said, "Judge, I can't talk with you. You are an educated non-Christian, and I have no learning. I simply want to say that if you are ever converted, I want you to let me know."

The judge replied: "Yes, young man, if I am ever converted, I will let you know."

The conversation ended. The clerks snickered louder when the zealous, young Christian left the office, but the judge was converted within a year. Mr. Moody, visiting the town again, asked the judge to explain how it came about. The judge said:

> One night, when my wife was at prayer meeting, I began to grow very uneasy and miserable. I did not know what was the matter with me, but I finally retired before my wife came home. I could not sleep all that night. I got up early, told my wife that I would eat no breakfast, and went down to the office. I told the clerks they could take a holiday and shut myself up in the inner office. I kept growing more and more miserable, and finally I got down and asked God to forgive my sins. But I would not say "for Jesus' sake" because I was a Unitarian and did not believe in the Atonement. I kept praying, "God forgive my sins," but no answer came. At last, in desperation, I cried, "O God, for Christ's sake, forgive my sins" and found peace at once.

The judge had no access to God until he came in the name of Christ. When he finally came in the name of Jesus, he was heard and answered at once.

Knowing God's Will through His Word

Great light is thrown on the subject "How to Pray" by 1 John 5:14–15:

> *Now this is the confidence that we have in Him, that if we ask anything according to His will, He hears us. And if we know that He hears us, whatever we ask, we know that we have the petitions that we have asked of Him.*

This passage clearly teaches that if we are to pray correctly, we must pray according to God's will. Then, we will, beyond a shadow of a doubt, receive the thing we ask of Him. But can we know the will of God? Can we know that any specific prayer is according to His will?

We most surely can. How? First by the Word. God has revealed His will in His Word. When anything is definitely promised in the Word of God, we know that it is His will to give that thing. If, when I pray, I can find some definite promise of God's Word and lay that promise before God, I know that He hears me. And if I know that He hears me, I know that I have the petition that I have asked of Him. For example, when I pray for wisdom, I know that it is the will of God to give me wisdom, for He said so in James 1:5: *"If any of you lacks wisdom, let him ask of God, who gives to all liberally and without reproach, and it will be given to him."* So when I ask for wisdom, I know that the prayer is heard and that wisdom will be given to me. In like manner, when I pray for the Holy Spirit, I know that it is God's will, that my prayer is heard, and that I have the petition that I have asked of Him: *"If you then, being evil, know how to give good gifts to your children, how much more will your heavenly Father give the Holy Spirit to those who ask Him!"* (Luke 11:13).

Some years ago, a minister came to me at the close of an address on prayer at a YMCA Bible school and said, "You have given those young men the impression that they can ask for definite things and get the very things that they ask."

I replied that I did not know whether that was the impression I had given or not, but that was certainly the impression I desired to give.

"But," he replied, "that is not right. We cannot be sure, for we don't know God's will."

I turned at once to James 1:5, read it to him, and said, "Is it not God's will to give us wisdom, and if you ask for wisdom do you not know that you are going to get it?"

"Ah!" he said, "we don't know what wisdom is."

I said, "No, if we did, we would not need to ask. But whatever wisdom may be, don't you know that you will get it?"

Certainly it is our privilege to know. When we have a specific promise in the Word of God, if we doubt that it is God's will or if we doubt that God will do what we ask, we make God a liar. (See 1 John 5:10.)

Here is one of the greatest secrets of prevailing prayer: Study the Word to find what God's will is as revealed there in the promises. Then, simply take these promises and claim them before God in prayer with the absolutely unwavering expectation that He will do what He has promised in His Word.

Knowing God's Will by His Spirit

Another way in which we may know the will of God is by the teaching of His Holy Spirit. There are many things that we need from God that are not covered by any specific promise. But we are not in ignorance of the will of God even then. In Romans 8:26–27, we are told:

Likewise the Spirit also helps in our weaknesses. For we do not know what we should pray for as we ought, but the Spirit Himself makes intercession for us with groanings which cannot be uttered. Now He who searches the hearts knows what the mind of the Spirit is, because He makes intercession for the saints according to the will of God.

Here we are distinctly told that the Spirit of God prays in us, draws out our prayers, according to God's will. When we are thus led out by the Holy Spirit in any direction, to pray for any given object, we may do it in all confidence that it is God's will. We are to be assured that we will receive the very thing we ask of Him, even though there is no specific promise to cover the case. Often, by His Spirit, God lays a heavy burden of prayer for some given individual on our hearts. We cannot rest. We pray for him *"with groanings which cannot be uttered."* Perhaps the man is entirely beyond our reach, but God hears the prayer. And, in many cases, it is not long before we hear of his definite conversion.

The passage in 1 John 5:14–15 is one of the most abused passages in the Bible:

This is the confidence that we have in Him, that if we ask anything according to His will, He hears us. And if we know that He hears us, whatever we ask, we know that we have the petitions that we have asked of Him.

Undoubtedly, the Holy Spirit put this passage into the Bible to encourage our faith. It begins with *"this is the confidence that we have in Him,"* and closes with *"we know that we have the petitions that we have asked of Him."* But one of the most frequent usages of this passage, which was so clearly given to bring confidence, is to introduce an element of uncertainty into our prayers. Often, when a person is confident in prayer, some cautious brother will come and say, "Now, don't be too confident. If it is God's will, He will do it. You should add, 'If it be Your will.'"

Doubtless, there are many times when we do not know the will of God, and submission to the excellent will of God should be the basis for all prayer. But when we know God's will, there need be no *if*s. This passage was not put into the Bible so that we could introduce *if*s into all our prayers, but so that we could throw our *if*s to the wind and have *"confidence"* and *"know that we have the petitions that we have asked of Him."*

Chapter 5

Praying in the Spirit

O ver and over again, we have seen our dependence on the Holy Spirit in prayer. This is stated very clearly in Ephesians 6:18, *"Praying always with all prayer and supplication in the Spirit,"* and in Jude 20, *"Praying in the Holy Spirit."* Indeed, the whole secret of prayer is found in these three words, *"in the Spirit."* God the Father answers the prayers that God the Holy Spirit inspires.

The disciples did not know how to pray as they should, so they came to Jesus and said, *"Lord, teach us to pray"* (Luke 11:1). We also do not know how to pray as we should, but we have another Teacher and Guide right at hand to help us. (See John 14:16–17.) *"The Spirit also helps in our weaknesses"* (Rom. 8:26). He teaches us how to pray. True prayer is prayer in the Spirit; that is, the prayer the Spirit inspires and directs. When we come into God's presence, we should recognize our infirmities, our ignorance of what we should pray for or how we should pray for it. In the consciousness of our utter inability to pray properly, we should look to the Holy Spirit, casting ourselves completely on Him to direct our prayers. He must lead our desires and guide our expressions of them.

Nothing can be more foolish in prayer than to rush heedlessly into God's presence and ask the first thing that comes into our minds. When we first come into God's presence, we should be silent before Him. We should look to Him to send His Holy Spirit to teach us how to pray. We must wait for the Holy Spirit and surrender ourselves to the Spirit. Then, we will pray correctly.

Often, when we come to God in prayer, we do not feel like praying. What should we do in such a case? Stop praying until we feel like it? Not at all. When we feel least like praying is the time when we most need to pray. We should wait quietly before God and tell Him how cold and prayerless our hearts are. We should look to Him, trust Him, and expect Him to send the Holy Spirit to warm our hearts and draw us out in prayer. It will not be long before the glow of the Spirit's presence will fill our hearts. We will begin to pray with freedom, directness, earnestness, and power. Many of the most blessed seasons of prayer I have ever known have begun with a feeling of utter deadness and prayerlessness. But in my helplessness and coldness, I have cast myself on God and looked to Him to send His Holy Spirit to teach me to pray. And He has always done it.

When we pray in the Spirit, we will pray for the right things in the right way. There will be joy and power in our prayers.

Praying with Faith

If we are to pray with power, we must pray with faith. In Mark 11:24, Jesus said, *"Therefore I say to you, whatever things you ask when you pray, believe that you receive them, and you will have them."* No matter how positive any promise of God's Word may be, we will not enjoy it unless we confidently expect its fulfillment. James said, *"If any of you lacks wisdom, let him ask of God, who gives to all liberally and without reproach, and it will be given to him"* (James 1:5). Now, that promise is as positive as a promise can be. The next two verses add:

> *But let him ask in faith, with no doubting, for he who doubts is like a wave of the sea driven and tossed by the wind. For let not that man suppose that he will receive anything from the Lord.* (James 1:6–7)

There must then be confident, unwavering expectation.

But there is a faith that goes beyond expectation. It believes that prayer is heard and that the promise is granted. This comes out in Mark 11:24: *"Therefore I say to you, whatever things you ask when you pray, believe that you receive them, and you will have them."* But how can one have this kind of faith?

303

Let us say with all emphasis, it cannot be forced. A person reads this promise about the prayer of faith and then asks for things that he desires. He tries to make himself believe that God has heard the prayer. This only ends in disappointment. It is not real faith, and the thing is not granted. At this point, many people lose faith altogether by trying to create faith by an effort of their will. When the thing they made themselves believe they would receive is not given, the very foundation of faith is often undermined.

But how does real faith come? Romans 10:17 answers the question: *"So then faith comes by hearing, and hearing by the word of God."* If we are to have real faith, we must study the Word of God and discover what is promised. Then, we must simply believe the promises of God. Faith must have God's sanction. Trying to believe something that you want to believe is not faith. Believing what God says in His Word is faith. If I am to have faith when I pray, I must find some promise in the Word of God to rest my faith on.

Furthermore, faith comes through the Spirit. The Spirit knows the will of God. If I pray in the Spirit and look to the Spirit to teach me God's will, He will lead me in prayer according to the will of God. He will give me faith that the prayer is to be answered. But in no case does real faith come by simply determining that you are going to receive what you want. If there is no promise in the Word of God and no clear leading of the Spirit, there can be no real faith. There should be no scolding for your lack of faith in such a case. But if the thing desired is promised in the Word of God, we may well scold ourselves for lack of faith if we doubt, for we are making God a liar by doubting His Word.

Chapter 6

Always Praying and Not Fainting

◆——————

I n the Gospel of Luke, Jesus emphasized the lesson that men should always pray and not faint (Luke 18:1 KJV). The first parable is found in Luke 11:5–8 and the other in Luke 18:1–8.

And He said to them, "Which of you shall have a friend, and go to him at midnight and say to him, 'Friend, lend me three loaves; for a friend of mine has come to me on his journey, and I have nothing to set before him'; and he will answer from within and say, 'Do not trouble me; the door is now shut, and my children are with me in bed; I cannot rise and give to you'? I say to you, though he will not rise and give to him because he is his friend, yet because of his persistence he will rise and give him as many as he needs."
(Luke 11:5–8)

Then He spoke a parable to them, that men always ought to pray and not lose heart, saying: "There was in a certain city a judge who did not fear God nor regard man. Now there was a widow in that city; and she came to him, saying, 'Get justice for me from my adversary.' And he would not for a while; but afterward he said within himself, 'Though I do not fear God nor regard man, yet because this widow troubles me I will avenge her, lest by her continual coming she weary me.'" Then the Lord said, "Hear what the unjust judge said. And shall God not avenge His own elect who cry out day and night to Him, though He bears long with them? I tell you that He will avenge them speedily. Nevertheless, when the Son of Man comes, will He really find faith on the earth?"
(Luke 18:1–8)

In the former of these two parables, Jesus sets forth in a startling way the necessity of persistence in prayer. The word translated *"persistence"* literally means *shamelessness.* Jesus wants us to understand that God desires us to draw near to Him with a determination to obtain the things we seek that will not be put to shame by any seeming refusal or delay on God's part. God delights in the holy boldness that will not take no for an answer. It is an expression of great faith, and nothing pleases God more than faith.

Jesus seemed to deal with the Syro-Phoenician woman almost with rudeness. But she would not give up that easily, and Jesus looked on her shameless persistence with pleasure. He said, *"O woman, great is your faith! Let it be to you as you desire"* (Matt. 15:28). God does not always give us things at our first efforts. He wants to train us and make us strong by compelling us to work hard for the best things. Likewise, He does not always give us what we ask in answer to the first prayer. He wants to train us and make us strong people of prayer by compelling us to pray hard for the best things. He makes us pray through.

I am glad that this is so. There is no more blessed training in prayer than what comes through being compelled to ask again and again, over long periods of time, before obtaining what we seek from God. Many people call it submission to the will of God when God does not grant them their requests at the first or second asking. They say, "Well, perhaps it is not God's will."

As a rule, this is not submission but spiritual laziness. We do not call it submission to the will of God when we give up after one or two efforts to obtain things by action. We call it lack of strength of character. When the strong man or woman of action starts out to accomplish a thing and does not accomplish it the first or second or one-hundredth time, he or she keeps hammering away until it is accomplished. The strong person of prayer keeps on praying until he prays through and obtains what he seeks. We should be careful about what we ask from God. But when we do begin to pray for a thing, we should never give up praying for it until we receive it or until God makes it very clear and very definite that it is not His will to give it.

Some people like us to believe that it shows unbelief to pray twice for the same thing. They think we ought to claim the answer the first time we ask. Doubtless, there are times when we are able, through faith in the Word or the leading of the Holy Spirit, to claim the first time what we have asked of God. But beyond question, there are other times when we must pray again and again for the same thing before we receive our answers. Those who are beyond praying twice for the same thing are beyond following their Master's example. (See Matthew 26:44.)

George Müller prayed for two men daily for more than sixty years. Although both were eventually converted, one turned to the Lord shortly before George Müller's death, I think at the last service that George Müller held. The other was converted within a year after Müller's death. One of the great needs of the present day is for men and women who will not only start out to pray for things, but will pray on and on until they obtain what they seek from the Lord.

Chapter 7

Abiding in Christ

The whole secret of prayer is found in these words of our Lord: *"If you abide in Me, and My words abide in you, you will ask what you desire, and it shall be done for you"* (John 15:7). Here is prayer that has unbounded power: *"Ask what you desire, and it shall be done for you."*

There is a way, then, of asking and receiving precisely what we ask. Christ gives two conditions for this all-prevailing prayer. The first condition is *"If you abide in Me."* What does it mean to abide in Christ? Some explanations are so mystical or so profound that many children of God think they mean practically nothing at all. But what Jesus meant was really very simple.

He had been comparing Himself to a vine and His disciples to the branches in the vine. Some branches continued in the vine in living union so that the sap or life of the vine constantly flowed into the branches. They had no independent life of their own. Everything in them was simply the outcome of the life of the vine flowing into them. Their buds, leaves, blossoms, and fruit were not really theirs, but the buds, leaves, blossoms, and fruit of the vine. Other branches were completely severed from the vine, or the flow of the sap or life of the vine was in some way hindered.

For us to abide in Christ is to bear the same relationship to Him that the first sort of branches bear to the vine. That is to say, to abide in Christ is to renounce any independent lives of our own. We must give up trying to think our own thoughts, form our own resolutions, or cultivate our own feelings. We must simply and constantly look to Christ to think His thoughts in us, to form His purposes in us, to feel His emotions and affections in us. It is to renounce all life independent of Christ and constantly look to Him for the inflow of His life into us and the outworking of His life through us. When we do this, our prayers will obtain what we seek from God.

This must necessarily be so, for our desires will not be our own desires but Christ's. And our prayers will not in reality be our own prayers, but Christ praying in us. Such prayers will always be in harmony with God's will, and the Father always hears Him. When our prayers fail, it is because they are indeed our prayers. We have conceived the desire and offered our own petitions, instead of looking to Christ to pray through us.

To abide in Christ, one must already be in Christ through the acceptance of Christ as an atoning Savior from the guilt of sin. Christ must be acknowledged as a risen Savior from the power of sin and as Lord and Master over all the believer's life. Once we are in Christ, all that we have to do to abide in Christ is simply to renounce our self-life. We must utterly renounce every thought, purpose, desire, and affection of our own and continually look for Jesus Christ to form His thoughts, purposes, affections, and desires in us. Abiding in Christ is really a very simple matter, though it is a wonderful life of privilege and of power.

Christ's Words in Us

Another condition is stated in John 15:7, though it is really involved in the first: *"and My words abide in you."* If we are to receive from God all we ask from Him, Christ's words must abide in us. We must study His words and let them sink into our thoughts and hearts. We must keep them in our memories, obey them constantly in our lives, and let them shape and mold our daily lives and all our actions.

This is really the method of abiding in Christ. It is through His words that Jesus imparts Himself to us. The words He speaks to us are spirit and life (John 6:63). It is vain to expect power in prayer unless we meditate on the words of Christ and let them sink deeply and find a permanent abode in our hearts. Many wonder why they are so powerless in prayer. The very simple explanation of it all is found in their neglect of the words of Christ. They have not hidden His words in their hearts (Ps.

119:11); His words do not abide in them. It is not by moments of mystical meditation and rapturous experiences that we learn to abide in Christ. It is by feeding on His Word, His written word in the Bible, and looking to the Spirit to implant these words in our hearts to make them a living thing in our hearts. If we thus let the words of Christ abide in us, they will stir us up to prayer. They will be the mold in which our prayers are shaped. And our prayers will necessarily be consistent with God's will and will prevail with Him. Prevailing prayer is almost an impossibility where there is neglect of the study of God's Word.

Mere intellectual study of the Word of God is not enough; there must be meditation on it. The Word of God must be revolved over and over in the mind with a constant looking to God and His Spirit to make that Word a living thing in the heart. The prayer that is born of meditation on the Word of God is the prayer that soars upward to God's listening ear.

George Müller, one of the mightiest men of prayer, would begin praying by reading and meditating on God's Word until a prayer began to form itself in his heart. Thus, God Himself was the real Author of the prayer, and God answered the prayer that He Himself had inspired.

The Word of God is the instrument through which the Holy Spirit works. It is the *"sword of the Spirit"* (Eph. 6:17) in more senses than one. The person who wants to know the work of the Holy Spirit in any direction must feed on the Word. The person who desires to pray in the Spirit must meditate on the Word so that the Holy Spirit may have something through which He can work. The Holy Spirit works His prayers in us through the Word. Neglect of the Word makes praying in the Holy Spirit an impossibility. If we seek to feed the fire of our prayers with the fuel of God's Word, all our difficulties in prayer will disappear.

Chapter 8

Praying with Thanksgiving

◆

Two words are often overlooked in the lesson about prayer that Paul gives us in Philippians 4:6–7:

Be anxious for nothing, but in everything by prayer and supplication, with thanksgiving, let your requests be made known to God; and the peace of God, which surpasses all understanding, will guard your hearts and minds through Christ Jesus.

The two important words often disregarded are *"with thanksgiving."*

In approaching God to ask for new blessings, we must never forget to thank Him for blessings already granted. If we would just stop and think about how many prayers God has answered and how seldom we have thanked Him, I am sure we would be overwhelmed. We should be just as definite in returning thanks as we are in making our requests. We come to God with very specific petitions, but when we thank Him, our thanksgiving is indefinite and general.

Doubtless one reason why so many of our prayers lack power is because we have neglected to thank God for blessings already received. If anyone were to constantly ask us for help and never say "Thank you" for the help given, we would soon get tired of helping one so ungrateful. Indeed, our respect for the one we were helping would stop us from encouraging such rank ingratitude. Doubtless our heavenly Father, out of wise regard for our highest welfare, often refuses to answer our prayers in order to bring us to a sense of our ingratitude. We must be taught to be thankful.

God is deeply grieved by the thanklessness and ingratitude of which so many of us are guilty. When Jesus healed the ten lepers and only one came back to give Him thanks, in wonderment and pain, He exclaimed, *"Were there not ten cleansed? But where are the nine?"* (Luke 17:17). How often He looks down on us in sadness at our forgetfulness of His repeated blessings and frequent answers to prayer.

Returning thanks for blessings already received increases our faith and enables us to approach God with new boldness and new assurance. Doubtless the reason so many have so little faith when they pray is because they take so little time to meditate on and thank God for blessings already received. As one meditates on the answers to prayers already granted, faith grows bolder and bolder. In the very depths of our souls, we come to feel that nothing is too hard for the Lord. As we reflect on the wondrous goodness of God on the one hand and on the little thanksgiving offered on the other hand, we may well humble ourselves before God and confess our sins.

The mighty men of prayer in the Bible, and those throughout the ages of the church's history, have been men who were devoted to offering thanksgiving and praise. David was a mighty man of prayer, and his psalms abound with thanksgiving and praise. The apostles were mighty men of prayer. We read that they *"were continually in the temple praising and blessing God"* (Luke 24:53). Paul was a mighty man of prayer. Often in his epistles, he burst out in specific thanksgiving to God for definite blessings and definite answers to prayers.

Jesus is our model in prayer as in everything else. In the study of His life, His manner of returning thanks at the simplest meal was so noticeable that two of His disciples recognized Him by this act after His resurrection. Thanksgiving is one of the inevitable results of being filled with the Holy Spirit. One who does not learn to *"give thanks in all circumstances"* (1 Thess. 5:18 NIV) cannot continue to pray in the Spirit. If we want to learn to pray with power, we would do well to let these two words sink deeply into our hearts: *"with thanksgiving."*

Chapter 9

Hindrances to Prayer

◆

We have very carefully studied the positive conditions of prevailing prayer, but there are some things that hinder prayer. God has made these obstacles very plain in His Word.

Selfish Prayers

The first hindrance to prayer is found in James 4:3: *"You ask and do not receive, because you ask amiss, that you may spend it on your pleasures."* A selfish purpose in prayer robs prayer of power. Many prayers are selfish. These may be prayers for things for which it is perfectly proper to ask, for things which it is the will of God to give, but the motive of the prayer is entirely wrong, so the prayer falls powerless to the ground. The true purpose in prayer is that God may be glorified in the answer. If we ask any petition merely to receive something to use for our pleasure or gratification, we *"ask amiss"* and should not expect to receive what we ask. This explains why many prayers remain unanswered.

For example, a woman is praying for the conversion of her husband. That certainly is a most proper thing to ask. But her motive in asking for the conversion of her husband is entirely improper; it is selfish. She desires that her husband may be converted because it would be so much more pleasant for her to have a husband who sympathized with her. Or it is so painful to think that her husband might die and be lost forever. For some such selfish reason as this, she desires to have her husband converted. The prayer is purely selfish. Why should a woman desire

313

the conversion of her husband? First and above all, that God may be glorified. It should be her desire because she cannot bear the thought that God the Father would be dishonored by her husband.

Many pray for a revival. That certainly is a prayer that is pleasing to God and in line with His will. But many prayers for revivals are purely selfish. Some churches desire revivals so that their membership may be increased or so that their church may have more power and influence in the community. Some churches want revival so that the church treasury may be filled or so that a good report may be made at the presbytery, conference, or association. For such low purposes as these, churches and ministers are often praying for a revival, and God does not answer the prayer.

We should pray for a revival because we cannot endure the dishonor of God caused by the worldliness of the church, the sins of unbelievers, and the proud unbelief of the day. We should pray for revival because God's Word is being made void. We should pray for revival so that God may be glorified by the outpouring of His Spirit on the church of Christ. For these reasons, first and above all, we should pray for revival.

Many prayers for filling by the Holy Spirit are selfish requests. It certainly is God's will to give the Holy Spirit to those who ask Him. He has told us so plainly in His Word. (See Luke 11:13.) But many prayers for filling by the Holy Spirit are hindered by the selfishness of the motive behind the prayer. Men and women pray for the Holy Spirit so that they may be happy, saved from the wretchedness of their lives, have power as Christian workers, or for some other self-centered reason. We should pray for the Holy Spirit in order that God may no longer be dishonored by the low level of our Christian lives and by our ineffective service. We should pray for the Holy Spirit so that God may be glorified in the new beauty that comes into our lives and the new power that comes into our service.

Sin Hinders Prayer

The second hindrance to prayer is seen in Isaiah 59:1–2:

314

Behold, the Lord's hand is not shortened, that it cannot save; nor His ear heavy, that it cannot hear. But your iniquities have separated you from your God; and your sins have hidden His face from you, so that He will not hear.

Sin hinders prayer. Perhaps a man prays and prays and receives no answer to his prayers. Perhaps he is tempted to think that it is not the will of God to answer, or he may think that the days when God answered prayer are over. This is what the Israelites seem to have thought. They thought that the Lord's hand was shortened, that it could not save, and that His ear could no longer hear.

"Not so," said Isaiah. "God's ear is just as open to hear as ever; His hand is just as mighty to save. But there is a hindrance. That hindrance is your own sins. Your iniquities have separated you and your God. Your sins have hid His face from you so that He will not hear."

It is the same today. A man is crying to God in vain, simply because of sin in his life. It may be some sin in the past that has been unconfessed and unjudged. It may be some sin in the present that is cherished. Very likely, it is not even looked on as sin. But the sin is there, hidden away somewhere in the heart or in the life, and God *"will not hear."*

Anyone who finds his prayers unanswered should not think that what he asks of God is not according to His will. Instead, he should go alone to God with the psalmist's prayer, *"Search me, O God, and know my heart; try me, and know my anxieties; and see if there is any wicked way in me"* (Ps. 139:23–24). He should wait before Him until He puts His finger on the thing that is displeasing in His sight. Then, this sin should be confessed and renounced.

I well remember a time in my life when I was praying for two definite things that I thought I must have, or God would be dishonored. But the answer did not come. I awoke in the middle of the night in great physical suffering and distress of soul. I cried to God for these things, reasoned with Him as to how necessary it was that I get them, and get them at once. Still no answer came. I asked God to show me if there was anything wrong in my own life. Something came to my mind that had often come

315

to it before—something definite, which I was unwilling to confess as sin. I said to God, "If this is wrong, I will give it up." Still no answer came. Though I had never admitted it, in my innermost heart, I knew it was wrong.

At last I said, "This is wrong. I have sinned. I will give it up." I found peace, and in a few moments, I was sleeping like a child. In the morning, the money that was needed so much for the honor of God's name came.

Sin is an awful thing. One of the most awful things about it is the way it hinders prayer. It severs the connection between us and the source of all grace, power, and blessing. Anyone who desires power in prayer must be merciless in dealing with his own sins. *"If I regard iniquity in my heart, the Lord will not hear"* (Ps. 66:18). As long as we hold on to sin or have any controversy with God, we cannot expect Him to heed our prayers. If there is anything that is constantly coming up in your moments of close communion with God, that is the thing that hinders prayer. Put it away.

Who Comes First?

The third hindrance to prayer is found in Ezekiel 14:3: *"Son of man, these men have set up their idols in their hearts, and put before them that which causes them to stumble into iniquity. Should I let Myself be inquired of at all by them?"* Idols in the heart cause God to refuse to listen to our prayers.

What is an idol? An idol is anything that takes the place of God, anything that is the ultimate object of our affections. God alone has the right to the supreme place in our hearts. Everything and everyone else must be subordinate to Him.

Suppose a man makes an idol of his wife. Not that a man can love his wife too much, but he can put her in the wrong place. He can put her before God. When a man regards his wife's pleasure before God's pleasure, when he gives her first place and God second place, his wife is an idol. God cannot hear his prayers.

Suppose a woman makes an idol of her children. Not that we can love our children too much. The more dearly we love Christ, the more dearly we love our children. But we can put our children in the wrong place; we can put them before God and their interests before God's interests. When we do this, our children become our idols.

Many make an idol of their reputations or careers. If these things come before God, God cannot hear the prayers of such people.

If we really desire power in prayer, we must answer the question: "Is God absolutely first?" Is He before our wives, before our children, before our reputations, before our careers, before our own lives? If not, prevailing prayer is impossible.

God often calls our attention to the fact that we have an idol by not answering our prayers. Thus, He leads us to inquire as to why our prayers are not answered. And so, we discover the idol, renounce it, and then God hears our prayers.

Give in order to Receive

The fourth hindrance to prayer is found in Proverbs 21:13: *"Whoever shuts his ears to the cry of the poor will also cry himself and not be heard."* There is perhaps no greater hindrance to prayer than stinginess, the lack of generosity toward the poor and toward God's work. It is the one who gives generously to others who receives generously from God:

> *Give, and it will be given to you: good measure, pressed down, shaken together, and running over will be put into your bosom. For with the same measure that you use, it will be measured back to you.* (Luke 6:38)

The generous man is the mighty man of prayer. The stingy man is the powerless man of prayer.

One of the most wonderful statements about prevailing prayer is made in direct connection with generosity toward the needy: *"And whatever we ask we receive from Him, because we keep His commandments and do those things that are pleasing in His sight"* (1 John 3:22). We are told in the context of the verse that when we love, not *"in word or in tongue, but in deed and in truth"* (v. 18), when we open our hearts toward the *"brother in need"* (v. 17), that God hears us. It is only then that we have confidence toward God in prayer.

317

Many men and women are seeking to find the secret of their powerlessness in prayer. They need not seek far. It is nothing more nor less than downright stinginess. George Müller was a mighty man of prayer because he was a mighty giver. What he received from God never stuck to his fingers. He immediately passed it on to others. He was constantly receiving because he was constantly giving. When one thinks of the selfishness of the professing church today, it is no wonder that the church has so little power in prayer. If we want to receive from God, we must give to others. Perhaps the most wonderful promise in the Bible in regard to God's supplying our needs is Philippians 4:19, *"And my God shall supply all your need according to His riches in glory by Christ Jesus."* This glorious promise was made to the Philippian church and made in immediate connection with their generosity.

An Unforgiving Spirit

The fifth hindrance to prayer is found in Mark 11:25: *"And whenever you stand praying, if you have anything against anyone, forgive him, that your Father in heaven may also forgive you your trespasses."*

An unforgiving spirit is one of the most common hindrances to prayer. Prayer is answered on the basis that our sins are forgiven. However, God cannot deal with us on the basis of forgiveness while we are harboring ill will against those who have wronged us. Anyone who is nursing a grudge against another has closed the ear of God against his own petition. How many are crying to God for the conversion of their husband, children, or friends and are wondering why it is that their prayers are not answered. The whole secret to their dilemma is some grudge that they have in their hearts against someone who has injured them. Many mothers and fathers allow their children to go through to eternity unsaved for the miserable gratification of hating somebody.

Husband and Wife Relationship

The sixth hindrance to prayer is found in 1 Peter 3:7:

Husbands, likewise, dwell with [your wives] with under-standing, giving honor to the wife, as to the weaker vessel, and as being heirs together of the grace of life, that your prayers may not be hindered.

Here we are plainly told that a wrong relationship between husband and wife is a hindrance to prayer.

In many cases, the prayers of husbands are hindered because of their failure in duty toward their wives. On the other hand, without a doubt, it is true that the prayers of wives are hindered because of their failure in duty toward their husbands. If husbands and wives diligently seek to find the cause of their unanswered prayers, they will often find it in their relationship to one another.

Many men make great claims of holiness and are very active in Christian work but show little consideration in the treatment of their wives. It is often unkind, if not brutal. Then they wonder why their prayers are not answered. The verse that we have just read explains the seeming mystery. On the other hand, many women are very devoted to the church and very faithful in attendance, yet they treat their husbands with the most unpardonable neglect. They are cross and peevish toward them and wound them by the sharpness of their speech and unruly temper. Then they wonder why they have no power in prayer.

Other things in the relationship between husbands and wives cannot be spoken of publicly but are often hindrances in approaching God in prayer. There is much sin covered up under the holy name of marriage. This sin is a cause of spiritual deadness and of powerlessness in prayer. Men or women whose prayers seem to bring no answer should spread their whole married life out before God. They should ask Him to put His finger on anything that is displeasing in His sight.

Believe His Word Absolutely

The seventh hindrance to prayer is found in James 1:5–7:

If any of you lacks wisdom, let him ask of God, who gives to all liberally and without reproach, and it will be given to him. But let him ask in faith, with no doubting, for he who doubts is like a wave of the sea driven and tossed by the wind. For let not that man suppose that he will receive anything from the Lord.

Prayers are hindered by unbelief. God demands that we believe His Word absolutely. To question it is to make Him a liar. (See 1 John 5:10.) Many of us do that when we plead His promises. Is it any wonder that our prayers are not answered? How many prayers are hindered by our wretched unbelief? We go to God and ask Him for something that is positively promised in His Word, and then we only half expect to get it. *"Let not that man suppose that he will receive anything from the Lord."*

Chapter 10

When to Pray

◆────────────────◆

If we want to know the fullness of blessing in our prayer lives, it is important not only to pray in the right way but also at the right time. Christ's own example is full of suggestions as to the right time for prayer. In the first chapter of Mark, we read: *"Now in the morning, having risen a long while before daylight, He went out and departed to a solitary place; and there He prayed"* (v. 35).

Prayer in the Morning

Jesus chose the early morning hour for prayer. Many of the mightiest men of God have followed the Lord's example in this. In the morning hour, the mind is fresh and at its very best. It is free from distraction. That absolute concentration that is essential to the most effective prayer is most easily possible in the early morning hours. Furthermore, when the early hours are spent in prayer, the whole day is sanctified. Power is then obtained for overcoming life's temptations and for performing its duties. More can be accomplished in prayer in the first hours of the day than at any other time. Every child of God who wants to make the most out of his life for Christ should set apart the first part of the day to meet with God in the study of His Word and in prayer. The first thing we do each day should be to get alone with God. We can then face the duties, the temptations, and the service of that day and receive strength from God for all. We should get victory before the hour of trial, temptation, or service comes. The secret place of prayer is the place to fight our battles and gain our victories.

Nights of Prayer

In Luke, we find further light regarding the right time to pray: *"Now it came to pass in those days that He went out to the mountain to pray, and continued all night in prayer to God"* (Luke 6:12). Here we see Jesus praying at night, spending the entire night in prayer. Of course, we have no reason to suppose that this was the constant practice of our Lord, nor do we even know how common this practice was. But there were certainly times when the whole night was given up to prayer. Here, too, we would do well to follow in the footsteps of the Master.

Of course, there is a way of setting apart nights for prayer in which there is no profit. It is pure legalism. But the abuse of this practice is no reason for neglecting it altogether. One should not say, "I am going to spend a whole night in prayer," thinking that there is any merit that will win God's favor in such an exercise. That is legalism. But we often do well to say, "I am going to set apart this night for meeting God and obtaining His blessing and power. If necessary, and if He so leads me, I will give the whole night to prayer." Often, we will have prayed things through long before the night has passed. Then we can retire and enjoy more refreshing and invigorating sleep than if we had not spent the time in prayer. At other times, God will keep us in communion with Himself way into the morning. When He does this in His infinite grace, these hours of night prayer are blessed indeed.

Nights of prayer to God are followed by days of power with men. In the night hours, the world is hushed in slumber. We can easily be alone with God and have undisturbed communion with Him. If we set apart the whole night for prayer, there will be no hurry. There will be time for our own hearts to become quiet before God. There will be time for the whole mind to be brought under the guidance of the Holy Spirit. There will be plenty of time to pray things through. A night of prayer should be put entirely under God's control. We should lay down no rules as to how long we will pray or what we will pray about. Be ready to wait on God for as short or as long a time as He may lead. Be ready to be led in one direction or another as He sees fit.

Prayer before and after a Crisis

Jesus Christ prayed before all the great crises in earthly life. He prayed before His entrance into His public ministry. (See Luke 3:21–22.) He prayed before choosing the twelve disciples. (See Luke 6:12–13.) He prayed during His public ministry. (See, for example, Mark 1:35–38.) He prayed before announcing to the Twelve His approaching death (see Luke 9:18, 21–22) and before the great consummation of His life on the cross. (See Luke 22:39–46.) He prepared for every important crisis by a lengthy season of prayer. We should do likewise. When any crisis of life is seen to be approaching, we should prepare for it by a season of very definite prayer to God. We should take plenty of time for this prayer.

Christ prayed not only before the great events and victories of His life, but also after its great achievements and important crises. When He had fed the five thousand with the five loaves and two fishes, the multitude desired to take Him and make Him king. Having sent them away, He went up into the mountain to pray and spent hours there alone with God. (See Matthew 14:23; John 6:15.) So He went on from victory to victory.

It is more common for most of us to pray before the great events of life than it is to pray after them. But the latter is as important as the former. If we prayed after the great achievements of life, we might go on to still greater accomplishments. As it is, we are often either exalted or exhausted by the things that we do in the name of the Lord, and so we advance no further. Often, a man, in answer to prayer, has been endued with power and has thus worked great things in the name of the Lord. When these great things were accomplished, instead of going alone with God and humbling himself before Him, giving God the glory, he has congratulated himself. He has become arrogant, and God has been obliged to lay him aside. The great things done were not followed by humility and thanks to God. Thus, pride entered, and the man was stripped of his power.

Never Too Busy

Jesus Christ gave special time to prayer when He was unusually busy. He would withdraw from the multitudes that thronged about Him and go into the wilderness to pray. For example, we read in Luke 5:15–16:

> *However, the report went around concerning Him all the more; and great multitudes came together to hear, and to be healed by Him of their infirmities. So He Himself often withdrew into the wilderness and prayed.*

Some men are so busy that they find no time for prayer. Apparently, the busier Christ's life was, the more He prayed. Sometimes He had no time to eat. (See Mark 3:20.) Sometimes He had no time for needed rest and sleep. (See Mark 6:31, 33, 46.) But He always took time to pray. The more the work increased, the more He prayed.

Many mighty followers of God have learned this secret from Christ. And when the work has increased more than usual, they have set an unusual amount of time apart for prayer. Other people of God, once mighty, have lost their power because they did not learn this secret. They allowed increasing work to crowd out prayer.

Years ago, it was my privilege, with other theological students, to ask questions of one of the most helpful Christian men of the day. I was led to ask, "Will you tell us something of your prayer life?"

The man was silent a moment, and then, turning his eyes earnestly upon me, replied: "Well, I must admit that I have been so swamped with work lately that I have not given the time I should to prayer."

Is it any wonder that man lost power? The great work he was doing was curtailed in a very marked degree. Let us never forget that the more work pressures us, the more time we must spend in prayer.

Pray at All Times

Jesus Christ prayed before the great temptations of His life. As He drew nearer and nearer to the cross and realized that the great final test of His life was imminent, Jesus went out into the Garden to pray. He came *"to a place called Gethsemane, and said to the disciples, 'Sit here while I go and pray over there'"* (Matt. 26:36). The victory of Calvary was won that night in the Garden of Gethsemane. The calm majesty with which He bore the awful onslaughts of Pilate's Judgment Hall and Calvary resulted from the struggle, agony, and victory of Gethsemane. While Jesus prayed, the disciples slept. He stood fast while they fell dishonorably.

Many temptations come on us suddenly and unannounced. All we can do is lift a cry to God for help then and there. But many temptations of life we can see ahead of time, and in such cases, the victory should be won before the temptation really reaches us.

In 1 Thessalonians 5:17, we read: *"Pray without ceasing,"* and in Ephesians 6:18: *"Praying always."* Our whole lives should be lives of prayer. We should walk in constant communion with God. There should be a constant looking upward to God. We should walk so habitually in His presence that even when we awake in the night, it would be the most natural thing for us to speak to Him in thanksgiving or petition.

Chapter 11

The Need for a General Revival

◆

If we are to pray correctly in such a time as this, many of our prayers should be for a general revival. If there was ever a need to cry to God in the words of the psalmist, *"Will You not revive us again, that Your people may rejoice in You?"* (Ps. 85:6), it is now. It is surely time for the Lord to work, for men have nullified His law. The voice of the Lord given in the written Word is made void both by the world and the church. This is not a time for discouragement: the man who believes in God and the Bible should never be discouraged. But it is a time for Jehovah Himself to step in and work. The intelligent Christian, the alert watchman on the walls of Zion, may well cry with the psalmist, *"It is time for You to act, O LORD, for they have regarded Your law as void"* (Ps. 119:126). The great need of the day is for a general revival. Let us consider first what a general revival is.

A revival is a time of quickening or impartation of life. As God alone can give life, a revival is a time when God visits His people. By the power of His Spirit, He imparts new life to them. Through them, He gives life to sinners *"dead in trespasses and sins"* (Eph. 2:1). We have spiritual enthusiasm contrived by the cunning methods and hypnotic influence of the professional evangelist. But these are not revivals and are not needed. They are the Devil's imitations of a revival. New life from God—that is a revival. A general revival is a time when this new life from God is not confined to scattered localities. It is general throughout Christendom and the earth.

The reason why a general revival is needed is that spiritual desolation and death affect everyone. They are not confined to any one country, though they may be more manifest in some countries than in others. They are found in mission fields as well as at home. We have had local revivals. The life-giving Spirit of God has breathed on this minister and that, this church and that, this community and that, but we sorely need a widespread, general revival.

Let us look at the results of a revival. These results are apparent in ministers of the church and in the unsaved.

Revival in Ministers

When ministers experience revival, they have a new love for souls. We ministers, as a rule, have an inadequate love for souls. We fall short of loving people as Jesus does or even Paul did. But when God visits His people, the hearts of ministers are heavily burdened for the unsaved. They go out in great longing for the salvation of their fellowmen. They forget their ambition to preach great sermons and to acquire fame; they simply long to see sinners brought to Christ.

Along with a renewed love for others, ministers receive a new love for and faith in God's Word. They cast away their doubts and criticisms of the Bible and start preaching it. They especially preach Christ crucified. Revivals make ministers who have become lax in their doctrines orthodox. A genuine, widespread revival is needed to set things right.

Revivals bring new liberty and power in preaching to ministers. It is no weeklong grind to prepare a sermon, and no nerve-consuming effort to preach it after it has been prepared. Preaching is a joy and refreshment. There is power in preaching during times of revival.

Revival in Christians

The results of a revival in Christians generally are as noticeable as its results on the ministry. In times of revival, Christians come out from the world and live separated lives. Christians who have been amused with the world and its pleasures give them up. These things are found to be incompatible with increasing life and light.

In times of revival, Christians receive a new spirit of prayer. Prayer meetings are no longer a duty but become the necessity of a hungry, persistent heart. Private prayer is followed with new zest. The voice of earnest prayer to God is heard day and night. People no longer ask, "Does God answer prayer?" They know He does, and they besiege the throne of grace day and night.

In times of revival, Christians go to work to find lost souls. They do not go to meetings simply to enjoy themselves and get blessed. They go to meetings to watch for souls and to bring them to Christ. They talk to people on the street and in their homes. The cross of Christ, heaven, and hell become the subjects of conversation. Politics, the weather, news, and the latest novels are forgotten.

In times of revival, Christians have new joy in Christ. Life is joy, and new life is new joy. Revival days are glad days, days of heaven on earth.

In times of revival, Christians receive a new love for the Word of God. They want to study it day and night. Revivals are bad for bars and theaters, but they are good for bookstores and Bible publishers.

Revival's Influence on the Unsaved

Revivals also have a decided influence on the unsaved world. First of all, they bring deep conviction of sin. Jesus said that when the Spirit comes, He convicts the world of sin (John 16:8). Revival is a coming of the Holy Spirit; therefore, there must be a new conviction of sin, and there always is. If you see something that people call a revival and there is no conviction of sin, you may know immediately that it is not a revival. A lack of Holy Spirit conviction is a sure sign that there is no revival.

Revivals also bring conversion and regeneration. When God refreshes His people, He always converts sinners as well. The first result of Pentecost was new life and power to the one hundred and twenty disciples in the Upper Room. The second result was three thousand conversions in a single day. It is always so. I am constantly reading of revivals where Christians were greatly encouraged but there were no conversions. I have my doubts about that kind of revival. If Christians are truly refreshed, they will influence the unsaved by prayer, testimony, and persuasion. And there will be conversions.

Why General Revival Is Needed

We know what a general revival is and what it does. Let us now face the question of why it is needed at the present time. I think that the mere description of what it is and what it does shows why it is sorely needed. Let us look at some specific conditions that exist today that demonstrate the need for revival. In showing these conditions, one is likely to be called a pessimist. If facing the facts is pessimistic, I am willing to be called a pessimist. If in order to be an optimist one must shut his eyes and call black white, error truth, sin righteousness, and death life, I do not want to be an optimist. But I am an optimist all the same. Pointing out the real conditions will lead to better conditions.

Look again at the ministry. Many of us who profess to be orthodox ministers are practically non-believers. That is plain speech, but it is also indisputable fact. There is no essential difference between the teachings of the liberal Tom Paine and the teachings of some of our theological professors. The latter are not so blunt and honest about it. They phrase their beliefs in more elegant and studied sentences, but they mean the same. Much of the so-called new learning and higher criticism is simply Tom Paine's infidelity sugarcoated. A German professor once read a statement of some positions, then asked if they fairly represented the scholarly criticism of the day. When it was agreed that they did, he startled his audience by saying: "I am reading from Tom Paine's *Age of Reason.*"

There is little new in the higher criticism. Some of our future ministers are being educated under immoral professors. Being immature when they enter college or the seminary, they naturally come out non-believers in many cases. Then they go forth to poison the church.

Even when our ministers are orthodox—as, thank God, so very many are—they are not always people of prayer. How many modern ministers know what it is to wrestle in prayer, to spend a good share of a night in prayer? I do not know how many, but I do know that many do not.

Some ministers have no love for souls. How many preach because they must preach? How many preach because they feel that men everywhere are perishing, and by preaching they hope to save some? How many follow up their preaching, as Paul did, by beseeching men everywhere to be reconciled to God?

Perhaps enough has been said about us ministers. But it is evident that a revival is needed for our sakes. If not, some of us will have to stand before God overwhelmed with confusion in an awful day of reckoning that is surely coming.

Look now at the doctrinal state of the church. It is bad enough. Many do not believe in the whole Bible. They think that the book of Genesis is a myth, Jonah is an allegory, and even the miracles of the Son of God are questioned. The doctrine of prayer is old-fashioned, and the work of the Holy Spirit is scorned. Conversion is unnecessary, and hell is no longer believed in. Look at the fads and errors that have sprung up out of this loss of faith. Christian Science, Unitarianism, Spiritualism, Universalism, Metaphysical Healing, etc., a perfect pandemonium of the doctrines of the Devil.

Look at the spiritual state of the church. Worldliness is rampant among church members. Many church members are just as eager as any to become rich. They use the methods of the world in their efforts to accumulate wealth. And they hold on to it just as tightly once they have gotten it.

Prayerlessness abounds among church members on every hand. Someone has said that Christians, on the average, do not spend more than five minutes a day in prayer. Neglect of the Word of God goes hand in hand with neglect of prayer to God. Many Christians spend twice as much time everyday engrossed in the daily papers as they do bathing in the cleansing Word of God. How many Christians average an hour a day in Bible study?

A lack of generosity goes along with neglect of prayer and the Word of God. Churches are rapidly increasing in wealth, but the treasuries of missionary societies are empty. Christians do not average a dollar a year for missions. It is simply appalling.

Then, there is the increasing disregard for the Lord's Day. It is fast becoming a day of worldly pleasures, instead of a day of holy service. The Sunday newspaper with its mundane rambling and scandals has replaced the Bible. Recreational activities have replaced Sunday school and church services. Christians mingle with the world in all forms of questionable amusements. The young man or young woman who does not believe in wearing immodest clothing, participating in wild parties, and attending the theater with its ever increasing appeal to lewdness is considered an old fogy.

How small a proportion of our membership has really entered into fellowship with Jesus Christ in His burden for souls! Enough has been said of the spiritual state of the church. Now look at the state of the world. Note how few conversions there are. Here and there a church has a large number of new members joining by confession of faith, but these churches are rare. Where there are such new members, in very few cases are the conversions deep, thorough, and satisfactory.

There is lack of conviction of sin. Seldom are men overwhelmed with a sense of their awful guilt in dishonoring the Son of God. Sin is regarded as a misfortune, infirmity, or even as good in the making. Seldom is it considered an enormous wrong against a holy God.

Unbelief is rampant. Many regard it as a mark of intellectual superiority to reject the Bible as well as faith in God and immortality. It is often the only mark of intellectual superiority many possess. Perhaps that is the reason they cling to it so dearly.

Hand in hand with this widespread atheism goes gross immorality, as has always been the case. Atheism and immorality are Siamese twins. They always exist and increase together. This prevailing immorality is found everywhere.

Look at the legalized adultery that we call divorce. Men marry one wife after another and are still admitted into good society, and women do likewise. Thousands of supposedly respectable men in America live with other men's wives. And there are thousands of supposedly respectable women living with other women's husbands.

This immorality is found in much modern theater. Many questionable characters of the stage rule the day. And the individuals who degrade themselves by appearing in such off-color plays are defended in the newspapers and welcomed by supposedly respectable people.

Much of our literature is rotten, but decent people will read bad books because they are popular. Art is often a mere covering for shameless indecency. Women are induced to cast modesty to the wind so that the artist may perfect his art and defile his morals.

Greed for money has become an obsession with the rich and poor. The multimillionaire will often sell his soul and trample the rights of his fellowmen in the hope of becoming a billionaire. The working man will often commit murder to increase the power of the union and keep up wages. Wars are waged and men shot down like dogs to improve commerce and to gain political prestige for unprincipled politicians who parade as statesmen.

The licentiousness of the day lifts its serpent head everywhere. You see it in the newspapers, on the billboards, in advertisements for cigars, shoes, bicycles, medicines, and everything else. You see it on the streets at night. You see it just outside the church door. You find it in the awful ghettos set apart for it in great cities. And it is crowding farther and farther up our business streets and into the residential portions of our cities. Alas! Every so often you find it, if you look closely, in supposedly respectable homes. Indeed it will be borne to your ears by the confessions of brokenhearted men and women. The moral condition of the world is disgusting, sickening, and appalling.

Pray for Revival

We need a revival—deep, widespread, and general—in the power of the Holy Spirit. It is either a general revival or the dissolution of the church, of the home, and of the state. A revival, new life from God, is the cure—the only cure. Revival will halt the awful tide of immorality and unbelief. Mere argument will not do it. But a wind from heaven, a new outpouring of the Holy Spirit, a true God-sent revival will. Atheism, higher criticism, Christian Science, Spiritualism, Universalism, all will go down before the outpouring of the Spirit of God. It was not discussion but the breath of God that banished non-believers of old to the limbo of forgetfulness. We need a new breath from God to send the current, radical non-Christians to keep those non-believers of old company. I believe that breath from God is coming.

The great need of today is a general revival. The need is clear. It allows no honest difference of opinion. What then must we do? Pray. Take up the psalmist's prayer, *"Will You not revive us again, that Your people may rejoice in You?"* (Ps. 85:6). Pray Ezekiel's prayer, *"Come from the four winds, O breath* [breath of God], *and breathe on these slain, that they may live"* (Ezek. 37:9). Hark, I hear a noise! Behold a shaking! I can almost feel the breeze on my cheek. I can almost see the great living army rising to their feet. Will we not pray and pray and pray until the Spirit comes, and God revives His people?

Chapter 12

Prayer before and during Revivals

◆

No treatment of the subject "How to Pray" would be at all complete if it did not consider the place of prayer in revivals. The first great revival of Christian history had its origin on the human side in a ten-day prayer meeting. We read of that handful of disciples: *"These all continued with one accord in prayer and supplication"* (Acts 1:14). The result of that prayer meeting is in the second chapter of the Acts of the Apostles: *"They were all filled with the Holy Spirit and began to speak with other tongues, as the Spirit gave them utterance"* (v. 4). Further in the chapter, we read that on *"that day about three thousand souls were added to them"* (v. 41). This revival proved genuine and permanent. The converts *"continued steadfastly in the apostles' doctrine and fellowship, in the breaking of bread, and in prayers"* (v. 42). *"And the Lord added to the church daily those who were being saved"* (v. 47).

Testimonies of Answered Prayer

Every true revival from that day to this has had its earthly origin in prayer. The great revival under Jonathan Edwards in the eighteenth century began with his famous call to prayer. The marvelous work of grace among the Indians under Brainerd began in the days and nights that he spent before God in prayer for an anointing of *"power from on high"* (Luke 24:49) for this work.

A most remarkable and widespread display of God's reviving power was the revival in Rochester, New York, in 1830, under the labors of Charles G. Finney. It spread not only throughout the state, but ultimately to Great Britain as well.

Mr. Finney himself attributed the power of this work to the spirit of prayer that prevailed. He described it in his autobiography in the following words:

When I was on my way to Rochester, as we passed through a village, some thirty miles east of Rochester, a brother minister whom I knew, seeing me on the canal-boat, jumped aboard to have a little conversation with me, intending to ride but a little way and return. He, however, became interested in conversation, and upon finding where I was going, he made up his mind to keep on and go with me to Rochester. We had been there but a few days when this minister became so convicted that he could not help weeping aloud at one time as we passed along the street. The Lord gave him a powerful spirit of prayer, and his heart was broken. As he and I prayed together, I was struck with his faith in regard to what the Lord was going to do there. I recollect he would say, "Lord, I do not know how it is; but I seem to know that Thou art going to do a great work in this city." The spirit of prayer was poured out powerfully, so much so that some people stayed away from the public services to pray, being unable to restrain their feelings under preaching.

And here I must introduce the name of a man, whom I shall have occasion to mention frequently, Mr. Abel Clary. He was the son of a very excellent man, and an elder of the church where I was converted. He was converted in the same revival in which I was. He had been licensed to preach; but his spirit of prayer was such, he was so burdened with the souls of men, that he was not able to preach much, his whole time and strength being given to prayer. The burden of his soul would frequently be so great that he was unable to stand, and he would writhe and groan in agony. I was well acquainted with him, and knew something of the wonderful spirit of prayer that was upon him. He was a very silent man, as almost all are who have that powerful spirit of prayer.

The first I knew of his being in Rochester, a gentleman who lived about a mile west of the city called on me one day and asked me if I knew a Mr. Abel Clary, a minister. I told him that I knew him well.

"Well," he said, "he is at my house, and has been there for some time. I don't know what to think of him."

I said, "I have not seen him at any of our meetings."

"No," he replied, "he cannot go to meetings, he says. He prays nearly all the time, day and night, and in such agony of mind that I do not know what to make of it. Sometimes he cannot even stand on his knees, but will lie prostrate on the floor, and groan and pray in a manner that quite astonishes me."

I said to the brother, "I understand it: please keep still. It will come out right; he will surely prevail."

I knew at the time a considerable number of men who were exercised in the same way....This Mr. Clary and many others among the men, and a large number of women, partook of the same spirit, and spent a great part of their time in prayer. Father Nash, as we called him who in several of my fields of labor came to me and aided me, was another of those men that had such a powerful spirit of prevailing prayer. This Mr. Clary continued in Rochester as long as I did, and did not leave it until after I had left. He never, that I could learn, appeared in public, but gave himself wholly to prayer.

I think it was the second Sabbath that I was at Auburn at this time, I observed in the congregation the solemn face of Mr. Clary. He looked as if he was borne down with an agony of prayer. Being well acquainted with him, and knowing the great gift of God that was upon him, the spirit of prayer, I was very glad to see him there. He sat in the pew with his brother, a doctor, who was also a professor of religion, but who had nothing by experience, I should think, of his brother Abel's great power with God.

At intermission, as soon as I came down from the pulpit, Mr. Clary and his brother met me at the pulpit stairs and invited me to go home with them and spend the intermission and get some refreshments. I did so.

After arriving at his house we were soon summoned to the dinner table. We gathered about the table, and Dr. Clary turned to his brother and said, "Brother Abel, will you ask the blessing?" Brother Abel bowed his head and began, audibly, to ask a blessing. He had uttered but a sentence or two when he broke instantly down, moved suddenly back from the table, and fled to his chamber. The doctor supposed he had been taken suddenly ill, and rose up and followed him. In a few moments he came down and said, "Mr. Finney, Brother Abel wants to see you."

Said I, "What ails him?"

Said he, "I do not know but he says you know. He appears in great distress, but I think it is the state of his mind."

I understood it in a moment, and went to his room. He lay groaning upon the bed, the Spirit making intercession for him, and in him, with groanings that could not be uttered. I had barely entered the room, when he made out to say, "Pray, Brother Finney." I knelt down and helped him in prayer, by leading his soul out for the conversion of sinners. I continued to pray until his distress passed away, and then I returned to the dinner table.

I understood that this was the voice of God. I saw the Spirit of prayer was upon him, and I felt His influence upon myself, and took it for granted that the work would move on powerfully. It did so. The pastor told me afterward that he found that in the six weeks that I was there, five hundred souls had been converted.

Persistent Prayer Results

Mr. Finney in his lectures on revivals told of other remarkable awakenings in answer to the prayers of God's people. He said:

A clergyman...told me of a revival among his people, which commenced with a zealous and devoted woman in the church. She became anxious about sinners, and went to praying for them; she prayed, and her distress increased; and she finally came to her minister, and talked with him, and asked him to appoint an anxious meeting, for she felt that one was needed. The minister put her off, for he felt nothing of it. The next week she came again, and besought him to appoint an anxious meeting; she knew there would be somebody to come, for she felt as if

God was going to pour out His Spirit. He put her off again. And finally she said to him, "If you do not appoint an anxious meeting I shall die, for there is certainly going to be a revival." The next Sabbath he appointed a meeting, and said that if there were any who wished to converse with him about the salvation of their souls, he would meet them on such an evening. He did not know of one, but when he went to the place, to his astonishment he found a large number of anxious inquirers.

In still another place, Finney said:

The first ray of light that broke in upon the midnight which rested on the churches in Oneida county, in the fall of 1825, was from a woman in feeble health, who I believe had never been in a powerful revival. Her soul was exercised about sinners. She was in agony for the land. She did not know what ailed her, but she kept praying more and more, till it seemed as if her agony would destroy her body. At length she became full of joy and exclaimed, "God has come! God has come! There is no mistake about it, the work is begun, and is going over all the region!" And sure enough, the work began, and her family was almost all converted, and the work spread all over that part of the country.

The great revival of 1857 in the United States began in prayer and was carried on by prayer more than by anything else. Dr. Cuyler in an article in a religious newspaper some years ago said:

Most revivals have humble beginnings, and the fire starts in a few warm hearts. Never despise the day of small things. During all my own long ministry, nearly every work of grace has had a similar beginning. One commenced in a meeting gathered at a few hours' notice in a private house. Another commenced in a group gathered for Bible study by Mr. Moody in our mission chapel. Still another—the most powerful of all—was kindled on a bitter January evening at a meeting of young Christians under my roof. That profound Christian, Dr. Thomas H.

Skinner of the Union Theological Seminary, once gave me an account of a remarkable coming together of three earnest men in his study when he was the pastor of the Arch Street church in Philadelphia. They wrestled in prayer. They made a clean breast in confession of sin, and humbled themselves before God. One and another church officer came in and joined them. The heaven-kindled flame soon spread through the whole congregation in one of the most powerful revivals ever known in that city.

Prayer Knows No Boundaries

In the early part of the sixteenth century, there was a great religious awakening in Ulster, Ireland. The lands of the rebel chiefs, which had been forfeited to the British crown, were settled by a class of colonists who were governed by a spirit of wild adventure. Authentic righteousness was rare. Seven ministers, five from Scotland and two from England, settled in that country, the earliest arrivals being in 1613. A contemporary of one of these ministers named Blair recorded: "He spent many days and nights in prayer, alone and with others, and was vouchsafed great intimacy with God." Mr. James Glendenning, a man of very meager natural gifts, was a man similarly minded in regard to prayer. The work began under this man Glendenning. The historian of the time said:

> He was a man who never would have been chosen by a wise assembly of ministers, nor sent to begin a reformation in this land. Yet this was the Lord's choice to begin with him the admirable work of God which I mention on purpose that all may see how the glory is only the Lord's in making a holy nation in this profane land, and that it was *"not by might, nor by power, but by my spirit, saith the LORD of hosts"* (Zech. 4:6 KJV).

In his preaching at Oldstone, multitudes of hearers felt great anxiety and terror of conscience. They looked on themselves as altogether lost and damned and cried out, "Men and women, what will we do to be saved?" They were stricken and became faint by the power of His Word. In one day, a dozen were carried out of doors as dead. These were not cowards, but some of the boldest spirits of the neighborhood, "some who had formerly feared not with their swords to put a whole market town into a fray." Concerning one of them, the historian wrote, "I have heard one of them, then a mighty strong man, now a mighty Christian, say that his end in coming into church was to consult with his companions how to work some mischief."

This work spread throughout the whole country of Ireland. By the year 1626, a monthly concert of prayer was held in Antrim. The work spread beyond the bounds of Down and Antrim to the churches of the neighboring counties. The spiritual interest became so great that Christians would come thirty or forty miles to the communions. They would continue from the time they came until they returned without wearying or making use of sleep. Many of them neither ate not drank, and yet some of them professed that they "went away most fresh and vigorous, their souls so filled with the sense of God." This revival changed the whole character of northern Ireland.

Another great awakening in Ireland in 1859 had a somewhat similar origin. By many who were unaware, it was thought that this marvelous work came without warning and preparation. But Rev. William Gibson, moderator of the General Assembly of the Presbyterian church in Ireland in 1860, in his history of the awakening, told how there had been two years of preparation. There had been constant discussion in the General Assembly of the low state of spiritual fervor and the need of a revival. There had been special sessions for prayer. Finally, four young men, who became leaders in the origin of the great work, began to meet together in an old schoolhouse. Around the spring of 1858, a work of power began to manifest itself. It spread from town to town, from county to county. The congregations became too large for the buildings, and the meetings were held outside. They were often attended by many thousands of people. Many hundreds of people were frequently convicted of sin in a single meeting. In some places, the criminal courts and jails were closed for lack of occupation. There were manifestations of the Holy Spirit's power of a most remarkable character. This clearly proves that the Holy Spirit is as ready to work today as in apostolic days. He will do so when ministers and

Christians really believe in Him and begin to prepare the way by prayer.

Mr. Moody's wonderful work in England, Scotland, and Ireland, then afterwards in America, originated in prayer. Moody made little impression until men and women began to cry to God. Indeed, his going to England at all was in answer to the persistent cries to God by a bedridden saint. While the spirit of prayer continued, the revival grew in strength. But in the course of time, less and less was made of prayer, and the work fell off in power. One of the great secrets of the superficiality and unreality of many of our modern, so-called revivals is that more dependence is put on man's machinery than on God's power. His power must be sought and obtained by earnest, persistent, believing prayer. We live in a day characterized by the multiplication of man's machinery and the decrease of God's power. The great cry of our day is work, new organizations, new methods, and new machinery. The great need of our day is prayer.

Church—Wake Up!

It was a masterstroke of Satan when he got the church to so generally lay aside this mighty weapon of prayer. Satan is perfectly willing that the church multiply its organizations and contrive machinery for the conquest of the world for Christ if it will only give up praying. He laughs as he looks at the church today and says to himself, "You can have your Sunday schools and your Young People's Societies. Enjoy your Young Men's and Women's Christian Associations. Continue your institutional churches, your industrial schools, and your Boys' Brigades. Worship with your grand choirs, your fine organs, your brilliant preachers, and your revival efforts, too. But don't bring the power of almighty God into them by earnest, persistent, believing, mighty prayer." Prayer could work as marvelously today as it ever could, if the church would only take up the call.

There seem to be increasing signs that the church is awaking to this fact. God is laying a burden of prayer on individual ministers and churches like they have never known before. Less dependence is being placed on human instrumentality and more on God. Ministers are crying to God day and night for power. Churches and groups are meeting together in the early morning and the late night hours crying to God for the *"latter rain"* (Deut. 11:14). There is every indication of the coming of a mighty, widespread revival. There is every reason why, if a revival should come in any country at this time, it should be more widespread in its extent than any revival of history. There is the closest and swiftest communication among all parts of the world. A true fire of God kindled in America would soon spread to the uttermost parts of the earth. The only thing needed to bring this fire is prayer.

It is not necessary that the whole church begins praying at first. Great revivals always begin in the hearts of a few men and women whom God arouses by His Spirit to believe in Him as a living God. They believe He is a God who answers prayer. He lays a burden on their hearts from which no rest can be found except in persistent crying to God.

May God use this book to arouse many others to pray so that the greatly needed revival will come, and come quickly. Let us pray!

How to Study the Bible

CONTENTS

Introduction

The Bible contains golden nuggets of truth, and anyone willing to dig for biblical truth is certain to find it.

Those reading this book for the first time must not become frightened at the elaborate methods I will suggest. They are not difficult. Their fruitfulness has been tested with those who have varying degrees of education, and the results have been found to be practical. As you use the methods I will recommend, you will soon find your ability to study the Bible rapidly increasing, until you will accomplish more in fifteen minutes than you once could in an hour.

Although the Bible is read much, comparatively, it is studied little. The methods you will learn are the same methods being used in highly technical fields, such as science and medicine. First, you will make a careful analysis of the facts. Then, you will learn how to classify those facts. While we cannot all be students of technology, we can all be profound students of Scripture. No other book than the Bible offers the opportunity for intellectual development by its study. People who have studied few books besides the Scriptures have astonished and amazed scholars and theologians.

The truths you will find as you study Scripture will far transcend any other study in inspiration, helpfulness, and practical value. They will, in fact, become life-changing.

Chapter 1

Conditions for Profitable Bible Study

◆

While you will be learning profitable methods for Bible study, there is something more important than the best procedures. The secret lies in meeting certain fundamental conditions before you begin to study God's Word. If you meet these conditions, you will get more out of the Bible, even while pursuing the poorest methods, than the one who does not meet them while he pursues the best methods. What you will need is far deeper than a new and better technique.

Obtaining Spiritual Understanding

The most essential of these conditions is that *"you must be born again"* (John 3:7). The Bible is a spiritual book. It combines spiritual concepts with spiritual words. Only a spiritual man can understand its deepest and most precious teachings. *"The natural man does not receive the things of the Spirit of God, for they are foolishness to him; nor can he know them, because they are spiritually discerned"* (1 Cor. 2:14).

Spiritual discernment can be obtained in only one way: by being born again—*"Unless one is born again, he cannot see the kingdom of God"* (John 3:3). No mere knowledge of the human languages in which the Bible was written, however extensive and accurate it may be, will qualify one to understand and appreciate the Bible. One must comprehend the divine language in which it was written as well as the language of the Holy Spirit.

A person who understands the language of the Holy Spirit but who does not understand a word of Greek, Hebrew, or Aramaic will get more out of the Bible than one who knows all about ancient languages but is not born again. Many ordinary men and women who possess no knowledge of the original languages in which the Bible was written have a knowledge of the real contents of the Bible. Their understanding of its actual teaching and its depth, fullness, and beauty far surpasses that of many learned professors in theological seminaries.

One of the greatest follies today is to allow an unregenerate person to teach the Bible. It would be just as unreasonable to allow someone to teach art because he had an accurate, technical knowledge of paints. An aesthetic sense is required to make a person a competent art teacher. Likewise, it requires spiritual sense to make a person a competent Bible teacher.

One who has aesthetic discernment but little or no technical knowledge of paint would be a far more competent critic of works of art than one who has extensive technical knowledge of paint but no aesthetic discernment. Similarly, the person who has no technical knowledge of biblical languages but who has spiritual discernment is a far more competent critic of the Bible than the one who has a rare knowledge of Greek and Hebrew but no spiritual discernment.

It is unfortunate that more emphasis is often placed on a knowledge of Greek and Hebrew in training for the ministry than is placed on the spiritual life and its consequent spiritual discernment. Unregenerate people should not be forbidden to study the Bible because the Word of God is the instrument the Holy Spirit uses in the new birth. (See 1 Peter 1:23; James 1:18.) But it should be distinctly understood that while there are teachings in the Bible that the natural man can understand, its most distinctive, characteristic teachings are beyond his grasp. Its highest beauties belong to a world in which he has no vision.

The first fundamental condition for profitable Bible study, then, is *"You must be born again"* (John 3:7). You cannot study the Bible to the greatest profit if you have not been born again. Its best treasures are sealed to you.

Gaining a Spiritual Appetite

The second condition for profitable study is to have a love for the Bible. A person who eats with an appetite will get far more good out of his meal than one who eats from a sense of duty. A student of the Bible should be able to say with Job, *"I have treasured the words of His mouth more than my necessary food"* (Job 23:12), or with Jeremiah, *"Your words were found, and I ate them, and Your word was to me the joy and rejoicing of my heart; for I am called by Your name, O LORD God of hosts"* (Jer. 15:16).

Many come to the table God has spread in His Word with no appetite for spiritual food. Instead of getting their fill of the feast God has prepared, they grumble about everything. Spiritual indigestion results from much of the modern criticism of the Bible.

But how can one acquire a love for the Bible? First of all, by being born again. Where there is life, there is likely to be appetite. A dead man never hungers. But going beyond this, the more there is of vitality, the more there is of hunger. Abounding life means abounding hunger for the Word.

Study of the Word stimulates love for the Word. I remember when I had more appetite for books about the Bible than I had for the Bible itself; but with increasing study, there has come increasing love for the Book. Bearing in mind who the Author of the Book is, what its purpose is, what its power is, and what the riches of its contents are will go far toward stimulating a love and appetite for the Book.

Digging for Treasures

The third condition is a willingness to work hard. Solomon gave a graphic picture of the Bible student who receives the most profit from his study:

> *My son, if you receive my words, and treasure my commands within you, so that you incline your ear to wisdom, and apply your heart to understanding; yes, if you cry out for discernment, and lift up your voice for understanding, if you seek her as silver and search for her as for hidden treasures; then you will understand the fear of the LORD, and find the knowledge of God.* (Prov. 2:1–5)

Seeking for silver and searching for hidden treasure mean hard work, and the one who wishes to get not only the silver but also the gold out of the Bible must make up his mind to dig. It is not glancing at the Word but studying the Word, meditating on the Word, and pondering the Word that will bring the richest yield.

The reason many people get so little out of their Bible reading is simply that they are not willing to think. Intellectual laziness lies at the heart of a large percent of fruitless Bible reading. People are constantly crying for new methods of Bible study, but what many of them want is simply some method of Bible study where they can get the most without much work.

If someone could tell lazy Christians some method of Bible study whereby they could use the sleepiest ten minutes of the day, just before they go to bed, for Bible study and get the most profit that God intends, that would be what they desire. But it can't be done. We must be willing to work and work hard if we wish to dig out the treasures of infinite wisdom, knowledge, and blessing that He has stored up in His Word.

A business friend once asked me in a hurried call to tell him "in a word" how to study his Bible. I replied, "Think." The psalmist pronounced that the man who *"meditates day and night" "in the law of the LORD"* is *"blessed."* (See Psalm 1:1–2.) The Lord commanded Joshua to *"meditate in it day and night"* and assured him that as a result of this meditation, *"you will make your way prosperous, and then you will have good success"* (Josh. 1:8). In this way alone can one study the Bible to the greatest profit.

One pound of beef well-chewed, digested, and assimilated will give more strength than tons of beef merely glanced at; and one verse of Scripture chewed, digested, and assimilated will give more strength than whole chapters simply skimmed. Weigh every word you read in the Bible. Look at it. Turn it over and over. The most familiar passages take on new meaning in this way. Spend fifteen minutes on each word in Psalm 23:1 or Philippians 4:19, and see if it is not so.

Finding the Treasure's Keys

The fourth condition is a will wholly surrendered to God: *"If anyone wants to do His will, he shall know concerning the doctrine"* (John 7:17). A surrendered will gives that clearness of spiritual vision necessary to understand God's Book. Many of the difficulties and obscurities of the Bible arise simply because the will of the student is not surrendered to the will of the Author of the Book.

It is remarkable how clear, simple, and beautiful passages that once puzzled us become when we are brought to that place where we say to God, "I surrender my will unconditionally to Yours. I have no will but Yours. Teach me Your will." A surrendered will does more than a university education to make the Bible an open book. It is simply impossible to get the most profit out of your Bible study until you surrender your will to God. You must be very definite about this.

Many will say, "Oh, yes, my will is surrendered to God," but it is not. They have never gone alone with God and said intelligently and definitely to Him, "O God, I here and now give myself to You, for You to command me, lead me, shape me, send me, and do with me absolutely as You will." Such an act is a wonderful key to unlock the treasure-house of God's Word. The Bible becomes a new Book when a person surrenders to God. Doing this brought a complete transformation in my own theology, life, and ministry.

Use It or Lose It

The fifth condition is very closely related to the fourth. The student of the Bible who desires to receive the greatest profit out of his studies must be obedient to its teachings as soon as he sees them. It was good advice James gave to early Christians and to us: *"Be doers of the word, and not hearers only, deceiving yourselves"* (James 1:22).

Many who consider themselves Bible students are deceiving themselves in this way today. They see what the Bible teaches, but they do not do it; soon, they lose their power to see it. Truth obeyed leads to more truth. Truth disobeyed destroys the capacity for discovering truth.

There must be not only a general surrender of the will but also a specific, practical obedience to each new word of God discovered. In no place is the law more joyously certain on the one hand and more sternly inexorable on the other than in the matter of using or refusing the truth revealed in the Bible: *"To everyone who has, more will be given, and he will have abundance; but from him who does not have, even what he has will be taken away"* (Matt. 25:29). Use and you get more; refuse and you lose all.

Do not study the Bible for the mere gratification of intellectual curiosity but to find out how to live and how to please God. Whatever duty you find commanded in the Bible, do it at once. Whatever good you see in any Bible character, imitate it immediately. Whatever mistake you note in the actions of Bible men and women, scrutinize your own life to see if you are making the same mistake; if you find you are, correct it immediately.

James compared the Bible to a mirror. (See James 1:23–24.) The chief purpose of a mirror is to show you if anything is out of place about you. If you find there is, you can set it right. Use the Bible in that way.

You already see that obeying the truth will solve the enigmas in the verses you do not yet understand. Disobeying the truth darkens the whole world of truth. This is the secret of much of the skepticism and error of the day. People saw the truth but did not do it, and now it is gone.

I once knew a bright and promising young minister who made rapid advancement in the truth. One day, however, he said to his wife, "It's nice to believe this truth, but we do not need to speak so much about it." He began to hide his testimony. Not long after this, his wife died, and he began to drift. The Bible became a sealed book to him. His faith reeled, and he publicly renounced his belief in the fundamental truths of the Bible. He seemed to lose his grip even on the doctrine of immortality. What was the cause of it all? Truth flees when it is not lived and stood for. That man was admired by many and applauded by some, but light gave place to darkness in his soul.

Come as a Child

The sixth condition is a childlike mind. God reveals His deepest truths to babes. No time more than our own needs to take to heart the words of Jesus: *"I thank You, Father, Lord of heaven and earth, that You have hidden these things from the wise and prudent and have revealed them to babes"* (Matt. 11:25).

How can we be babes if God is to reveal His truth to us, and we are to understand His Word? By having a childlike spirit. A child is not full of his own wisdom. He recognizes his ignorance and is ready to be taught. He does not oppose his own notions and ideas to those of his teachers.

It is in this spirit that we should come to the Bible if we are to get the most profit out of our study. Do not come to the Bible seeking confirmation for your own ideas. Come rather to find out what God's ideas are as He has revealed them. Do not come to find confirmation for your own opinions but to be taught what God may be pleased to teach. If a person comes to the Bible just to find his own ideas taught there, he will find them. But if he comes, recognizing his own ignorance just as a little child seeks to be taught, he will find something infinitely better than his own ideas; he will find the mind of God.

Thus, we see why many people cannot see things that are plainly taught in the Bible. They are so full of their own ideas that there is no room left for what the Bible actually teaches.

An illustration of this is given in the lives of the apostles at one stage in their training. In Mark 9:31, we read: *"For He taught His disciples and said to them, 'The Son of Man is being betrayed into the hands of men, and they will kill Him. And after He is killed, He will rise the third day.'"* Now this is as plain and definite as language can make it, but it was utterly contrary to the apostles' ideas of what would happen to Christ.

We read in the next verse: *"They did not understand this saying"* (v. 32). Is this any different than our own inability to comprehend plain statements in the Bible when they run counter to our preconceived notions?

You must come to Christ like a child to be taught what to believe and do, rather than coming as a full-grown person who already knows it all and must find some interpretations of Christ's words that will fit into his mature and infallible philosophy. Many people are so full of unbiblical theology that it takes a lifetime to get rid of it and understand the clear teaching of the Bible. "Oh, what can this verse mean?" many bewildered

355

individuals cry. It means what it clearly says. But these people are not after the meaning God has clearly put into it, but the meaning they can, by some ingenious tricks of explanation, twist to make fit into their own interpretations.

Don't come to the Bible to find out what you can make it mean but to find out what God intended it to mean. People often miss the real truth of a verse by saying, "But that can be interpreted this way." Oh, yes, so it can, but is that the way God intended it to be interpreted?

We all need to pray, "O, God, make me like a little child. Empty me of my own notions. Teach me Your own mind. Make me ready to receive all that You have to say, no matter how contrary it is to what I have thought before." How the Bible opens up to one who approaches it in this way! How it closes to the fool who thinks he knows everything and imagines he can give points to Peter, Paul, and even to God Himself!

I was once talking with a ministerial friend about what seemed to be the clear teaching of a certain passage. "Yes," he replied, "but that doesn't agree with my philosophy." This man was sincere, yet he did not have the childlike spirit essential for productive Bible study. We have reached an important point in Bible study when we realize that an infinite God knows more than we, that our highest wisdom is less than the knowledge of the most ignorant babe compared with His, and that we must come to Him to be taught as children.

We are not to argue with Him. But we so easily and so constantly forget this point that every time we open our Bibles, we should bow humbly before God and say, "Father, I am but a child; please teach me."

Believing God's Word

The seventh condition of studying the Bible for the greatest profit is that we study it as the Word of God. The apostle Paul, in writing to the Thessalonians, thanked God *"without ceasing"* (1 Thess. 2:13) that when they received the Word of God, they *"welcomed it not as the word of men, but as it is in truth, the word of God"* (v. 13). Paul thanked God for that, and so may we thank God when we get to the place where we receive the Word of God as *the* Word of God.

He who does not believe the Bible is the Word of God should be encouraged to study it. Once I doubted that the Bible was the Word of God, but the firm confidence that I have today that the Bible is the Word of God has come more from the study of the Book itself than from anything else. Those who doubt it are more usually those who study about the Book rather than those who dig into the actual teachings of the Book.

Studying the Bible as the Word of God involves four things. First, it involves the unquestioning acceptance of its teachings when they are definitely understood, even when they may appear unreasonable or impossible. Reason demands that we submit our judgment to the statements of infinite wisdom. Nothing is more irrational than rationalism. It makes finite wisdom the test of infinite wisdom and submits the teachings of God's omniscience to the approval of man's judgment. Conceit says, "This cannot be true, even though God says it, for it does not approve itself to my reason." *"O man, who are you to reply against God?"* (Rom. 9:20).

Real human wisdom, when it finds infinite wisdom, bows before it and says, "Speak what You will and I will believe." When we have once become convinced that the Bible is God's Word, its teachings must be the end of all controversy and discussion. A "Thus says the Lord" will settle every question. Yet many who profess to believe that the Bible is the Word of God will shake their heads and say, "Yes, but I think so and so," or "Doctor ——— or Professor ——— or our church doesn't teach it that way." There is little advantage to that sort of study.

Second, studying the Bible as the Word of God involves absolute reliance on all its promises in all their length and breadth. The person who studies the Bible as the Word of God will not discount any one of its promises one iota. A student who studies the Bible as the Word of God will say, "God who cannot lie has promised," and he will not try to make God a liar by trying to make one of His promises mean less than it says. (See 1 John 5:10.) The one who studies the Bible as the Word of God will be on the lookout for promises. As soon as he finds one, he should seek to discover what it means and then place his entire trust on its full meaning.

This is one of the secrets of profitable Bible study. Hunt for promises and appropriate them as fast as you find them by meeting the conditions and risking all upon them. This is the way to make all the fullness of God's blessing your own. This is the key to all the treasures of God's grace. Happy is the one who has learned to study the Bible as God's Word and is ready to claim for himself every new promise as it appears and to risk everything on it.

Next, studying the Bible as the Word of God involves prompt obedience to its every precept. Obedience may seem hard and impossible; but God has commanded it, and you have nothing to do but to obey and leave the results with God. To get results from your Bible study, resolve that from this time on, you will claim every clear promise and obey every plain command. When the meaning of promises and commands is not yet clear, try to discern their meaning immediately.

Finally, studying the Bible as the Word of God involves studying it in God's presence. When you read a verse of Scripture, hear the voice of the living God speaking directly to you in these written words. There is new power and attractiveness in the Bible when you have learned to hear a living, present Person—God our Father—talking directly to you in these words.

One of the most fascinating and inspiring statements in the Bible is *"Enoch walked with God"* (Gen. 5:24). We can have God's glorious companionship any moment we please by simply opening His Word and letting the living, ever present God speak to us through it. With what holy awe and strange and unutterable joy one studies the Bible if he studies it in this way! It is heaven come down to earth.

The Key to Understanding

The last condition for profitable Bible study is prayerfulness. The psalmist prayed, *"Open my eyes, that I may see wondrous things from Your law"* (Ps. 119:18). Everyone who desires productive study needs to offer a similar prayer each time he undertakes to study the Word. A few keys open many treasure chests of prayer. A few clues unravel many difficulties. A few microscopes disclose many beauties hidden from the eye of the ordinary observer. What new light often shines from familiar texts as you bend over them in prayer!

I believe in studying the Bible many times on your knees. When you read an entire book through on your knees—and this is easily done—that book takes on a new meaning and becomes a new book. You should never open the Bible without at least lifting your heart to God in silent prayer that He will interpret it and illumine its pages by the light of His Spirit. It is a rare privilege to study any book under the immediate guidance and instruction of the author, and this is the privilege of us all in studying the Bible.

When you come to a passage that is difficult to understand or interpret, instead of giving up or rushing to some learned friend or some commentary, lay that passage before God and ask Him to explain it. Plead God's promise, *"If any of you lacks wisdom, let him ask of God, who gives to all liberally and without reproach, and it will be given to him. But let him ask in faith, with no doubting"* (James 1:5–6).

Harry Morehouse, one of the most remarkable Bible scholars among unlearned men, used to say that whenever he came to a passage in the Bible that he could not understand, he would search through the Bible for another passage that threw light on it and place it before God in prayer. He said he had never found a passage that did not yield to this treatment.

Some years ago, I took a tour of Switzerland with a friend, visiting some of the more famous caves. One day, the country letter carrier stopped us and asked if we would like to see a cave of rare beauty and interest away from the beaten tracks of travel. Of course, we said yes. He led us through the woods and underbrush to the mouth of the cave. As we entered, all was dark and eerie. He expounded greatly on the beauty of the cave, telling us of altars and fantastic formations, but we could see absolutely nothing. Now and then he uttered a note to warn us to be careful since near our feet lay a gulf whose bottom had never been discovered. We began to fear that we might be the first discoverers of its depth.

There was nothing pleasant about the whole affair. But as soon as a magnesium taper was lit, all became different. Stalagmites rose from the floor to meet the stalactites descending from the ceiling. The great altar of nature that has been ascribed to the skill of ancient worshippers and the beautiful and fantastic formations on every hand all glistened in fairylike beauty in the brilliant light.

I have often thought it was like a passage of Scripture. Others tell you of its beauty, but you cannot see it. It looks dark, intricate, forbidding, and dangerous; but when God's own light is kindled there by prayer, how different it all becomes in an instant! You see a beauty that language cannot express. Only those who have stood there in the same light can appreciate it. He who desires to understand and love the Bible must pray much. Prayer will do more than a college education to make the Bible an open and glorious book.

Chapter 2

Individual Book Study

◆

The first method of Bible study that we will consider is the study of individual books. This method of study is the most thorough and the most difficult, but the one that yields the most permanent results. We examine it first because, in my opinion, it should occupy the greater portion of our time.

How to Begin

The first step is selecting the correct book of the Bible to study. If you make an unfortunate selection, you may become discouraged and give up a method of study that might have been most fruitful.

For your first book study, choose a short book. Choosing a long book to begin with leads to discouragement. The average student will give up before the final results are reached.

Choose a comparatively easy book. Some books of the Bible are harder to understand than others. You may want to meet and overcome these later, but they are not recommended work for a beginner. When you are more familiar with Scripture as a whole, then you can tackle these books successfully and satisfactorily. You will find yourself floundering if you begin the more difficult books too soon.

The first epistle of Peter is an exceedingly precious book, but a few of the most difficult passages in the Bible are in it. If it were not for these hard passages, it would be a good book to recommend to the beginner. In view of these difficulties, it is not wise to undertake it until later.

Choose a book that is rich enough in its teaching to illustrate the advantage of this method of study and thus give a keen appetite for further studies of the same kind. Once you have gone through one reasonably large book by the method of study about to be described, you will have an eagerness that will encourage you to find time for further studies.

A book that meets all the conditions stated is the first epistle of Paul to the Thessalonians. It is quite short, has no great difficulties in interpretation, and is exceedingly rich in its teaching. It has the further advantage of being the first of the Pauline Epistles. The first epistle of John is also a good book to begin with and is not difficult.

Possessing the Truths

The second step is to master the general contents of the book. The method is very simple. It consists in merely reading the book through without stopping, then reading it through again and again, say a dozen times in all, at a single sitting. To one who has never tried this, it does not seem as if that would amount to much. But any thoughtful man who has ever tried it will tell you quite differently.

It is simply wonderful how a book takes on new meaning and beauty. It begins to open up. New relationships between different parts of the book begin to disclose themselves. Fascinating lines of thought running through the book appear. The book is grasped as a whole, and a foundation is laid for an intelligent study of those parts in detail.

Rev. James M. Gray of Boston, a prominent teacher and a great lover of the Bible, said that for many years of his ministry he had "an inadequate and unsatisfactory knowledge of the Bible." The first practical idea he received in the study of the Bible was from a layman. The brother possessed an unusual serenity and joy in his Christian experience, which he attributed to his reading of the letter to the Ephesians.

Gray asked him how he read it. The man said that he had taken a pocket copy of the Scriptures into the woods one Sunday afternoon and read Ephesians through at a single sitting, repeating the process a dozen times before stopping. When he arose, he had gained possession of the epistle or, rather, its wondrous truths had gained possession of him. This was the secret, simple as it was, that Gray had been waiting and praying for. From that time on, he studied his Bible in this way, and it became a new Book to him.

Practical Principles for Study

The third step is to prepare an introduction to the book. Write down at the top of separate sheets of paper or cards the following questions:

- Who wrote this book?
- To whom was it written?
- Where did the author write it?
- When did he write it?
- What was the occasion of his writing?
- What was the purpose for which he wrote?
- What were the circumstances of the author when he wrote?
- What were the circumstances of those to whom he wrote?
- What glimpses does the book give into the life and character of the author?
- What are the leading ideas of the book?
- What is the central truth of the book?
- What are the characteristics of the book?

Having prepared your sheets of paper with these headings, lay them side by side on your study table. Go through the book slowly, and as you come to an answer to any one of these questions, write it down on the appropriate sheet of paper. It may be necessary to go through the book several times to do the work thoroughly and satisfactorily, but you will be amply rewarded. After you have completed this process, and not until then, it would be good to refer to commentaries to compare your results with those reached by others.

The introduction you prepare for yourself will be worth many times more to you than anything you can gain from the research of others. Your study will be a rare education of the facilities of perception, comparison, and reasoning.

Seeing the Big Picture

Sometimes the answers to our questions will be found in a related book. For example, if you are studying one of the Pauline Epistles, the answers to your questions may be found in the Acts of the Apostles or in another letter. Of course, all the questions given will not apply to every book in the Bible.

If you are not willing to give the time and effort necessary, this introductory work can be omitted but only at a great sacrifice. Single passages in an epistle can never be correctly understood unless we know to whom they were written. Much false interpretation of the Bible arises from taking a local application and applying it as universal authority. Also, false interpretations often arise from applying to the unbeliever what was intended for the believer.

Note the occasion of the writing. It will clear up the meaning of a passage that would otherwise be obscure. Bearing in mind the circumstances of the author as he wrote will frequently give new force to his words. The jubilant epistle to the Philippians contains repeated phrases, such as *"rejoice in the Lord"* (Phil. 3:1; 4:4), *"trust in the Lord"* (Phil. 2:19, 24), and *"be anxious for nothing"* (Phil. 4:6). Remember that these words were written by a prisoner awaiting a possible sentence of death, and then they will become more meaningful to you.

If you will remember the main purpose for which a book was written, it will help you to interpret its incidental exhortations in their proper relationship. In fact, the answers to all the questions will be valuable in all the work that follows, as well as valuable in themselves.

Divide and Conquer

The fourth step is to divide the book into its proper sections. This procedure is not indispensable, but still it is valuable. Go through the book, and notice the principal divisions among the thoughts. Mark them. Then go through these divisions, find if there are any natural subdivisions, and mark them. In organizing your studies, work from a version of the Bible that is divided according to a logical plan.

Having discovered the divisions of the book, proceed to give each section an appropriate caption. Make this caption as precise a statement of the general contents of the section as possible. Also, make it as brief and as impressionable as you can so that it will fix itself in your mind. Create captions for the subdivisions to connect with the general caption of the division. Do not attempt too complicated a division at first.

The following division of 1 Peter, without many marked subdivisions, will serve as a simple illustration:

Chapter 1:1–2: Introduction and salutation to the pilgrims and sojourners in Pontus, etc.

Chapter 1:3–12: The inheritance reserved in heaven and the salvation ready to be revealed for those pilgrims who, in the midst of manifold temptations, are kept by the power of God through faith.

Chapter 1:13–25: The pilgrim's conduct during the days of his pilgrimage.

Chapter 2:1–10: The high calling, position, and destiny of the pilgrim people.

Chapter 2:11–12: The pilgrim's conduct during the days of his pilgrimage.

Chapter 2:13–17: The pilgrim's duty toward the human governments under which he lives.

Chapter 2:18–3:7: The duty of various classes of pilgrims.

2:18–25: The duty of servants toward their masters—enforced by an appeal to Christ's conduct under injustice and reviling.

3:1–6: The duty of wives toward their husbands.

3:7: The duty of husbands toward their wives.

Chapter 3:8–12: The conduct of pilgrims toward one another.

Chapter 3:13–22: The pilgrim suffering for righteousness' sake.

Chapter 4:1–6: The pilgrim's separation from the practices of those among whom he spends the days of his pilgrimage.

Chapter 4:7–11: The pilgrim's sojourning drawing to a close and his conduct during the last days.

Chapter 4:12–19: The pilgrim suffering for and with Christ.

Chapter 5:1–4: The duty and reward of elders.

Chapter 5:5–11: The pilgrim's walk—humble, trustful, watchful, and steadfast—and a doxology.

Chapter 5:12–14: Conclusion and benediction.

Taking Bite-Size Pieces

The fifth step is to take each verse in order and study it. In this verse-by-verse study of the book, derive the exact meaning of the verse. How is this to be done? Three steps lead to the meaning of a verse.

First, try to get the exact meaning of the words used. You will find two classes of words: those whose meaning is perfectly apparent and those whose meaning is doubtful. It is quite possible to find the precise meaning of these doubtful words. This is not done, however, by consulting a dictionary. That is an easy, but dangerous, method of finding the scriptural significance of a word. The only safe and sure method is to study the usage of the word in the Bible itself and particularly by the Bible writer whom you are studying.

To study the Bible usage of words, you must have a concordance. In my opinion, the best concordance is *Strong's Exhaustive Concordance of the Bible*. The next best is *Young's Analytical Concordance*. *Cruden's Complete Concordance* will also do if you are on a limited budget. When you are studying a particular word, all the passages in which the word occurs should be found and examined. In this way, the precise meaning of the word will be determined.

Many important Bible doctrines will change the meaning of a word. For example, two schools of theology are divided on the meaning of the word *justify*. The critical question is, does the word *justify* mean "to make righteous," or does it mean "to count or declare righteous"? The correct interpretation of many passages of Scripture hinges on the sense that we give to this word. Look up all the passages in the Bible in which the word is found, and then you will have no doubt as to the Bible usage and meaning of the word. Deuteronomy 25:1; Exodus 23:7; Isaiah 5:23; Luke 16:15; Romans 2:13, 3:23–24, 4:2–8; and Luke 18:14 will serve to illustrate the biblical usage of the word *justify*.

By using *Strong's* or *Young's Concordance,* you will see that the same word may be used in the English version for the translation of several Greek or Hebrew words. Of course, in determining the biblical usage, we should give special attention to those passages in which the English word examined is the translation of the same word in Greek or Hebrew. Either of these concordances will enable you to do this, even though you are not acquainted with Greek or Hebrew. It will be much easier to do, however, with *Strong's Concordance* than with *Young's.*

It is surprising how many knotty problems in the interpretation of Scripture are solved by the simple examination of the biblical usage of words. For example, one of the burning questions of today is the meaning of 1 John 1:7. Does this verse teach that *"the blood of Jesus Christ"* cleanses us from all the guilt of sin; or does it teach us that *"the blood of Jesus Christ"* cleanses us from the very presence of sin so that, by the blood of Christ, indwelling sin is itself eradicated?

Many of those who read this question will answer it offhand at once, one way or the other. But the spur-of-the-moment way of answering questions of this kind is a bad way. Take your concordance and look up every passage in the Bible in which the word *cleanse* is used in connection with blood, and the question will be answered conclusively and forever.

Never conclude that you have the right meaning of a verse until you have carefully determined the meaning of all doubtful words in it by an examination of Bible usage. Even when you are fairly sure you know the meaning of the words, it is good not to be too sure until you have looked them up.

Look Behind and Ahead

Now try to ascertain the meaning of a verse by carefully noticing the context (what goes before and what comes after). Many verses, if they stood alone, might be capable of several interpretations. But when the context is considered, all the interpretations except one are seen to be impossible.

For example, in John 14:18, Jesus said, *"I will not leave you orphans; I will come to you."* What did Jesus mean when He said, *"I will come to you"*? One commentator said, "He refers to

His reappearance to His disciples after His resurrection to comfort them." Another said, "He refers to His second coming." Another said, "He refers to His coming through the Holy Spirit's work to manifest Himself to His disciples and make His abode with them."

So what did Jesus mean? When doctors disagree, can an ordinary layman decide? Yes, very often. Certainly in this case. If you will carefully note what Jesus was talking about in the verses immediately preceding (vv. 15–17) and immediately following (vv. 19–26), you will have no doubt as to what coming Jesus referred to in this passage. You can see this by trying it for yourself.

Look at Comparison Verses

To ascertain the correct and precise meaning of a verse, examine parallel passages—passages that deal with the same subject. For example, study other verses that give another account of the same event or passages that are evidently intended as a commentary on the passage at hand.

Very often, after having carefully studied the context, you may still be in doubt as to which interpretation the writer intended. In this case, there is probably a passage somewhere else in the Bible that will settle this question. In John 14:3, Jesus said, *"I will come again and receive you to Myself; that where I am, there you may be also."* A careful consideration of the words used in their relation to one another will help to determine the meaning of this passage.

Still, among commentators, we find four different interpretations. First, the coming referred to here is explained as Christ's coming at death to receive the believer to Himself, as in the case of Stephen. Another commentator interprets this as the coming again at the Resurrection. A third sees the coming again through the Holy Spirit. The last defines this passage to be when Christ returns personally and gloriously at the end of the age.

Which of these four interpretations is the correct one? What has already been said about verse eighteen might seem to settle the question, but it does not. It is not at all clear that the coming in verse three is the same as in verse eighteen. What is said in connection with the two comings is altogether different. In the one case, it is a coming of Christ to *"receive you to Myself; that where I am, there you may be also"* (v. 3). In the other case, it is a coming of Christ to manifest Himself to us and make His abode with us.

Fortunately, there is a passage that settles the question. It is found in 1 Thessalonians 4:16–17. This will be clearly seen if we arrange the two passages in parallel columns.

John 14:3	1 Thessalonians 4:16–17
I will come again	*The Lord Himself will descend from heaven...*
and receive you to Myself;	*we...shall be caught up... to meet the Lord...*
that where I am,	*we shall always be*
there you may be also.	*with the Lord.*

The two passages clearly match exactly in the three facts stated. Beyond a doubt, they refer to the same event. Look closely at 1 Thessalonians 4:16–17. There can be no doubt as to what coming of our Lord is referred to here.

These three steps lead us to the meaning of a verse. They require work, but it is work that anyone can do. When the meaning of a verse is settled, you can arrive at conclusions that are correct and fixed. After taking these steps, it is wise to consult commentaries to compare your conclusions to those of others.

Before we proceed to the next step, let me say that God intended to convey definite truth in each verse of Scripture. With every verse, we should ask what it was *intended* to teach, not what it can be *made* to teach; we should not be satisfied until we have settled this question. Of course, I admit a verse may have a primary meaning and then other more remote meanings. For example, a prophecy may have its primary fulfillment in some personage or event near at hand, such as Solomon, with a more remote and complete fulfillment in Christ.

Analyzing the Verse

We are not finished with a verse when we have determined its meaning. The next thing to do is to analyze the verse. The way to do it is this: Look steadfastly at the verse and ask your-self, "What does this verse teach?" Then begin to write down: This verse teaches first ———, second ———, third ———, etc. At first glance, you will see one or two things the verse teaches; but as you look again and again, the teachings will begin to mul-tiply. You will wonder how one verse could teach so much, and you will have an ever growing sense of the divine Author of the Book.

I was once told the story of a professor who had a young man come to him to study ichthyology. The professor gave him a fish to study and told him to come back to get another lesson when he had mastered that fish. In time the young man came back and told the professor what he had observed about the fish. When he had finished, to his surprise, he was given the same fish again and told to study it further. He came back again, having observed new facts about the fish. But again he was given the same fish to study; and so it went on, lesson after les-son, until that student had been taught what his perceptive fac-ulties were for and also how to do thorough work.

We should study the Bible in the same way. We ought to come back to the same verse of the Bible again and again until we have examined, as far as it is possible to us, all that is in the verse. The probability is that when we come back to the same verse several months later, we will find something we did not see before.

An illustration of this method of analysis will be helpful. Look at 1 Peter 1:1–2. (Here is an instance in which the verse division of the King James Version is so clearly illogical that in our analysis we cannot follow it but must take the two verses together. This will often be the case.)

These verses teach:

1. This epistle was written by Peter.

2. The Peter who wrote this epistle was an apostle of Jesus Christ. (*Apostle* is Greek for the word *missionary*.)

3. Peter delighted to think and speak of himself as one sent by Jesus Christ. (Compare 2 Peter 1:1.)

4. The name Jesus Christ is used twice in these two verses. Its significance:

    a. Savior.

b. Anointed One.

c. Fulfiller of the messianic predictions of the Old Testament. It has special reference to the earthly reign of Christ.

5. This epistle was written to the elect, especially to the elect who are sojourners of the dispersion in Pontus, i.e., Paul's old field of labor.

6. Believers are:

a. Elect or chosen by God.

b. Foreknown by God.

c. Sanctified by the Spirit.

d. Sprinkled by the blood of Jesus Christ.

e. Sojourners or pilgrims on earth.

f. Subjects of multiplied grace.

g. Possessors of multiplied peace.

7. Election. Who are the elect? Believers. (Compare verse five.) To what are they elect? Obedience and the sprinkling of the blood of Jesus. According to what are they elect? The foreknowledge of God. (Compare Romans 8:29–30.) In what are they elect? Sanctification of the Spirit. The test of election is obedience. (Compare 2 Peter 1:10.) The work of the three persons of the Trinity in election is this: the Father foreknows, Jesus Christ cleanses sin by His blood, and the Spirit sanctifies.

8. God is the Father of the elect.

9. The humanity of Christ is seen in the mention of His blood.

10. The reality of the body of Jesus Christ is seen in the mention of His blood.

11. It is by His blood and not by His example that Jesus Christ delivers from sin.

12. Peter's first and great wish and prayer for those to whom he wrote was that grace and peace might be multiplied.

13. It is not enough to have grace and peace. One should have multiplied grace and peace.

14. That one already has grace and peace is no reason to cease praying for them but rather an incentive to pray that they may have more grace and peace.

15. Grace precedes peace. Compare all passages where these words are found together.

This is simply an illustration of what is meant by analyzing a verse. The whole book should be gone through in this way.

Three rules must be observed, however, in this analytical work. First, do not put anything into your analysis that is not clearly in the verse. One of the greatest faults in Bible study is reading into passages what God never put into them. Some people have their pet doctrines; they see them everywhere, even where God does not see them. No matter how true, precious, or scriptural a doctrine is, do not put into your analysis what is not in the verse. Considerable experience in this kind of study leads me to emphasize this rule.

Second, find all that is in the verse. This rule can only be carried out relatively. Much will escape you because many of the verses of the Bible are so deep. But do not rest until you have dug and dug and dug, and there seems to be nothing more to find.

Then, state what you do find just as accurately and exactly as possible. Do not be content with putting into your analysis something similar to what is in the verse, but state in your analysis precisely what is in the verse.

Classifying Your Results

Through your verse-by-verse analysis, you have discovered and recorded a great number of facts. The work now is to get these facts organized. To do this, go carefully through your analysis, and note the various subjects in the epistle. Write these subjects down as fast as you find them. Having made a complete list of the subjects dealt with in the book, write these subjects on separate cards or sheets of paper. Then, go through the analysis again and copy each point in the analysis on its appropriate sheet of paper. For example, write every point regarding God the Father on one card or sheet of paper.

This general classification should be followed by a more thorough and minute subdivision. Suppose that you are studying 1 Peter. Having completed your analysis of the epistle and gone over it carefully, you will find that the following subjects are dealt with in this epistle:

- God
- Jesus Christ

- The Holy Spirit
- The Believer
- Wives and Husbands
- Servants
- The New Birth
- The Word of God
- Old Testament Scripture
- The Prophets
- Prayer
- Angels
- The Devil
- Baptism
- The Gospel
- Salvation
- The World
- Gospel Preachers and Teachers
- Heaven
- Humility
- Love

These will serve as general headings. After the material found in the analysis is arranged under these headings, you will find it easier to divide it into numerous subdivisions. For example, the material under the heading *God* can be divided into these subdivisions:

His names: The material under this heading is quite rich.

His attributes: This should be subdivided again into His holiness, His power, His foreknowledge, His faithfulness, His long-suffering, His grace, His mercy, His impartiality, and His severity.

God's judgments.

God's will.

What is acceptable to God?

What is due to God?

God's dwelling place.

God's dominion.

God's work or what God does.

The things of God: For example, *"the mighty hand of God"* (1 Pet. 5:6), *"the house of God"* (1 Pet. 4:17), *"the gospel of God"*

(v. 17), *"the flock of God"* (1 Pet. 5:2), *"the people of God"* (1 Pet. 2:10), the *"bondservants of God,"*(v. 16), *"the word of God"* (1 Pet. 1:23), *"the oracles of God"* (1 Pet. 4:11), etc.

To illustrate the classified arrangement of the teaching of a book on one doctrine will probably show you better how to do this work than any abstract statement. It will also illustrate in part how fruitful this method of study is. Look again at 1 Peter and its teachings regarding the believer.

The Believer's Privileges

His election
> He is foreknown by the Father, 1:2.
> He is elect or chosen by God, 1:2.
> He is chosen by God according to His foreknowledge, 1:2.
> He is chosen to obedience, 1:2.
> He is chosen for the sprinkling of the blood of Jesus, 1:2.
> He is chosen in sanctification by the Spirit, 1:2.

His calling
> By whom called: God, 1:15; and the God of all grace, 5:10.
> To what called: the imitation of Christ in the patient taking
> of suffering for well doing, 2:20–21; to render blessing
> for reviling, 3:9; out of darkness into God's marvelous
> light, 2:9; to God's eternal glory, 5:10.
> In whom called: in Christ, 5:10.
> The purpose of his calling: that he may show forth the
> praises of Him who called, 2:9; that he may inherit a
> blessing, 3:9.

His regeneration
> Of God, 1:3.
> To a living hope, 1:3.
> To an inheritance incorruptible, undefiled, and that does
> not fade away, reserved in heaven, 1:4.
> By the resurrection of Jesus Christ, 1:3.
> Of incorruptible seed by the Word of God that lives, 1:23.

His redemption
> Not with corruptible things, such as silver and gold, 1:18.

With precious blood, even the blood of Christ, 1:19.
From his vain manner of life, handed down from his father, 1:18.
His sins have been borne by Christ, in His own body, on the tree, 2:24.

His sanctification by the Spirit, 1:2.

His cleansing by the blood, 1:2.

His security
He is guarded by the power of God, 1:5.
He is guarded to a salvation ready, or prepared, to be revealed in the last time, 1:5.
God cares for him, 5:7.
He can cast all his anxiety upon God, 5:7.
The God of all grace will perfect, establish, and strengthen him after a brief trial of suffering, 5:10.
None can harm him if he is zealous of what is good, 3:13.
He will not be put to shame, 2:6.

His joy
The character of his joy. Presently, it is an unspeakable joy, 1:8; a joy full of glory, 1:8. This present joy cannot be hindered by being put to grief because of many temptations, 1:6. His future joy is exceeding, 4:13.
He rejoices in the salvation prepared to be revealed in the last time, 1:5; in his faith in the unseen Jesus Christ, 1:8; and in fellowship in Christ's sufferings, 4:13.
What he will rejoice in: the revelation of Christ's glory, 4:13. Present joy in fellowship with the sufferings of Christ is the condition of exceeding joy at the revelation of Christ's glory, 4:13.

His hope
Its character: a living hope, 1:3; a reasonable hope, 3:15; an inward hope, 3:15.
In whom his hope lies: God, 1:21. The foundation of his hope is in the resurrection of Jesus Christ, 1:3–21.

His salvation
A past salvation: he has been redeemed, 1:18–19; and he has been healed, 2:24. By baptism, like Noah by the flood,

the believer has passed out of the old life of nature into
the new resurrection life of grace, 3:21.
A present salvation: he is now receiving the salvation of
his soul, 1:9.
A growing salvation: through feeding on His Word, 2:2.
A future salvation: ready or prepared to be revealed in the
last time, 1:5.

The believer's possessions
God as his Father, 1:17.
Christ as his Sin-Bearer, 2:24; example, 2:21; fellow sufferer,
4:13.
A living hope, 1:3.
An incorruptible, undefiled, and unfading inheritance
reserved in heaven, 1:4.
Multiplied grace and peace, 1:2.
Spiritual milk without guile for his food, 2:2.
Gifts for service—each believer has some gift, 4:10.

What believers are
Sojourners or strangers, 1:1.
A sojourner on his way to another country, 2:1.
A holy priesthood, 2:5.
Living stones, 2:5.
A spiritual house, 2:5.
A chosen generation, 2:9.
A royal priesthood, 2:9.
A holy nation, 2:9.
Partakers of, or partners in, Christ's sufferings, 4:13.
Representatives of Christ, 4:16.
The house of God, 4:17.
Partakers of, or partners in, the glory to be revealed, 5:1.
The flock of God, 5:2.

The believer's possibilities
He may die to sin, 2:24.
He may live for righteousness, 2:24.
He may follow in Christ's steps, 2:21.
He may cease from sin, 4:1.
He may cease from living for the lusts of men, 4:2.
He may live for the will of God, 4:2.

What was for the believer
> The ministry of the prophets was in his behalf, 1:12.
> The preciousness of Jesus is for him, 2:7.

Unclassified
> The Gospel has been preached to him in the Holy Spirit, 1:12.
> Grace is to be brought to him at the revelation of Jesus Christ, 1:3. (Compare Ephesians 3:7.)
> He has tasted that the Lord is gracious, 2:3.

The Believer's Sufferings and Trials

The fact of the believer's sufferings and trials, 1:6

The nature of the believer's sufferings and trials
> He endures grief, suffering wrongfully, 2:19.
> He suffers for righteousness' sake, 3:14.
> He suffers for doing good, 3:17; 2:20.
> He suffers as a Christian, 4:16.
> He is subjected to many temptations, 1:6.
> He is put to grief in manifold temptations, 1:6.
> He is spoken against as an evildoer, 2:12.
> His good manner of life is reviled, 3:16.
> He is spoken evil of because of his separated life, 4:4.
> He is reproached for the name of Christ, 4:14.
> He is subjected to fiery trials, 4:12.

Encouragement for believers undergoing fiery trials and suffering
> It is better to suffer for doing good than for doing evil, 3:17.
> Judgment must begin at the house of God. The present judgment of believers through trial is not comparable to the future end of those who do not obey the Gospel, 4:17.
> Blessed is the believer who suffers for righteousness' sake, 3:14. (Compare Matthew 5:10–12.)
> Blessed is the believer who is reproached for the name of Christ, 4:14.
> The Spirit of Glory and of God rests upon the believer who is reproached for the name of Christ, 4:14.

The believer's grief is for a little while, 1:6.

Suffering for a little while will be followed by God's glory in Christ, which is eternal, 5:10.

The suffering endured for a little while is for the testing of faith, 1:7.

The fiery trial is for a test, 4:12.

The faith thus proved is more precious than gold, 1:7.

Faith proven by manifold temptations will be found to praise and honor and glory at the revelation of Jesus Christ, 1:7.

His proved faith may result in praise, glory, and honor at the revelation of Jesus Christ, when the believer is for a little while subjected to many temptations, 1:7.

It is pleasing to God when a believer takes persecution patiently, when he does well and suffers for it, 2:20.

Through suffering in the flesh, we cease from sin, 4:1.

Those who speak evil of us will give account to God, 4:5.

Sufferings are being shared by fellow believers, 5:9.

Christ suffered for us, 2:21.

Christ suffered for sins once for all, the righteous for the unrighteous, so that He might bring us to God, being put to death in the flesh, but enlivened by the spirit, 3:18.

Christ left the believer an example that he should follow in His steps, 2:21.

In our fiery trials, we are made partakers of, or partners in, Christ's sufferings, 4:13.

When His glory is revealed, we will be glad with exceeding joy, 4:13.

How the believer should meet his trials and sufferings

The believer should not regard his fiery trials as a strange thing, 4:12.

The believer should expect fiery trials, 4:12.

When the believer suffers as a Christian, he should not be ashamed, 4:16.

When the believer suffers as a Christian, he should glorify God in this matter, 4:16.

When the believer suffers, he should not return reviling with reviling, or suffering with threatening, but commit himself to God who judges righteously, 2:23.

When the believer suffers, he should commit the keeping of his soul to God, as to a faithful Creator, 4:19.

The Believer's Dangers

The believer may fall into fleshly lusts that war against the soul, 2:11.

The believer may sin, 2:20.

The believer may fall into sins of the gravest character, 4:15. (Note in this verse the awful possibilities that lie dormant in the heart of a sincere, professed believer.)

The believer's prayers may be hindered, 3:7.

The believer is in danger that his high calling and destiny may tempt him to despise human laws and authority, 2:13. The believer is in danger that his high calling may lead him to lose sight of his lowly obligations to human masters, 2:18.

Young believers are in danger of disregarding the will and authority of older believers, 5:5.

The Believer's Responsibility

Each believer has an individual responsibility, 4:10.

Each believer's responsibility is for the gift he has received, 4:10.

The Believer's Duties

What the believer should be
> Be holy in all manner of living because God is holy, 1:15; and because it is written, *"Be holy, for I am holy"* (v. 16).
> Be like Him who called him, 1:15–16.
> Be sober, or of a calm, collected, thoughtful spirit, 1:13; 4:7; 5:8.
> Be serious in prayer, 4:7.
> Be of a sound mind; the end of all things is approaching, 4:7.
> Be watchful, 5:8.

Be steadfast in the faith, 5:9.
Be subject to every ordinance of man for the Lord's sake,
2:13; to the king as supreme, 2:13; to government officials
who are sent by the king to punish evildoers and to praise
those who do well, 2:14; because this is God's will, 2:15.
Be of one mind, 3:8.
Be compassionate, 3:8.
Be tenderhearted, 3:8.
Be courteous, 3:8.
Be ready always to give an answer to everyone who asks a
reason for the hope that is in him, with meekness and
fear, 3:15; in order to put to shame those who revile his
good conduct in Christ, 3:16.
Be not troubled, 3:14.

What the believer should not do
The believer should not conform himself to the lusts of
the old life of ignorance, 1:14.
The believer should not return evil for evil, 3:9.
The believer should not return reviling for reviling, 3:9.
The believer should not be afraid of the world's threats,
3:14.
The believer should not live his remaining time in the
flesh for the lusts of men, 4:2.

What the believer should do
Live as a child of obedience, 1:14.
Pass the time of his sojourning here in fear of the Lord,
1:17.
Abstain from fleshly lusts that war against the soul, 2:11.
Observe God's will as the absolute law of life, 2:15.
Let his conscience be governed by the thought of God and
not by the conduct of men, 2:19.
Sanctify Christ in his heart as Lord, 3:15. (Compare Isaiah
8:13.)
Live his remaining time in the flesh to the will of God, 4:2.
Put away all malice, 2:1; all deceit, 2:1; hypocrisy, 2:1;
envy, 2:1; all evil speaking, 2:1.
Come to the Lord as to a living stone, 2:4.
Proclaim the praises of Him who called him out of darkness
into His marvelous light, 2:9.

Arm himself with the mind of Christ, i.e., to suffer in the flesh, 4:1.

Cast all his care upon God because He cares for him, 5:7.

Stand fast in the true grace of God, 5:12.

Resist the Devil, 5:9.

Humble himself under the mighty hand of God: because God resists the proud and gives grace to the humble, 5:5; so that God may exalt him in due time, 5:6.

Glorify God when he suffers as a Christian, 4:16.

See to it that he does not suffer as a thief, an evildoer, or a meddler in other people's matters, 4:15.

Rejoice in fiery trials, 4:13.

Toward various persons: toward God—fear, 2:17; toward the king—honor, 2:17; toward masters—be in subjection with all fear (not only to the good and gentle, but also to the harsh) 2:18; toward the brethren—love, 1:22; 2:17; 4:8; toward his revilers—blessing for reviling, 3:9; toward the Gentiles—honorable conduct, 2:12 (that God may be glorified); toward foolish men—by doing good, put to silence their ignorance, 2:15; and toward all people—honor, 2:17.

Desire the pure milk of the Word, 2:2.

Gird up the loins of his mind, 1:13.

Grow, 2:2.

Hope fully on the grace that is to be brought to him at the revelation of Jesus Christ, 1:13.

The Believer's Characteristics

His faith and hope are in God, 1:21.

He believes in God through Jesus Christ, 1:21.

He calls on God as Father, 1:17.

He believes in Christ, though he has never seen Him, 1:8.

He loves Christ, though he has never seen Him, 1:8.

He has returned to the Shepherd and Overseer of his soul, 2:25.

He has purified his soul in obedience to the truth, 1:22.

He has sincere love for the brethren, 1:22.

He has good conduct, 3:16.

He does not run with the Gentiles among whom he lives, to the same excess of riot, but lives a separated life, 4:4.

He refrains his tongue from evil, 3:10, and refrains his lips so that they speak no deceit, 3:10.

He turns away from evil, 3:11.

He does good, 3:11.

He seeks peace, 3:11.

He pursues peace, 3:11.

The Believer's Warfare

The believer has a warfare before him, 4:1.

The mind of Christ is the proper armament for this warfare, 4:1.

The warfare is with the Devil, 5:8–9.

Victory is possible for the believer, 5:9.

Victory is won through steadfastness in the faith, 5:9.

How to Retain Your Studies

At first thought, it may seem that when we had completed our classification of results, our work was finished, but this is not so. These results are for use: first, for personal enjoyment and appropriation, and afterward to give to others. To obtain results, you must meditate on them.

We are no more through with a book when we have carefully and fully classified its contents than we are through with a meal when we have arranged it in an orderly way on the table. It is there to eat, digest, and assimilate.

One of the greatest failures in Bible study today is at this point. There is observation, analysis, classification, but no meditation. Perhaps nothing is as important in Bible study as meditation. (See Joshua 1:8; Psalm 1:2–3.)

Take your classified teachings and go slowly over them. Ponder them, point by point, until these wonderful truths live before you, sink into your soul, and become part of your life. Do this again and again. Nothing will go further than meditation to make you become a great, fresh, and original thinker and speaker. Very few people in this world are great thinkers.

The method of study outlined in this chapter can be shortened to suit the time and vocation of the student. For example, you can omit the verse-by-verse study and proceed at once to go through the book as a whole and note its teachings on different doctrines. This will greatly shorten and lighten the work. It will also greatly detract from the richness of the results, however, and will not be as thorough, accurate, or as scholarly. But anyone can be, if he will, a scholar, at least in the most important work: that of biblical study.

Chapter 3

Topical Study

◆———————————

A second method of Bible study, perhaps the most fascinating, is the topical method. This consists in searching through the Bible to find out what its teaching is on various topics. The only way to master any subject is to go through the Bible and find what it has to teach on that topic. Almost any great subject will take a remarkable hold on the heart of a Christian, if he will take time to go through the Bible from Genesis to Revelation and note what it has to say on that topic. He will have a fuller, more correct understanding of that specific area than he ever had before.

D. L. Moody once said that he studied the word *grace* in this way. Day after day, he went through the Bible, studying what it had to say about *grace*. As the Bible doctrine unfolded before his mind, his heart began to burn, until at last, full of the subject and on fire with the subject, he ran onto the street. Taking hold of the first man he met, he said, "Do you know grace?"

"Grace who?" was the reply.

"The grace of God that brings salvation."

Then he poured out his soul on that subject.

If any child of God will study grace, love, faith, prayer, or any other great Bible doctrine in this way, his soul, too, will become filled with it. Jesus evidently studied the Old Testament Scriptures in this way. *"Beginning at Moses and all the Prophets, He expounded to them in all the Scriptures the things concerning Himself"* (Luke 24:27). This method of study made the hearts of the two who walked with Him burn within them. (See Luke 24:32.) Paul seemed to have followed his Master in this method of study and teaching. (See Acts 17:2–3.)

Watch Out for Imbalance

This method of topical study has its dangers, however. Many are drawn by the fascination of this method to give up all other methods of study, and this is a great misfortune. A well-rounded, thorough knowledge of the Bible is not possible by one method of study alone.

But the greatest danger lies in this: everyone is almost certain to have some topics in which he is especially interested. If he studies his Bible topically, unless he is warned, he is more than likely to focus on certain topics repeatedly. Thus, he will be very strong in certain areas of truth, but other topics of equal importance may be neglected, and he may become one-sided.

We never know one truth correctly until we know it in its proper relationship to other truths. I know of people, for example, who are interested in the great doctrine of the Lord's second coming. Therefore, almost all their Bible studies are on that line. Now this is a precious doctrine, but there are other doctrines in the Bible that a person needs to know; it is folly to study this doctrine alone.

I know others whose whole interest and study seem to focus on the subject of divine healing. One man confided to a friend that he had devoted years to the study of the number seven in the Bible. This is doubtless an extreme case, but it illustrates the danger in topical study. It is certain that we will never master the whole range of Bible truth if we pursue the topical method alone. A few rules concerning topical study will probably be helpful to you.

Don't follow your fancy in the choice of topics. Don't take up any topic that happens to suggest itself. Make a list of all the subjects you can think of that are touched on in the Bible. Make it as comprehensive and complete as possible. Then study these topics one by one in logical order. The following list of subjects is given as a suggestion. Each person can add to the list for himself and separate the general subjects into proper subdivisions.

List of Topics

God
> God as a Spirit

The unity of God
The eternity of God
The omnipresence of God
The personality of God
The omnipotence of God
The omniscience of God
The holiness of God
The love of God
The righteousness of God
The mercy or lovingkindness of God
The faithfulness of God
The grace of God

Jesus Christ

The divinity of Christ
The subordination of Christ to God
The human nature of Jesus Christ
The character of Jesus Christ
    His holiness
    His love for God
    His love for man
    His love for souls
    His compassion
    His prayer life
    His meekness and humility
The death of Jesus Christ
    The purpose of Christ's death
    Why did Christ die?
    For whom did Christ die?
    The results of Christ's death
The resurrection of Jesus Christ
    The fact of the resurrection
    The results of the resurrection
    The importance of the resurrection
    The manner of the resurrection
The ascension and exaltation of Christ
The return or coming again of Christ
    The fact of His coming again
    The manner of His coming again

The purpose of His coming again
The result of His coming again
The time of His coming again
The reign of Jesus Christ

The Holy Spirit

The personality of the Holy Spirit
The deity of the Holy Spirit
The distinction of the Holy Spirit
The subordination of the Holy Spirit
The names of the Holy Spirit
The work of the Holy Spirit
In the universe
In man in general
In the believer
In the prophet and apostle
In Jesus Christ

Man

His original condition
His fall
His standing before God
The future destiny of unbelievers
Justification
The new birth
Adoption
The believer's assurance of salvation
The flesh
Sanctification
Cleansing
Consecration
Faith
Repentance
Prayer
Thanksgiving
Praise
Worship
Love for God
Love for Jesus Christ

Love for man
The future destiny of believers

Angels

Their nature and position
Their number
Their abode
Their character
Their work
Their destiny

Satan or the Devil

His existence
His nature and position
His abode
His work
Our duty regarding him
His destiny

Demons

Their existence
Their nature
Their work
Their destiny

For the student who has the perseverance to carry it through, it might be recommended to begin with the first topic on a list like this and go right through to the end, searching for everything the Bible has to say on these topics. I have done this and, thereby, gained a fuller knowledge of truth than I ever obtained by extended studies in systematic theology.

Many, however, will stagger at the seeming immensity of the undertaking. To such, it is recommended to begin by selecting those topics that seem more important, but sooner or later, settle down to a thorough study of what the Bible has to teach about God and man.

Be Thorough

Whenever you are studying any topic, do not be content with examining some of the passages in the Bible that pertain to the subject. As far as possible, find every passage in the Bible that relates to this subject. As long as there is a single passage in the Bible on any subject that you have not considered, you have not yet acquired a thorough knowledge of that subject.

How can you find all the passages in the Bible that relate to any subject? First, by the use of a concordance. Look up every passage that has the word in it. Then look up every passage that has synonyms of that word in it. If, for example, you are studying the subject of prayer, look up every passage that has the word *pray* and its derivatives in it and also every passage that has such words as *cry, call, ask, supplication, intercession,* etc.

You may also use a topical Bible, such as *Nave's Topical Bible: A Digest of the Holy Scriptures.* This book arranges the passages of Scripture by the subjects discussed.

Finally, passages not discovered by the use of either a concordance or topical guide will come to light as you study by books or as you read the Bible through. In this way, the number of topics we deal with will be ever broadening.

Getting the Exact Meaning

Study each passage in its context and find its meaning in the way suggested in the chapter on "Individual Book Study."

Topical study is frequently carried on in a very careless fashion. Passages taken out of context are strung or huddled together because of some superficial connection with one another without regard to their real sense and teaching.

This has brought the whole method of topical study into disrepute. But it is possible to be as exact and scholarly in topical study as in any other method when the results are instructive and gratifying and not misleading. But the results are sure to be misleading and unsatisfactory if the work is done in a careless, inexact way.

How to Arrange Your Notes

In studying any large subject, you will obtain a large amount of written material. Having obtained it, it must now be organized into a logical study form. As you look it over carefully, you will soon see the facts that belong together. Arrange them together in a logical order. For instance, perhaps you have accumulated much material on the deity of Jesus Christ. An example of topical study may be arranged as follows:

Jesus Christ: His Deity

Divine names

"The Son of God" (Luke 22:70). This name is given to Christ forty times. Additionally, the synonymous expression, *His Son* or *My Son* frequently occur. This name of Christ is a distinctly divine name that indicates Jesus' relationship with God, His Father. (See John 5:18.)

"The only begotten Son" (John 1:18). This name occurs five times. It is not true when people say that Jesus Christ is the Son of God only in the same sense that all men are sons of God. (Compare Mark 12:6.) Here Jesus Himself, having spoken of all the prophets as servants of God, speaks of Himself as *"one son, his beloved."*

"The First and the Last" (Rev. 1:17). (Compare Isaiah 41:4; 44:6.) In these latter passages, it is *"the LORD of hosts,"* who is *"the First and the Last"* (Isa. 44:6).

"The Alpha and the Omega" or "the Beginning and the End" (Rev. 22:13). In Revelation 1:8, it is the Lord who is *"the Alpha and the Omega."*

"The Holy One" (Acts 3:14). In Hosea 11:9 and many other passages, it is God who is *"The Holy One."*

"The Lord." (See, for example, Malachi 3:1; Luke 2:11; Acts 9:17; John 20:28; Hebrews 1:10.) This name or title is used of Jesus several hundred times. He is spoken of as "the Lord" just as God is. (Compare Acts 4:26 with 4:33. Note also Matthew 22:43–45, Philippians 2:11, and Ephesians 4:5.) If anyone doubts the attitude of the apostles of Jesus toward Him as divine, they would do well to read one after another the passages that speak of Him as Lord.

"Lord of all" (Acts 10:36).

"The Lord of glory" (1 Cor. 2:8). In Psalm 24:10, it is *"the Lord of hosts"* who is *"the King of glory."*

"Wonderful," "Counselor," "Mighty God," "Everlasting Father," and "Prince of Peace" (Isa. 9:6).

"God" (Heb. 1:8). In John 20:28, Thomas calls Jesus *"my God"* and is gently rebuked for not believing it before. (See verse 29.)

"God with us" (Matt. 1:23).

"Our great God" (Titus 2:13).

"Eternally blessed God" (Rom. 9:5).

Conclusion: Sixteen names clearly implying deity are used of Christ in the Bible, some of them over and over again, the total number of passages reaching into the hundreds.

Divine Attributes

Omnipotence
> Jesus has power over disease. It is subject to His word. (See Luke 4:39.)
> The Son of God has power over death. It is subject to His word. (See Luke 7:14–15; 8:54–55; John 5:25.)
> Jesus has power over the winds and sea. They are subject to His word. (See Matthew 8:26–27.)
> Jesus the Christ, the Son of God, has power over demons. They are subject to His word. (See Matthew 8:16; Luke 4:35–36, 41.)
> Christ is far above *all* principality, power, might, dominion, and every name that is named, not only in this world but also in the one to come. All things are in subjection under His feet. All the hierarchies of the angelic world are under Him. (See Ephesians 1:20–23.)
> The Son of God upholds *all* things by the word of His power. (Hebrews 1:3.)

Conclusion: Jesus Christ, the Son of God, is omnipotent.

Omniscience

Jesus knows men's lives, even their secret histories. (See John 4:16–19.)

Jesus knows the secret thoughts of men. He knew all men. He knew what was in man. (See Mark 2:8; Luke 5:22; John 2:24–25.)

Jesus knew from the beginning that Judas would betray Him. Not only men's present thoughts, but also their future choices were known to Him. (See John 6:64.)

Jesus knew what men were doing at a distance. (See John 1:48.)

Jesus knew the future regarding not only God's acts, but also the minute, specific acts of men. (See Luke 5:4–6; Luke 22:10–12; John 13:1.)

Jesus knew all things. In Him are hidden all the treasures of wisdom and knowledge. (See John 16:30; 21:17; Colossians 2:3.)

Conclusion: Jesus Christ is omniscient.

Omnipresence

Jesus Christ is present in every place where two or three are gathered together in His name. (See Matthew 18:20.)

Jesus Christ is present with everyone who goes forth into any part of the world to make disciples, etc. (See Matthew 28:19–20.)

Jesus Christ is in each believer. (See John 14:20; 2 Corinthians 13:5.)

Jesus Christ fills all in all. (See Ephesians 1:23.)

Conclusion: Jesus Christ is omnipresent.

Eternal

Jesus is eternal. (See Isaiah 9:7; Micah 5:2; John 1:1; John 17:5; Colossians 1:17; Hebrews 13:8.)

Conclusion: The Son of God was from all eternity.

Immutable

Jesus Christ is unchangeable. He not only always is, but always is *the same*. (See Hebrews 1:12; 13:8.)

Conclusion: Five or more distinctively divine attributes are ascribed to Jesus Christ, and all the fullness of the Godhead is said to dwell in Him. (See Colossians 2:9.)

Divine Offices

The Son of God, the eternal Word, the Lord, is Creator of all created things. (See John 1:3; Colossians 1:16; and Hebrews 1:10.)

The Son of God is the preserver of all things. (See Hebrews 1:3.)

Jesus Christ had power on earth to forgive sins. (See Mark 2:5–10; Luke 7:48–50.)

Jesus Christ raised the dead. (See John 6:39–44; 5:28–29.) Question: Did not Elijah and Elisha raise the dead? No, God raised the dead in answer to their prayers, but Jesus Christ will raise the dead by His own word. During the days of His humiliation, it was by prayer that Christ raised the dead.

Jesus Christ will fashion anew the body of our humiliation into the likeness of His own glorious body. (See Philippians 3:21.)

Christ Jesus will judge the living and the dead. (See 2 Timothy 4:1.)

Jesus Christ is the giver of eternal life. (See John 10:28; 17:2.)

Conclusion: Seven distinctively divine offices belong to Jesus Christ.

Old Testament Statements Made Distinctly about Jehovah God Refer to Jesus Christ in the New Testament

Numbers 21:6–7. Compare 1 Corinthians 10:9.

Psalm 23:1; Isaiah 40:10–11. Compare John 10:11.

Psalm 102:24–27. Compare Hebrews 1:10–12.

Isaiah 3:10; 6:1. Compare John 12:37–4 1.

Isaiah 8:12–13. Compare I Peter 3:14–15.

Isaiah 8:13–14. Compare 1 Peter 2:7–8.

Isaiah 40:3–4. Compare Matthew 3:3; Luke 1:68–69, 76.

Isaiah 60:19; Zechariah 2:5. Compare Luke 2:32.

Jeremiah 11:20; 17:10. Compare Revelation 2:23.

Ezekiel 34:11–12,16. Compare Luke 19:10.

"Lord" in the Old Testament always refers to God except when the context clearly indicates otherwise. "Lord" in the New Testament always refers to Jesus Christ except where the context clearly indicates otherwise.

Conclusion: Many statements in the Old Testament made distinctly of Jehovah God are taken in the New Testament to refer to Jesus Christ. In New Testament thought and doctrine, Jesus Christ occupies the place that Jehovah occupies in Old Testament thought and doctrine.

Names of God the Father and Jesus Christ the Son Coupled Together

2 Corinthians 13:14.

Matthew 28:19.

1 Thessalonians 3:11.

1 Corinthians 12:4–6.

Titus 3:4–5. Compare Titus 2:13.

Romans 1:7. (See all the Pauline Epistles.)

James 1:1.

John 14:23, "We," i.e., God and Jesus Christ.

2 Peter 1:1.

Colossians 2:2.

John 17:3.

John 14:1. Compare Jeremiah 17:5–7.

Revelation 7:10.

Revelation 5:13. Compare John 5:23.

Conclusion: The name of Jesus Christ is coupled with that of God the Father in numerous passages in a way in which it would be impossible to couple the name of any finite being with that of the deity.

Divine Worship Is to Be Given to Jesus Christ

Jesus Christ accepted without hesitation a worship that good men and angels declined with fear (horror). (See Matthew 4:9–10; Matthew 14:33; Matthew 28:8–9; Luke 24:52. Compare Acts 10:25–26 and Revelation 22:8–9.)
Prayer is to be made to Christ. (See Acts 7:59; 1 Corinthians 1:2; and 2 Corinthians 12:8–9.)
It is God the Father's will that all men pay the same divine honor to the Son as to Himself. (See Psalm 45:11; John 5:23. Compare Revelation 5:8–9, 12–13.)
The Son of God, Jesus, is to be worshipped as God by angels and men.

Conclusion: Jesus Christ is a person to be worshipped by angels and men even as God the Father is worshipped.

General Conclusion: By the use of numerous divine names, by attributing all the distinctively divine attributes, by the affirmation of several divine offices, by referring statements that in the Old Testament distinctly name Jehovah God as their subject to Jesus Christ in the New Testament, by coupling the name of Jesus Christ with that of God the Father in a way in which it would be impossible to couple that of any finite being with that of the deity, and by the clear teaching that Jesus Christ should be worshipped even as God the Father is worshipped—in all these unmistakable ways—God's Word distinctly proclaims that Jesus Christ is a divine being and is indeed God.

One suggestion remains in regard to topical study: choose further subjects for topical study from your own book studies.

Chapter 4

Biographical Study

◆

A third method of study is the biographical study, which consists in studying the life, work, and character of various people mentioned in Scripture. It is a special form of topical study that can be particularly useful to ministers as they prepare their sermons. The following suggestions will help those who are not already experienced in this line of work.

Using *Strong's Concordance,* collect all the passages in the Bible that mention the person to be studied.

Analyze the character of the person. This will require a repeated reading of the passages in which he is mentioned. This should be done with pen in hand so that any characteristic may be noted at once.

Note the elements of power and success.

Note the elements of weakness and failure.

Note the difficulties overcome.

Note the helps to success.

Note the privileges abused.

Note the opportunities neglected.

Note the opportunities improved.

Note the mistakes made.

Note the perils avoided.

Make a sketch of the life in hand. Make it as vivid, living, and realistic as possible. Try to reproduce the subject as a real, living person. Note the place and surroundings of the different events, e.g., Paul in Athens, Corinth, or Philippi. Note the time relationships of different events. Very few people take notice of the rapid passage of time when they read the Acts of the Apostles. They regard events that are separated by years as following one another in close sequence. In this connection, note the age or approximate age of the subject at the time of the events recorded.

Summarize the lessons we should learn from the story of this person's life.

Note the person's relationship to Jesus as a type of Christ (Joseph, David, Solomon, and others), a forerunner of Christ, a believer in Christ, an enemy of Christ, a servant of Christ, a brother of Christ (James and Jude), or a friend, etc.

Begin with some person who does not occupy too much space in the Bible, such as Enoch or Stephen. Of course many of the points mentioned above cannot be applied to some characters.

Chapter 5

Study of Types

———◆———

A fourth method is the study of types. Both an interesting and instructive method, it shows us precious truths buried away in seemingly dry and meaningless portions of the Bible. This method of study is, however, greatly abused and overdone by some people. But that is no reason why we should neglect it altogether, especially when we remember that not only Paul, but also Jesus, was fond of this method of study. The following principles may guide us in this study.

Be sure you have a biblical authority for your supposed type. If one gives free rein to his suppositions, he can imagine types everywhere, even in places that neither the human nor the divine Author of the book intended. Never say something is a type unless you can point to some clear passage of Scripture where types are definitely taught.

Begin with simple and evident types, such as the Passover (compare Exodus 12 with 1 Corinthians 5:7), the high priest, or the tabernacle.

Guard against an overstrained imagination. Anyone blessed with imagination and quickness of typical discernment will find his imagination running away unless he holds it in check.

In studying any passage where types may be suggested, look up all scriptural references in a reliable concordance. Study carefully the meaning of the names of people and places mentioned. Bible names often have a deep and far-reaching suggestiveness. For example, Hebron, which means "joining together," "union," or "fellowship," is deeply significant when taken in connection with its history, as are all the names of the cities of refuge. Was it accidental that Bethlehem, the name of the place where the Bread of Life was born, means "house of bread"?

Chapter 6

Study of Biblical and Chronological Order

◆———————

A fifth method of Bible study is the old-fashioned method of biblical order, beginning at Genesis and going right on through to Revelation. This method has some advantages that no other methods of study possess. Start at the beginning of this library of sixty-six books and read right through. It is important to master the Bible as a whole in order to understand the separate books in it.

There are advantages to studying the Bible in scriptural order. First, it is the only method by which you will get an idea of the Book as a whole. The more you know of the Bible as a whole, the better prepared you will be to understand any individual portion of it. Second, it is the only method by which you are likely to cover the whole Book and so take in the entire scope of God's revelation. This is a time-consuming but rewarding way to study the Bible.

Every part of God's Word is precious. Hidden away in the most unexpected places, such as 1 Chronicles 4:10, you will find priceless gems. It is also the best method to enable one to get hold of the unity of the Bible and its organic character.

The Bible is a many-sided book. It clearly teaches the deity of Christ and insists on His real humanity. It exalts faith and demands works. It urges to victory through conflict and asserts most vigorously that victory is won by faith.

If you become too one-sided with any line of truth, the daily, orderly study of the Bible will soon bring you to some contrasted line of truth and back to proper balance. Some people have become mentally distracted through too much occupation with a single line of truth. Thoughtful study of the whole Bible is a great corrective to this tendency.

It would be good to have three methods of study in progress at the same time: first, the study of a particular book; second, the study of topics (perhaps topics suggested by the book being studied); third, the study of the Bible in a progressive and organized fashion. Every other method of study should be supplemented by studying the Bible in biblical order. Some years ago I determined to read a different version of the Bible and the New Testament in Greek through every year. It proved exceedingly profitable in my own studies.

Studying by Chronological Order

Another method of study closely related to the above method has advantages of its own. It is studying the various portions of the Bible in their chronological order. In this way, the Psalms are read in their historical settings, as are prophecies, epistles, and so on.

Chapter 7

Study for Practical Use in Dealing with People

◆

The last method of Bible study is for use in dealing with people. To study the Bible in this way, make as complete a classification as possible of all the different personalities that you find in the world today. Write the names of these various types at the head of separate sheets of paper or cards. Then begin reading the Bible through slowly. When you come to a passage that seems likely to prove useful in dealing with a certain personality type, write it down on the appropriate sheet. Go through the entire Bible in this way. Use special Bible markers in different colored inks or use different letters or symbols to represent the personalities. The best book is the one you organize yourself. My book entitled *How To Bring Men To Christ* may give you some suggestions on how to begin.

The following list of types of people are suggestions to which you can add.

1. The careless and indifferent.
2. Those who wish to be saved but do not know how.
3. Those who know how to be saved but have difficulties. They may be further categorized with statements, such as:
   "I am too great a sinner."
   "My heart is too hard."
   "I must become better before I become a Christian."
   "I am afraid I can't hold out."
   "I am too weak."
   "I have tried before and failed.
   "I cannot give up my evil ways."
   "I will be persecuted if I become a Christian."
   "It will hurt my business."

"There is too much to give up."
"The Christian life is too hard."
"I am afraid of ridicule."
"I will lose my friends."
"I have no feeling."
"I have been seeking Christ but cannot find Him."
"God won't receive me."
"I have committed the unpardonable sin."
"It is too late."
"Christians are so inconsistent."
"God seems to me unjust and cruel."
"There are so many things in the Bible that I can't understand."
"There is someone I can't forgive."

Perhaps you will meet people who are cherishing false hopes. Their hope lies in being saved by a righteous life or by being saved by "trying to be a good Christian." They may "feel saved" because of a profession of religion or church membership.

Others on your list may include those who wish to put off the decision to be saved, such as Jews, Spiritualists, or Christian Scientists. You may also add to your list: the sorrowing, the persecuted, the discouraged, the despondent, or the worldly Christian.

The results of this work will be of incalculable value. You will get a new view of how perfectly the Bible is adapted to everyone's need. Familiar passages of the Bible will take on new meaning as you see their relationship to people's needs. In seeking food for others, you will get a vast amount of material to use in sermons, in teaching, and in personal work. You will acquire a rare working knowledge of the Bible.

Chapter 8

Final Suggestions

———◆———

S ome suggestions remain to be given before I close this book. First of all, study the Bible regularly. Regularity counts more in Bible study than most people can imagine. The spasmodic student who sometimes gives a great deal of time to the study of the Word and at other times neglects it for days does not achieve the same results as the one who plods on faithfully day by day. The Bereans were wise as well as *"fairminded"* in that they *"searched the Scriptures daily"* (Acts 17:11).

A well-known speaker among Christian college students once remarked that he had been at many conventions and had received great blessings from them, but the greatest blessing he had ever received was from a convention where only three people gathered together with him. These four had covenanted together to spend a certain portion of every day in Bible study. Since that day, much of his time had been spent in cars, in hotels, and at conventions, but he had kept that covenant. The greatest blessing that had come to him in his Christian life had come through this daily study of the Word.

Anyone who has tried it realizes how much can be accomplished by setting apart a fixed portion of each day for Bible study. You may study as little as fifteen or thirty minutes, but it is better to have an hour kept sacredly for that purpose under all circumstances.

Many will say, "I cannot spare the time." It will not do to study the Bible only when you feel like it or when you have leisure. You must have fixed habits if you are to study the Bible profitably. Nothing is more important than daily Bible study, and less important things must not take its place. What regularity in eating is to physical life, regularity in Bible study is to spiritual life. Decide upon some time, even if it is no more than fifteen minutes to start with, and hold to it until you are ready to set a longer period.

Select the Correct Time

Don't put off your Bible study until nearly bedtime when your mind is drowsy. It is good to meditate on God's Word as you retire, but this is not the time for study. Bible study demands a clear mind. Don't take the time immediately after a heavy meal when you are mentally and physically sluggish. It is almost the unanimous opinion of those who have given this subject careful attention that the early hours of the day are the best for Bible study, if they can be free from interruption. Wherever possible, lock yourself in and lock the world out to concentrate fully on the Word of God.

Look for Jesus

We read of Jesus that *"beginning at Moses and all the Prophets, He expounded to them in all the Scriptures the things concerning Himself"* (Luke 24:27). Jesus Christ is the subject of the whole Bible, and He pervades the entire Book. Some of the seemingly driest portions become infused with a new life when we learn to see Christ in them. I remember in my early reading what a dull book Leviticus seemed, but it all became different when I learned to see Jesus in the various offerings and sacrifices, in the high priest and his garments, in the tabernacle and its furniture, and indeed everywhere. Look for Christ in every verse you study, and even the genealogies and the names of towns will begin to have beauty and power.

Memorize Scripture

The psalmist said, *"Your word I have hidden in my heart, that I might not sin against You!"* (Ps. 119:11). There is nothing better to keep one from sinning than this. By the Word of God hidden in His heart, Jesus overcame the Tempter. (See Matthew 4:4, 7, 10.)

But the Word of God hidden in the heart is good for other purposes than victory over sin. It is good to meet and expose error. It is good to enable one *"to speak a word in season to him who is weary"* (Isa. 50:4). It is good for manifold uses, even *"that the man of God may be complete, thoroughly equipped for every good work"* (2 Tim. 3:17).

Memorize Scripture by chapter and verse. It is just as easy as memorizing a few words, and it is immeasurably more useful for practical purposes. Memorize Scripture in systematic form. Do not have a chaotic heap of texts in your mind, but pigeonhole the Scripture you store in memory under appropriate titles. Then you can bring it out when you need it, without racking your brain. Many can stand up without a moment's warning and speak coherently and convincingly on any vital theme because they have a vast fund of wisdom in Scripture texts stored away in their mind in systematic form.

Utilize Spare Moments

Most of us waste too much time. Time spent traveling, waiting for appointments, or waiting for meals can be utilized in Bible study if you will carry a pocket Bible or pocket Testament. You can also utilize the time to meditate on texts already stored away in memory.

Henry Ward Beecher read one of the larger histories of England through while waiting day after day for his meals to be brought to the table. How many books of the Bible could be studied in the same way? A friend once told me about a man who had, in some respect, the most extraordinary knowledge of the Bible of any man he knew. This man was a junk dealer in a Canadian city. He kept a Bible open on his shelves; during intervals of business, he pondered the Book of God. His Bible became black from handling in such surroundings, but I have little doubt his soul became correspondingly white. No economy pays as does the economy of time, but there is no way of economizing time so thriftily as putting wasted moments into the study of or meditation on the Word of God.

Difficulties in
the Bible

Contents

Introduction

◆

In this book filled with scriptural insight, R. A. Torrey considers the difficulties in the Bible that are often puzzling to many Christians, and that are more often confusing to non-Christians. No attempt is made to consider in detail every possible difficulty that could be found in the Scriptures; it would take many volumes to do so. However, readers will likely find in the following pages detailed solutions to difficulties that have been the most perplexing or the most frequently pondered in their own lives.

Of course, the solutions provided here by Torrey are meant to be timeless, yet the words *modern science* may leave readers questioning not only a particular difficulty, but also its solution. This results from the fact that the scientific world and its body of knowledge are constantly undergoing transformation. Since the writing of this book, many more discoveries have been made; therefore, today's readers have at their disposal more scientific knowledge than Torrey had.

With much success, Torrey attempted in this book to tie together his God-given understanding of the Word of God with the scientific discoveries of his time. Even so, he never hesitated to point out that the Scriptures are, indeed, the true Word of God. As Torrey wrote in his book, *Talks to Men about the Bible and the Christ of the Bible,* "The Bible contains nothing but truth, [and it] contains more truth than all other books put together." Certainly, if Torrey had known then what is known today in the scientific world, he would have been equally successful at harmonizing modern science with the immutable Word of God.

---

*Published by Whitaker House under the title *Powerful Faith.*

Chapter 1

A General Statement

◆───────◆

E very careful student and every thoughtful reader of the Bible finds that the words of the apostle Peter concerning the Scriptures, *"in which are some things hard to understand, which untaught and unstable people twist to their own destruction"* (2 Pet. 3:16), are abundantly true. Has any one of us not found things in the Bible that have puzzled us, that in our early Christian experience have led us to question whether the Bible was, after all, the Word of God?

We find some things in the Bible that seem impossible to reconcile with other things in the Bible. Some things seem incompatible with the thought that the whole Bible is of divine origin and absolutely free from error. It is not wise to attempt to conceal the fact that these difficulties exist. It is the duty of wisdom, as well as of honesty, to face them frankly and consider them. I can say several things concerning these difficulties that every thoughtful student will eventually encounter.

We Can Expect Difficulties

The first thing I have to say about these difficulties in the Bible is that, from the very nature of the case, difficulties are to be expected. Some people are surprised and staggered because there are difficulties in the Bible. For my part, however, I would be more surprised and staggered if there were not.

What is the Bible? It is a revelation of the mind, will, character, and being of an infinitely great, perfectly wise, and absolutely holy God. God Himself is the Author of this revelation, but to whom is the revelation made? To finite beings; to those who are imperfect in intellectual development and in knowledge; and to those who are also imperfect in character and, consequently, in spiritual discernment. The wisest person measured on the scale of eternity is only a babe, and the holiest person compared with God is only an infant in moral development. As a result, from the very necessities of the case, there must be difficulties in such a revelation, from such a Source, made to such people.

When the finite tries to understand the infinite, there is bound to be difficulty. When the ignorant contemplate the utterances of One perfect in knowledge, there must be many things hard to understand, and some things that appear absurd to their immature and inaccurate minds. When beings, whose moral judgment regarding the hatefulness of sin and the awfulness of the penalty that it demands is blunted by their own sinfulness, listen to the demands of an absolutely holy being, they are bound to be perplexed at some of His demands; when they consider His dealings, they are bound to be staggered by some of them. These dealings will appear too severe, too stern, too harsh, too horrible.

It is clear that there must be difficulties for us in a revelation such as the Bible. If someone were to hand me a book that was as simple to me as the multiplication table and say, "This is the Word of God. In it, God has revealed His whole will and wisdom," I would shake my head and say, "I cannot believe it; that is too easy to be a perfect revelation of infinite wisdom." In any complete revelation of God's mind, will, character, and Being, there must be things hard for the beginner to understand; and the wisest and best of us are but beginners.

Difficulty Does Not Equal Falsehood

The second thing to be said about these difficulties is that a difficulty in a doctrine, or a grave objection to a doctrine, does not, in any way, prove the doctrine to be untrue. Many thoughtless people imagine that it does. If they come across some difficulty in the way of believing in the divine origin and absolute inerrancy and infallibility of the Bible, they at once conclude that the doctrine is discredited. That is very illogical.

Stop a moment and think; learn to be reasonable and fair. There is scarcely a doctrine in science generally believed today that has not had some great difficulty in becoming accepted. When the Copernican theory, now so universally accepted, was first proclaimed, it encountered a great deal of difficulty. If this theory was true, the planet Venus should have phases as the moon has, but no phases could be discovered by the best telescope then in existence. Even so, the positive argument for the theory was so strong that it was accepted in spite of this apparently unanswerable objection. When a more powerful telescope was made, it was found that Venus had phases after all. The whole difficulty arose, as almost all of those in the Bible arise, from man's ignorance of some of the facts in the case.

If we apply to Bible study the commonsense logic recognized in every department of science (with the exception of biblical criticism, if that is a science), then we must demand that if the positive proof of a theory is conclusive, it must be believed by rational men, in spite of any number of difficulties in minor details. He is a very shallow thinker indeed who gives up a well-tested truth because there are some apparent facts that he cannot reconcile with that truth. And he is a very shallow Bible scholar who gives up his belief in the divine origin and inerrancy of the Bible because there are some supposed facts that he cannot reconcile with that doctrine. Unfortunately, there are many shallow thinkers of that kind in the theological world today.

Greater Difficulties Exist

The third thing to be said about the difficulties in the Bible is that there are many more, and much greater, difficulties in the doctrine that holds the Bible to be of human origin, and hence fallible, than there are in the doctrine that holds the Bible to be of divine origin, hence infallible. Often a person will bring you some difficulty and say, "How do you explain that, if the Bible is the Word of God?" Perhaps you may not be able to answer him satisfactorily.

Then he thinks he has you, but not at all. Turn to him, and ask, "How do you account for the fulfilled prophecies of the Bible if it is of human origin? How do you account for its marvelous unity? How do you account for its inexhaustible depth? How do you account for its unique power in lifting men to God?" and so on. For every insignificant objection he can bring to your view of the Bible, you can bring many more deeply significant objections to his view of the Bible. Any really candid, honest man who desires to know and obey the truth will have no difficulty in deciding between the two views.

Some time ago, a young man who had a bright mind and was unusually well-read in skeptical, agnostic literature told me he had given the matter a great deal of candid and careful thought; as a result, he could not believe the Bible was of divine origin. I asked him, "Why not?" He pointed to a certain teaching of the Bible that he could not and would not believe to be true.

I replied, "Suppose for a moment that I could not answer that specific difficulty. My inability would not prove that the Bible was not of divine origin. Yet I can present many things to you, things far more difficult to account for on the hypothesis that the Bible *is not* of divine origin, than this is on the hypothesis that the Bible *is* of divine origin. You cannot deny the fact of fulfilled prophecy. How do you account for it if the Bible is not God's Word?

"You cannot shut your eyes to the marvelous unity of the sixty-six books of the Bible, written under such divergent circumstances and at periods of time so remote from one another. How do you account for it, if God is not the real Author of the Book, behind the forty or more human authors? You cannot deny that the Bible has the power to save men from sin, to bring men peace and hope and joy, to lift men to God, that all other books taken together do not possess. How do you account for these things if the Bible is not the Word of God?"

The objector did not answer. The difficulties that confront one who denies that the Bible is of divine origin and authority are far more numerous and much more weighty than those that confront the one who believes it to be of divine origin and authority.

Solutions Do Not Depend on Us

The fourth thing to be said about the difficulties in the Bible is this: the fact that you cannot solve a difficulty does not prove it cannot be solved, and the fact that you cannot answer an objection does not prove at all that it cannot be answered. It is remarkable how often we overlook this very evident fact. Many, when they meet a difficulty in the Bible and give it a little thought and can see no possible solution, jump at once to the conclusion that a solution is impossible by anyone, so they throw up their hands and forget their faith in the inerrancy and divine origin of the Bible.

It seems that everyone should have enough modesty, which is fitting for beings so limited in knowledge as we all undeniably are, to say, "Though I see no possible solution to this difficulty, someone a little wiser than I might easily find one." If we would bear in mind that we do not know everything, and that a great many things that we cannot solve now we could very easily solve if we only knew a little more, it would save us from all this folly.

Above all, we must never forget that infinite wisdom may have a very easy solution to what appears absolutely unexplainable to our finite wisdom—or ignorance. What would we think of a beginner in algebra, who, having tried in vain for half an hour to solve a difficult problem, declared that there was no possible solution to the problem because he could not find one?

One day, a man of unusual experience and ability left his work and came a long distance to see me. He was greatly perturbed in spirit because he had discovered what seemed to him to be an outright contradiction in the Bible. He had lain awake all night thinking about it. It had defied all his attempts at reconciliation; but when he had fully stated the case to me, in a very few moments I showed him a simple and satisfactory solution to the difficulty. He went away with a happy heart.

Why had it not occurred to him at the outset, though it appeared absolutely impossible to him to find a solution, that a solution might easily be discovered by someone else? He supposed that the difficulty was entirely new, but it was one that had been faced and answered long before either of us was born.

Difficulties versus Excellencies

The fifth thing to be said about the difficulties in the Bible is that the seeming defects of the Book are insignificant when

417

compared to its many and marvelous excellencies. It certainly reveals great perversity of both mind and heart that men spend so much time discussing and writing about such insignificant points that they consider defects in the Bible, while the incomparable beauties and wonders that adorn and glorify almost every page pass absolutely unnoticed.

Even in some prominent institutions of learning, where men are supposed to be taught to appreciate and understand the Bible, and where they are sent to be trained to preach its truth to others, much more time is spent on minute and insignificant points that seem to point toward an entirely human origin of the Bible than is spent in studying, understanding, and admiring the unparalleled glories that make this Book stand apart from all other books. What would we think of a person who, in studying some great masterpiece of art, concentrated his whole attention on what looked like a flyspeck in the corner?

A large proportion of the much vaunted critical study of the Bible is a laborious and scholarly investigation of supposed flyspecks. The man who is not willing to squander the major portion of his time in this erudite investigation of flyspecks, but prefers to devote it to the study of the unrivaled beauties and majestic splendors of the Book, is considered by some people as not being "scholarly and up-to-date."

The Superficial versus the Profound

The sixth thing to be said about the difficulties in the Bible is that they have far more weight with superficial readers than with profound students. Take that class of modern preachers who read the Bible for the most part for the sole purpose of finding texts to serve as pegs to hang their own ideas on. To such superficial readers of the Bible, these difficulties seem immensely important.

On the other hand, to the one who has learned to meditate on the Word of God day and night, they have scarcely any weight at all. That rare man of God, George Müller, who had carefully studied the Bible from beginning to end more than one hundred times, was not disturbed by any difficulties he encountered; but to the man who is reading it through for the first or second time, many things perplex and stagger.

The Role of Careful Study

The seventh thing to be said about the difficulties in the Bible is that they rapidly disappear upon careful and prayerful study. How many things in the Bible once puzzled and confused me, but have since been perfectly cleared up and no longer present any difficulty whatever! Every year of study finds these difficulties disappearing more and more rapidly. At first they go by ones and twos, then by dozens, and then by scores. Is it not reasonable, therefore, to suppose that the difficulties that still remain will all disappear upon further study? Then let us look at some of these difficulties in greater detail.

Chapter 2

Classes of Difficulties

◆

All the difficulties found in the Bible can be included under ten general headings. In this chapter, I will proceed to explain in detail the nature of each class of difficulties.

Imperfect Manuscripts

The first class of difficulties is those that arise from the text from which our English Bible was translated. No one, as far as I know, believes that the English translation of the Bible is absolutely infallible and inerrant. The doctrine held by many is that the Scriptures as *originally given* were absolutely infallible and inerrant, and that our English translation is a *substantially accurate* rendering of the Scriptures as originally given.

We do not possess the original manuscripts of the Bible. These original manuscripts were copied many times with great care and exactness, but naturally some errors crept into the copies that were made. We now possess so many good copies that by comparing one with another, we can tell with great precision just what the original text was. Indeed, for all practical purposes, the original text is now settled. There is not one important doctrine that depends on any doubtful reading of the text.

However, when our King James Version was made, some of the best manuscripts were not within reach of the translators, and the science of textual criticism was not so well understood as it is today; thus, the translation was made from an imperfect text. Not a few of the apparent difficulties in the Bible arise from this source. For example, we are told in John 5:4 (KJV):

An angel went down at a certain season into the pool, and troubled the water: whosoever then first after the troubling of the water stepped in was made whole of whatsoever disease he had.

This statement for many reasons seems improbable and difficult to believe, but upon investigation, we find that it is all a mistake of the copyist. Some early copyist, reading John's account, added in the margin an explanation of the healing properties of the intermittent medicinal spring. A later copyist incorporated this marginal note in the body of the text, and so it came to be handed down and got into our Bibles. Very properly, it has been omitted from the Revised Version.

The discrepancies in figures in different accounts of the same events, as, for example, the differences in the ages of some of the kings as given in the text of Kings and Chronicles, doubtless arise from the same cause: errors of copyists. Such an error in the matter of numerals would be very easy to make, especially since the Hebrew numbers are made by letters, and letters that appear very much alike have a very different value as numbers.

For example, the first letter in the Hebrew alphabet denotes one; and with two little points above it, not larger than flyspecks, it denotes a thousand. The twenty-third, or last, letter of the Hebrew alphabet denotes four hundred, but the eighth letter of the Hebrew alphabet, which looks very much like it and could be easily mistaken for it, denotes eight. A very slight error of the copyist would therefore make a drastic change in the value of the numbers. The remarkable thing, when one contemplates the facts in the case, is that so few errors of this kind have been made.

Inaccurate Translations

The second class of difficulties is those that arise from inaccurate translations. For example, in Matthew 12:40 (KJV), Jonah is spoken of as being in the whale's belly. Many a skeptic has had a good laugh over the thought of a whale, with the peculiar construction of its mouth and throat, swallowing a man;

but if the skeptic had only taken the trouble to look the matter up, he would have found the word translated "whale" really means "sea monster," without any definition as to the character of the sea monster. I will take this up in more detail in considering the story of Jonah.

So the whole difficulty arose from the translator's mistake and the skeptic's ignorance. Many skeptics today are extremely ignorant of matters clearly understood by many Sunday school children that they are still harping in the name of scholarship on this supposed error in the Bible.

False Interpretations

The third class of difficulties is those that arise from false interpretations of the Bible. What the Bible teaches is one thing, and what men interpret it to mean is often something widely different. Many difficulties that we have with the Bible arise not from what the Bible actually says, but from what men interpret it to mean.

A striking illustration of this is found in the first chapter of Genesis. If we were to believe the interpretation that is put upon this chapter by many interpreters, it would be very difficult indeed to reconcile it with much that modern science regards as established. Even so, the difficulty is not with what the first chapter of Genesis says, but with the interpretation that is put upon it; for, in actuality, there is no contradiction whatever between what is proven by science and what is said in the first chapter of Genesis. This will come out clearly in the next chapter of this book.

Another difficulty of the same character is with Jesus' statement that He would be three days and three nights in the heart of the earth (Matt. 12:40). Many interpreters would have us believe that He died Friday night and rose early Sunday morning, and the time between these two is far from being three days and three nights. We will see later that it is a matter of biblical interpretation, and the trouble is not with what the Bible actually says, but with the interpretation that men place on it.

Wrong Ideas about the Bible

The fourth class of difficulties is those that arise from a wrong conception of the Bible. Many think that when you say the Bible is the Word of God, of divine origin and authority, you mean that God is the speaker in every utterance it contains, but this is not at all what is meant. Often God simply records what others say: what good men say, what bad men say, what inspired men say, what uninspired men say, what angels and demons say, and even what the Devil himself says. The record of what they said is from God and absolutely true, but what those other people are recorded as saying may or may not be true. It is true that they said it, but what they said may not be true.

For example, the Devil is recorded in Genesis 3:4 as saying, *"You will not surely die."* It is true that the Devil said it, yet what the Devil said is not true, but an infamous lie that shipwrecked our race. God's Word is that the Devil said it, yet what the Devil said is not God's Word but the Devil's word. It is God's Word that this was the Devil's word. Many careless readers of the Bible do not notice who is talking—God, good men, bad men, inspired men, uninspired men, angels, or devils. They will tear a verse right out of its context, regardless of the speaker, and say, "There, God said that," but God said nothing of the kind. God said that the Devil said it, or a bad man said it, or a good man, or an inspired man, or an uninspired man, or an angel said it.

What God says is true, but what others said may or may not be true. It is very common to hear men quote what Eliphaz, Bildad, or Zophar said to Job, as if it were necessarily God's Word because it is recorded in the Bible, in spite of the fact that God disavows their teaching and says to them, *"You have not spoken of Me what is right"* (Job 42:7). It is true that these men said the things that God records them as saying, but often they gave the truth a twist and said what is not right.

Many difficulties arise from not noticing who is speaking. The Bible always tells us, and we should always note. In the Psalms, we sometimes have what God said to man, and that is always true; on the other hand, we often have what man said to God, and that may or may not be true. Sometimes, and far more often than most of us see, it is the voice of the speaker's personal vengeance or despair. This vengeance may be, and often is, prophetic; but it may be the wronged man committing his cause to the One to whom vengeance belongs (see Romans 12:19), and we are not obliged to defend all that he said.

Also in the Psalms, we have seen a record of what the fool said: *"There is no God"* (Ps. 14:1). Now, it is true that the fool said it, but the fool lied when he said it. It is God's Word that the fool said it; however, what God reports the fool as saying is not God speaking, but the fool's own words. So in studying our Bible, if God is the speaker, we must believe what He says; if an inspired man is the speaker, we must believe what he says; if an uninspired man is the speaker, we must judge for ourselves: it is perhaps true, perhaps false. If it is the Devil who is speaking, we do well to remember that he was a liar from the beginning (John 8:44), but even the Devil may tell the truth sometimes.

The Original Language

The fifth class of difficulties is those that arise from the language in which the Bible was written. The Bible is a book for all ages and for all kinds of people; therefore, it was written in the language that is understood by all: the language of the common people and of appearances. It was not written in the terminology of science. For example, what occurred at the battle of Gibeon (see Joshua 10:12–14) was described in the way it appeared to those who saw it, and in the way it would be understood by those who read about it. There is no talk about the refraction of the sun's rays, etc., but the sun is said to have "stood still" or "tarried" in the midst of heaven.

It is one of the perfections of the Bible that this account was not written in the terminology of modern science. If it had been, it would never have been understood until the present day, and even now it would be understood only by a few. Furthermore, since science and its terminology are constantly changing, the Bible, if written in the terminology of the science of today, would be out-of-date in a few years; but being written in just the language chosen, it has proved to be the Book for all ages, all lands, and all conditions of men.

Other difficulties from the language in which the Bible was written arise from the fact that large portions of the Bible are written in the language of poetry—the language of feeling, passion, and imagination. If a man is hopelessly prosaic, he will inevitably find difficulties with these poetic portions of the inspired Word. For example, in Psalm 18 we have a marvelous description of a thunderstorm; but let the dull, prosaic fellow get hold of the eighth verse, for example, and he will be head over heels in difficulty at once. Nevertheless, the trouble is not with the Bible, but with his own lack of appreciation for poetic beauty.

Our Lack of Knowledge

The sixth class of difficulties is those that arise from our defective knowledge of the history, geography, and customs of Bible times. For example, in Acts 13:7, Luke spoke of *"the proconsul"* of Cyprus. Roman provinces were of two classes, imperial and senatorial. The ruler of an imperial province was called a "propraetor"; the ruler of a senatorial province was called a "proconsul." Up to a comparatively recent date, according to the best information we had, Cyprus was an imperial province; therefore, its ruler would be a propraetor, but Luke calls him a proconsul.

This certainly seemed like a clear case of error on Luke's part, and even the conservative commentators felt forced to admit that Luke was in slight error. The destructive critics were delighted to find this "mistake." However, further and more thorough investigation has brought to light that, just at the time of which Luke wrote, the senate had made an exchange with the emperor, whereby Cyprus had become a senatorial province; therefore, its ruler was a proconsul. Luke was right after all, and the literary critics were themselves in error.

Time and time again, further research and discoveries— geographical, historical, and archaeological—have vindicated the Bible and put its critics to shame. For example, the book of Daniel has naturally been one of the books that infidels and destructive critics have hated most. One of their strongest arguments against its authenticity and veracity was that such a person as Belshazzar was unknown to history. They argued that all historians agreed that Nabonidus was the last king of Babylon, and that he was absent from the city when it was captured; so Belshazzar must be a purely mythical character, and the whole story legendary and not historical. Their argument seemed very strong. In fact, it seemed unanswerable.

However, Sir Henry Rawlinson discovered at Mugheir and other Chaldean sites clay cylinders, on which Belshazzar (Belzarazur) is named by Nabonidus as his eldest son. Doubtless he reigned as regent in the city during his father's absence, an indication of which we have in his proposal to make Daniel third ruler in the kingdom (Daniel 5:16)—he himself being second ruler in the kingdom, Daniel would be next to him.

So the Bible was vindicated, and the critics put to shame. It is not so long since the destructive critics asserted most positively that Moses could not have written the Pentateuch, because writing was unknown in his day, but recent discoveries have proved beyond a doubt that writing far antedates the time of Moses. Therefore, the critics have been compelled to give up their argument, though they have had the bad grace to hold on stubbornly to their conclusion.

Ignorance about Conditions

The seventh class of difficulties is those that arise from the ignorance of conditions under which books were written and commands given. For example, God's commands to Israel to exterminate the Canaanites seem cruel and horrible to one ignorant of the conditions; but when one understands the moral condition to which these nations had sunk, the utter hopelessness of reclaiming them, and the weakness of the Israelites themselves, their extermination seems to have been an act of mercy to all succeeding generations and to themselves. We will go into this more fully in the chapter on the slaughter of the Canaanites.

Our One-Sidedness

The eighth class of difficulties is those that arise from the many-sidedness of the Bible. The most broad-minded man is yet one-sided, but the truth is many-sided, and the Bible is all-sided. So to our narrow thought, one part of the Bible seems to contradict another. For example, men as a rule are either Calvinistic or Arminian in their mental makeup, and some portions of the Bible are decidedly Calvinistic and present great difficulties to the Arminian type of mind, whereas other portions of the Bible are decidedly Arminian and present difficulties to the Calvinistic type of mind. Yet both sides are true.

Many people in our day are broad-minded enough to be able to grasp at the same time the Calvinistic and the Arminian side of the truth, but some are not. And so the Bible perplexes, puzzles, and bewilders them; yet the trouble is not with the Bible, but with their own lack of capacity for comprehensive thought. So, too, Paul seems to contradict James, and James seems sometimes to contradict Paul, and what Paul said in one place seems to contradict what he said in another place. Nevertheless, the whole trouble is that our narrow minds cannot take in God's large truth.

Our Finite Minds

The ninth class of difficulties is those that arise from the fact that the Bible has to do with the infinite, and our minds are finite. It is as difficult to put the facts of infinite being into the limited capacity of our finite intelligence as it is to put the ocean into a pint cup. To this class of difficulties belong those connected with the Bible doctrine of the Trinity, and with the Bible doctrine of the divine-human nature of Christ.

To those who forget that God is infinite, the doctrine of the Trinity seems like the mathematical monstrosity of making one equal three. However, when one bears in mind that the doctrine of the Trinity is an attempt to put the facts of infinite Being into forms of finite thought, and the facts of the Spirit into material forms of expression, the difficulties vanish.

Our Dull Spiritual Perceptions

The tenth class of difficulties is those that arise from the dullness of our spiritual perceptions. The man who is farthest

427

advanced spiritually is still so immature that he cannot expect to see everything as an absolutely holy God sees it, unless he takes it on simple faith in Him. To this class of difficulties belong those connected with the Bible doctrine of eternal punishment. It often seems to us as if this doctrine cannot be true, must not be true, but the whole difficulty arises from the fact that we are still so spiritually blind that we have no adequate conception of the awfulness of sin, and especially the awfulness of the sin of rejecting the infinitely glorious Son of God. Yet when we become so holy, so like God that we see the enormity of sin as He sees it, we will have no difficulty whatever with the doctrine of eternal punishment.

As we look back over the ten classes of difficulties, we see that they all arise from our imperfection and not from the imperfection of the Bible. The Bible is perfect, but we, being imperfect, have difficulty with it. Even so, as we grow more and more into the perfection of God, our difficulties will become ever less and less; thus, we are forced to conclude that when we become as perfect as God is, we will have no more difficulties whatever with the Bible.

Chapter 3

How Should We Deal with Difficulties in the Bible?

◆

Before taking up those specific difficulties and "contradictions" in the Bible that have caused the most trouble to seekers of truth, let us first consider how difficulties in general should be dealt with.

With Honesty

First of all, let us deal with them honestly. Whenever you find a difficulty in the Bible, frankly acknowledge it. Do not try to obscure it; do not try to dodge it. Look it squarely in the face. Admit it frankly to whoever mentions it. If you cannot give a good, honest explanation, do not attempt any at all.

Untold harm has been done by those, who in their zeal for the infallibility of the Bible, have attempted explanations of difficulties that do not commend themselves to the honest, fair-minded man. People have concluded that if these are the best explanations, then there are really no explanations at all. And the Bible, instead of being helped, has been injured by the unintelligent zeal of foolish friends. If you are really convinced that the Bible is the Word of God, you can far better afford to wait for an honest solution to a difficulty than you can afford to attempt a solution that is evasive and unsatisfactory.

With Humility

Second, let us deal with them humbly. Recognize the limitations of your own mind and knowledge, and do not for a moment imagine that there is no solution just because you have not found one. There is, in all probability, a very simple solution, even when you can find no solution at all.

With Determination

Next, deal with the difficulties determinedly. Make up your mind that you will find the solution, if you can, by any amount of study and hard thinking. The difficulties of the Bible are our heavenly Father's challenge to us to set our brains to work. Do not give up searching for a solution because you cannot find one in five or ten minutes. Ponder over it and work over it for days, if necessary. The work will do you more good than the solution does. There is a solution somewhere, and you will find it if you will only search for it long enough and hard enough.

Without Fear

In the fourth place, deal with the difficulties fearlessly. Do not be frightened when you find a difficulty, no matter how unanswerable or how insurmountable it appears at first sight. Thousands have found just such difficulties before you were born. They were seen hundreds of years ago, and still the old Book stands.

The Bible that has stood so many centuries of rigid examination and incessant and awful assault is not likely to go down before your discoveries or before the discharges of any modern critical guns. To one who is at all familiar with the history of critical attacks on the Bible, the confidence of those modern destructive critics who think they are going to annihilate the Bible at last is simply amusing.

With Patience

Fifth, deal with the difficulty patiently. Do not be discouraged because you do not solve every problem in a day. If some difficulty persistently defies your very best efforts at a solution, lay it aside for a while. Very likely when you come back to it, it will have disappeared, and you will wonder how you were ever perplexed by it.

According to Scripture

Furthermore, deal with the difficulties scripturally. If you find a difficulty in one part of the Bible, look for other Scriptures to throw light on it and dissolve it. Nothing explains Scripture like Scripture. Time and again people have come to me and asked for a solution to some difficulty in the Bible that had greatly staggered them, and I have been able to give a solution by simply asking them to read some other chapter and verse. In the end, the simple reading of that verse has thrown such a light on the passage in question that all the mists have disappeared, and the truth has shone out as clear as day.

With Prayer

Finally, deal with the difficulty prayerfully. It is simply wonderful how difficulties dissolve when we look at them on our knees. Not only does God open our eyes in answer to prayer to *"see wondrous things from* [His] *law"* (Ps. 119:18), but He also opens our eyes to look straight through a difficulty that seemed impenetrable before we prayed. One great reason why many modern Bible scholars have learned to be destructive critics is that they have forgotten how to pray.

Having considered how the difficulties in the Bible should be dealt with, let us now examine in more detail the difficulties and seeming contradictions that have baffled so many students of the Scriptures.

Chapter 4

Genesis 1: Historical and Scientific?

◆——————

There is no part of the Bible that the more scholarly opponents of its divine origin are more fond of attacking than the very first chapter in the Book. Time and again we have been assured that the teachings of this chapter are in hopeless conflict with the best established conclusions of modern science. Even a prominent theological teacher in a supposedly Christian university has said that "no one who knows what history or science are would think of calling the first chapter of Genesis either historical or scientific."

Yet in spite of this confident assertion, men who have gained a name as historians beyond anything that this teacher of theology can expect assure us that Genesis 1 is not only historical, but also the very foundation of history. Other men who have secured for themselves a position in the scientific world to which I can never hope to aspire assure us that this chapter agrees absolutely with everything that is known scientifically of the origin and early history of the earth. For example, Lord Kelvin, who is greatly admired in the scientific world, said, "Physical science has nothing to say against the order of creation as given in Genesis."

The Length of a Day

This being said, let us come to the specific difficulties in the first chapter of Genesis. The objector is fond of telling us that "the first chapter of Genesis says that the world was created in six days of twenty-four hours each, when everyone who is familiar with modern science knows that the world as it now stands was millions of years in the making." This objection sounds good to the ear, but the one who makes it displays a hopeless ignorance of the Bible.

Anyone who is at all familiar with the Bible and the way the Bible uses words knows that the use of the word *day* is not limited to periods of twenty-four hours. It is frequently used to denote a period of time of an entirely undefined length. For example, in Joel 3:18–20, the millennial period is spoken of as a day. In Zechariah 2:10–13, the millennial period is again spoken of as a day, and again in Zechariah 13:1–2 and 14:9. Even in the second chapter of Genesis, the whole period covered by the six days of the first account is spoken of as a day (Gen. 2:4).

There is no necessity whatever for interpreting the days of Genesis 1 as solar days of twenty-four hours each. They may be vast periods of undefined length. Yet someone may say, "This is twisting the Scriptures to make them fit the conclusions of modern science." The one who says so simply displays his ignorance of the history of biblical interpretation. St. Augustine, as far back as the fourth century, centuries before modern science and its conclusions were dreamed of, interpreted the days of Genesis 1 as periods of time, just as the word means in many places elsewhere in the Bible.

The Order of Creation

Another point urged against the truth and accuracy in the account of Creation given in Genesis 1 is that it speaks of there being light before the sun existed. Some people will say, "It is absurd to think of light before the sun, the source of light." The one who says this displays his ignorance of modern science. Anyone who is familiar with the nebular hypothesis, commonly accepted among scientific men today, knows that there was cosmic light ages before the sun became differentiated from the general luminous nebulous mass as a separate body. Nevertheless, the objector further urges, against the scientific accuracy of Genesis 1, that the order of creation in Genesis 1 is not the order determined by the investigations of modern science, but this is an assertion that cannot be proven.

It was my privilege to study geology under that prince of geologists, who has been pronounced by competent authorities to be the greatest scientific thinker of the nineteenth century with the exception of Charles Darwin, namely, Professor James D. Dana of Yale. Professor Dana once said in my presence that one reason he believed the Bible to be the Word of God was the marvelous accord of the order of creation given in Genesis with that worked out by the best scientific investigation. Note also what Lord Kelvin is quoted as saying earlier in this chapter.

It must be said, however, that men of science are constantly changing their views of what was the exact order of creation. Very recently, discoveries have been made that have overthrown creation theories held by many men of science. Their theories did not seem at first to harmonize with the order as given in the first chapter of Genesis, but these recent discoveries have brought the theories into harmony with the order set forth in that first chapter of the Scriptures.

A Refitting of the World

There is no need of going into great detail concerning this order of creation as taught by modern science and taught in Genesis 1. In fact, there is considerable reason to doubt that anything in Genesis 1, after verse 1, relates to the original creation of the universe. All the verses after the first seem rather to refer to a *refitting* of the world that had been created and had afterwards been plunged into chaos by the sin of some pre-Adamic race, to be the abode of the present race that inhabits it, the Adamic race.

Waste and Void

The reasons for thinking this way are, first, that the words translated *"without form, and void"* (Gen. 1:2) are used everywhere else in the Bible to describe the state of affairs that God brought upon people and places as a punishment for sin. For example, in Isaiah 34:11, we read of the judgment that God would bring upon Edom as a punishment for their sins in these words: *"He shall stretch out over it the line of confusion and the stones of emptiness."* The Hebrew words translated *"confusion"* and *"emptiness"* are the same that are translated *"without form, and void"* in Genesis 1:2.

We read again in Jeremiah 4:23: *"I beheld the earth, and indeed it was without form, and void."* In both instances, the words *"without form, and void"* refer to a ruin that God had sent as a punishment for sin, and the assumption is very strong that they have a similar significance in Genesis 1.

Not Created in Vain

The second reason for this interpretation is stronger yet, namely, that the Bible expressly declares that God did not create the earth *"in vain"* (Isa. 45:18). The word translated *"in vain"* in this passage is precisely the one translated *"without form"* in Genesis 1:2.

Here, then, is a plain and specific declaration in the Bible that God did not create the earth *"without form,"* so it is plain that Genesis 1:2 cannot refer to the original creation. The word translated *"was"* in Genesis 1:2 can, with perfect propriety, be translated "became"; then Genesis 1:2 would read: "And the earth became waste and void."

In that case, in Genesis 1:1, we have the actual account of Creation. It is very brief, but wonderfully expressive, instructive, and suggestive. In Genesis 1:2, we have a brief but suggestive account of how the earth became involved in desolation and emptiness, presumably through the sin of some pre-Adamic race. Then, everything after verse two does not describe the original Creation of the earth, but its fitting up anew for the new race God was to bring upon the earth—the Adamic race. Even if we allow the word *was* to stand in Genesis 1:2, and do not substitute the word *became*, it does not materially affect the interpretation.

If this is the true interpretation of the chapter (and the argument for this interpretation seems conclusive), then, of course, this record cannot by any possibility come into conflict with any discoveries of geology as yet made or to be made, for the geological strata lie prior to the period here described. The agreement of the order as set forth in Genesis 1, with the order as discovered by science, would be accounted for by the fact that God always works in orderly progress from the lower to the higher.

Chapter 5

The Antiquity of Man

◆

One of the questions that is greatly puzzling to many Bible scholars today is how to reconcile the chronology of the Bible with discoveries that are being made as to the antiquity of man. It is said that the Bible chronology only allows about four thousand years from Adam to Christ, but the Egyptian and Babylonian civilizations were highly developed before four thousand years before Christ. If there were only four thousand years from Adam to Christ, there would, of course, be only about six thousand years for the whole age of the whole human race, and historians and scientists have traced the history of the race back ten thousand or more years. How are we to reconcile these apparent discrepancies?

Uncertain Data

In the first place, let it be said that the dates commonly accepted by many historians are not at all certain. For example, in figuring out the dates of Egyptian dynasties, the data on which conclusions are built can hardly be considered decisive. Discoveries have been made of ancient records that assert that the dynasties preceding them covered certain vast periods of time that are named, but anyone who is at all familiar with the ancient and Oriental habit of exaggeration should receive these assertions regarding the length of these dynasties with a great deal of caution. While these views of the vast antiquity of the ancient Egyptian civilization, as well as the ancient civilizations of Nineveh and Babylon, are widely accepted, they are not by any means proven. We can afford to wait for more light.

The Genealogies of Scripture

In fact, it is not at all definite that there were only about four thousand years from Adam to Christ. Bishop Ussher's chronology, which is found in the margin of most reference Bibles, is not, of course, a part of the Bible itself, and its accuracy is altogether doubtful. It is founded on the supposition that the genealogies of Scripture are intended to be complete; but a careful study of the genealogies of Scripture clearly shows that they are not intended to be complete, that they often contain only some outstanding names.

For example, the genealogy in Exodus 6:16–24, if it were taken as a complete genealogy containing all the names, would make Moses the great-grandson of Levi, though 480 years intervened. Again, there is reason to question whether the lists of names in Genesis 5 and 11 are complete. One might say that the total length of time from Adam to the Flood, and from the Flood to Abraham, is never mentioned in Scripture, although the period from Joseph to Moses (Exod. 12:40) and the time from the Exodus to the building of the temple (1 Kings 6:1) are mentioned.

The fact that there are just ten names in each list also suggests that a similar arrangement may have been used in the first chapter of Matthew. The regular formula is "A lived ——— years and begat B. And A lived ——— years after he begat B and begat sons and daughters. B lived ——— years and begat C," etc.

The word translated "begat" is sometimes used not of an immediate descendant but of succeeding generations. For example, Zilpah is said to have borne her great-grandchildren (Gen. 46:18). The Hebrew word translated "bare" in this passage is the same word translated "begat" in the other passages. Bilhah is said to have borne her grandchildren (Gen. 46:25). Canaan is said to have begotten whole nations (Gen. 10:15–18).

So we see that in the formula quoted above, the meaning is not necessarily that B is the literal son of A. Rather, B may be his literal son or a distant descendant. Many centuries may have intervened between A and B. Of course, no chronology is intended by these figures. Their purpose is not at all to show the age of the world. We see, therefore, that there is no real and necessary conflict between real Bible chronology and any modern historical discoveries as to the antiquity of man.

Archaeological Discoveries

It should be said further that these ancient civilizations, which are being discovered in the vicinity of Nineveh and elsewhere, may be the remains of the pre-Adamic race already mentioned. There are passages in the Bible that seem to hint that there were some existing even in Bible times who may have belonged to these pre-Adamic races. Such may have been the Rephaim, the Zamzummin, and the Emim.

Take a look at Genesis 14:5 and Deuteronomy 2:20–21; 3:11. The hints given in those passages are somewhat obscure, but they seem to suggest the remains of a race other than the Adamic race. If such was the case, these earlier civilizations that are now being uncovered may have been theirs. No one need have the least fear of any discoveries that the archeologists may make; for if it should be found that there were early civilizations thousands of years before Christ, it would not come into any conflict whatever with what the Bible really teaches about the antiquity of man, the Adamic race.

Chapter 6

Where Did Cain Get His Wife?

◆

In almost every place that I have visited in going around the world, I have given people an opportunity to ask questions at one or two meetings. I do not think that I have ever held a meeting at which someone has not put in the question: "Where did Cain get his wife?" This seems to be a favorite question with unbelievers. I have also met young Christians who have been greatly puzzled and perplexed over this question. Yet if one will study his Bible carefully and note exactly what it says, there is really no great difficulty in this question.

Unbelievers constantly assert that the Bible says that "Cain went into the land of Nod and took to himself a wife." In fact, it says nothing of the kind. An unbeliever in Edinburgh came to me with the assertion that the Bible did say this, and when I told him it did not, he offered to bet me one hundred pounds that it did. What the Bible does say is that *"Cain went out from the presence of the LORD and dwelt in the land of Nod on the east of Eden. And Cain knew his wife; and she conceived and bore Enoch"* (Gen. 4:16–17).

What the Bible means by *"knew"* in such connection, any-one can discover for himself by taking his concordance and looking it up. He will discover that the word *knew* in this context does not mean "to get acquainted with," but it is connected with the procreation of the species. (See, for example, Genesis 4:1; Judges 11:39; 1 Samuel 1:19; Matthew 1:25.) Cain doubtless had his wife before going to the Land of Nod and took her there with him.

In either case, who was she, and where did he get her? In Genesis 5:3–5, we learn that Adam in his long life of 930 years fathered many sons and daughters. There can be little doubt that Cain married one of those numerous daughters as his wife.

Yet someone will say, "In that case Cain married his own sister." Yes, that was, of course, a necessity. If the whole Adamic race was to descend from a single pair, the sons and daughters had to intermarry. However, as the race increased, it remained no longer necessary for men to marry their own sisters; and the practice, if continued, would result in great mischief to the race.

Indeed, even the intermarriage of cousins in the present day is laden with frightful consequences. There are parts of the globe where the inhabitants have been largely shut out from contact with other people; the intermarriages of cousins have been frequent, and the physical and mental results have been very bad. But in the dawn of human history, such an intermarriage was not surrounded with these dangers. As late as the time of Abraham, that patriarch married his half sister. (See Genesis 20:12.)

However, as the race multiplied and such intermarriages became unnecessary, and as they were accompanied with great dangers, God by special commandment forbade the marriage of brother and sister (Lev. 18:9); such marriages now would be sin because of this commandment of God. Yet it was not sin in the dawn of the race, when the only male and female inhabitants of the earth were brothers and sisters. Such marriages today would be a crime, the crime of incest, but we cannot reasonably carry back the conditions of today into the time of the dawn of human history and judge actions performed then by the conditions and laws existing today.

If we were to throw the Bible account overboard and adopt the evolutionary hypothesis as to the origin of the human race, we would not relieve matters at all, for in that case our early ancestors would have been beasts, and the father and mother of the human race would be descendants of the same pair of beasts, brother and sister beasts. Take whatever theory of the origin of the human race that we may, we are driven to the conclusion that in the early history of the race, there was the necessary intermarriage of the children of the same pair.

To sum it all up, Cain married one of the many daughters of Adam and Eve, and the impenetrable mystery that some fantastic occurrence surrounds the question of where Cain got his wife is found to be no mystery at all.

Chapter 7

God's Command to Abraham

◆——————————

One of the most frequent objections made to the Bible is that "the Bible says that God commanded Abraham to offer his son as a burnt offering." It is claimed that this story justifies the horrible practice of human sacrifices. Not many years ago, when an insane man actually did slay his son as a sacrifice to God, infidels proclaimed that the Bible, in its story of Abraham and Isaac, was responsible for the action.

Many Christians have been bewildered and distressed by this story. How can one remove this apparent difficulty? It can be easily answered in the same way that most Bible difficulties may be understood, namely, by noting exactly what the Bible says.

"Offer Him," Not "Slay Him"

Notice, in the first place, that the Bible nowhere says that God commanded Abraham to slay Isaac. It is constantly said by enemies of the Bible that the Bible commanded Abraham to slay Isaac, but this is not what the Bible says. Exactly what the Bible says is that God commanded Abraham to *"offer him there as a burnt offering"* (Gen. 22:2). Literally translated, God commanded Abraham to "make him go up [that is, upon the altar] for a burnt offering."

Abraham was merely commanded to lay Isaac on the altar as an offering to God. Whether God would require him to go further and slay his son, once he was laid on the altar and presented to God, Abraham did not know. All that God commanded was for him to *"offer him"* (Gen. 22:2), ready to be slain and burned if God should so require.

Did God so require? The record expressly declares that He did not. On the contrary, God plainly forbade the actual slaughter

441

of Isaac (v. 12). That the original command was not to kill Isaac, but merely to *"offer him,"* is clear from the fact that we are explicitly told that Abraham did exactly what God told him to do, that is, *"By faith Abraham...offered up Isaac"* (Heb. 11:17). Abraham did exactly what he was told to do, but Abraham did not slay Isaac—he was not told to do *that*.

The divine commandment to offer was not a command to slay. The story as told in the Bible is not that God had first commanded Abraham to slay and burn Isaac, and that, afterwards, when He saw that Abraham was willing to do even this, He took it back and provided a lamb to take Isaac's place. The Bible story is that God commanded Abraham to make his son Isaac ascend the altar to be presented to God as a whole offering, and that Abraham actually did what he was commanded to do. This did not, either in God's original intention or in the execution of the command, involve the slaughter of Isaac.

The Forbiddance of Human Sacrifice

This story, then, in no way justifies human sacrifice. On the contrary, the whole force of the narrative is against such sacrifice. Instead of being commanded, it is explicitly forbidden. It does, however, justify the offering of ourselves to God wholly, as *"a living sacrifice"* (Rom. 12:1).

The Bible tells us that when Abraham was about to slay his son, God intervened and positively forbade it. Jehovah sent His own angel to speak in an audible voice from heaven, forbidding the shedding of Isaac's blood:

> *Do not lay your hand on the lad, or do anything to him; for now I know that you fear God, since you have not withheld your son, your only son, from Me.* (Gen. 22:12)

This story, then, far from encouraging human sacrifice, positively and explicitly forbids it in the most solemn manner. All our difficulty with this narrative disappears when we look carefully with open eyes at the record and note precisely what is said.

Chapter 8

Pharaoh's Hard Heart

◆━━━━━━━━━━◆

Various statements made in the Scriptures in regard to God's hardening Pharaoh's heart have perplexed many young Christians and have frequently been used by unbelievers in their attacks on the Bible. It is said that if God hardened Pharaoh's heart, and in consequence of this hardening of Pharaoh's heart, Pharaoh rebelled against God, then God Himself was responsible for Pharaoh's sin. In that case, how could it be just to hold Pharaoh accountable for his rebellion and to punish him for it?

In Exodus 4:21, we read:

And the LORD said to Moses, "When you go back to Egypt, see that you do all those wonders before Pharaoh which I have put in your hand. But I will harden his heart, so that he will not let the people go."

From reading this passage, along with Exodus 7:3 and 14:4, it does seem at first glance as if there were some ground for criticism of God's action in this matter, or at least of the Bible account of it. Yet when we study carefully exactly what the Bible says, exactly what God is reported as saying, and the circumstances under which He said it, the difficulty disappears.

If God were to take a man who really desires to know and do His will and harden his heart and thus incline him not to do His will, it would indeed be an action on God's part that would be difficult or impossible to justify. However, when we read God's utterances on this matter in their context, we find this is not at all what God did with Pharaoh. Pharaoh was not a man who wished to obey God.

443

The whole account begins not with God hardening Pharaoh's heart, but rather with Pharaoh hardening his own heart. In Exodus 4:21, we have a prophecy of what God would do with Pharaoh, a prophecy that God made, fully knowing beforehand what Pharaoh would do before He hardened his heart. In Exodus 9:12, and in later passages, we have the fulfillment of this prophecy; but before God does here harden Pharaoh's heart, we have a description of what Pharaoh himself did.

In Exodus 5:1–2, we are told that Moses and Aaron appeared in the presence of Pharaoh with Jehovah's message:

> *Thus says the* LORD *God of Israel: "Let My people go, that they may hold a feast to Me in the wilderness." And Pharaoh said, "Who is the* LORD, *that I should obey His voice to let Israel go? I do not know the* LORD, *nor will I let Israel go."*

Here, Pharaoh definitely and defiantly refuses to recognize or obey God. In truth, he hardened his own heart. This was before God hardened his heart. Then follows a description of how Pharaoh gave himself over to crueler oppression of the Israelites than ever (vv. 3–9).

In Exodus 7:10 and following, we see Moses and Aaron coming into the presence of Pharaoh and performing signs before him as proof that they were messengers sent from God, but Pharaoh would not listen. In the thirteenth verse, we read: *"And Pharaoh's heart grew hard, and he did not heed them, as the* LORD *had said."* It does not say as yet that the Lord hardened his heart.

The fact, then, is that Pharaoh was a cruel and oppressive tyrant, subjecting the people of Israel to horrible bondage, suffering, and death. God looked on His people, heard their cries, and in His mercy determined to deliver them (Exod. 2:25; 3:7–8). He sent Moses, as His representative, to Pharaoh to demand the deliverance of His people, and Pharaoh in proud rebellion defied Him and gave himself up to even crueler oppression of the people. It was then, and only then, that God hardened his heart.

This was simply in pursuance of God's universal method of dealing with men. God's universal method is, if men choose error, He gives them up to error (2 Thess. 2:9–12); if they choose sin, at last He gives them over to sin (Rom. 1:24–28). This is stern dealing, but it is also just dealing.

If there is any difficulty that still remains in the incident, it all disappears when we consider the manner in which God hardened Pharaoh's heart. It was, of course, not a physical act. God was not dealing with Pharaoh's heart as a part of his body. He was dealing with Pharaoh's heart in the sense of the supposed seat of intelligence, emotion, and will.

The will cannot be coerced by force. The will can no more be moved by force than a train of cars can be drawn by an argument or an inference. The way in which God hardened Pharaoh's heart was by sending to him a series of demonstrations of His own existence and power and a series of judgments. If Pharaoh had taken the right attitude toward these revelations of God's existence, if he had recognized God's power in these judgments that God sent upon him, they would have led to his repentance and salvation. Yet, by willingly and willfully taking the wrong attitude toward them, he was hardened by them.

Nothing God sends us is more merciful than the judgments that He sends upon our sins. If we take these judgments correctly, they will soften our hearts and lead us to repentance and entire surrender to God, and thus bring us salvation. However, if we rebel against them, they will harden our hearts and bring us eternal ruin. The fault is not with God, and the fault is not with His judgments; rather, the fault is with us and with the attitude we take toward His judgments and toward the truth of God itself. The Gospel is the *"fragrance of Christ"* (2 Cor. 2:15) to those who receive it aright, but it is the *"aroma of death"* (v.16) to those who reject it.

The trouble is not with the Gospel, which is *"the power of God to salvation for everyone who believes"* (Rom. 1:16). The trouble is with the man who rejects the Gospel and who is thus hardened, condemned, and destroyed by it. To him it becomes the *"aroma of death leading to death"* (2 Cor. 2:16).

Often the same sermon brings life to one person and death to another. It brings life, pardon, and peace to the one who believes it and acts on it; it brings condemnation and death to the one who rejects its truth. It softens the heart of one; it hardens the heart of the other. Jesus Christ Himself came into the world, not to condemn the world, but to save the world (John 3:17); but to the one who does not believe, He brings condemnation and eternal ruin (vv. 18, 36).

Chapter 9

The Slaughter of the Canaanites

◆━━━━━◆

There are few things in the Bible over which more intelligent readers have stumbled, and over which infidels have more frequently gloated and gloried, than God's command that certain peoples should be utterly exterminated, sparing neither gender nor age. Men, women, and children were to be slain.

For example, we read in Deuteronomy 20:16–17 this command of God to the people of Israel:

> *But of the cities of these peoples which the LORD your God gives you as an inheritance, you shall let nothing that breathes remain alive, but you shall utterly destroy them: the Hittite and the Amorite and the Canaanite and the Perizzite and the Hivite and the Jebusite, just as the LORD your God has commanded you.*

In regard to other cities, it was commanded that if they pleaded for peace, peace was to be granted and all the inhabitants spared; but if they made war, the adult males were to be slain, but the women and children were to be spared. (See Deuteronomy 20:10–15.) These were the cities that were far away, but the inhabitants of the cities of the lands that the Israelites themselves were to inhabit were to be utterly exterminated.

We are asked, "How can we reconcile such appallingly harsh commands as these with the doctrine so plainly taught in the New Testament that *'God is love'* (1 John 4:8)?" It is said that these commands cannot have come from God, and that the Old Testament is certainly wrong when it says that they were from God. What can we say in reply to this charge?

Sin Made It Necessary

Let us say, first of all, that it is certainly appalling that any people should be utterly put to the sword, not only the men of war, but old men and old women, as well as young women and children. Yet there is something more appalling than even this when one stops to think about the matter; that is that the iniquity of any people should have become so full, their rebellion against God so strong and so universal, their moral corruption and debasement so utter and so pervasive, even down to babes just born, as to make such treatment absolutely necessary in the interests of humanity.

This was precisely the case with the nations in question. We learn, not only from the Bible but also from other sources, how unfathomable were the depths of moral pollution to which these nations had sunken. They had become a moral cancer threatening the very life of the whole human race. That cancer had be cut out in every fiber if the body was to be saved. Removing a cancer is a dreadful operation, an operation from which any kind-hearted surgeon must shrink, but often the cutting out of the cancer is the kindest thing the surgeon can do under existing circumstances. Similarly, the kindest thing that God could do for the human race was to cut out this cancer in every root and every fiber.

For the Good of the Whole Race

Let us say, in the second place, that God certainly has a right to visit judgment on individuals and on nations immersed in sin. The only wonder, when one stops to think about it, is that He is so longsuffering and that He does not visit judgment on individuals and on nations sooner. When one really comes to understand His holiness on the one hand, and on the other hand the depths of covetousness, greed, lust, sin, vileness, lawlessness, and contempt for God to which certain cities even today have sunk, and how even young children go astray into unmentionable vileness, one almost wonders why He does not blot them out, as He commanded the Israelites to do with the Canaanites of old.

The command to exterminate the Canaanites was a command filled with mercy and love. It was mercy and love to the Israelites. Unless the Canaanites were exterminated, the Israelites would themselves be exterminated. In fact, the Israelites were contaminated for the very reason that they did not carry out God's stern decree to its fullest extent. They stopped short of what God commanded them to do, to their own lasting loss.

"But what about the women; could not they have been spared?" The answer is very clear. The women were often the prime source of contamination (Num. 31:15–16). Though true women are nobler than true men, depraved women are far more dangerous than depraved men. "But what about the children? Could not they have been spared?" Anyone who has had experience with the children of the depraved knows how the vices bred for generations in the ancestors reappear persistently in the children, even when they are taken away from their evil surroundings and brought up in the most favorable environment.

By the regenerating power of the Gospel, it is possible to correct all this, but we must remember that the case with which we are dealing was centuries before the Gospel proclamation. Love and mercy for Israel demanded just what God commanded; love and mercy for the whole race demanded it. God's purpose in Israel was not merely to bless Israel. Through Israel, He planned to bless the whole race. He was training a people in the seclusion of centuries in order that when the training was completed they might come out of the cloister and carry benediction, salvation, and life to all nations.

God's Plans Are beyond Our Scrutiny

Let it be said, in the third place, that God's plans are not only beneficent, but also vast, and it takes centuries to work them out. We creatures of a day, in our little conceit, look at some little fragment of God's infinite plan and presume to judge the whole, of which we know little or nothing. It would be well if we could only learn that God is infinite and we infinitesimal; and so out of scientific and philosophic necessity, *"how unsearchable are His judgments and His ways past finding out!"* (Rom. 11:33). A child never appears a greater fool than when criticizing a philosopher, and a philosopher never appears a greater fool than when criticizing God.

An Act of Mercy toward the Children

In the fourth place, the extermination of the Canaanite children was not only an act of mercy and love to the world at large, but it was also an act of love and mercy to the children themselves. What awaited these children, if they had been allowed to live, was something vastly worse than death.

What awaited them in death, it is impossible to be dogmatic about; but unless one accepts the wholly unbiblical and improbable doctrine of the damnation of all unbaptized infants, we need have no fears. Even today I could almost wish that all the babes born in the darkness of heathenism might be slain in infancy, were it not for the hope that the church of Christ would awaken and carry to them the saving Gospel of the Son of God.

Someone may still say, "Yes, I can see it was an act of mercy to blot out people so fallen, but why was it not done by pestilence or famine, rather than by the slaying hand of the Israelites?" The answer is very simple. The Israelites themselves were in training. They were constantly falling into sin, and they needed the solemn lesson that would come to them through their being made the executioners of God's wrath against the wickedness and vileness of the Canaanites. A deep impression would thus be produced of God's holiness and hatred of sin.

The Israelites were distinctly told, before they carried into execution God's judgment upon the Canaanites, that the reason they were to utterly destroy the Canaanites was *"lest they teach you to do according to all their abominations which they have done for their gods, and you sin against the LORD your God"* (Deut. 20:18). The whole proceeding is an impressive illustration of the exceeding hatefulness of sin in God's sight. It says to us that sin persisted in is a thing so grievous and ruinous as to necessitate the utter destruction of the entire race, male and female, young and old, that persist in it. It is simply the lesson that the whole Bible teaches, and that all history teaches, written in characters of fire: *"The wages of sin is death"* (Rom. 6:23).

Consciousness of Our Own Sin

Let it be said, in the fifth place, that those who regard sin lightly, and who have no adequate conception of God's holiness, will always find insurmountable difficulty in this command of God. On the other hand, those who have come to see the awfulness of sin, have learned to hate it with the infinite hate it deserves, have caught some glimpses of the infinite holiness of God, and have been made in some measure partakers of that holiness, will, after mature reflection, have no difficulty whatever with this command. It is consciousness of sin in our own hearts and lives that makes us rebel against God's stern dealings with sin.

The Sparing of the Women

One more thing needs to be said. The sneering objection is sometimes made by infidels to the sparing, in certain cases, of the women as recorded in Deuteronomy 20:10–15, and also the sparing of the women in Numbers 31:21–35, 40, that the women were to be spared for immoral purposes. One writer has asked, "Am I to understand that God approved of taking as tribute in spoils of war a number of virgins, for a use that is only too obvious?" Words of similar import are to be found in a number of infidel books.

Of course, what the questioner meant to imply is that these women were taken for immoral purposes. This is the use that is "only too obvious" to the objector. Even so, this is not at all obvious to any pure-minded person who reads the actual Scripture account. There is in the Scripture account not the slightest intimation that the virgins were preserved for the use suggested. To the one whose own heart is evil and impure, of course it will always be obvious that if women are preserved alive and taken as tribute, they are taken for this purpose; but this will not even occur to the pure-minded man.

The whole context of the passage in Numbers 31, which is the one most frequently cited in this connection by unbelievers, is a solemn warning against immorality of this kind. Far from this passage being a suggestion that God sanctions impurity of this character, it shows how sternly God dealt with this impurity.

In Numbers 25, we are told how the men of Israel gave themselves up to impurity with the daughters of Moab, but how in consequence *"the anger of the LORD was aroused against* [them]" (v. 3), and how God visited their impurity with the sternest judgment (vv. 5, 8–9). In the very chapter in question, every woman who had been guilty of impurity was slain (Num. 31:17). In fact, it is suggested, at least by verse eighteen, that it was only the female children who could be spared.

It was certainly an act of mercy on God's part to deliver these *"young girls"* (v. 18) from their evil surroundings, and hand them over to Israel for training, where they would be brought in contact with a pure religion and trained to become pure women. So, according to the record, far from being handed over to the Israelites for immoral purposes, they were entrusted to them for the highest purposes of all.

Chapter 10

The Sun Stands Still

◆

One of the greatest difficulties in the Bible to many students is found in the story recorded in Joshua 10:12–14, about which Bishop Colenso wrote, "The miracle of Joshua is the most striking instance of Scripture and science being at variance." This Scripture reads:

> *Then Joshua spoke to the LORD in the day when the LORD delivered up the Amorites before the children of Israel, and he said in the sight of Israel: "Sun, stand still over Gibeon; and Moon, in the Valley of Aijalon." So the sun stood still, and the moon stopped, till the people had revenge upon their enemies. Is this not written in the Book of Jasher? So the sun stood still in the midst of heaven, and did not hasten to go down for about a whole day. And there has been no day like that, before it or after it, that the LORD heeded the voice of a man; for the LORD fought for Israel.*

It is said by destructive critics and infidels that this story cannot possibly be true; that if the sun were to stand still in the way recorded here, it would upset the whole course of nature. Whether that is true or not, no one can tell. It is simply a supposition. Yet certainly the God who made the earth and the sun and the whole universe could maintain it even if the sun stood still, or to speak more accurately, if the earth stood still on its axis and the sun appeared to stand still.

Nevertheless, by a careful study of the Hebrew, we find that the sun is not said to have stood still. The command of Joshua in verse twelve, which says, *"Sun, stand still,"* literally translated means "be silent," and the words rendered *"stood still"* in verse thirteen literally translated mean "was silent." Nine times in the Bible it is translated as "keep silence"; five times at least, "be still"; in another passage, "held his peace"; in another, "quiet oneself"; in another, "tarry"; in another, "wait"; and in another, "rest." These renderings occur some thirty times, but it is never translated "stand still" except in this one passage.

Indeed, in the very passage in which it is rendered *"wait"* (1 Sam. 14:9), the words *stand still* do occur, but as the translation of an entirely different Hebrew word. The word translated *"stopped"* in Joshua 10:13 is sometimes translated "stand still." It means literally "to stand" or "stand up," but it is used of tarrying or remaining in any place, state, or condition, as, for example, in 2 Kings 15:20 or in Genesis 45:1.

So, then, what the sun and moon are said to have done in the passage is to have *tarried,* tarried from disappearing, not that they stood absolutely still, but that their apparent motion, or their disappearance, was slowed up or delayed. Furthermore, the Hebrew words translated *"in the midst of heaven"* (Josh. 10:13) mean literally "in the half of heaven." The word translated *"midst,"* in considerably more than one hundred cases, is translated "half." In only five or six cases is it rendered *"midst,"* and in one of these cases (Dan. 9:27) the Revised Version has changed *midst* to *half.* In the remaining cases it would be as well, or better, if it were *half* (for example, Psalm 102:24).

What Joshua bade the sun to do, then, was to linger in the half of the heavens, and that is what the sun is recorded as doing. There are two halves to the heavens, the half that is visible to us and the other half visible on the other side of the globe. The Hebrew preposition rendered *"about"* (Josh. 10:13) means primarily "as" or "so." Therefore, put these facts together, and what the story tells us is that the sun continued or tarried above the visible horizon for a whole day.

Apparently, this means that an event occurred on this day near Gibeon, in the valley of Aijalon, that occurs many days every year at the North Pole, namely, that the sun remained visible for the entire twenty-four hours. We are not told the method by which this was accomplished. It might be by a slight dip of the pole, or possibly by a refraction of the rays of light, or in other ways that we cannot conjecture. It certainly would not necessitate such a crash in the physical universe as objectors have imagined.

As to whether such a thing happened or not is a question of history. The history in the book of Joshua, which we have reason to believe is authentic, says that it did. It is a remarkable fact that we also have a suggestion of the same thing in history outside the Bible. Herodotus, the great Greek historian, tells us that the priests of Egypt showed him a record of a long day. The Chinese writings state that there was such a day in the reign of their emperor Yeo, who is thought to have been a contemporary of Joshua. The Mexicans also have a record that the sun stood still for one entire day in the year that is supposed to correspond with the exact year in which Joshua was warring in Palestine.

There is really nothing of any weight to prove that there was no such day. So, on careful examination, this "most striking instance of Scripture and science being at variance" is found to be in no sense whatever an instance of Scripture and science, or even Scripture and history, being at variance.

The theory has been advanced that the words rendered *"stand still"* (v. 12), which mean literally "be silent," should be interpreted as meaning that Joshua commanded the sun to be silent in the sense of withholding its light, and that what occurred on this occasion was not the prolongation of a day, but a dark day, so that Joshua had the advantage of fighting practically at night, though it was really the time of the day that should have been light.

Of course, if this is the true interpretation of *"stand still,"* all difficulty with the passage disappears. Yet, while this interpretation might be admissible, it is difficult to see how some other portions of the narrative can be reconciled with this theory. And, as already seen, this particular theory is not necessary to remove all difficulties in the passage.

Of course, in any event, it was a miracle, but no one who believes in a God who is the Creator of the entire material universe, and a God who is historically proven to have raised Jesus Christ from the dead, ever stumbles at the mere fact of a miracle. We believe in a miracle-working God.

Chapter 11

Deborah's Praise of a Murderess

◆

I t is frequently urged against the divine origin of the Bible that it defends and glorifies the treacherous murder of Sisera by Jael, and that any book that defends so violent, cruel, and deceitful an action as this cannot have God for its author.

The very simple answer to this objection is that the Bible neither defends nor glorifies the action of Jael. The Bible simply records the act in all its details. It also records the fact that Deborah, the prophetess who judged Israel at that time (Judg. 4:4), predicted that the Lord would sell Sisera into the hand of a woman (v. 9). It also records the fact that Deborah and Barak, in their joyful song of praise to the Lord after their deliverance from the cruel oppression of Sisera, did say, *"Most blessed among women is Jael, the wife of Heber the Kenite; blessed is she among women in tents"* (Judg. 5:24).

However, nowhere is it hinted in the biblical account that Deborah and Barak were speaking by divine inspiration in this song of thanksgiving and praise. The Bible, by speaking of Deborah as a prophetess, no more endorses every action and every utterance of Deborah than it endorses every action and every utterance of Balaam, of whom it likewise refers to as a *"prophet"* (2 Pet. 2:15–16). In the very passage in which it speaks of Balaam as a prophet, it speaks about his being rebuked for his iniquities.

It is not the teaching of the Bible that every utterance of every prophet is the inspired Word of God. On the contrary, the Bible teaches that a prophet may tell lies. (See 1 Kings 13:11–18.) The Bible nowhere justifies Jael's action. It simply records the action. It records Deborah and Barak's praise of the action, but it nowhere endorses this praise. We are under no necessity, therefore, of trying to justify all the details of Jael's conduct, nor indeed of trying to justify her conduct at all.

On the other hand, we must not unjustly judge Jael. We cannot judge her in the light of New Testament ethics, for she lived some three hundred years before Christ. She lived in a cruel age. Furthermore, she had to deal with a cruel oppressor, who was working ruin among the people. It was a time of war—war not conducted according to modern ideas of war—and we must judge her in the light of the conditions in which she lived. Nevertheless, even if her conduct were absolutely without excuse, it does not in the least affect the proven fact of the divine origin of the Bible. That Book makes absolutely no attempt to defend her conduct; it simply describes it.

Chapter 12

The Sacrifice of Jephthah's Daughter

◆

The story of Jephthah's daughter, as recorded in the Bible, has presented a great difficulty to many superficial students of the Bible, as well as to many critics of it. "How can we possibly justify Jephthah's burning of his daughter as a sacrifice to Jehovah?" we are often asked.

In reply we would say, in the first place, nowhere are we told that Jephthah did burn his daughter. We are told that Jephthah vowed the following:

> *Whatever comes out of the doors of my house to meet me, when I return in peace from the people of Ammon, shall surely be the Lord's, and I will offer it up as a burnt offering.* (Judg. 11:31)

The word translated *"burnt offering"* does not necessarily involve the idea of burning. There is no record that Jephthah's daughter was actually slain and burned. The passage that relates what actually was done with her is somewhat obscure, and many think that she was devoted by her father, as an offering to God, by her living a life of perpetual virginity. (See Judges 11:37–39.)

Even supposing that she was slain and burned—as many candid Bible students believe, though the Bible does not actually say she was—even in this case, there is no necessity for defending Jephthah's action. We are not in any way required to defend any wrong action of all the imperfect instruments that God, in His wondrous grace and mercy, has seen fit to use in helping His people.

The Bible itself nowhere defends Jephthah's action. If Jephthah really did slay his daughter, he simply made a vow in haste, without any command or warrant from God for doing so; having made this vow, he went forth in his wrongdoing and carried that rash vow into execution. In that case, the whole story, instead of being a warrant for human sacrifice, is intended to be a lesson on the exceeding folly of hasty vows made in the impulsivity of the flesh.

Chapter 13

"Impure" Bible Stories

◆

An old and favorite objection to the Bible on the part of un-believers is that the Bible contains "chapters that reek with obscenity from beginning to end." Of course, we have no desire to deny that there are chapters in the Bible that de-scribe scenes that cannot be dealt with wisely in a mixed audi-ence, but these chapters are not obscene.

To speak of sin—even the vilest of sins—in its plainest terms, is not obscenity. It is purity in one of its highest forms. Whether the story of sin is obscene or not depends entirely on how it is told and for what purpose it is told. If the story is told in order to make a joke of sin, or in order to palliate or excuse sin, it is obscene. On the other hand, if a story is told in order to make people hate sin, to show them the hideousness of sin, to induce them to keep sin as far away as possible, and to show their need of redemption, it is not obscene; rather, it is morally wholesome.

Now, this is precisely the way in which sin is portrayed in the Bible. It is true that adultery and similar offenses against purity are mentioned by name without any attempt to mince words. Revolting deeds of this character are plainly described and their awful results related, but everything is told so as to make one recoil from these horrid and disgusting sins.

Beyond a doubt, many have been kept back from the prac-tice of these sins by the plain things the Bible has said about them. Many others, who have already fallen into these sins, have been led by the Bible stories to see the enormity of their consequences, and have been led to forsake them by what the Bible says about them. I am not speculating about this, but I write from a broad range of experiences with men and women who have been tempted to these sins and have been held back by what the Bible says regarding them. I also write from a large experience with others who have already fallen and who have been lifted up and saved by the truth of what is contained in the Bible on these subjects.

It is said, "There is much in the Bible that is not fit to read in public," and this is brought forward as if it were an argument against the Bible. Yet it is an exceedingly foolish argument. Many passages in the very best and most valuable medical works are not fit to be read in public; they are not even fit for a father to read to his children. Even so, he would be a fool who would cut these passages out of these medical works on that account, and he is equally a fool who objects to the Bible because there are passages in it that are invaluable in their place but were not intended for public reading.

The Bible is like a book of moral anatomy and spiritual therapeutics, and it would be a great defect in the book—in fact, an indication that it was not from God—if it did not deal with these frightful facts about man as he is and with the method of healing these foul diseases of morals.

I, for one, thank God that these passages are in the Bible. There are things that every boy and girl needs to know at a comparatively early age about some forms of sin. Many have fallen into these forms of sin before they realized their loathsome character, simply because they were not warned against them. Ignorance about them is a misfortune. I know of no better way for young men and women to become acquainted with the effects of sins that they need to know about, than for them to read, during their time alone with God, what the Bible has to say about these sins.

Instead of finding fault with the Bible for these things in it, we ought to praise God for putting them there. For example, there are things in the first chapter of Romans that one cannot dwell on in a public address; as a rule, we often omit two verses in the public reading of this chapter. However, these two verses have been of great value in dealing with the heathen, and they have saved many in so-called Christian lands from the loathsome sins that are exposed and denounced there.

An infidel, in one of his works, challenged Christians to know if they "dare to pick up the Bible and read from the book of Genesis the fact of Onan." (See Genesis 38:8–9.) He seemed to think that this is a conclusive argument against the Bible; but it is simply silly. It might not be wise to read this chapter in public, but a private reading of that very story has saved many from the practice of a like sin. Indeed, this whole chapter, which is a favorite point of attack with infidels, has been greatly used in exposing lust and its appalling consequences.

It has also been said by an objector to the Bible, "Part of the holy writings consist of history and the narration of facts of a kind that cannot be mentioned in the presence of a virtuous woman without exciting horror. Should a woman be permitted to read in her room what one would tremble to hear at her dinner table?" This, too, is considered a logical argument against the Bible; yet when one looks carefully at it and considers it, it is seen to be utter folly.

Most assuredly, a woman should be permitted to read in her room what she would "tremble to hear" at her dinner table. Every wise woman does it. I know of books that would be most desirable for every woman to read in private, which, if they were read at the dinner table, would cause her to wish to rise from the table in embarrassment and leave the room.

There are many things that men and women should think about, and must think about, in private, that they would not for a moment discuss in public. There are books on the proper conduct of women in certain sacred relations of life that are as holy as any and that can be entered into in the presence of a holy God with no question of His approval, but that cannot be mentioned in public. It is strange that intelligent men and women should use arguments so childish as this.

That the Bible is a pure book is evidenced by the fact that it is not a favorite book in dens of infamy. On the other hand, books that try to make the Bible seem like an obscene book, and that endeavor to keep people from reading it, are favorite books in dens of infamy. Both men and women of unholy thinking were devoted admirers of a brilliant man who attacked what he called the "obscenity of the Bible." These people do not frequent Bible lectures but do frequent infidel lectures.

These infidel objectors, who refer to the Book as an "obscene Book," constantly betray their insincerity and hypocrisy. Colonel Ingersoll, in one passage where he dealt with this subject, objected to the Bible for telling these vile deeds "without a touch of humor." In other words, he did not object to telling stories of vice, if only a joke was made of the sin. Thank God, that is exactly what the Bible does not do—make a joke of sin. It makes sin hideous, so that men who are obscene in their own hearts think of the Bible as being an obscene book.

Some of those who make the most of the so-called "obscenity of the Book" are themselves notorious tellers of offensive stories. One of the men who led the attack on the Bible on the ground of its obscenity was employed by the publishers of obscene literature to defend their case. Another man, who was a leader in his city in sending out attacks on the Bible, challenging Christians to read in public certain portions of Scripture that were said to be immoral, was shortly afterwards found dead by his own hand in a Boston hotel, side by side with a young woman who was not his wife.

A man who says, "I protest against the Bible being placed in the hands of the young because its pages reek with filth," and who does not wish people to read these "vile portions" of Scripture lest their minds be defiled, takes great care to give a catalog of the passages that he does not wish to be read. He even asks his readers to look them up. Can anything exceed the hypocrisy of that?

I found in one city where I was holding meetings that a man who kept interrupting a service by calling out portions of the Scripture that he regarded as improper and immoral had himself been arrested and convicted for publishing obscene literature. The truth is, these men hate the Bible. They hate it because it denounces sin and makes them uneasy in sin.

To sum it all up, there are descriptions of sins in the Bible that cannot wisely be read in every public assembly, but these descriptions of sin are morally wholesome in the places where God, the Author of the Book, intends them to be read. The child who is brought up to read the Bible as a whole, from Genesis to Revelation, will come to know, in the very best way possible, what a child ought to know very early in life if he is to be safeguarded against the perils that surround our modern life. A child who is brought up on a constant, thorough reading of the whole Bible is more likely than any other child to be free from the vices that are undermining the mental, moral, and physical strength of our young men and young women.

But the child who is brought up on ungodly literature and conversation is the easiest prey there is for the seducer and the prostitute. The next easiest is the one who, through neglect of the Bible, is left in ignorance of the awful pitfalls of life.

Chapter 14

David's Sin

―――――――◆―――――――

In 2 Samuel 11, we read the story of one of the saddest downfalls of a man of God recorded anywhere in history, and at the same time, the record of one of the most contemptible and outrageous sins that anyone ever committed against a faithful friend. We read how David committed against Uriah, his faithful servant, one of the most outrageous offenses that one man can commit against another, and how, in order to cover up his sin, he stained his hands with the blood of this man. After the deed was done, God in His great mercy sent His prophet to David, declaring to him, *"By this deed you have given great occasion to the enemies of the LORD to blaspheme"* (2 Sam. 12:14).

History has proven the truth of this declaration. There is scarcely anything in the Bible that has caused more of the enemies of the Lord to blaspheme than this treacherous crime of King David. The enemies of the Lord are constantly bringing it up and making it the target of pitiless ridicule.

Some of those who desire to defend the Bible have thought it necessary to defend David's action, or at least to try to make it appear that it was not as heinous as it looks at first glance. Yet why should we seek to defend David's action? The Bible nowhere seeks to defend it. On the contrary, God rebuked it in the sternest terms. It was punished by a series of frightful calamities, the kind of which have seldom overtaken any other man.

It is true that David is spoken of in the Scriptures as *"a man after* [God's] *own heart"* (1 Sam. 13:14; Acts 13:22); but this does not mean that David was an absolutely faultless man. It simply means that, in distinction from Saul, who was constantly disposed to go his own way, David was a man who

465

sought in all things to know God's will and to do it exactly. Therefore, he was a man after God's own heart.

Although this was the abiding attitude of David's mind and heart toward God, it was still possible for him to fall prey to sin—just as it is possible for us today. Even a person whose will on the whole is entirely surrendered to God can step out of his position of absolute surrender to God and, in a moment of weakness and folly, commit an act so hideous in the sight of God that it will bring upon him the sternest judgment of the Lord.

The recording of David's sin, without any attempt in the Scripture to make light of it, is one of the many proofs of the divine origin and absolute reliability of the Bible. David was the great hero of his times. Unless his Bible biographers had been guided by the Holy Spirit, they certainly would have concealed, or at least have sought to palliate, this awful fault of David; but in fact, they did nothing of the kind. The Holy Spirit, who guided them in their record, led them to portray this event in all its hideousness.

Here is a radical difference between Bible biographers and all other biographers. Even the heroes of the Bible, when they fall, are not whitewashed; no excuses are offered for their sins. Their sins are not concealed from the public eye. They are recorded with fullness of detail, and the sinner is held up as a warning to others. In this particular matter, David *"despised the commandment of the LORD, to do evil in His sight"* (2 Sam. 12:9), and the Bible plainly says so.

"The thing that David had done displeased the LORD" (2 Sam. 11:27), and God set him forth before the whole world as an adulterer and a murderer (2 Sam. 12:9). The whole story is too horrible for public recital, but if one will read it in private with earnest prayer, he may find exceedingly precious lessons in it. It was one of the most treacherous crimes of history, but I am glad that it is recorded in the Bible. The record of it and its consequences have held many people back from contemplated sin.

The Best Men Can Still Fall

The story of David's sin abounds in great lessons. The first lesson that it teaches us is that an exceptionally good man, yes, a man "after God's own heart," if he gets his eyes off God and His words, may easily fall into very gross sin. Anyone *"who trusts in his own heart is a fool"* (Prov. 28:26). Anyone who imagines that he is a match for the Devil in his own wisdom and strength is badly deceived.

David was one of the noblest men of his day. He was brave; he was generous; he had a single-hearted purpose to do the will of God; but he allowed himself to trifle with temptation, and he went down to the deepest depths of vileness, baseness, and dishonor.

God Is Not Partial

The story also teaches us that God never looks on anyone's sin with the least degree of approval. God has no favorites (Rom. 2:11), in the sense that He allows some people's sins to go unpunished. God loved David. He had given David remarkable proofs of His love. But when David sinned, God dealt with his sin with the sternest and most relentless judgment. He allowed David's sin to plague him and to embitter his life to his dying day.

God forgave David's sin and restored him to fellowship and the joy of his salvation (Ps. 51:12), but God let David drink deeply of the bitter cup he had mixed for himself. One of his sons followed him into adultery, the burden of which came on David's own daughter. (See 2 Samuel 13:1–14.) Another son followed him into murder (see 2 Samuel 13:28–29); and as David had rebelled against his heavenly Father, his own son rebelled against him. (See 2 Samuel 15:13–14.) David was left to reap what he had sown. David cried over this rebellious son as he lay before David, silent in death: *"O my son Absalom; my son, my son Absalom; if only I had died in your place! O Absalom my son, my son!"* (2 Sam. 18:33).

Yet David knew full well that Absalom's wandering and Absalom's death were simply the fruit of his own sin.

Full Pardon for All Sinners

But there is another precious lesson for us, too, in the history of David's sin, and it is that there is full and free pardon for

467

even the vilest sinner. David's sin was black, black as midnight; it was appalling; it was inexcusable; but David found pardon, full and free. David said, *"I have sinned against the LORD,"* and God said through Nathan, His prophet, *"The LORD also has put away your sin"* (2 Sam. 12:13).

David himself told us, in one of his most beautiful psalms, the story of his pardon (Ps. 32:1–6). God is a holy God. He hates sin with infinite hatred. He will not look on the smallest sin with the least bit of consent. Yet God is also a God of pardoning love. He stands ready to forgive the vilest sinner. He is ever calling to men and women who have sinned:

> *Let the wicked forsake his way, and the unrighteous man his thoughts; let him return to the LORD, and He will have mercy on him; and to our God, for He will abundantly pardon.* (Isa. 55:7)

There are those who think they have sinned too deeply to ever find pardon, but it is not so. It would be hard to find one who had sinned more deeply than David. He committed the greatest wrong one man can commit against another, and he stained his hands with the blood of his victim, yet still he found pardon. I thank God for this story of David. It gives me hope for everyone. In the light of it as told in the Bible, I do not care who comes and asks me, "Is there salvation for me?" because I will not hesitate to answer, "Yes, David found mercy and so can you."

One night I was speaking to a man under deep conviction of sin. He had stained his hands with the blood of a fellowman. He had shot another to death. He said there could be no pardon for him. I took him to David's prayer in Psalm 51:14 and showed him that David was delivered from bloodshed and that there was pardon for him, too.

Chapter 15

The Imprecatory Psalms

A frequent objection urged against the Bible is some of the utterances in the so-called "Imprecatory Psalms," or the Psalms that seem to be full of curses and prayers for injury to fall upon others. Many of these statements have greatly perplexed earnest-minded Christians who have carefully studied the New Testament teachings regarding the forgiveness of enemies.

Three passages in the Psalms are especially cited by a recent writer as showing that the Bible is not the Word of God. The first is Psalm 58:6: *"Break their teeth in their mouth, O God!"* It is said that this utterance exhibits so much vindictive passion that it could not possibly have been written under the inspiration of the Holy Spirit.

The second passage objected to is Psalm 109:10: *"Let his children continually be vagabonds, and beg; let them seek their bread also from their desolate places."* The third passage is Psalm 137:8–9: *"O daughter of Babylon, who are to be destroyed, happy the one who repays you as you have served us! Happy the one who takes and dashes your little ones against the rock!"* What can we say about these passages?

A Record of What Was Said

The first thing we have to say is what we have already said in chapter two, namely, that God often simply records what others said—bad men, good men, inspired men, and uninspired men, etc.—and the things people have said may or may not be true. On the other hand, we sometimes have in the Psalms what God said to man, and that is always true.

469

All three passages I have cited are what men said to God. They are the inspired record of men's prayers. To God they breathe out the agony of their hearts, and to God they cry for vengeance on their enemies. Judged even by Christian standards, this was far better than taking vengeance into their own hands.

Leaving Vengeance to God

Indeed, this is exactly what the New Testament commands us to do regarding those who wrong us. Vengeance belongs to God, and He will repay (Rom. 12:19); instead of taking vengeance into our own hands, we should put it in His hands. There is certainly nothing wrong in asking God to break the teeth of wicked men who are using those teeth to tear the upright.

The first prayer is taken from a psalm that there is every reason to suppose is Davidic, as is also the second passage quoted. However, it is a well-known fact that David, in his personal dealings with his enemies, was most generous, for when he had his bitterest, most dangerous enemy in his hand, an enemy who persistently sought his life, he not only refused to kill him, but also refused to let another kill him (1 Sam. 26:5–9). Even when he did so small a thing to Saul as to cut off the hem of Saul's robe, his heart smote him (1 Sam. 24:5), even for that slight indignity offered to his bitterest, most implacable enemy.

How much better we would be if, instead of taking vengeance into our own hands, we would breathe out the bitterness of our hearts to God, and then treat our enemies, in actual fact, as generously as David did. Even though David prayed to Jehovah in Psalm 109:10, *"Let his children continually be vagabonds, and beg; let them seek their bread also from their desolate places,"* he later asked, when he was in a place of power, *"Is there still anyone who is left of the house of Saul, that I may show him kindness?"* (2 Sam. 9:1). He found a grandson of Saul's and had him eat at his table as one of his own sons (vv. 2–11).

A Prophecy, Not a Prayer

O daughter of Babylon, who are to be destroyed, happy the one who repays you as you have served us! Happy the one who takes and dashes your little ones against the rock!

(Ps. 137:8–9)

The utterance in Psalm 137:8–9 does sound very cruel, but the utterance is a prophecy rather than a prayer. It is the declaration of awful judgment that will come upon Babylon because of the way in which Babylon had treated the people of God. Babylon was to reap what it had sown. (See Galatians 6:7.) They were to be served by others as they had served the people of God. It was a literal prophecy of what actually occurred afterward in Babylon. We find in Isaiah 13:15–18 a similar, but even more awful, prophecy of the coming doom of Babylon.

So when we study these Imprecatory Psalms in the light that is thrown on them from other passages of Scripture, all the supposed difficulties disappear, and we find that there is nothing here that is not in perfect harmony with the thought that the whole Bible is God's Word. Of course, in some instances, what is recorded as being said may not in itself be right, but the record of what is said is correct and exact. It is God's Word that man said it, though what man was recorded as saying may not be God's Word.

Chapter 16

Lying and Evil Spirits

◆

One of the most puzzling passages in the Bible is found in 1 Kings 22, and in the parallel account in 2 Chronicles 18. In these passages, the prophet Micaiah is reported as saying, *"Hear the word of the LORD"* (1 Kings 22:19). In the same verse, he goes on to tell how he *"saw the LORD sitting on His throne, and all the host of heaven standing by, on His right hand and on His left."*

Jehovah, in this passage, is pictured as asking the assembled host who would go and persuade Ahab to go up to Ramoth Gilead. Then, a lying spirit is represented as coming forth and standing before the Lord and saying, *"I will go forth, and I will be a lying spirit in the mouth of all his prophets"* (v. 22 KJV). Jehovah is represented as saying to the lying spirit, "Thou shalt persuade him, and prevail also: go forth, and do so" (v. 22 KJV).

At first glance, it appears here as if the Lord sanctioned and took a part in lying and deception. What is the explanation? It is clearly given in the context. Micaiah, speaking by the Holy Spirit, is seeking to dissuade Ahab and Jehoshaphat from going up to Ramoth Gilead. All the false prophets have told the two kings that they would go up to victory. Micaiah, the messenger of the Lord, tells them on the contrary that they will go up to defeat and to the certain death of Ahab. He tells them that the spirit that had spoken by the false prophets was a lying spirit. He puts this in a highly pictorial way.

Although the picture is exceedingly vivid, it does not teach error, but truth, and teaches it in a most forcible way, namely, that it was a lying spirit that was in the mouth of the false prophets. It is clear in the narrative, if we take it as a whole, that Jehovah was not really a party to the deception. Far from being a party to the deception, He sends His own prophet to warn them that the spirit that spoke by the false prophets was a lying spirit, and to tell them the exact facts in the case as to what the issue of the battle would be. If they chose to listen to God and His prophet, they would be saved from calamity; but if they would not listen to God and His prophet, then God would give them over to *"strong delusion, that they should believe the lie"* (2 Thess. 2:11). But He would not do this without abundant warning.

This is God's universal method, not only as taught in the Bible, but also as taught in experience: He allows every man to choose either to listen to Him and know the truth or to turn a deaf ear to Him and be given over to *"strong delusion."* If men will not receive *"the love of the truth, that they might be saved"* (v. 10), then God gives them over to *"strong delusion, that they should believe the lie"* (v. 11). If men want lies, God gives them their fill of them.

In other passages of the Bible, it seems to be taught that God sends evil spirits to men, and the question arises, "How can we believe that a good God, a God of love, sends evil spirits to men?" Let us turn to a passage in which this is taught, and we will soon find an answer to the difficulty. In 1 Samuel 16:14 (KJV), we read: *"But the spirit of the LORD departed from Saul, and an evil spirit from the LORD troubled him."*

What is meant by *"an evil spirit"*? The context clearly shows that it was a spirit of discontent, unrest, and depression. The circumstances were these: Saul had proved untrue to God; he had deliberately disobeyed God (see 1 Samuel 15:4–35, especially verses 22–23); consequently, God had withdrawn His Spirit from him, and a spirit of discontent and unrest had come upon him.

This was not an unkind act on God's part. There was nothing kinder that God could have done. It is one of the most merciful provisions of our heavenly Father, when we disobey Him and wander from Him, that He makes us unhappy and discontented in our sin. If God should leave us to continue to be happy in sin, it would be the cruelest thing He could do. But God, in His great mercy, will win every sinner possible back to Himself; and if we

473

sin, God, for our highest good, sends to us deep depression and unrest in our sin. If we make the right use of this spirit of unrest and depression that God sends us, it brings us back to God and to the joy of the Holy Spirit.

Saul made the wrong use of it. Instead of allowing his unrest of heart to bring him to repentance and back to God, he allowed the distress to embitter his soul against one whom God favored. The sending of the evil spirit was an act of mercy on God's part. The misuse of this act of mercy resulted in Saul's utter ruin.

Today, many who once knew something about the Spirit of the Lord and the joy of the Holy Spirit have fallen into sin; God, in His great love and mercy, is sending them *"a distressing spirit"* (1 Sam. 16:14)—a spirit of unrest, dissatisfaction, deep discontent, or even of abject misery. Let them thank God for it. Let them inquire, humbly on their faces before God, in what respect they have sinned against God and lost the joy of their salvation. Let them renounce and confess their sins and return to God and have renewed unto them the joy of God's salvation. (See Psalm 51:12.)

An evil spirit of unrest and discontent was sent to David, too, when he sinned; but when, after some resistance, David confessed his sin to the Lord, the Lord blotted it out and brought him into a place of gladness and joy in the Lord, where he could instruct and teach others in the way they should go (Ps. 32:4–8; 51:9–13).

Chapter 17

Jonah and the Whale

◆

The story of Jonah and the whale has for many years been a favorite target of ridicule with unbelievers, and it has also been the cause of much perplexity with those who are *"untaught and unstable"* (2 Pet. 3:16). The story is quite generally discredited by the destructive critics, and they question whether or not it is actually historical. They attempt to explain it as an allegory or as a parable.

Those who desire to discredit the full inspiration and absolute veracity of the Bible have again and again assured us, with a great display of scientific knowledge, that the structure of a whale's mouth and the configuration of its throat are such that it would be impossible for a full-grown man to pass either through the sieve in its mouth or the narrow orifice of its throat, to say nothing of his coming out again alive and whole. What can we say to all this?

A Sea Monster

First of all, let us notice the fact that the Bible nowhere tells us that Jonah was swallowed by a whale. In Jonah 1:17, we are told that *"the LORD had prepared a great fish to swallow Jonah. And Jonah was in the belly of the fish three days and three nights."* There is no mention here whatever of this great fish being a whale, with its peculiarly constructed mouth and throat. It may have been either a fish prepared especially for the occasion or a fish already existing sent providentially for the purpose God had in mind.

In Jesus' reference to this historical event, He said that Jonah was three days and three nights in *"the whale's belly"* (Matt.

12:40 KJV), but we read in the margin of the Revised Version that the Greek word rendered "whale" is actually "sea monster." One cannot help wondering, since the Greek word means "sea monster," why the translators would continue to put "whale" in the text. In the Septuagint translation of the book of Jonah, *"a great fish"* is rendered by a Greek adjective meaning "great" and the same word that is used in Matthew 12:40 and translated "whale."

The word *whale* was in the minds of the translators and not in the word spoken by Jesus, so in neither the Old Testament nor the New Testament account is it said that Jonah was swallowed by a "whale," but by *"a great fish,"* or sea monster. Consequently, we see that "scholarly critics" have spent much time and effort in proving the absurdity of something the Bible did not say, and that they would have known it did not say if they had been as "scholarly" as they supposed.

As to what the great fish was, we are not told; but it is a well-known fact that these sea monsters—that is, dog sharks, large enough to swallow a man or horse whole—exist, or have existed until recent times in the Mediterranean Sea, where the recorded event seems to have taken place. In fact, it is recorded that a man fell overboard in the Mediterranean and was swallowed by one of these sea monsters; the monster was killed and the man rescued alive. A whole horse was taken out of the belly of another.

A Particular Species of Whale

Furthermore, even if the Bible had said that the great fish was a whale, there would be none of the difficulty with the narrative that has been supposed by unbelievers and the uninformed. While it is true that there are some kinds of whales whose mouths and throats are of such a formation that it would be impossible for a full-grown man to pass through, it is not true of all kinds of whales.

Frank Bullen, in his book *The Cruise of the Cachalot,* said that "a shark fifteen feet in length has been found in the stomach of a cachalot." He wrote further that "when dying, the cachalot, or sperm whale, always ejected the contents of its stomach." His book tells us of one whale that was caught and killed:

The ejected food from whose stomach was in masses of enormous size, some of them estimated to be the size of our hatch-house, which is about 8 x 6 x 6 ft.

Of course, such a whale would have no difficulty in swallowing a man, so the whole objection to the Bible narrative from the standpoint that a whale could not swallow a man is not founded on superior knowledge, but on ignorance.

"But," someone may say, "the action of the gastric juices would kill a man within a whale, or in any other sea monster, for that matter." Yet this leaves God out of the picture, whereas in the Bible story God is very prominent in the whole transaction. The God who made the monster, the man, and the gastric juices could quite easily control the digestive process and preserve the man. I am not trying to suggest that the transaction was not miraculous in any event, but those who really believe in God and have had any large experience with God have no trouble with the miraculous.

It should be added, moreover, that the Bible does not tell us that Jonah remained alive during the period that he was in the belly of the great fish. There are things in the narrative as recorded in the book of Jonah that make it appear as if he did not remain alive. (See Jonah 2:2, 5–7.) There seems to be a strong probability that Jonah actually did die and was raised from the dead. If Jonah did die, this only adds one more to the resurrections recorded in the Bible and makes Jonah a still more remarkable type of Christ.

To those who believe in God, there is no difficulty in believing in a resurrection, if it is sufficiently well-attested. Why should it be thought incredible that God would raise the dead? There are numerous instances on record of at least resuscitation of men and women who, from all appearances, had been dead for some days. The historicity of this event with Jonah and the great fish is endorsed by Jesus Christ Himself (Matt. 12:40). To think of it as being merely allegory or parable is to discredit the words of Jesus.

On careful examination of what the Scriptures say and of the facts of history, all the difficulties supposed to exist in the story of Jonah and "the whale" are found to disappear.

Chapter 18

"Contradictions" in the Bible

---◆---

I am constantly meeting people who say that the Bible is full of
contradictions. When I ask them to show me one, they reply,
"It is full of them." When I press them to point one out, usually they have no more to say. But now and then, I meet an infidel who does know enough about the Bible to point out some
apparent contradictions. In this chapter, we will consider some
of these.

Can We See God?

One of the objections most frequently brought forward is
the apparent contradiction between John 1:18, where we read:
"No one has seen God at any time," and Exodus 24:10, where we
are told that Moses, Aaron, Nadab, Abihu, and seventy of the
elders of Israel *"saw the God of Israel."* (There are also other
passages in which men are said to have seen God.) Now, this
certainly looks like an outright contradiction, and many besides
skeptics and infidels have been puzzled by it. Indeed, one of the
most devout men I ever knew was so puzzled by it that he left
his place of business and came miles in great perturbation of
spirit to ask me about it. The solution of this apparently unanswerable difficulty is, in reality, very simple.

We must remember, first of all, that whenever two statements utterly contradict one another in terms, both may still be
absolutely true, because the terms used in the two statements
are not used in the same sense. For example, if any man were to
ask me if I ever saw the back of my head, I might answer, "No, I
never saw the back of my head," and this statement would be

strictly true. Or I might answer, " Yes, I have seen the back of my head," and this statement would also be true, though the two statements appear to contradict one another completely. I have never truly seen the back of my head, but I have seen it more than once when looking into a mirror with another mirror behind me.

My answer depends entirely on what the person means when he asks me the question. If he means one thing, I answer, "No," and that is true. If he means another thing, I answer, "Yes, I have seen the back of my head," and that is equally true. Even so, someone may object, "In the latter case you did not really see the back of your head. What you saw was a reflection of the back of your head in the mirror." But to this I would reply, "Neither do you see the back of anyone's head when you are looking right at it. What you see is the reflection of that person's head on the retina of your eye."

But everyone knows what you mean when you use language in this commonsense, everyday way. They would know that when you said you saw the back of another man's head, that you meant you saw a reflection of it on the retina of your eye; and they would know when you said you saw the back of your own head in the mirror, that you meant you saw the reflection of the back of your head in the mirror. In the one case, you see the reflection; in the other case, you see the reflection of the reflection; in both cases, what you actually see is the thing that was reflected.

Now, in this case before us in the Bible, it is all very similar to this illustration. God in His eternal essence is *"invisible"* (1 Tim. 1:17). No man has seen Him, nor can we see Him (1 Tim. 6:16). He is spirit, not form (John 4:23–24). In John 1, we are told this profound and wondrous truth: *"No one has seen God at any time. The only begotten Son, who is in the bosom of the Father, He has declared Him"* (v. 18).

That is, this *"invisible"* (unseeable) God is unfolded to us, interpreted to us (the word translated here "declared" is the word from which our word *exegesis* is derived) in the words and in the person of Jesus Himself. So fully is He declared, not only in the words of Jesus, but in His person, that Jesus said, *"He who has seen Me has seen the Father"* (John 14:9).

Nonetheless, this essentially invisible God has been pleased in His great grace to show Himself again and again in bodily form. Moses and the seventy elders saw such a manifestation of God when they were on the mountain (Exod. 24:9–10). Isaiah saw such a manifestation in the temple (Isa. 6:1), and in describing it, he properly declared, *"I saw the Lord."* Job saw such a manifestation and was so humbled by the actual coming face-to-face with God Himself that he cried, *"I abhor myself, and repent in dust and ashes"* (Job 42:6).

It was God who was manifested in these theophanies, and so it was God they saw. We see, then, that both of these apparently contradictory statements—that *"No one has seen God at any time"* (John 1:18), and that Moses and the others *"saw the God of Israel"* (Exod. 24:10)—are perfectly true.

Jesus Christ Himself was the crowning manifestation of God: *"For in Him dwells all the fullness of the Godhead bodily* [that is, in bodily form]*"* (Col. 2:9). So Jesus said to Philip with perfect propriety, *"He who has seen Me has seen the Father"* (John 14:9). The time is coming when all the pure in heart will behold God permanently manifested in a bodily form (Matt. 5:8).

The form in which Jesus existed in His preexistent state of glory was *"the form of God"* (Phil. 2:6). The Greek word that is translated *"form"* in this passage means "the form by which a person or thing strikes the vision; the external appearance" (*Thayer's Greek-English Lexicon of the New Testament*), so we are clearly taught that the external appearance of Jesus in His preexistent form was the external appearance of God—that is, the invisible God, who is a spirit in His essential essence, manifests Himself in an external, visible form.

The Inscriptions on the Cross

A second "contradiction" of which infidels make a great deal and by which many believers are puzzled is that found in the four accounts of the inscriptions on the cross. We read in Matthew 27:37: *"And they put up over His head the accusation written against Him: THIS IS JESUS THE KING OF THE JEWS."* We read in Mark 15:26: "And the inscription of His accusation was written above: THE KING OF THE JEWS." We read in Luke 23:38: *"And an inscription also was written over Him in letters of Greek, Latin, and Hebrew: THIS IS THE KING OF THE JEWS."* And we read in John 19:19: *"Now Pilate wrote a title and put it on the cross. And the writing was: JESUS OF NAZARETH, THE KING OF THE JEWS."*

Now, no two of these verses agree absolutely in the words used. It is asked by the objector, "How can all four possibly be right?" It is said that at least three must be wrong, at least in part. A great deal is made of this difficulty by those who argue against the verbal inspiration of the Scriptures.

I am surprised that anyone should make so much of it, for the answer is found so plainly stated in the very passages cited; it is surprising that any careful student should have overlooked it. John told us in John 19:20 that the charge on which Jesus was crucified was written in Hebrew, in Latin, and in Greek, in order that all the different nationalities present might read it: in Hebrew for the common people; in Latin for the Romans; and in Greek, the universal language. The substantial part of the charge was that Jesus claimed to be "the King of the Jews" and was crucified for making this claim. That explains why the words *the King of the Jews* appear in Hebrew, Latin, and Greek, and why they also appear in all four accounts of the Gospels.

Matthew would naturally report the inscription as it appeared in Hebrew; Mark would be likely to give it as it appeared in Latin; and Luke as it appeared in Greek. Presumably, John gives it in the full Roman form, "Jesus of Nazareth" being a full and explicit statement of who Jesus is, and the charge being "King of the Jews."

The only thing that is left to account for, then, is the difference between Mark and John; but if we carefully read Mark 15:26, we will see that Mark did not claim to give the full wording that appeared on the cross. He simply said, *"The inscription of His accusation was written above."* The accusation was "The King of the Jews," and this Mark gave, and this alone. The words, "This is Jesus of Nazareth," were not the accusation, but the name of the accused. So all this difficulty, of which so much is made, disappears altogether when we notice exactly what is said and all that is said.

Paul's Conversion

Another "contradiction" of which a great deal is made is what seems to exist between two different accounts of the conversion of Saul of Tarsus. We are told in Acts 9:7 that those who journeyed with Saul to Damascus heard a voice that spoke to Saul, but they did not see anyone. On the other hand, Paul, in relating to the Jews in Jerusalem the story of his conversion, said, *"And those who were with me indeed saw the light and were afraid, but they did not hear the voice of Him who spoke to me"* (Acts 22:9).

These two statements seem to contradict one another outright. Luke, in recounting the conversion, said that the men who journeyed with Paul heard the voice, but Paul himself in recounting his conversion said that they did not hear the voice. Could there possibly be a more obvious contradiction than this?

Even so, this apparent contradiction disappears entirely when we look at the Greek of the two passages. The Greek word translated "heard" governs two cases, the genitive, or possessive, and the accusative. The genitive case is used when a person or thing is spoken of and when the *sound of the voice* is heard. However, when the *message* that is heard is spoken of, the accusative case is used. Often, there is a difference of a mere letter at the end of the word between the two cases. In Acts 9:7, the genitive is used. They did hear the voice, that is, the sound of it. In Acts 22:9, the words translated "the voice" are in the accusative. They did not hear, or hear with understanding, the message of the One who spoke.

The word rendered "voice" also has two meanings: first, "a sound, a tone," and second, "a sound of uttered words" (*Thayer's Greek-English Lexicon of the New Testament*). The voice, as mere sound, they heard. The voice as the "sound of uttered words," the message, they did not hear. So another seeming difficulty entirely disappears when we look exactly at what the Bible in the original says. Instead of having an objection to the Bible, we have another illustration of its absolute accuracy, not only down to a word, but down to a single letter that ends a word and by which a case is indicated.

Accounts of the Resurrection

A great deal is made by some who deny the accuracy of the Bible about the apparent contradictions in the various accounts of the resurrection of Jesus Christ from the dead. A very prominent unbeliever once sent to the daily papers the following problem for me to solve.

> The account of the visit to the grave is entirely different in the four Gospels. In one case, two of the Gospels state that the women saw two angels at the grave; and two of the other Gospels state that they saw only one angel.

What is the solution of this apparent difficulty?

First of all, let it be said that the objector does not truly state the facts in the case. It is true that Matthew said that they saw an angel (Matt. 28:1–5) and Mark said, *"They saw a young man"* (presumably an angel, Mark 16:5–7), but neither Matthew nor Mark said that "they saw only one angel." Saying that they saw one does not rule out the possibility of their seeing two. So far from its being true that two of the Gospels state that "they saw only one angel," not even *one* of the Gospels states that there was only one angel to be seen.

Furthermore, let it be noticed that it is not true, as stated by the objector, that two of the Gospels state that the women saw two angels at the grave. It is true that Luke said that after they had entered the tomb, two men (presumably angels) stood by them in dazzling apparel (Luke 24:3–4). However, this apparently does not refer to the incident that Matthew referred to, for the angel mentioned there was an angel who was outside the tomb.

Nor does it seem to refer to the same fact of which Mark speaks, for the young man (or angel) in Mark's gospel was one who was sitting on the right side of the sepulchre. This angel may have been joined later by the one who was on the outside, and these two together may have stood by the women. This seems more likely, as the message uttered by the two in Luke is in part the same as that spoken by the angel outside the sepulchre in Matthew, and by the young man inside the sepulchre in Mark. (See Luke 24:5–6; Matthew 28:5–7; Mark 16:5–7.)

The very simple solution of it all is that there was an angel outside the tomb when the women approached, and they saw another one sitting inside. The one outside entered and the one sitting arose and, standing by the women, together, or after one another, they uttered the words recorded in Matthew, Mark, and Luke.

Yet what about the account in John? John told us that there were two angels in white sitting, one at the head and one at the feet where the body of Jesus had lain (John 20:12–13). How can we reconcile that with the other three? Very easily. It was not the *group of women* at all that saw these two angels, but we are distinctly told it was Mary alone (v. 1). Mary started out with the other women to the sepulchre, got a little ahead of the group, was the first to see the stone rolled away from the tomb (v. 1), immediately jumped to the conclusion that the tomb had been rifled, and ran at the top of her speed to the city to carry the news to Peter and John (v. 2).

While she was going into the city, the other women reached and entered the tomb, and the things recorded in Matthew, Mark, and Luke occurred. These women left the sepulchre before Mary reached it the second time. Peter and John had also left it when Mary reached the sepulchre, and two angels, the one who had been on the outside and the one who at first had been sitting on the inside, were now both sitting, one at the head and the other at the feet where the body of Jesus had lain.

All the other apparent contradictions in the four accounts of the Resurrection (and they are quite numerous) also disappear on careful study. These apparent contradictions are themselves proof of the truth and the accuracy of the accounts. It is evident that these four accounts are separate and independent accounts. If four different people had sat down in collusion to make up a story of a resurrection that never occurred, they would have made their four accounts appear to agree, at least on the surface. Whatever contradictions there might be in the four accounts would come out only after minute and careful study.

However, in the Gospels, just the opposite is the case. It is all on the surface that the apparent contradictions occur. It is only by careful and protracted study that the real agreement shines forth. It is just the kind of harmony that would not exist between four accounts fabricated in collusion. It is just the kind of agreement that would exist in four independent accounts of substantially the same circumstances—each narrator telling the same story from his own standpoint, relating the details that impressed him, omitting other details that did not impress him but that did impress another narrator to the point of relating them.

Sometimes two accounts seem to contradict one another, but a third account comes in and unintentionally reconciles the apparent discrepancies between the two. This is precisely what we have in the four accounts of the resurrection of Jesus Christ. We may heartily thank God that there are these apparent discrepancies among them. And even if we cannot find the solution to some apparent discrepancies, the fact that we do by careful study find a solution of what appeared to be an inexplicable contradiction will suggest to us the certainty that if we knew all the facts in the case, we could also find a solution to the apparent discrepancies that as yet we cannot reconcile.

The more one studies the four accounts of the Resurrection, the more he will be convinced, if he is candid about the matter, that they are separate, independent accounts and a truthful narration of what actually occurred. They could not have been fabricated in collusion with one another; the discrepancies prove this. Much less could they have been fabricated independently of one another. Four men sitting down independently of one another to fabricate an account of something that never occurred would nowhere have agreed with one another. But the more we study the four accounts, the more clearly do we discover how marvelously the four accounts fit together.

What has been said about the apparent discrepancies among the four accounts of the Resurrection will apply also to other apparent discrepancies in the different gospel narratives of the same event. They are very numerous, and to take them all in detail would require a much larger volume than this; but the illustration given above will serve to prove how these apparent discrepancies can be reconciled one by one if we examine them thoroughly. And if there are any that still refuse to yield to our hardest study, we may be confident that if we knew all the facts in the case, the apparent discrepancy could be readily reconciled.

Does God Change His Mind?

Another apparent contradiction of the Scriptures, of which a great deal is made and that has puzzled a great many believers, is the following. We read in Malachi 3:6: *"For I am the LORD, I do not change,"* and in James 1:17:

> *Every good gift and every perfect gift is from above, and comes down from the Father of lights, with whom there is no variation or shadow of turning.*

And in 1 Samuel 15:29, we read: *"And also the Strength of Israel will not lie nor relent. For He is not a man, that He should relent."*

However, in an apparently outright contradiction of these verses, we read in Jonah 3:10:

> *Then God saw their works, that they turned from their evil way; and God relented from the disaster that He had said He would bring upon them, and He did not do it.*

Additionally, Genesis 6:6 says, *"And the LORD was sorry that He had made man on the earth, and He was grieved in His heart."* Now, this appears to be an outright contradiction. What is the explanation?

The explanation is this: what the first set of passages says is completely true, that God is absolutely unchangeable. He is *"the same yesterday, today, and forever"* (Heb. 13:8). But what the second group of passages says is also true, for if God does remain the same in character—absolutely unchangeable, infinitely hating sin, and in His purpose to visit sin with judgment—then if any city or any person changes in his attitude toward sin, God must necessarily change in His attitude toward that person or city.

If God remains the same, if His attitude toward sin and righteousness is unchanging, then His dealings with men must change as they turn from sin to repentance. His character ever remains the same, but His dealings with men change as they turn from the position that is hateful to His unchanging hatred of sin, to one that is pleasing to His unchanging love of righteousness.

We may illustrate this by the position of a railway station, which remains in one place relative to the train that moves along the track in front of the station. When the train begins to move, it is to the east of the station, but as the train moves westward, it is soon west of the station. The only way in which the station can maintain the same direction from the moving train is by moving as the train moves. Yet if the station is unchangeable in its position, its direction relative to the train must change as the train moves.

So it is with God's attitude toward man. If God remains unchangeable in His character, His purpose, and His position, then as man moves from sin to righteousness, God's attitude relative to that man must change. The very fact that God does not repent (change His mind), that He remains always the same in His attitude toward sin, makes it necessary that God should repent in His conduct (change His dealings with men) as they turn from sin to righteousness.

As to Jehovah's repenting of having made man on the earth and its grieving Him at His heart, this, too, is necessitated by the unchanging attitude of God toward sin. If God does not repent (change His mind about or His attitude toward sin), if man's wickedness becomes great, then God's unrepenting, unchanging hatred of sin necessitates that the man whom He has created, who has fallen into sin so great and so abhorrent to Himself, should become the object of great grief to Him, and that He should turn from His creative dealings with man to His destructive dealings with man.

This was necessitated by man's sin. An unchangeably holy God must destroy man who has become so hopelessly fallen in sin. The only condition on which He could spare him would be if God Himself were to change from the holiness of His character as it was when God created man to become an unholy God. Again we see that what appears at first to be a flat-out contradiction is really no contradiction at all, but an entire agreement in fact and thought among passages that seem to contradict in words.

Who Led David to Number Israel?

Another apparent contradiction of Scripture that is frequently discussed is found in 2 Samuel 24:1, compared with 1 Chronicles 21:1. In 2 Samuel 24:1, we read that the *"anger of the LORD was aroused against Israel, and He moved David against them to say, 'Go, number Israel and Judah.'"* But in 1 Chronicles 21:1 we read: *"Now Satan stood up against Israel, and moved David to number Israel."* In one passage, we are told that Jehovah moved David against the people when he said, *"Go, number Israel and Judah."* In the other passage, we are told that Satan moved David to number Israel. Which is the correct account?

The very simple answer to this question is that both accounts are correct. We do not even need to suppose that an error has crept into the text and that "He" appears instead of "Satan." In that case, what really was recorded in 2 Samuel would be, "And again the anger of the LORD was kindled against Israel, and Satan moved David against them," meaning that the anger of the Lord was kindled because He yielded to Satan's moving David.

Of course, it is possible that such an error may have crept into the text, or it is possible that the pronoun *he* really refers to Satan, who is not mentioned. Or the *he* might be interpreted "one" without any designation as to who the "one" was. If this were so, of course there would be no difficulty whatever in the passage; but there is no insurmountable difficulty in any case to anyone who understands the Bible teaching regarding God's relation to temptation and the attitude that He takes toward Satan.

In 2 Corinthians 12:7, we are told by Paul that *"lest [he] should be exalted above measure by the abundance of the revelations, a thorn in the flesh was given to [him], a messenger of Satan to buffet [him], lest [he] be exalted above measure."* Now, the purpose of this *"thorn in the flesh,"* this *"messenger of Satan,"* was beneficial, to keep Paul from being unduly exalted. Evidently, it was God who gave the thorn, the messenger of Satan, but the messenger was nonetheless a messenger of Satan.

In other words, God, for our good, uses Satan, evil as he is, for our moral discipline. Just as God makes the wrath of man to praise Him (Ps. 76:10), so He makes even the wrath of Satan to praise Him. What Satan intends only for evil, God uses for our good. In the case of David's numbering Israel, it was Satan who tempted David, but it was by God's permission that Satan tempted him. God was behind the testing and consequent failure of David and the beneficial humiliation of David that came out of it. In this sense, it was God who moved David to the act, so that David might discover through his failure what was in his own heart.

Chapter 19

"Mistakes" in the Bible

◆

The Bible is said not only to be full of contradictions, but also to contain mistakes. One of the mistakes most constantly referred to by destructive critics is found in Matthew 27:9–10.

> *Then was fulfilled what was spoken by Jeremiah the prophet, saying, "And they took the thirty pieces of silver, the value of Him who was priced, whom they of the children of Israel priced, and gave them for the potter's field, as the LORD directed me."*

The passage referred to here by Matthew is found in the prophecy ascribed in the Old Testament to Zechariah (Zech. 11:12–13). At first sight this appears as if Matthew had made a mistake and ascribed to Jeremiah a prophecy that was really made by Zechariah. Even John Calvin seems to have thought that Matthew made a mistake, for he said:

> How the name of Jeremiah crept in, I confess I do not know, nor do I give myself much trouble to inquire. The passage itself plainly shows the name of Jeremiah has been put down by mistake instead of Zechariah; for in [the book of] Jeremiah we find nothing of this sort, nor anything that even approaches it.

This passage has been presented as proof that the gospel narratives are not necessarily "historical accounts" of what actually occurred. Must we admit that Matthew was mistaken? No, there is not the slightest necessity of admitting that.

490

The Words of the Prophets

In the first place, in some manuscripts, the word *Jeremiah* does not appear, but the passage reads, "Then was fulfilled what was spoken by the prophet," without any mention as to who the prophet was. In still another reading, *Zechariah* appears instead of *Jeremiah*. Westcott and Hort do not accept the reading without *Jeremiah*, nor the reading that substitutes *Zechariah* for *Jeremiah*, but they do mention these readings, especially the first, as "noteworthy rejected readings." Mrs. Lewis says that some of the earliest and best manuscripts omit the word *Jeremiah*; so the apparent mistake here may be due to the error of a copyist.

However, the best textual critics all accept reading the word *Jeremiah* in this passage, and it seems to me that this is probably the correct reading. If in the gospel of Matthew, as originally written, Matthew used the word *Jeremiah* here, was it not a mistake? Not necessarily. That these words, or words very similar to them, are found in the prophecy that in our Old Testament bears the name of Zechariah, is unquestionably true. But it does not follow at all from this that Jeremiah did not speak them, for it is a well-known fact that the later prophets of the Old Testament often quoted the predictions of earlier prophets. For example, Zechariah himself in Zechariah 1:4 quoted a prophecy known to be Jeremiah's (Jer. 18:11); and in the passage that we are now considering, Zechariah may also have quoted from the prophecy of Jeremiah.

There is no record in the book of Jeremiah, as we now have it in the Old Testament, of Jeremiah's having uttered this prophecy, but there is no reason whatever to think we have in the book of Jeremiah all the prophecies that Jeremiah ever uttered. Zechariah may easily have had access to prophecies of Jeremiah not recorded in the book of Jeremiah.

Furthermore, Zechariah himself said in Zechariah 7:7, *"Should you not have obeyed the words which the LORD proclaimed through the former prophets"*; so it is evident that Zechariah regarded it as part of his mission to recall the prophecies of the prophets who had gone before him. He would have been especially inclined to recall the prophecies of Jeremiah, for it was a saying among the Jews that "the spirit of Jeremiah was upon Zechariah." We see that this much-vaunted "mistake" of Matthew does not appear to have been a mistake at all when we closely examine it.

Perhaps it ought to be added that there has been much question by the critics as to whether the closing chapters of the book of Zechariah were really a portion of the prophecies of Zechariah. There is nothing in the chapters themselves to indicate that they were. It is true that for centuries they have been attached to the prophecies of Zechariah, but nowhere in the Bible does it state that they were by Zechariah, and it has been held that they were in reality not by Zechariah, but by Jeremiah.

This, however, is a question for the critics. If it should prove to be so, it would simply be an additional confirmation of the accuracy of Matthew's statement. But even if it is not so, if Zechariah is the author of this prophecy (Zech. 11:11–13) as we find it in the Bible, it does not at all prove that Jeremiah may not have uttered a similar prophecy to which Zechariah referred and that Matthew quoted accurately. The critics will have to search further if they wish to prove Matthew to have been in error.

Records of Purchases

A second alleged mistake in the Bible is the statement of Stephen in Acts 7:16:

> *And they were carried back to Shechem and laid in the tomb that Abraham bought for a sum of money from the sons of Hamor, the father of Shechem.*

On the other hand, Genesis 23:17–18 states:

> *So the field of Ephron which was in Machpelah, which was before Mamre, the field and the cave which was in it...were deeded to Abraham as a possession.*

According to this second verse, Stephen seems to have been mistaken in his statement that Abraham bought the sepulchre from the sons of Emmor (known as Hamor in the Old Testament).

Let me put the supposed mistake in the words of a prominent Doctor of Divinity. He says:

> According to Luke's report, Stephen says Abraham bought a sepulchre of the sons of Emmor, the father of Sychem (Acts 7:16 KJV). But Genesis 23:17–18 says Abraham bought it of Ephron, the Hittite, and Genesis 33:19 says that Jacob bought it of the sons of Hamor....John Calvin says, "Stephen evidently made a mistake." Dr. Hackett admits that Stephen appears to have confounded the two transactions...but what do those say about it...who maintain the absolute inerrancy of the Bible?

This seems like a puzzler until one notices exactly what the three passages referred to say; then the puzzle is solved. The very simple solution is as follows:

First, Genesis 23:17–18 does not say what the objector says it does; that is, it does not say that Abraham bought from Ephron, the Hittite, *this sepulchre to which Stephen refers*. It does state that Abraham bought a field from Ephron, the Hittite, in which there was a cave, and that Abraham buried his wife Sarah in this cave.

However, there is no good reason for supposing that this was the sepulchre in which Jacob and the patriarchs were buried. There is no reason for supposing that Abraham in his long lifetime bought only one burial place. I myself have purchased two: one where my brother is buried, in Chicago, and one where my daughter is buried, in Northfield, Massachusetts. And I am thinking of buying a third in Brooklyn, where my father, mother, and other brother are buried.

There is not the slightest hint in the Scriptures that these two sepulchres mentioned in Genesis 23:17–18 and Acts 7:16 are the same. As to the passage in Genesis 33:19, where, according to the objector, it is said that Jacob, and not Abraham (as Stephen put it), bought the sepulchre, this passage does not, in fact, say that Jacob bought *the sepulchre*. It says he bought "*a parcel of land...from the children of Hamor*" (the people of whom Stephen said Abraham bought the actual sepulchre).

The presumption in this case is that Abraham had already purchased the sepulchre at an earlier date, and Jacob, in his day, purchased the ground (*"a parcel of land"*) in which the sepulchre was located. When Abraham purchased a tomb in which to bury Sarah, he took the precaution of buying the field as well as the sepulchre; but in the latter case, he seems to have purchased the sepulchre without buying the whole piece of ground, which Jacob himself therefore bought at a later date. It is altogether likely that Abraham would have purchased a sepulchre in this spot in his later life, for it was a place dear to him by many memories. (See Genesis 12:6–7.)

So, after all, the mistake was not Stephen's, but the mistake of the commentators, who were not careful to note exactly what Stephen said and what is said in the two passages in Genesis. Joshua stated that it was in this parcel of ground that Jacob bought, which presumably contained the sepulchre that Abraham had bought at an earlier date, that the bones of Joseph were buried (Josh. 24:32). Apparently Stephen was a more careful student of Old Testament Scripture than some of his critics.

But even allowing for the moment that Stephen was mistaken in this case, it would prove nothing against the divine origin of the Bible or its absolute inerrancy, for Stephen is not one of the authors of the Bible. He was neither a prophet nor an apostle. It is true he was a Spirit-filled man, but he was not the writer of a book in the Bible.

The inspired author of the Acts of the Apostles records that Stephen said these words, and if these words that Stephen spoke had been mistaken, the record that he said them would still be correct. It would be God's Word that Stephen said this, but what Stephen said would not be God's Word. The one who contends for the divine origin of the Bible and its absolute accuracy is under no obligation whatever to prove the accuracy of every statement that every speaker in the Bible, or even every Spirit-filled speaker, is recorded as saying.

The Teaching Regarding Strong Drink

Another alleged mistake in the Bible is found in Proverbs 31:6–7:

Give strong drink to him who is perishing, and wine to those who are bitter of heart. Let him drink and forget his poverty, and remember his misery no more.

It is said that these verses advocate the use of intoxicating liquor under certain conditions; therefore, since the use of intoxicating liquor under any and all circumstances is wrong, this teaching of the Bible is a mistake. But the difficulty disappears, as many other difficulties will disappear, if we do not rip the verses out of their context, but study them, as any passage in any book should be studied, in their context.

The whole section of Proverbs 31 from verses one to nine is a protest against kings (and, by implication, people in any place of responsibility) using wine or strong drink at all. It is plainly taught that any use of wine has a tendency to make them forget the law and to pervert judgment. Verses six and seven themselves go on to add that wine and strong drink should only be used in cases of extreme physical weakness and despondency, when the man is so far gone that he is *"ready to perish"* (v. 6 KJV), and is consequently in the deepest depths of despondency.

The words are addressed to the king; and the king who was able to buy wine, instead of using it for himself, is advised to give it to those who are in a physical condition that requires it. The one in this condition would be stimulated by the wine and lifted out of his depression by the generosity of the king who gave the wine, so that he would be enabled to *"forget his poverty"* (v. 7), which would naturally prevent him from buying the wine for himself. The whole passage goes on to urge the king's attention to *"the cause of the poor and needy"* (v. 9).

So there remains no difficulty in this passage except for those who believe that all use of intoxicating liquors is wrong under any circumstances. But there are many who believe that in extreme cases of physical weakness, the use of wine is wise and permissible. We do not need to go into the question as to whether the wine and strong drink in this case were alcoholic. Those who urge that "strong drink" in the Old Testament often refers to a heavy, sweet, unfermented wine, have a good deal to say in favor of their position. Of course, if this interpretation were true, it would remove all difficulty from the passage. In either case, there is really no difficulty here at all for anyone who believes that there are circumstances in which the use of alcoholic stimulants is advisable.

There was a time in my life when the doctors had all given me up to die, and when my life was sustained by a prescription of an old nurse, one of the main ingredients of the prescription being brandy. Therefore, I am naturally disposed to think there are cases mentioned in the Bible when the use of strong drink is warranted. However, I thoroughly agree with the context of the passage that teaches that all use of wine should be renounced by people in health, strength, and prosperity.

Turning the Water into Wine

A stock objection against the Bible—not only against the Bible, but also against Jesus Christ Himself—is found in the story of Jesus turning the water into wine at the marriage festival at Cana of Galilee, as recorded in John 2:1–11. But there does not need to be any difficulty in this action of Jesus, even for the extreme teetotaler, if we would carefully consider exactly what is said and precisely what Jesus did.

The wine provided for the marriage festivities at Cana ran out. A cloud was about to fall over the joy of what is properly a festive occasion. Jesus came to the rescue. He provided wine, but there is not a hint that the wine He made was intoxicating. It was a freshly made wine. Newly made wine is never intoxicating, until some time after the process of fermentation, the process of decay, has set in. There is not a hint that our Lord produced alcohol, which is a product of decay or death. He produced a living wine, uncontaminated by fermentation. It is true it was better wine than they had been drinking, but that does not show for a moment that it was more fermented than what they had been previously served.

I am an absolute teetotaler. I do not believe at all in the use of alcoholic stimulants, even in cases of sickness, except in the most extreme cases, and even then only with the greatest caution. But I do not have the slightest objection, nor do I think that any reasonable person can have the slightest objection, to anyone's drinking newly made wine—the fresh juice of the grape. It is a wholesome drink. Even if some of the guests were already drunk, or had drunk freely of wine that may have been intoxicating, there would be no harm, but good, in substituting an unintoxicating wine for the intoxicating drink that they had been drinking.

Our Lord, as far as this story goes, at least, did not make *intoxicating* liquor for anybody to drink, but simply saved a festive occasion from disaster by providing a pure, wholesome, nonalcoholic drink. By turning the water into a wholesome wine, He showed His creative power and manifested His glory.

Chapter 20

"Contradictory" Genealogies of Jesus

◆————————

Those who deny the divine origin and inerrancy of the Bible frequently attack what appear to be two varying genealogies of Jesus Christ. Not only is this a favorite point of attack by unbelievers, but it is also a question that often puzzles earnest students of the Bible. It is perfectly clear that the two genealogies differ widely from one another, yet each of them is given as the genealogy of Christ. How can they possibly both be true?

One person has recently written me on this question in these words: "Two genealogies of Jesus are given, one in Matthew and one in Luke, and one is entirely different from the other. How can both be correct?" There is a very simple answer to this apparently difficult question.

Written for Two Audiences

The genealogy given in Matthew is the genealogy of Joseph, the reputed father of Jesus, and His father in the eyes of the law. The genealogy given in Luke is the genealogy of Mary, the mother of Jesus, and is the human genealogy of Jesus Christ in actual fact. The gospel of Matthew was written for the Jews. All through it, Joseph is prominent, and Mary is scarcely mentioned. In Luke, on the other hand, Mary is the chief personage in the whole account of the Savior's conception and birth. Joseph is brought in only incidentally because he was Mary's husband. In all of this, of course, there is a deep significance.

Our Redeemer, Our Brother

In Matthew, Jesus appears as the Messiah; in Luke, as "the Son of Man," our Brother and Redeemer, who belongs to the whole race and claims kindred with all kinds and conditions of men. So the genealogy in Matthew descends from Abraham to Joseph and Jesus, because all the promises touching the Messiah are fulfilled in Him. However, the genealogy in Luke ascends from Jesus to Adam, because the genealogy is being traced back to the head of the whole race, to show the relation of the Second Adam to the first.

The Royal Line

Joseph's line is the strictly royal line from David to Joseph. In Luke, though the line of descent is from David, it is not the royal line. In this, Jesus is descended from David through Nathan, David's son indeed, but not in the royal line, and the list follows a line quite distinct from the royal line.

The Lineal Descendent

The Messiah, according to prediction, was to be born of the seed of David (2 Sam. 7:12–16; Ps. 89:3–4, 34–37; 132:11; Acts 2:30; 13:22–23; Rom. 1:3; 2 Tim. 2:8). These prophecies are fulfilled by Jesus being the Son of Mary, who was a lineal descendant of David, though not in the royal line. Joseph, who was of the royal line, was not His father according to the flesh, but was His father in the eyes of the law.

Joseph, the Son of Heli

Mary was a descendant of David through her father, Heli. It is true that Luke 3:23 says that Joseph was the son of Heli. The simple explanation of this is that since Mary was a woman, her name, according to Jewish usage, could not come into the genealogy. Males alone formed the line, so Joseph's name is introduced in the place of Mary's. Because Joseph was Mary's husband, Heli was his father-in-law; thus, Joseph is called the son of Heli, and the line is completed. While Joseph was the son-in-law of Heli, according to the flesh, he was actually the son of Jacob (Matt. 1:16).

The Legal and the Natural

Two genealogies are absolutely necessary to trace the lineage of our Lord and Savior Jesus Christ, one the royal and legal, the other the natural and literal. We find these two genealogies in the Gospels: the legal and royal in Matthew's gospel, the gospel of law and kingship; and the natural and literal in Luke's, the gospel of humanity.

The Seed of Coniah

We are told in Jeremiah 22:30 that any descendant of Coniah (also called Jeconiah) could not come to the throne of David, and Joseph was of this line. Yet while Joseph's genealogy furnishes the royal line for Jesus, his son before the law, nevertheless, Jeremiah's prediction is fulfilled to the very letter, for Jesus, strictly speaking, was not Joseph's descendant; therefore, he was not of the seed of Coniah. If Jesus had been the son of Joseph in reality, He could not have come to the throne. But He is Mary's son and can come to the throne legally through Nathan by her marrying Joseph, thus clearing His way legally to it.

As we study these two genealogies of Jesus carefully and read them in the light of Old Testament prediction, we find that, far from constituting a reason for doubting the accuracy of the Bible, they are rather a confirmation of the minutest accuracy of that Book. It is amazing how one part of the Bible fits into another part when we study it closely. We need no longer stumble over the two genealogies, but discover and rejoice in the deep meaning represented by those genealogies.

Chapter 21

Did Jesus Go to the Heart of the Earth?

◆

I n the twelfth chapter of Matthew's gospel, Jesus is reported as saying, *"As Jonah was three days and three nights in the belly of the great fish, so will the Son of Man be three days and three nights in the heart of the earth"* (v. 40). According to the commonly accepted tradition of the church, Jesus was crucified on Friday, dying at 3 P.M., or somewhere between 3 P.M. and sundown, and was raised from the dead very early in the morning of the following Sunday. Many readers of the Bible are puzzled to know how the interval between late Friday afternoon and early Sunday morning can be figured out to be three days and three nights. It seems rather to be two nights, one day, and a very small portion of another day.

The solution proposed by many commentators to this apparent difficulty is that "a day and a night" is simply another way of saying, "a day," and that the ancient Jews counted a fraction of a day as a whole day. So they say there was a part (a very small part) of Friday (or a day and a night); all of Saturday, another day (or a day and a night); and part of Sunday (a very small part), another day (or a day and a night). This solution does not altogether satisfy many people, and I confess it does not satisfy me at all. It seems to me to be a makeshift answer, and a very weak one at that. Is there any solution that is altogether satisfactory? There is.

The first fact noticed in the proper solution is that the Bible nowhere says or implies that Jesus was crucified on Friday. It is said that Jesus was crucified on *"the day before the Sabbath"* (Mark 15:42). As the Jewish weekly Sabbath came on Saturday, beginning at sunset the evening before, the conclusion is naturally drawn that since Jesus was crucified the day before the Sabbath, He must have been crucified on Friday.

However, it is a well-known fact, to which the Bible bears abundant testimony, that the Jews had other Sabbaths besides the weekly Sabbath that fell on Saturday. The first day of the Passover week, no matter on what day of the week it came, was always a Sabbath (Exod. 12:16; Lev. 23:7; Num. 28:16–18). The question therefore arises whether the Sabbath that followed Christ's crucifixion was the weekly Sabbath (Saturday) or the Passover Sabbath, falling on the fifteenth day of Nisan, which came that year on Thursday.

The Bible does not leave us to speculate which Sabbath is meant in this instance, for John tells us in so many words, in John 19:14, that the day on which Jesus was tried and crucified was *"the Preparation Day of the Passover."* In other words, it was not the day before the weekly Sabbath, Friday, but it was the day before the Passover Sabbath, which came that year on Thursday—that is to say, the day on which Jesus Christ was crucified was Wednesday. John makes this as clear as day.

The gospel of John was written later than the other Gospels, and scholars have for a long time noticed that in various places there was an evident intention to correct false impressions that one might get from reading the other Gospels. One of these false impressions was that Jesus ate the Passover with His disciples at the regular time of the Passover. To correct this false impression, John clearly states that He ate it the evening before, and that He Himself died on the cross *at the very moment* the Passover lambs were being slain "between the two evenings" on the fourteenth day of Nisan. (See Exodus 12:6 in the Hebrew.)

God's real Paschal Lamb, Jesus, of whom all other paschal lambs offered through the centuries were only types, was therefore slain at the very time appointed by God. Everything about the Passover Lamb was fulfilled in Jesus. First, He was a Lamb without blemish and without spot (Exod. 12:5). Second, He was chosen on the tenth day of Nisan (v. 3), for it was on the tenth day of the month, the preceding Saturday, that the triumphal entry into Jerusalem was made.

We know this because He came from Jericho to Bethany six days before the Passover (John 12:1). That would be six days before Thursday, which would be Friday. Furthermore, it was on the next day that the entry into Jerusalem was made (v. 12 and following), that is, on Saturday, the tenth day of Nisan. It was also on this same day that Judas went to the chief priests and offered to betray Jesus for thirty pieces of silver (Matt. 26:6–16; Mark 14:3–11). Since it was after the supper in the house of Simon the leper, and since the supper occurred late on Friday or early on Saturday, after sunset, after the supper would necessarily be on the tenth of Nisan.

The price set on Him by the chief priests represented, of course, the buying or taking to them of a lamb, which according to law must occur on the tenth day of Nisan. Furthermore, they put the exact value on the Lamb that Old Testament prophecy predicted (Zech. 11:12; Matt. 26:15).

Third, not a bone of His was broken when He was killed (John 19:36; Exod. 12:46; Num. 9:12; Ps. 34:20). Fourth, He was killed on the fourteenth of Nisan, between the evenings, just before the beginning of the fifteenth day, at sundown (Exod. 12:6). If we take exactly what the Bible says, that Jesus was slain before the Passover Sabbath, the type is marvelously fulfilled in every detail; but if we accept the traditional theory that Jesus was crucified on Friday, the type fails at many points.

Furthermore, if we accept the traditional view that Jesus was crucified on Friday and ate the Passover on the regular day of the Passover, then the journey from Jericho to Bethany, which occurred six days before the Passover (John 12:1), would fall on a Saturday—that is, the Jewish Sabbath. Such a journey on the Jewish Sabbath would be contrary to Jewish law.

Of course, it was impossible for Jesus to take such a journey on the Jewish Sabbath because his triumphal entry into Jerusalem was on the Jewish Sabbath, Saturday. This was altogether possible, for the Bible elsewhere tells us that Bethany was a Sabbath day's journey from Jerusalem (Acts 1:12; Luke 24:50).

It has also been figured out by astronomers that in the year A.D. 30, which is the commonly accepted year for the crucifixion of our Lord, the Passover was observed on Thursday, April 6, the moon being full that day. The chronologists who have supposed that the Crucifixion took place on Friday have been greatly perplexed by this fact that in the year A.D. 30, the Passover occurred on Thursday.

One writer, in seeking a solution to the difficulty, has suggested that the Crucifixion may have been in the year A.D. 33. Although the full moon was on a Thursday that year also, the time was only two and a half hours from being Friday. Consequently, he thinks that perhaps the Jews may have observed the Passover on Friday, instead, and that the Crucifixion therefore took place on Thursday. However, when we accept exactly what the Bible says—namely, that Jesus was not crucified on the Passover day but on *"the Preparation Day of the Passover"* (John 19:14), and that He was to be three days and three nights in the grave—then the fact that *"the Preparation Day of the Passover"* that year was on a Wednesday and His resurrection early on the first day of the week allows exactly three days and three nights in the grave.

In summary, Jesus died just about at sunset on Wednesday. Seventy-two hours later, exactly three days and three nights, at the beginning of the first day of the week, Saturday at sunset, He arose again from the grave. When the women visited the tomb in the morning just before dawn, they found the grave already empty.

From this, we are not driven to the makeshift explanation that any small portion of a day is counted as a whole day and night, but we find that the statement of Jesus was literally true. Three days and three nights His body was dead and lay in the tomb. While His body lay dead, He Himself, being *"made alive by the Spirit"* (1 Pet. 3:18), went into the heart of the earth and preached to the spirits that were in prison (v. 19).

The two men on the way to Emmaus early on the first day of the week, that is, Sunday, said to Jesus, in speaking of the Crucifixion and events accompanying it, *"Besides all this, today is the third day since these things happened"* (Luke 24:21). Some people have objected to this verse, saying that if the Crucifixion took place on Wednesday, Sunday would be the fourth day since these things were done; but the answer is very simple.

These things were done at sunset, just as Thursday was beginning. They were therefore completed on Thursday, and the first day since Thursday would be Friday, the second day since

Thursday would be Saturday, and *"the third day since"* Thursday would be Sunday, the first day of the week. So the supposed objection in reality supports the theory. On the other hand, if the Crucifixion took place on Friday, by no manner of accounting could Sunday be made *"the third day since"* these things were done.

Many passages in the Scriptures support the theory advanced above and make it necessary to believe that Jesus died late on Wednesday. Some of them are as follows:

> *For as Jonah was three days and three nights in the belly of the great fish, so will the Son of Man be three days and three nights in the heart of the earth.* (Matt. 12:40)

> *This fellow said, "I am able to destroy the temple of God and to build it in three days."* (Matt. 26:61)

> *You who destroy the temple and build it in three days, save Yourself!* (Matt. 27:40)

> *Sir, we remember, while He was still alive, how that deceiver said, "After three days I will rise."* (v. 63)

> *The Son of Man must suffer many things, and be rejected by the elders and chief priests and scribes, and be killed, and after three days rise again.* (Mark 8:31)

> *The Son of Man is being betrayed into the hands of men, and they will kill Him. And after He is killed, He will rise the third day.* (Mark 9:31)

> *They will mock Him, and scourge Him, and spit on Him, and kill Him. And the third day He will rise again.* (Mark 10:34)

> *I will destroy this temple made with hands, and within three days I will build another made without hands.* (Mark 14:58)

> *Aha! You who destroy the temple and build it in three days, save Yourself, and come down from the cross!* (Mark 15:29–30)

> *Besides all this, today is the third day since these things happened.* (Luke 24:21)

> *Jesus answered and said to them, "Destroy this temple, and in three days I will raise it up." Then the Jews said, "It has taken forty-six years to build this temple, and will You raise it up in three days?" But He was speaking of the temple of His body. Therefore, when He had risen from the dead, His disciples remembered that He had said this to them; and they believed the Scripture and the word which Jesus had said.* (John 2:19–22)

There is absolutely nothing in favor of a Friday crucifixion, but everything in the Scripture is perfectly harmonized by a Wednesday crucifixion. It is remarkable how many prophetic passages of the Old Testament are fulfilled and how many seeming discrepancies in the gospel narratives are straightened out when we once come to understand that Jesus died on Wednesday and not on Friday.

Chapter 22

Did Jesus Commend an Unrighteous Steward?

◆

A very puzzling passage in the Bible to many is the story of the unrighteous steward, recorded in Luke 16:1–14. Once, when this lesson was appointed by the International Sunday School Lesson, a lady told me that she had made up her mind not to teach it. She said, "The three points of difficulty are these: first, that Jesus should hold this dishonest scoundrel up for our imitation; second, that the Lord should commend the unrighteous steward; and third, that Jesus should tell His disciples to make themselves *'friends of the mammon of unrighteousness'*" (Luke 16:9).

We will take these three points in order. By noticing exactly what is said, we will soon see that in each point, if we adhere strictly to the words of Jesus, the difficulties will disappear, and the incident, instead of staggering us, will be profoundly instructive.

An Example to Christians?

First, why did Jesus "hold this dishonest scoundrel up for our imitation"? The answer is found in the text itself. Jesus did not hold him up for imitation. He held him up, first of all, as a warning of what would overtake unfaithful stewards, how they would be called to give account of their stewardship, and how their stewardship would be taken from them.

Having taught this solemn and beneficial lesson—one that is much needed today—Jesus goes on to show how the *"sons of this world are more shrewd in their generation than the sons of*

507

light" (Luke 16:8). They are wiser in that they used their utmost ingenuity and put forth their utmost effort to make present opportunities count for the hour of future need.

"The sons of light" often do not do that. Indeed, how many present-day sons of light, who profess to believe that eternity is all and that time is nothing in comparison, are using their cleverness and putting forth their best efforts to make the opportunities of the present life count most for the needs of the great eternity that is to follow? The average professing Christian today uses his skills and puts forth his best efforts to bring things to pass in business and other affairs of this brief, present world; but when it comes to matters that affect eternity, he is content with the exercise of the least possible amount of ingenuity and with the putting forth of the smallest effort that will satisfy his conscience.

Jesus did not point to the steward's dishonesty to stir our emulation. Jesus plainly rebuked his dishonesty. But Jesus did point to his common sense in using the opportunity of the present to provide for the necessities of the future. God wants us to learn to use the opportunities of the present to provide for the necessities of the future—the eternal future. Even in pointing out the steward's common sense, Jesus carefully guarded His statement by saying that the unjust steward was *"more shrewd in* [his] *generation"* (Luke 16:8). He knew only the life that is now; and from that narrow and imperfect standpoint, he was wiser than the *"sons of light"* (v. 8), who are not wise enough to live wholly for eternity.

There are other utterances of our Lord and Savior where wicked and selfish men are held up by way of contrast to show how much more godly men, or even God Himself, may be expected to act in the way suggested. (See Luke 11:5–8; 18:6–7; Matthew 12:11–12.) The first difficulty in the passage, then, has disappeared on careful scrutiny of exactly what is said. Let us move to the second difficulty.

The Lord of the Steward

Why did the Lord "commend the unrighteous steward"? The answer to this, too, is very simple, namely, that the Lord

Jesus did not commend the unrighteous steward. This is evident by a single glance at verse eight. It reads, *"The lord commended the unjust steward"* (KJV). Now, if we were to leave it standing that way, there might be some possible doubt as to whether *"the lord"* meant was the lord of the steward or whether it was the Lord Jesus, who relates the parable.

Newer versions remove this possible ambiguity from this verse by translating it to read *"the master* [that is, the steward's lord] *commended the unjust steward."* It was not the Lord Jesus who commended him, but his own lord, and he only commended his shrewdness. That this interpretation is the correct interpretation of the verse is beyond dispute, for the Lord Jesus is the speaker, and it is He who speaks about the one who does the commending as *"the lord"* (*"the master"* in NKJV), evidently not speaking about Himself, but about the lord of the unjust steward. It is only by a very careless reading of the passage that anyone could make "the lord" of this passage the Lord Jesus.

Far from commending him, the Lord Jesus candidly called him *"the unjust steward"*; furthermore, He warned against unfaithfulness in stewardship in the verses that follow (Luke 16:10–11). So the second difficulty entirely disappears on a careful look at what is said. In that case, let us consider the third difficulty.

The Wise Use of Money

Why did Jesus say to His disciples to *"make friends for yourselves by unrighteous mammon"* (v. 9)? This difficulty disappears when we discover the accurate biblical definition of the terms used. First, what does *"unrighteous mammon"* mean? It means nothing more nor less than money. Money is called *"unrighteous mammon"* because it is such a constant agent of sin and selfishness (as, for example, in the case of the scoundrel previously mentioned), and because *"the love of money is a root of all kinds of evil"* (1 Tim. 6:10). Jesus warned against the perils of money by speaking of it as *"unrighteous mammon"* (Luke 16:9). He often packed a whole sermon into a single phrase.

In the second place, what does the *of* mean when our Lord tells us to make *"friends of the mammon of unrighteousness"* (v. 9

KJV)? The answer to this question is found in the Revised Version, where the *of* is properly translated "by means of." So then, what Jesus told His disciples to do (and what he tells us to do) was to make themselves friends by means of money. That is, they were to use the money God entrusted to them in the present life, so as to make friends for themselves among God's poor and needy ones by their use of it. As the context shows, they would make friends who, in turn, would go to the *"everlasting home"* (v. 9) and be ready to give us, their benefactors who had used our money to bless them, a royal welcome when our lives here on earth have ended and our money has run out.

In other words, Jesus simply put into a new and striking form His oft-repeated teaching not to keep our money hoarded (Matt. 6:19–21), not to spend it on ourselves, but to spend it in doing good (1 Tim. 6:17–19), especially to God's needy ones (Matt. 25:40; Prov. 19:17). By this kind of use, we invest it in heavenly and abiding securities (Matt. 19:21, 29). That this teaching of Jesus was clearly understood by His hearers is proven by verse fourteen that follows. In this verse, we are told that the Pharisees, who were lovers of money, heard all these things and scoffed at Him.

So the third and last difficulty has disappeared, and this passage stands out in glorious light, teaching with great force a lesson that our day needs to learn: that money is a stewardship; that the one who seeks to enjoy it now rather than spending it in a way that will bring him interest for all eternity is a great fool; and that even the petty shrewdness of the *"sons of this world"* (Luke 16:8) rebukes him.

Chapter 23

A "Mistake" about the Second Coming

◆

It is constantly taught not only by unbelievers, but even in many Christian pulpits and in some of our theological seminaries, that Jesus and Paul were mistaken as to the time of our Lord's return. In an interesting little pamphlet published by the Boston American Unitarian Association, in which five ministers tell how they came to be Unitarians after having preached in orthodox churches, one writer said:

> But in a lecture one day on Thessalonians, our professor remarked that Paul evidently was mistaken as to the time of the coming of Christ. I was thunderstruck and stared rigidly at the speaker, while my pencil dropped from my fingers. It is true, then, after all the denunciation of the preachers, Higher Criticism wasn't the false, shallow thing that it was made out to be. I can hear yet, after many years, the echo of that slamming book in the vacant library, and that cedar pencil clattering to the floor.

Evidently, this young man was easily shaken. If a professor in a theological seminary said anything, that settled it for him. The professor must certainly be correct, and all other professors who taught differently, and all others who studied the Bible for themselves, must be wrong. The fact that the professor made such a remark as this was positive proof to this young man that Higher Criticism was not "the false, shallow thing that it was made out to be."

I do not wonder that such a young man became a Unitarian preacher. Yet even theological professors are sometimes mistaken, and this professor certainly was mistaken. The mistake was altogether the professor's, and not at all Paul's, as we will see in this chapter.

Interpreting What Jesus Meant

Let us begin with Jesus, and not with Paul. Was Jesus mistaken as to the time of His own return? As proof that He was, Matthew 24:34, and parallel passages in the other gospels (Mark 13:30; Luke 21:32), are constantly cited. Our Lord is here reported as saying, *"Assuredly, I say to you, this generation will by no means pass away till all these things take place"* (Matt. 24:34). And it is claimed that Jesus plainly taught here that the generation living on earth at the time that He spoke these words would not have passed away before all the things recorded in the preceding verses had come to pass, so of course this would be a mistake.

However, if anybody will read the entire passage carefully, he will see that Jesus said nothing of the kind. In the context, He taught how rapidly things will culminate at the end, that when certain signs begin to appear, events will ripen so fast that the generation living when these signs appear will not have passed away until all things belonging to that particular epoch will have come to be.

These signs mentioned as indicating the speedy close of the age are found in Matthew 24:29: *"The sun will be darkened, and the moon will not give its light; the stars will fall from heaven, and the powers of the heavens will be shaken."* These signs did not occur while our Lord was on earth, nor in that generation; but when they do occur, then things will ripen so fast that the sign of the Son of Man will be seen in heaven, and the Son of Man will come in clouds with power and great glory before the generation then existing passes away. That this is the true interpretation of the passage is evident when Jesus says distinctly, *"When you see all these things, know that it is near; at the doors!"* (v. 33).

Jesus taught that just as the putting forth of tender shoots and young leaves is an indication that summer is nigh, so the appearing of these signs will be an indication that the Lord is near—so near that that generation will not pass away until the

Lord actually comes. And *"this generation"* (v. 34) clearly refers, if taken in context, to the generation existing when these signs appear.

The connection is just the same in Mark 13, where similar words are found. If possible, it is even clearer in Luke 21:25–32, where the words are found again. So the whole difficulty is not with what Jesus actually said, but with the failure of expositors to carefully notice exactly what Jesus had in mind when He spoke the words to which objection has been made.

Another interpretation of this verse has been offered that is full of suggestion, namely, that the word rendered "generation" in this passage means often "race" or "family" or "men begotten of the same stock," and this doubtless is one meaning of the word that is used. In fact, this is given as the second meaning of the word in *Thayer's Greek-English Lexicon of the New Testament*, and "age" (or "generation") is the fourth meaning given. Taking this as the meaning of the word, the passage is interpreted to mean that this "race" ("generation"), that is, the Jewish race, will not pass away, that is, will maintain its race identity, until the coming of the Lord.

It is a remarkable fact that, though the Jews have for centuries been driven from their native land and scattered throughout all the nations, they have always retained their race identity. This thought may also have been in Jesus' mind, and His words may have been pregnant with meaning that cannot be exhausted by one interpretation. Nevertheless, from the context, the primary meaning seems to be the one given in the first explanation above.

Another passage urged to show that Jesus was mistaken about the time of His return is Matthew 16:28, although parallel passages, including Mark 9:1 and Luke 9:27, may also be used here.

> *Assuredly, I say to you, there are some standing here who shall not taste death till they see the Son of Man coming in His kingdom.* (Matt. 16:28)

It is believed that in this passage Jesus taught that His coming again would be before some of those standing there would die. Here, again, the solution of the difficulty is found in the context.

It is my opinion that there should not be a chapter division where Matthew 17 begins. (Of course, chapter divisions are not part of the original Scriptures.) We should read right on as we do in the parallel passages in Mark and Luke; for if we read right on and see what is said, the meaning of Jesus' words becomes as clear as day. The words were spoken as a prophecy of the Transfiguration, the account of which immediately follows.

Three of those standing with Jesus when He spoke the words were to go up with Him to the mount; there on the mountain, they were to see His true glory shining forth in His face, in His person, in the very raiment He wore (Matt. 17:2). In fact, they were to hear the Father declare, *"This is My beloved Son, in whom I am well pleased"* (v. 5). In all this, they saw *"the Son of Man coming in His kingdom"* (Matt. 16:28).

If events had been allowed to take their natural course, Jesus then and there would have been manifested to the world as He was to the disciples as the King. But Jesus chose rather, in order that men might be saved, to go down from this Mount of Transfiguration—where He was manifested in His glory as coming in His kingdom, where the kingdom of God came with power (Mark 9:1), where Peter, James, and John saw the kingdom of God (Luke 9:27)—to die as an atoning sacrifice on the cross of Calvary. It is a significant fact in this connection that the subject of which Moses and Elijah spoke, who appeared talking with Him on the mountain, was *"of His decease which He was about to accomplish at Jerusalem"* (Luke 9:31).

Here again, then, we see that the mistake was not on Jesus' part, but on the part of the interpreter, who was careless and overlooked the context in which the words of Jesus are found. The difficulty also arises from the interpretation that is placed on the words by the writers themselves, immediately after they have recorded them. So all these arguments of the destructive critics built on our Lord's being mistaken as to the time of His own return fall to the ground.

Interpreting What Paul Meant

However, was Paul mistaken? By those who contend against the verbal accuracy of the New Testament writings, it is constantly said that he was. It is frequently repeated that "Paul evidently was mistaken in his early writings as to the time of the coming of Christ."

In defense of this contention, the words of Paul in 1 Thessalonians 4:15–18 are brought forward. Paul said in verse 15:

For this we say to you by the word of the Lord, that we who are alive and remain until the coming of the Lord will by no means precede those who are asleep.

It is said here that these words make it evident that Paul expected to be alive when the Lord came. What Paul may have expected, I do not know. Very likely he did hope to be alive when the Lord came, but he certainly did not teach that he would be alive. And no one holds any theory of inspiration that maintains that the Bible writers did not entertain mistaken hopes.

The theory of inspiration and absolute veracity and accuracy of Bible teaching is simply the theory that the Bible writers nowhere taught error. That they may have entertained erroneous notions on a great many things, no one questions. However, if they had such mistaken notions, the Holy Spirit kept them from teaching them, and this is what is maintained. Paul certainly did not teach here that he would be alive when the Lord came.

On the other hand, he did teach that some people would have fallen asleep and others would be alive. As he was still alive, he naturally put himself in the class to which he belonged at the time of writing, those *"who are alive"* (v. 15). He certainly was alive at the time of writing. He certainly was one of those left at that time. That he should continue to be alive, however, he does not say. Very likely he hoped to be. Every believer who has a true understanding of the doctrine of the coming of the Lord naturally entertains a hope that he may be alive when the Lord comes.

I hope that I may be alive when He comes, but not for a moment do I venture to teach that I will be. I do know that I am alive at this moment; I know that I am not one of those who have as yet fallen asleep; and if I were differentiating between the two classes—those who are alive and those who are asleep—I would certainly put myself with those who are alive and would not be mistaken in doing so.

Paul put himself with those who were alive at that time. He had not yet fallen asleep. Paul knew perfectly well that the Lord Himself had taught, long before he wrote these words to the Thessalonians, that it is not for us *"to know times or seasons which the Father has put in His own authority"* (Acts 1:7). He did not attempt to know times or seasons that his Master had so distinctly taught were not for him, nor for us, to know, but he did teach the following:

> *The Lord Himself will descend from heaven with a shout, with the voice of an archangel, and with the trumpet of God. And the dead in Christ will rise first. Then we who are alive and remain shall be caught up together with them in the clouds to meet the Lord in the air. And thus we shall always be with the Lord.* (1 Thess. 4:16–17)

In verses thirteen through fifteen, Paul urged those who were alive at that time not to sorrow over those who had already died. As Paul was among the class that were alive, he naturally and properly put himself with them and not with those who had already fallen asleep. So in this passage, instead of finding that the Holy Spirit left Paul to make mistakes, we find, in fact, that the Holy Spirit kept him from making a mistake, even in regard to the matter about which in his own longing he might have entertained a mistaken hope.

The whole passage, then, instead of being an argument against the verbal accuracy of the Scriptures, is an argument for it. The passage shows how the men chosen by the Holy Spirit to be the vehicles of His revelation to us were kept absolutely from putting into their teaching any mistaken hope that they might have entertained. Our critical friends, who are hunting so persistently for some mistake in the teaching of Paul, will have to carry their search further.

Perhaps the young theological student who was so thunderstruck by his professor's saying that Paul was mistaken as to the time of the coming of Christ, and who therefore launched forth into Unitarianism, may be a lesson to the critics to be cautious lest their teaching prove equally disastrous to some other weak-minded young people.

Chapter 24

Did Jesus Go to the Abode of the Dead?

◆

think I have never had a question box in any city into which someone did not put the question, "What does 1 Peter 3:18–20 mean when it says that Jesus went and preached to the spirits in prison?" A very simple answer to this question is that it means just what it says, but let us notice carefully exactly what it does say.

> *For Christ also suffered once for sins, the just for the un-just, that He might bring us to God, being put to death in the flesh but made alive by the Spirit, by whom also He went and preached to the spirits in prison, who formerly were disobedient, when once the Divine longsuffering waited in the days of Noah, while the ark was being pre-pared, in which a few, that is, eight souls, were saved through water.* (1 Pet. 3:18–20)

For many people, the point of difficulty with this passage is that it seems to convey the idea that Jesus actually went into the abode of the dead and preached there to the spirits in prison. To these people, this idea seems to imply that there is an opportunity for repentance after death. Many have attempted to explain the verses in order to avoid this conclusion, by saying that the spirit here in which Jesus was quickened is the Holy Spirit. They say that, in the Holy Spirit, Jesus Christ preached through Noah (while the ark was being prepared) to the spirits who were then disobedient and who consequently are now in prison.

One writer, Mr. William Kelly, has argued for this interpretation with a great deal of ability and skill and with a large display of knowledge of Greek grammar. Of Mr. Kelly's unusual knowledge of Greek, there can be no question; nevertheless, I think he fails to make his case stand. After all that has been said, it seems to me that his interpretation is an evasion.

The "spirit" in verse eighteen cannot mean "the Holy Spirit." A contrast is being drawn between the two parts of Christ's nature: the flesh in which He was put to death, and the spirit in which He was made alive at the time He was put to death in the flesh. In His spirit in which He was made alive, while the body lay motionless in death, He went and preached to the spirits in prison. It seems to me that this is the only fair interpretation to put on the words; and if we are to take the Scriptures as meaning exactly what they say, this is what we must take them to mean.

Even so, does this not involve a second probation for those who have died in disobedience to God and who consequently have gone to the place of penalty and suffering? Even if it did, we should not dodge it on that account. Rather, we ought to be fair with the Scriptures whether they conform to our theories or not.

But, in fact, this does not in any way involve a second probation for those who have died in disobedience, and who consequently have gone to the place of penalty and suffering. This is apparent if we notice three things: first, if we notice to whom Jesus preached; second, if we notice what He preached to them; and, third, if we notice what the results of His preaching were.

To Whom Did Jesus Preach?

First of all, then, to whom did Jesus preach? You will answer, "The spirits in prison." But who were these spirits in prison? Were they the spirits of departed, wicked men? There is nothing whatever to indicate that they were. The word *spirits* is never used in this unqualified way of the spirits of departed men, but it is used constantly of angelic or supernatural beings. (See Hebrews 1:7, 14; Matthew 10:1; Mark 3:11; Luke 6:18; 7:21; Acts 19:12; 1 John 4:1; and many other places.) The only place in Scripture where *spirits* is used of men in any way analogous to this is Hebrews 12:23. It is certainly more consistently used for angels or other supernatural beings.

If we interpret it here to refer to supernatural beings, then of course the preaching was not at all to men who had been wicked in the days of Noah, but to supernatural beings who had been disobedient in the days of Noah and who were now in prison as a consequence of this disobedience. Are there any passages of Scripture that hint that there were supernatural beings who were disobedient in the days of Noah and who were consequently now in prison? There are.

In Genesis 6:2, we are told that *"the sons of God saw the daughters of men, that they were beautiful; and they took wives for themselves of all whom they chose."* Many commentators understand the *"sons of God"* in this passage to be the descendants of Seth, a godly man; but if we are to interpret Scripture by Scripture, they seem rather to have been angelic beings. There seems to be a clear reference to this passage in Jude 1:6, where we are told of *"angels who did not keep their proper domain, but left their own abode,"* and in consequence were kept in *"everlasting chains under darkness for the judgment of the great day."* In the next verse, we are told that Sodom and Gomorrah *"in a similar manner to these"* [that is, these angels] gave themselves over to fornication and went after *"strange flesh."*

From this verse, it seems clear that the sin of the angels was going after *"strange flesh,"* the very sin mentioned in Genesis 6:1–3. Furthermore, we read that *"God did not spare the angels who sinned, but cast them down to hell and delivered them into chains of darkness, to be reserved for judgment"* (2 Pet. 2:4). The clear implication of all this is that the spirits to whom Jesus preached, when He went to the abode of the dead, were the angels that sinned in the days of Noah, and who were now in prison as a consequence of that sin.

What Did He Preach?

Let us notice next what the word translated "preach" in 1 Peter 3:18–20 means. There are two words in constant use in the New Testament that are translated "preach." One of them means "to preach the Gospel." The other means "to herald" (to announce a king or his kingdom). It is the latter of these two words that is used in this passage.

There is not a suggestion in the passage that the Gospel, with its offer of salvation, was preached to anyone. The King and the kingdom were heralded. So then, even if we take *"the spirits in prison"* (v. 19) to mean the spirits of men who had died in sin, there is not a hint of another probation. We are simply told that the King and the kingdom were declared to them. Christ has been proclaimed as King in heaven, in earth, and in hell.

The Results of His Preaching

In the third place, notice the results of this preaching. There is not a word of suggestion that any of the spirits in prison were converted by it. If they were, we must learn it from sources other than this passage, but there is not a single passage anywhere in the Scriptures that suggests that there were any conversions or any salvation resultant from this preaching. The purpose of the preaching was evidently not the salvation of those already lost, but the proclamation of the kingdom and the King throughout the universe.

The time is coming when *"every knee should bow, of those in heaven, and of those on earth, and of those under the earth, and that every tongue should confess that Jesus Christ is Lord, to the glory of God the Father"* (Phil. 2:10–11). Yet that enforced confession of Christ on the part of disobedient men and angels will bring them no salvation. We must all take our choice of either confessing and accepting Christ of our own free will now and obtaining salvation thereby, or of confessing Him and acknowledging Him against our will in the world to come.

We must confess Him at some time. We must someday bow before Him. Happy is the man who gladly bows before Jesus now in this time of probation and confesses that Jesus Christ is Lord to the glory of God the Father. Happy is the man who does not wait until that day when he is forced to do it, and when the confession will bring him no salvation.

How to Witness
to Anyone

Contents

Introduction

n a compelling passage of Scripture in the book of Matthew, Jesus told His disciples, *"The harvest truly is plentiful, but the laborers are few. Therefore pray the Lord of the harvest to send out laborers into His harvest"* (Matt. 9:37–38).

When Christians answer the call to work in God's harvest field, they may be sent across the street to witness to a neighbor or across the ocean to a different culture. These workers must be prepared to answer a variety of questions and arguments when they confront people with the truth about heaven, hell, and eternity.

Through His Word, God has revealed Himself and given the answer to every doubt and every need in the hearts of men. *How to Witness to Anyone* conveniently groups Scriptures according to topics, providing Christians with a valuable tool for ministry. The subjects and Scriptures correspond to R. A. Torrey's larger and more detailed work, *How to Bring Men to Christ*.

Study these Scriptures, and prepare your heart to testify about the Lord Jesus Christ. Then, when someone with whom you are sharing the Gospel says, "I can't give up my evil ways," or "I will lose my friends if I come to Christ," you can reply using God's own Word. Allow God to use you in the glorious ministry of reconciliation.

Chapter 1

You Can Be a Soulwinner

Certain requirements must be fulfilled for real success in leading lost souls to Christ. Fortunately, these are few and simple, and anyone can meet them.

First, be a born-again believer. If you desire to bring others to Christ, you must turn away from all sin, worldliness, and selfishness, allowing Jesus to be Lord over your entire life.

Second, truly love others and long for their salvation. If you have no love for other souls, your efforts will be mechanical and powerless; however, if you, like Paul, have great heaviness and continual pain in your heart for the unsaved (Rom. 9:2), the earnestness in your tone and manner will impress even the most uninterested person. Furthermore, you will be watching for opportunities to tell people about Jesus.

Third, have a working knowledge of the Bible. The Word of God is the *"sword of the Spirit"* (Eph. 6:17), which God uses to convict people of sin, to reveal Christ, and to regenerate the lost. You must use the Bible to bring people to Christ.

Fourth, pray frequently. Pray about whom you should speak to, what you should say, and that you will speak powerfully.

Fifth, be baptized in the Holy Spirit. After Jesus gave His disciples the Great Commission, He told them: *"But you shall receive power when the Holy Spirit has come upon you; and you shall be witnesses to Me in Jerusalem, and in all Judea and Samaria, and to the end of the earth"* (Acts 1:8).

The next two chapters contain promises from God's Word that explain His plan of salvation. Several chapters that follow give specific verses to answer the many objections that unbelievers have to God's plan. Then, there are chapters containing verses to help the new believer to become stronger and to weather difficult times. The final chapter gives valuable hints for you, the soulwinner.

Chapter 2

The Promise of Salvation

1. All Have Sinned

There is no difference; for all have sinned and fall short of the glory of God. (Rom. 3:22–23)

If we say that we have no sin, we deceive ourselves, and the truth is not in us....If we say that we have not sinned, we make Him a liar, and His word is not in us. (1 John 1:8, 10)

You shall love the LORD your God with all your heart, with all your soul, and with all your mind. This is the first and great commandment. (Matt. 22:37–38)

If You, LORD, should mark iniquities, O Lord, who could stand? (Ps. 130:3)

2. The Consequences of Sin and Unbelief

But the wicked are like the troubled sea, when it cannot rest, whose waters cast up mire and dirt. "There is no peace," says my God, "for the wicked." (Isa. 57:20–21)

Jesus answered them, "Most assuredly, I say to you, whoever commits sin is a slave of sin." (John 8:34)

For as many as are of the works of the law are under the curse; for it is written, "Cursed is everyone who does not

528

continue in all things which are written in the book of the law, to do them." (Gal. 3:10)

He who believes in the Son has everlasting life; and he who does not believe the Son shall not see life, but the wrath of God abides on him. (John 3:36)

He who believes in Him is not condemned; but he who does not believe is condemned already, because he has not believed in the name of the only begotten Son of God. (John 3:18)

For the wages of sin is death, but the gift of God is eternal life in Christ Jesus our Lord. (Rom. 6:23)

The Lord Jesus is revealed from heaven with His mighty angels, in flaming fire taking vengeance on those who do not know God, and on those who do not obey the gospel of our Lord Jesus Christ. These shall be punished with everlasting destruction from the presence of the Lord and from the glory of His power. (2 Thess. 1:7–9)

You will die in your sins; for if you do not believe that I am He, you will die in your sins. (John 8:24)

But the cowardly, unbelieving, abominable, murderers, sexually immoral, sorcerers, idolaters, and all liars shall have their part in the lake which burns with fire and brimstone, which is the second death. (Rev. 21:8)

Anyone who has rejected Moses' law dies without mercy on the testimony of two or three witnesses. Of how much worse punishment, do you suppose, will he be thought worthy who has trampled the Son of God underfoot, counted the blood of the covenant by which he was sanctified a common thing, and insulted the Spirit of grace? (Heb. 10:28–29)

3. God's Love for Man

For God so loved the world that He gave His only begotten Son, that whoever believes in Him should not perish but have everlasting life.   (John 3:16)

For when we were still without strength, in due time Christ died for the ungodly....God demonstrates His own love toward us, in that while we were still sinners, Christ died for us.   (Rom. 5:6, 8)

But He was wounded for our transgressions, He was bruised for our iniquities; the chastisement for our peace was upon Him, and by His stripes we are healed. All we like sheep have gone astray; we have turned, every one, to his own way; and the LORD has laid on Him the iniquity of us all.   (Isa. 53:5–6)

And being in agony, He prayed more earnestly. Then His sweat became like great drops of blood falling down to the ground.   (Luke 22:44)

And about the ninth hour Jesus cried out with a loud voice, saying, "Eli, Eli, lama sabachthani?" that is, "My God, My God, why have You forsaken Me?"
                    (Matt. 27:46)

Christ has redeemed us from the curse of the law, having become a curse for us (for it is written, "Cursed is everyone who hangs on a tree").   (Gal. 3:13)

Knowing that you were not redeemed with corruptible things, like silver or gold, from your aimless conduct received by tradition from your fathers, but with the precious blood of Christ, as of a lamb without blemish and without spot.   (1 Pet. 1:18–19)

Chapter 3

Dealing with the Openhearted

◆

1. Jesus—Our Sin-Bearer

All we like sheep have gone astray; we have turned, every one, to his own way; and the LORD has laid on Him the iniquity of us all. (Isa. 53:6)

Who Himself bore our sins in His own body on the tree, that we, having died to sins, might live for righteousness; by whose stripes you were healed. (1 Pet. 2:24)

In this is love, not that we loved God, but that He loved us and sent His Son to be the propitiation for our sins. (1 John 4:10)

And He Himself is the propitiation for our sins, and not for ours only but also for the whole world. (1 John 2:2)

For it pleased the Father that in Him all the fullness should dwell, and by Him to reconcile all things to Himself, by Him, whether things on earth or things in heaven. (Col. 1:19–20)

In Him we have redemption through His blood, the forgiveness of sins, according to the riches of His grace. (Eph. 1:7)

For when we were still without strength, in due time Christ died for the ungodly. For scarcely for a righteous man will one die; yet perhaps for a good man someone would even dare to die. But God demonstrates His own love toward us, in that while we were still sinners, Christ died for us. Much more then, having now been justified by His blood, we shall be saved from wrath through Him. For if when we were enemies we were reconciled to God through the death of His Son, much more, having been reconciled, we shall be saved by His life. And not only that, but we also rejoice in God through our Lord Jesus Christ, through whom we have now received the reconciliation. (Rom. 5:6–11)

2. Jesus—Our Risen Savior

Moreover, brethren, I declare to you the gospel which I preached to you, which also you received and in which you stand, by which also you are saved, if you hold fast that word which I preached to you; unless you believed in vain. For I delivered to you first of all that which I also received: that Christ died for our sins according to the Scriptures, and that He was buried, and that He rose again the third day according to the Scriptures. (1 Cor. 15:1–4)

And she will bring forth a Son, and you shall call His name JESUS, for He will save His people from their sins. (Matt. 1:21)

Now if I do what I will not to do, it is no longer I who do it, but sin that dwells in me. I find then a law, that evil is present with me, the one who wills to do good. For I delight in the law of God according to the inward man. But I see another law in my members, warring against the law of my mind, and bringing me into captivity to the law of sin which is in my members. O wretched man that I am! Who will deliver me from this body of death? I thank God; through Jesus Christ our Lord! So then, with the mind I myself serve the law of God, but with the flesh the law of sin. (Rom. 7:20–25)

[He] is able to keep you from stumbling, and to present you faultless before the presence of His glory with exceeding joy. (Jude 24)

[We] are kept by the power of God through faith for salvation ready to be revealed in the last time. (1 Pet. 1:5)

3. Jesus—Our Ever Living Intercessor

My little children, these things write I to you, so that you may not sin. And if anyone sins, we have an Advocate with the Father, Jesus Christ the righteous. (1 John 2:1)

Who is he who condemns? It is Christ who died, and furthermore is also risen, who is even at the right hand of God, who also makes intercession for us. (Rom. 8:34)

Therefore He is also able to save to the uttermost those who come to God through Him, since He always lives to make intercession for them. (Heb. 7:25)

4. Believing, Receiving, and Confessing Jesus

But as many as received Him, to them He gave the right to become children of God, to those who believe in His name. (John 1:12)

Believe on the Lord Jesus Christ, and you will be saved, you and your household. (Acts 16:31)

For God so loved the world that He gave His only begotten Son, that whoever believes in Him should not perish but have everlasting life. (John 3:16)

Look to Me, and be saved, all you ends of the earth! For I am God, and there is no other. (Isa. 45:22)

If you confess with your mouth the Lord Jesus and believe in your heart that God has raised Him from the

*dead, you will be saved. For with the heart one believes
unto righteousness, and with the mouth confession is
made unto salvation.* (Rom. 10:9–10)

*He who believes in the Son has everlasting life; and he
who does not believe the Son shall not see life, but the
wrath of God abides on him.* (John 3:36)

*To Him all the prophets witness that, through His
name, whoever believes in Him will receive remission of
sins.* (Acts 10:43)

*And by Him everyone who believes is justified from all
things from which you could not be justified by the law
of Moses.* (Acts 13:39)

Chapter 4

Dealing with Difficulties

◆

1. I am too great a sinner.

This is a faithful saying and worthy of all acceptance, that Christ Jesus came into the world to save sinners, of whom I am chief. (1 Tim. 1:15)

For when we were still without strength, in due time Christ died for the ungodly....God demonstrates His own love toward us, in that while we were still sinners, Christ died for us. (Rom. 5:6, 8)

"Come now, and let us reason together," says the LORD, "though your sins are like scarlet, they shall be as white as snow; though they are red like crimson, they shall be as wool." (Isa. 1:18)

To Him all the prophets witness that, through His name, whoever believes in Him will receive remission of sins. (Acts 10:43)

For the Son of Man has come to seek and to save that which was lost. (Luke 19:10)

All that the Father gives Me will come to Me, and the one who comes to Me I will by no means cast out.
(John 6:37)

2. I am afraid of failure.

And I give them eternal life, and they shall never perish; neither shall anyone snatch them out of My hand. My Father, who has given them to Me, is greater than all; and no one is able to snatch them out of My Father's hand. (John 10:28–29)

Fear not, for I am with you; be not dismayed, for I am your God. I will strengthen you, Yes, I will help you, I will uphold you with My righteous right hand....For I, the LORD your God, will hold your right hand, saying to you, "Fear not, I will help you." (Isa. 41:10, 13)

[We] are kept by the power of God through faith for salvation ready to be revealed in the last time. (1 Pet. 1:5)

For this reason I also suffer these things; nevertheless I am not ashamed, for I know whom I have believed and am persuaded that He is able to keep what I have committed to Him until that Day. (2 Tim. 1:12)

Be strong and courageous; do not be afraid nor dismayed before the king of Assyria, nor before all the multitude that is with him; for there are more with us than with him. With him is an arm of flesh; but with us is the LORD our God, to help us and to fight our battles. (2 Chron. 32:7–8)

Who are you to judge another's servant? To his own master he stands or falls. Indeed, he will be made to stand, for God is able to make him stand. (Rom. 14:4)

But the Lord is faithful, who will establish you and guard you from the evil one. (2 Thess. 3:3)

No temptation has overtaken you except such as is common to man; but God is faithful, who will not allow you to be tempted beyond what you are able, but with the temptation will also make the way of escape, that you may be able to bear it. (1 Cor. 10:13)

3. I am too weak.

And He said to me, "My grace is sufficient for you, for My strength is made perfect in weakness." Therefore most gladly I will rather boast in my infirmities, that the power of Christ may rest upon me. Therefore I take pleasure in infirmities, in reproaches, in needs, in persecutions, in distresses, for Christ's sake. For when I am weak, then I am strong. (2 Cor. 12:9–10)

I can do all things through Christ who strengthens me. (Phil. 4:13)

For what the law could not do in that it was weak through the flesh, God did by sending His own Son in the likeness of sinful flesh, on account of sin: He condemned sin in the flesh, that the righteous requirement of the law might be fulfilled in us who do not walk according to the flesh but according to the Spirit. (Rom. 8:3–4)

He gives power to the weak, and to those who have no might He increases strength. Even the youths shall faint and be weary, and the young men shall utterly fall, but those who wait on the LORD shall renew their strength; they shall mount up with wings like eagles, they shall run and not be weary, they shall walk and not faint. (Isa. 40:29–31)

Your word I have hidden in my heart, that I might not sin against You! (Ps. 119:11)

For whatever is born of God overcomes the world. And this is the victory that has overcome the world; our faith. (1 John 5:4)

Be sober, be vigilant; because your adversary the devil walks about like a roaring lion, seeking whom he may devour. Resist him, steadfast in the faith, knowing that the same sufferings are experienced by your brotherhood in the world. But may the God of all grace, who called us to His eternal glory by Christ Jesus, after you have suffered a while, perfect, establish, strengthen, and settle you. (1 Pet. 5:8–10)

4. I can't give up my evil ways and bad habits.

Do not be deceived, God is not mocked; for whatever a man sows, that he will also reap. For he who sows to his flesh will of the flesh reap corruption, but he who sows to the Spirit will of the Spirit reap everlasting life. (Gal. 6:7–8)

I can do all things through Christ who strengthens me. (Phil. 4:13)

If the Son makes you free, you shall be free indeed. (John 8:36)

5. I will be persecuted if I become a Christian.

Yes, and all who desire to live godly in Christ Jesus will suffer persecution. (2 Tim. 3:12)

Blessed are those who are persecuted for righteousness' sake, for theirs is the kingdom of heaven. Blessed are you when they revile and persecute you, and say all kinds of evil against you falsely for My sake. Rejoice and be exceedingly glad, for great is your reward in heaven, for so they persecuted the prophets who were before you. (Matt. 5:10–12)

For whoever desires to save his life will lose it, but whoever loses his life for My sake and the gospel's will save it....For whoever is ashamed of Me and My words in this adulterous and sinful generation, of him the Son of Man also will be ashamed when He comes in the glory of His Father with the holy angels.

(Mark 8:35, 38)

For I consider that the sufferings of this present time are not worthy to be compared with the glory which shall be revealed in us. (Rom. 8:18)

Continue in the faith...[for] we must through many tribulations enter the kingdom of God. (Acts 14:22)

And when they had called for the apostles and beaten them, they commanded that they should not speak in the name of Jesus, and let them go. So they departed from the presence of the council, rejoicing that they were counted worthy to suffer shame for His name.

(Acts 5:40–41)

If we endure, we shall also reign with Him. If we deny Him, He also will deny us. (2 Tim. 2:12)

Looking unto Jesus, the author and finisher of our faith, who for the joy that was set before Him endured the cross, despising the shame, and has sat down at the right hand of the throne of God. For consider Him who endured such hostility from sinners against Himself, lest you become weary and discouraged in your souls.

(Heb. 12:2–3)

For what credit is it if, when you are beaten for your faults, you take it patiently? But when you do good and suffer, if you take it patiently, this is commendable before God. For to this you were called, because Christ also suffered for us, leaving us an example, that you should follow His steps. (1 Pet. 2:20–21)

6. I will lose my friends.

The fear of man brings a snare, but whoever trusts in the LORD shall be safe. (Prov. 29:25)

He who walks with wise men will be wise, but the companion of fools will be destroyed. (Prov. 13:20)

Blessed is the man who walks not in the counsel of the ungodly, nor stands in the path of sinners, nor sits in the seat of the scornful; but his delight is in the law of the LORD, and in His law he meditates day and night. (Ps. 1:1–2)

That which we have seen and heard we declare to you, that you also may have fellowship with us; and truly our fellowship is with the Father and with His Son Jesus Christ. (1 John 1:3)

Adulterers and adulteresses! Do you not know that friendship with the world is enmity with God? Whoever therefore wants to be a friend of the world makes himself an enemy of God. (James 4:4)

7. I have too much to give up.

For what will it profit a man if he gains the whole world, and loses his own soul? (Mark 8:36)

But seek first the kingdom of God and His righteousness, and all these things shall be added to you. (Matt. 6:33)

For the LORD God is a sun and shield; the LORD will give grace and glory; no good thing will He withhold from those who walk uprightly. (Ps. 84:11)

He who did not spare His own Son, but delivered Him up for us all, how shall He not with Him also freely give us all things? (Rom. 8:32)

Do not love the world or the things in the world. If anyone loves the world, the love of the Father is not in him. For all that is in the world; the lust of the flesh, the lust

of the eyes, and the pride of life; is not of the Father but is of the world. And the world is passing away, and the lust of it; but he who does the will of God abides forever.
(1 John 2:15–17)

By faith Moses, when he became of age, refused to be called the son of Pharaoh's daughter, choosing rather to suffer affliction with the people of God than to enjoy the passing pleasures of sin, esteeming the reproach of Christ greater riches than the treasures in Egypt; for he looked to the reward.   (Heb. 11:24–26)

But what things were gain to me, these I have counted loss for Christ. Yet indeed I also count all things loss for the excellence of the knowledge of Christ Jesus my Lord, for whom I have suffered the loss of all things, and count them as rubbish, that I may gain Christ.
(Phil. 3:7–8)

The ground of a certain rich man yielded plentifully. And he thought within himself, saying, "What shall I do, since I have no room to store my crops?" So he said, "I will do this: I will pull down my barns and build greater, and there I will store all my crops and my goods. And I will say to my soul, 'Soul, you have many goods laid up for many years; take your ease; eat, drink, and be merry.'" But God said to him, "Fool! This night your soul will be required of you; then whose will those things be which you have provided?" So is he who lays up treasure for himself, and is not rich toward God.
(Luke 12:16–21)

For my yoke is easy, and my burden is light.
(Matt. 11:30)

8. I don't have the right feelings.

God does not demand that we feel sorry for our sins, but that we turn from sin and receive Christ.

For with the heart one believes unto righteousness, and with the mouth confession is made unto salvation.
(Rom. 10:10)

Let the wicked forsake his way, and the unrighteous man his thoughts; let him return to the LORD, and He will have mercy on him; and to our God, for He will abundantly pardon. (Isa. 55:7)

But as many as received Him, to them He gave the right to become children of God, to those who believe in His name. (John 1:12)

Believe on the Lord Jesus Christ, and you will be saved, you and your household. (Acts 16:31)

9. I am seeking Christ but cannot find Him.

And you will seek Me and find Me, when you search for Me with all your heart. (Jer. 29:13)

What man of you, having a hundred sheep, if he loses one of them, does not leave the ninety-nine in the wilderness, and go after the one which is lost until he finds it? And when he has found it, he lays it on his shoulders, rejoicing. And when he comes home, he calls together his friends and neighbors, saying to them, "Rejoice with me, for I have found my sheep which was lost!" I say to you that likewise there will be more joy in heaven over one sinner who repents than over ninety-nine just persons who need no repentance. Or what woman, having ten silver coins, if she loses one coin, does not light a lamp, sweep the house, and search carefully until she finds it? And when she has found it, she calls her friends and neighbors together, saying, "Rejoice with me, for I have found the piece which I lost!" Likewise, I say to you, there is joy in the presence of the angels of God over one sinner who repents.
(Luke 15:4–10)

*For the Son of Man has come to seek and to save that
which was lost.*   (Luke 19:10)

Also read the passages under Jesus—Our Sin-Bearer.

10. My heart is too hard.

*I will give you a new heart and put a new spirit within
you; I will take the heart of stone out of your flesh and
give you a heart of flesh. I will put My Spirit within you
and cause you to walk in My statutes, and you will keep
My judgments and do them.*   (Ezek. 36:26–27)

11. God will not receive me.

*All that the Father gives Me will come to Me, and the
one who comes to Me I will by no means cast out.*
                                        (John 6:37)

Whoever calls on the name of the LORD shall be saved.
                                        (Rom. 10:13)

*Manasseh was twelve years old when he became king,
and he reigned fifty-five years in Jerusalem. But he did
evil in the sight of the LORD, according to the abominations of the nations whom the LORD had cast out before
the children of Israel....And the LORD spoke to
Manasseh and his people, but they would not listen.
Therefore the LORD brought upon them the captains of
the army of the king of Assyria, who took Manasseh
with hooks, bound him with bronze fetters, and carried
him off to Babylon. Now when he was in affliction, he
implored the LORD his God, and humbled himself
greatly before the God of his fathers, and prayed to Him;
and He received his entreaty, heard his supplication,
and brought him back to Jerusalem into his kingdom.
Then Manasseh knew that the LORD was God.*
                                (2 Chron. 33:1–2, 10–13)

12. I have committed the unpardonable sin.

What is the unpardonable sin?

Therefore I say to you, every sin and blasphemy will be forgiven men, but the blasphemy against the Spirit will not be forgiven men. Anyone who speaks a word against the Son of Man, it will be forgiven him; but whoever speaks against the Holy Spirit, it will not be forgiven him, either in this age or in the age to come.
(Matt. 12:31–32)

For it is impossible for those who were once enlightened, and have tasted the heavenly gift, and have become par-takers of the Holy Spirit, and have tasted the good word of God and the powers of the age to come, if they fall away, to renew them again to repentance since they cru-cify again for themselves the Son of God, and put Him to an open shame. (Heb. 6:4–6)

This passage describes one who renounces Christianity and returns to the things of this world, not one who merely falls into sin, even deep sin, as Peter did.

13. It is too late.

When you are in distress, and all these things come upon you in the latter days, when you turn to the LORD your God and obey His voice (for the LORD your God is a merciful God), He will not forsake you nor destroy you, nor forget the covenant of your fathers which He swore to them. (Deut. 4:30–31)

The Lord is not slack concerning His promise, as some count slackness, but is longsuffering toward us, not will-ing that any should perish but that all should come to repentance. (2 Pet. 3:9)

And the Spirit and the bride say, "Come!" And let him who hears say, "Come!" And let him who thirsts come. Whoever desires, let him take the water of life freely.

(Rev. 22:17)

14. I must become a better person first.

Those who are well have no need of a physician, but those who are sick. But go and learn what this means: "I desire mercy and not sacrifice." For I did not come to call the righteous, but sinners, to repentance.

(Matt. 9:12–13)

I will arise and go to my father, and will say to him, "Father, I have sinned against heaven and before you."...And he arose and came to his father. But when he was still a great way off, his father saw him and had compassion, and ran and fell on his neck and kissed him. And the son said to him, "Father, I have sinned against heaven and in your sight, and am no longer worthy to be called your son." But the father said to his servants, "Bring out the best robe and put it on him, and put a ring on his hand and sandals on his feet. And bring the fatted calf here and kill it, and let us eat and be merry; for this my son was dead and is alive again; he was lost and is found.   (Luke 15:18, 20–24)

Two men went up to the temple to pray, one a Pharisee and the other a tax collector. The Pharisee stood and prayed thus with himself, "God, I thank You that I am not like other men; extortioners, unjust, adulterers, or even as this tax collector. I fast twice a week; I give tithes of all that I possess." And the tax collector, standing afar off, would not so much as raise his eyes to heaven, but beat his breast, saying, "God, be merciful to me a sinner!" I tell you, this man went down to his house justified rather than the other; for everyone who exalts himself will be humbled, and he who humbles himself will be exalted.   (Luke 18:10–14)

I have blotted out, like a thick cloud, your transgressions, and like a cloud, your sins. Return to Me, for I have redeemed you. (Isa. 44:22)

Chapter 5

Dealing with the Self-Righteous

◆————————◆

1. I'm no worse than anybody else.

Knowing that a man is not justified by the works of the law but by faith in Jesus Christ, even we have believed in Christ Jesus, that we might be justified by faith in Christ and not by the works of the law; for by the works of the law no flesh shall be justified. (Gal. 2:16)

Now we know that whatever the law says, it says to those who are under the law, that every mouth may be stopped, and all the world may become guilty before God. Therefore by the deeds of the law no flesh will be justified in His sight, for by the law is the knowledge of sin. (Rom. 3:19–20)

For as many as are of the works of the law are under the curse; for it is written, "Cursed is everyone who does not continue in all things which are written in the book of the law, to do them." (Gal. 3:10)

For whoever shall keep the whole law, and yet stumble in one point, he is guilty of all. (James 2:10)

Unless your righteousness exceeds the righteousness of the scribes and Pharisees, you will by no means enter the kingdom of heaven. (Matt. 5:20)

And He said to them, "You are those who justify your-selves before men, but God knows your hearts. For what is highly esteemed among men is an abomination in the sight of God. (Luke 16:15)

God will judge the secrets of men by Jesus Christ, according to my gospel. (Rom. 2:16)

Man looks at the outward appearance, but the LORD looks at the heart. (1 Sam. 16:7)

But without faith it is impossible to please Him, for he who comes to God must believe that He is, and that He is a rewarder of those who diligently seek Him.
(Heb. 11:6)

Anyone who has rejected Moses' law dies without mercy on the testimony of two or three witnesses. Of how much worse punishment, do you suppose, will he be thought worthy who has trampled the Son of God underfoot, counted the blood of the covenant by which he was sanctified a common thing, and insulted the Spirit of grace?
(Heb. 10:28–29)

2. God is too good to damn anyone.

Or do you despise the riches of His goodness, forbear-ance, and longsuffering, not knowing that the goodness of God leads you to repentance? But in accordance with your hardness and your impenitent heart you are treas-uring up for yourself wrath in the day of wrath and revelation of the righteous judgment of God.
(Rom. 2:4–5)

If you do not believe that I am He, you will die in your sins. (John 8:24)

The Lord is not slack concerning His promise, as some count slackness, but is longsuffering toward us, not willing that any should perish but that all should come to repentance. But the day of the Lord will come as a thief in the night, in which the heavens will pass away with a great noise, and the elements will melt with fervent heat; both the earth and the works that are in it will be burned up. Therefore, since all these things will be dissolved, what manner of persons ought you to be in holy conduct and godliness? (2 Pet. 3:9–11)

I have no pleasure in the death of the wicked, but that the wicked turn from his way and live. Turn, turn from your evil ways! For why should you die, O house of Israel? (Ezek. 33:11)

For if God did not spare the angels who sinned, but cast them down to hell and delivered them into chains of darkness, to be reserved for judgment; and did not spare the ancient world, but saved Noah, one of eight people, a preacher of righteousness, bringing in the flood on the world of the ungodly; and turning the cities of Sodom and Gomorrah into ashes, condemned them to destruction, making them an example to those who afterward would live ungodly...then the Lord knows how to deliver the godly out of temptations and to reserve the unjust under punishment for the day of judgment. (2 Pet. 2:4–6, 9)

Unless you repent you will all likewise perish. (Luke 13:3)

He who believes in Him is not condemned; but he who does not believe is condemned already, because he has not believed in the name of the only begotten Son of God. (John 3:18)

3. I'm trying to be a good Christian.

We are saved by trusting what Jesus has done and will do, not by any effort of our own.

For all have sinned and fall short of the glory of God, being justified freely by His grace through the redemption that is in Christ Jesus, whom God set forth as a propitiation by His blood. (Rom. 3:23–25)

For what does the Scripture say? "Abraham believed God, and it was accounted to him for righteousness." Now to him who works, the wages are not counted as grace but as debt. But to him who does not work but believes on Him who justifies the ungodly, his faith is accounted for righteousness. (Rom. 4:3–5)

But as many as received Him, to them He gave the right to become children of God, to those who believe in His name. (John 1:12)

Behold, God is my salvation; I will trust, and not be afraid: for the LORD JEHOVAH is my strength and my song; he also is become my salvation. (Isa. 12:2 KJV)

4. I feel that I am saved.

There is a way that seems right to a man, but its end is the way of death. (Prov. 14:12)

He who believes in the Son has everlasting life; and he who does not believe the Son shall not see life, but the wrath of God abides on him. (John 3:36)

5. I belong to a church.

Pursue peace with all people, and holiness, without which no one will see the Lord. (Heb. 12:14)

Do you not know that the unrighteous will not inherit the kingdom of God? Do not be deceived. Neither fornicators, nor idolaters, nor adulterers, nor homosexuals, nor sodomites, nor thieves, nor covetous, nor drunkards, nor revilers, nor extortioners will inherit the kingdom of God. (1 Cor. 6:9–10)

They profess to know God, but in works they deny Him, being abominable, disobedient, and disqualified for every good work. (Titus 1:16)

What does it profit, my brethren, if someone says he has faith but does not have works? Can faith save him? (James 2:14)

Jesus answered and said to him, "Most assuredly, I say to you, unless one is born again, he cannot see the kingdom of God." (John 3:3)

If you know that He is righteous, you know that everyone who practices righteousness is born of Him. (1 John 2:29)

But the cowardly, unbelieving, abominable, murderers, sexually immoral, sorcerers, idolaters, and all liars shall have their part in the lake which burns with fire and brimstone, which is the second death. (Rev. 21:8)

Chapter 6

Dealing with the Uncertain
and with Backsliders

◆

1. How can I know I am saved?

*These things I have written to you who believe in the
name of the Son of God, that you may know that you
have eternal life.*   (1 John 5:13)

*Most assuredly, I say to you, he who hears My word and
believes in Him who sent Me has everlasting life, and
shall not come into judgment, but has passed from
death into life.*   (John 5:24)

*And this is the testimony: that God has given us eternal
life, and this life is in His Son. He who has the Son has
life; he who does not have the Son of God does not have
life.*   (1 John 5:11–12)

*I am the light of the world. He who follows Me shall not
walk in darkness, but have the light of life.*   (John 8:12)

*Let the wicked forsake his way, and the unrighteous
man his thoughts; let him return to the LORD, and He
will have mercy on him; and to our God, for he will
abundantly pardon.*   (Isa. 55:7)

2. I don't care about serving God anymore.

*What injustice have your fathers found in Me, that they
have gone far from Me, have followed idols, and have*

become idolaters?....For My people have committed two evils: they have forsaken Me, the fountain of living waters, and hewn themselves cisterns; broken cisterns that can hold no water....Your own wickedness will correct you, and your backslidings will rebuke you. Know therefore and see that it is an evil and bitter thing that you have forsaken the LORD your God, and the fear of Me is not in you, says the Lord GOD of hosts.

(Jer. 2:5, 13, 19)

"I overthrew some of you, as God overthrew Sodom and Gomorrah, and you were like a firebrand plucked from the burning; yet you have not returned to Me," says the LORD. "Therefore thus will I do to you, O Israel; because I will do this to you, prepare to meet your God, O Israel!"

(Amos 4:11–12)

The backslider in heart will be filled with his own ways, but a good man will be satisfied from above.

(Prov. 14:14)

3. I want to come back to the Lord.

Go and proclaim these words toward the north, and say: "Return, backsliding Israel," says the LORD; "I will not cause My anger to fall on you. For I am merciful," says the LORD; "I will not remain angry forever. Only acknowledge your iniquity, that you have transgressed against the LORD your God, and have scattered your charms to alien deities under every green tree, and you have not obeyed My voice," says the LORD...."Return, you backsliding children, and I will heal your backslidings." "Indeed we do come to You, for You are the LORD our God."

(Jer. 3:12–13, 22)

O Israel, return to the LORD your God, for you have stumbled because of your iniquity; take words with you, and return to the LORD. Say to Him, "Take away all iniquity; receive us graciously, for we will offer the sacrifices

553

of our lips. Assyria shall not save us, we will not ride on horses, nor will we say anymore to the work of our hands, 'You are our gods.' For in You the fatherless finds mercy." I will heal their backsliding, I will love them freely, for My anger has turned away from him.
(Hos. 14:1–4)

But you have not called upon Me, O Jacob; and you have been weary of Me, O Israel....You have bought Me no sweet cane with money, nor have you satisfied Me with the fat of your sacrifices; but you have burdened Me with your sins, you have wearied Me with your iniquities. I, even I, am He who blots out your transgressions for My own sake; and I will not remember your sins.
(Isa. 43:22, 24–25)

I have blotted out, like a thick cloud, your transgressions, and like a cloud, your sins. Return to Me, for I have redeemed you. (Isa. 44:22)

For I know the thoughts that I think toward you, says the LORD, thoughts of peace and not of evil, to give you a future and a hope. Then you will call upon Me and go and pray to Me, and I will listen to you. And you will seek Me and find Me, when you search for Me with all your heart. (Jer. 29:11–13)

And there you will serve gods, the work of men's hands, wood and stone, which neither see nor hear nor eat nor smell. But from there you will seek the LORD your God, and you will find Him if you seek Him with all your heart and with all your soul. When you are in distress, and all these things come upon you in the latter days, when you turn to the LORD your God and obey His voice (for the LORD your God is a merciful God), He will not forsake you nor destroy you, nor forget the covenant of your fathers which He swore to them. (Deut. 4:28–31)

If My people who are called by My name will humble themselves, and pray and seek My face, and turn from their wicked ways, then I will hear from heaven, and will forgive their sin and heal their land.

(2 Chron. 7:14)

If we confess our sins, He is faithful and just to forgive us our sins and to cleanse us from all unrighteousness.

(1 John 1:9)

But when in their trouble they turned to the LORD God of Israel, and sought Him, He was found by them.

(2 Chron. 15:4)

And not many days after, the younger son gathered all together, journeyed to a far country, and there wasted his possessions with prodigal living. But when he had spent all, there arose a severe famine in that land, and he began to be in want. Then he went and joined himself to a citizen of that country, and he sent him into his fields to feed swine. And he would gladly have filled his stomach with the pods that the swine ate, and no one gave him anything. But when he came to himself, he said, "How many of my father's hired servants have bread enough and to spare, and I perish with hunger! I will arise and go to my father, and will say to him, 'Father, I have sinned against heaven and before you, and I am no longer worthy to be called your son. Make me like one of your hired servants.'" And he arose and came to his father. But when he was still a great way off, his father saw him and had compassion, and ran and fell on his neck and kissed him. And the son said to him, "Father, I have sinned against heaven and in your sight, and am no longer worthy to be called your son." But the father said to his servants, "Bring out the best robe and put it on him, and put a ring on his hand and sandals on his feet. And bring the fatted calf here and kill it, and let us eat and be merry; for this my son was dead and is alive again; he was lost and is found." And they began to be merry. (Luke 15:13–24)

Chapter 7

Dealing with Skeptics

◆

1. The Bible and God's plan of salvation seem foolish to me.

For the message of the cross is foolishness to those who are perishing, but to us who are being saved it is the power of God. (1 Cor. 1:18)

But even if our gospel is veiled, it is veiled to those who are perishing, whose minds the god of this age has blinded, who do not believe, lest the light of the gospel of the glory of Christ, who is the image of God, should shine on them. (2 Cor. 4:3–4)

The Lord Jesus is revealed from heaven with His mighty angels, in flaming fire taking vengeance on those who do not know God, and on those who do not obey the gospel of our Lord Jesus Christ. (2 Thess. 1:7–8)

Then the lawless one will be revealed....The coming of the lawless one is according to the working of Satan, with all power, signs, and lying wonders, and with all unrighteous deception among those who perish, because they did not receive the love of the truth, that they might be saved. And for this reason God will send them strong delusion, that they should believe the lie, that they all may be condemned who did not believe the truth but had pleasure in unrighteousness. (2 Thess. 2:8–12)

He who believes and is baptized will be saved; but he who does not believe will be condemned. (Mark 16:16)

2. I've tried, but I can't believe.

If anyone wants to do His will, he shall know concerning the doctrine, whether it is from God or whether I speak on My own authority. (John 7:17)

But the natural man does not receive the things of the Spirit of God, for they are foolishness to him; nor can he know them, because they are spiritually discerned.

(1 Cor. 2:14)

Philip found Nathanael and said to him, "We have found Him of whom Moses in the law, and also the prophets, wrote; Jesus of Nazareth, the son of Joseph." And Nathanael said to him, "Can anything good come out of Nazareth?" Philip said to him, "Come and see." Jesus saw Nathanael coming toward Him, and said of him, "Behold, an Israelite indeed, in whom is no deceit!" Nathanael said to Him, "How do You know me?" Jesus answered and said to him, "Before Philip called you, when you were under the fig tree, I saw you." Nathanael answered and said to Him, "Rabbi, You are the Son of God! You are the King of Israel!" (John 1:45–49)

Now Thomas, called the Twin, one of the twelve, was not with them when Jesus came. The other disciples therefore said to him, "We have seen the Lord." So he said to them, "Unless I see in His hands the print of the nails, and put my finger into the print of the nails, and put my hand into His side, I will not believe." And after eight days His disciples were again inside, and Thomas with them. Jesus came, the doors being shut, and stood in the midst, and said, "Peace to you!" Then He said to Thomas, "Reach your finger here, and look at My hands; and reach your hand here, and put it into My side. Do not be unbelieving, but believing." And Thomas answered and said to Him, "My Lord and my God!" Jesus said to him, "Thomas, because you have seen Me, you have believed. Blessed are those who have not seen and yet have believed." (John 20:24–29)

The officers answered, "No man ever spoke like this Man!" (John 7:46)

Have I been with you so long, and yet you have not known Me, Philip? He who has seen Me has seen the Father; so how can you say, "Show us the Father"? Do you not believe that I am in the Father, and the Father in Me? The words that I speak to you I do not speak on My own authority; but the Father who dwells in Me does the works. Believe Me that I am in the Father and the Father in Me, or else believe Me for the sake of the works themselves. (John 14:9–11)

If I had not done among them the works which no one else did, they would have no sin; but now they have seen and also hated both Me and My Father (John 15:24)

He who is of God hears God's words; therefore you do not hear, because you are not of God. (John 8:47)

For God did not send His Son into the world to condemn the world, but that the world through Him might be saved. He who believes in Him is not condemned; but he who does not believe is condemned already, because he has not believed in the name of the only begotten Son of God. And this is the condemnation, that the light has come into the world, and men loved darkness rather than light, because their deeds were evil. For everyone practicing evil hates the light and does not come to the light, lest his deeds should be exposed. But he who does the truth comes to the light, that his deeds may be clearly seen, that they have been done in God. (John 3:17–21)

And truly Jesus did many other signs in the presence of His disciples, which are not written in this book; but these are written that you may believe that Jesus is the Christ, the Son of God, and that believing you may have life in His name. (John 20:30–31)

3. I don't believe there is a God.

What may be known of God is manifest in them, for God has shown it to them. For since the creation of the world His invisible attributes are clearly seen, being understood by the things that are made, even His eternal power and Godhead, so that they are without excuse, because, although they knew God, they did not glorify Him as God, nor were thankful, but became futile in their thoughts, and their foolish hearts were darkened. Professing to be wise, they became fools. (Rom. 1:19–22)

The heavens declare the glory of God; and the firmament shows His handiwork. (Ps. 19:1)

The fool has said in his heart, "There is no God." They are corrupt, they have done abominable works, there is none who does good. (Ps. 14:1)

4. Is the Bible the Word of God?

[You make] the word of God of no effect through your tradition which you have handed down. And many such things you do. (Mark 7:13)

Heaven and earth will pass away, but My words will by no means pass away. (Matt. 24:35)

Till heaven and earth pass away, one jot or one tittle will by no means pass from the law till all is fulfilled. (Matt. 5:18)

Beginning at Moses and all the Prophets, He expounded to them in all the Scriptures the things concerning Himself....Then He said to them, "These are the words which I spoke to you while I was still with you, that all things must be fulfilled which were written in the Law of Moses and the Prophets and the Psalms concerning Me." (Luke 24:27, 44)

For this reason we also thank God without ceasing, because when you received the word of God which you heard from us, you welcomed it not as the word of men, but as it is in truth, the word of God, which also effectively works in you who believe. (1 Thess. 2:13)

And so we have the prophetic word confirmed, which you do well to heed as a light that shines in a dark place, until the day dawns and the morning star rises in your hearts; knowing this first, that no prophecy of Scripture is of any private interpretation, for prophecy never came by the will of man, but holy men of God spoke as they were moved by the Holy Spirit.
(2 Pet. 1:19–21)

He who believes in the Son of God has the witness in himself; he who does not believe God has made Him a liar, because he has not believed the testimony that God has given of His Son. (1 John 5:10)

He who is of God hears God's words; therefore you do not hear, because you are not of God. (John 8:47)

5. Is Jesus the Son of God?

The word which God sent to the children of Israel, preaching peace through Jesus Christ; He is Lord of all; that word you know. (Acts 10:36–37)

But we speak the wisdom of God in a mystery, the hidden wisdom which God ordained before the ages for our glory, which none of the rulers of this age knew; for had they known, they would not have crucified the Lord of glory. (1 Cor. 2:7–8)

But to the Son He says: "Your throne, O God, is forever and ever; a scepter of righteousness is the scepter of Your Kingdom." (Heb. 1:8)

And Thomas answered and said to Him, "My Lord and my God!" Jesus said to him, "Thomas, because you have seen Me, you have believed. Blessed are those who have not seen and yet have believed." (John 20:28–29)

But these are written that you may believe that Jesus is the Christ, the Son of God, and that believing you may have life in His name. (John 20:31)

All should honor the Son just as they honor the Father. He who does not honor the Son does not honor the Father who sent Him. (John 5:23)

Therefore God also has highly exalted Him and given Him the name which is above every name, that at the name of Jesus every knee should bow, of those in heaven, and of those on earth, and of those under the earth. (Phil. 2:9–10)

Who is a liar but he who denies that Jesus is the Christ? He is antichrist who denies the Father and the Son. Whoever denies the Son does not have the Father either; he who acknowledges the Son has the Father also. (1 John 2:22–23)

Whoever believes that Jesus is the Christ is born of God, and everyone who loves Him who begot also loves him who is begotten of Him....Who is he who overcomes the world, but he who believes that Jesus is the Son of God? (1 John 5:1, 5)

You will die in your sins; for if you do not believe that I am He, you will die in your sins. (John 8:24)

Chapter 8

Dealing with Objections

◆──────────────

1. God is unjust and cruel to create men and then damn them.

> *But indeed, O man, who are you to reply against God? Will the thing formed say to him who formed it, "Why have you made me like this?"* (Rom. 9:20)

> *"For My thoughts are not your thoughts, nor are your ways My ways," says the LORD. "For as the heavens are higher than the earth, so are My ways higher than your ways, and My thoughts than your thoughts."* (Isa. 55:8–9)

> *Shall the one who contends with the Almighty correct Him? He who rebukes God, let him answer it.* (Job 40:2)

> *"My son, do not despise the chastening of the LORD, nor be discouraged when you are rebuked by Him; for whom the LORD loves He chastens, and scourges every son whom He receives."...Now no chastening seems to be joyful for the present, but painful; nevertheless, afterward it yields the peaceable fruit of righteousness to those who have been trained by it.* (Heb. 12:5–6, 11)

2. The Bible has too many contradictions, and I can't understand it.

> *Open my eyes, that I may see wondrous things from Your law.* (Ps. 119:18)

*But the natural man does not receive the things of the
Spirit of God, for they are foolishness to him; nor can he
know them, because they are spiritually discerned.*

(1 Cor. 2:14)

*Oh, the depth of the riches both of the wisdom and
knowledge of God! How unsearchable are His judgments and His ways past finding out!* (Rom. 11:33)

*When I was a child, I spoke as a child, I understood as a
child, I thought as a child; but when I became a man, I
put away childish things. For now we see in a mirror,
dimly, but then face to face. Now I know in part, but
then I shall know just as I also am known.*

(1 Cor. 13:11–12)

*In all his epistles, [Paul spoke] in them of these things,
in which are some things hard to understand, which
untaught and unstable people twist to their own destruction, as they do also the rest of the Scriptures. You therefore, beloved, since you know this beforehand, beware
lest you also fall from your own steadfastness, being led
away with the error of the wicked; but grow in the grace
and knowledge of our Lord and Savior Jesus Christ. To
Him be the glory both now and forever. Amen.*

(2 Pet. 3:16–18)

3. There are too many hypocrites in church.

So then each of us shall give account of himself to God.
(Rom. 14:12)

*Therefore you are inexcusable, O man, whoever you are
who judge, for in whatever you judge another you condemn yourself; for you who judge practice the same
things. But we know that the judgment of God is according to truth against those who practice such things.
And do you think this, O man, you who judge those
practicing such things, and doing the same, that you*

will escape the judgment of God? Or do you despise the riches of His goodness, forbearance, and longsuffering, not knowing that the goodness of God leads you to repentance? But in accordance with your hardness and your impenitent heart you are treasuring up for yourself wrath in the day of wrath and revelation of the righteous judgment of God. (Rom. 2:1–5)

Judge not, that you be not judged. For with what judgment you judge, you will be judged; and with the measure you use, it will be measured back to you. And why do you look at the speck in your brother's eye, but do not consider the plank in your own eye? Or how can you say to your brother, "Let me remove the speck from your eye"; and look, a plank is in your own eye? Hypocrite! First remove the plank from your own eye, and then you will see clearly to remove the speck from your brother's eye. (Matt. 7:1–5)

4. I'll accept Christ some time in the future.

Seek the LORD while He may be found, call upon Him while He is near. (Isa. 55:6)

Do not boast about tomorrow, for you do not know what a day may bring forth. (Prov. 27:1)

He who is often rebuked, and hardens his neck, will suddenly be destroyed, and that without remedy. (Prov. 29:1)

Therefore you also be ready, for the Son of Man is coming at an hour you do not expect. (Matt. 24:44)

And while they went to buy, the bridegroom came, and those who were ready went in with him to the wedding; and the door was shut. Afterward the other virgins came also, saying "Lord, Lord, open to us!" But he answered and said, "Assuredly, I say to you, I do not know you."

Watch therefore, for you know neither the day nor the hour in which the Son of Man is coming.
(Matt. 25:10–13)

And I will say to my soul, "Soul, you have many goods laid up for many years; take your ease; eat, drink, and be merry." But God said to him, "Fool! This night your soul will be required of you; then whose will those things be which you have provided?" (Luke 12:19–20)

And Elijah came to all the people, and said, "How long will you falter between two opinions? If the LORD is God, follow Him; but if Baal, follow him." But the people answered him not a word. (1 Kings 18:21)

Come now, you who say, "Today or tomorrow we will go to such and such a city, spend a year there, buy and sell, and make a profit"; whereas you do not know what will happen tomorrow. For what is your life? It is even a vapor that appears for a little time and then vanishes away. (James 4:13–14)

Strive to enter through the narrow gate, for many, I say to you, will seek to enter and will not be able. When once the Master of the house has risen up and shut the door, and you begin to stand outside and knock at the door, saying, "Lord, Lord, open for us," and He will answer and say to you, "I do not know you, where you are from." (Luke 13:24–25)

A little while longer the light is with you. Walk while you have the light, lest darkness overtake you; he who walks in darkness does not know where he is going.
(John 12:35)

But seek first the kingdom of God and His righteousness, and all these things shall be added to you.
(Matt. 6:33)

Behold, now is the accepted time; behold, now is the day of salvation. (2 Cor. 6:2)

Today, if you will hear His voice, do not harden your hearts. (Heb. 3:15)

Remember now your Creator in the days of your youth, before the difficult days come, and the years draw near when you say, "I have no pleasure in them." (Eccl. 12:1)

He who is not with Me is against Me, and he who does not gather with Me scatters abroad. (Matt. 12:30)

5. I don't want you to talk to me about Christ.

Anyone who has rejected Moses' law dies without mercy on the testimony of two or three witnesses. Of how much worse punishment, do you suppose, will he be thought worthy who has trampled the Son of God underfoot, counted the blood of the covenant by which he was sanctified a common thing, and insulted the Spirit of grace? (Heb. 10:28–29)

See that you do not refuse Him who speaks. For if they did not escape who refused Him who spoke on earth, much more shall we not escape if we turn away from Him who speaks from heaven. (Heb. 12:25)

He who believes and is baptized will be saved; but he who does not believe will be condemned. (Mark 16:16)

Because they hated knowledge and did not choose the fear of the LORD, they would have none of my counsel and despised my every rebuke. Therefore they shall eat the fruit of their own way, and be filled to the full with their own fancies. For the turning away of the simple will slay them, and the complacency of fools will destroy them; but whoever listens to me will dwell safely, and will be secure, without fear of evil. (Prov. 1:29–33)

6. There is someone I can't forgive.

But if you do not forgive men their trespasses, neither will your Father forgive your trespasses.   (Matt. 6:15)

Therefore the kingdom of heaven is like a certain king who wanted to settle accounts with his servants. And when he had begun to settle accounts, one was brought to him who owed him ten thousand talents. But as he was not able to pay, his master commanded that he be sold, with his wife and children and all that he had, and that payment be made. The servant therefore fell down before him, saying, "Master, have patience with me, and I will pay you all." Then the master of that servant was moved with compassion, released him, and forgave him the debt. But that servant went out and found one of his fellow servants who owed him a hundred denarii; and he laid hands on him and took him by the throat, saying, "Pay me what you owe!" So his fellow servant fell down at his feet and begged him, saying, "Have patience with me, and I will pay you all." And he would not, but went and threw him into prison till he should pay the debt. So when his fellow servants saw what had been done, they were very grieved, and came and told their master all that had been done. Then his master, after he had called him, said to him, "You wicked servant! I forgave you all that debt because you begged me. Should you not also have had compassion on your fellow servant, just as I had pity on you?" And his master was angry, and delivered him to the torturers until he should pay all that was due to him. So My heavenly Father also will do to you if each of you, from his heart, does not forgive his brother his trespasses.
(Matt. 18:23–35)

And be kind to one another, tenderhearted, forgiving one another, just as God in Christ forgave you.
(Eph. 4:32)

Chapter 9

Special Texts for Special People

◆

1. I'm a Roman Catholic.

Jesus answered and said to him, "Most assuredly, I say to you, unless one is born again, he cannot see the kingdom of God....Most assuredly, I say to you, unless one is born of water and the Spirit, he cannot enter the kingdom of God....Do not marvel that I said to you, 'You must be born again.'" (John 3:3, 5, 7)

Whosoever has been born of God does not sin, for His seed remains in him; and he cannot sin, because he has been born of God....We know that we have passed from death to life, because we love the brethren. He who does not love his brother abides in death. Whoever hates his brother is a murderer, and you know that no murderer has eternal life abiding in him. By this we know love, because He laid down His life for us. And we also ought to lay down our lives for the brethren. But whoever has this world's goods, and sees his brother in need, and shuts up his heart from him, how does the love of God abide in him? (1 John 3:9, 14–17)

But to him who does not work but believes on Him who justifies the ungodly, his faith is accounted for righteousness. (Rom. 4:5)

For there is one God and one Mediator between God and men, the Man Christ Jesus. (1 Tim. 2:5)

I acknowledged my sin to You, and my iniquity I have not hidden. I said, "I will confess my transgressions to the LORD," and You forgave the iniquity of my sin.
(Ps. 32:5)

These things I have written to you who believe in the name of the Son of God, that you may know that you have eternal life, and that you may continue to believe in the name of the Son of God. (1 John 5:13)

And by Him everyone who believes is justified from all things from which you could not be justified by the law of Moses. (Acts 13:39)

You search the Scriptures, for in them you think you have eternal life; and these are they which testify of Me.
(John 5:39)

Therefore, laying aside all malice, all deceit, hypocrisy, envy, and all evil speaking, as newborn babes, desire the pure milk of the word, that you may grow thereby.
(1 Pet. 2:1–2)

But evil men and impostors will grow worse and worse, deceiving and being deceived. But you must continue in the things which you have learned and been assured of, knowing from whom you have learned them, and that from childhood you have known the Holy Scriptures, which are able to make you wise for salvation through faith which is in Christ Jesus. All Scripture is given by inspiration of God, and is profitable for doctrine, for reproof, for correction, for instruction in righteousness, that the man of God may be complete, thoroughly equipped for every good work. (2 Tim. 3:13–17)

And in vain they worship Me, teaching as doctrines the commandments of men. For laying aside the commandment of God, you hold the tradition of men; the washing of pitchers and cups, and many other such things you do....[You make] the word of God of no effect through your tradition which you have handed down. And many such things you do. (Mark 7:7–8, 13)

You are mistaken, not knowing the Scriptures nor the power of God. (Matt. 22:29)

2. I'm a Jew.

Who has believed our report? And to whom has the arm of the LORD been revealed? For He shall grow up before Him as a tender plant, and as a root out of dry ground. He has no form or comeliness; and when we see Him, there is no beauty that we should desire Him. He is despised and rejected by men, a Man of sorrows and acquainted with grief. And we hid, as it were, our faces from Him; He was despised, and we did not esteem Him. Surely He has borne our griefs and carried our sorrows; yet we esteemed Him stricken, smitten by God, and afflicted. But He was wounded for our transgressions, He was bruised for our iniquities; the chastisement for our peace was upon Him, and by His stripes we are healed. All we like sheep have gone astray; we have turned, every one, to his own way; and the LORD has laid on Him the iniquity of us all. He was oppressed and He was afflicted, yet He opened not His mouth; He was led as a lamb to the slaughter, and as a sheep before its shearers is silent, so He opened not His mouth. He was taken from prison and from judgment, and who will declare His generation? For He was cut off from the land of the living; for the transgressions of My people He was stricken. And they made His grave with the wicked; but with the rich at His death, because He had done no violence, nor was any deceit in His mouth. Yet it pleased the LORD to bruise Him; He has put Him to grief. When You make His soul an offering for sin, He shall see His seed, He shall prolong His days, and the pleasure of the LORD shall prosper in His hand. He shall see the labor of His soul, and be satisfied. By His knowledge My righteous Servant shall justify many, for He shall bear their iniquities. Therefore I will divide Him a portion with the great, and He shall divide the spoil with the strong, because He poured out His soul unto death, and He was numbered with the transgressors, and He bore the sin of many, and made intercession for the trans-gressors. (Isa. 53)

And I will pour on the house of David and on the in-habitants of Jerusalem the Spirit of grace and supplica-tion; then they will look on Me whom they pierced. Yes, they will mourn for Him as one mourns for his only son, and grieve for Him as one grieves for a firstborn. (Zech. 12:10)

And after the sixty-two weeks Messiah shall be cut off, but not for Himself; and the people of the prince who is to come shall destroy the city and the sanctuary. The end of it shall be with a flood, and till the end of the war desolations are determined. (Dan. 9:26)

3. I'm a spiritualist.

And when they say to you, "Seek those who are mediums and wizards, who whisper and mutter," should not a people seek their God? Should they seek the dead on be-half of the living? To the law and to the testimony! If they do not speak according to this word, it is because there is no light in them. (Isa. 8:19–20)

Beloved, do not believe every spirit, but test the spirits, whether they are of God; because many false prophets have gone out into the world. By this you know the Spirit of God: Every spirit that confesses that Jesus Christ has come in the flesh is of God, and every spirit that does not confess that Jesus Christ has come in the flesh is not of God. And this is the spirit of the Anti-christ, which you have heard was coming, and is now already in the world. (1 John 4:1–3)

Give no regard to mediums and familiar spirits; do not seek after them, to be defiled by them: I am the LORD your God. (Lev. 19:31)

And the person who turns to mediums and familiar spirits, to prostitute himself with them, I will set My face against that person and cut him off from his people.
(Lev. 20:6)

There shall not be found among you anyone who makes his son or his daughter pass through the fire, or one who practices witchcraft, or a soothsayer, or one who interprets omens, or a sorcerer, or one who conjures spells, or a medium, or a spiritist, or one who calls up the dead. For all who do these things are an abomination to the LORD, and because of these abominations the LORD your God drives them out from before you.
(Deut. 18:10–12)

And then the lawless one will be revealed, whom the Lord will consume with the breath of His mouth and destroy with the brightness of His coming. The coming of the lawless one is according to the working of Satan, with all power, signs, and lying wonders, and with all unrighteous deception among those who perish, because they did not receive the love of the truth, that they might be saved. And for this reason God will send them strong delusion, that they should believe the lie, that they all may be condemned who did not believe the truth but had pleasure in unrighteousness. (2 Thess. 2:8–12)

So Saul died for his unfaithfulness which he had committed against the LORD, because he did not keep the word of the LORD, and also because he consulted a medium for guidance. But he did not inquire of the LORD; therefore He killed him, and turned the kingdom over to David the son of Jesse. (1 Chron. 10:13–14)

Chapter 10

Becoming a Mature Believer

◆

1. Confessing Christ before the World

Therefore whoever confesses Me before men, him I will also confess before My Father who is in heaven. But whoever denies Me before men, him I will also deny before My Father who is in heaven. (Matt. 10:32–33)

If you confess with your mouth the Lord Jesus and believe in your heart that God has raised Him from the dead, you will be saved. For with the heart one believes unto righteousness, and with the mouth confession is made unto salvation. (Rom. 10:9–10)

Nevertheless even among the rulers many believed in Him, but because of the Pharisees they did not confess Him, lest they should be put out of the synagogue; for they loved the praise of men more than the praise of God. (John 12:42–43)

For whoever is ashamed of Me and My words in this adulterous and sinful generation, of him the Son of Man also will be ashamed when He comes in the glory of His Father with the holy angels. (Mark 8:38)

2. The Bible—God's Message to Man

As newborn babes, desire the pure milk of the word, that you may grow thereby. (1 Pet. 2:2)

So now, brethren, I commend you to God and to the word of His grace, which is able to build you up and give you an inheritance among all those who are sanctified. (Acts 20:32)

Therefore lay aside all filthiness and overflow of wickedness, and receive with meekness the implanted word, which is able to save your souls. But be doers of the word, and not hearers only, deceiving yourselves. (James 1:21–22)

All Scripture is given by inspiration of God, and is profitable for doctrine, for reproof, for correction, for instruction in righteousness, that the man of God may be complete, thoroughly equipped for every good work. (2 Tim. 3:16–17)

And take the helmet of salvation, and the sword of the Spirit, which is the word of God. (Eph. 6:17)

How can a young man cleanse his way? By taking heed according to Your word....Your word I have hidden in my heart, that I might not sin against You!...The entrance of Your words gives light; it gives understanding to the simple. (Ps. 119:9, 11, 130)

Blessed is the man who walks not in the counsel of the ungodly, nor stands in the path of sinners, nor sits in the seat of the scornful; but his delight is in the law of the LORD, and in His law he meditates day and night. (Ps. 1:1–2)

This Book of the Law shall not depart from your mouth, but you shall meditate in it day and night, that you may observe to do according to all that is written in it. For then you will make your way prosperous, and then you will have good success. (Josh. 1:8)

These were more fair-minded than those in Thessalonica, in that they received the word with all readiness, and searched the Scriptures daily to find out whether these things were so. (Acts 17:11)

3. The Privilege of Prayer

You lust and do not have. You murder and covet and cannot obtain. You fight and war. Yet you do not have because you do not ask. (James 4:2)

So I say to you, ask, and it will be given to you; seek, and you will find; knock, and it will be opened to you. For everyone who asks receives, and he who seeks finds, and to him who knocks it will be opened. If a son asks for bread from any father among you, will he give him a stone? Or if he asks for a fish, will he give him a serpent instead of a fish? Or if he asks for an egg, will he offer him a scorpion? If you then, being evil, know how to give good gifts to your children, how much more will your heavenly Father give the Holy Spirit to those who ask Him! (Luke 11:9–13)

Is anyone among you suffering? Let him pray. Is anyone cheerful? Let him sing psalms. Is anyone among you sick? Let him call for the elders of the church, and let them pray over him, anointing him with oil in the name of the Lord. And the prayer of faith will save the sick, and the Lord will raise him up. And if he has committed sins, he will be forgiven. Confess your trespasses to one another, and pray for one another, that you may be healed. The effective, fervent prayer of a righteous man avails much. Elijah was a man with a nature like ours, and he prayed earnestly that it would not rain; and it did not rain on the land for three years and six months. And he prayed again, and the heaven gave rain, and the earth produced its fruit. (James 5:13–18)

Why do you sleep? Rise and pray, lest you enter into temptation. (Luke 22:46)

But those who wait on the LORD shall renew their strength; they shall mount up with wings like eagles, they shall run and not be weary, they shall walk and not faint. (Isa. 40:31)

Evening and morning and at noon I will pray, and cry aloud, and He shall hear my voice. (Ps. 55:17)

Now when Daniel knew that the writing was signed, he went home. And in his upper room, with his windows open toward Jerusalem, he knelt down on his knees three times that day, and prayed and gave thanks before his God, as was his custom since early days. (Dan. 6:10)

And when [Jesus] had sent them away, He departed to the mountain to pray. (Mark 6:46)

Now it came to pass in those days that [Jesus] went out to the mountain to pray, and continued all night in prayer to God. (Luke 6:12)

Pray without ceasing. (1 Thess. 5:17)

4. Living a Holy Life

Do not be unequally yoked together with unbelievers. For what fellowship has righteousness with lawlessness? And what communion has light with darkness? And what accord has Christ with Belial? Or what part has a believer with an unbeliever? And what agreement has the temple of God with idols? For you are the temple of the living God. As God has said: "I will dwell in them and walk among them. I will be their God, and they shall be My people." Therefore "come out from among them and be separate, says the Lord. Do not touch what is unclean, and I will receive you. I will be a Father to you, and you shall be My sons and daughters, says the LORD Almighty." Therefore, having these promises,

beloved, let us cleanse ourselves from all filthiness of the flesh and spirit, perfecting holiness in the fear of God.
(2 Cor. 6:14–7:1)

No one can serve two masters; for either he will hate the one and love the other, or else he will be loyal to the one and despise the other. You cannot serve God and mammon.
(Matt. 6:24)

Do not love the world or the things in the world. If anyone loves the world, the love of the Father is not in him. For all that is in the world; the lust of the flesh, the lust of the eyes, and the pride of life; is not of the Father but is of the world. And the world is passing away, and the lust of it; but he who does the will of God abides forever.
(1 John 2:15–17)

Do you not know that friendship with the world is enmity with God? Whoever therefore wants to be a friend of the world makes himself an enemy of God....But He gives more grace. Therefore He says: "God resists the proud, but gives grace to the humble." Therefore submit to God. Resist the devil and he will flee from you. Draw near to God and He will draw near to you. Cleanse your hands, you sinners; and purify your hearts, you double-minded.
(James 4:4, 6–8)

Pursue peace with all people, and holiness, without which no one will see the Lord.
(Heb. 12:14)

As obedient children, not conforming yourselves to the former lusts, as in your ignorance; but as He who called you is holy, you also be holy in all your conduct, because it is written, "Be holy, for I am holy." And if you call on the Father, who without partiality judges according to each one's work, conduct yourselves throughout the time of your stay here in fear; knowing that you were not redeemed with corruptible things, like silver or gold, from your aimless conduct received by tradition from your

577

fathers, but with the precious blood of Christ, as of a lamb without blemish and without spot. (1 Pet. 1:14–19)

For the time has come for judgment to begin at the house of God; and if it begins with us first, what will be the end of those who do not obey the gospel of God? Now "if the righteous one is scarcely saved, where will the ungodly and the sinner appear?" (1 Pet. 4:17–18)

Now the ones that fell among thorns are those who, when they have heard, go out and are choked with cares, riches, and pleasures of life, and bring no fruit to maturity. (Luke 8:14)

But take heed to yourselves, lest your hearts be weighed down with carousing, drunkenness, and cares of this life, and that Day come on you unexpectedly. For it will come as a snare on all those who dwell on the face of the whole earth. Watch therefore, and pray always that you may be counted worthy to escape all these things that will come to pass, and to stand before the Son of Man. (Luke 21:34–36)

I beseech you therefore, brethren, by the mercies of God, that you present your bodies a living sacrifice, holy, acceptable to God, which is your reasonable service. And do not be conformed to this world, but be transformed by the renewing of your mind, that you may prove what is that good and acceptable and perfect will of God. (Rom. 12:1–2)

I have fought the good fight, I have finished the race, I have kept the faith. Finally, there is laid up for me the crown of righteousness, which the Lord, the righteous Judge, will give to me on that Day, and not to me only but also to all who have loved His appearing. (2 Tim. 4:7–8)

5. Working for Christ

It is like a man going to a far country, who left his house and gave authority to his servants, and to each his work, and commanded the doorkeeper to watch. Watch therefore, for you do not know when the master of the house is coming; in the evening, at midnight, at the crowing of the rooster, or in the morning; lest, coming suddenly, he find you sleeping. And what I say to you, I say to all: Watch! (Mark 13:34–37)

Therefore you also be ready, for the Son of Man is coming at an hour you do not expect. Who then is a faithful and wise servant, whom his master made ruler over his household, to give them food in due season? Blessed is that servant whom his master, when he comes, will find so doing. Assuredly, I say to you that he will make him ruler over all his goods. But if that evil servant says in his heart, "My master is delaying his coming," and begins to beat his fellow servants, and to eat and drink with the drunkards, the master of that servant will come on a day when he is not looking for him and at an hour that he is not aware of, and will cut him in two and appoint him his portion with the hypocrites. There shall be weeping and gnashing of teeth. (Matt. 24:44–51)

The kingdom of heaven is like a man traveling to a far country, who called his own servants and delivered his goods to them. And to one he gave five talents, to another two, and to another one, to each according to his own ability; and immediately he went on a journey. Then he who had received the five talents went and traded with them, and made another five talents. And likewise he who had received two gained two more also. But he who had received one went and dug in the ground, and hid his lord's money. After a long time the lord of those servants came and settled accounts with them. So he who had received five talents came and brought five other talents, saying, "Lord, you delivered to me five talents; look, I have gained five more talents besides them." His lord said to him, "Well done, good and faithful servant; you were faithful over a few things, I will make you ruler over many things. Enter into the joy of your lord." He also who had received two talents came and said, "Lord, you delivered to me two talents; look, I have gained two more talents besides them." His lord said to him, "Well done, good and faithful servant; you have been faithful over a few things, I will make you ruler over many things. Enter into the joy of your lord." Then he who had received the one talent came and said, "Lord, I knew you to be a hard man, reaping where you have not sown, and gathering where you have not scattered seed. And I was afraid, and went and hid your talent in the ground. Look, there you have what is yours." But his lord answered and said to him, "You wicked and lazy servant, you knew that I reap where I have not sown, and gather where I have not scattered seed. So you ought to have deposited my money with the bankers, and at my coming I would have received back my own with interest. Therefore take the talent from him, and give it to him who has ten talents. For to everyone who has, more will be given, and he will have abundance; but from him who does not have, even what he has will be taken away. And cast the unprofitable servant into the outer darkness. There will be weeping and gnashing of teeth." (Matt. 25:14–30)

Therefore those who were scattered went everywhere preaching the word. (Acts 8:4)

That we should no longer be children, tossed to and fro and carried about with every wind of doctrine, by the trickery of men, in the cunning craftiness of deceitful plotting, but, speaking the truth in love, may grow up in all things into Him who is the head; Christ; from whom the whole body, joined and knit together by what every joint supplies, according to the effective working by which every part does its share, causes growth of the body for the edifying of itself in love. (Eph. 4:14–16)

Therefore He says: "Awake, you who sleep, arise from the dead, and Christ will give you light." See then that you

580

walk circumspectly, not as fools but as wise, redeeming the time, because the days are evil. Therefore do not be unwise, but understand what the will of the Lord is. And do not be drunk with wine, in which is dissipation; but be filled with the Spirit, speaking to one another in psalms and hymns and spiritual songs, singing and making melody in your heart to the Lord, giving thanks always for all things to God the Father in the name of our Lord Jesus Christ, submitting to one another in the fear of God. (Eph. 5:14–21)

Let him know that he who turns a sinner from the error of his way will save a soul from death and cover a multitude of sins. (James 5:20)

Those who are wise shall shine like the brightness of the firmament, and those who turn many to righteousness like the stars forever and ever. (Dan. 12:3)

And behold, I am coming quickly, and My reward is with Me, to give to every one according to his work. (Rev. 22:12)

Chapter 11

Strength for Difficult Times

◆

1. Victory over Temptation

My brethren, count it all joy when you fall into various trials, knowing that the testing of your faith produces patience. But let patience have its perfect work, that you may be perfect and complete, lacking nothing.

(James 1:2–4)

Blessed is the man who endures temptation; for when he has been approved, he will receive the crown of life which the Lord has promised to those who love Him.

(James 1:12)

Be sober, be vigilant; because your adversary the devil walks about like a roaring lion, seeking whom he may devour. Resist him, steadfast in the faith, knowing that the same sufferings are experienced by your brotherhood in the world. But may the God of all grace, who called us to His eternal glory by Christ Jesus, after you have suffered a while, perfect, establish, strengthen, and settle you. (1 Pet. 5:8–10)

No temptation has overtaken you except such as is common to man; but God is faithful, who will not allow you to be tempted beyond what you are able, but with the temptation will also make the way of escape, that you may be able to bear it. (1 Cor. 10:13)

And He said to me, "My grace is sufficient for you, for My strength is made perfect in weakness." Therefore most gladly I will rather boast in my infirmities, that the power of Christ may rest upon me. Therefore I take pleasure in infirmities, in reproaches, in needs, in persecutions, in distresses, for Christ's sake. For when I am weak, then I am strong.   (2 Cor. 12:9–10)

Pray without ceasing.   (1 Thess. 5:17)

Every spirit that does not confess that Jesus Christ has come in the flesh is not of God. And this is the spirit of the Antichrist, which you have heard was coming, and is now already in the world. You are of God, little children, and have overcome them, because He who is in you is greater than he who is in the world.   (1 John 4:3–4)

I can do all things through Christ who strengthens me.
(Phil. 4:13)

I have written to you, fathers, because you have known Him who is from the beginning. I have written to you, young men, because you are strong, and the word of God abides in you, and you have overcome the wicked one.
(1 John 2:14)

How can a young man cleanse his way? By taking heed according to Your word.   (Ps. 119:9)

2. Rejoicing in Persecution

Blessed are those who are persecuted for righteousness' sake, for theirs is the kingdom of heaven. Blessed are you when they revile and persecute you, and say all kinds of evil against you falsely for My sake. Rejoice and be exceedingly glad, for great is your reward in heaven, for so they persecuted the prophets who were before you.
(Matt. 5:10–12)

Beloved, do not think it strange concerning the fiery trial which is to try you, as though some strange thing happened to you; but rejoice to the extent that you partake of Christ's sufferings, that when His glory is revealed, you may also be glad with exceeding joy. If you are reproached for the name of Christ, blessed are you, for the Spirit of glory and of God rests upon you. On their part He is blasphemed, but on your part He is glorified. (1 Pet. 4:12–14)

Yet if anyone suffers as a Christian, let him not be ashamed, but let him glorify God in this matter.
(1 Pet. 4:16)

For to this you were called, because Christ also suffered for us, leaving us an example, that you should follow His steps...who, when He was reviled, did not revile in return; when He suffered, He did not threaten, but committed Himself to Him who judges righteously.
(1 Pet. 2:21, 23)

For it is better, if it is the will of God, to suffer for doing good than for doing evil. For Christ also suffered once for sins, the just for the unjust, that He might bring us to God, being put to death in the flesh but made alive by the Spirit. (1 Pet. 3:17–18)

Yes, and all who desire to live godly in Christ Jesus will suffer persecution. (2 Tim. 3:12)

If we endure, we shall also reign with Him. If we deny Him, He also will deny us. (2 Tim. 2:12)

Continue in the faith...[for] we must through many tribulations enter the kingdom of God. (Acts 14:22)

And when they had called for the apostles and beaten them, they commanded that they should not speak in the name of Jesus, and let them go. So they departed from the presence of the council, rejoicing that they were counted worthy to suffer shame for His name. And daily in the temple, and in every house, they did not cease teaching and preaching Jesus as the Christ.

(Acts 5:40–42)

Therefore we also, since we are surrounded by so great a cloud of witnesses, let us lay aside every weight, and the sin which so easily ensnares us, and let us run with endurance the race that is set before us, looking unto Jesus, the author and finisher of our faith, who for the joy that was set before Him endured the cross, despising the shame, and has sat down at the right hand of the throne of God. For consider Him who endured such hostility from sinners against Himself, lest you become weary and discouraged in your souls. You have not yet resisted to bloodshed, striving against sin. (Heb. 12:1–4)

Do not fear any of those things which you are about to suffer. Indeed, the devil is about to throw some of you into prison, that you may be tested, and you will have tribulation ten days. Be faithful until death, and I will give you the crown of life. (Rev. 2:10)

3. Persevering through Trial

An inheritance incorruptible and undefiled and that does not fade away,[is] reserved in heaven for you, who are kept by the power of God through faith for salvation ready to be revealed in the last time. In this you greatly rejoice, though now for a little while, if need be, you have been grieved by various trials, that the genuineness of your faith, being much more precious than gold that perishes, though it is tested by fire, may be found to praise, honor, and glory at the revelation of Jesus Christ. (1 Pet. 1:4–7)

Therefore humble yourselves under the mighty hand of God, that He may exalt you in due time, casting all your care upon Him, for He cares for you. (1 Pet. 5:6–7)

God is our refuge and strength, a very present help in trouble. Therefore we will not fear, even though the earth be removed, and though the mountains be carried into the midst of the sea; though its waters roar and be troubled, though the mountains shake with its swelling.
(Ps. 46:1–3)

Yea, though I walk through the valley of the shadow of death, I will fear no evil; for You are with me; Your rod and Your staff, they comfort me. (Ps. 23:4)

Many are the afflictions of the righteous, but the LORD delivers him out of them all. (Ps. 34:19)

Call upon Me in the day of trouble; I will deliver you, and you shall glorify Me. (Ps. 50:15)

The righteous cry out, and the LORD hears, and delivers them out of all their troubles. (Ps. 34:17)

The LORD is my light and my salvation; whom shall I fear? The LORD is the strength of my life; of whom shall I be afraid? When the wicked came against me to eat up my flesh, my enemies and foes, they stumbled and fell. Though an army may encamp against me, my heart shall not fear; though war should rise against me, in this I will be confident. One thing I have desired of the LORD, that will I seek: That I may dwell in the house of the LORD all the days of my life, to behold the beauty of the LORD, and to inquire in His temple. For in the time of trouble He shall hide me in His pavilion; in the secret place of His tabernacle He shall hide me; He shall set me high upon a rock. And now my head shall be lifted up above my enemies all around me; therefore I will offer sacrifices of joy in His tabernacle; I will sing, yes, I will sing praises to the LORD....I would have lost heart, unless I had believed that I would see the goodness of the LORD in the land of the living. Wait on the LORD; be of good courage, and He shall strengthen your heart; wait, I say, on the LORD! (Ps. 27:1–6, 13–14)

Come to Me, all you who labor and are heavy laden, and I will give you rest. Take My yoke upon you and learn from Me, for I am gentle and lowly in heart, and you will find rest for your souls. (Matt. 11:28–29)

4. Comfort in Time of Loss

Let not your heart be troubled; you believe in God, believe also in Me. In My Father's house are many mansions; if it were not so, I would have told you. I go to prepare a place for you. And if I go and prepare a place for you, I will come again and receive you to Myself; that where I am, there you may be also....Peace I leave with you, My peace I give to you; not as the world gives do I give to you. Let not your heart be troubled, neither let it be afraid. (John 14:1–3, 27)

Be still, and know that I am God. (Ps. 46:10)

Then I heard a voice from heaven saying to me, "Write: 'Blessed are the dead who die in the Lord from now on.'" "Yes," says the Spirit, "that they may rest from their labors, and their works follow them." (Rev. 14:13)

But I do not want you to be ignorant, brethren, concerning those who have fallen asleep, lest you sorrow as others who have no hope. For if we believe that Jesus died and rose again, even so God will bring with Him those who sleep in Jesus. For this we say to you by the word of the Lord, that we who are alive and remain until the coming of the Lord will by no means precede those who are asleep. For the Lord Himself will descend from heaven with a shout, with the voice of an archangel, and with the trumpet of God. And the dead in Christ will rise first. Then we who are alive and remain shall be caught up together with them in the clouds to meet the Lord in the air. And thus we shall always be with the Lord. Therefore comfort one another with these words. (1 Thess. 4:13–18)

So we are always confident, knowing that while we are at home in the body we are absent from the Lord. For we walk by faith, not by sight. We are confident, yes, well pleased rather to be absent from the body and to be present with the Lord. (2 Cor. 5:6–8)

For I am hard pressed between the two, having a desire to depart and be with Christ, which is far better.
(Phil. 1:23)

For this corruptible must put on incorruption, and this mortal must put on immortality. So when this corruptible has put on incorruption, and this mortal has put on immortality, then shall be brought to pass the saying that is written: "Death is swallowed up in victory. O Death, where is your sting? O Hades, where is your victory?" The sting of death is sin, and the strength of sin is the law. But thanks be to God, who gives us the victory through our Lord Jesus Christ. Therefore, my beloved brethren, be steadfast, immovable, always abounding in the work of the Lord, knowing that your labor is not in vain in the Lord. (1 Cor. 15:53–58)

Chapter 12

Helpful Soul-Winning Hints

1. Generally deal with people of your own gender and those who are close to your own age.

2. Whenever it is possible, talk to the person alone.

3. Rely completely on the Spirit of God.

4. Do not merely quote or read passages from the Bible, but have the one with whom you are speaking read them for himself.

5. Emphasize a single passage of Scripture, repeating and discussing it until the inquirer cannot forget it. He will hear it ringing in his memory long after you have ceased talking.

6. Always hold the person to the main point of accepting Christ. Many opportunities for repentance have been lost by an inexperienced worker allowing himself to become involved in an argument over some side issue.

7. Be courteous. Some overzealous workers cause the people they approach to become defensive and to put up barriers that are impossible to penetrate.

8. Be earnest. Genuine earnestness means more than any skill learned in a training class or even from a book such as this.

9. Never lose your temper.

10. Never interrupt anyone else who is leading someone to Christ.

11. Don't be in a hurry.

12. Ask the person to pray with you. Difficulties can disappear during prayer, and many stubborn people yield when they are brought into the presence of God.

13. Whenever you seem to fail, go home, pray about it, and find out why you failed. Then go back, if you can, and try again.

14. Be sure to give the new believer definite instructions concerning how to succeed in the Christian life.

15. Spend time with the new believer regularly to encourage him and to help him grow as a Christian.

Heaven or Hell

Contents

Chapter 1

Come out of Hiding

◆——————————

The first question that God ever asked of man is recorded in Genesis 3:9: *"Where are you?"* God asked the question of Adam on the evening of that awful day of the first sin. The voice of God in its majesty rolled down the avenues of the Garden of Eden. Until that day, the voice of God had been the sweetest music to Adam. He knew no greater joy than that of glad communion with his Creator and his heavenly Father. But now all was different. As the voice of God was heard in the Garden, Adam was filled with fear and tried to hide himself.

This is the history of every son of Adam from that day until now. Every sinner is trying to hide from the presence and the all-seeing eyes of God. This accounts for a large share of the skepticism, agnosticism, and atheism of our day. It is sinful man trying to hide from a holy God.

True Reasons for Unbelief

People will give many reasons why they are skeptics, agnostics, or atheists. But in the majority of cases, the real reason is this: they hope to hide themselves from the discomfort of God's presence by denying that He exists. This also accounts for much of the neglect of the Bible. People will tell you that they do not read their Bibles because they have so much else to read or because they are not interested in the Bible. They declare that it is a dull and boring book to them. But the true cause of man's neglect of Bible study is this: the Bible brings God near to us as no other book does, and men are uneasy when they become conscious of the presence of God. Therefore, they neglect the book that brings God near.

This also accounts for much of the absenteeism from the house of God and its services. People give many reasons why they do not attend church. They will tell you they cannot dress well enough to attend church or that they are too busy and too tired. They will complain that the services are dull and uninteresting. But the reason why men and women, old and young, are habitually absent from church is because the house of God brings God near and makes them uncomfortable in their sin.

No one ever succeeded in hiding from God. God said to Adam, *"Where are you?"* Adam had to come from his hiding place to meet God face-to-face and make full confession of his sin. Sooner or later, no matter how carefully they hide themselves from God, all men and women will have to come from their hiding places and meet Him face-to-face. They will have to make a full declaration of where they stand in His presence.

God puts this question to every Christian and to everyone who is not a Christian: *"Where are you?"* Where do you stand concerning spiritual and eternal things? Where do you stand concerning God, heaven, righteousness, Christ, and eternity? *"Where are you?"*

Knowing Where You Stand

Every truly intelligent person desires to know just where he is. Every wise businessman desires to know where he stands financially. In our country, every careful businessman periodically takes an inventory of his stock, examines his accounts, finds out precisely what are his credits and debits, and how much his assets exceed or fall below his liabilities.

He may discover as a result of his scrutiny that he does not stand as well as he thought he did. If that is true, he wants to know it in order that he may conduct his business accordingly. Many have failed in business through unwillingness to face facts and find out just where they stood.

I knew a very brilliant businessman who was truly gifted in a certain type of business enterprise. But his affairs got into a tangled condition.

His wise business friends came to him and advised him to go through his books and find out just where he stood. They said to him, "If you are in bad shape, we will help you out."

But the man was too proud to take their advice. He was too proud to admit that his business was in danger of failure, so he refused to look into it. He resolutely tried to plunge through. But instead of plunging through, he sunk into utter financial ruin. Although he was an exceptionally brilliant man in some areas, he experienced complete financial shipwreck. He never got on his feet again. When he died, he did not have enough money to pay for his funeral expenses, simply because he was not willing to humble his pride and face facts.

Many people are too proud to confess that they are morally and spiritually bankrupt. So they are going to grit their teeth and plunge through. They will fall into utter and eternal ruin. Everyone wants to know where he stands physically. He wants to know the condition of his lungs, heart, stomach, and nerves. He may be worse off than he thinks he is. He may think his heart is sound when it is defective. But he wants to know it, because then he will not subject it to the strain that otherwise he would. Many lie in a premature grave who might be doing good work on earth if they had been willing to find out what their real condition was and to act accordingly.

Every man at sea wishes to know where his vessel is, its exact latitude and longitude. When crossing the Atlantic Ocean some years ago, I sailed for days beneath clouds and through fogs. The sailors were unable to take an observation by the sun and had been sailing blindly. One night I happened to be on deck, when suddenly there was a rift in the clouds, and the North Star appeared. Word was sent below, and the captain of the vessel hurried on deck. I remember how he nearly laid across the compass as he carefully took an observation by the North Star in order to know exactly where we were.

In life, we are all sailing across a perilous sea toward an eternal port. All intelligent men and women will desire to know just where they are—their exact spiritual longitude and their exact spiritual latitude.

How to Evaluate the Question

Let us consider this weighty question of where we are. We should consider it seriously. It is not a question to trifle with. It is amazing that men and women may be sensible about everything else and would not think of trifling with the great financial questions of the day or with great social problems. But they treat this great question of eternity as a joke.

One evening I bought a paper from a little newsboy on the street. As he handed me my change, I asked him, "My boy, are you saved?" The boy treated it as a joke. That might be all you could expect of a poor, uneducated newsboy on the street. But it is not what you would expect of thinking men and women when you come to these great eternal problems of God, eternity, salvation, heaven, and hell.

Anyone who trifles with questions like these is a fool. I don't care about your culture, social position, or reputation. Unless you face the great question of your spiritual condition with the most profound earnestness and seriousness, you are playing the part of a fool.

We should consider this question honestly. Many people today try to deceive themselves, others, and even God. They know in their innermost hearts that they are wrong, but they try to persuade themselves, others, and God that they are right.

You cannot deceive God. It will do you no good to deceive anybody else, and it is the height of folly to deceive yourself. The biggest fool on earth is the man who fools himself. Be honest. If you are lost, admit it; if you are on the road to hell, acknowledge it; if you are not a Christian, say so. If you are an enemy of God, face the facts. If you are a child of the Devil, realize it. Be honest with yourself, honest with your fellowmen, and honest with God.

We should consider the question thoroughly. Many people are honest and serious to a certain point, but they don't go to the bottom of things. They are superficial. They give these tremendous questions a few moments' thought, and then their weak minds grow weary. They say, "I guess I am all right; I will take my chances."

No one can afford to guess on questions like these. We must be absolutely certain. It will not satisfy me to hope I am saved; I must know that I am saved. It will not satisfy me to hope that I am a child of God; I must know that I am a child of God. It will not satisfy me to hope that I am bound for heaven; I must know that I am bound for heaven. Do not lay these questions down until you have gone to the bottom of them and know for certain just where you stand.

We should consider these questions prayerfully. God tells us in His Word, and we know from experience, that *"the heart is deceitful above all things, and desperately wicked"* (Jer. 17:9). There is nothing that the human heart is as deceitful about as our moral and spiritual conditions. Every man and woman is by nature sharp-sighted to the faults of others and blind to their own faults. We need to face this question in prayer. You will never know where you stand until God shows you.

We must pray like David, *"Search me, O God, and know my heart; try me, and know my anxieties; and see if there is any wicked way in me"* (Ps. 139:23–24). Only when God sheds the light of His Holy Spirit into our hearts and shows us ourselves as He sees us will we ever know ourselves as we truly are. To see ourselves in the light of God's presence, as God sees us, will only be in answer to definite and earnest prayer.

Are You a Religious Person?

One morning I met the minister of a church that formerly I had pastored. He said to me, "Brother Torrey, I had an awful experience this morning."

I said, "What was it, Brother Norris?" He mentioned a member of the church.

"You know she is dying. She sent for me to come and see her this morning. I hurried to her home. The moment I opened the door and entered the room she cried from her bed, 'Oh, Brother Norris, I have been a professing Christian for forty years. I am now dying and have just found out that I was never saved at all.'"

The horror of it! To be a professing Christian for forty years and never find out until your life is at an end that you have never really been a Christian at all. It is better to find it out today than in eternity.

Many men and women have been professing Christians for years but were never saved. In a paper edited by a clergyman, I read a letter complaining about our meetings. The writer said,

599

"These men produced the impression that some of our church members are not saved." Well, that is the impression we tried to produce, for that is the truth of God. In churches throughout the world, you will find many men and women who are unsaved.

Once more we should consider this question scripturally, according to the Book. God has given to you and me only one safe chart and compass to guide us on our voyages through life toward eternity. That chart and compass is the Bible. If you steer your course according to the Book, you will steer safely. If you steer according to your own feelings, according to the speculation of the petty philosopher or the theologian, according to anything but the clear declaration of the Word of God, you steer your course to shipwreck. Any hope that is not founded on the clear, unmistakable teaching of God's Word is absolutely worthless.

You Can Be Sure

In one of my pastorates, a young married couple had a sweet little child entrusted to them by the heavenly Father. Then one day, that little child went home to be with the Lord. In the hour of their sorrow, I went to call on the grieving parents. Taking advantage of their tenderness of heart, I pointed them to the Savior with whom their child was safely at home. They promised to accept Jesus as their Savior.

After some days and weeks had passed and the first shock of the sorrow had gone, they began to drift back into the world again. I called on them to speak with them. Only the wife was at home. I began by talking about the little child and how safe and happy he was in the arms of Jesus. She gladly assented to all of this. Then I turned the topic a little bit and said to her, "Do you expect to see your child again?"

"Oh," she said, "certainly. I have no doubt that I will see my child again."

I said, "Why do you expect to see your child again?"

"Because the child is with Jesus, and I expect when I die I will go to be with Him, too."

I said, "Do you think you are saved?"

"Oh, yes," she replied, "I think I am saved."

"Why do you think you are saved?"

"Because I feel so," she said.

"Is that your only ground of hope?"

"That is all."

I said, "Your hope is not worth anything." That seemed cruel, didn't it? But it was kind. I asked her, "Can you put your finger on anything in the Word of God that proves you have everlasting life?"

"No," she said, "I cannot."

"Well, then," I said, "your hope is absolutely worthless." Then she turned on me, which she had a perfect right to do. It is quite right to talk back to preachers. I believe in it, and she began to talk back.

"Do you expect to go to heaven when you die?"

I responded, "Yes, I know I will."

"When you die, do you expect to be with Christ?"

"Yes," I said, "I know I will."

"Do you think you have everlasting life?"

"Yes," I said, "I know I have."

"Can you put your finger on anything in the Word of God that proves you have eternal life?"

I said, "Yes, thank God, John 3:36: *'He who believes in the Son has everlasting life.'* I know I believe in the Son of God. On the sure ground of God's Word, I know I have everlasting life."

Chapter 2

Where Do You Stand?

◆————————

Choose for yourselves this day whom you will serve.
—Joshua 24:15

A few suggestions will help you in considering this question: Where are you? Are you saved or are you lost? You are one or the other. Unless you have been definitely saved by a deliberate acceptance of Jesus Christ, you are definitely lost. Only two classes exist—lost sinners and saved sinners. To which class do you belong?

Are you on the road to heaven or the road to hell? You are on one or the other. The Lord Jesus tells us that there are only two roads—the broad road that leads to destruction and the narrow road that leads to life everlasting. (See Matthew 7:13–14.) Which road are you on? Are you on the road that leads to God, heaven, and glory? Or are you on the road that leads to Satan, sin, shame, and hell?

Some years ago, an English sailor came into a mission in New York City. As he left the church not very much affected, a worker at the door put a little card into his hand. These words were printed on this card: "If I would die tonight, I would go to ————." The place was left blank, and underneath was written, "Please fill in the blank and sign your name."

The sailor, without even reading the card, put it in his pocket and went down to the steamer. During the journey back to England, he was thrown from the rigging and broke his leg. His fellow sailors took him down to his berth, and as he lay there day after day, that card stared him in the face. "If I would die tonight, I would go to ———— ."

"Well," he said, "if I filled that out honestly, I would have to write *hell*. If I would die tonight, I would go to hell. But I won't fill it out that way." Lying there in his berth, he accepted Jesus Christ as his Lord and Savior and filled out the card: "If I would die tonight, I would go to heaven." One day he went back to New York. He walked into the mission and handed in the card with his name signed to it.

Suppose you had such a card to complete. "If I would die tonight, I would go to ———— ." What would you answer? Are you a child of God or a child of the Devil?

We live in a day in which many superficial thinkers are telling us that all men are the children of God. That is not the teaching of the Bible, and it is not the teaching of Jesus Christ. Jesus Christ said distinctly in John 8:44, talking to certain Jews, *"You are of your father the devil."* We are told in 1 John 3:10, *"In this the children of God and the children of the devil are manifest: whoever does not practice righteousness is not of God."* And we are told distinctly in John 1:12, *"As many as received Him, to them He gave the right to become children of God."* Every one of us is either a child of God or a child of the Devil. Which are you?

When I was speaking in Ballarat, Australia, a large group of educated men sat listening to the sermon. I was preaching on the difference between the children of God and the children of the Devil. The next night when I gave the invitation, almost the entire group of educated men came to the front. When they got up to give their testimony, one of them said, "The reason I came tonight and accepted Christ was this: I was here last night and heard Dr. Torrey say that everyone was a child of God or a child of the Devil. I knew I was not a child of God; therefore, I knew I must be a child of the Devil. I made up my mind I would be a child of the Devil no longer. I have come forward tonight to take Jesus Christ."

Are you a Christian in name only, or are you a real Christian? You know there are two kinds. Are you one of these people who call themselves Christians, go to the house of God on Sunday, take Communion, and perhaps even teach a Sunday school class? But the rest of the week, do you run around drinking, carousing, and participating in all the frivolity and foolishness of the world?

Are you one of these Christians who are trying to hold on to Jesus Christ with one hand and the world with the other? Or are you a real Christian who has renounced the world with your whole heart and given yourself to Jesus Christ, a Christian who can sing and mean it, "I surrender all"? What kind of a Christian are you?

Are you for Christ or against Him? You are either one or the other. We read Jesus' words in Matthew 12:30: *"He who is not with Me is against Me."* Either you are with Jesus wholeheartedly and openly, or you are against Him. Are you for Christ or against Him?

Taking a Stand

In my first pastorate, year after year, there came an outpouring of God's Spirit. In one of these gracious outpourings, many of the leading businessmen of the area were converted. It was a small town, but one of the businessmen would not take a stand. He was one of the most exemplary men in the community. He was an amiable, upright, regular attender at church. He was a member of my Bible class and the choir, but he was one of those men who wanted to please both sides. He was identified with friends in business, in community action groups, and elsewhere, who were not committed Christians. He was afraid that he would offend them if he came out boldly and honestly for Christ.

The weeks passed by. One Sunday morning, he was leaving my Bible class and passed by the superintendent of the Sunday school, who was his intimate friend. They had been in the army together. As he passed by, his friend turned to him and said, "George?"

"Well, what is it, Porter?" said the other, calling him by his first name.

"George, when are you going to take a stand?"

He said, "Ring the bell."

Promptly the superintendent stepped up to the bell and rang it. The congregation turned in surprise, wondering what was going to happen. George stepped to the front of the platform. It was a community where everybody knew everybody else by their first name, and everybody was curious.

"Friends," he said, "I have heard it said time and time again during these meetings that a man must either be for Jesus Christ or against Him. I want you all to know that from this time on, my wife and I are for Christ."

Many people have been involved in a church for years, but they have never taken an open stand for Christ. Take it now. Say, *"As for me and my house, we will serve the LORD"* (Josh. 24:15).

It is important to face the question, "Where are you?" Where you are today may determine where you will spend eternity.

Meeting the Chief Physician

A story is told of Dr. Forbes Winslow, an eminent pathologist in diseases of the mind. A young French nobleman came to London bringing letters of introduction from leading Frenchmen. The letters introduced him to Dr. Winslow and requested the doctor's best care for the young man. He presented his letters, and Dr. Winslow said, "What is your trouble?"

"Dr. Winslow, I cannot sleep. I have not had a good night's sleep for two years. Unless something is done for me, I will go insane."

Dr. Winslow said, "Why can't you sleep?"

"Well," said the young man, "I can't tell you."

Dr. Winslow said, "Have you lost any money?"

"No," he said, "I have lost no money."

"Have you lost friends?"

"No, I have lost no friends recently.

"Have you suffered in honor or reputation?"

"Not that I know of."

"Well then," said the doctor, "why can't you sleep?"

The young man said, "I would rather not tell you."

"Well," said Dr. Winslow, "if you don't tell me, I can't help you."

"Well," he said, "if I must tell you, I will. I am an agnostic. My father was an agnostic before me. Every night when I lie down to sleep, I am confronted with the question, 'Where will I spend eternity?' All night that question rings in my ears. If I succeed in getting off to sleep, my dreams are worse than my waking hours, and I awaken again."

Dr. Winslow said, "I can't do anything for you."

"What!" said the young Frenchman. "Have I come all the way over here from Paris for you to help me, and you dash my hopes to the ground? Do you mean to tell me that my case is hopeless?"

Dr. Winslow repeated, "I can do nothing for you, but I can tell you about a Physician who can." He walked across his study, took up his Bible from the center of the table, and opened it to Isaiah 53:5–6. He began to read:

> *He was wounded for our transgressions, He was bruised for our iniquities; the chastisement for our peace was upon Him, and by His stripes we are healed. All we like sheep have gone astray; we have turned, every one, to his own way; and the LORD has laid on Him the iniquity of us all.*

Looking at the Frenchman, he said, "He is the only Physician in the world who can help you."

There was a curl of scorn on the man's lips. He said, "Dr. Winslow, do you mean to tell me that you, an eminent scientist, believe in that worn-out superstition of the Bible and Christianity?"

"Yes," said Dr. Winslow. "I believe in the Bible. I believe in Jesus Christ. And believing in the Bible and believing in Jesus Christ has saved me from becoming what you are today."

The young fellow thought for a moment. Then he said, "Dr. Winslow, if I am an honest man, I should at least be willing to consider it, correct?"

"Yes, sir."

"Well," he said, "will you explain it to me?"

The eminent physician sat down with his open Bible, and for several days, he showed the young Frenchman the way of eternal life. He saw Christ as his divine, atoning Savior, put his trust in Him, and went back to Paris with peace of mind. He had solved the great question of eternity and where he would spend it, for he would spend it with Christ in glory. Where will you spend eternity?

Chapter 3

Why Do You Not Believe?

◆

*He who believes in Him is not condemned; but he who does not
believe is condemned already because he has not believed in the
name of the only begotten Son of God.*
—John 3:18

The failure to put faith in Jesus Christ is not a mere misfortune. It is a sin—a grievous sin, an appalling sin, a damning sin. Men will tell you very lightly, as if it were something of which they were quite proud, "I do not believe in Jesus Christ." Few men are foolish, blind, or utterly depraved enough to tell you proudly, "I am a murderer" or "I am an adulterer" or "I am a habitual liar." Yet none of these is a sadder or darker confession than "I am an unbeliever in Jesus Christ."

Believing or not believing in Jesus Christ is largely a matter of the will. Some people imagine it is wholly a matter of intellectual conviction. The one who assumes this is a very superficial thinker. Few people do not have sufficient evidence that Jesus is the Son of God and the Savior of those who believe in Him. They must only be willing to yield themselves to the evidence.

Men and women who believe in Jesus Christ have decided to yield to the truth. They believe in Him who is clearly proven to be God's Son. Those who do not believe because of the love of sin, or for some other reason, will not yield to the truth and accept Him as Savior and Lord.

Your refusal to accept Jesus Christ is not because you have honest reasons for believing that He is not who He claims to be. You know it is because you do not want to accept Him and surrender your life to Him. This is a great sin—greater than any sin you can commit against any person by lying to him, stealing from him, or killing him.

Facing the Truth

Don't try to ignore the truth. If you do, you will do it to your eternal ruin. If I am right in this matter, and if the Bible is right, it is infinitely important that you know it. Therefore, read carefully and be honest with yourself.

Unbelief in Jesus Christ is an appalling sin because of the dignity of the person of Jesus Christ. Jesus is the Son of God in a sense that no other person is the Son of God. Consider these Scriptures: *"Who being the brightness of His glory, and the express image of His person"* (Heb. 1:3); *"For in Him dwells all the fullness of the Godhead bodily"* (Col. 2:9); *"When He again brings the firstborn into the world, He says: 'Let all the angels of God worship Him'"* (Heb. 1:6); *"That all should honor the Son just as they honor the Father"* (John 5:23).

A dignity belongs to Jesus Christ that belongs to no angel or archangel and to none of the *"principalities and powers in the heavenly places"* (Eph. 3:10). His is the *"name which is above every name, that at the name of Jesus every knee should bow... and...every tongue should confess that Jesus Christ is Lord"* (Phil. 2:9–11).

An injury done to Jesus Christ is a sin of vastly greater magnitude than a sin done to man. A mule has rights, but its rights are unimportant when compared with the rights of a man. The law recognizes the rights of a mule, but the killing of a mule is not regarded as serious as the putting out of a man's eye. But the rights of a man, even of the purest, noblest, greatest of men, pale into insignificance before the rights of the infinite God and His Son, Jesus Christ.

God's Majesty and Our Sin

To realize the enormity of a sin committed against Jesus Christ, we must strive for an adequate understanding of His dignity and majesty. When we do, we see that our unbelief robs this infinitely glorious Person of the honor due Him.

What was it that struck conviction into the hearts of three thousand men on the Day of Pentecost and made them cry out in agony, *"Men and brethren, what shall we do?"* (Acts 2:37). It was this: Peter, filled with the Spirit, told them who Jesus was. He said, *"Therefore let all the house of Israel know assuredly that God has made this Jesus, whom you crucified, both Lord and Christ"* (v. 36). Their eyes were opened at last to see the glory, dignity, and majesty of the Person they had so outrageously wronged. All the sins of their lifetime instantly seemed to be nothing in comparison with this sin.

If you permit God to open your eyes to see who Jesus is, to see His infinite dignity, glory, and majesty, you will see that every wrong done to any mere man is nothing compared to the wrong done to this holy and majestic Person. You may refuse to let God open your eyes to the infinite glory of Jesus. You may say, "I don't see that He is essentially greater than other men or that His rights are more sacred than those of Longfellow, Lincoln, Washington, or my next-door neighbor. But the day will come when you will have to see.

The full glory of Jesus will be unveiled to the whole universe. If you will not repent now and receive pardon for your awful sin of unbelief, you will be overwhelmed with eternal shame. You will cry for the rocks and the hills to fall on you and hide you from the wrath of the One who sits upon the throne of the universe. (See Revelation 6:15–17.) You will wish to run from the presence of glory into eternal darkness if only you could escape the presence of Him whom you have so grievously wronged. On and on you will wish to flee from the outraged Son of God.

One night God gave me a vision of the glory of Jesus Christ. I saw the appalling nature of sin against Him, this infinitely glorious One. You may not have had such a vision, and you do not need to have it. You know what God's testimony regarding Jesus is. That testimony is in His Word. In that testimony, you will find that the most grievous wrongs against man—theft, adultery, murder—are as nothing. For this reason our text says, *"He who believes in Him is not condemned; but he who does not believe is condemned already, because he has not believed in the name of the only begotten Son of God."*

Unbelief in Jesus Christ is an appalling sin because faith is the supreme thing He is entitled to receive. Jesus is worthy of many things. He is worthy of our admiration, our attention, our obedience, our service, and our love—all these things are His due. Not to give Him these things is to rob Him of what is rightly His.

Above all else, Jesus Christ is worthy of faith. Man's confidence belongs in Jesus Christ. He is infinitely worthy of the surrender of our intellects, our feelings, and our wills. It is right for you to go to Him and say, "Lord Jesus, infinite Son of God, I surrender to You my faith, the confidence of my heart, and my will." If you refuse to do that, you have robbed Jesus Christ. You have robbed this glorious, divine Person of His first and greatest right, robbed a divine Person of His supreme due. So it is written in our text, *"He who believes in Him is not condemned; but he who does not believe is condemned already, because he has not believed in the name of the only begotten Son of God."*

Unbelief in Jesus Christ is an appalling sin because He is the incarnation of all the infinite moral perfections of God's own being. *"God is light and in Him is no darkness at all"* (1 John 1:5). This infinite, absolute light and this infinite holiness, love, and truth are incarnate in Jesus Christ. The refusal to accept Him is the refusal of light and the choice of darkness. The one who rejects Him loves darkness rather than light. Nothing more clearly reveals a man's heart than what he chooses and what he rejects. A man who chooses dirty books, indecent pictures, and worldly friends is a foul man despite what he pretends to be. A man who rejects the good, the pure, and the true is bad, impure, and false. To reject Christ is to reject the infinite light of God. It reveals a corrupt heart that loves darkness rather than light.

Unbelief in Jesus Christ is an appalling sin because it is trampling underfoot the infinite love and mercy of God. Jesus Christ is the supreme expression of God's love and mercy to sinners. The Bible tells us: *"For God so loved the world that He gave His only begotten Son, that whoever believes in Him should not perish but have everlasting life"* (John 3:16).

Although we have all broken God's holy laws and brought the wrath of the Holy One upon ourselves, God still loves us. Instead of banishing us forever from His presence into the darkness where there is only agony and despair, He provided salvation for us at infinite cost to Himself. His saving love had no limit, and it stopped at no sacrifice. He gave His best—His only begotten Son—to redeem us. All that we need to do to be saved is to believe in God's Son and put our trust in the pardoning mercy and love of God.

But instead of believing and obtaining eternal life, what are you doing? You are not believing; you are rejecting the love and its provision. You are despising and trampling underfoot the salvation that God purchased with the blood of His Son and offered to you. Unbelief in Jesus Christ scorns and insults infinite pardoning love. Men and women, young and old, who do not place the faith of their whole beings in Jesus Christ and receive Him as their Lord and Savior are guilty of scorning and insulting the infinite, pardoning love of God.

Some even go beyond that. They try to make themselves believe that Jesus is not the Son of God and that there is no need for an atonement. They laugh at the sacrifice the loving Father has made in order that His guilty, hell-deserving subjects might be saved. One sometimes wonders why the love of God does not turn to blazing wrath and why God does not blast the world of Christ-rejecting men with the breath of His mouth.

There are other reasons why unbelief in Jesus Christ is an appalling sin, but these four significant reasons are enough:

1. Because of the infinite dignity of His person.

2. Because faith is rightly His, and withholding it robs a divine Person of His supreme due.

3. Because Jesus Christ is the incarnation of all the infinite moral perfection of God's own being.

4. Because it tramples underfoot the infinite love and mercy of God.

Unbelief in Jesus Christ is an appalling sin. Theft is a gross sin, adultery is worse, and murder is shocking. But all these are nothing compared to the violation of the dignity and majesty of Jesus Christ, the only begotten Son of God, by our unbelief. How God must abhor the sin of unbelief! How all holy men and women must despise the sin of unbelief!

Not only the agnostic and the skeptic are guilty of this sin, but also everyone who holds back from the wholehearted surrender of his mind, affections, and will. All who fail to gladly welcome Jesus as Savior and Lord are guilty of this appalling sin. Do you cry out as the three thousand at Pentecost did, *"What shall we do?"* (Acts 2:37). Soften your hearts of stone; publicly confess your awful sin, and forsake it forever. Don't rest another day under such awful guilt.

We see why unbelief leads to eternal doom. No matter how many good things a person may do, he must forever perish if he refuses to believe in Jesus Christ. Give up your unbelief in Jesus Christ and receive Him now.

Chapter 4

The Reality of Hell

◆

If your right eye causes you to sin, pluck it out and cast it from
you; for it is more profitable for you that one of your members
perish, than for your whole body to be cast into hell.
—Matthew 5:29

If I were able to choose my own subject to write about, I certainly would never choose hell. It is an awful subject, but a minister of God has no right to choose his own subjects. He must go to God for them and faithfully teach what God has commanded.

I wish that I could believe that there was no hell. That is, I wish that I could believe that all men would repent and accept Christ, and that hell would therefore be unnecessary. Of course, if men persist in sin and persist in the rejection of Christ, it is right that there should be a hell.

If men choose sin, it is for the good of the universe and the glory of God that there is a hell to confine them in. But I wish with all my heart that all men would repent and render hell unnecessary. But I cannot believe it if it is not true. I would rather believe unpleasant truth than to believe pleasant error. As awful as the thought is, I have been driven to the conclusion that there is a hell.

Once, I honestly believed and taught that all men, and even the Devil, would ultimately come to repentance, and that hell would one day cease to be. But I could not honestly reconcile this position with the teaching of Christ and the apostles. I finally decided that I must either give up my Bible or give up my eternal hope.

I could not give up the Bible. I had become thoroughly convinced that the Bible, beyond a doubt, was the Word of God. I could not twist and distort the Scriptures to make them agree with what I wanted to believe. As an honest man, there was only one thing left for me to do: give up my opinion that all men would ultimately come to repentance and be saved.

The Painful Truth

I know that if a man stands squarely on the teaching of Christ and the apostles and declares it without fear, he will be called narrow, harsh, and cruel. But I have no desire to be any broader than Jesus Christ was. Is it cruel to tell men the truth? The kindest thing that one can do is to declare the whole counsel of God (Acts 20:27) and show men the full measure of their danger.

Suppose I was walking down railroad tracts knowing that far behind me there was a train coming loaded with happy travelers. I come to a place where I had supposed that there was a bridge across the chasm. But to my horror, I find that the bridge is out. I say to myself, "I must go back at once, as far as possible up the tracks and stop that oncoming train."

My awful warning that the bridge is out and that the passengers are in peril of a frightful disaster spoils the merriment of the evening. Would that be cruel? Would it not be the kindest thing that I could do?

Suppose when I found the bridge out, I had said, "These people are so happy. I cannot bear to disturb their lightheartedness and pleasure. That would be too cruel. I will sit down here and wait until the train comes." Then I sit down while the train comes rushing on and leaps unwarned into that awful abyss. Soon I would hear the despairing shrieks and groans of the wounded and mangled as they crawl out from among the bodies of the dead. Would that be kind? Would it not be the cruelest thing that I could do? If I acted that way, I would be arrested for manslaughter.

I have been down the tracks of life. I thought that there was a bridge across the chasm, but I have found that the bridge is out. Many of you who are now full of laughter are rushing on unaware of the awful fate that awaits you. I have come back up the track to warn you. I may destroy your present merriment, but by God's grace, I will save you from the awful doom. Is that cruel?

I would much rather be called cruel for being kind than be called kind for being cruel. The cruelest man on earth is the man who believes the stern things we are told in the Word of God about the future penalties of sin but avoids declaring them because they are unpopular.

The Danger of Man's Philosophies

I will not give you my own speculations about the future destiny of those who refuse to repent. Man's speculations on such a subject are absolutely worthless. God knows; we don't. But God has told us much of what He knows about it. Let us listen to Him. One ounce of God's revelation about the future is worth a hundred tons of man's speculation. What difference does it make what you or I think? The question is this: What does God say? His Word says, *"If your right eye causes you to sin, pluck it out and cast it from you; for it is more profitable for you that one of your members perish, than for your whole body to be cast into hell."*

It is absolutely certain that there is a hell. People will tell you that all scholarly ministers and clergymen have given up their belief in hell. This simply is not so. This kind of argument is a favorite with those who know that they have a weak case. They try to bolster it with strong assertions.

It is true that some scholarly ministers have given up belief in hell, but they never gave it up for reasons of Greek or New Testament scholarship. They give it up for purely sentimental and speculative reasons. If a person goes to the New Testament to find out the truth and not to see how he can twist it into conformity with his speculations, he will find the reality of hell in the New Testament.

But suppose that every scholarly minister had given up belief in hell. It would not prove anything. Everybody who is familiar with the history of the world and the history of the church knows that time and time again some scholars have given up belief in doctrines that in the final outcome proved to be true.

There were no scholars in Noah's day who believed there would be a flood. But the flood came just the same. No scholars in Lot's day believed that God would destroy Sodom and Gomorrah, but He did. Jeremiah and one friend were the only leading men in all of Jerusalem who believed what Jeremiah taught about the coming destruction of Jerusalem under Nebuchadnezzar. But history outside the Bible, as well as history in the Bible, tells us that it came true to the very letter.

Every leading school of theological thought in the days of Jesus Christ—the Pharisees, the Sadducees, the Herodians, and the Essenes—every one of the four scoffed at Jesus Christ's prediction about the coming judgment of God upon Jerusalem. But secular history tells us that, in spite of the dissent of all the scholars, it came true just as Jesus predicted.

Nearly every leading scholar in the days of Luther and Huss had given up faith in the doctrine of justification by faith. Luther and his colleagues had to establish a new university to stand for the truth of God. But today we know that Martin Luther was right, and every university of Germany, France, England, and Scotland was wrong. So even if it every scholarly preacher on earth had given up belief in the doctrine of hell, it would not prove anything.

What the Bible Says

Hell is certain. Why? First of all, because Jesus Christ said so, the apostles said so, and God says so. Jesus Christ said, *"Then He will also say to those on the left hand, 'Depart from Me, you cursed, into the everlasting fire prepared for the devil and his angels'"* (Matt. 25:41). Paul wrote:

> *The Lord Jesus is revealed from heaven with His mighty angels, in flaming fire taking vengeance on those who do not know God, and on those who do not obey the gospel of our Lord Jesus Christ. These shall be punished with everlasting destruction from the presence of the Lord and from the glory of His power.* (2 Thess. 1:7–9)

John recorded in Revelation 20:15, *"And anyone not found written in the Book of Life was cast into the lake of fire."* Peter
wrote:

> *God did not spare the angels who sinned, but cast them
> down to hell and delivered them into chains of darkness, to
> be reserved for judgment;...The Lord knows how to deliver
> the godly out of temptations and to reserve the unjust un-
> der punishment for the day of judgment.*   (2 Pet. 2:4, 9)

And in Jude, we read:

> *Behold, the Lord comes with ten thousands of His saints,
> to execute judgment on all, to convict all who are ungodly
> among them of all their ungodly deeds which they have
> committed in an ungodly way, and of all the harsh things
> which ungodly sinners have spoken against Him.*
> (Jude 14–15)

After Jesus had died and come up again from the abode of
the dead, He ascended to the right hand of His Father. He said:

> *But the cowardly, unbelieving, abominable, murderers,
> sexually immoral, sorcerers, idolaters, and all liars shall
> have their part in the lake which burns with fire and brim-
> stone, which is the second death.*   (Rev. 21:8)

Hell is certain because Jesus Christ and the apostles said it
is and because God says it is through them. The only thing
against it is the speculation of theologians and dreams of poets.
The words of Christ have stood the test of the centuries and always prove true in the final outcome. When I have Christ on one
side and speculative theologians on the other, it doesn't take me
long to decide which to believe.

Experience, observation, and common sense prove that
there is a hell. One of the most certain acts of every man's experience is this: where there is sin, there must be suffering. We all
know that. The longer a man continues in sin, the deeper he
sinks into ruin, shame, agony, and despair. There are hundreds

and thousands of men and women in the world living in a very real hell, and the hell is getting worse every day. You may not know how to reconcile what these men and women suffer with the doctrine that God is love. But no intelligent man gives up facts because he cannot explain the philosophy behind them.

Now, if this process keeps going on, sinking ever deeper into ruin, shame, and despair, when the time of possible repentance has passed, what is left but an everlasting hell? The only thing against it are the dreams of poets and the speculations of would-be philosophers. But the speculations of philosophers have proven to be misleading from the dawn of history. When we have the sure teaching of the Word of God, the case is settled.

There is a hell. It is more certain that there is a hell than that you will wake again tomorrow morning. You probably will; you may not. But it is absolutely certain that there is a hell. The next time you buy a book, no matter how skillfully it is written, and that author wants to prove to you that there is no hell, you will have paid to be made a fool of. There is a hell.

Chapter 5

A Picture of Hell

◆

Fear Him who is able to destroy both soul and body in hell.
—Matthew 10:28

We know that hell is a real place, but what is it like? What kind of people are there? Will they really remain in hell forever? Hell is a place of extreme bodily suffering. This is plain from the teaching of the New Testament. The words commonly used to express the doom of unrepenting sinners are *death* and *destruction*.

What do death and destruction mean? God has carefully defined His terms. In Revelation 17:8, we are told that the beast will go into *"perdition."* The word translated *perdition* is translated elsewhere *destruction*.

In Revelation 19:20, you will read that the beast and the false prophet were cast into a *"lake of fire burning with brimstone."* One thousand years after the beast and the false prophet have been thrown into the lake of fire, the Devil also is cast in. They will be *"tormented day and night forever and ever"* (Rev. 20:10). By God's definition, *perdition* or *destruction* is a place in a lake of torment forever.

Now let us took at God's definition of death. *"The cowardly, unbelieving, abominable, murderers, sexually immoral, sorcerers, idolaters, and all liars shall have their part in the lake which burns with fire and brimstone, which is the second death"* (Rev. 21:8). God's definition of *death* is a portion in the *"lake of fire burning with brimstone"* (Rev. 19:20), the same as His definition of *perdition*.

"Oh," you may respond, "that is all highly figurative." Remember God's descriptions stand for facts. When some people come to something unwelcome in the Bible, they will say it is figurative and imagine that they have done away with it. You cannot do away with God's Word by calling it figurative. God is no liar, and God never overstates the facts. Hell means at least this much: bodily suffering of the most intense kind.

Furthermore, in the next life, we do not exist as disembodied spirits. This theory is man's philosophy and not New Testament teaching. According to the Bible, in the world to come, the spirit has a radically different body, but it is the perfect counterpart of the spirit that inhabits it and partakes in punishment or reward.

Even in this life, inward spiritual sin often causes outward bodily pain. Many are suffering the most severe pain because of inward sin. Hell is the place of punishment for the incurables of the universe, where people exist in awful and perpetual pain.

Painful Memories

But physical pain is the least significant feature of hell. Hell is a place of memory and remorse. In the picture Christ gave us of the rich man in hell, Abraham said to the rich man, *"Remember"* (Luke 16:25). The rich man brought little that he had on earth with him, but he had taken one thing—his memory.

If you choose to go on in sin and spend eternity in hell, you won't take much with you that you own, but you will take your memory. Men will remember the women whose lives they have ruined, and women will remember the time squandered in frivolity, fashion, and foolishness, when they might have been living for God. They will remember the Christ they rejected and the opportunities for salvation they despised.

There is no torment like the torment of an accusing memory. I have seen strong men weeping like children. What was the matter? Memory. One of the strongest, most intelligent men I ever knew threw himself on the floor of my office and sobbed hysterically. What was the matter? Memory. I have had men and women hurry to me at the close of a service with pale faces and haunted eyes, begging for a private conversation. What was the matter? Memory.

You will take your memory with you. The memory and the conscience that are not set at peace in this life by the atoning blood of Christ and the pardoning grace of God never will be. Hell is the place where men remember and suffer.

When D. L. Moody was a boy, one day he was hoeing corn along with an elderly man. Suddenly the man stopped hoeing and began striking a stone with his hoe. Young Moody stared at him. Tears were rolling down the man's cheeks, and he said, "Dwight, when I was a lad like you, I left home to make a living for myself. As I came out of the front gate, my mother handed me a Bible and said, 'My boy, *"seek first the kingdom of God and His righteousness, and all these things shall be added to you"'"* (Matt. 6:33). He took a deep breath and continued, "I went to the next town. I went to church on Sunday, and the minister got up to preach. He announced his text: Matthew 6:33. He looked right down at me pointed his finger at me and said, 'Young man, *"seek first the kingdom of God and His righteousness, and all these things shall be added to you."'* I went out of the church and had an awful struggle! It seemed as if the minister was talking to me. I decided, 'No; I will get settled in life first and then I will become a Christian.' I found no work in that town, but I went to another town and found a job. I went to church, as was my custom, Sunday after Sunday. After a few Sundays, the minister stood up in the pulpit and announced his text: Matthew 6:33. '*Seek first the kingdom of God and His righteousness, and all these things shall be added to you.'*"

The old man began to tremble violently. "Dwight, that minister seemed to look right at me and point his finger right at me. I got up and went out of the church. I went to the cemetery behind the church and sat down on a tombstone. I had an awful fight, but at last I said, 'No, I will not become a Christian until I get settled in life.'" He paused for a moment and then said, "Dwight, from that day to this the Spirit of God has left me, and I have never had the slightest inclination to be a Christian."

Mr. Moody said, "I did not understand it then. I was not a Christian myself. I went to Boston and was converted. Then I understood. I wrote to my mother to ask her what had become of the old man. She answered, "Dwight, he has gone insane, and they have taken him to the Brattleboro Insane Asylum."

I went to Brattleboro and called on him there. As I went into his cell, he glared at me, pointed his finger at me, and said, "Young man, *'seek first the kingdom of God and His righteousness.'"*

I could do nothing with him. I went back to Boston. After some time, I came home again. I asked my mother where he was now. "Oh!" she said, "he is home, but he is a helpless imbecile."

I went up to his house. There he sat in a rocking chair, a white-haired man. As I went into the room, he pointed his finger at me and said, "Young man, *'seek first the kingdom of God and His righteousness.'"* He had gone crazy with memory. Hell is the madhouse of the universe, where men and women remember.

Desires Forever Denied

Hell is a place of insatiable and tormenting desire. Remember what Jesus told us of the rich man in hell. The rich man said, *"Send Lazarus that he may dip the tip of his finger in water and cool my tongue; for I am tormented in this flame"* (Luke 16:24).

You will carry into the next world the desires that you build up here. Hell is the place where desires and passions exist in their highest potency, and where there is nothing to gratify them. Men and women who are living in sin and worldliness are developing passions and desires for which there is no gratification in hell. Happy are those people who set their affections on things above. Those who cultivate power, passions, and desires for which there is no gratification in the next world will spend eternity in severe torment.

Hell is a place of shame. Oh, the awful, heartbreaking agony of shame! It can cause depression, illness, and even death. A bank cashier was in a hurry to get rich, so he appropriated the funds of the bank and invested them, intending to pay them back. But his investment failed. For a long time, he managed to conceal his theft from the bank examiner. One day the embezzlement was discovered. The cashier had to acknowledge his crime. He was arrested, tried, and sent to prison.

He had a beautiful wife and a lovely child, a sweet little girl. Some time after his arrest and imprisonment, the little child came home sobbing. "Oh," she said, "Mother, I can never go back to that school again. Send for my books."

Thinking it was some childish whim, the mother said, "Of course you will go back."

"No," the child insisted, "I can never go back. Send for my books."

"Darling, what is the matter?"

She said, "Another little girl said to me today, 'Your father is a thief.'"

Oh, the cruel stab! The mother saw that her child could not go back to school. The wound was fatal. That fair blossom began to fade. A physician was called, but her illness surpassed all the capacities of his skill. The child grew weaker every day until they laid her on her bed. The physician said, "Madam, I am powerless in this case. The child's heart has given way with the agony of the wound. Your child will probably die."

The mother went in and said to her dying child, "Darling, is there anything you would like to have me do for you?"

"Oh yes, Mother, send for Father. Let him come home and lay his head down on the pillow beside mine as he used to do."

But the father was behind iron bars. They spoke to the governor, and he said, "I have no power in the matter." They spoke to the warden of the prison. He said, "I have no power in the matter."

But hearts were touched by the girl's condition. The judge and the governor made an arrangement so that the father was permitted to come home under a deputy-warden. He reached his home late at night and entered his house. The physician was waiting. He said, "I think you had better go in tonight, for I am afraid your child will not live until morning."

The father went to the door and opened it. The child looked up quickly. "Oh," she said, "I knew it was you, Father. I knew you would come. Come and lay your head beside mine on the pillow just as you used to do."

The strong man went and laid his head on the pillow. The child lovingly patted his cheek and died. She was killed by shame. Hell is the place of shame, where everybody is dishonored.

No Parties in Hell

Hell is a place of vile companionships. The society of hell is described in Revelation 21:8: *"The cowardly, unbelieving, abominable, murderers, sexually immoral, sorcerers, idolaters, and all liars shall have their part in the lake which burns with fire and brimstone, which is the second death."* Some may say, "Many who are brilliant and gifted are going there." It may be, but how long will it take the most gifted man or woman to sink in such a world as that? I can take you to skid row and show you men who were once physicians, lawyers, congressmen, college professors, leading businessmen, and even ministers of the Gospel. But now they are living with thugs, prostitutes, and everything that is vile and bad. How did they get there? They began to sink.

Many years ago, my father was one of the delegates to the Presidential convention in Chicago. We then lived in New York. He took us children to a quiet country town in Michigan and went on to the convention. On the way home, we got on a Hudson River ferry, filled with the leading Democratic politicians. Many gifted orators stood up and spoke to the crowd, but there was one man who eclipsed everyone else. Everybody was spellbound by the power of his eloquence.

Years passed. One day I saw someone lying on our front lawn, covered with vomit, sleeping heavily, snoring like an overfed hog. When I went up to him, I found it was the same man whose gift of speaking had carried away everyone on that ferry. He died in a psychiatric ward from alcoholism.

During the World's Fair, there was a women's commission appointed to receive the dignitaries and the members of the royalty of other countries. A woman stood near the chairman of the commission, dazzling people by her beauty and wit.

Several years later, some friends of mine were in the slums of Chicago hunting for forlorn people that they might help. They found a poor creature with nails grown like claws, with long, tangled hair twisted full of filth, a face that had not been washed for weeks, clad in a single filthy garment—a wreck! When they began to talk with her, they found it was that woman who had belonged to the women's commission during the World's Fair. She had destroyed herself with cocaine.

A Place without Hope

Finally, hell is a world without hope. There are those who tell you that the Greek word *aionios,* translated "everlasting," does not always means everlasting. The meaning must be determined by the context. In Matthew 25:46, we read: *"And these will go away into everlasting punishment, but the righteous into eternal life."* If it means everlasting in one part of the verse, it must mean the same in the other part of the verse. In other words, those who are cast into hell because of their sins will receive eternal or everlasting punishment while those who are redeemed will receive eternal or everlasting reward. Scriptures must be carefully interpreted in their context with an honest attempt to discover their true meaning, and not to make them fit a theory.

There is another expression used often in the Bible: "To the ages of the ages." It is used twelve times in one book—eight times describing the existence of God and the duration of His reign, once referring to the duration of the blessedness of the righteous, and in every remaining instance referring to the punishment of the beast, the false prophet, and the unrepentant. It is the strongest known expression for absolute endlessness.

I have searched my Bible for one ray of hope for those who die without repentance. I have failed to find one after years of searching. The New Testament does not contain one ray of hope for men and women who die without Christ. "Forever and ever" is the endless wail of that restless sea of fire. Hell is a place of bodily anguish, a place of agony of conscience, a place of insatiable torment and desire, a place of evil companionship, a place of shame, and a place without hope.

Escape from Hell

There is only one way to escape hell—accept Jesus Christ as your personal Savior, surrender to Him as your Lord and Master, confess Him openly before the world, and live obediently according to His Word. The Bible is perfectly plain about this. Examine the following verses:

There is no other name under heaven given among men by which we must be saved. (Acts 4:12)

He who believes in the Son has everlasting life; and he who does not believe the Son shall not see life, but the wrath of God abides on him. (John 3:36)

Therefore whoever confesses Me before men, him will I also confess before My Father who is in heaven. But whoever denies Me before men, him I will also deny before My Father who is in heaven. (Matt. 10:32–33)

The Lord Jesus is revealed from heaven with His mighty angels, in flaming fire taking vengeance on those who do not know God, and on those who do not obey the gospel of our Lord Jesus Christ. These shall be punished with ever-lasting destruction from the presence of the Lord and from the glory of His power. (2 Thess. 1:7–9)

The question is this: Will you accept Christ now? Hell is too awful to risk it for a year, a month, or even a day. Your eternal destiny may be settled right now.

I know what the Devil is whispering to you. He is saying, "Don't be a coward; don't be frightened into repentance." Is it cowardice to be moved by rational fear? Is it heroism to rush into unnecessary danger? Suppose I looked up and saw a building on fire. A man is sitting near an upper window, reading a book carelessly. I see his peril, and I call out, "Flee for your life! The house is on fire!" Then suppose that man leans out of the window and shouts back, "I am no coward. You can't frighten me." Would he be a hero or a fool?

One night I went to see my parents at home. As I stepped off the train, I stepped on to another track. Unknown to me, an express train was coming down that other track. A man saw my peril and cried, "Mr. Torrey, there is a train coming! Get off the track!" I did not shout back, "I am no coward. You can't scare me." I was not such a fool. I got off the track, or I would not be telling you the story.

If you are on the track toward hell, listen to the thunder and rumble of the wrath of God as it comes hurrying on. I beg you to get off the track! Receive Christ now!

Chapter 6

Obstacles on the Road to Hell

◆

*The Lord is not...willing that any should perish but that all
should come to repentance.*
—2 Peter 3:9

f any man or woman is lost and goes to hell, it won't be God's
fault. If God had His way, every man and woman in the world
would be saved at once. God is doing everything in His power
to bring you to repentance.

Of course, He cannot save you if you will not repent. You
can have salvation if you want to be saved from sin, but sin and
salvation can never go together. There are people who talk
about a scheme of salvation where man can continue in sin and
yet be saved. It is impossible. Sin is damnation, and if a man will
go on everlastingly in sin, he will be everlastingly lost.

But God is doing everything in His power to turn you away
from the path of sin and destruction toward the path of righteousness and everlasting life. God has filled the path of sin, which
leads to hell, with obstacles. He has made it hard and bitter.

A great many people are saying today, "The Christian life is
so hard." It is not. Jesus said, *"For My yoke is easy and My burden is light"* (Matt. 11:30). God tells us in His Word, *"The way
of the unfaithful is hard"* (Prov. 13:15). God has filled it full of
obstacles, and you cannot go on in it without surmounting one
obstacle after another.

The Power in God's Word

The first obstacle is the Bible. You cannot get very far in
the path of sin without finding the Bible in your way. The Bible

is one of the greatest hindrances to sin in the world. It contains warnings, invitations, and descriptions of the character and consequences of sin. It gives us representations of righteousness, its beauty and its reward. With its pictures of God and God's love, the Bible always stands as a great hindrance to sin. This is the reason many people hate the Bible. They are determined to sin, and the Bible makes them uneasy in sin, so they hate the Book.

People sometimes say to me, "I object to the Bible because of its immoral stories." But when I look into their lives, I find that their lives are immoral. The Bible paints sin in its true colors with stories that make sin hideous. Their objections are not to the stories but to the uneasiness the Bible causes them in their sinful ways.

People have often been turned back from the path of sin by a single verse in the Bible. Hundreds have been turned from the path of sin by Romans 6:23: *"For the wages of sin is death, but the gift of God is eternal life in Jesus Christ our Lord."* Thousands have been turned away from sin by Amos 4:12: *"Prepare to meet your God."* Tens of thousands have been turned from the path of sin by John 3:16, *"For God so loved the world that He gave His only begotten Son, that whoever believes in Him should not perish but have everlasting life."* John 6:37 contains the promise, *"The one who comes to Me I will by no means cast out."*

Several years ago a man who had not been in a house of worship for fifteen years came into our church in Chicago. He was a strong agnostic and proud of it. I don't know why he came in that night. I suppose he saw the crowd coming and was curious to know what was going on. He sat down, and I began to preach. In my sermon, I quoted John 6:37, *"The one who comes to Me I will by no means cast out."* It went like an arrow into that man's heart.

When the meeting was over, he got up and went out and tried to forget that verse, but could not. He went to bed but could not sleep. *"The one who comes to Me I will by no means cast out"* kept ringing in his mind. The next day it haunted him at work; for days and weeks, that verse troubled him, but he refused to come to Christ. He came back to the street where our church stands, walked up and down the sidewalk, stamped his foot, and cursed the text, but he could not get rid of it.

Six weeks had passed when he came into our prayer meeting. He stood up and said, "I was here six weeks ago and heard your minister preach. I heard the text, John 6:37, and I have tried to forget it, but it has haunted me night and day. I have walked up and down the sidewalk in front of your church and cursed the text, but I can't get rid of it. Pray for me." We did, and he was saved. One text from God's Word turned him from the path of sin and ruin.

The Miracle of a Mother's Prayers

The second obstacle that God has put in the path of sin is a mother's holy influence and teaching. Hundreds of men and women who are not yet Christians have tried to be unbelievers and plunge into sin. But their mother's holy influence and Christian teaching won't let them go. Sometimes it is years later that a mother's teaching does its work.

A young fellow went west to Colorado to work in the mines. He worked during the day and gambled at night, but he spent more money gambling than he made in the mines. One night he was at the gambling table. He lost his last cent. Then he used some of his employer's money and lost that. He felt he was ruined. He rose from the table, went up into the mountains, drew his revolver, and held it to his temple. He was about to pull the trigger when the words that his mother had spoken to him years before came to his mind: "My son, if you are ever in trouble, think of God." And there, standing in the moonlight, with a revolver pressed against his temple, and his finger on the trigger, he remembered what his mother had said and dropped on his knees. He cried to God and was saved.

In the desperate hardness of our hearts, we often trample our mothers' teachings underfoot, but we find it very hard to get over their prayers. Often at the last moment, people are saved because of their mothers' prayers.

In my church in Chicago, a man used to stand outside with a container of beer. As the people came out of the meeting, he offered them a drink. He was hard, desperate, and wicked, but he had a praying mother in Scotland.

One night after he went home from the meeting where he had caused trouble, he was awakened and saved without getting out of bed. He went back to Scotland to see his mother. He had a brother who was a sailor in the China seas, and the mother and the saved son knelt down and prayed for the wandering boy. That same night while they prayed, the Spirit of God came upon that sailor, and he was saved. He later became a missionary to India—a man saved by a mother's prayers.

When I was rushing headlong in the path of sin and ruin, my mother's prayers arose, and I could not get over them. I used to think that nobody had anything to do with my salvation. I had gone to bed one night with no more thought of becoming a Christian than I had of jumping over the moon. In the middle of the night, I climbed out of bed and decided to end my miserable life, but something came upon me. I dropped on my knees. In five minutes from the time I got out of bed to take my life, I had surrendered to God.

I thought no one had anything to do with it. But I found out later that my mother was four hundred twenty-seven miles away praying. Although I had gotten over sermons, arguments, churches, and everything else, I could not get over my mother's prayers. Do you know why some people are not in hell right now? Their mothers' prayers have kept them out of hell.

Faithful Preaching and Teaching

Another obstacle on the road to hell is the sermons we hear. Many thousands of people are turned from sin to God by sermons that they hear or read. Sometimes the sermon does its work years later.

In my first pastorate, I prepared a sermon on the parable of the ten virgins. There was one member of my congregation who was very much on my heart. I prayed she might be saved by that sermon. I went and preached; but when I gave the invitation, she never made a sign. I went home and did not know what to make of it. I said, "I prayed for her conversion by that sermon and fully expected her conversion, but she is not converted."

Years later, when I had gone to another pastorate, I heard that this woman was converted. I revisited the place, called on her, and said, "I am very glad to hear you have been converted."

She said, "Would you like to know how I was converted?" I said I would. "Do you remember preaching a sermon years ago on the ten virgins? I could not get your words out of my mind. I felt I must accept Christ that night, but I would not. That sermon followed me, and I was converted years later by it."

Another obstacle is a Sunday school teacher's influence and teaching. A faithful Sunday school teacher is one of God's best instruments on earth for the salvation of the perishing. In Mr. Moody's first Sunday school in Chicago, he had a class of very unruly girls. Nobody could manage them. Finally, he found a young man who could keep the class under control. One day this young man came to Mr. Moody and said, "Mr. Moody," as he suddenly burst into tears.

Mr. Moody said, "What is the matter?"

"The doctor says I have tuberculosis and that I must go to California at once or die." He sobbed as if his heart would break.

Mr. Moody tried to comfort him and said, "Suppose that is true, you have no reason to feel so bad. You are a Christian."

"It is not that, Mr. Moody; I am perfectly willing to die, but I have had this Sunday school class all these years and not one of them is saved. I am going off to leave them, every one unsaved." He sobbed like a child.

Mr. Moody said, "Wait, I will get a carriage, and we will drive around and visit them. One by one you can lead them to Christ."

He took the sickly teacher in the carriage, and they drove around to the homes of the girls. He talked to them about Christ until he was so tired that he had to be taken home. The next day they went out again, and they went out every day until every one of these women but one was saved. They met for a prayer meeting before he went away. One after another led in prayer, and at last the one unsaved girl prayed too and accepted Christ.

He left by the early train the next morning, and Mr. Moody went to see him off. As they were waiting, one by one the girls came to say goodbye. He spoke a few words of farewell to them. As the train pulled out of the station, he stood on the back platform of the car with his finger pointing heavenward, telling his Sunday school class to meet him in heaven.

Kindness Is Never Wasted

Sometimes God throws a kind word or act as an obstacle to sin. A lady, standing at a window looking out on a New York street, saw a drunkard. He had been the mayor of a Southern city, but now he was a penniless drunkard on the streets of New York. He had made up his mind to commit suicide. He started for the river, but then he thought, "I will go into a bar and have one more drink. I have spent a lot of money in that bar, and I can certainly get one drink without paying for it."

He went in, asked for a drink, and told the man he had no money. The man came around from behind the bar and threw him out into the street. The woman who was looking out of the window saw the poor man picking himself up out of the gutter. She hurried over to him, wiped the mud off his face with her handkerchief, and said, "Come over to our meeting. It is bright and warm, and you will be welcome." He followed her over and sat on the bench. The meeting began, and one after another gave his testimony. After the meeting, that lady came and spoke to him about his soul. His heart was touched, and he was saved.

He got a job, and then a better one, and finally was made manager of one of the largest publishing houses in New York City. One day he came to the woman who had found him in the gutter and said, "I have some friends at a hotel who I want you to meet." She went to the hotel, and he introduced her to a fine-looking, middle-aged woman and a lovely young lady. He said, "This is my wife and daughter." They were beautiful, refined, cultured ladies whom he had left when he had gone down to the gates of hell. But a kind act and a word of invitation to Christ reached him and placed him on the path that leads to glory. Oh, let us go as missionaries of God's grace and block the path of sinful men and women with kind deeds and turn them to righteousness and to God!

The Voice of the Spirit

Another obstacle that God puts in the path of sin and ruin is the Holy Spirit. You and I have experienced the Holy Spirit's working, perhaps without realizing it. Perhaps we were right in the midst of a party, when a strange feeling came into our hearts. It was a feeling of unrest, dissatisfaction with the life we were living, or a longing for something better. The feeling would be accompanied by memories of home, church, mother, Bible, and God.

One night a man was at a gambling table. He was a wild, reckless spendthrift. Suddenly the voice of God's Spirit spoke to his heart. He thought he was about to die. He sprang up from the table, threw down his cards, and rushed to his room. There was someone in the room. He thought at first, "I won't pray while the maid is in the room." But he was so much in earnest that he did not care what anybody might think. He dropped down by his bed and called on God for Christ's sake to forgive his sins. The man was Brownlow North. He did a great work for God in Ireland and Scotland in the 1800s.

If you have ever been in a nightclub when there came into your heart a wretchedness, a sense of disgust, a longing for something better, a calling to a purer life, that was God's Spirit. If you have ever felt a stirring in your heart, you might have said to yourself, "I wonder if I had better become a Christian now?" God is sending His Spirit to block the road to hell. Listen to God's Spirit. Yield and accept Christ.

Facing the Cross

God has put one other obstacle in the road as blockade in the path to hell: the cross of Christ. No man can get very far down the path of sin and ruin before he sees the cross looming before him. On that cross hangs a Man, the Son of Man, the Son of God. You see Him hanging with nails in His hands and feet, and a voice says, "It was for you. I bore this for you. I died for you." In the pathway of every man and woman stands the cross with Christ upon it. If you choose to continue in sin, you will have to step over the cross and over the crucified form of the Son of God.

I heard of a godly old man who had a worthless son. That son was more anxious to make money than he was for honor or anything else. He decided to go into the liquor business.

Anyone who is willing to make money out of selling alcoholic beverages will profit from the tears of brokenhearted wives and the groans and sighs of an alcoholic's sons and daughters. The abuse of liquor is sending thousands of people every year to premature graves. It causes more sorrow, more ruined homes, more wretchedness than perhaps anything else on earth. Every tavern owner, bartender, barmaid, and professed Christian who holds stocks in breweries or distilleries is a part of the crime.

Once I knew of a man who was going to open a tavern. His father was deeply grieved and tried to reason with his son. He said, "My boy, you bear an honorable name that has never been disgraced before. Don't disgrace it by putting it up over a bar." But the son was so determined to get rich that he would not listen to his father.

The day came to open the bar. The father was one of the first on hand. He stepped up to every man who approached the door and told him of the miseries that come from alcohol. One after another, they turned away. The son looked out of the window to see why he was getting no customers. He saw his father outside, turning his customers away. He came outside and said, "Father, go home. You are ruining my business."

He said, "I can't help it, my boy. I won't have my name dishonored by this business. If you are determined to go on with it, I will stand here and warn every man that comes to enter your door.

Finally, the son lost his temper. He struck his old father in the face. The father turned to him without any anger. He said, "My son, you can strike me if you will. You can kill me if you will, but no man will enter your bar unless he goes over my dead body."

No man or woman will ever enter hell unless they go over the dead body of Jesus Christ. No man or woman can refuse Christ and persist in sin without trampling underfoot the One who was crucified on the cross of Calvary for us.

God has piled the obstacles high in His patient love. Don't try to surmount them. Turn back. Turn away from the path of sin; turn toward the path of faith in Jesus Christ. Turn now!

Chapter 7

Catching a Glimpse of Heaven

———————◆———————

He waited for the city which has foundations,
whose builder and maker is God.
—Hebrews 11:10

For here we have no continuing city,
but we seek the one to come.
—Hebrews 13:14

Heaven was the city Abraham sought, the *"city which has foundations."* This is the *"continuing city"* that we are seeking instead of the fleeting and perishable cities and homes of earth. What sort of a place is this city? What sort of a place is heaven?

In answer to the question, I am not going to discuss the sort of a place I imagine heaven to be. I care very little about my speculations or any other man's speculations and fancies on this point. I am going to tell you something that is certain. I am going to tell you what God plainly teaches in His Word.

Many think we know nothing about heaven and that it is all guesswork. This is not so. God has revealed much about it. What He has revealed is very encouraging. It will awaken in every wise and true heart a desire to go there.

If we thought more about heaven, it would help us to bear our burdens here more bravely. We would want to live holier lives and be delivered from the power of greed and lust that often attacks us. Our lives would be filled with joy and sunshine.

Shallow philosophers tell us that our business is to live this present life and let the future take care of itself. You might as well tell the schoolboy that his business is to live today without considering his future. True thoughts of the life that is to come clothe the life that now is with new beauty and strength.

The Reality of Heaven

Jesus said, *"I go to prepare a place for you"* (John 14:2). Some will tell you that heaven is merely a state or condition. Doubtless it is more important to be in a heavenly state or condition than in a heavenly place. But heaven is a real place. We are not to be merely in a heavenly state of mind, but in a heavenly city as well, *"a city which has foundations,"* a *"continuing city."*

Christ has already entered into heaven to appear in the presence of God for us. (See Hebrews 9:24.) He has gone to prepare a place for us and is coming back to take us there. We will not be disembodied spirits in the world to come, but redeemed spirits, in redeemed bodies, in a redeemed universe.

Heaven is a place of incomparable beauty. This is obvious from the description we have in Revelation 21 and 22. The God of the Bible is a God of beauty. He made this world beautiful. Its beauty has been marred by sin. The weed, the thorn, and the brier spring up. The insect devours the roses, and the lilies fade. Decay and death bring loathsome sights and foul smells.

All of creation, together with fallen man, groans and travails in pain until now (Rom. 8:22). But enough is left of the original creation to show us how intensely God loves beauty. He has told us in His Word that the creation will be delivered from the bondage of corruption into the glorious liberty of the children of God. (See verses 21–23.)

There will be perfection of beauty in heaven. Perfection of form, color, and sound will be combined into a beauty that will be indescribable. All earthly comparisons fail. Every sense of perception in our present state is clouded by sin. But in our redemption bodies, every sense will be enlarged and exist in perfection.

Some of us have seen beautiful visions on earth. We have seen the mountains rearing their snowcapped heads through the clouds, the vista of rolling hills and verdant valleys, winding rivers and forests with their changing colors, lakes and oceans dancing and tossing and rolling in the moonlight, the heavens in the clear wintry night jeweled with countless stars. We have caught the fragrances that float through the summer night in parks and gardens. We have listened to the indescribable harmonies of piano and violin as they responded to the touch of the master's hand and the more matchless music of the human voice. But all these are nothing compared to the beauty of sight and sound and fragrance that will greet us in that fair city of eternity.

The Best Companions

But the beauty of heaven, as good and attractive as it is, will be its least important characteristic. Heaven will be a place of high and holy companionships. The best, wisest, and noblest people of all ages, such as Abraham, Isaac, and Jacob, will be there: *"And I say to you that many will come from east and west, and sit down with Abraham, Isaac, and Jacob in the kingdom of heaven"* (Matt. 8:11). Heaven is the home of Moses, Elijah, Daniel, Paul, John, Rutherford, and Brainerd. All the purest, noblest, most unselfish people the world has ever known are there because they have trusted in the atoning blood of Christ.

"For we know that if our earthly house, this tent, is destroyed, we have a building from God, a house not made with hands, eternal in the heavens" (2 Cor. 5:1). All the dear ones who believed in and loved the Lord Jesus will be there.

Many desire to get into the most exclusive social circles. That is all right if it is not merely the society of wealth, fashion, and foolishness that is so strangely called "the best society." But the most select group of this world will be nothing compared to the society of heaven. The joys we find in the companionship of noble, unselfish, thoughtful people here give only the faintest conception of the joys of heaven's companionships.

The angels are there. *"And the angel answered and said to him, 'I am Gabriel, who stands in the presence of God, and was sent to speak to you and bring you these glad tidings'"* (Luke 1:19). *"I say to you that likewise there will be more joy in heaven over one sinner who repents than over ninety-nine just persons*

638

who need no repentance....Likewise, I say to you, there is joy in the presence of the angels of God over one sinner who repents" (Luke 15:7, 10). We will enjoy the companionship of these lofty beings—Gabriel, Michael, and the whole angelic host.

God Himself is there, too. In a sense, He is everywhere, but heaven is the place of His unique presence and manifestation of Himself. Scripture says, *"Then hear from heaven Your dwelling place"* (2 Chron. 6:30); *"Your kingdom come. Your will be done on earth as it is in heaven"* (Matt. 6:10).

We will hold communion with Him. Jesus Christ is there. Stephen said, *"Look! I see the heavens opened and the Son of Man standing at the right hand of God!"* (Acts 7:56). *"Seeing then that we have a great High Priest who has passed through the heavens, Jesus the Son of God, let us hold fast our confession"* (Heb. 4:14). *"Now this is the main point of the things we are saying: We have such a High Priest, who is seated at the right hand of the throne of the Majesty in the heavens"* (Heb. 8:1).

To Paul, being with Jesus was one of the most attractive thoughts about heaven. He wrote, *"For I am hard pressed between the two, having a desire to depart and be with Christ, which is far better. Nevertheless to remain in the flesh is more needful for you"* (Phil. 1:23–24).

There will be no unpleasant or degrading companions in heaven. The Devil will not be there. The lewd, the vulgar, and the obscene will not be there. The greedy, the scheming, and the selfish will not be there. The liar, the slanderer, the backbiter, the meddler, and the gossip will not be there. The mean, the contemptible, and the hypocrite will not be there. The profane, the blasphemer, and the scoffer will not be there . No money, influence, or cunning will get them in. *"But there shall by no means enter it anything that defiles, or causes an abomination or a lie, but only those who are written in the Lamb's Book of Life"* (Rev. 21:27).

There are limitations to the joys of the dearest earthly companionships. It will not be so in heaven. We can perfectly open our hearts to one another there, as we often long to do here but are unable. *"For now we see in a mirror, dimly, but then face to face. Now I know in part, but then I shall know just as I also am known"* (1 Cor. 13:12).

Heaven will be a place of glad reunions. *"Then we who are alive and remain shall be caught up together with them in the clouds to meet the Lord in the air. And thus we shall always be with the Lord"* (1 Thess. 4:17). The bereaved wife will meet again the husband she has missed so long, and the son will see the mother whose departure left his life so desolate. What glad days those coming days will be when we meet again, never to part!

The Most Glorious Freedom

Heaven will be a place that is free from everything that curses or mars our lives here. The world we live in would be a happy place if there were no sin, sickness, pain, poverty, or death. But these things ruin the present world.

There will be none of these things in heaven. There will be no sin. Everyone will perfectly obey the will of God. There will be no poverty. Everyone will have all the inexhaustible wealth of God at his disposal. *"And if children, then heirs; heirs of God and joint heirs with Christ, if indeed we suffer with Him, that we may also be glorified together"* (Rom. 8:17).

There will be no grinding labor. When I see the men and women who rise at dawn and go forth to another day of back-breaking labor, I rejoice that there is a place where the weary can rest. *"There remains therefore a rest for the people of God"* (Heb. 4:9).

There will be no sickness or pain. *"And God will wipe away every tear from their eyes; there shall be no more death, nor sorrow, nor crying. There shall be no more pain, for the former things have passed away"* (Rev. 21:4). There will be no more aching limbs, no more throbbing temples, and no more darting pains. Weakness, sighs, groans, nights of tossing in sweltering rooms, and tears will become vague memories from a distant past. There will be no death in heaven.

Heaven will be a place of universal and perfect knowledge. On this earth, the wisest of us sees through a glass darkly, but there, we will see face-to-face. Here we know in part, but there we will know even as we are known. (See 1 Corinthians 13:12.) The wisest scientist or philosopher on earth knows very little. Sir Isaac Newton, the famous physicist, said to one who praised his wisdom, "I am as a child on the seashore picking up a pebble here and a shell there, but the great ocean of truth still lies before me."

In heaven, the most uneducated of us will have fathomed that great ocean of truth. We will have perfect knowledge of all things. The great perplexing problems of God and man, of time and eternity, will be solved. No doubts, questions, uncertainties, or errors will trouble us. Faith will be swallowed up in sight.

Heaven will be a place of universal love. *"Beloved, now we are children of God; and it has not yet been revealed what we shall be, but we know that when He is revealed, we shall be like Him, for we shall see Him as He is"* (1 John 3:2). We will be like our God, and He is love. *"He who does not love does not know God, for God is love"* (1 John 4:8).

What a place to live, where everyone loves each other with a perfect love! Happy is the home where love is triumphant. It may be a very plain place, but it is a happy place. *"Better is a dinner of herbs where love is, than a fatted calf with hatred"* (Prov. 15:17).

All is love in heaven. And the love there will not be like that of earth—hesitating, suspicious, selfish, now so cold and then so warm. It will be pure, unbounded, unfaltering, unchanging, and Christlike. What a world that will be! The universal brotherhood of which we read and talk so much and see so little will find its perfect realization there.

Heaven will be a place of praise:

After these things I looked, and behold, a great multitude which no one could number, of all nations, tribes, peoples, and tongues, standing before the throne and before the Lamb, clothed with white robes, with palm branches in their hands, and crying out with a loud voice, saying, "Salvation belongs to our God who sits on the throne, and to the Lamb!" All the angels stood around the throne and the elders and the four living creatures, and fell on their faces before the throne and worshiped God, saying:

"Amen! Blessing and glory and wisdom, thanksgiving and honor and power and might, be to our God forever and ever. Amen." (Rev. 7:9–12)

Men will have open eyes to see God as He is. Souls will burst forth with praise. Suppose we were to catch one glimpse of God as He is, one view of Jesus Christ as He is. A burst of song like the world has never heard would be our response.

Melody will ring out all day long in heaven. Some people ask me in a critical way, "Why do you have so much music in your evangelistic meetings?" I answer, "Because we wish them to be as much like heaven as possible." Heaven will be a very musical place. There will be far more singing than preaching there.

Heaven will be a *"city which has foundations,"* a *"continuing city."* Earth's greatest cities and fairest homes do not endure; they crumble into dust. The so-called "eternal city" of the past is trodden underneath the feet of the beggars of modern Rome.

The world itself does not abide. *"The world is passing away"* (1 John 2:17). Heaven does abide. Eternity rolls on, but heaven abides in its beauty, glory, joy, and love; and we abide with it.

The Way to Heaven

Is your heart stirred with a longing for that abiding city? Who would not rather have an entrance there than have the fleeting possessions of any of earth's millionaires? If I had my choice between having everything that money could buy and then missing heaven in the end or living in the most wretched tenement but gaining heaven at last, it would not take long to decide which to choose.

When we reach that fair home, the trials of earth will seem small and trifling indeed. *"I consider that the sufferings of this present time are not worthy to be compared with the glory which shall be revealed in us"* (Rom. 8:18).

We may all gain an entrance there. There is only one way, but it is simple and open to all. In John 14:6, *"Jesus said to [Thomas], 'I am the way, the truth, and the life. No one comes to the Father except through Me.'"* In John 10:9, Jesus said, *"I am the door. If anyone enters by Me, he will be saved, and will go in and out and find pasture."*

Christ is the door to heaven; Christ is the way to God. Accept Christ as your Savior, your Master, and your Lord. Do it now. If you stood outside the door of some beautiful mansion where all inside was beauty and love, and the owner said cordially, "Come in," would you risk waiting for a second invitation? Jesus swings heaven's door open wide and says, "Come in." Accept Him at once and gain a right to enter and live forever in heaven.

A godless father had a sweet little child who was an earnest Christian. The young daughter became ill and died. The father was angry at God. After the funeral, he raged about his room, cursing God and blaming Him for taking his beloved child. At last, utterly worn out, he threw himself on the bed and fell asleep.

In his slumber, he dreamed that he stood beside a dark river. He saw a beautiful land on the far side. As he gazed across the river, he saw children coming toward him. One fair child came forth, whom he recognized as his little daughter. She was beckoning to him and calling, "Come over here, Father! Come over here."

He awoke and burst into tears. He gave up his rebellion against God, accepted Christ, and prepared to meet his child in the fair land beyond the river.

Voices of loved ones who have gone before are calling, "Come over here, Father." "Come over here, Son." "Come over here, Husband." Come over here, Wife." Accept Christ at once and gain the right to enter heaven and live there forever.

Chapter 8

The New Birth

―――――◆―――――

You must be born again.
—John 3:7

No one can be saved unless he is born again by the power of God's Holy Spirit. Jesus said, *"You must be born again."* The necessity is absolute. He did not merely say, "You may be born again if you think that you want to be," but *"You must be born again."*

Nothing else will take the place of the new birth. Neither baptism nor confirmation can be substituted for it. Simon, in the eighth chapter of Acts, was baptized and taken into the early church. But when Peter and John came down and saw his heart, Peter said to him, *"You have neither part nor portion in this matter, for your heart is not right in the sight of God....For I see that you are poisoned by bitterness and bound by iniquity"* (Acts 8:21, 23). He was a baptized, lost sinner!

I often ask people to come to Christ, but they say, "I have been baptized; I have been confirmed." Have you been born again? *"You must be born again."*

No performance of religious duties will take the place of the new birth. Many people are depending on the fact that they say their prayers, read their Bibles, go to church, receive Communion, and perform other duties. But all of that will not take the place of the new birth. *"You must be born again."*

No Substitutes

Strict adherence to faith will not take the place of the new birth. Many people are saying, "I believe the Apostles' Creed; I hold the right views about Christ, the right views about the Bible, the right views about the Atonement."

You can be orthodox regarding every doctrine and still be lost forever. The Devil is as orthodox a person as there is. The Devil knows the truth about the Bible. He hates it and loves to get others to believe something else, but he believes it himself. The Devil knows the truth about Christ. He believes in the divinity of Christ. He tries to keep others from believing in it, but he believes in it himself. The Devil believes the truth about hell. No one knows better than the Devil that there is an everlasting hell. The Devil is perfectly orthodox, but he is lost. *"You must be born again."* Culture, refinement, and outward morality will not take the place of the new birth. The trouble with us is not merely in our outward lives. The trouble is in the heart. The corruption is in the heart, in the very depths of our inner lives. Merely to reform your outward life will not save you. The change does not go deep enough.

Suppose I had a rotten apple. I could take that apple to an artist and have him put a coating of wax around it, and then paint it until it was beautiful in appearance. But it would be just as rotten as ever. If you would take one bite of it, you would bite into the decay.

Without Christ, people are rotten at the heart. Culture, refinement, respectability, and reform simply put a coating of wax on the outside. We must be changed down to the depths of our beings. We need the power of God going down to the deepest depths of our souls, banishing death and bringing in life, banishing corruption and bringing in the holiness of God.

Without holiness, no one will see God. (See Hebrews 12:14.) It is only by the regenerating power of the Spirit of God that any man or woman can become holy. *"You must be born again."*

The necessity of the new birth is universal. No one will ever see the unless he is born again. There is no exception. I do not care how refined, how highly educated, how amiable, or how attractive you are. You will never see the kingdom of God unless you are born again.

If anybody could have entered the kingdom of God without the new birth, it was Nicodemus. He was an upright man, honored by everyone. He moved in the best society as a man of wealth and culture. He belonged to the orthodox party. He was a man of deep religious earnestness, sincerely desiring to know the right way. He prayed and studied his Bible and went to the synagogue several times a week. The Lord Jesus looked him right in the face, and He said, "Nicodemus, *'you must be born again.'*" No exceptions.

Have you been born again? I do not ask if you are a church member or if you believe the truth. I do not ask if you say your prayers or read your Bible. I do not ask if you go to church. I do not ask if you have a liberal heart toward the poor or if you give to missions. Have you been born again?

Born Again Defined

What does it mean to be born again? A good definition is given in 2 Corinthians 5:17: *"If anyone is in Christ, he is a new creation; old things have passed away; behold, all things have become new."* The new birth is a new creation. It involves a radical transformation by the power of the Spirit of God in the depths of our beings. We receive a new will, new desires, and new thoughts. We were born with a perverted will, corrupted affections, and a blinded mind. By the power of the Holy Spirit, in regeneration, God transforms our wills, our affections, and our tastes. He transforms our way of looking at things.

Every man and woman by nature has a perverted will that is set on pleasing self. What pleases us may not be evil in itself. Perhaps we do not get drunk or swear or lie or do anything vicious or vulgar. But our minds are bent on pleasing ourselves.

When God, by His Spirit, imparts to us His nature and life, our wills are changed along with the whole purpose of our lives. Instead of pleasing self, our wills are surrendered to God, and we live to please Him. We may do a great many of the things we did before, but now we do them because they please God.

Our desires are corrupt by nature. We love the things we should not love and hate the things we should love. For example, many women love to read romantic novels more than they love to read the Bible. If a great many Christian women told the truth they would say, "I would rather read a good love story any day of the week than read the Bible."

You love to go to nightclubs, which God hates. I don't say God hates the people in the nightclubs—He loves them, but He hates the nightclubs. Perhaps you would rather go to the theater than to the gathering of God's children. If you had your choice between going to a first-class opera or to a place where God's Spirit was present in power, would you choose the opera? Would you go to a card party rather than to a quiet meeting of God's people where they knelt down and prayed for the outpouring of the Holy Spirit?

When God, through the power of the Spirit, gives you a new nature, you will love the Bible more than any other book in the world. You will love the places where God manifests Himself better than any places of worldly entertainment. You will love the company of God's people better than you love the pleasures of this world. The beautiful thing is that in a moment of time, by the power of God's Holy Spirit, the change comes. New tastes and new desires take the place of old tastes and old desires.

All Things Become New

Nobody loves worldly entertainment more than I once did. I used to attend four to six dances a week. I played cards every day of my life except on Sundays. You could not pay me to do those things today. I would never go to a nightclub unless I went there to get some poor soul out. I love the things I once hated, and I hate the things I once loved. In those days, I would rather have read any novel than read the Bible. Today I have more joy in reading this Book than in any other book on earth. I love it. My greatest intellectual joy is to study the wonderful pages of this Book of God.

Many people are blind to the divine authority of the Bible. They believe all the nonsense that people try to tell them about the contradictions in it. When you are born again, your mind will be so in tune with the mind of God that you will believe everything His Word says, in spite of what others might say.

Some people cannot believe that Jesus took our sins in His own body on the cross (1 Pet. 2:24). The preaching of this doctrine is *"foolishness to those who are perishing"* (1 Cor. 1:18). But when you are born again, the doctrine that the Son of God died on the cross of Calvary will be one of the sweetest doctrines to you in all the universe.

Being born again means having a new will set on pleasing God instead of pleasing self. You will have a new desire to love the things that God loves and to hate the things that God hates. Your mind and heart will believe the truth of God.

Have you been born again? If not, you are not saved. *"Most assuredly, I say to you, unless one is born again, he cannot see the kingdom of God"* (John 3:3).

How can we tell whether we have been born again or not? *"If you know that He is righteous, you know that everyone who practices righteousness is born of Him"* (1 John 2:29). If you have been born of God, you will do as God does. God does righteousness. If you are born of God, righteousness will be the practice of your life.

To do righteousness means to do the things that are right in God's sight. A man who is born of God will study the Word of God to find out what God's will is as revealed in His Word. When he finds out, he will do it. Are you studying the Word of God daily to find out what God wants you to do? When you find out what God wants you to do, are you doing it?

"Whoever has been born of God does not sin, for His seed remains in him; and he cannot sin, because he has been born of God" (1 John 3:9). That is, he does not make a practice of sin. To commit sin is to do something you know to be contrary to God's will. The man of God will not, when he knows God's will, disobey it. He may make mistakes. He may do something that he did not think was against God's will. But when he learns that it was wrong, he will confess it as sin. Or he may be overtaken by a sudden temptation and fall. But as soon as he sees it, he will confess it. He will not go on day after day doing what he knows to be contrary to the will of God. Anybody who is making a practice of something that he knows is contrary to the will of God has reason to doubt whether he is born again.

A young man stopped me on the street and asked, "If a man is born again and lives and dies in sin, will he be saved?"

"Why," I said, "a man who is born again will not live in sin. He may fall into it, but he will not stay there."

Do you know the difference between a hog and a sheep? A hog will fall into the mud, and he will stay there. A sheep may fall into the mud, but he gets up as quickly as he can. Many people who we think are Christ's sheep are only washed hogs. A hog that is washed will return to the mire, but a sheep will not stay in the mud. (See 2 Peter 2:22.)

If you are only outwardly reformed and externally converted, in a few weeks you will go back to your sin and your worldliness. You are only a washed hog. The person who is outwardly converted, but not inwardly transformed, will give up after a little while. But if you have been born again, you are transformed from a hog into a sheep, and you will never wallow in sin again.

The Test of Love

Proof of regeneration is the love of the brethren. *"We know that we have passed from death to life, because we love the brethren. He who does not love his brother abides in death"* (1 John 3:14). Our love should include everybody who belongs to Christ, regardless of his social position, race, or color. The nature of God is love, and if God has imparted His nature to you, you have a heart full of love.

I once went to a Communion service where the church was receiving new members. When the people stood up to receive the new members, a lady near me remained seated. When the meeting was over, I said to her, "Why didn't you stand up to receive the new members?"

She replied, "I was not going to stand up for them. They are our charity cases. I am not going to love and watch over and care for them."

They were poor, and she was rich. She loved rich Christians. A child of God will love the poorest person who is born of God just as much as if he were a millionaire.

Practical love shows itself by reaching into the pocket. People will get up in a prayer meeting sometimes and say, "I know I have passed from death to life because I love the brethren." After the meeting, someone says, "Mrs. Smith is in trouble. She needs a little help, and we are taking up a collection for her.

Won't you give something?" The reply is, "I cannot do it. Christmas is coming, and I have to get presents for my sisters, children, and cousins, and I cannot give to everybody." You can if you are a child of God.

The proof of the new birth is love. If you have a penny left in your pocket, you will go and share it with your poor brothers and sisters, if you are born again.

"Whoever believes that Jesus is the Christ is born of God" (1 John 5:1). You say, "I believe that Jesus is the Christ." Do you? It is not mere religion; it is true belief. *Christ* means King. If you believe in Christ as King, you will set Him up as King in your heart. Does Christ sit upon the throne of your heart? Does Christ rule your life? If He does, you are born of God. If He doesn't, you are not.

"For whatever is born of God overcomes the world" (v. 4). There are two classes of people in the world—those who are overcoming the world, and those who are being overcome by the world. To which class do you belong? Are you getting the victory over the world, or is the world getting the victory over you?

A great many people come to me and say, "I know this is not right, but it is what everybody does, and so I do it." The world is getting the victory over you. If you are born of God, you will get the victory over the world. You won't ask what the world does. You will ask what Christ says, and you will obey Christ, your King, and get the victory over the world, even if you have to stand alone.

How to Be Born Again

God tells us exactly what we must do to be born again. *"But as many as received Him, to them He gave the right to become children of God, to those who believe in His name"* (John 1:12). We are born again by God's Holy Spirit, through His Word, the moment we receive Christ. When you take Christ into your heart, you take the life of God into your heart. Christ comes and reigns and transforms you completely in a moment. It does not matter how worldly you are, how sinful you are, or how unbelieving you are. Anyone can throw his heart open and let Jesus come in to rule and reign. Anyone can take Christ as his Savior and Deliverer from the power of sin. The moment you surrender the control of your life to Him, God, by the power of His Holy Spirit, will make you a new creature.

Let us compare two people: one who has been carefully taught to observe the outward forms of Christianity, and another who has gone down into the depths of sin. We may look at the religious person and say, "She will surely be easily led to accept Christ. But this person who has gone down into the depths of sin probably won't be saved right now."

Why not? If that moral, refined, beautiful girl takes Christ, God by His Holy Spirit will impart His nature to her and make her a child of God. But if the most immoral woman takes Christ, God by His Holy Spirit will impart His nature to her and make her His child in exactly the same way.

The most highly educated, most upright, most attractive person will never be saved until the Holy Spirit makes him a new creation in Christ. The most hopeless, abandoned person can be born again and made a new creature the moment he accepts Christ.

We are all saved the same way—by the acceptance of Christ and the power of the Holy Spirit. Have you been born again? If not, will you receive Jesus right now and be born again?

Chapter 9

Refuges of Lies

◆

The hail will sweep away the refuge of lies.
—Isaiah 28:17

E very one of us needs a refuge from four things: the accusations of our own conscience, the power of sin, the displeasure of God, and the wrath to come. The trouble is not that
people have no refuge, but that they have a false one. Our text
characterizes it as a refuge of lies.

God announces to us that there is a day coming for testing
the refuges of men. In that day of testing, the hail will sweep
away the refuge of lies. Is your refuge a true one or a false one?
Is it a refuge that will stand the test of the hour that is coming,
or is it a refuge that will go down in a day of storm?

There are four tests that you can apply to every hope that
will show clearly whether it is a true hope or a refuge of lies.
First, a true refuge must meet the highest demands of your conscience. If it is not a refuge from the accusations of your conscience, it is probably not a refuge from the displeasure of God.
*"For if our heart condemns us, God is greater than our heart,
and knows all things"* (1 John 3:20).

Second, trust in your refuge must make you a better person.
If that refuge you trust in is not making you a better person
from day to day, it is not a refuge from the power of sin or from
the wrath to come. Any hope that does not save you from the
power of sin in this life can never save you from the consequences of sin in the life that is to come.

Third, it must stand the test of the dying hour. A refuge that only comforts you when you are well and strong, but fails when you are face-to-face with death, is absolutely worthless.

Finally, it must be a refuge that will stand the test of the Judgment Day. You may say you have a refuge that satisfies you, but will it satisfy God on Judgment Day? That's the question.

Our Own Righteousness

The first refuge of lies is trust in our own morality, our own goodness, or our own character. When you approach a person on the subject of becoming a Christian, he may reply, "No, I don't feel any need of Christ. I am trusting in my own character. Of course, I am not perfect, but I believe that the good in my life will more than make up for the evil. I am trusting in my own good deeds."

Let us apply our four tests. Does your goodness meet the highest demands of your conscience? In talking with highly moral people, I have met only two men who maintained that their own goodness came up to the highest demands of their consciences. You may think that they must have been remarkably good men. No, they had remarkably poor consciences.

I met one of these men when crossing the Atlantic Ocean. I started to talk to him one day about becoming a Christian, and he said to me, "I feel no need of a Savior."

I said, "Do you mean to tell me that you have never sinned?"

"Never," he said.

"Never fallen below the highest demand of your own conscience?"

"Never."

"Never done anything that you regretted afterward?"

"Never."

"Well," you say, "he must have been a good man indeed." Far from it. He was so mean that before we reached New York City, he was the most unpopular man on the ship.

Apply the second test: Is trust in your own goodness making you a better person? As you go on talking about your own morality and trusting in it, do you find that you are grow-ing more unselfish, more kind, more considerate of others, more helpful, and more humble? I have known a great many men who trusted in their own morality. Every one of them grew more cross, critical, self-centered, and proud.

Apply the third test: Will it stand the test of the dying hour? In days of health and strength, a man will boast of his own goodness. But when he comes near death, he wishes that he had a living faith in Christ.

In one of my pastorates, there was the most self-righteous man I ever knew. He had no use for the church, the Bible, Jesus Christ, or ministers. He had a particular grudge against me be-cause of something I had once done that he misunderstood. But he was perfectly confident that he was the best man in the community.

After many years, a cancer appeared on that man's scalp. It spread and ate its way through the scalp until it reached the skull. Little by little, it ate its way through the skull until there was only a thin film of skull between the cancer and the brain. He knew he would soon die. In that hour he said, "Send for Mr. Torrey. I must speak to him."

I hurried to his home at once, sat down beside his bed, and he said, "Oh, Mr. Torrey, tell me how to be saved. Tell me how to become a Christian."

I took my Bible and explained to him as simply as I knew how what to do to be saved. But somehow, he could not grasp it. I sat with him hour after hour. When night came, I said to his wife and family, "You have sat up with him night after night. You go to bed, and I will sit up with him all night and minister to him." They gave me instructions what to do and retired for the night.

All night long I sat by him, except when I had to go into the other room to get something for him to eat or drink. Every time when I returned to the room where he was lying, there came a constant groan from his bed, "Oh, I wish I was a Christian!" And so the man died.

Will your own goodness stand the test of the Judgment Day? Someday you will stand face-to-face with God. That all-seeing, holy eye will look you through and through, the eye of the One who knows all your past, all your secret thoughts, and every hidden imagination. Will you look into His face and say, "O God, Holy One, All-seeing One, I stand here today confident that my own righteousness will satisfy You"? Never!

See if it will stand the test of the Word of God. We know that it will not. Paul warned us about trying to be saved by our own doings. *"As many as are of the works of the law are under the curse; for it is written, 'Cursed is everyone who does not continue in all things which are written in the book of the law, to do them'"* (Gal. 3:10). We are told in Romans 3:20, *"By the deeds of the law no flesh will be justified in His sight."*

Looking Good by Comparison

The second refuge of lies is trust in other people's badness. Some people make their boast in their own goodness; others make their boast in the badness of others. When you urge someone like this to come to Christ, he says, "No, I don't pretend to be very good, but I am just as good as a lot of other folks who are your church members."

Does it satisfy your conscience to say, "Well, I am not very good, but I am no worse than somebody else"? If it does, you must have an insensitive conscience. Is trust in other people's badness making you a better person? I have known many people who talked much of other people's badness, but I have yet to find anyone who was made better by the practice.

Show me a man who is always talking about the faults of others, and I will show you a man who is rotten at the heart. Show me a man who calls every other man a thief, and I will show you a man you can't trust with your wallet. Show me a man who thinks every other man is impure, and I will show you an adulterer. Show me a man or woman who is always talking about others' faults, and I will show you a man or woman who you cannot trust. It never fails.

In one of my Bible classes, I had a woman who was notoriously dishonest in business. One day she said to me, "Brother Torrey,"—she loved to use the word *brother*—Brother Torrey, don't you think that everybody in business is dishonest?"

I looked at her and replied, "When anybody in business accuses everybody in business of being dishonest, he or she convicts at least one person." She was furious! But why should she be? I only told her the truth.

Will you stand the test of the Judgment Day? Face-to-face with God who knows you, will you look into His face and say, "I have never been good, but I am no worse than others"? Never! In that day, God tells us distinctly, *"Each of us shall give account of himself to God"* (Rom. 14:12).

God's Mercy and Judgment

The third refuge of lies is universalism, the belief that God is too good to condemn anyone, that there is no hell, and no future punishment for sin. How common a refuge this is today! When you urge people to come to Christ, they answer, "I believe in the mercy and goodness of God. I believe God is love and too good to condemn anyone. I don't believe in hell."

Does that satisfy the demands of your own conscience? When your conscience points out your sin and demands a change in your life, does it satisfy you to say, "Yes, I know my life is not right, but God is love; therefore, I am going right on trampling His laws underfoot, because He is so good and so loving." Is that the kind of conscience you have? Shame on you! Don't ever do it again. God's infinite love gave His Son to die for you on the cross of Calvary.

Will your misinterpretation of God's goodness stand the test of the dying hour? A certain young man who was not a Christian became suddenly and seriously ill. His family saw that the illness might result in death, and they sent for their pastor. When he came into the room, this young fellow was tossing on a bed of sickness. The pastor hurried to his side and tried to present to him the consolation of the Gospel.

He said, "Pastor, I can't listen to you. I have heard it over and over again. I would not listen to it in times of health and strength. I am now very ill. I will die soon. I can't repent in my last hour."

His father paced the room in great anxiety. Finally, he said, "My son, there is nothing for you to be so anxious about. You have not been a bad boy, and there is no hell. You have nothing to fear."

His dying son turned to him and said, "Father, you have deceived me all through my life. If I had listened to Mother instead of to you, I would not be here now. She tried to get me to go to church and Sunday school, but you took me fishing instead. You told me that there was no hell, and I believed you. You have deceived me up to this time, but you can't deceive me any longer. I am dying and going to hell, and my blood is on your soul." Then he turned his face to the wall and died.

Fathers, you who are undermining the teaching of godly wives, the day is coming when your sons will curse you. Will your universalism stand the test of the dying hour?

Is universalism making you a better man? Oh, with many it is simply an excuse for sin! In many of our churches, the world is sweeping in like a flood! All separation is gone, and professed Christians are running after the world, the flesh, and the Devil. They have accepted the eternal hope nonsense that is robbing the church of its devotion and beauty. The church is becoming so like the world that you can't tell the two apart. People have grown comfortable in a life of sin, giving up their separation to God.

Will universalism stand the test of the Judgment Day? When you meet God, will you look into His face and say, "O God, I know my life has not been right, but I thought that You were a God of love. I thought You were too good to punish sin. I did not think there was any hell, so I didn't bother to obey Your laws"?

The Danger of Unbelief

The next refuge of lies is infidelity. Let us apply the tests. Does your unbelief meet the highest demands of your own conscience? When conscience points out your sin and demands a new life, do you reply, "Well, I don't believe in the Bible, and I don't believe in God. I don't believe that Jesus Christ is the Son of God"? If that satisfies your conscience, you are not fit to be called a human being.

Is your unbelief making you a better person? My ministry has been largely a ministry to skeptics and agnostics. I have yet to meet the first unbeliever who was made better by his unbelief, but I have known many whose characters have been undermined by a lack of faith. I have had young men come to me with breaking hearts and with sad confessions of immorality and ruin. They tell me that the first step was listening to some ungodly lecturer or reading an ungodly book. Trifling with spiritual matters undermines the foundations of sound character. Unbelief is filling the world with wickedness.

In my own church in Chicago, to which a good many infidels come, one of them said to me, "We come over here to hear you. You don't spare us, but we like men who take a stand. That is the reason we come." There are always a lot of them every Sunday. Thank God, many of them become converted.

Will unbelief stand the test of the dying hour? How often it fails! A friend of mine who was in the army said that in the same company with him was a man who was a very outspoken unbeliever. On the second day of battle, he said to his fellow soldiers, "I have a strange feeling that I am going to be shot today."

"Nonsense," they said. "It is nothing but superstition. You are not going to be shot."

"Well," he said, "I feel very strange. I feel as if I am going to be shot."

At last they were lined up waiting for the word of command. "Forward, march!" They went up the hill, and just as they reached the summit, a volley came from the enemy's guns. A bullet pierced this man near the heart. He cried as they carried him to the rear, "O God, just give me time to repent." It only took one bullet to take the doubt out of that man. It should take less than that to take the nonsense out of you.

Will it stand the test of the Judgment Day? Will you go into God's presence and be ready to say, "God, my answer is this: I was an unbeliever; I was an agnostic; I was a skeptic; I was an atheist"? Do you think you will? Get down on your knees and try to tell Him. You can talk nonsense to your fellowmen, but when you talk to God, it will take the nonsense out of you.

Hiding behind Religion

One more refuge of lies is religion. It may surprise you that religion is as much a refuge of lies as morality, other people's badness, universalism, or infidelity. Religion never saved anybody. It is one thing to trust in religion; it is something entirely different to trust in the living Christ.

You may tell people about Christ, and they may say, "Oh, I am very religious. I go to church. I say my prayers every morning and night. I read my Bible. I go to Communion. I have been baptized. I have been confirmed. I give a tenth of my income to the poor. I am very religious." Well, you can do every bit of that and go straight to hell. Religion never saved anybody.

Is your religion making you a better man or woman? A great deal of religion will not make men or women one bit better. Many religious people will lie as fast as anybody. They will go around slandering their neighbors. Men who are prominent religious businessmen will cut you as wide open in a business deal as any man in town. They turn a deaf ear to the cry of the aged and the needy, unless it is going to get into the papers that they gave them something. Many men are very religious and are perfect scoundrels.

I met a man who seemed to be most religious. He made his employees gather together at a certain hour every day for prayer, and he held religious services with them every Sunday so that they would not have to go to church. But this pious hypocrite was paying the women who worked for him starvation wages. His employees were the palest, most sickly crowd of women I have ever seen. That kind of religion will send a man to the deepest part of hell.

Will your religion stand the test of the dying hour? A great many religious people are as badly scared as anybody when they come to die. I have heard them groan and sigh and weep in the dying hour. Their hollow religion doesn't stand the test of great crisis.

Will it stand the test of the Judgment Day? The Lord Jesus Christ said:

> *Many will say to Me in that day, "Lord, Lord, have we not prophesied in Your name, cast out demons in Your name, and done many wonders in Your name?" And then I will declare to them, "I never knew you; depart from Me, you who practice lawlessness!"* (Matt. 7:22–23)

Religion is a refuge of lies, and if that is what you are trusting in, you will be lost forever.

The Sure Foundation

Is there no true refuge? Yes, there is. God says, *"Behold, I lay in Zion a stone for a foundation, a tried stone, a precious cornerstone, a sure foundation; whoever believes will not act hastily"* (Isa. 28:16).

This sure foundation stone is Jesus Christ. *"For no other foundation can anyone lay than that which is laid, which is Jesus Christ"* (1 Cor. 3:11). It is one thing to trust in religion and something entirely different to trust with a living faith in a crucified and risen Christ.

Will this refuge stand the test of our own consciences? When my conscience points to my sin, I have an answer that satisfies it. Jesus bore my sins on the cross. Will it make people better people? Yes. A living faith in a crucified and living Christ will make everyone who has it more like Christ every day. If you have a faith that is not making you like Christ, you do not have a real faith.

Will it stand the test of the Judgment Day? Yes. If it is God's will, I am willing to face Him tonight in judgment. You say, "What! Have you never sinned?" Certainly I have. You will never know how deeply I have sinned. But when God asks for my answer, I will say one word—*Jesus*—and this answer will satisfy God. *"The hail will sweep away the refuge of lies."* Throw them all away, and come to Christ. Be ready for life, ready for death, and ready for eternity.

Chapter 10

Found Out

———◆———

Be sure your sin will find you out.
—Numbers 32:23

No one can escape his sins. Every sin we commit will find us out, call us to account, and make us pay. No man ever committed a sin that he did not pay for in some way. The most serious folly of which a man can be guilty is for him to imagine that he can ever gain anything by doing wrong. Whether you hurt anyone else by your own wrongdoing or not, you are sure to hurt yourself.

If a man puts his hand in the fire, he will be burned. If a man sins, he will certainly suffer for each sin he commits. You may escape the laws of men, but you cannot escape the law of God. No man can hide where his sin will not find him.

Men's sins find them out by the execution of human laws. The execution of law in society is necessarily imperfect, yet it is astonishing how often men who break the laws are sooner or later punished for their crimes. A man may successfully elude the meshes of the law for months or even years, but he is all the time weaving a net that will almost certainly entrap him at last. It is a marvelous thing how crime comes to light. A man's sin finds him out and exposes him at last to the contempt of the whole world.

Men's sins find them out in their own bodies. When a man does not pay the penalty of his sin in human courts, he pays it in a court where there is no possibility of bribery—the court of physical retribution for moral offenses. In a general way, there is an intimate connection between morality and health. All sins have physical consequences. The consequences of some sins are often not immediate or definitely traceable to specific sins, but it remains true that every sin has some physical consequences.

Young men see others suffering the terrible consequences of transgressing God's law, yet they go right on as an ox to the slaughter. They suppose that they will be an exception. There are no exceptions to physical law. Any action that is unnatural or immoral is bound to be visited with penalty. Why are there so many men with broken bodies and shattered intellects? Why so many broken-down women? The answer is the violation of God's law: their sins are finding them out.

Of course, disease may be hereditary or the result of accident or misfortune. But if we were to eliminate all the sickness that is the direct or indirect result of our own sins, we would be surprised at the relatively small amount of sickness left.

Consider a sin such as anger. Does it affect an individual's body? It causes disorders in the blood, stomach, brain, and nerves. It is obviously unhealthy in every case and may even lead to paralysis and death. It is amazing the many ways, some direct and some indirect, in which our sins find us out in our own bodies. If you are contemplating sin, just stop and think of this: *"Be sure your sin will find you out."*

Damaging to Character and Conscience

For every sin you commit, you will suffer in character. Sin breeds a moral ulcer. A diseased character is worse than a diseased body. You can't tell a lie without your moral blood being poisoned by it and your moral health undermined.

Do you think you can cheat a man in business and not suffer in your character more than he suffers in his pocket? Do you think you can wrong an employee in his wages and not suffer more in what you become than he suffers in what he gets? Do you think you can wrong a man regarding his wife and not have a deadly cancer develop in your own character? Do you think you can read an impure book or listen to an obscene story and not breed corruption in your own moral nature? Do you think you can violate those laws of purity that God has written in His Word and on your heart and not reap the consequences in your own character? Sin always finds people out in their characters—in what they become.

Again, your sin will find you out in your own conscience. You can hide your sin from everyone but yourself. You are so constructed by God that to know you are a sinner means self-condemnation and agony. Many suffer from the bitter consciousness of sins that no one else knows anything about. No physical torments can match the torments of an accusing conscience. An accusing conscience means hell on earth. No earthly prosperity, no human love, no mirth, music, fun, or intoxication can dispel its clouds or assuage the agony of its gnawing tooth. That sin you are contemplating looks inviting and harmless. It won't look so tempting or innocent after it is committed. It will find you out, and you will suffer.

Your sin will find you out in the lives of your children. One of the most awful things about sin is that its curse falls not only on us, but also on our children. You may complain about this as much as you like, but it is an unquestionable fact.

I remember a man who was a constant, but moderate drinker. He had three sons. I don't think that man was ever drunk in his life. He despised a drunkard, but he laughed at total abstainers. Each one of his three sons became alcoholics. A wise friend of mine says he never has known a man in the liquor business where the curse sooner or later did not strike his own home.

Facing Eternity

There is one more place where your sin will find you out: your sin will find you out in eternity. This present life is not all that there is. Our acts and their consequences will follow us into our future life. If your sin does not find you out here, it will there. You may be absolutely sure of that. In eternity, we will reap the consequences of every sin we sowed here on earth.

Life sometimes seems to go on here to the end without justice. Men defraud their employees, they rob the needy, they condemn other men and their families to poverty in order to increase their already enormous wealth. No one seems to call them to account. It will not always be so. God will call them to strict account. A few thousands or millions of their ill-gotten wealth given to charity will not blind the eyes of a holy God. They will suffer.

Men sometimes lay traps for foolish girls, bringing ruin to their reputations. Yet no one seems to hold the man accountable. He continues to be accepted in the "best society" and is loaded with honors. His sin will find him out, however, if not in this world, then, in the next. He will stand before the universe exposed, dishonored, and condemned to everlasting contempt.

Men despise God, laugh at His Word, and trample underfoot His Son (Heb. 10:29), yet God still lets them live. He does not seem to call them to account. But it will not be always so. *"Be sure your sin will find you out."*

You cannot sin without suffering for it. Your sin will find you out in the court of law, in your own body, in your character, in your conscience, in your children, in eternity, or in all of these put together. You will suffer. You will pay an awful price.

> *The Lord Jesus is revealed from heaven with His mighty angels, in flaming fire taking vengeance on those who do not know God, and on those who do not obey the gospel of our Lord Jesus Christ. These shall be punished with everlasting destruction from the presence of the Lord and from the glory of His power.* (2 Thess. 1:7–9)

All of us have sinned (Rom. 3:23), and for some, our sins are finding us out now. What shall we do? There is only one way of escape from the penalties of the law—the grace of the Gospel. *"Christ has redeemed us from the curse of the law, having become a curse for us"* (Gal. 3:13). He calls, *"Come to Me, all you who labor and are heavy laden, and I will give you rest"* (Matt. 11:28).

Chapter 11

Salvation Is for You

◆

Who then can be saved?
—Mark 10:26

The disciples asked Jesus this question. Jesus had just told them how hard it was for a rich man to enter the kingdom of heaven. The disciples seem to have held the same opinion that most men do today—a rich man can get anywhere. But Jesus said, *"It is easier for a camel to go through the eye of a needle than for a rich man to enter the kingdom of God"* (Mark 10:25).

"Who then can be saved?" Jesus went on to tell them that although it was impossible through man's power for a rich man to be saved, God, with whom all things are possible, could save even a rich man. But only God could.

We come, then, to the question again: *"Who then can be saved?"* The Bible answers the question clearly. The Bible tells us that there are some people who cannot be saved, and that there are some people who can be saved.

Who Cannot Be Saved?

No one can be saved who will not give up his sin. We read in Isaiah 55:7: *"Let the wicked forsake his way, and the unrighteous man his thoughts; let him return to the LORD, and He will have mercy on him; and to our God, for He will abundantly pardon."*

Every man and woman has to choose between sin and salvation. You cannot have both. If you won't give up sin, you must give up salvation. Absurd schemes of salvation propose to save a man while he continues in sin. We read in Matthew 1:21 concerning our Savior: *"You shall call His name JESUS, for He will save His people from their sins."* Sin is damnation; holiness is salvation. The reason some people are not saved is that they do not want to give up sinning. Some will not give up drunkenness or adultery or profanity or lying or bad tempers. You cannot be saved if you want to sin. If you persist in sinning, you will be lost forever.

No man can be saved who trusts in his own righteousness and is not willing to admit that he is a lost sinner. Thousands of lost sinners are proud of their own morality. They are not willing to humble themselves and say, "I am a poor, vile, worthless, miserable sinner." You can never be saved while you trust in your own righteousness.

Jesus told us that two men went up to the temple to pray. One was a Pharisee, one of the most respectable religious men in the community. The other was a tax collector, a man whom everybody looked down on. The Pharisee talked about his own goodness when he prayed. He looked up and said, *"God, I thank You that I am not like other men; extortioners, unjust, adulterers, or even as this tax collector"* (Luke 18:11). His contempt for the tax collector was obvious. The Pharisee continued in his prayer: *"I fast twice every week; I give tithes of all that I possess"* (v. 12). Jesus said that this man went out of the temple an unforgiven, hopelessly lost sinner.

But the tax collector, the outcast, the man everybody looked down on, would not so much as lift his eyes to heaven. He felt he was a miserable, worthless sinner. He beat his breast and said, *"God, be merciful to me a sinner!"* (v. 13). Jesus said that this man returned to his house justified (v. 14). Anybody can be saved who will take the sinner's place and cry for mercy.

The World's Largest Family

One day a friend of mine, an old Scotsman, was walking through the country when a man came along and stopped beside him. The man started up a conversation with the old Scotsman, curious about his background. My friend said, "I will tell you who I am, and I will tell you what my business is. I have a very strange business. I am hunting for heirs."

The other man said, "What?"

"I am hunting for heirs to a great estate. I represent a very great estate, and I am hunting heirs for it. There are a good many in this neighborhood."

The other said, "Do you mind telling me their names?"

"No," he said. "It is a very large family. Their name begins with *S*."

"Oh," said the man. "Smith, I suppose?"

"No," the old man replied, "a much larger family than the Smith family."

"Larger than the Smith family! Who are they?"

The old Scotsman said, "They are the sinner family. The estate I represent is the kingdom of God; the inheritance is incorruptible, undefiled, and does not fade away. The heirs to it are the sinners who are willing to take the family name, admit that they are sinners, and look to God for pardon."

Do you belong to the sinner family? If you do, you can be saved. If you are not willing to admit that you do, you cannot be saved. You are lost forever.

No man or woman can be saved who is not willing to accept salvation as a free gift. We are told in Ephesians 2:8, *"For by grace you have been saved through faith, and that not of yourselves; it is the gift of God." "The gift of God is eternal life in Christ Jesus our Lord"* (Rom. 6:23).

Salvation is a free gift. Anybody can have it for nothing; nobody can have it any other way. If you are not willing to take it as a free gift, you cannot have it at all.

My wife was talking to a young man, a son of the richest man in the neighborhood. There seemed to be some difficulty about his accepting Christ. Finally my wife said to him, "The trouble with you is you are not willing to accept salvation as a free gift."

"Mrs. Torrey, that is just it. I am not willing to accept salvation as a free gift. If I could earn it, if I could work for it, if I could deserve it, then it would be different. I am willing to earn it, but I am not willing to take it as a free gift."

Nobody can earn it; nobody can merit it; nobody can deserve it. Unless you are willing to take it as a free gift, you will never get it at all. The richest man on earth who gets saved will have nothing more to boast about when he reaches heaven than the lowliest beggar who is saved.

Sincerely Wrong

Nobody can be saved who will not accept Jesus Christ as his Savior. *"There is no other name under heaven given among men by which we must be saved"* (Acts 4:12). Anybody can be saved in Christ; nobody can be saved in any other way. An infidel once said to a friend of mine, "If I cannot be saved without accepting Christ, I won't be saved." Well, then, he won't be saved. That is all there is to it.

If you ever go to Sydney, Australia, you will soon find that every citizen in that city is very proud of the harbor. You won't be in Sydney long before somebody will ask you, "What do you think of our harbor?" They should be proud of it. It is one of the finest harbors in the world, but it has only one entrance. There is one enormous rock called the North Head and another called the South Head. The only channel, wide and deep, is between these two heads. A little south of the South Head is another promontory, called Jacob's Ladder.

One night, many years ago, a vessel called the *Duncan Dunbar,* with hundreds of people on board, came outside of Sydney harbor after dark. The captain saw the South Head and thought it was the North Head. He saw Jacob's Ladder and thought it was the South Head. He steered, put on full speed, steamed in between the two lights, and ran onto the rocks. Every one of the hundreds on board perished, except one man who was thrown up into a cave on the face of the rock.

That captain was perfectly sincere. There never was a more sincere man on earth, but he was mistaken, and he was lost. People say it does not make any difference what you believe if you are only sincere. But the more sincerely you believe error, the worse off you are. There is just one channel into salvation, and that is Christ. Try to go any other way, no matter how sincere you are, and you will be wrecked and lost eternally.

Who Can Be Saved?

Sinners can be saved, even the most depraved. Paul wrote, *"This is a faithful saying and worthy of all acceptance, that Christ Jesus came into the world to save sinners, of whom I am chief"* (1 Tim. 1:15). He has already saved the chief of sinners, and He is able to do it again.

In the city where I used to live, a young girl of thirteen became pregnant. Her father and mother disowned her. Her brothers rejected her, and I doubt if they were any better than she. They cast this poor girl of only thirteen years of age into the streets to fend for herself. She soon became the companion of thieves, robbers, murderers, of everything that was disreputable. She lost the baby because of her poor health and became a member of two of the worst gangs, at different times, in New York and Chicago.

A friend of mine met her one night and said, "If you are ever sick of this life, come to me, and I will help you out of it." A time came when she was thoroughly sick of it, and she went to this gentleman's house. He was a very wealthy man, who used all his money for God. He showed her the way of life, and she was saved. That young woman went on to occupy a high position of great responsibility and honor in her city. There is scarcely anyone who even knows her past life. God has covered it up, though she still has the same name.

A few years ago I was in her town. She came to me and said, "I hope, Mr. Torrey, that you won't think it necessary to tell the people here my story." My wife and I were the only ones there that knew her past record. She had been in our house in the days of her trouble.

I said, "Most assuredly, we shall not." Why should you tell a saved woman's story, when it is underneath the blood of Jesus? It is no longer her story. It is blotted out. Jesus Christ not only saved her out of the depths of sin, but He covered up her past as well.

Depending on His Power

Any person who is too weak to resist sin in his own strength can be saved. It is not a question of human strength, but of

Christ's strength. *"Now to Him who is able to keep you from stumbling, and to present you faultless before the presence of His glory with exceeding joy"* (Jude 24). *"Who are kept by the power of God through faith for salvation ready to be revealed in the last time"* (1 Pet. 1:5). Jesus Christ can keep the weakest man or woman just as well as the strongest.

I have seen men start out in the Christian life who talk this way in testimony meetings: "Friends, you know me; I am a man with great strength of character. When I make up my mind to do anything, I always follow through. I have started out in this Christian life, and I want you to understand that I am not going to backslide as so many do. I am going through." Whenever I hear a man talking that way, I know he is going to backslide within six weeks.

Another man will stand up trembling, hesitant, and he will say, "You all know me. You know I have no willpower left. I have tried to quit my sin time and time again. As you know, I have failed every time. I have absolutely no confidence in myself. But God says in Isaiah 41:10, *'Fear not, for I am with you; be not dismayed, for I am your God. I will strengthen you, yes, I will help you, I will uphold you with My righteous right hand.'* I am trusting in Him." When I hear a man talking that way, I know he is going to stand every time.

One day somebody came to me in Chicago and said, "We have to find a place for this woman to stay. Her husband got drunk last night and tried to kill her with a knife. It is not safe for her or her child, so she has left him. We must do something to provide for her."

I said, "You are right to provide for her; that is just what we should do."

A few days later, her husband came to me and said, "Mr. Torrey, do you know where my wife is?"

I said, "I do."

"Will you please tell me where she is?"

"I will not. You tried to kill her. You do not deserve to have a wife. I am not going to tell you where she is so that you may go and kill her."

He said, "If you do not tell me, I will commit suicide."

"Very well," I said. "You will go to hell if you do." A man like him never commits suicide. He kept getting drunk instead. He could not help it, poor fellow. Every now and then, he would come to me for a few dollars, saying that he was going to get a job in a shoe factory. I always knew that the money was going for whiskey. He was always saying that he was going to quit drinking. I knew he was not. He meant to. He would say that he was hunting for work. But I knew he was looking for another drink.

That went on for years. One day I said to God, "Heavenly Father, if you will give me this man, I will never despair of the salvation of another man as long as I live." Very soon afterward, he got his feet on the Rock, Christ Jesus, and never fell again.

Years passed, and he became an honored member of that church. When I returned for a visit, among those who came to welcome me was this man, his wife, and a child, a happy family in Jesus Christ. The Christ who saved the lying, habitual, hopeless drunkard can save anyone who will trust in Him.

Power for Deliverance

Anyone can be saved who thinks he has committed the unpardonable sin, if he is willing to come to Jesus Christ. Jesus said, *"All that the Father gives Me will come to Me, and the one who comes to Me I will by no means cast out"* (John 6:37). I think I have never gone anywhere in my life where somebody has not said, "I have committed the unpardonable sin." Almost every one, if not every one, has gone away rejoicing in Jesus.

One time I received a brokenhearted letter from a father who was a Presbyterian minister. He wrote that he had a son who was in deep spiritual darkness. The son thought that he had committed the unpardonable sin, and he was plunged into absolute despair. Would I take him into the Bible Institute? I replied that, though I had every sympathy for him in his sorrow, the Bible Institute was not for the purpose of helping cases like this one, but to train men and women for Christian service.

The father continued to write, begging me to take his son, and he got other friends to plead for him. Finally, I consented to take the young man. He was sent to me under guard, to prevent him from doing something rash on the way.

671

When he was brought to my office, I showed him to a seat. As soon as the others had left the room, he began the conversation by saying, "I am possessed of the Devil."

"I think quite likely you are," I replied, "but Christ is able to cast out devils."

"You do not understand me," he said. "I mean that the Devil has entered into me as he did into Judas Iscariot."

"That may be," I answered, "but Christ came to destroy the works of the Devil. He says in John 6:37, *'The one who comes to Me I will by no means cast out.'* If you will just come to Him, He will receive you and set you free from Satan's power."

The conversation went on in this way for some time. He constantly asserted the absolute hopelessness of his case, and I constantly claimed the power of Jesus Christ and His promise, *"The one who comes to Me I will by no means cast out."*

Days and weeks passed, and we had many conversations, always on the same line. One day I met him in the hall of the Institute and made up my mind that the time had come to have the battle out. I invited him to my office and told him to sit down. "Do you believe the Bible?" I asked.

"Yes," he replied, "I believe everything in it."

"Do you believe that Jesus Christ told the truth when He said, *'The one who comes to Me I will by no means cast out'*?"

"Yes, I do. I believe everything in the Bible."

"Well, then, will you come to Christ?"

"I have committed the unpardonable sin."

I replied, "Jesus does not say, 'The one who has not committed the unpardonable sin who comes to Me I will in no wise cast out.' He says, *'The one who comes to Me I will by no means cast out.'*"

"But I have sinned willfully after I have received the knowledge of the truth."

"Jesus does not say, 'The one who has not sinned willfully after he received the knowledge of the truth who comes to Me I will in no wise cast out.' He says, *'The one who comes to Me I will by no means cast out.'*"

"But I have been enlightened and tasted the heavenly gift and have fallen away. It is impossible to renew me again unto repentance."

"Jesus does not say, 'The one who has not tasted of the heavenly gift, and has not fallen away, if he comes to Me I will in no wise cast him out.' He says, *'The one who comes to Me I will by no means cast out.'*"

He continued with his excuses. "But I am possessed of the Devil. The Devil has entered into me as he did into Judas Iscariot. My heart is hard as a millstone."

I answered every one of his protests with the same Scripture, John 6:37, until his excuses were exhausted. I looked him square in the face and said, "Now, will you come? Get down on your knees, and quit your nonsense." He knelt, and I knelt by his side. "Now," I said, "follow me in prayer."

"Lord Jesus," I said, and he repeated, "Lord Jesus." "My heart is as hard as a millstone. I have no desire to come to You. But You said in Your Word, *'The one who comes to Me I will by no means cast out.'* I believe this statement of Yours. Therefore, though I don't feel it, I believe You have received me."

When he had finished, I said, "Did you really come to Jesus?"

He replied, "I did."

"Has He received you?"

"I do not feel it," he replied.

"But what does He say?"

"The one who comes to Me I will by no means cast out."

"Is this true? Does Jesus tell the truth, or does He lie?"

"He tells the truth."

"What, then, must He have done?"

"He must have received me."

"Now," I said, "go to your room. Stand firmly on this promise of Jesus Christ. The Devil will give you an awful conflict, but just answer him every time with John 6:37. Stand right there, believing what Jesus says in spite of your feelings, in spite of what the Devil may say, in spite of everything."

He went to his room. The Devil did give him an awful conflict, but he stood firmly on John 6:37 and came out of his room triumphant and radiant.

Years have passed since then. Though the Devil tried again and again to plunge him into despair, he stood firmly on John

6:37. He was used of God to do larger work for Christ than al-most any man I know. He is the author of that hymn:

> Years I spent in vanity and pride,
> Caring not my Lord was crucified,
> Knowing not it was for me He died On Calvary.
> Mercy there was great, and grace was free,
> Pardon there was multiplied to me,
> There my burdened soul found liberty,
> At Calvary.

Anyone can be saved who will come to Jesus. *"The Spirit and the bride say, 'Come!' And let him who hears say, 'Come!' And let him who thirsts come. Whoever desires, let him take the water of life freely"* (Rev. 22:17).

Chapter 12

How to Find Rest

———————◆———————

*Come to Me, all you who labor and are heavy laden, and I will
give you rest. Take My yoke upon you and learn from Me, for I am
gentle and lowly in heart, and you will find rest for your souls.*
—Matthew 11:28–29

What this world needs is rest. What every person who is
not already in Christ needs is rest. Millions of people
work hard for small pay and go home night after night
to wretched homes, worn out, without any fit place to sleep.
Millions more have no rest for their hearts, no rest for their
souls.

There is One who can give rest to every tired heart. His
name is Jesus Christ. He stands with extended hands and says,
*"Come to Me, all you who labor and are heavy laden, and I will
give you rest."*

Those are either the words of a divine Being or the words of
a lunatic. If the Lord Jesus Christ offers rest and gives it, He is
a divine Being. If He offers rest and cannot give it, He is a lunatic. If any man, even the greatest and the best that the world
ever saw, held out his hands to this sorrowing, grief-stricken,
burdened world of ours and said, "Come to me, and I will give
you rest," you would know at once that the man had gone crazy,
for no man could do it. But Jesus offers to do it, and He does it.
Millions throughout the centuries have accepted Christ's offer.
Nobody who ever accepted it failed to find rest.

Whom Did Jesus Call?

There was a great throng when the Lord Jesus spoke that
day. That crowd represented lives filled with misery. Multitudes

of the poor were there—the penniless, the sick, the demonic, and the outcast—a mass of misery. The Lord Jesus Christ cast His loving eyes over that great multitude that represented so much misery, and His great heart went out to them. He said, "Come, come to Me, every one of you who has a burden, every one who has a sorrow, every one who has a broken heart. Come to Me, and I will give you rest."

He extends His hands to all men and all women in all ages who are burdened, downtrodden, oppressed, wretched, broken-hearted, and filled with despair. He invites all who labor and are heavy laden to come to Him.

Some commentators have tried to tone down the words of our Lord. They tell us that He meant all who were burdened with the many requirements of the Mosaic law. Others tell us He meant all who were burdened by a consciousness of sin, a sense of guilt. Jesus means just what He says. *"Come to Me, all you who labor"*—every person who has a burden, a sorrow, a heartache, a trouble, a problem of any kind; Jesus invites you to come.

He invites all who are burdened with a sense of sin and shame. Perhaps you feel that your life is disgraceful. You are ashamed of yourself, and you can hardly lift up your head. You are saying to yourself, "My life is simply shameful," and you are crushed by the sense of your sin. Jesus says to you, *"Come to Me...and I will give you rest."*

A Woman Transformed

That day when our Lord Jesus spoke these words in Capernaum, on the outskirts of the crowd, there was a woman who was a prostitute, an outcast despised by everyone. As she stood there, I have no doubt many women who prided themselves on their morality turned and looked at her with scorn. But soon Jesus looked at her, too—not with scorn, but with pity, with compassion, with tenderness, with yearning, and with love. She saw that He was speaking directly to her. He seemed to lose sight of everybody else as He stretched His hands out toward her and said, *"Come to Me, all you who labor and are heavy laden, and I will give you rest."*

That woman said in amazement, "He means me!" When the crowd broke up, she followed at a distance to see where Jesus went. Jesus went to the house of Simon, the Pharisee, who had invited Him to dinner. She hurried to her home, took a very costly box of ointment, the most expensive thing that she had, and hurried back to Simon's house. As Jesus reclined there, she came up behind Him, bent over His feet, and began to bathe them with her tears.

The other guests looked on in scorn. They grumbled, "This man pretends to be a prophet. He is no prophet, or He would not allow that woman to touch Him. If He were a prophet, He would know what kind of woman she is. She is a sinner."

Well, He did know. He knew better than any of them did, not only that she was a sinner, but also that she was a repentant sinner. While His feet were still wet with her tears, she wiped them with the long tresses of her beautiful hair. Then she broke open her alabaster box of precious ointment and anointed His feet with the fragrant oil. The Lord Jesus turned to her and said, *"Your sins are forgiven"* (Luke 7:48). Then He spoke again to her and said, *"Your faith has saved you. Go in peace"* (v. 50). That woman, who stood on the outskirts of the crowd with a breaking heart, left that house with the peace of God in her soul. (See Luke 7:36–50.)

Freedom from Bondage

The Lord Jesus invites every man and woman who is burdened by the bondage of sin. Some of you are in bondage to alcohol. You want to be sober and to lead an upright life. You have tried again and again to give up drinking but have failed. Others are burdened with the desire for drugs. You have tried to be free from your bondage. The Lord Jesus says to you, *"Come to Me...and I will give you rest."*

You may be burdened with impurity or some disgusting sin. You have tried to break away time and time again, until at last you have given up. You are utterly discouraged, crushed by the power of your sin. If you could read the secret sorrow of every heart, you would find hundreds of people crushed to the earth by the power of sin. The Lord Jesus says to everyone, *"Come to*

Me, all you who labor and are heavy laden, and I will give you rest."

I have a dear friend who was carefully reared by a godly mother. His father had been an alcoholic. His mother was afraid that her son would become a drunkard, so she made him promise that he would never touch a drop of liquor. He lived for eighteen years without tasting it.

One day he was on a business trip with a friend. On the way back, the man bought some alcohol and asked him to have a drink. "No," he said, "I promised my mother never to drink."

"Well," he said, "if you don't drink you will insult me." That elderly man worked on that boy until he got him to drink his first glass of whiskey. It was as though a demon in him was set on fire. From that time on, he became a drunkard. He lost one job after another and at last was a wrecked man in New York City. He wrote one hundred and thirty-eight bad checks against his last employer, and the officers of the law were looking for him.

One awful night, he went into a bar and for a long time sat there in a drunken stupor. He suddenly began to feel all the horrors of delirium tremens coming over him. He thought he was going to die. He went up to the bar and ordered a drink. Then he threw down the glass and said, "Men, hear me, hear me; I shall never drink another glass of whiskey, even if it kills me."

They all laughed at him. He went out of the bar and down to the police station. He said to the sergeant at the desk, "Lock me up; I am going to have the tremors; lock me up!" The sergeant took him down to the cell and locked him up.

He spent a night and a day in awful agony. The next evening, somebody said to him, "Why don't you go to the city mission?" In an awful condition, he went down to the mission and listened to one man after another give his testimony of how he was saved. When the minister asked all who wanted to receive Christ to come to the front, he went up to the front, knelt down, and said, "Pray for me."

The minister responded, "Pray for yourself."

"Oh," he said, "I don't know how to pray. I have forgotten how to pray."

The minister softly repeated, "Pray for yourself." That wrecked and ruined man lifted up his broken heart to Jesus. Jesus met him and took the bondage of alcohol from him that same night. That man became one of the most respected men in New York City.

Are you burdened? Have you fought again and failed? Have you tried again and again, perhaps signed pledge after pledge, only to break it? Are you burdened with the weight of an overcoming sin? Jesus holds out His hand to you. *"Come to Me, all you who labor and are heavy laden, and I will give you rest."*

There is a cure for every sorrow at the feet Jesus. I have a beautiful family Bible that my mother gave to my grandmother at the time of my grandfather's death. On the flyleaf of the Bible in my mother's own beautiful handwriting are the words, "Earth hath no sorrow that heaven cannot heal." That is true, but something better is that earth has no sorrow that Jesus cannot heal right now, before we get to heaven.

Lifting the Burden of Doubt

The Lord Jesus invites all who are burdened by doubt and unbelief. To some men, doubt and unbelief are not a burden. They are glad that they are skeptics. They are proud of their doubts. But to a man of any real moral earnestness, doubt is a burden, a heavy load. He is never proud of doubt. An earnest-minded man wants truth, not uncertainty, and knowledge of God to replace agnosticism.

There are some who honestly doubt, and their doubt is a burden. Jesus says, *"Come to Me, all you who labor and are heavy laden, and I will give you rest."*

Am I suggesting that a skeptic should come to Christ, an unbeliever come to Christ, an agnostic come to Christ? Certainly; He is the best One you can come to.

Thomas was a skeptic. The other disciples had seen our Lord after His resurrection. Thomas was not present. When Thomas came back, the other disciples said, *"We have seen the Lord"* (John 20:25). He said, "I don't believe it. I don't believe you have seen the Lord, and I won't believe it unless I see Him with my own eyes, put my fingers into the prints of the nails in His hands, and thrust my hand into His side."

But Thomas was an honest doubter. When he thought that perhaps the Lord Jesus would be around the next Sunday evening, He was there. He came to Jesus with his doubts. Jesus scattered every one of them, and Thomas cried, *"My Lord and my God!"* (v. 28).

Nathaniel was an honest doubter and a thorough skeptic. Philip came to him and said, *"We have found Him of whom Moses in the law, and also the prophets, wrote; Jesus of Nazareth, the son of Joseph"* (John 1:45).

Nathaniel said, "I don't believe He is the Messiah. He came from Nazareth. Can any good thing come out of Nazareth?"

Philip said, "You come and see." This is the thing to do—come and see. Nathaniel said, "I will come." He came along with Philip. He met the Lord, and he had not been with the Lord ten minutes when all his doubts were gone. Nathaniel cried, *"You are the Son of God! You are the King of Israel!"* (v. 49).

If you are burdened with doubt, bring your doubts to Jesus. Whatever your burden is, Jesus invites you, every burdened one, every heavyhearted one, to come to Him.

Come Only to Jesus

Jesus says, *"Come to Me,"* not "Come to the church." The church cannot give you rest. I believe in the church; I believe every converted person should be a member of some church, but the church never gave anybody rest. The church is full of people who have never found rest. They have come to the church instead of coming to Jesus Himself.

Jesus does not say, "Come to a creed." I believe in creeds. I think every person should have a creed. A creed is simply an intelligent, systematic statement of what a person believes. A man should believe something and be able to state intelligently what he believes. If he is an intelligent, studious man, his creed will be getting longer all the time. But there was never a creed written or printed that would give anybody rest. It is not going to a creed that brings peace and forgiveness; it is going to the personal Savior.

The Lord Jesus does not say, "Come to the priest" or "Come to the preacher" or "Come to the evangelist" or "Come to any other man." He says, *"Come to Me."* No preacher can give you rest; no priest can give you rest; no man can give you rest. Jesus says, *"Come to Me."*

I have sometimes asked people if they have come to Jesus, and they say, "Oh, I am a Protestant." Well, that never saved anybody. There will be lots of Protestants in hell. Others say, "I am a Roman Catholic." That never saved anybody either. There will be lots of Roman Catholics in hell. When a man says, "I am a Roman Catholic," I say, "I am not asking you that. Have you come to Jesus?" It is not a question of whether you are a Roman Catholic or a Protestant. Have you come to Jesus? If you have not, will you come now?

Come to Jesus, take His yoke, and surrender absolutely to Him. Commit all your sins to Him to pardon; commit all your doubts to Him to remove; commit all your thoughts to Him to teach; commit yourself to believe in Him, to learn from Him, to obey Him, to serve Him. The moment you come to Him with all your heart and cast yourself upon Him, He will give you rest. You can have rest right now.

One night in my church in Chicago, one of the officers of my church went to the upper balcony after I was through preaching. He stepped up to a gentleman and said, "Are you saved?"

"Yes, sir," he said, "I am saved." He was very positive about it.

"How long have you been saved?"

He said, "About five minutes."

"When were you saved?"

He motioned toward the platform and said, "While that man was preaching." He did not wait until I had finished my sermon. He came to Jesus right then, and Jesus saved him right there.

Will you come? Lose sight of everyone else, and see the Lord Jesus standing there, holding out His hands to you with a heart bursting with love, breaking with pity and compassion. He says to every heavyhearted man and woman, *"Come to Me, all you who labor and are heavy laden, and I will give you rest."* Will you come?

Chapter 13

JOY UNSPEAKABLE

◆

Though now you do not see Him, yet believing, you rejoice with joy inexpressible and full of glory.
—1 Peter 1:8

Christians are the happiest people in the world. According to our text they *"rejoice with joy inexpressible and full of glory,"* and nobody else does. Why are Christians so happy?

First of all, Christians are happy because they know that their sins are all forgiven. *"Everyone who believes is justified from all things"* (Acts 13:39). Christians know their sins are forgiven because the Holy Spirit bears witness of forgiveness in their hearts.

The apostle Peter preached about Jesus in the household of Cornelius. He said, *"To Him all the prophets witness that, through His name, whoever believes in Him will receive remission of sins"* (Acts 10:43). Cornelius and his whole household believed it, and the Spirit of God came upon them immediately.

When you and I believe in Jesus, His Spirit comes into our hearts, bearing witness with our spirits that our sins are all forgiven and that we are children of God. There is no joy on earth like the joy of knowing that God has forgiven and blotted out every sin you ever committed.

Suppose a person was in prison for some crime, and someone brought him a pardon. Don't you think he would be happy? But that is nothing compared to knowing that God has forgiven all your sins. Oh, the joy that comes into the heart when a man knows that every sin he ever committed is blotted out and that God has absolutely nothing against him!

A great king wrote a song of joy that has lived through the centuries. That king had been a great sinner, and God had forgiven his sin. He had much to be happy about. He was the greatest king of his day. He had great wealth and great armies. He was the greatest general of the time, and he had a great palace. But when he wrote his song of joy he did not say, "Happy is the man who has a beautiful palace" or "Happy is the man who has great armies" or "Happy is the man who is loved by his people." He said, *"Blessed is he whose transgression is forgiven, whose sin is covered. Blessed is the man to whom the LORD does not impute iniquity, and in whose spirit there is no deceit"* (Ps. 32:1–2). Every man who receives the Lord Jesus as his Savior will have his sins forgiven and will have the joy of knowing that every sin is blotted out.

Sons of the King

Christians are happy because they are set free from sin's power. Everybody who sins is a slave to sin (John 8:34). Since ancient times, many nations and races have been subject to the harshness of slavery. Some of the masters were kind, and some were cruel. But there was never a slaveholder who was such a cruel master as Satan, and there was never a bondage as awful as the bondage of sin.

Every person who is not in Christ is a slave. But when you come to Jesus Christ, He sets you free. *"If you abide in My word, you are My disciples indeed. And you shall know the truth, and the truth shall make you free....Therefore if the Son makes you free, you shall be free indeed"* (John 8:31–32, 36). The Lord Jesus Christ takes every man and woman who believes in Him and sets him or her free from the power of every sin.

Christians are happy because they know that they are children of God. It is a wonderful thing to know that you are a child of God. No one knows it but the Christian, for only the Christian is a child of God.

How does the Christian know that he is a child of God? Because God says so. *"As many as received Him, to them He gave the right to become children of God, to those who believe in His name"* (John 1:12).

The moment you accept the Lord Jesus Christ, you will be a child of God and know that you are a child of God. Isn't that enough to be happy about? Suppose you knew that you were the son of some great man or the son of a millionaire or the son of a king. Don't you think you would be happy? But being the son of any king is nothing compared to being the son of God, the King of Kings.

One day, many years ago, an English duke lay dying. He called his younger brother to his bedside and said, "Brother, in a few hours you will be a duke, and I will be a king." He was a Christian. He was a child of the King, and he knew that when he left this world, he would get a kingdom in heaven. The moment anyone receives Jesus Christ, even if he is the poorest man on earth, he can lift up his head and say, "I am a child of the King. I know I am a child of God."

Sometimes, as I travel around the world, people will point out a man to me and say, "That man is the son of a great man." What of it? Suppose he is a child of a king? I am a child of God. That is better than being a child of a king.

We read in the Bible that the Gospel was preached to the poor. I believe in preaching to the rich. They need it as much as anybody. But I would rather be a poor man who is a child of God than a rich man who is a child of the Devil.

Nothing to Fear

Christians are happy because they are delivered from all fear. A Christian who believes the Bible, studies it, and remembers it is not afraid of anything or anybody. A great many wealthy people have all their joy spoiled because they are constantly thinking that some calamity may overtake them. People who have all the comforts of life do not enjoy them because they fear that some calamity may come and sweep the comforts away. Those with very little, who are perhaps barely getting by, do not enjoy what they have because they fear they may be thrown out of work and not be able to make a living. The true Christian is delivered from all those fears.

There is one verse in the Bible that will take away all anxiety as long as you live. *"And we know that all things work together for good to those who love God"* (Rom. 8:28).

If a person believes the Bible and keeps it in mind, he is not afraid of calamity; nor is he afraid of any man. Many people are afraid of men and tormented by the fear of men. They want to take a stand as a Christian, but they are afraid of being laughed at or persecuted at home or on their jobs. But a Christian is not afraid of man. The Christian reads Romans 8:31 and says, *"If God is for us, who can be against us?"* A Christian does not fear any man or woman on earth.

In Chicago a man came to me and said, "You had better look out. There is a man who says he has it in for you." He told me who the man was—a very desperate man, a man willing to do almost anything. I was not troubled a bit. I did not lie awake a single night. I was not worried for two seconds. I said, "That is all right. I know he is quite powerful, and I have reason to believe he will do anything, but I know that I am right with God. God is on my side, and that man can't touch me." A living faith in Jesus Christ takes away all fear of man forever.

It takes away the fear of death. People's lives are shadowed and darkened by the fear of death. Right in the middle of health and strength they say, "Oh, what if I have some terrible disease!" But death has lost all its terror for the Christian. A Christian knows that what men call death is for him simply to depart and be with Christ.

There is one word that fills the heart of the Christian with joy but fills the heart of the unsaved with terror. That word is *eternity*. In eternity, sorrow, separation, sickness, and death are over forever. All is eternal sunshine. A Christian is delivered from fear of eternity. To people who do not know Christ, eternity is a dreadful thing to think about. But for people in Christ, eternity is the sweetest thing there is to think about.

Write out a card with these words, "Where will you spend eternity?" If you hand it to a person who is not a Christian, it will make him mad. But hand it to a Christian, and he will rejoice. He will answer, "Why, I will spend eternity with Christ in glory!"

The Joy of Everlasting Life

Christians are happy because they know they will live forever. It is a wonderful thing to know that you will never die, that throughout the endless ages you will live on and on. *"And the world is passing away, and the lust of it; but he who does the will of God abides forever"* (1 John 2:17). *"He who believes in the Son has everlasting life; and he who does not believe the Son shall not see life, but the wrath of God abides on him"* (John 3:36).

Before I was a Christian, I did not like to look into the future, but how I love to look into the future now! It is a great joy to preach, but oh, what joy it is to be able to stand and look down through the coming ages and see them roll on, age after age, and know that I am going to live for all eternity in happiness and joy ever increasing! I am not surprised that Christians are happy. I don't wonder that they have *"joy inexpressible and full of glory."*

Christians know that they are heirs of God and joint heirs with Jesus Christ (Rom. 8:17). They know that they have *"an inheritance incorruptible and undefiled and that does not fade away, reserved in heaven for* [them]*"* (1 Pet. 1:4). When someone rides down beautiful country roads and looks out at the beautiful mansions and sees the lakes, forests, parks, and the gardens, he may say, "It must be very pleasant to live there." I suppose it is, but how long will those people live there? They will soon be gone. But every man, woman, and child who takes Jesus will have an inheritance that will last forever. Every earthly inheritance soon fails. Even the richest man on earth won't keep his property very long. But the poorest man who will take Jesus Christ will receive an inheritance that will last forever.

One day a poor English girl was traveling by train and looking out the window. The train passed by beautiful farms and mansions. Every once in a while the poor girl said with a smile, "That belongs to my Father." She would come to a farm and would say, "That belongs to my Father"; to a beautiful mansion, "That belongs to my Father, too"; then she would pass a castle and would say, "That belongs to my Father."

Finally, the man who was listening turned to her and said, "Well, Miss, you must have a rich father."

She said, "He is. I am a child of God." She was very rich.

You may be having a hard time in this world. You may have to work long hours for small pay. Perhaps your home is not very comfortable. Well, you won't have to live here very long. If you receive Christ, you are going to a mansion such as this earth never saw and to an inheritance like none ever inherited on this earth. If you will accept Jesus Christ as your Savior, you will know that you are an heir to all that God has. The whole world belongs to Him—even *"the cattle on a thousand hills"* (Ps. 50:10). If you are a child of God, if you will take Christ, you will be heir to all that He is and all that He has.

The Holy Spirit Living Within

Christians are happy because God gives them the Holy Spirit to dwell in their hearts. When the Holy Spirit dwells in the heart, He fills it with sunshine, gladness, and joy unspeakable.

One Monday morning a woman came to my door, rang the bell, and said she wanted to see me. My daughter said, "You know he sees no one on Monday." She said, "I know it, but I have got to see him." When I came down, I saw one of the members of my church, a poor woman who had to work hard for her living.

"Oh," she said, "Mr. Torrey, I knew you didn't see anybody on Monday, and I didn't like to trouble you, but I received the Holy Spirit last night. I could not sleep all night, and I made up my mind that I was going to give up one day's work and just come and tell you how happy I was. I just had to. I can't very well afford to give up a day's work, but my heart is so full of joy I could not keep still. I had to tell somebody, and I didn't know anybody else I wanted to tell as much as I wanted to tell you. Though I knew you didn't see anybody on Monday, I thought you would be glad to have me come and tell you."

"Yes," I said, "I am glad." That woman was so happy that she could not work; her heart was full of joy.

I don't care how discouraged your heart is today or how full of sadness you are. I don't care if you think your situation is hopeless. If you will take Jesus as your Savior and surrender your whole heart and your whole life to Him, your heart will be filled with a sweetness above anything to be known this side of heaven.

A Christian can *"rejoice with joy inexpressible and full of glory"* (1 Pet. 1:8). But you have to be a true Christian. Just going to church won't do it; just saying your prayers won't do it; just reading the Bible or a prayer book won't do it; just being baptized and confirmed won't do it; just going to the Lord's Supper won't do it. But if you take Jesus into your heart to be your Savior to rule and reign there and surrender all to Him, you will get a joy that is heaven on earth.

People say to me, "Do you expect to go to heaven?" Yes, I know I am going to heaven, but I am in heaven now. I now have a present heaven to live in until I go to the future heaven. Thank God, I feel like singing all the time. I used to be one of the most depressed men on earth. I was despondent; I was gloomy; I used to sit and have the blues by the hour. But I never have had the blues since I accepted the Lord Jesus. I have had trouble. I have had trials. I have seen the time when I had a wife and four children and not a penny to buy them another meal. But it came in time, for I knew where to go—right to God, and He provided. I knew whom I trusted (2 Tim. 1:12). I knew He could get me out somehow, and He did.

If you want darkness turned into sunshine, if you want sadness turned into joy, if you want despair turned into glory, if you want defeat turned into victory, if you want all that is bad turned into all that is good, receive the Lord Jesus Christ, and receive Him right now.

Chapter 14

The Fear of Man

The fear of man brings a snare, but whoever
trusts in the LORD shall be safe.
—Proverbs 29:25

Two paths extend before us: one of ruin, the other of salvation. *"The fear of man brings a snare, but whoever trusts in the LORD shall be safe."* The way of salvation is trust in Jehovah. Even if you do not believe another verse in the Bible, you know this verse is true. I don't care how much of an unbeliever a man may be, he knows that the fear of what others will think brings a snare.

Once a young fellow came to Chicago who was too much of a man to gamble. But he liked an occasional innocent game of cards. One night, he was playing cards with his friends, and someone suggested that they put up a dollar to make it interesting. "Oh," they said, "we don't care for the money, but it is just to lend interest to the game."

"No," he said. "I never gamble. I think gambling is stealing." He is right, for gambling is stealing. No self-respecting man wants another man's money. I don't see how a man who has taken another man's money by gambling can look in the mirror.

He insisted, "No. Gambling is rank dishonesty; I never gamble."

"Oh," they said, "it is not gambling; it is just for a little amusement. You better go home and go to Sunday school. Go and sit with your mother." They ridiculed him into his first game of cards for money. The gambler's passion—a harder passion to overcome then the appetite for drink ever was—seized him. He ended up behind prison bars because he gambled until he took his employer's money to gamble with. The fear of man brought snare that landed him in prison.

Afraid to Take a Stand

The fear of man ensnares Christians into a denial of their Lord. It did Peter. He told his Lord, *"Even if I have to die with You, I will not deny You!"* (Matt. 26:35). But when the servant girl accused him of being a follower of Jesus of Nazareth, he said, *"I do not know the Man!"* (v. 72). A few moments later, he repeated his denial, and an hour after, with oaths and cursings, frightened by what a servant girl might do or say, he denied his Lord. (See Matthew 26:69–75.)

Many of you are doing the same every day. In your office or shop or factory, Jesus Christ is ridiculed. Hard things are said about the Bible; the name of the Lord who died upon the cross of Calvary for you is taken in blasphemy, and you are not man enough or woman enough to stand up and say, "I am a Christian. I believe in that Christ whom you are ridiculing. I believe in that Bible you are laughing at." You are afraid to be laughed at, and the fear of man has ensnared you into a denial of the Lord who died on the cross for you.

The fear of man ensnares professed Christians into a guilty compromise with the world. Are you doing things in your family life, social life, or business life that you know are wrong? Your best moral judgment condemns you every time you do them, but you say, "Well, everybody does them. I will be considered odd if I don't do them."

A Christian man living in one of the suburbs of Chicago said to me, "My daughter is practically ostracized because she won't drink." Thank God, she was woman enough, though she was still a young girl, to be willing to be ostracized rather than compromise. Many people are not.

Would you rather not participate in worldly entertainment? You know you don't feel happy or comfortable there. But you are not brave enough to stand for modesty, purity, and God. The fear of man has entangled you in a snare that has robbed you by your compromise of every bit of real power for Jesus Christ.

Slothful Silence

The fear of man ensnares Christians into a guilty silence and inactivity. When the invitation is given for Christians to go to work and speak to the unsaved, few want to do it. Oh, you would like to lead someone to Christ. What a joy it would be to you! But you say, "Suppose I talk to somebody and they don't like it; suppose they laugh at me; suppose they say some hard things to me." The fear of man in your home, in your shop, in your hotel, everywhere you go, is shutting your mouth and robbing you of the joy of leading others to Jesus Christ.

Suppose they do laugh at you. They spat in your Master's face. They won't spit in yours. They struck Him with their fists. They probably won't strike you. They nailed Him to the cross. Are you not willing to be laughed at for a Master like that?

I believe that the fear of man that keeps Christians from giving their testimony for Christ and working to bring others to Christ does far more to hinder the work of God than any other cause. Men are being saved by the thousands, but if Christians would abandon their fears and have the boldness to witness and work for their Master, people would be saved by the tens of thousands.

The fear of man ensnares those who are not Christians into the rejection of Jesus Christ. Hundreds of men and women would like to be Christians. They see the joy of it. But they are afraid that if they accept Christ, somebody will ridicule them. The fear of man shuts them out of the acceptance of Jesus Christ. I believe that more people are kept from accepting Christ by the fear of what someone will say or do than by any other cause. If we could get rid of this fear, there would be thousands saved every night at evangelistic crusades instead of two or three.

The fear of man ensnares those who think they have accepted Christ into not making a public confession of Him. Jesus says distinctly, *"Whoever confesses Me before men, him I will also confess before My Father who is in heaven. But whoever denies Me before men, him I will also deny before My Father who is in heaven"* (Matt. 10:32–33).

Paul said distinctly, *"With the heart one believes unto right-eousness, and with the mouth confession is made unto salvation"* (Rom. 10:10). Yet a host of men and women are trying to be Christians and never stand up to say so. "I don't believe in this publicity. I don't believe in this standing-up business. I believe in doing things more quietly. I don't believe in excitement." You can give a thousand and one reasons, but if you were honest with yourself, as you will have to be honest with God some day, you would say, "It is because I am afraid to do it."

A fine looking young fellow came to me one day and said, "I am a fool."

I said, "What is the matter?"

He said, "I thought I accepted Christ here the other night, and I have not been man enough to tell another man in the office what I have done. I am a fool."

Well, he was. So are you. You professed to receive Jesus Christ, but to this day you have not told the other people in your office, in your home, in your hotel, in your shop. The fear of man has sealed your mouth, made you a coward, and robbed you of all the joy that there is in a bold Christian experience.

The fear of man ensnares those who start out in the Christian life from going on in it, because somebody says something discouraging. One night two young men both professed to accept Christ at a crusade meeting. One of the men went to his pastor and told him what he had done. His pastor encouraged him in his new walk with Christ.

The other man's pastor was one of those convivial pastors, a man whose chief function is to serve as a figurehead at large banquets where he joins in and encourages the frivolity. The young convert went to this preacher and told him what he had done. His preacher said, "Don't you believe a word they are saying up there." He discouraged him. There must be a deep spot in hell for the man who bears the name of minister and dares to discourage a young convert in his first aspirations toward God.

The poor young fellow was discouraged entirely. A minister of the Gospel had laughed at him and snared him into wretched backsliding and maybe even into hell. If you are starting out in the Christian life, no matter who approves or disapproves, you are on the right track. Go on in spite of everybody.

Eternal Consequences

The fear of man ensnares people to their eternal ruin. Many men and women lie in Christless graves and will spend a Christless eternity because the fear of man kept them from the acceptance of Christ. One night after speaking, I gave the altar call. Among those who were moved by the Spirit of God was a young woman. She rose to her feet and started to come to the front. The young man who sat beside her touched her arm. He was engaged to marry her. He said, "Don't go tonight. If you will wait for a few days, I may go with you." For fear of offending her fiancé, she sat down.

I went back the next week to speak at the same place. At the close of the meeting two young women came and said, "Oh, Mr. Torrey, just as soon as you can get away from the meeting here, come with us. There is a young lady who was going to come forward the other night, but the young man to whom she is engaged asked her to wait. She did wait, and now she has scarlet fever. She probably won't live until morning. Come to see her just as soon as you can get away from the meeting."

I left as soon as I could. I entered her home and went into the room where the poor girl lay dying, hardly recognizable as the same person, but perfectly conscious. I urged her to accept Christ. "No," she said, "I was about to receive Him the last time you were here. I didn't repent then. I am dying; I can't repent now."

I begged her. I knew it was her last hour. I did everything, but she would not yield. When I left that room of awful darkness, a young man in the hallway grasped me by the hand. He was shaking like a leaf. "Oh," he said, "Mr. Torrey, I am engaged to marry that girl. Now she is dying without Christ. She is lost, and I am to blame. I am to blame."

The Spirit of God is moving on this earth with mighty power. Many of you are on the verge of a decision for Christ. Don't let the fear of man frighten you from taking your stand now.

Trusting the Lord

Our text in Proverbs 29:25 promises, *"Whoever trusts in the LORD shall be safe."* He will be safe from all danger of yielding to sin and temptation. If you trust God, temptation has no power over you. A man cannot yield to temptation without distrusting God. Every act of sin is an act of distrust of God. He who trusts God will do right even though the heavens fall.

I knew a businessman who lost nearly everything he owned and had to sell everything else in order to pay his debts. He paid all his debts, but it left him practically penniless. Then he was offered a job with a manufacturing firm. He came to me and said, "What should I do? This is an excellent company to work for. They said they will promote me quickly, but if I take this post, I must work on Sundays. What should I do?"

I said, "Well, you will have to decide for yourself, but if you can't do it with a clear conscience, you can't afford to do it."

He said, "I can't do it with a clear conscience." He refused the position, although he did not know what he was to do to support himself and his wife and family of three children. A day or two later, he got a job at very low wages. A few weeks after that, he got a position at several hundred dollars per month. He went on to become the controller of one of the biggest mercantile establishments in the Northwest—all because he trusted God.

When I was home one summer, I found that a young Jewish woman had been converted while I was away. She was a very talented woman, but she had to work hard for her living to support the family. After she was converted, she was full of love for Christ. She went out to the place where she worked, a very large company, and she began talking about Christ to the other employees. Some of them did not like it. They went to the head of the firm and said, "She is constantly talking to us about Christ. We don't like it."

The managers called her in and said, "We have no objection to Christianity, and no objection to your being a Christian. It is a good thing, but you must not talk about it at this company."

"Very well," she said. "I won't work where I can't take Christ with me and talk for my Master."

"Well, then," they said, "you will have to lose your job."

"Very well," she said, "I will give up my position before I will be disloyal to Jesus Christ."

They said, "Go back to work, and we will tell you our decision later." She went back to work.

At the end of the week, she got a letter from the firm. She said, "Here is my discharge," and she tore it open. The letter read: "We have a position with great responsibility, with a much larger salary than you are getting. We think you are the woman for the position, and we offer it to you." They saw she could be trusted. Businessmen are looking for men and women whom they can trust.

Facing Persecution

Whoever trusts in the Lord will be safe from danger of every kind. We read in Romans 8:31: *"If God is for us, who can be against us?"* Men will persecute you. They will ridicule you. They will do all they can to harm you. Jesus said in John 15:20, *"If they persecuted Me, they will also persecute you."* But it won't do you any harm.

Some people are frightened at the thought of being persecuted. But it is one of the greatest privileges on earth for converts to be persecuted for Jesus Christ. Jesus said:

> *Blessed are you when they revile and persecute you, and say all kinds of evil against you falsely for My sake. Rejoice and be exceedingly glad, for great is your reward in heaven, for so they persecuted the prophets who were before you.* (Matt. 5:11–12)

When I was in Australia, an organized gang came to break up our meeting. I had said some rather plain things about living a holy life before God that angered a number of people. This gang that came to break up the meetings was seated in the far balcony. The power of God came down, and two ringleaders walked right up from that balcony the whole length of the hall and came down to the front. They turned and faced the crowd and said, "We accept Jesus Christ."

The next day, some friends of the ringleader of the gang met him on the street. They knocked him down and pounded him to make him swear and curse God. But God had taken all the swearing out of him. Instead of swearing, he wrote one of the most beautiful letters to a friend of his, who sent it to me. He wrote about the joy of suffering for Jesus' sake.

They may persecute you. They may pound you, they may hound you, but they can't hurt you if you are right with God. The man who trusts in the Lord is eternally safe.

Jesus said in John 10:28–29:

And I give them eternal life, and they shall never perish; neither shall anyone snatch them out of My hand. My Father, who has given them to Me, is greater than all; and no one is able to snatch them out of My Father's hand.

If you trust in the Lord, God Almighty's hand is underneath you and around you; Christ the Son's hand is over you and around you. You are in between the almighty hand of God the Father and God the Son, and all the devils in hell can't get you.

Throw away your fear of man. In place of it, put trust in Jehovah. You compromising Christians, throw away your compromise. Be radical for Jesus; be a clean, straight Christian for God. Throw away your guilty silence. Go to work to bring others to Christ, and keep it up tomorrow, the next day, and the day after that. Throw away your guilty silence about unpopular truth, and declare the whole counsel of God, even though some say you are old-fashioned because you tell the truth. Don't worry about what anybody says, but stand up boldly and confess Christ before the world.

The Time for Harvest

In the early days of Mr. Moody's work in Chicago, there was a man who regularly attended the church. He seemed to be on the point of decision for Christ. At last Mr. Moody went to him and urged him to decide at once. He replied that he could not take a stand for Christ. There was a man with whom he worked who would ridicule him, and he could not endure his ridicule. As Mr. Moody kept urging him to make a decision, the man at last became irritated and ceased attending the church.

Some months later, when the man had quite dropped out of sight, Mr. Moody received an urgent call to go and see the man.

He found him very ill, apparently dying, and in great anxiety about his soul. Mr. Moody showed him the way of life, and the man professed to accept Christ. His soul seemed at rest. To everyone's surprise, he took a turn for the better, and full recovery seemed sure.

Mr. Moody called on him one day and found him sitting out in the sunshine. Mr. Moody said, "Now that you have accepted Christ, and God has raised you up, you must come and confess Him publicly as soon as you are able to come to church."

To Mr. Moody's astonishment, the man replied, "No, not now. I don't dare admit I am a Christian in Chicago. But I intend to move to Michigan soon. As soon as I get over there, I will come out publicly and take my stand for Christ." Mr. Moody told him that Christ could protect him in Chicago as well as in Michigan, but the man's fear of his friend held him back. Mr. Moody was greatly disappointed and left.

One week from that day, the man's wife called Mr. Moody and begged him to come at once and see her husband. He had suffered a relapse, was worse than ever, and a council of physicians agreed that there was no possibility of recovery.

"Did he send for me to come?" asked Mr. Moody.

"No. He says that he is lost, and that there is no hope for him. He does not wish to see you or speak to you, but I cannot let him die this way. You must come."

Mr. Moody hastened to the house and found the man in a state of utter despair. To all Mr. Moody's pleas for him to take Christ, he would reply that it was too late, that he was lost, that he had thrown away his day of opportunity, and that he could not be saved now. Mr. Moody said, "I will pray for you."

"No," said the man, "don't pray for me. It is useless. I am lost. Pray for my wife and children. They need your prayers."

Mr. Moody knelt down by his side and prayed, but his prayers did not seem to go higher than his head. He could not get hold of God for this man's salvation. When he arose, the man said, "There, Mr. Moody, I knew that prayer would do no good. I am lost."

With a heavy heart, Mr. Moody left the house. All afternoon the man kept repeating, "The harvest is past, the summer is ended, and I am not saved." (See Jeremiah 8:20.) Just as the sun

697

was setting behind the western prairies, the man passed away. In his last moment, they heard him murmuring, "The harvest is past, the summer is ended, and I am not saved." Another soul went out into eternity unprepared, snared into eternal perdition by the fear of man. Throw away your fear of man, and put your trust in the Lord and be saved.

Chapter 15

How God Loves the World

---◆---

For God so loved the world that He gave His only begotten Son,
that whoever believes in Him should not perish
but have everlasting life.
—John 3:16

Thousands of people have been saved by this wonderful verse, tens of thousands, hundreds of thousands—by simply reading it in the Bible. This one verse tells us some very important things about the love of God. It tells us that our salvation begins in God's love. We are not saved because we love God; we are saved because God loves us. Our salvation begins in God's loving us, and it ends in our loving God.

The first thing our text teaches us about the love of God is that the love of God is universal. *"God so loved the world"*—not some part of it, not some elect people or some select class. God loves the rich, but God loves the poor, too. The rich need to hear the Gospel just as much as the poor, and they are not nearly as likely to. If some poor man who did not even know where he was going to sleep tonight stood up to receive Christ, many people would not think it amounted to much. But God would be just as pleased to see the poorest man or woman accept Christ as He would be to see the richest millionaire come to Him. God loves the man who can't read or write as much as He loves the most brilliant scientist or philosopher on earth.

If some university professor were converted, some people would be delighted. They would say, "Oh, a wonderful thing happened. One of our learned professors was converted." But if an illiterate person accepted Christ, some people would not be nearly as impressed. The most wonderful thing of all is this: God loves the poor as much as the rich, the uneducated as much as the educated, and the unrighteous as much as the righteous.

One night I was visiting one of the members of my church, and his little girl was playing in the room. The child did something naughty, and her father called out, "Don't be naughty. If you are a good girl, God will love you, but if you are not, God won't love you."

I said, "Charlie, what nonsense are you teaching that child of yours? That is not what my Bible teaches. It teaches that God loves the sinner just as truly as He loves the saint."

It is hard to make people believe that God loves the sinner and the outcast. The Bible emphasizes this truth the most.

Christ Died for Sinners

I was preaching one hot summer's night; it was so hot that the windows were all opened at the back to let in the fresh air. The room was packed. At the back of the room, a man sat on the windowsill. When I asked for all who wished to be saved that night to hold up their hands, that man raised his hand. But as soon as I pronounced the benediction, he started for the door. I forgot about the meeting to follow. All I saw was that man starting for the door, and I went after him. I caught him just as he turned to descend the stairway. I laid my hand on his shoulder and said to him, "My friend, you held up your hand to say you wanted to be saved."

"Yes, I did."

"Why didn't you stay, then, for the second meeting?"

He said, "It is no use."

I said, "God loves you."

"You don't know who you are talking to. I am the worst thief in this town."

"Well, even if you are, I can prove to you from the Bible that God loves you." I opened my Bible to Romans 5:8, and I read: *"But God demonstrates His own love toward us, in that while we were still sinners, Christ died for us."*

I said, "If you are the worst thief in town, you are certainly a sinner, and that verse says that God loves sinners."

It broke the man's heart, and he began to weep. I took him to my office where we sat down, and he told me his story. He said, "I was released from prison this morning. I had started out this evening with some companions to commit one of the most daring burglaries ever committed in this city. By tomorrow morning, I would either have had a big stake of money or a bullet in my body.

"But as we were going down the street together, we passed the corner where you were holding that open-air meeting. A Scotsman was speaking. My mother was Scotch, and when I heard that familiar accent, it reminded me of my mother.

"I had a dream about her the other night in prison. I dreamed that she came to me and begged me to give up my wicked life. When I heard that Scotsman talk, I stopped to listen. My two pals said, 'Come along,' and cursed me. I said, 'I am going to listen to what this man says.' Then they tried to drag me across the street, but I would not go. What that man said touched my heart. When he invited everyone to this meeting, I came, and that is why I am here."

I opened my Bible and showed him that God loves sinners, that Christ had died for sinners, and that he could be saved by simply accepting Christ. He did accept Christ. We knelt down side by side, and that man offered the most wonderful prayer I ever heard in all my life.

Are you a thief? God loves you. Are you an unbeliever? God loves you. Are you a blasphemer? God loves you. You can't find in all the earth anyone whom God doesn't love.

The Character of God's Love

The second thing our text teaches about the love of God is that God's love is a holy love. *"God so loved the world that He gave His only begotten Son"* (John 3:16). A great many people cannot understand that. They say, "If God loves me, I cannot see why He doesn't forgive my sins outright without His Son dying in my place. I cannot see the necessity of Christ's death. If God is love, and if God loves me and everybody else, why doesn't He take us to heaven right away without Christ dying for us?"

The text answers the question, *"God so loved."* That *so* brings out the character of God's love. God could not and would not pardon sin without an atonement. God is a holy God. God's holiness must manifest itself in some way. It must either manifest itself in the punishment of the sinner, that is, in our eternal banishment from His presence, or it must manifest itself in some other way.

The death of Jesus Christ on the cross of Calvary was God providing atonement for sinful man. But some people say, "That is not fair. Are you saying that God took the sin of man and laid it on Jesus Christ, an innocent third person? That is not fair."

But Jesus Christ was not a third person. *"God was in Christ reconciling the world to Himself"* (2 Cor. 5:19). The atoning death of Jesus Christ on the cross is not God taking my sin from me and laying it on a third person. It is God the Father taking the penalty of my sin into His own heart and dying in His Son, in my place. Jesus Christ was not merely the first Person. He was the second Person, too. Jesus Christ was the Son of Man, the Second Adam, the representative Man. No ordinary man could have died for you and me. It would have been of no value. But Jesus Christ was the Second Adam, your representative and mine. When Christ died on the cross of Calvary, I died in Him, and the penalty of my sin was paid.

If you do not believe in the deity of Christ, the Atonement becomes irrational. If you remove the humanity of Christ and believe He is merely divine, the Atonement becomes irrational. But take all that the Bible says—that God was in Christ, and that in Christ the Word became God manifest in the flesh—and the Atonement is the most profound and wonderful truth the world has ever seen.

God's love is a holy love. In His perfect righteousness, perfect justice, perfect holiness, and perfect love, Christ, through His atoning death, provided pardon to save the vilest of sinners. When you are awakened to a proper sense of your sinfulness, when you see yourself as you really are and see God as He really is, nothing will satisfy your conscience but the doctrine that God, the Holy One, substituted His atoning action for His punitive action. In the death of Jesus Christ on the cross of Calvary, your sins and mine were perfectly settled forever.

Thank God, the law of God has no claim on me. I broke it, I admit, but Jesus Christ kept it. He satisfied its punitive claim by dying for those who had not kept it. On the ground of that atoning death, there is pardon for the vilest sinner.

You may have gone deeper into sin than you realize yourself, but while your sins are as high as the mountains, the Atonement that covers them is as high as the heavens. While your sins are as deep as the ocean, the Atonement that swallows them up is as deep as eternity. On the ground of Christ's atoning death, there is pardon for the vilest sinner on earth.

God's Infinite Love

The third thing our text teaches us about the love of God is the greatness of that love. We see His love in the greatness of the gift He offers us—eternal life. It means a life that is perfect and divine in its quality as well as endless in its duration. *"God so loved the world that He gave His only begotten Son, that whoever believes in Him should not perish but have everlasting life."*

I thank God for a life that is perfect in quality and that will never end. Most of us will have to die before long, as far as our physical life is concerned. Eighty years from now, you and most of your family and friends will be gone, unless the Lord comes back first. You may say that eighty years is a long time. No, it is not. It sounds long to young people, but when you get to be older, it looks very short. When the eighty years are up, what then? Suppose I had a guarantee that I was going to live two hundred years in perfect health, strength, and prosperity. Would that satisfy me? No, it would not. For when the two hundred years are up, what then? I want something that never ends, and thank God, in Christ, I have something that never ends—eternal life! Who can have it? Anybody. *"Whoever believes in Him should not perish but have everlasting life."*

Somebody asked a little boy, "What does *whoever* mean?" The little fellow answered, "It means you and me and everybody else." When I read that *"God so loved the world that He gave His only begotten Son, that whoever believes in Him should not perish but have everlasting life,"* I know that means me. Thank God it does, and that it includes everybody else.

703

The Measure of Love

The text tells us a second way in which the greatness of the love of God shows itself: in the sacrifice that God made for us. *"God so loved the world that He gave His only begotten Son."* The measure of love is sacrifice. You can tell how much anybody loves you by the sacrifice that he is willing to make for you. God has shown the measure of His love by the sacrifice He made. He gave His very best, the dearest that He had.

No earthly father ever loved his son as God loved Jesus Christ. I have an only son; how I love him! But suppose some day I should see that boy of mine arrested by the enemies of Christ; and suppose they blindfolded him, spat in his face, beat him, and then made a crown of big, cruel thorns and put it on his brow, causing the blood to pour down his face on either side. How do you suppose I would feel?

Then suppose they stripped his garments from him, tied him to a post, and beat him with a stick that had long lashes of leather twisted with bits of brass and lead, until his back was all torn and bleeding. How do you think I would feel?

Suppose they threw him down on a cross laid on the ground, stretched his right hand out on the arm of the cross, put a nail in the hand, lifted the heavy hammer, and drove the nail through the hand; then they stretched his left arm on the other arm of the cross, put a nail in the palm of that hand, lifted the heavy hammer, and sent the nail through that hand; then they drove the nail through his feet. Finally, they took that cross and plunged it into a hole and left him hanging there while the agony grew worse every minute. Suppose they left him to die beneath the burning sun. How do you suppose I would feel if I stood and looked on as my only boy died in awful agony on a cross?

That is just what God saw. He loved His only begotten Son, as you and I never imagined loving our sons. He saw His Son hanging there, aching, all His bones out of joint, tortured in every part of His body! God looked on. Why did He permit it? Because He loves you and me, and it was the only way by which we could be saved.

Your Response to God's Love

How are you going to repay this love? Some people will repay it with hatred. They hate God. They have never said it, but it is true.

A friend of mine was preaching one time in Connecticut. He was staying with a physician who had a beautiful, amiable daughter. She had never made a profession of faith, but she was such a beautiful person that people thought she was a Christian. One night, after the meetings had been going on for some time, my friend said to this young lady, "Are you going up to the meeting tonight?"

She said, "No, I am not."

He said, "I think you had better go."

"I will not go."

"Why," he said, "don't you love God?"

She said, "I hate God." She had never realized it before. I think she would have said she loved God up to that time, but when the demands of God were pressed home by the Holy Spirit, she was not willing to obey. She found out that she hated God.

Some of you have never found out that you hate God, but it is true. How have you used the name of God today? You have used it many times. In prayer? No, in profanity. Why? Because you hate God.

If a woman receives Christ, she may find that her husband makes her life unbearable. Why? Because he hates God, and he wants to make his wife miserable for accepting His Son. If someone in your business accepts Christ, do you laugh at him? If you do, it is because you hate God. Some people will read every heretical book they can get and go to every ungodly lecture. They are trying to convince themselves that the Bible is not God's Word. If anybody comes along and brings up some smart objection to the Bible, they laugh and rejoice in it. Why? Because they hate God and want to get rid of God's Book.

Some people love to hold up their heads and say, "I don't believe in the divinity of Christ. I don't believe He is the Son of God." Why? Because they hate God, and if they can rob His divine Son of the honor that belongs to Him, they will do it. They are repaying the wondrous love of God with hatred.

Perhaps you refuse to accept Christ. You heard God's message of salvation many times. When people speak to you about committing your life to the Lord, you get angry. You say, "I wish you would not talk to me. It is none of your business whether I am a Christian or not." Why do you respond like this? Because you hate God.

Some people so bitterly hate God that they try to find fault with the doctrine of the Atonement. They try to make themselves believe that Christ did not die on the cross for their salvation. They say, "I cannot understand the philosophy of it." A person who loved God would not stop to ask the philosophy of it. He would lift his heart in simple gratitude and praise to God for His great love and mercy.

Conquered by Love

There is one other thing that our text teaches us about the love of God: the conquering power of God's love. The love of God conquers sin, death, and wrong, and gives everlasting life. The love of God conquers where everything else fails.

The first time I ever preached in Chicago, I noticed a young woman who did not come forward when the rest came. I went down to where she was standing and urged her to come forward. She laughed and said, "No, I am not going forward," and sat down again.

The next night was not an evangelistic service, but a convention meeting. I was president of the convention. As I looked over the audience, I saw that young woman sitting in the back. She was elegantly dressed. I called somebody else to the platform and slipped around to the back part of the building. When the meeting was dismissed, I made my way to where that young lady was sitting. I sat down beside her and said, "Won't you accept Christ tonight?"

"No," she said. "Would you like to know the kind of life I am living?" She was living in the best society, honored and respected. Then she told me a sad story of immorality and laughed as if it were a good joke.

I simply took my Bible and opened it to John 3:16. I passed it over to her and said, "Won't you please read that?" She had to hold it very near her eyes to see the small print, and she began in a laughing way. *"God so loved—her* laughter subsided—*the world"*—there was nothing like a laugh now—*"that He gave His only begotten Son."* She burst into tears, and the tears flowed down on the elegant silk dress she was wearing. Hardened and shameless as she was, trifling as she was, one glimpse of Jesus on the cross of Calvary for her had broken her heart.

One night I was preaching, and we had an after-meeting. The leading soprano in the choir was not a Christian. She was a respectable girl, but very worldly and frivolous. She decided to stay for the after-meeting. Her mother stood up in the congregation and said, "I wish you would all pray for the conversion of my daughter." I did not turn to took at the choir, but I knew perfectly well how that young woman looked. I knew her cheeks were burning, I knew her eyes were flashing, and I knew that she was angry from the crown of her head to the soles of her feet.

As soon as the meeting was over, I hurried down to the door. As she came along, I walked toward her, held out my hand, and said, "Good evening, Cora." Her eyes flashed, and her checks burned. She did not take my hand. She stamped her foot and said, "Mr. Torrey, my mother knows better than to do what she has done tonight. She knows it will only make me worse."

I said, "Cora, sit down." The angry girl sat down, and I opened my Bible to Isaiah 53:5 and handed it to her. I said, "Won't you please read it?" She read: *"He was wounded for our transgressions, He was bruised for our iniquities; the chastisement for our peace was upon Him."* She did not get any further; she burst into tears. The love of God revealed in the cross of Christ had broken her heart, and she received Christ into her life.

Let the love of God conquer your stubborn, wicked, foolish, sinful, worldly, careless heart. *"God so loved the world that He gave His only begotten Son, that whoever believes in Him should not perish but have everlasting life."* Yield to that love now.

Chapter 16

Today and Tomorrow

◆

The Holy Spirit says: "Today, if you will hear His voice."
—Hebrews 3:7

Do not boast about tomorrow.
—Proverbs 27:1

Today is the wise man's day; tomorrow is the fool's day. The wise man sees what ought to be done and does it today. The foolish man says, "I will do it tomorrow." Those who always do the thing that should be done today are successful for time and for eternity. Those who put off until tomorrow what should be done today will fail for time and eternity. *"The Holy Spirit says: 'Today.'"* Man, in the folly of his heart, says, "Tomorrow."

I have no doubt that thousands of men and women intend to be Christians at some time, but they keep saying, "Not yet, not today." I am going to tell you not merely why you should become a Christian, but why you should become a Christian today.

The sooner you come to Christ, the sooner you will find the wonderful joy that is found in Him. In Jesus, there is an immeasurably better joy than there is in the world, a purer joy, a holier joy, a more satisfying joy.

This fact is not open to dispute. Everyone knows that it is true. Go to any person who followed the ways of the world and then tried Christ, and ask him, "Which joy is better—the joy that the world gave or the joy that you have found in Christ?" You will get the same answer every time. The joy found in the world cannot for a moment compare to the joy that is found in Christ.

If ever a person had an opportunity to try what this world can give, I had it, and I tried it. I tried all that could be found in the world; then I turned to Christ and tried Him. My testimony is the testimony of millions of others who have found that the joy of the world is not real joy. The joy of Christ is everything.

Anyone who has really found Christ will tell you there is a joy in Christ that is higher, deeper, broader, wider, and more wonderful in every way than the joy that the world gives. The sooner you come to Christ, the sooner you will have that joy.

Deep and Abiding Peace

The sooner you come to Christ, the sooner you will escape the wretchedness and misery that there is away from Christ. First of all, there is the misery of an accusing conscience. No one out of Christ has peace of mind.

One night I was preaching to an audience of men and women to whom twenty dollars would have been a great help. As I was preaching, I took out the money and held it up and said, "Now, is there a anyone in this audience who does not know Christ who has peace in his heart, deep, abiding satisfaction and rest? If he will come up here and say so, I will give him this twenty-dollar bill."

Nobody came up. When the meeting was over, I went down and stood at the door with the twenty dollar bill, for I thought some might be timid about coming up in front for it. I said, "If anybody can claim this twenty dollars by saying, 'I have peace of conscience and heart. My heart is satisfied without Christ,' he can have this twenty dollar bill." They filed out, and nobody claimed the money. Finally, a man came along, and I said, "Don't you want this money?" He answered, "I cannot claim it on those conditions." Neither can you.

Another night I was preaching in Chicago, and I asked everybody in the building who had found rest and perfect satisfaction through the acceptance of Christ to stand up. More than a thousand men and women rose to their feet. I asked them to sit down, and then I said, "If there is an unbeliever in this house who can say he has found rest, peace, and perfect satisfaction of heart, will he please stand?" Many agnostics and skeptics were there. One man stood up in the balcony, and I said, "I see there is a gentleman up there. I am glad that he has the courage of his convictions, and I would like to speak with him after the meeting."

He came to the after-meeting. I said, "You stood up in the meeting tonight to say that you had perfect rest and peace of heart without Christ, and that your soul was satisfied with your unbelief. Is that true?"

"Oh," he said, "Mr. Torrey, that will have to be qualified." I guess it will. *"'There is no peace,' says the LORD, 'for the wicked'"* (Isa. 48:22).

There is slavery in sin. *"Whoever commits sin is a slave of sin"* (John 8:34). Away from Christ is apprehension of what may happen, fear of disaster, fear of what man may do, fear of what may be found beyond the grave. When you come to Christ, you get rid of the fear of man. You have no fear of misfortune, for you are able to say, *"All things work together for good to those who love God"* (Rom. 8:28). You have no fear of death, for what men call death is simply to depart and be with Christ. The moment you accept Christ, you get rid of the accusations of conscience, the slavery of sin, all fear of disaster, and the dread of death.

Why not get rid of it all right now? Suppose you were on the seashore and saw in the distance a wreck of a ship and a man clinging to a piece of board. If you went to rescue him, do you think he would say, "I think I can hold on until morning. Come out again then, and I will get into the boat and come ashore." You would say, "Man, are you mad? Will you stay out here tonight when you can come ashore now?"

Men and women, out on the wreck of life, the cold waves break over you with all the wretchedness of an accusing conscience, the bondage of sin, the fear of death, and all the multiplied wretchedness of the soul away from God. Why cling to the wreck another night? You can come ashore to safety and joy now, if you will climb right into the lifeboat.

Working for the Lord

The moment a person is saved he can begin to do something for the Master. The sooner you come to Christ, the more you can do for Him. If you are saved a year from now, you can begin to work for Christ, but there will be one year gone that will never come back. You are associated with friends now who you can lead to Christ. A year from now, they may be past your reach. I had a friend who lived in the same building as I before I was converted. Had I been a Christian then, I could have led him to Christ. Three years later, after I had accepted Christ, we had gone our separate ways.

One day, I picked up the *New York Times* and began to read about a young man who was out playing ball. The man in center field threw the ball in. This young man's back was toward center field, and he was struck at the base of the brain. He never regained consciousness. My father said, "Isn't that your old friend?" I took the paper and read it and said, "Yes, it is my old friend." He was called into eternity without a moment's warning, and my opportunity of bringing him to Christ was gone forever! In the years that have come since, God has used me to lead others to Christ, but I have often thought of Frank. In spite of all those who are now coming to Christ, Frank has gone, and my opportunity of leading him to Christ is lost forever. If you postpone accepting Christ for thirty days, people whom you might have reached during those thirty days will have passed beyond your reach forever.

In my first pastorate, a woman a little over fifty years of age, who had been a backslider, recommitted her life to the Lord. She became the best worker in the community. But her two sons had grown up during the years that she was far from God. They had both married and passed beyond her reach. Although she has been used to bring many to Christ, she was never able to bring these sons to her Lord. Her day of opportunity for them was while she was living in the world. Fathers and mothers living far from God, if you are not saved now, you may be some other day. But your sons and daughters will very likely have passed beyond your reach forever. The sooner you come to Christ, the more people you can bring with you.

The sooner you come to Christ, the richer will be your eternity. We are saved by grace, but we are rewarded according to our works. Every day after a man is saved, he lays up treasures in heaven. (See Matthew 6:20.) Every day you live for Christ, you will be that much richer for all eternity.

Some people have an idea that a man can be saved on his deathbed and have just as abundant an entrance into the kingdom of God as he could have if he had been saved forty years. Neither common sense nor the Bible supports that thought. A man may be saved on his deathbed, but he is saved *"so as through fire"* (1 Cor. 3:15). His works are all burned up, and he enters heaven penniless. The man who is saved forty years before he dies and serves Christ for those years makes his deposits for which he will be richer throughout all eternity. *"Lay up for yourselves treasures in heaven"* (Matt. 6:20).

If you come to Christ while you are still young, you can enter the kingdom of God with much fuller hands. I thank God I was converted when I was young, but what would I give for those wasted years while I deliberately resisted the Spirit of God! But I can't call them back.

The Day of Salvation

The sooner you come to Christ, the surer you are to come to Christ. If you are not saved today, you may be saved tomorrow, but you may not be saved. I believe there are scores of people who will be saved now or never. People think they can turn to Christ when they decide that they want to, but when the Spirit of God is moving on your heart, it is a solemn moment. To say yes, means life; to say no, means death. To say yes, means heaven; to say no, means hell.

Often a man will be near the kingdom, and he will say, "I am so interested now that I will certainly be just as interested tomorrow." But the critical hour has come, and if he does not yield now, he will have no interest tomorrow.

I once received a message from a wealthy young fellow saying that he wished to see me that night at Mr. Moody's meeting. I went and met him at the close of the meeting. He was on the verge of a decision. As we stood talking on the sidewalk, a bell rang out a late hour. I said to myself, "He is so near a decision, I can leave him safely until tomorrow morning." So I said, "Good night, Will. I will be around to your room tomorrow morning at ten."

It was one of the most fatal mistakes I have ever made. I was there at ten and he was there, but his convictions had all left him. He was hard as stone. His opportunity had come and gone. You may be very near a decision at this moment, on the very borders of the kingdom, but if you say no, tomorrow will be forever too late. Who of us can tell who will be called out of the world into eternity in a moment?

You have a chance now. Don't throw it away. The sooner you accept Christ, the surer you will be to receive Him. Ask Him into your heart now. You can have the joy of salvation at this moment; why wait a week? You can be saved from a life of wretchedness at once; why bear it another hour? The sooner you come to Christ, the more you can do for Him, and the richer you will be throughout all eternity.

Come to Him today and begin to lay up treasures in the bank of heaven. The sooner you come to Christ, the surer it is that you will come. Come now. *"The Holy Spirit says: 'Today, if you will hear His voice, do not harden your hearts"* (Heb. 3:7–8). *"Do not boast about tomorrow, for you do not know what a day may bring forth"* (Prov. 27:1). *"Behold, now is the accepted time; behold, now is the day of salvation"* (2 Cor. 6:2).